POWER & BALANCE
an introduction
to American
constitutional government

W9-BJD-987

Property of
FAMILY OF FAITH
LIBRARY

Family of Faith Library

Property of
FAMILY OF FAITH
LIBRARY

Power & Balance

an introduction to American constitutional government

IRA H. CARMEN
University of Illinois
at Urbana-Champaign

Under the General Editorship of
James David Barber, Duke University

HARCOURT BRACE JOVANOVICH, INC.
New York San Diego Chicago San Francisco Atlanta

© 1978 by Harcourt Brace Jovanovich, Inc.

All rights reserved. No part of this publication may be reproduced or transmitted in any form or by any means, electronic or mechanical, including photocopy, recording, or any information storage and retrieval system, without permission in writing from the publisher.

ISBN: 0-15-570753-1

Library of Congress Catalog Card Number: 77-20746

Printed in the United States of America

Chapter-opening illustrations by Hal Just

To my parents,
Jacob and Lida Carmen

preface

The past ten years have been a turbulent time for American national government. Every week, newspapers carried provocative headlines signaling examination of the basic powers of statecraft and the basic liberties of citizens: "Civil Rights Workers Arrested"; "Court Bans Pornography"; "Draft Cards Burned on Street Corner"; "Nixon Withholds Tapes"; "School Busing Plan Approved." Today our political climate is somewhat more serene. But the fundamental issues remain unresolved, for the root inquiries are as old as the nation itself: What policies and rules can public authority ordain under our Constitution? What freedoms do individuals possess under our Constitution? What *is* our Constitution? This book focuses on these questions in the context of contemporary politics.

Power and Balance is an introduction to American government. It is addressed to the undergraduate who has a passion for politics but who may well perceive the current dialogue—whether in or out of the classroom—as colorless and futile. I have found my students at the University of Illinois to be profoundly interested in such concepts as liberty, equality, national security, the criminal justice system, voting, and race relations—in all the facets of political life that the "Living Constitution" in some manner entails. To these students, to other concerned observers, and to my colleagues in the academic field, I wish to convey my conception of American government—one that emphasizes *constitutional politics.* And by "constitutional politics" I mean the power relations flowing from explicit and implicit "rules of the game," norms commonly accepted yet sometimes incapable of providing both reasoned accommodation and equitable solution.

The footnoting scheme I have adopted bears witness to my dual role as political scientist and teacher. The numbered references, at the end of each chapter, include not only the profusion of scholarly materials I have found indispensable but also definitions of terms, hypothetical questions, informational updates, explorations of arguments, and personal asides. The lettered references, which appear at the bottom of the pages, include primarily extensions of remarks found in the text; I hope that they will make more lucid either what I have said or why I have said it.

I would like to thank the following people, who have in one way or another contributed significantly to either my work or my state of mind during the past several years of research and writing: Harrison C. Griffin, who persuaded me to write this book; Professor Benjamin I. Page of the University of Chicago, who read the manuscript and kept my biases from running amok; Joanne D. Daniels, who guided the work to fruition; Gail Goldey, whose skillful editing is an integral aspect of my prose; Ruth Burnham, who typed these many pages in highly professional style; Professor Clarence A. Berdahl, my long-time office mate, who bore my fits and starts with good humor and understanding; and, especially, my wife and children, who often wondered whether my labors would ever cease.

IRA H. CARMEN

contents

4

The Congress: Paper Tiger? 107

8

9

POWER & BALANCE
an introduction
to American
constitutional government

1

the american constitution: architectural design?

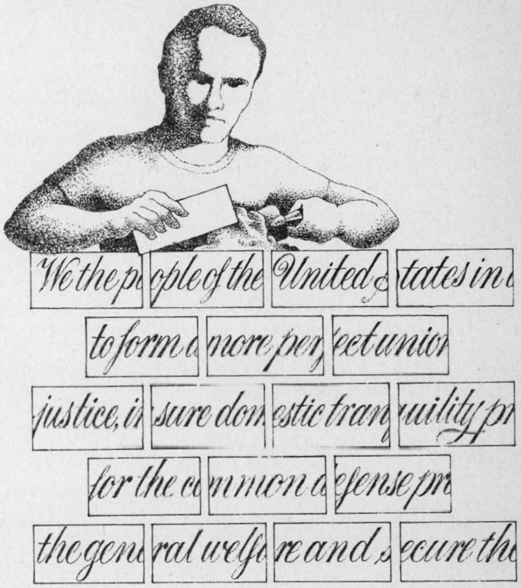

Our social landscape is dotted with groups and organizations: play groups, hobby groups, fraternities and sororities, vocational groups, political groups. If the group possesses any degree of formality, it almost always has a *constitution.* Look at the college campus. There are language clubs and sports clubs and Greek-letter clubs. Isn't it curious that virtually every one of these has a constitution stored away in somebody's file cabinet? And don't the Elks have a constitution? And the New York Stock Exchange? And the N.A.A.C.P.?

Obviously the best-known and most revered constitution in the land is the United States Constitution. Of course, some people don't know we have a Constitution. And many others would disagree as to what's *in* the Constitution. And still others would argue: "The Constitution is OK, but we don't live up to it." Nevertheless, the salient facts are these: we think our important group activities should be governed by constitutions; we think our country should be governed by a constitution; and we are devoted to the constitution we have taken for our own.

Of laws and constitutions

How can we explain this romance with constitutionalism? The answer requires a deep understanding of our history. Moreover, both the major purposes underlying our Constitution and the particular form that our Constitution displays developed out of experiences and ideas about the glories of government by constitution.

For generations, philosophers had talked of putting a rein on arbitrary rule by kings and princes.[1] But as Europe moved into the seventeenth century, only England had made substantial progress toward attaining this goal. Her feudal lords had long since forced King John to sign the famous Magna Carta (1215), an overt declaration of monarchical restraint. Furthermore, Parliament had become a viable political force, supplying a strong legislative antidote to the sovereign's potentially despotic acts. But the single most effective weapon that had been developed to meet tyranny was the *common law.* This was a set of legal rules laid down by judges who were responsible for arbitrating disputes among citizens. In dispensing their authority, the courts applied both generally accepted customs of proper conduct and good, old-fashioned standards of "reasonable" behavior. As time went by, an elaborate structure of precedent piled on precedent slowly evolved, and the common law came to be known as virtually the "rights of Englishmen." Of course, this entire baggage of liberties and duties was brought across the Atlantic by the colonists and became incorporated in their new governmental structures.

Think of what the common law must have meant to these people, the confidence they must have felt that their legal rights and obligations embraced the virtues of *certainty, uniformity,* and *predictability.* The law was certain because it was a known quantity, not something that changed with the mood of the most powerful; the law was uniform because it applied to everyone on an equal basis; and the law was predictable because it served as a road map, enabling people to chart their future plans with knowledge of what was permissible. No wonder these rules symbolized the entire tradition of struggle against oppression.

But a constitution is *more* than law. It is special law; it is *higher* law. A constitution is law that can be changed only by adopting some unusual procedure; thus, to *amend* the constitution of the local chamber of commerce or trade union chapter might require a two-thirds vote of eligible members. How did the adoration of law, then, lead to the adoration of *constitutional* law?

If this process could somehow be ascribed to the doings of one person—an artificial explanation, by definition—he would be Sir Edward Coke (1552–1634), a leading English judge during the early colonial period. What Coke did was to articulate and propagandize notions of law and politics that had been fermenting for several centuries. The common law, he argued, was *superior* to the will of Parliament or the will of the king. The common law was rooted in Magna Carta, a visible, tangible document attesting to an unbreakable contractual obligation between monarch and subjects. This parchment rendered certain liberties and freedoms impregnable to governmental assault. So the entire fabric of the common law constituted a justice and an equity inherent in English citizenship. Clearly, the intellectual roots of our commitment to the written constitution as a political necessity were planted here.

However, the germinal stage of this romance had its intensely practical aspects, too. Without question, the earliest American governmental forms gave the eventual acceptance of constitutionalism a healthy boost. Most of the colonies, such as Virginia and the Massachusetts Bay community, were owned by private trading companies interested in reaping a financial harvest. They had gone to the king and obtained charters giving them rights of exploitation. When faced with the troublesome task of setting up political institutions in the New World (that is, of establishing "constitutions"), these businessmen merely employed the familiar organizational patterns they had devised to run their own companies. Each colony was to have a governor and a lawmaking council. Eventually, in order to attract settlers, colonial assemblies were provided for; these might be likened to the stockholders' meetings used by today's corporations.

After the trading companies went bankrupt, the king assumed control but made few noteworthy changes. However, the authority to appoint colonial executive officers did revert to him, and much of the pre-Revolutionary War strife between mother country and overseas communities was essentially a struggle for power between royal governors and colonial assemblies. The hard-won prerogatives these popularly chosen representatives wielded came to be perceived by their constituents as "constitutional rights." Moreover, the political structures used in the *royal colonies* also served as a model for the *proprietary colonies.* Here the king simply handed over a parcel of land to some favorite, such as William Penn. But the governing charters (contracts?) required the fiefholders to institute political schemes along the lines of those in lands where the monarch held sway. Finally, we have the *charter colonies,* which were established without the king's permission in Plymouth, Rhode Island, and Connecticut. The first public acts authorized in these communities took the form of contractual agreements ordaining government *by the consent of the governed.* In Connecticut, an elaborate, full-blown constitution was actually drafted. Don't the notions of separation of powers, bicameralism, written constitutionalism, government by contract, and popular sovereignty lurk throughout these various arrangements?

A second English philosopher whose writings had a profound impact on the establishment of constitutional government was John Locke (1634–1704). His works were published about eighty years after the founding of the colonies and about eighty years prior to the American Revolution. Essentially, Locke's aim was to justify the Glorious Revolution, in which the English staged a successful insurrection against King James II. This autocrat was one of the last monarchs to advocate the absolute supremacy of royal commands; he argued, in fact, that his power stemmed from divine origins. Locke maintained that humans possess *natural rights*—that is, rights acquired at birth. Furthermore, while individuals are essentially good and therefore are bound to honor the rights of others, they possess complete freedom to decide when their liberties are being compromised and when they may resist their fellow citizens through the use of force. This "state of nature" endures until and unless members of the "community" sit down and draft a contract establishing some mutually acceptable governmental scheme. Locke called such an agreement a "social compact."

Many colonial thinkers found this emphasis on individual liberties appealing, and they likened the Mayflower Compact and the first constitution of Connecticut to "social compacts." In Locke's "best state," an elected legislature wields sovereign power. Yet not even a majority in this body could exercise arbitrary power. In other words, some rights occupy such lofty status that they are immune from state regulation; after all, the social compact creates only the right to govern, *not the right to tyrannize.* If a legislature sought to compromise these freedoms, it could be thrown out either by ballot or, when necessary, by force. The "right of revolution," then, is clearly part of Locke's approach, and the angry colonists of later years could hardly overlook it. Note that Locke's "natural rights" represent the functional equivalent of a constitutional "higher law," which ordinary statutes must not abridge; but, as in the state of nature, one person's "freedoms" might be another person's "duties," so the "right of revolution" is strictly a subjective assessment.

There was a final link in the chain that helped establish our early passion for constitutionalism: the colonists were people of strong religious conviction. Some were Puritan-type Calvinists, who believed the charters given their forebears to be in the nature of sacred covenants. (Remember: It took centuries to slay the "divine right of kings" doctrine.) Others saw social compacts as moral agreements, because Protestant sects generally were thought to arise via a kind of contractual consensus among fellow believers. This was a theme Martin Luther had emphasized in his teachings. Still others, including several of the leading figures of the Revolutionary period, were Deists, who believed that human behavior ought to be forged in the pattern of certain immutable moral standards. An enlightened citizenry should use its God-given rational faculties to discern these rules, whether they resided in Coke's common law or in Locke's natural rights. In sum, the important point is this: to most colonists, there was a "higher" constitutional law, and this law possessed theological meaning as well.[2]

As revolution approached, these diffuse ideas began to coalesce. The belief grew in the necessity of a constitution which would provide a list of fundamental rules constraining the powers of the state. (England, the argument ran, did not possess a constitution because no limits were placed on Parliament's authority.) Moreover, in order to survive the winds of governmental caprice, a constitution should be armed with a special source of power. That source would be official citizen ratification of the fundamental law.

What results did this line of thinking spawn when the moment of truth arrived? Because Parliament's supremacy had become conventional wisdom in England, colonial leaders were obliged to contend that this body had no right whatsoever to levy stamp acts and tea taxes overseas. In their eyes, since the representatives they elected sat in the colonies and not in Parliament, the only bond between the two quite different political entities was the monarchy itself. The Declaration of Independence points up these distinctions. It comprises a set of grievances lodged against the king and considers him morally and legally responsible for the impending split. Parliament is ignored entirely.

So our infatuation with constitutions lies at the very root of our politics; it is inherent in our understanding of personal rights; and it bears witness to our belief in a moral law transcending human opinion.

The Articles of Confederation

Important though legal rules may be to an understanding of government, there are two political concepts that possess far greater scope than law, that underlie *every* country of long standing, no matter how democratic or despotic it may be. To understand the process by which this land became a constitutional republic, we must first understand how these two elements combined to make us a nation.

The first of these notions is *sovereignty,* a term generally defined as "supreme temporal power."[3] In every political community, some person, group, or organization has authority to make the big, far-reaching political decisions. Certain countries feature a sovereign power *whose actions are bound by law;* others feature a sovereign power *whose actions are bound by no law.* Louis XIV and Stalin were not constrained by any rules that we would label "law." From their decisions no appeal was permissible.

The second basic element in nation-statehood is *community consciousness*—implicit bonds of loyalty holding a people together. Japan, Norway, Algeria, and Bulgaria owe their political integrity not only to the fact that they possess a sovereign authority commanding obedience but also to the fact that the people consider themselves Japanese, Norwegians, Algerians, and Bulgarians. The same goes for any other country.

Unpredictable consequences—sometimes most unfortunate ones—usually arise when a political grouping possesses one but not the other of these two qualities. The Roman Empire, for instance, attempted to exert its sovereignty on many neighboring peoples, with considerable short-term success. State citizenship was even accorded to various conquered nations. But, in the end, the device failed. The Romans were never really able to build a worldwide "Roman consciousness," and this failure was one reason the Caesars eventually fell by the wayside. It was this feeling of "oneness" shared by Jews around the world that led to the establishment of Israel after centuries of sovereign incapacity.

But what about the independent colonies of post-Revolutionary War America? Did not Cornwallis's surrender at Yorktown lead to the creation of one autonomous sovereign community? It certainly fostered an aura of patriotism; yet the evidence is mostly to the contrary. This can be seen plainly when we review the growth and development of American political institutions prior to the ratification of the Constitution itself.

Crucial in evaluating the "state of American union" at that time is an understanding of the powers and duties of the Continental Congresses. After George III disbanded the elected assemblies in a fit of pique, the leading political figures throughout the colonies organized Committees of Correspondence. These informal gatherings virtually governed their particular jurisdictions until the war was won, and it was the committees that had sent delegates to the First Continental Congress, in 1774. This body passed a number of resolutions calling for the boycott of English merchandise; its members also signed a document called The Association, designed to put these declarations into practice. But nothing this Congress did could have been implemented with vigor unless the local committees executed the dirty work. Indeed, such implementation was approved specifically by The Association. The Second Continental Congress, however, exercised considerable authority during the war. It appointed Washington to his post of commanding general, conducted negotiations with foreign powers, and printed money. Still, all this was based on revolutionary fiat; the Second Congress was given no lawmaking or law-enforcement tasks by anyone.

As political orchestrator of insurrectionist strategies, the Congress assigned to Thomas Jefferson the job of writing a Declaration of Independence, the opening paragraph of which is familiar prose:

> We hold these Truths to be self-evident, that all Men are created equal, that they are endowed by their Creator with certain unalienable Rights, that among these are Life, Liberty and the Pursuit of Happiness.—That to secure these rights, Governments are instituted among Men, deriving their just powers from the consent of the governed,—That whenever any Form of Government becomes destructive of these ends, it is the Right of the People to alter or to abolish it, and to institute new Government, laying its foundation on such principles and organizing its Powers in such form, as to them shall seem most likely to effect their Safety and Happiness.

Notice that John Locke's ideas—social compact theory, inherent prerogatives of revolution, natural rights colored by theological gloss—are all present and accounted for. Seen in the light of the power struggle then being waged—rather than as the "sacred text" it has since become—Jefferson's rhetoric should be understood and judged as propaganda. The Declaration was an inspiring defense of individual freedom written in the heat of armed insurrection, but it certainly did not represent the thinking of all important and influential activists once the smoke had cleared and a national polity had to be fashioned. Furthermore, it most certainly did not dispel the oppressive yoke of British authority, which could be done only on the battlefield. Even more important, it contained no suggestion of a *national* American sovereignty; it spoke only of the *colonies* that were and of the independent *states* that would be. In fact, once the individual colonies had assumed the role of states and drafted their own constitutions, they took over responsibility for appointing delegates to the Congress and, without exception, forced these representatives to follow specific instructions upon pain of recall.

That the states held sovereign power is demonstrated graphically by the Articles of Confederation, the first attempt by Americans to construct a permanent constitutional apparatus. It was written by the Continental Congress, whose demise was inevitable after British capitulation. The key word is "confederation," meaning a loose alliance in which each individual entity retains ultimate control over its own destiny. And the wording of the Articles themselves makes clear where authority resided. Article II says with finality: "Each state retains its sovereignty, freedom and independence." Article III calls the entire document a "league of friendship," which the states had entered into for their common protection against alien aggressors.

The Articles' provisions must be inspected with care. First of all, there was no president. After long and bitter experience with royalty, the prevailing opinion was to make it impossible for any tyrant to find a foothold here. Nor was there a national judicial system. For anyone who wanted to press a legal claim, it would be necessary to use the state court machinery. Not surprisingly, then, personal liberties were guaranteed by the state constitutions alone; in effect, it was these charters that, for the moment at least, had become the repositories of the "higher law" principle so dear to early Americans. The only governmental institution created by the Articles was a one-chamber Congress. Since Parliament had also been an adversary, this legislative body was given minimal functions. Nevertheless, it did hold a portion of what we label today "sovereign power." Congress could make war, conduct foreign affairs, see to defense needs, draft treaties, and regulate the currency. But it possessed no *implied* power; that is, if authority were not delegated in so many words, then it could not be assumed. Nor was this assembly permitted to levy taxes; its only hope for funding lay in *asking* the states to chip in. Finally, congressmen voted by state delegation ("one state—one vote"); an extraordinary majority of *nine* states (out of thirteen) was required to pass any law; and nothing in the Articles could be changed unless Congress itself proposed amendments and *every* state concurred. Indeed, the document lacked binding force until unanimous affirmation by the state legislatures had carried. It was four years before the last holdout, Maryland, finally acquiesced.

The substance of this first constitution (perhaps "treaty" is the more accurate word) raises one resonant question about the political state of mind then current among Americans: Why did they bother? If the states were hell-bent on retaining their preserves of power free from constraint, then why provide for confederation at all? One reason, of course, was fear. Standing alone, they could be plucked like ripe apples by some European despot. The Articles at least laid a foundation for security in the international arena. But this explanation is insufficient. The root cause was *community consciousness.* In fact, a country had already come into being, but the people and their leaders did not really understand the political ramifications of what had happened. The rudiment of this new nationhood was a feeling of empathy, a mutual understanding that had begun more than a century earlier, when the colonies were first settled. This feeling of kinship had as its basis the long voyage across the ocean, the taming of a primeval hinterland far removed from the mother country, the building up of local cultures, incessant warfare with Indian tribes, and, finally, the struggle against an English imperialism perceived as a gross violation of natural- and common-law tradition.[4] The Articles of Confederation reflected the first glimmer of comprehension that the destinies of the revolutionaries were commingled. But the political sophistication needed to forge a sovereign America had not yet materialized.

It did not take long for most to see the glaring weaknesses in this first, ill-fated effort. Under the Articles, the Congress was absolutely powerless to maintain financial solvency. The states were derelict in handing over monies to the national regime, so funds had to be borrowed. Later on, interest payments accruing from these debts began to pile up. In the area of trade relations, states discriminated against one another by passing tariffs favorable to their own producers.[a] Of course, if the Congress had possessed the power to enact laws regulating commerce among the many states, uniform rules could have been adopted. But the national legislature had been given no authority here; hence, trade barriers proliferated, and each state became more and more an economic island.

Some prominent men of affairs saw even more substantial reasons for recasting the Articles. Military necessities weighed heavily in their thinking. Both the English and the Spanish hovered ominously on the states' doorsteps, and neither country harbored any affection for the embryonic confederation. Abroad, Congress was a laughingstock because European leaders thought treaties could not be carried out in the face of state resistance. With no army or navy or political autonomy to speak of, the new nation's word lacked impact, and an open invitation to imperialism was everything but engraved.[5] Domestic factors, as well as foreign relations, also were crucial. Deep divisions among the revolutionaries, obscured by the fight against England, resurfaced. Some rhapsodized over the egalitarian rhetoric of the Jeffersons and the Tom Paines. Others—"conservatives"[6]—tended to perceive the American Revolution as a *constitutional* remedy invoked against a king who had emasculated their rights under *English* law, and they deemphasized the *natural-rights* elements of revolutionary philosophy. To them, the French Revolution was a kind of bestiality: Robespierre and Bastille-storming epitomized *unconstitutional* action because the social fabric of the entire community was rent asunder.[7] These people believed that the Articles failed to provide sufficient protection for property rights. They were men of means: mercantilists, landowners, creditors. The Congress owed them money and couldn't pay its debts. Inexpensive foreign merchandise was being imported, and Congress had no authority to erect tariff barriers. These people felt that the state legislatures were meddling with contractual obligations by passing laws making it more difficult to collect payments from debtors. All this reached a climax with Shays's Rebellion. A group of poor Massachusetts farmers, unable to meet pressing financial commitments, marched to the local courthouse—pitchforks in hand—and refused to allow

[a] If, say, Pennsylvania farmers couldn't compete on equal terms with out-of-state farmers, then the Pennsylvania legislature would either be obligated to place a tax on imports or face boiling-mad constituents in the next election. And if Pennsylvania could pass a tariff on commodities shipped from New York and New Jersey, so could those states retaliate against Pennsylvania merchandise.

foreclosures on their mortgages. This outburst was quickly scotched; yet, to those who saw private-property ownership as a cornerstone of individual liberty, such lawlessness bordered on anarchy.

Nor was Jeffersonian theory insensitive to these constitutional travails. The Declaration of Independence postulates negative and positive aspects of revolution: "the Right of the People to alter or to abolish" tyrannical government *and* the right "to institute new Government." Conditions under the Articles had forced the United States to confront directly Jefferson's second stage. The time had come to tighten the bonds of union—to complete the Revolution of 1776.

The Constitution: who?

The document we have come to call *the* Constitution was written in Philadelphia in 1787. But before we consider what was done there and why, the stage must be set. Who were present at the creation, and how did they obtain credentials for admission?

The state legislatures got the ball rolling by appointing delegates to meet in convention and overhaul the malfunctioning Articles. But Congress was worried. Perhaps this assembly might undermine the very Confederation itself and, along the way, create competing centers of national authority. The lawmakers deemed it prudent to cooperate—but only with considerable circumspection. They requested the states to send representatives for the sole and express purpose of improving the Articles, and they reminded the legislatures that any amendments adopted would not take effect unless first approved by the Congress and then ratified by *all* thirteen participants.

What kinds of men were selected? It is important to note, first, who was *not* there. Samuel Adams and Tom Paine were absent. So also were John Hancock and Thomas Jefferson. In fact, only eight of the fifty-six notables who had signed the Declaration of Independence attended. It is true that some of these worthies had conflicting obligations, while others (Patrick Henry, for example) declined to participate because they feared that the Convention would greatly expand the scope of national power. Still, there is little doubt the states themselves wanted renewal; thus, they chose people ready and willing to vote for change. The "radicals," who had stood in the forefront of rebellion and succeeded, had tried their hand at constitution-writing and failed. So the emerging consensus looked to new talents and new heads. Now the message was clear: throwing off the mantle of repression required certain skills, but forging a viable national *political* apparatus was a completely different ball game.

The standard composite of the Founding Fathers is that they were wealthy; they were aristocrats, born to positions of power and social grace; they were landowners, traders, moneylenders, and lawyers; they possessed intimate knowledge of such theorists as Locke, Montesquieu, and the Greeks. There is some truth to the characterization, of course. John Q. Public was not invited to take part in these proceedings. He was working on the farm or toiling in the shop trying to make ends meet. But the profile tends to blur significant individual differences. It turns the Framers into a homogeneous group of provincials who were simply doing their duty. Moreover, the description treats them as Bicentennial curiosities, "antidemocrats" who were doing then what only popular forces could do today.

By way of contrast, I want to point up the diversity of talent, experience, background, political outlook, and *convention role* that distinguish a few selected participants and their impact on the final result:

George Washington. "Gentleman farmer" and landowner, Washington was skilled in surveying, a craft that sent him into the Virginia hinterlands and fired his interest in westward expansion. Extraordinarily courageous in combat, he came close to death on numerous occasions. Washington was a stern disciplinarian, who, it is alleged, flogged disobedient soldiers at Valley Forge. In spite of being a mediocre military strategist, he turned brigades of civilians into an army that held out for four years until Yorktown. The Convention took on real authority when, as our first national hero, he agreed to participate. Elected presiding officer, Washington, who had little training or interest in philosophical rhetoric, joined in debate only once, but behind the scenes he worked hard for a sovereign regime that could withstand the pressures of international strife.

Benjamin Franklin. As a scientist, he made important discoveries in the field of electricity. He was also a self-made man who preached "pseudo-Calvinist" homilies in his *Autobiography,* instructing readers how to get ahead in the world. As a diplomat, Franklin was considered the "first civilized American" by the French. At the age of eighty-one, he came to Philadelphia with a reputation second only to Washington's. His ideas were too democratic to be taken seriously, but he played a key role in compromising "large-state" and "small-state" differences. He moved, successfully, that the delegates approve unanimously their final draft so as to emphasize agreement.

Edmund Randolph. This lawyer, experienced in convention politics because he played a leading role in drafting his state's constitution, was governor of Virginia and a strong advocate of "large-state" interests. Yet he refused to sign the Constitution as written because it did not provide enough protection for individual and states' rights. Ideologically elusive, with a penchant for the middle-of-the-road, he reversed field and supported ratification at home.

Gouverneur Morris. In the parlance of present-day politics, he was a reactionary on economic and social issues but a liberal with regard to personal rights. He advocated a strong central government controlled by the rich, and believed there should be a president who would serve for life and who would appoint senators to hold life tenure also. Morris led the fight to include a provision guaranteeing religious toleration in the first New York Constitution, favored the immediate abolition of slavery, got the presidential veto approved, and helped to defeat legislative selection of the chief executive. A great stylist, he wrote the Constitution as we now know it.

Alexander Hamilton. The illegitimate son of socially prominent parents, Hamilton married well in an attempt to achieve the wealth and influence he felt he deserved. He was a financier, extremely well read on questions of economics and business. As Washington's aide-de-camp, Hamilton served with valor during wartime, while as a writer of pamphlets he drummed up early support for the Revolution. He was infatuated with British government; hence he favored a unitary system in which the central administration would have sovereignty and states would be appendages. His approach had little impact, as the states would never have approved such drastic measures. He was rarely present at the Convention and was constantly outvoted by his New York colleagues when he did appear.

James Madison. Like Washington, his forebears owned large Virginia estates; like Randolph, he played a key role in writing the Virginia Constitution. He was a profound student of ancient and modern governmental systems and was probably unique in that he came to the Convention with a clearly defined blueprint of what the new constitution should encompass. Madison saw confederations as inherently fallible because national government must be able to coerce people. Realizing that a unitary arrangement was "inexpedient," he advocated federalism as the only "middle ground," an alternative the Convention ultimately adopted. He was also an implacable foe of slavery. At the Convention, he spoke frequently and kept the most complete firsthand account we have of what transpired.

The Constitution: what?

The first decision made by the delegates was undoubtedly their most important. They voted to *throw out* the Articles and start from scratch, to draft an entirely new constitution, and to inter forever the notion of state sovereignty.[8]

The Framers also decided early on to conduct their meetings behind closed doors. Was this decision democratic? It depends on how one defines "democracy." The delegates were obviously not committed to popular participation or observation, but they were committed to representative government whose basics would require popular *ratification,* and this they achieved. Closing their meetings to the public allowed them the flexibility to advance extreme positions, push hard for various reforms, and, finally, adopt practical approaches, free from second-guessing and intimidation.

With the meeting underway, Virginia—under Madison's influence—came to the front by offering a thoroughgoing plan of reform. The Virginia Plan, a natural outgrowth of the decision to scrap the Articles, proposed to set up three independent branches of government—legislative, executive, judicial—each to be supreme in its particular area of competence. The key idea was to eliminate the political improprieties of confederation by shackling the "individual independence of the states." But to do so, the Plan had to cope with fear of consolidation. One branch of the national government might be acceptable so long as its powers were limited; but if a central *coercive* apparatus with real force were to be established, then political power had better be divided, else tyranny might soon follow.

The salient points in this proposal should be understood. Congress was to be bicameral: the dominant branch would be elected at the ballot box and would serve as agents of the "people" (that is, the more densely populated states were allotted greater representation); the other chamber would simply be chosen by the first body. Powers held by this new two-headed legislative assembly were awesome. Naturally, it possessed authority already granted under the Articles, but it could also accomplish anything the states were "incompetent" to do. Furthermore, the lawmakers would appoint the president, and they could disallow all *state* statutes that they felt trespassed upon areas of national responsibility. The only check on this Congress was a veto given to the new chief executive and a new Supreme Court. In evaluating the Virginia Plan, we cannot ignore one intensely practical consideration: the populous, large states, *such as Virginia,* would control the Congress and, for all practical purposes, the new ship of state.

The "small" states (the more sparsely settled ones, that is) were not prepared to be placed on a sacrificial altar, however. Rising nationalism had not yet slain the idea of state equality. Hence, they rallied around a counterproposal, the so-called New Jersey Plan. Under this scheme, Congress was to perform its traditional legislative tasks along with the powers to tax and to control interstate commerce. A plural executive (*two* presidents) was to be established, with Congress to appoint both of them. Obviously, the small-state delegations were still traumatized by the last effective chief of state they had encountered, King George III. A Supreme Court was provided for, to enforce federal laws and treaties. Of singular importance, all enactments ordained by national authority were to be considered the *supreme law of the land,* and no state provisions could supplant or alter them.

The New Jersey Plan is generally perceived as a warmed-over Articles of Confederation. Congress would continue to vote by state delegations, and each of the thirteen blocs would retain its lone voice in balloting. Therefore, the plan is considered indicative of a deep-seated cleavage between the large and small states. But there is evidence on the other side. The New Jersey proposal made the Constitution and federal law enacted under its provisions superior to state law. Also, the small states envisioned a national administration acting directly on individuals, for the new regime could levy taxes on citizens and could rely on a responsive independent judicial system to enforce its directives.[9]

The crucial bone of contention obviously was: What would be the makeup and constituency of Congress? Virginia's strongest argument emphasized a need to bury state sovereignty—to assure against congressional impotence—while New Jersey's trump card was that ratification would be impossible should the large states bulldoze the Convention. The outcome was the creation of a select committee to effect some accommodation. The delegates did not designate the intellectual Madison or the brilliant legal mind James Wilson to sit on this group; they leaned toward practical politicians who could be counted on to minimize ideological dogma.[b] The end product of their labors was the "Great Compromise," which barely carried the entire assembly—five states favorable to four states opposed.

There would be a bicameral Congress consisting of a House of Representatives and a Senate; House members would be chosen by and would represent voters (Virginia Plan); two senators would be selected by and would represent each state (New Jersey Plan); all taxation measures would have to originate in the "people-oriented" House (nightmares of tea and sugar duties continued to haunt the Framers); no state could be deprived of its equal representation in the Senate *even by constitutional amendment* unless the state concurred (New Jersey Plan, with a vengeance); but members of the Senate would vote as individuals, not by state delegations (a sop to critics of state autonomy). Madison has been called "Father of the Constitution," but he fought this proposal to the end. The man who wanted a strong and vigorous central government could not reconcile himself to a Senate that perpetuated the concept of state parity in the *national* political arena, what we call today "states' rights."

A second important compromise, necessitated by the large state-small state split, concerned the selection of a President. Madison and his allies saw the executive as responsible to Congress; others wanted the states to play a key role in the process. The result was another blue-ribbon committee, more haggling by inventive and prudent spokesmen, and, finally, an agreement calling for a special agency—the Electoral College—to make the choice. Again, each important faction in the dialogue got a piece of the action. Members named to the College would be chosen in any way a state's legislature desired (small-state preference); if a state had a larger population, it would have greater representation (large-state preference); College participants would vote as individuals (large-state preference); should no person receive a majority of the votes, the House of Representatives would decide (large-state preference), but voting in the House for this purpose would be by *states*, each with one ballot (small-state preference).

We may note one last and rather complicated compromise—this time arising out of a Northern states-Southern states dispute. Naturally, slavery was the fly in the ointment. The question was not whether involuntary servitude should be kept or abolished. What later became a great moral issue was, in 1787, simply a lever for attempting to maximize rights and minimize duties. The South wanted slaves classified as people for purposes of apportioning seats in the House of Representatives, but it did not want slaves counted as people for taxation purposes. The North, of course, wanted the reverse. (In those days, it was thought that Congress would raise monies mostly through levies that could

[b] The notion that the Framers were a homogeneous group of pragmatists committed to democratic consensus under a nationalist umbrella is defended vigorously in John P. Roche, "The Founding Fathers: A Reform Caucus in Action," *The American Political Science Review* 55 (1961), pp. 799-816. But I must state a reservation. Somehow, the Founders emerge from this piece as Franklin Roosevelts, Hubert Humphreys, and Lyndon Johnsons clothed in garters, knickers, and lace. Again and again, I will stress an *a priori* which I suspect is too often neglected in the literature: 1787 is not 1977.

be apportioned among the states according to their population. If slaves were *people,* a Southern state's tax would be considerably higher.) Somehow the magic figure turned out to be 60 percent. That is, three-fifths of the slaves in each state would count for both taxes imposed and House members allotted.

A corollary issue arose over foreign commerce. Everyone realized Congress must be able to regulate commercial relations with other nations, but the Southern states had twin fears: (1) that statutes might be passed inhibiting the importation of slaves and (2) that treaties might be enacted lessening the South's status as chief exporter and enhancing the North's position as chief importer. But the Founders' fertile imagination was more than equal to this squabble. Congress was specifically prohibited from tampering with the international traffic in slaves until 1807, and the ratification of treaties was toughened by requiring two-thirds approval in the state-dominated Senate.

The Framers made one final decision that cannot be bypassed here. Very early in their debates and almost without dissent, they committed themselves to revising the process through which the Articles of Confederation could be changed. Recall the binding constitutional constraint: unanimous approval by the states was necessary. This meant that intransigent "Rogues Island" could veto the entire operation. The delegates faced this obvious peril by derailing it. The new Constitution, they said, would be considered officially endorsed if *three-fourths* of the states went along, and ratification proceedings were to be held in special conventions called only for this purpose. The latter condition, of course, was designed to circumvent the thirteen legislatures, bastions of state-sovereignty sentiment.

Such lawless defiance of unequivocal procedural norms did not create much hue and cry, even among opponents of ratification. To many prominent Americans the Articles seemed only a quasi-constitution anyway. But more important, the country was going downhill, and a constitutional face-lifting was mandatory.[10] The fact is that the American Revolution had not yet been completed. Now the sovereign apparatus needed to consummate nationhood was being put into place.

The Constitution: why?

Anyone who attempts to identify and explain the motivations of the Philadelphia assembly is asking for trouble. Personality differences, divergent state interests, and common adherence to strong national political institutions were salient factors, as we have seen. There were other forces at work as well.[11] Single-variable explanations of the Founders' intentions are difficult to defend. But several have been formulated, and two of the more notable deserve mention.

Easily the most frequently cited theory was framed by Charles Beard.[12] His argument is neat and clean: the Constitution was the result of a *coup d'état* staged by the conventioneers, who were interested only in creating a governmental scheme responsive to their concerns, which were chiefly economic. The states had to be shackled, or the property rights of the wealthy, privileged classes would be diluted. Hence, the Articles had to be scrapped and "law and order" in the financial sphere maintained.

To support his case, Beard examined various provisions in the charter which, he claimed, were inserted to quash grassroots movements favorable to the broad mass of people. For instance, the Constitution forbids the states to make legal tender anything but gold and silver. Well, Beard said, these were precious metals. The idea behind this clause was to prevent states from debasing the value of financial reserves held by the wealthy Framers. The Constitution also prohibits states from impairing the obligation of contracts. Aha! The typical delegate was a creditor, not a debtor, Beard observed. And most politically volatile contracts were business arrangements between lender and borrower. If the states interfered with contracts, they would probably do so to help out the debtor class. Such relief could not be allowed. Finally, the Constitution held the new regime liable for all financial obligations assumed by Congress under the Articles. For Beard, this was salt on the wound. To whom did Congress owe this money? Why, in part, to rich Americans, the very ones rewriting the fundamental law.

It does not take much imagination to put Beard's theory into proper perspective. Naturally, he soft-pedaled the heterogeneity of the gathering from the standpoint not only of personal experience and philosophy but also of state affiliation and bias. He refused to wrestle with the central question of power and its impact on a group of nationalist-oriented pragmatists. Moreover, the same people who attended the Philadelphia meeting had been largely instrumental in formulating the first state constitutions; and, I reiterate, these people were selected by the very state legislatures that, supposedly, had forsaken any concern for stability and become revolutionary hotbeds. So the Convention was certainly no *putsch* organized by counterrevolutionaries. Those distinguished Americans absent from the Framers' ranks were not denied admittance because they were poor; rather, most were not selected because they lacked "feel" for constitution-building. Beard seemed to deplore a lack of popular participation; but, as a matter of fact, the representational scheme that was worked out for the House of Representatives was extraordinarily egalitarian by standards prevailing at that time. Furthermore, the constitutional provisions Beard emphasized can be defended as entirely consistent with the national interest. How could a sovereign political apparatus endure if each state were able to manipulate the worth of currency floated within its borders? And an auspicious beginning among the family of nations is hardly encouraged by repudiating one's debts at the outset.

A second oft-cited single-variable explanation of the Founders' motives is that they were thoughtful, intelligent men highly versed in Locke, Harrington, Montesquieu, and so on. The result was a document reflecting their dominant views. Evidence for this assertion is culled largely from *The Federalist,* a compilation of ninety-odd newspaper articles published in order to explain the Constitution and to advocate its ratification. Authorship was anonymous, but we now know that Madison and Hamilton wrote virtually all of them, and the articles they penned have even been authoritatively identified. If we scan these works, we find numerous references to the great philosophers. Obviously Madison and Hamilton were well acquainted with their doctrines, and certainly many of the other delegates did share that background.

However, this argument ignores reality in several ways. The papers themselves were propaganda tracts, of course, just as the Declaration of Independence was. They tried to show the Constitution in a favorable light; thus they drew on the best that had been thought and said, omitting the endless haggling and painful negotiation that actually transpired at the Convention. The importance of the papers stems from a tightness of reasoning and a depth of analysis rarely evidenced in dialogue among American political practitioners. Indeed, the "great philosophers" were almost never cited approvingly in Convention debates,[13] nor do their writings anywhere suggest anything remotely resembling the Virginia or New Jersey Plans. *The Federalist* probably paid extensive tribute to these theorists for two reasons: first, to rationalize the propriety of compromises made at the meetings, and, second, to buttress deeply held beliefs which the delegates generally shared with these thinkers about political life and the individual's relationship to the state.[14] But if one wants reasons why such notions as separation of powers, bicameralism, and the checks-and-balances scheme show up in the document, a more likely explanation is that these institutional arrangements were all political artifacts of the colonial experience. The Framers had firsthand knowledge of the strengths and weaknesses of these concepts and so they served as useful mechanisms for compromise.

Ratification[15]

The first step in obtaining support outside Convention halls was fraught with danger. Under the rules, all changes had to be forwarded to Congress for its endorsement. Considering the fact that the Founders were bent on abolishing the Articles and giving Congress itself a top-to-bottom face-lifting, chances must have seemed marginal at best. But Madison, who assumed control of post-Philadelphia strategy, structured the choice as an "either-or" dilemma: either take our Constitution or the country perishes! With the prestige of men like Washington behind this effort, Congress had to compromise. The legislators refused to vote on the charter, but they did send it along to the state conventions for their consideration.

It would be dramatic to characterize the nation as poised on the brink of a great debate. But Americans have a long tradition of political apathy, and things were no different then. More than 80 percent of adult white males were eligible to select convention delegates; however, only a small minority did so. The average citizen did *not* see the nation as imperiled by either anarchy or despotism. This being the case, the choice between the old and the new must have seemed murky indeed.

But while electoral apathy is an American trademark, so also is electoral invective. The Constitution was painted by some opponents as an aristocratic artifice endangering the liberties of the people. The "Antifederalists," on the other hand, were often depicted as shortsighted localists, having little conception of national welfare. And each faction impugned the other's patriotism. Critics of reform were able to score one telling point, however. Why was there no bill of rights in the Constitution? James Wilson and Alexander Hamilton struck back boldly. If a list had been prepared, they argued, something would have been left out; it was impossible to itemize everything. Besides, the charter spelled out all the rule-making authority given to Congress and the President. They couldn't abridge civil liberties because they possessed no such power. But Patrick Henry persisted. If the state constitutions contained guarantees of individual freedom, why didn't the national Constitution? On this issue an accommodation had to be reached, or ratification would likely have failed. The campaign managers for adoption agreed to support a roster of individual rights in the form of amendments to the document if the other side would first swallow the Constitution as written. This concession probably won over many fence-straddlers, though it proved unacceptable to hard-line opposition.

Advocates of ratification invoked this same strategy on other occasions also. Whenever critics scored a sharp point in debate, the constitutionalists would more than likely retort: "Your argument may have merit, but let's wait awhile; if experience demonstrates that we have blundered, all that need be done is to amend the charter." This approach bore fruit, because everyone realized a central weakness in the Articles was their virtual unamendability.

The smaller states generally were placated by their parity in the Senate and tended to ratify quickly. Battle lines formed in the larger states, however, and the Federalists were hard pressed all the way. Ultimately, they prevailed 187–168 in Massachusetts and squeaked through by even narrower tallies in Virginia and New York. Time had passed the Articles by, and now the propitious moment for burial had arrived.

The Constitution as mood music

There are as many ways to read the Constitution as there are to read a book. One is to read it word for word, ascribing meanings to each phrase. The layperson might ask: "What is a 'bill of attainder'?" "What is 'commerce among the states'?" This tool of analysis is clearly indispensable, and I will use it extensively. A second approach emphasizes rules. A constitution is a special kind of law, because it represents the framework for governmental decision-making; constitutions contain basic rules spelling out who can do what and when. Clearly, *the* Constitution delineates certain explicit rights, obligations, and procedures, and it is important to master such rules.

But there is a third way to translate the Constitution, perhaps the most rewarding, certainly the most difficult to manipulate. We now realize this document was written by certain kinds of people, living at a particular period in history, who had to wrestle with clear-cut, practical problems and who could not afford to be doctrinaire about solutions. Compromises were made, as we know. But scholars agree that the final product is not a series of random bargains bearing no relation to one another. Rather, the Constitution expresses the

Framers' commitment to deep, fundamental norms, *implicit* in the rules they wrote out. In other words, the charter communicates certain precepts that the Founders assumed valid, and these themes suffuse their handiwork. Such themes tend to create a mood or backdrop as important as the words and rules themselves. Somehow, they must be explicated, or the Constitution will be stripped of its larger philosophical heritage. The following list attempts to capture the essence of these moods:

1. *The "higher-law" theme.* The Framers accepted, as had their forebears, the existence of immutable laws that governed both relations among people and relations between people and government. Among these laws were the "social compact" idea, a belief in the individual's innate rationality, and an acceptance of fundamental personal rights. Constitutions were the most respected of legal codes; therefore, a viable, adhesive, truly national constitution must mirror these basic political and *ethical* truths. Indeed, such rules were perceived as the very essence of that intangible communal integrity binding us together as a people.[16] Our government is, in truth, one of laws and not of men. The supreme law is the Constitution itself.

2. *Popular sovereignty.* The "people" had written the Articles of Confederation, it was believed, but that effort was no longer adequate. The Preamble to the Constitution says: "In Order to form a *more* perfect Union," "*We the People*" have decided to draft a better statement of our ties with government (italics mine). So the Framers saw themselves as representing the entire social group. There existed, then, a kind of trust, or fiduciary, relationship, which held the Philadelphia assembly within the bounds of propriety. The delegates could make sweeping changes but only to effectuate what they honestly saw as the general welfare. Ultimate power to rework constitutions resides in the popular will.[17]

3. *Politics through peaceful change.* But does not the Constitution's "rule of law" clash with popular sovereignty? Suppose the state passed legislation the "people" would not support? Does not popular sovereignty even legitimize revolution as the final remedy? The Constitution is not an instrument for insurrection; indeed, what constitution is? The document looks to popular control of the political order through freedom of speech, the ballot box, and the amending process. So there is a dynamic tension between the supremacy of constitutional institutions and public opinion; that is, all systems are "go" when these two forces are constantly checking each other. But Jefferson's idea of frequent revolutions being the natural manure of liberty is no longer operational, unless methods for peaceful change are choked off.[18]

4. *National supremacy.* The United States could not survive, it was decided, unless institutions of national authority were established and state sovereignty dismantled. This new governmental layer would be supreme in its area of competence.

5. *Statecraft as the "art of the possible."* The Constitution presupposes a certain pessimism about human nature. People possess basic rights, to be sure, but they are capable of great excess in the name of self-interest. Once more, a kind of paradox stands out. The document may contain a strong ethical element; however, it was surely not meant to be an experiment in utopian deliverance. Individual freedom and national survival, the Founders believed, must be predicated on restraint.[19] (For those who know some political theory, the Constitution could have been written by a St. Thomas Aquinas but never by a St. Augustine.)

6. *Separation of powers.* Lord Acton coined the well-known aphorism: "Power tends to corrupt; absolute power corrupts absolutely." The Constitution is shot through with Actonitis. The phrase "separation of powers" is never used, but the intent of the assembly cannot be doubted. Legislative, executive, and judicial authority is demarcated at the federal level, and either the states or the people are to retain all powers not given to national bodies. Some have gone so far as to say that there are nice, tidy lines separating these various entities. But this theory violates the realistic, pragmatic tenor of the document. The guiding criterion might better be characterized by these two comments: First, "Where the whole power of one department is exercised by the same hands which possess the whole power of another department, the fundamental principles of a free constitution are subverted."[20] Second, "The great ordinances of the Constitution do not establish and divide fields of black and white. Even the more specific of them are found to terminate in a penumbra shading gradually from one extreme to the other."[21] In a very real sense, "separation of powers" is a misnomer; the powers given to national government are blended and fused.

7. *Checks and balances (politics).* This oft-cited term captures the ideological gyroscope of our constitutional system. Division of power among governmental units might prevent autocracy but invite political paralysis. To bring the units together in harmonious relationship, so-called checks were placed in the Constitution. In fact, it is hard to pinpoint a phase of significant governmental authority left *exclusively* in the hands of any one branch. The intent was to create a *balance* of political power—for the three constituent agencies with national jurisdiction to lie on the same plateau of coercive capability. For those who judge political processes by their problem-solving *efficiency,* this scheme is forever doomed to be a disappointment. Friction among the competing power centers is inevitable, and this was entirely intentional.

The principles of republicanism found in the Constitution also owe an intellectual debt to the "balance of forces" idea. By "republicanism" I mean simply representative government, and this model stands as a compromise between those who advocated democracy (large-scale popular control) and those who endorsed various elitist alternatives. But the spirit of this compromise is very much in tune with both Actonitis and theories of countervailing power groups.

8. *Checks and balances (economics).* The "balance of power" concept seems to have had a deeper meaning as well. Aristotle and Locke described property rights as intimately related to the individual's quest for freedom. People possessed divergent property interests because there existed a division of labor in society; different skills reaped different economic rewards. To rob people of their property interests was to strip them of a salient facet of their personality. The Framers not only accepted these teachings but considered the corollaries of a viable private-property system—free domestic markets, sound currency, contractual obligations lived up to—essential attributes of the nation-state that had successfully balanced liberty and authority. But property was also a source of *faction;* it was divisive. Cleavages resulting from the desire of some to get their hands on another's estate could destroy the entire community. Government, then, must establish a stable balance among the economic interests of the major classes.

Madison, in fact, took the thesis one step further when he defined factions to include not only economically oriented groups but *all groups.* By "group" he meant "a number of citizens . . . who are united and actuated by some common impulse of passion, or of interest, adverse to the right of other citizens, or to the permanent and aggregate interests of the community." These groups, of course, could use the power of persuasion to build a consensus favorable to their cause; nonetheless, the challenge of republican government was to *balance factionalism* by passing laws for the good of all. Factions were perceived as an inevitable attribute of individual liberties, but factions must be contained.[22] As the "republican principle" would shield the polity from minority factions, the greatest danger lay in factional sentiments enjoying majority support. And in the economic sphere, those sentiments would most likely be egalitarian. That is why a private-property "Bill of Rights" is an implicit attribute of our Constitution.

The Constitution as love object

In my earlier discussions, I tried to ascertain why Americans are attracted to the notion of constitutionalism. Now the question comes: Why are we so infatuated with *this* Constitution? A theory often expressed emphasizes the wave of prosperity that followed ratification. As the country expanded and grew stronger, the people, it is said, ascribed these successes to the new legal superstructure. But this thesis hardly explains how the Constitution came to be treated with blind reverence.[23]

A far more subtle approach is taken by Edmond Cahn. During the post-Revolutionary War period, he finds, Americans generally considered constitutions *perpetual, immutable,* and enforceable through *appeals to God.*[24] Put another way, constitutional agreements were supposed to last forever; they provided a scheme of unalterable moral rights and duties; and if they were broken, retaliatory action was justified on the part of aggrieved citizens, who would be sustained by divine sanction.

According to Cahn, the Constitutional Convention paved the way for changes in all three perceptions.[25] The idea of perpetuity was scrapped, and the notion of *practical efficiency* substituted. The Framers, pragmatic in their objectives, doubtless did not expect their accomplishments to survive endless centuries. Next, he argues, immutability was replaced by *adaptation.* Here he leans heavily on the updated process for amending the Constitution. The unanimity rule employed under the Articles had been consistent with the perpetuity and immutability themes. But now change would be encouraged, because the practical political approach undergirding the Philadelphia agreement could not be effective unless an infusion of new ideas was possible. All it took to alter the proposed Constitution, Hamilton had written approvingly,[26] was for two-thirds of the Congress to initiate amendments and for three-quarters of the states to ratify. And if Congress hesitated, the states themselves could mobilize change. If two-thirds of their number petitioned Congress to call a constitutional convention, new proposals might be drafted there and sent back to the states, where, once more, three-quarters could finalize matters. Cahn notes that the Bill of Rights in the form of ten propositions was quickly adopted through the revised procedure. This was clear evidence of the demise of immutability and the triumph of adaptability. The final link in his chain is the replacement of theologically inspired remedies by *judicial, or courtroom, remedies.* Under our system, judges shape and develop constitutional law; thus stability is constantly maintained as social conditions evolve. Cahn even conceives judicial decrees as substitutes for popularly inspired revolutionary fervor, because judges enforce the rules against those who would break them. Furthermore, the amending process has proven to be too slow; judicial remedies are more responsive, he contends.

While I think that Cahn's argument may account for the longevity of our Constitution, I do not think it can be invoked to explain our irrepressible affection for the Constitution, because the theory places a disproportionate reliance upon the document as an adaptable, practical, political instrument. People tend not to *venerate* these qualities. Rather, I confess to being struck by the realization that every society needs its totems and rituals. For us, I think, the vestments of religion surround the Constitution. It specifies rational, knowable principles in Ten Commandments style, and we like that. It endorses explicit norms of freedom and responsibility that are consistent with shared religious and ethical basics, and we like that. Finally, it was written by men who have the glamour of the "superstar," and we like that. So for Americans the Constitution is the embodiment of both change and stability, and we very much like the *balance* this symbolism affords.

The Constitution as living organism

Our emotional attachment to the Constitution has a tendency to evoke truisms, and one most often heard is that the Constitution is a "living document." If this phrase is to have meaning, the relevant questions, I submit, are these: (1) In what sense is the Constitution "alive"? (2) How does the Constitution maintain its lifelike qualities? Several explanations have been formulated to meet these inquiries, and each is predicated on some notion of evolutionary process. The universal premise seems to be that times change, and the Constitution will become a vestigial organ if it fails to change with the times.

The most traditional and straightforward thesis relies upon the amending process. Putting the Bill of Rights to one side (because, in a political sense, it is part and parcel of the original ratification compromise), the Constitution has been altered in this fashion on sixteen occasions. These revisions, it is said, demonstrate our willingness to adapt constitutional provisions to new ways of looking at things, thus keeping the larger framework of government in touch with reality.

We can test the argument by classifying these amendments and judging their impact. The sixteen changes fall rather nicely into six larger categories:

1. *Expansion of the right to vote.* Six alterations were designed to accomplish this goal. Four provisions prohibit government from discriminating on certain grounds when it designates eligible voters. Race and sex may no longer be used as criteria for electoral participation, nor can anyone over the age of seventeen, if otherwise qualified, be denied the vote. Poll taxes are no longer valid prerequisites for balloting in *federal* elections. A fifth addition permits residents of the District of Columbia, if otherwise qualified, to vote in presidential elections. Finally, the sixth gives voters an opportunity to choose U.S. senators.[27]

2. *Changes in selecting the President.* Three amendments fit this description. One requires Electoral College members to distinguish between their presidential and their vice presidential choices; another restricts the chief executive to two four-year terms, under normal circumstances; the last makes clearer what would transpire should a President be disabled and therefore incompetent to meet the responsibilities of the office.[28]

3. *Changes in selecting the Congress.* Only the Twentieth Amendment qualifies here. This addition wipes out the old "lame-duck sessions"; under the new rules, once general elections are held there is no opportunity for defeated representatives to return to Washington and pass on legislative business.[29]

4. *Reversing Supreme Court decisions.* Two constitutional changes meet this test. In an early flight of audacity, the judicial branch decided that states could be sued in federal court by citizens of other states. Needless to say, with the Articles of Confederation still lying warm in their grave, the states reacted swiftly and decisively by annulling this ruling. A century later, the Court entertained another gambit. It said an income tax was one of those levies that Congress must *apportion among the states according to population.* Since this was a practical impossibility, a constitutional amendment reversing the decision gained favor.[30]

5. *Expressions of moral outrage.* Three examples of this species of adaptation (to use Cahn's rhetoric) may be cited. The Thirteenth Amendment abolishes slavery; the Eighteenth Amendment abolishes the use of intoxicating beverages; the Twenty-first Amendment abolishes the Eighteenth Amendment.

6. *Changes in constitutional responsibility.* The Fourteenth Amendment, on its face, alters the federal balance of power in this country. The states are forbidden to violate specified individual rights, and national citizenship now takes priority over state citizenship.[31]

I do not doubt that each of these amendments represents an attempt to adjust the Constitution to changing conditions and help an eighteenth-century scheme of statecraft live and breathe in subsequent eras. But how many of them deal with the crucial questions of governance this land has faced over the years? Would we have needed the Twelfth Amendment if Aaron Burr had not violated the spirit of the Constitution by seeking to submarine his way into the White House during the presidential election of 1800? Would we have needed the Twenty-second Amendment had not Franklin Roosevelt violated the hitherto unbroken custom restraining a President from running for more than two terms? Is it fundamental to our system that citizens may vote for U.S. senators rather than having these officials chosen by state legislators, whom we have always elected?

I think it significant that virtually all these amendments relate to the *process* of government and not to the *substance* of what government does. We have made alterations in how democratic decisions should be arrived at, but this prescription for change has rarely been used to settle the problems themselves. The great questions of justice, domestic tranquility, common defense, general welfare, and the blessings of liberty (to cite again the language of the Constitution's Preamble) are rarely mentioned. The only exceptions involve categories 5 and 6. The Thirteenth Amendment was absolutely essential, or we could not survive today as a nation-state; the Eighteenth Amendment was so ill-conceived it required repudiation. The Fourteenth Amendment legitimized the passing of state sovereignty; its contribution both to the protection of individual liberties and to the rise of a meaningful nationalism can hardly be overrated. It is no coincidence that both the Thirteenth and Fourteenth resulted from our greatest nightmare, the Civil War.

So Americans instinctively realize the need to reserve issues of substance for the marketplace of normal debate and dispensation. The amending procedure is unsuitable for such overriding purposes unless nothing else will suffice. To sum up, if the Constitution "lives" only because of this formalized mechanism for change, it would constantly be in a state of oxygen deficiency.

A second approach to the problem relies on more informal methods of revision. Recall Cahn's observation, which surely is irrefutable, that the Framers put their trust in the amending procedure but that the Supreme Court has largely preempted this role. A few examples provide the necessary proof. Since

World War II, the Court has (1) invalidated segregation of the races in all public facilities, (2) invalidated all manner of prayer in the public schools, and (3) invalidated every state legislative scheme that fails to create voting districts of approximately equal populations. I could mention other decisions of gravity and visibility. What should be clear, though, is that these holdings far outstrip in significance any formalized constitutional amendments enacted during a comparable period. Without doubt, judicial interpretation is a much greater giver of life to the "Living Constitution." Indeed, most contemporary scholars define this important concept as including the document plus definitive Supreme Court interpretation of what it says.[32]

Informal modes of updating constitutional norms are not confined to courtroom pronouncements, however. Both Congress and the President also play crucial roles. This interpretive function is a by-product of their day-to-day problem-solving business. The laws they enact and the orders they issue are very often based on new and original elaborations of age-old constitutional doctrine.

Again, examples are instructive. The Congress has authority to pass laws "necessary and proper" for the implementation of its specifically assigned powers. In our time, this immense grant of discretion justifies antipoverty statutes, farm-income statutes, minimum-wage statutes, and civil rights statutes. There is no way any nineteenth-century constitutional scholar could have predicted the gigantic sweep this clause has been accorded.

With regard to the President, constitutional elaboration may be demonstrated by noting both past and present decisions of moment. When Thomas Jefferson came to the White House, he was confronted with an opportunity to buy the vast Louisiana Territory from a financially pressed Napoleon. But Jefferson had for years preached against a national government armed with generous political scope, fearing such flexibility might be used to undermine individual rights. Jefferson knew the country would benefit enormously from the transaction, but where, he pondered, did the Constitution specifically give the President power to negotiate land purchases? In the end, Jefferson the politician won out over Jefferson the ideologue. The purchase was consummated and a precedent established that today would not be challenged. More recently, Harry Truman had to decide whether the President, on his own authority, could send troops to South Korea for the purpose of resisting an invasion by North Korean forces. To be sure, Presidents had ordered military personnel to foreign countries on other occasions, but never had the commitment been so vast or the threat of confrontation with a "superpower" so proximate. Truman's decision was in the affirmative, and—rightly or wrongly—certainly had the effect of expanding greatly executive branch control over the armed services.

Judicial interpretation, congressional interpretation, and presidential interpretation would seem, at first glance, to comprise the sum and substance of informal constitutional manipulation and revision. Yet informal constitutional updating encompasses this and much more. There is to be reckoned with the whole range of custom and routine developed over almost two centuries.[33] Suppose a group of Martians alighted from their spaceship and asked to see a copy of our Constitution. Their attention might be drawn to the explicit rules for choosing a chief executive, and they would return to their planet thinking the Electoral College does it all. Of course, they wouldn't have a clue as to how the presidential selection process actually works. What does the Constitution say about political parties, national conventions, preferential primaries, and the rest? They could also read about the executive branch and never know there was a Cabinet; they could memorize the entire legislative article and never have an inkling about the power of congressional committees. But, in fact, these elements have become integral facets of our national governmental apparatus, for we would be hopelessly at sea without them.

These many formal processes and informal rituals make up the basis for Karl Llewellyn's notion of the "Living Constitution," a definition I believe is the most inclusive and sophisticated in the literature. He thinks it embraces those *basic* attributes of government that are both *regularized* in their function and considered by politically relevant participants to possess *"unquestioned rightness"* (italics mine).[34] Notice that his conception encompasses three elements: (1) The attribute must be fundamental (it has attained "rules of the game" stature). (2) The attribute must be used with consistency (its occurrence is patterned rather than random). And (3) the attribute must be legitimate (it possesses an ethical dimension). I think that the two-party system and senatorial principle of unlimited debate are excellent examples of "Living Constitutionalism." Needless to say, the many aspects of constitutional interpretation I have presented would ordinarily qualify.

But Llewellyn takes us one step further. He says the total constitutional system is an *institution.* It "involves ways of behavior deeply set and settled in the make-up [of the entire population, and includes] not patterns of doing . . . merely, but also accompanying patterns of thinking and of emotion—attitudes—toward the verbal symbol 'Constitution.' . . ."[35] At this point we are talking about phenomena clearly different from the basic, consistent, and legitimate norms of national government. The subject now is *public opinion* and *public behavior* relative to constitutional processes. The "Living Constitution" here encompasses the way segments of the population respond to these rules, and it would include not only their opinions on what the rules mean but also their strategies for using these rules. Specifically, Llewellyn has in mind the activities of pressure groups as they attempt to influence congressional or executive policy formation, the opinions of the public with respect to Supreme Court performance, and the rights particular groups (like women or Chicanos) think they deserve under the Constitution. These are only examples, of course, but obviously the common denominator here is the social fabric responding to and impinging upon the rules of statecraft rather than the rules of statecraft themselves. And these social forces, in order to be part of the "Living Constitution," must meet the threefold test mentioned earlier. That is, the public opinion and behavior we want to study must consist of *basic patterns* of belief or conduct with respect to constitutional processes, which participants think possess an *ethical* ingredient. The whole package, to repeat, is a kind of *institution* qualitatively distinct from the rest of the political system.

Throughout this book, I will use the Constitution as a barometer for understanding what American national government is all about. Sometimes I will be citing the Constitution as a *document.* But eventually we must get beyond this stage and focus on the "Living Constitution,"[36] making reference to precisely the factors Llewellyn has in mind. I will try to map out and utilize the Constitution as fundamental, regularized, legitimate norms invoked by our leaders; but I will also consider the Constitution as an institution, with everything this idea was meant to convey.

I must now introduce one other concept, the term "constitutional environment." The "Living Constitution" has not developed in a time-space vacuum, much less in a value-free culture. The fundamental political norms and rules we have adhered to over time and with the highest regard are, to a considerable extent, the product of larger environmental forces; indeed, these forces color our entire outlook on life. If I had to provide a shorthand enumeration, I would stress the following facets of our constitutional environment:

1. The United States has always been separated physically from the world's "superpowers." This phenomenon encourages an attention to domestic affairs and lessens concern over foreign affairs.

2. The United States has traditionally enjoyed an abundance of elbow room. Our tremendous growth would have been impossible without the frontier, and this potential has hardly been exhausted.

3. The United States—even as thirteen states—has been a diverse geographic community. Rivers and harbors, mountains, forests and plains—our great climatic and topographical variation has made for economic self-sufficiency.

4. The United States is "a nation of immigrants." If not a melting pot, we are a stew with countless ethnic ingredients. Such cultural heterogeneity has produced cultural richness.

5. The United States is a country of skilled practitioners. Our emphasis on doing enables us to maximize the benefits of the technological advances that are the legacy of modern society.

6. The United States was settled by Christians who were religious enough to share a common ethical heritage but diverse enough not to believe we should be a "Christian nation." The result has been a sometimes tenuous accommodation: we have combined a sense of rightness with a healthy skepticism toward theology as a prime instrument for social action.

The American Constitution specifies highly technical governmental "rules of the game"; it transmits values embodying the spirit of our intellectual tradition; it inspires fervent patriotism. In a very real sense, then, the Constitution is a grand design giving form and meaning to our political lives. But to equate the charter with some overarching scheme contrived by master builders would be to conceive our governmental enterprise in too rational a light. The Constitution also encompasses implicit norms of custom and usage, which have evolved over many decades in response to important political needs; and the Constitution also includes people striving to make the fundamental law more meaningful, given their precious beliefs and aspirations. These attributes—the first stressing institutional adjustment, the second stressing popular participation and conviction—impart to the Constitution a characteristic more basic even than that of architectural design. They make the Constitution a living organism.

NOTES

1. The following dialogue is based in considerable measure on the insights of Edward S. Corwin's, *The "Higher Law" Background of American Constitutional Law* (Ithaca: Cornell Univ. Press, 1957).

2. A "must" for understanding the colonists' conception of government by constitution is Bernard Bailyn, *The Ideological Origins of the American Revolution* (Cambridge, Mass.: Harvard Univ. Press, 1967). Read in tandem, Bailyn and Corwin (see note 1) capture beautifully the complexities of ideological commitment underlying the public debates during that period.

3. The word "temporal" means secular or worldly, as opposed to the religious authority of popes, rabbis, and other clergy.

4. A gripping description of this evolutionary process is found in C. H. Van Tyne, *The Causes of the War of Independence* (Boston and New York: Houghton Mifflin, 1922), Ch. 1.

5. William H. Riker, *Federalism* (Boston: Little, Brown, 1964), pp. 17-20.

6. How can a study like this one avoid forever the use of those elusive and hopelessly controversial terms "liberalism" and "conservatism"? Unless otherwise indicated, these concepts have reference to the manner in which particular people respond to *social change*. Thus, a liberal tends to favor change and reform; a conservative is inclined to resist change. The liberal is more willing to look for new and different solutions; when in doubt, liberals opt for a shake-up. A conservative, tending to believe that innovation will likely make things worse, is simply more respectful of tradition and established routine. These definitions approximate the original meanings the words had, and they were accepted long before "liberal" became a synonym for "socialist," and "conservative" became another word for "fossil" or "racist."

7. Philosophers love to debate the nature and justifiability of revolution. The best description of the American Revolution as a social process qualitatively different from, say, the French and Russian revolutions, is perhaps C. H. McIlwain, *The American Revolution* (New York: Macmillan, 1923). Of course, Jefferson et al. thought the Declaration of Independence was consistent with the colonists' constitutional rights, but they strongly supported both the American and French revolutions on grounds of abstract "natural" rights as well.

8. The Founders have been accused of violating their "legal" charge by proposing a wholly new charter of government. Without doubt, the delegates understood well the boldness of

their action, and they knew it ran counter to the spirit of the trust given them. They also realized, however, that public opinion was favorable to far-reaching constitutional adjustment, only if they could work out the particulars.

9. For an assessment of the Philadelphia meeting as a struggle between these two state factions, see Robert L. Schuyler, *The Constitution of the United States* (London: Macmillan, 1923).

10. Madison defended the Convention's departure by citing "the great principle of self-preservation" which underlies all political institutions. *The Federalist,* No. 43.

11. See the last sections of this chapter, where I describe the implicit norms emanating from the Constitution.

12. His persuasive book, which enthralled more than a generation of historians, is *An Economic Interpretation of the Constitution of the United States* (New York: Macmillan, 1913). The classical rebuttal is Robert E. Brown, *Charles Beard and the Constitution* (Princeton: Princeton Univ. Press, 1956).

13. Max Farrand, *Records of the Federal Convention* (New Haven: Yale Univ. Press, 1911).

14. For perceptive contemporary research on the place of these writings in our history and politics, see Benjamin F. Wright, *The Federalist* (Cambridge, Mass.: Harvard Univ. Press, 1961).

15. An excellent discussion of the dialogue surrounding ratification is found in Alpheus Thomas Mason, *The States Rights Debate: Antifederalism and the Constitution* (Englewood Cliffs, N.J.: Prentice-Hall, 1964), Ch. 3.

16. A somewhat similar point is made in Winton U. Solberg, *The Federal Convention and the Formation of the Union of the American States* (New York: Liberal Arts Press, 1958); see especially his introductory remarks.

17. John Marshall captures the essence of this theme with his usual trenchance. *McCulloch v. Maryland,* 4 Wheat. 316 (1819).

18. The constitutionality of revolutions in this country has been treated in like fashion by a plurality of Supreme Court justices. *Dennis v. United States,* 341 U.S. 494 (1951), opinion of Chief Justice Vinson. And see also John Marshall's views expressed in *Marbury v. Madison,* 1 Cr. 137 (1803).

19. B. F. Wright, "*The Federalist* on the Nature of Political Man," *Ethics* 59 (1949) no. 2, part II.

20. James Madison, *The Federalist,* No. 47.

21. *Springer v. Philippine Islands,* 277 U.S. 189 (1928), dissenting opinion of Mr. Justice Holmes.

22. James Madison, *The Federalist,* No. 10.

23. Corwin, *The "Higher Law" Background of American Constitutional Law,* pp. 2-3.

24. Edmond Cahn, ed., *Supreme Court and Supreme Law* (Bloomington: Indiana Univ. Press, 1954), p. 3.

25. Ibid., p. 12.

26. Alexander Hamilton, *The Federalist,* No. 85.

27. These are amendments 15, 17, 19, 23, 24, and 26.

28. These are amendments 12, 22, and 25.

29. Classifications such as this one should not be taken as hard-and-fast schemes. I suppose the Seventeenth Amendment, involving direct election of senators, could be placed under this heading, for instance, but I feel it is essentially a "voting rights" policy judgment.

30. These are amendments 11 and 16.

31. This is by far the most complicated and far-reaching revision of the lot. I am not prepared at this time to spell out even its general contours. All in good time!

32. This view is best articulated in Arthur N. Holcombe, *The Constitutional System* (Chicago: Scott, Foresman, 1964), Ch. 6, and Arthur S. Miller, "Notes on the Concept of the 'Living' Constitution," *The George Washington Law Review* 31 (1963), pp. 881-918.

33. This theme is explored fully in Herbert W. Horwill, *The Usages of the American Constitution* (London: Oxford Univ. Press, H. Milford, 1925).

34. Karl N. Llewellyn, "The Constitution as an Institution," *Columbia Law Review* 34 (1934), pp. 26, 28-30.

35. *Ibid.*, p. 18. Compare Glendon A. Schubert, "The Rhetoric of Constitutional Change," *Journal of Public Law* 16 (1967), pp. 23, 38, 50. I have also elevated the concept one notch by according it upper-case status. I think "Living Constitution," as used here has specific enough meaning to warrant capitals.

36. If there is something called the "Living Constitution," then there must also be something called "living law," a notion of far broader scope, including, I would think, all norms having the force of legal sanction plus society's "interpretation" of, and reaction to, those norms. The term "living law" is analyzed in Eugen Ehrlich, *Fundamental Principles of the Sociology of Law* (New York: Russell and Russell, 1962), especially Ch. XXI.

2
the supreme court: constitutional oracle?

In the preceding chapter, I described the Constitution as embodying a set of rules. But it would be a mistake for students of politics simply to flit from rule to rule, memorizing each, and trying to understand the document in this fashion. Under our system, the Supreme Court has authority to tell us what the Constitution *means;* for this reason alone, we must study the charter in the context of judicial behavior. Furthermore, and of greater relevance to "Living Constitutionalism," the Court's opinions are in considerable measure a product of what *it* is: the men who sit in judgment, the institutional norms and traditions that influence their responses to appeals, and the power they have available to resolve particular issues.

Let me begin by stating the obvious: the Supreme Court is a *court.* When we think of judges, we think of men who are neutral and impartial and *nonpolitical*—that is, removed from crass considerations of partisanship and power enhancement. This "aura of neutrality" is conveyed through many of the obvious trappings surrounding the Court's public image. The Justices wear long, black robes when they perform official duties, and when they meet in conference to discuss litigation, no one—not even the paid help—is allowed to enter the inner sanctum.[1] But the most visible example of detachment is found in the Court's opinions themselves. They are long, windy exercises in allegedly dispassionate logic, interrupted only by elaborate footnotes citing both high-flown legal research and the many precedents designed to buttress the Justices' convictions.[2]

This studied detachment reached incredibly grandiose proportions when students of jurisprudence preached—as they so often did until quite recently—that judges actually *found* the law. Indeed, one of the reasons the common law achieved so much prestige was its image as a package of right conduct *discovered* by legal wizards.[3] Consider the following assertion, written as recently as 1935:

> When an act of Congress is appropriately challenged in the courts as not conforming to the constitutional mandate the judicial branch of the Government has only one duty—to lay the article of the Constitution which is invoked beside the statute which is challenged and to decide whether the latter squares with the former.[4]

In other words, judges characterized themselves as members of the neuter gender; they were robots, machines programmed to determine whether a statute of known size and poundage exceeds a constitutional provision of known size and poundage. If it does, judicial decapitation must follow, for the Constitution is the highest of all laws.

Today we know courts are involved in politics simply because they dispense governmental power. And the Supreme Court is more involved than any other, for it can say with finality to both President and Congress: "You have violated the Constitution and your edicts therefore have no force or effect." Moreover, we now realize judges are human. They do not *find* the law; they *make* the law in the sense that they possess options and exercise value judgments. But still the Justices are not legislators. Their creativity and discretion are less sweeping, and there are at least three important reasons for the differences.

First, the strength of the Supreme Court lies in maintaining its neutral image; thus it must ordinarily be more restrained than most political bodies. At the least, this means the Court presumes in favor of precedent.[a] To be sure, precedents evolve over time, and on rare occasions they are even thrust aside entirely, but the Court's neutral image requires that it maintain a *consistent* theoretical rule structure wherein the precedents jibe with one another. Second, we consider ourselves a republic, and this means government by elected officials who can be thrown out if the spirit moves us, not by Justices who are appointed for life.[5] If the Court proceeds too fast, we begin to question its use of power. The yellow caution flag is forever up, and the Court has long understood the message.[6] Third, in theory at least, the Supreme Court is the weakest of the three branches of federal authority. It commands no army and prints and spends no currency. And so as we examine the work of this institution and the meaning it gives to constitutional rules, we must always look to the men on the bench; the options available to them; and the struggle for power among Congress, President, the public, and the Court itself, which is inherent in our politics.

[a] The technical term is *stare decisis,* which means "let the decision stand," and the posture of usually abiding by decided cases is common to all courts.

"Pure judicial review"

Nowhere does the Constitution clearly authorize the Justices to knock down presidential and congressional actions if they appear contrary to fundamental law. The term I use to label this unique instrument is "pure judicial review,"[7] and to understand how it became included in the Court's arsenal of weapons is really to understand how the Court became the important locus of power it has been in modern times.

As we have seen, the Framers were men from the right side of the tracks. They saw national government as the repository of their influence, and they could hardly envision the Thomas Jeffersons and Patrick Henrys—states' rights advocates at best and revolutionaries at worst—standing at the helm of their sovereign creation. But in 1800 Jefferson was elected President, and the Republican party, which he headed, won control of the Congress. Fearful of the chaos they felt would ensue, the "lame-duck" Federalist legislators[8] passed a law creating approximately fifty new federal judgeships, which outgoing President John Adams promptly staffed with loyal party members. The idea was simply to pack the courts. Any new statutes these judges perceived as unduly noxious would be interpreted in the least harmful manner, a tactic of judicial discretion accepted even then.[9]

Needless to say, Jefferson's legions were incensed and immediately abolished these offices by repealing the law creating them.[10] This probably would have ended the skirmish but for one William Marbury, a true-blue Federalist, who had been tapped to serve in the minor post of justice of the peace for the District of Columbia, under a statute the Jeffersonians had carelessly left unscathed. Due to a clerical slip-up, the certificate of office attesting to Marbury's appointment was never delivered to him; thus, he launched a suit against James Madison, Jefferson's Secretary of State, who was responsible for carrying out such duties but had no intention of consummating the nomination. The gist of Marbury's argument was simple enough: the law obligates Madison to give me my seal of responsibility, and I will get a decree from the Supreme Court making him obey the rules. Marbury's request—for an order called a *writ of mandamus*[11]—was based on the Judiciary Act of 1789, by which Congress had given the Court power to issue such directives.

Sitting on the Supreme Court waiting for Marbury's petition were a host of friendly Federalists, and their leader was another last-minute appointee, Chief Justice John Marshall. In addition to being a devout Hamiltonian, Marshall also detested Jefferson personally. A confrontation of the highest proportions loomed between Court and President, especially when it became clear that a ruling favorable to Marbury would never be honored.

The first portion of *Marbury v. Madison* bears out these forebodings. Marshall excoriated the President for denying plaintiff's legal rights. But the Chief Justice was no blind ideologue who would allow either doctrine or emotion to dictate his strategy. He knew the Court's prestige to be low,[12] that it had yet to issue a weighty decision of binding effect,[13] and he was not prepared to see the chief executive make a mockery of judicial decrees. Having scored his political points, Marshall suddenly threw up his arms and retreated. Unfortunately, he said, there is nothing we can do to aid the maligned petitioner, for *Congress had no power to vest the Supreme Court with the authority to issue writs of mandamus in the Court's original jurisdiction.* How come? Under "original jurisdiction" a case is brought directly to the Supreme Court, without first going through the lower courts. Original-jurisdiction cases fall into two categories, and these are specifically cited in the Constitution: (1) where a state is involved, or (2) where an ambassador or dignitary of equivalent status is a party. But now Congress had added a third, the issuance of mandamus. As between the will of Congress and the will of the Constitution, the statute—that is, this portion of the 1789 Judiciary Act—must be declared unenforceable.

The *Marbury* case[14] is like a good movie because it contains several layers of analysis. Marshall was not a great scholar, but he was a first-rate logician. His opinions have an irresistible lure, in part because of the writer's absolute confidence in his own premises. Marshall, we must remember, lived at a time when people thought the universe was governed by Sir Isaac Newton's static, enduring truths, which they could understand through the exercise of their own reason. And Marshall would *find* the correct constitutional rules according to the same slot-machine formula laid down for *finding* common-law rules. He perceived the following to be unquestionable:

Step 1. The Constitution is the supreme law of the land.

Step 2. It is the duty of judges to interpret the law.

Step 3. Any statute we find contradictory to the Constitution must fall.

Then what is political about this opinion? Obviously, there was the blast at Jefferson. Moreover, Marbury lost his case, and executive branch prerogatives remained unimpaired. The Court's decision, on the surface at least, had been a model of self-restraint. But behind this smoke screen of partisanship and abnegation, Marshall had vested in himself and his successors the power to read the Constitution and to limit the boundaries of congressional authority.

As a matter of sheer logic, there was in fact nothing in Marshall's opinion to justify the principle of pure judicial review. He demonstrated only that Congress was merely co-equal to the Court and could not expand the judicial power contrary to the Constitution. Congress could just as well have maintained that it then had the right to interpret the Constitution as it applied to *legislative* powers and responsibilities. As a matter of fact, this is exactly what Jefferson, when he regained his composure, did argue. And so did Andrew Jackson, and so did Abraham Lincoln. None of these men accepted the exclusivity of the Supreme Court's right to clarify constitutional meanings. They believed that the three branches could spell out for themselves the range of authority placed in their hands. Seen in this light, the decision in *Marbury* would still be defensible because the Court was resisting a compromise of its own powers; but the ruling would provide no precedent for judicial protection of individual liberties undermined by federal law.

Marshall's opinion, then, perhaps the most important in the history of American jurisprudence, was by and large a series of value judgments. He simply felt the Supreme Court—that branch of government most removed from popular control—was best suited to explicate the rules of our political game. The argument has been made, in fact, that *Marbury* was simply a naked grab for power; after all, the criticism runs, if the Framers had wanted judges to exercise a legislative veto, they would have said so. But the men who sat at Philadelphia and whose opinions can be gleaned on the matter tended to see judicial oversight à la *Marbury* in a favorable light. [15] Marshall, no innovator of theory, really did nothing more than adopt Hamilton's ideas set out in *The Federalist.* [16] In all likelihood, the Framers did not debate the pros and cons either because of negligence or because most delegates could not conceive of constitutional interpretation unless wielded by an elite cloistered from political winds.

It is hard to judge the significance of pure judicial review. Approximately 125 national laws and executive orders have been voided since *Marbury,* and in only two instances have the Court's findings been reversed by constitutional amendment. [17] But over the years the Court has generally acceded to the major policy initiatives advanced by executive and legislative officials. Rarely has it been intemperate enough to risk full-scale hostilities, because the "political branches" tend to represent the vast power of majority opinion—that is, what Madison would have called the dominant factional alignment. And much of its resistance has been in the nature of brushfire activity involving minor questions of constitutional propriety. What pure judicial review can do, however, is to keep both Congress and President on their toes and ever wary of judicial remonstrance, especially where power is divided and these two centers of influence do not share common conviction. Furthermore, the Justices can try to restrain the "governing alliance" from enforcing policy by methods that violate the "rules of the game." And, of course, pure judicial review adds even more luster to that most potent of all *political* weapons in the Supreme Court's repository: the prestige of neutral adjudicator that accrues to those who weave constitutional symbols and norms. [18]

Jurisdiction and standing

The Supreme Court, I have said, is first and foremost a court of law. As such, it operates at a marked disadvantage in the never-ending war of power politics. The Justices cannot reach out and make sweeping rules; they must wait for litigants to come before the bench armed with petitions requesting relief. It is important to know, then, who can use the federal courts and under what conditions. The key is *jurisdiction.*

In *Marbury* we learned about *original* jurisdiction and the two kinds of cases it entails. Far more important is the Supreme Court's *appellate* jurisdiction—that is, the various kinds of questions the Court may hear *on appeal.* The Framers went so far as to list what these *might* consist of. The possibilities divide into two groups. The first division is based on subject matter. The Court may hear litigation involving the meaning of a federal statute, treaty, executive order, or the Constitution itself. Second, there is the division based on the nature of the litigants. For example, a citizen of one state may sue a citizen of another state. A controversy involving the United States or any of its countless agencies is also amenable to resolution. Notice these two categories operate independently of one another. If the subject matter is appropriate, it makes no difference who the parties are; conversely, if the litigants can obtain access, it makes no difference what the issue is. But this checklist, I must emphasize, is only by way of recommendation, because the Constitution specifies that the Court's appellate jurisdiction is subject to "such Exceptions, and under such Regulations as the Congress shall make."[19]

This significant limitation on judicial power received direct attention in the unique *McCardle* decision.[20] Just after the Civil War, Congress passed a law to protect former slaves and Union sympathizers in the South. The statute allowed persons who were held illegally by government officials to obtain a Supreme Court order freeing them at once. Ironically, it was not a newly ordained black citizen but a white newspaperman with Confederate sympathies who invoked this protective device. He had written editorials highly critical of the alleged police-state regime created by Congress to govern the conquered states. Having been convicted by a military commission for the publication of these supposedly seditious pamphlets, he demanded that the Court release him and, in so doing, declare unconstitutional the Congress's Reconstruction laws under which he was imprisoned.

Now at this point in our history Congress was never stronger and the Supreme Court—because of its ruling in the notorious *Dred Scott* case—never weaker. And with the ill-fated Andrew Johnson in the White House, the vengeful Republicans who were orchestrating congressional decision-making would brook no judicial interference with their program of "rejuvenation" for the battered South.

On the other hand, the Court obviously had jurisdiction over the case. What to do? The Justices invited the parties to appear and present arguments. Then they stalled, awaiting congressional action. Fearing the worst for its programs, the legislature responded by repealing the law under which McCardle had requested a hearing. And the Court, in an act that could be labeled either acute prudence or blatant cowardice, went along with this action. Congress, it said, could revise or amend the Supreme Court's appellate jurisdiction any way it wished. With McCardle's legal basis removed, the Justices were without jurisdiction to proceed. Case dismissed.

In our time, the Court has made its greatest name in adjudicating civil liberties and civil rights cases. Almost all these decisions have stemmed from the exercise of appellate jurisdiction, so the lesson of *McCardle* is an important one. Congress, under prevailing constitutional theory, could put a tremendous dent in the Court's capacity to interpret the free speech clause of the First Amendment, the due process clause of the Fifth Amendment or, for that matter, the entire Bill of Rights.

Generally amicable relations between the branches, however, have almost always moved the lawmakers to use this authority as an aid to judicial independence. The controlling statute on the subject dates from 1925. It incorporates virtually the entire set of criteria for appellate jurisdiction found in the Constitution and then goes on to give the Court very great leeway in choosing the particular cases it may hear. So the policy in effect is based largely on whether the Justices think a novel and substantial federal question is involved.[21] As I noted earlier, courts that keep their political houses in order tend not to suffer political setbacks.

Only once since 1867 has there arisen a serious move to cut down the Supreme Court's appellate jurisdiction as a form of punishment. This occurred in the late 1950s, following a series of rulings limiting federal and state legislative attempts to regulate "subversive activities."[22] The proposal, among other things, would have made it impossible for the Court to hear litigation involving a congressional committee charged with abridging the constitutional rights of witnesses. Nor could the Court have exercised any control over executive policy with regard to employees accused of being security risks. Fear of legislative and executive autonomy in these sensitive areas, subject to *no* Supreme Court check, was evidently too much to swallow, however, and the Senate killed the bill by a 49-41 tally.

The term "jurisdiction" has a second and quite different meaning. As courts of law, the federal judiciary may hear only "cases and controversies," so the Constitution says.[23] In other words, the litigants must be true adversaries squared off against each other, and the Court is supposed to lay down rules no broader than necessary to resolve their claims. This procedure helps the Justices avoid the pitfalls stemming from needless rhetoric and decision-making, opinion and behavior that might undermine their delicate political role. For instance, the Court has always avoided rendering advisory opinions. When President Washington asked for a legal interpretation of certain treaty commitments, Chief Justice John Jay bluntly told him the Court would act when a proper lawsuit had been brought before it and not sooner.[24]

Congress has used more subtle approaches. It once passed a law giving persons the right to obtain financial awards from the Court if they could prove that the government owed them money; however, no debts were to be paid unless the Secretary of the Treasury approved. The Justices denounced the role assigned them, claiming their findings would be merely advisory opinions. They reminded Congress that their judgment did not depend on the concurrence of any other official; when the Court said monies must be paid, the decision was final.[25]

To sum up, the rule mandating an adversary relationship between contestants insulates the Court from both premature disclosures of opinion and precipitous action. On the other hand, the rule keeps "activist" jurists from playing "roving constitutional commissioners." But perhaps most important, the rule often makes the judiciary wait, and wait, and wait for a controversy to be formulated.

There is another criterion that limits access to the Supreme Court, a norm unspecified in the Constitution but very much a part of the "Living Constitution" because the Justices consider it fundamental. No one can obtain judicial review without *standing*. That is, plaintiff must establish a meaningful personal interest in the litigation. Take the case of Mrs. Frothingham. Congress had passed the Maternity Act of 1921, which disbursed money to states for the purpose of better protecting the health of both mothers and newborn babies. Frothingham claimed that Congress could not fund these expenses because they were a matter of state concern, and the effect of the appropriation would lead to an increase in her taxes. Thus, in her status as a taxpayer, she alleged standing to challenge the supposedly unconstitutional federal action. The Court rejected her petition.[26] For one thing, her interest was shared with citizens generally; it was, therefore, trivial and minute. Second, she could not show that her tax money was used in any way to support the program. The Court, then, had no intention of allowing taxpayers to challenge, on that basis alone, any federal action they believed invalid.

The *Frothingham* rule has an obvious basis in common sense, but it also has a weakness. In the 1970s the Congress has given the states a staggering amount of money to pay for highways, education, and all kinds of social welfare benefits. But if a taxpayer cannot sue, who will have standing to raise questions about the constitutionality of such grants? If the money were used to undermine precious individual rights, the Court would be powerless to act.

This inflexibility proved particularly frustrating with regard to federal aid to schools, including gifts to the parochial system. Many people saw these grants as governmental subsidies to certain churches, and a violation of the First Amendment, which makes governmental "establishment of religion" unconstitutional. In the *Flast* decision,[27] the Supreme Court painted itself out of this corner by refining its opposition to taxpayers' suits. Where the taxpayer claims federal funds are being spent in violation of some specific clause in the Constitution, then standing will have been established. This should not be seen as an attempt by a civil liberties-oriented Court to move against these aid programs. Rather, it was more likely an effort to reiterate the Court's position as reader of the Constitution, a role the Justices can hardly fulfill if they are unable to receive cases concerning such subjects.

Flast teaches that the standing issue is not a matter of dry, colorless procedure; interpretations of who has access to the Supreme Court are key policy matters. For further evidence, we may examine the *Sierra Club v. Morton* case,[28] which took form when Walt Disney Enterprises received approval from the federal government to construct a tourist complex in Mineral King Valley, a wildlife refuge in Sequoia National Forest.

The Sierra Club, one of the oldest and largest environmental pressure groups, argued before the Supreme Court that Mineral King's aesthetic beauty and ecological integrity would be altered drastically by Disney's plans. The Court's opinion took pains to recognize environmental concerns as an important element in the quality of national life; clearly, the damage alleged might very well form the basis of a proper appeal. But did the Sierra Club have standing to sue? Was it enough to say that a public question involving environmental use was at stake and that the Club was expert in defending these concerns? Here the Justices split 4–3 against the contention. To show standing, plaintiff must prove "injury in fact"; and to prove "injury in fact," plaintiff must show that its members actually used the Mineral King complex. The Club had not proven that the members spent time in the area at all, much less demonstrated a threat of meaningful deprivation resulting from Disney's facilities. If the Sierra Club need only show an authentic special interest to establish standing, the majority reasoned, why couldn't an individual with similar expertise also establish standing? The Court must protect itself, the majority Justices concluded, from becoming a forum for anyone who wished merely to vindicate a particular conviction.

Justices Douglas, Brennan, and Blackmun dissented. Douglas, the inveterate outdoorsman, argued that if a corporation, which is certainly not a real person, can sue when damaged sufficiently, so also can a mountain about to be despoiled or a river about to be polluted. All three dissenters would loosen the requirements for standing, so that knowledgeable environmentalists could represent the interests of threatened mountains and rivers. But the dissenters would not allow suits to be brought by people off the street, those who had no meaningful involvement in such matters.

So standing can be established through loss not only of a tangible (such as money) but also of an intangible (such as ecological integrity). But in *Sierra Club v. Morton* the Court did not understand how it could distinguish between a bona fide concern and a fly-by-night interest. Is the standing issue in this case just a function of the importance of environmental questions to particular judges? The two factors may be related, but manageable rules and workloads necessary to a responsible exercise of judicial power are also part of the picture. Furthermore, political influence is also a function of political information. The Court has learned that the best way to obtain relevant facts on important policy issues is to bring adversaries with direct, personal, and lively competing interests together and let them develop their claims to the fullest.

"Political questions"

In theory at least, if a case is presented, if the Court has authority to act, and if litigants can show direct personal interest, then the Court will move. But in fact Justices avoid some policy areas with determination. The Court calls these "political questions"; when they crop up, the Justices usually pin the label on them, explain the reasons why, and refuse to debate the constitutional merits. "Political questions," then, are another example of "Living Constitutional" judicial self-restraint.

An excellent example of this phenomenon is almost anything relating to foreign affairs. The Court considers itself incompetent to enter this domain, so the President has a pretty free constitutional hand. The most controversial instance arose during the Vietnam War. Could the chief executive unilaterally order troops into the fray? Did Congress's Gulf of Tonkin resolution constitute legislative approval for his actions? Or did our treaty commitments render such approval unnecessary? These are all questions pregnant with political substance, and several cases were presented that could have been used as stepladders for judicial intervention. In every instance, however, the Court simply refused to hear the appeal. Dodging and sidestepping, it avoided any comment whatsoever on the many constitutional facets of Southeast Asian military policy.[29]

Why the fancy judicial footwork? The courts cannot see themselves poring over intelligence reports and troop movements in order to assess whether these serve as reasonable justifications for political action. According to the prevailing logic, the President, armed with his confidential sources of information, should be second-guessed only by forces more reflective of public opinion.[30] But there is surely more to it than that. What the Court means by "political questions" are those issues better suited to either congressional or presidential resolution. But the Justices are also loath to involve the Court in issues that are the subject of overriding political controversy in the nation at large.[31] To avoid endangering its own prestige and authority, the Court must avoid seeming to "take sides" on such "hot" issues.[32]

Probably the classic decision in the "political questions" realm grew out of the Dorr Rebellion in Rhode Island during the 1840s. This insurrection was aimed at overthrowing a regime which at that late date limited suffrage to a relatively few property owners. The Constitution mandates the United States to guarantee a republican form of government in the states; and federal authorities must also protect states against domestic violence. As can be imagined, each of the warring factions said it represented republicanism—one group claimed it had been properly elected, while the other relied on its popularity with the average citizen.

In the case *Luther v. Borden,*[33] the Court found that the "political branches" should decide the meaning of a republican government. First, Congress has the power to seat, or refuse to seat, senators and representatives chosen in state elections. If it thinks these officials do not satisfy "republican principles" because they are part and parcel of an unsavory political machine, it can refuse to honor their credentials and send them home. Perhaps the Justices were wondering how they could implement a ruling that state X did not meet prescribed standards of republicanism. Second, Congress had, quite properly, given the President power to send forces to quash rebellions in the states. In this instance, John Tyler had furnished military aid to the established government, and this action had smashed the insurrection. The Court rejected as an exercise in futility any attempt to second-guess the President's determination of a republican regime. Again, the key ingredient of constitutional policy was military involvement, and, as before, the Justices steered very clear of any entanglement with their partners in government.

The 1840s decision provides a solid foundation for understanding the Court's response to a group of students at Kent State University who feared a repetition of the 1970 violence on their campus. They wanted the judiciary to oversee the training, weaponry, and command structure of the Ohio National Guard; where these procedures and techniques appeared to foster excessive and unreasonable coercion, the judges could substitute their own training requirements. The majority, relying on Congress's power to organize, arm and discipline these forces, as well as on the President's authority to nationalize them, rejected this alternative. In the Court's view, it was difficult to conceive of an area of policy-making less amenable to judicial scrutiny. The "political branches" were entrusted with control over military affairs; in a democracy the use of troops presupposed civilian supervision by elected officials—not judges.[34]

Over the last forty years, and particularly since the Second World War, the public has tended to rely increasingly on executive flexibility in military matters to protect the national interest. The decision in *Laird v. Tatum*[35] emphasizes graphically the spillover effect between military actions usually confined to overseas commitments and military orders that some contemporary Presidents have thought appropriate for the home front. Furthermore, it shows the possible relationship between the "political questions" doctrine and standing requirements.

Following the 1967 civil disorders in Detroit, in which federal troops were dispatched to maintain order, the Army launched a program of intelligence-gathering, made possible in part by surveillance of potential lawbreakers at public meetings and the storage of relevant information in a central computer. The program's alleged purpose was to enable the military to respond with greater effectiveness if the occasion should arise. When the program, begun by President Johnson and continued by President Nixon, became known to Senator Sam Ervin, his Subcommittee on Constitutional Rights held a series of hearings to look into the Army's activities. Perhaps as a response to the senator's searching inquiry, the Undersecretary of the Army announced a cutback in intelligence activities and the destruction of computerized information.

The American Civil Liberties Union filed a complaint against the Army's intelligence-gathering activities. No claim was made that specific injury had been done to the A.C.L.U. or its members, nor was any instance cited of illegal action, such as breaking and entering. Rather, the argument was that the armed forces lacked constitutional power to take part in surveillance activities and, furthermore, that the very existence of this investigatory network inhibited full and complete exercise of free speech. The gist of the allegation, then, was a charge of military Big Brotherism, *1984* politics on a small scale.

The Court, in an opinion endorsed by all four Nixon appointees as well as John Kennedy's former Assistant Attorney General, Byron White, combined deftly the "standing" and "political questions" doctrines to reject the A.C.L.U.'s claim. The Union had not demonstrated any direct personal injury; it merely disagreed with the executive branch both on the kinds of information necessary for the Army to perform its tasks effectively and on the choice of legal means necessary to accomplish this mission. The courts, they wrote, are not open to monitor the President's weighing of tactics and strategy. Congress, with its investigating committees wielding the power of the purse, was far better equipped to undertake appropriate supervision. The premise which seems to underlie this opinion is that the closer the Justices find themselves to "political questions," the more stringent the standing criterion becomes.[36]

The dissenters, on the other hand, claimed the Army had indulged in surveillance activities at least arguably beyond the constitutional powers assigned to noncivilian personnel. Since A.C.L.U. members were subjected to these investigations, standing had been established. Thus, the courts could decide whether the President's military tentacles had illegally abridged free expression.

"Political questions" doctrine should be seen as a spin-off of larger separation-of-powers theory. The Justices will not dispute legislative or executive action stemming from inherent attributes of either co-equal power center. The Court is not going to look foolish by applying judicial rules where they do not belong palpably—such as the battlefield. But beyond these generalities, there are juicy items of dispute, as *Laird v. Tatum* exemplifies. The unanswered question is simply this: Can the Congress and the President do a workmanlike job of checking and balancing the power of the other, or is it necessary, even in these situations of potential judicial impotence, for the Court to leap in and try to preserve the equilibrium?

The Court as power broker: the "unfolding" of constitutional doctrine[37]

In discussing the Court's awesome powers of constitutional interpretation and pure judicial review, the defensive posture inherent in its relations with the "political branches," and the rules of self-limitation it has honed to prevent possible embarrassment, I have taken the first steps toward understanding the Court as a political body. Now it is time to examine the Court's track record. What significant policies has it championed? What has been the ebb and flow of its power in dealing with other centers of authority? What important divisions among the Justices have influenced its work, and what have these disputes concerned? Which segments of society has it endeavored to represent, if any?

In retrospect, the political development of the Constitution divides itself nicely into three great eras: (1) from ratification to the Civil War, (2) from the Civil War to the Depression, and (3) from the Depression to our time. And these are the major symphonic divisions of Supreme Court policy-making as well, though there are movements within each era that must be distinguished.

Clearly, the period of Chief Justice John Marshall's dominance (1801–35) deserves special treatment. Before his time, the Court accomplished little, and when it did speak each member offered his own views. Under Marshall's leadership, the Justices learned "team play." Every judgment was supported by an opinion written on behalf of the Court itself. Any member who wouldn't "play ball" could dissent, of course, but the majority would be united. Marshall himself generally did the talking for the majority, and his leadership tactics proved effective. Even though political enemies such as Jefferson and Jackson placed allies on the bench to counteract his influence, the Court's key decisions were usually unanimous, and Marshall dissented against important constitutional rulings but once in thirty-four years! Most important of all, under Marshall's guidance the Supreme Court's judgments acquired a new institutional gloss; a holding did not simply reflect the opinions of individual judges but, rather, was the voice of one of the three great branches itself. Such consensus undoubtedly strengthened the symbolic authority and, therefore, the political power of the Justices as constitutional arbiters.

Marshall and his colleagues were, first and foremost, nationalists. The power of the Court, which they tried so hard to fortify in *Marbury,* was part of a larger principle, the supremacy of the Union. Therefore, congressional policies also deserved generous treatment. Could Congress establish a national bank? Of course, said Marshall. The Constitution didn't say so specifically, to be sure, but Congress did have the delegated power to control the currency. Furthermore, it could enact laws "necessary and proper" to enforce any and all delegated authority. A banking system was obviously an attempt to manage the dollar, so it was permissible.[38] What about the right to regulate commerce "among the several states" (Art. I, Sec. 8)? Did this allow Congress to control the flow of traffic from one state to another? Certainly, Marshall contended. In fact, commerce should be construed to mean *all* relations among states; "intercourse," he called these.[39] And, while this was not a period marked by unilateral presidential effort, it does not take much imagination to see Marshall upholding most of what there was—for instance, Jefferson's purchase of the Louisiana Territory.

The Supreme Court's enemy during these years was state action. With popular sovereignty riding high in the form of Jeffersonian and Jacksonian democracy, the layers of government "closest to the people" played a forceful political role. As Federalist and Unionist, Marshall fought the state legislatures and the "common man" on two fronts. First, attempts to undercut the supremacy of national authority and its great branches of government were to be stymied. For example, when Maryland levied a tax on the national bank, the Court said that a constituent member of the body politic could not control the actions of the Republic itself. If Maryland could tax the bank, then Maryland could tax the Mint, the Post Office, and all other federal agencies. We should never forget, Marshall warned, that the "power to tax is the power to destroy"; national power does not sit at the feet of state power.[40] Second, Marshall opposed state laws limiting personal liberties. As a champion of property rights he frowned on any attempt to regulate contractual obligations between individuals. The Framers, I have noted, placed in the Constitution a provision negating such state interference, and Marshall's Court enforced the "contract clause" (Art. I, Sec. 10) to the letter by thrusting several of these attempts aside.[41]

The duel with states' rights supporters lasted until Marshall's passing. The Court usually had the last word because it can also declare null and void any *state* law it thinks violates the Constitution. This concept may be called "federal judicial review," and it ranks with "pure judicial review" as one of the Court's primary weapons for construing our fundamental law.[42] That Marshall was chief architect of both doctrines is testament to a happy blend of political shrewdness and ideological persuasiveness that his successors could only hope to approach.

Marshall's successor as Chief Justice was the ill-starred Roger Taney, a Jacksonian by conviction but an advocate of compromise in practice. The Court under his direction could have been expected to roll back at least some of Marshall's policy thrusts, but its gestures were mostly piecemeal and oblique. A typical instance involved the debate over contract regulation. Suppose the state awarded a charter to some private company. Did this constitute an irrevocable contract that barred other businesses from entering the field even when the state thought such competition might be beneficial? Marshall would have said yes. But Taney did not believe that states could bargain away their powers to pass laws in the public interest by affixing their signatures to the usual charter of incorporation. He thought all contracts states had entered into should be interpreted in a manner favorable to legislative discretion wherever possible; individuals could tie the states' hands only when the agreements they had signed *specifically* supported their claims.[43] Taney's jurisprudence, then, constituted a period of respite from judicial activism and abetted the consolidation of judicial power.

But why didn't the Jacksonian populists attempt to rip down this nationalist, Federalist, elitist oligarchy established by Marshall and his peers? The explanation lies, in part, in Marshall's elongated tenure on the bench, the fact that with all his rhetoric he rarely challenged President and Congress directly, and in the economic prosperity and larger perspective that accompanied national growth and expansion. Moreover, the slavery question loomed larger and larger. The Court, inextricably bound to the cause of viable central government, could not give its unqualified support to the states, whose principal concern at that time was the maintenance of involuntary servitude free from national control. It was the politics of serendipity, rather than states' rights ideology, that led Taney's Court to throw off the yoke of restraint and leap into the fray.

The *Dred Scott* decision[44] is so important it should be described in detail. Congress had long thrashed over the nagging issue of whether slavery should be allowed in the territories—the lands owned by the federal government. The South was strongly favorable; the North was aghast. The acrimonious debate ended with passage of the Missouri Compromise in 1821. The southern reaches of this vast, unsettled area would be open to slavery, but the practice was banned north of an agreed-upon demarcation line. Naturally, the compromise rested on the understanding that Congress could regulate property rights (in this instance, slaves) within the territories it owned, just as states could regulate property rights within their various jurisdictions.

Dred Scott's claim presented to the Supreme Court was clear enough. John Emerson, a resident of Missouri, had taken him—a slave—into the Louisiana Territory for a visit. Because he had been brought onto free soil as specified by an act of Congress, Scott claimed he was a free man. If the Court had taken this road it would have infuriated the South, which at this late date saw any attempt by the federal government to impede slavery as an excessive limitation on both individual and states' rights. A possible alternative was to rule against Scott on the ground that his sojourn in federal territory was temporary; he was bound by Missouri law wherever he traveled with his owner. There is no doubt this course of action appealed to Taney, but it would have prompted a strong dissent from the minority bloc of antislave Justices, who wanted to uphold broad federal control over the federal government's own lands. The prospect of several colleagues taking such an intransigent nationalist view antagonized the majority, which really believed the Compromise unconstitutional yet was anxious to avoid open warfare on the bench.

From a larger perspective, however, the *Dred Scott* decision stemmed from the terrible dissension slavery was causing throughout the country. Congress had been unable to provide a remedy, the presidency was enfeebled, and both sides were growing more militant. Perhaps the Court, with its great prestige, could solve the problem. How could a patriot reject virtually the only chance for compromise still in the offing?

So Taney wrote the opinion for the majority. Dred Scott had no standing to sue because he was a member of the black race. Only United States citizens could use the federal courts, and the Framers of the Constitution did not consider blacks citizens. Nor did Congress have the power to vest freed slaves and their offspring with citizenship! For better or worse, this should have ended the decision, but it didn't. Taney went on to declare the Missouri Compromise unconstitutional. Slaves, as property, could not be kept out of the territories. Individual rights (of slaveholders) were paramount, and so Dred Scott was still chattel goods.

Even when assessed against the admittedly narrow standards of its effect on the Court's political prestige and power enhancement, *Dred Scott* is the worst decision the Justices have ever announced. They tried to adjudicate a social problem of immense proportions and came near to destroying their own good name. Years would pass before the stigma could be erased; in the meantime, the Court languished in obscurity, scorned by the forces of victorious Union as an ally of the infamous Confederate rebellion.

As one might anticipate, the Justices played no meaningful role during the Civil War. There is no more farcical sketch in our constitutional politics than Chief Justice Taney holding a general of the army in contempt because he would not release a Confederate sympathizer from Fort McHenry. The military, acting under President Lincoln's directive, had detained many such people, and Taney believed the whole procedure unconstitutional. Imagine the Chief Justice's consternation when a federal marshal rode up to the gates of the fort to bring the commanding officer before the bar of justice and was unceremoniously denied entry. No punishment was ever meted out![45]

The Court did not begin to make a comeback until it joined the dominant political consensus of the day. The first step was to allow the Republican majority in Congress to turn the Southern states into military districts. The

McCardle case discussed earlier bears witness to the bankruptcy of judicial influence in the late 1860s. As the years went by, the people would turn their attention away from the problems and frustrations raised by the war. They would become preoccupied with the nation's new industrial capacity and its application to the taming of the West. They would adopt as their guiding light the capitalist ethic of laissez faire—that government should not interfere with individuals as they seek to assert their personalities in the economic marketplace—and capitalism's root assumptions—that property rights are basic to the human condition and that worth is attained by those who have demonstrated their superiority in the natural competitive world of free enterprise. And the Justices were more than willing to pull their weight in making laissez faire meaningful.

To accomplish this, the Court went along with efforts to bury the consequences of the Civil War. First, it said the federal-state balance had not really been altered by the hostilities. The Fourteenth Amendment, added to the Constitution following the war, was a sweeping and controversial enactment that contained many provisions of singular importance. For instance, it said states couldn't deprive anyone of the "privileges and immunities" they possessed because of their American citizenship. What were these guarantees anyway? It is doubtful whether anyone really knew, but here was a perfect tool to make sure the states met minimal standards in dealing with the rights of the individual. Prior to the Civil War, no such check could be found in the Constitution; indeed, the real purpose of the conflict was to decide whether the states could be made to march to the tune of federal supervisory power. No matter. The Court said it would not play the role of "super-censor"; the phrase "privileges and immunities" meant only the right to travel around the country freely, to come to the seat of government and transact business with public officials, and the like.[46] Second, quandaries posed by the abolition of slavery must be shunted to the sidelines. The states were told to treat blacks on an equal basis but were not prevented from treating them on a separate basis.[47] Privately owned businesses and facilities did not have to service blacks at all if they didn't want to.[48] So racial segregation became constitutional doctrine.

In characterizing the Court's new role as legitimizer of capitalist economics, I want to stress the differences and similarities between its political base and Marshall's constituency. Defending property rights was certainly old stuff to the Justices. The function came naturally, because judges are invariably selected from the legal profession, and lawyers do not ordinarily make names for themselves by representing lower-class interests. But Marshall's clientele was the aristocratic, well-educated upper class that would manage the state for the good of all. The Court's clientele as the twentieth century approached was a nouveau riche upper-middle class, fearful that restrictions might be imposed on its economic freedom by small farmers and laborers who, armed now with the right to vote, could use government for their own "socializing" purposes.

When courts are influenced largely by gut political, economic, or philosophical preferences, they do not, of course, ordinarily come out and say so. They are sufficiently adept at the rituals of their trade to couch these values in specific constitutional language. This is a delicate, sometimes risky, business. The doctrine so expounded may not fit emerging trends, or it may run into unavoidable conflicting precedents. These factors contribute to the conservative nature of judicial policy-making. The method necessitates an inch-by-inch approach; thus, it is most difficult for forces of social reform to manipulate.

The "gay nineties" Court initially tried the commerce clause. As usual it was the state legislatures, still oriented toward Jeffersonian democracy, that first attempted regulatory legislation. But when Illinois determined that interstate railroads had to limit their fees, the Court said this was Congress's domain. If every state could place its own set of limitations on a transcontinental railroad, commerce among the states would be severely undermined.[49] And when Congress itself stepped into the picture by outlawing "combinations in restraint of trade," the Court said that the sugar industry, which was controlled almost entirely by one giant concern, was not affected by the law: if the statute were applied to the sugar monopoly, it would constitute regulation of production (manufacturing) rather than of the transport of the product in interstate commerce.[50]

However, a tool more sweeping in its scope than the commerce clause was needed, for if Congress set rules on the flow of goods or the states began to regulate manufacturing, the clause would be of little utility. The weapon that finally took shape was known as "substantive due process of law." To understand this concept, we must return first to the Bill of Rights (the Fifth Amendment, specifically), which says: "No person shall be . . . deprived of life, liberty, or property, without due process of law." This clause, with its roots in the early development of the English legal system, means that individuals cannot be fined, or imprisoned, or put to death unless they receive "due process"—a fair hearing in federal court. But if the *procedure* is fair, they can be subjected to whatever punishments the law allows. After the Civil War, the same phrase, with the same meaning intended, was placed in the Fourteenth Amendment and so became binding on the states.

What the Court did was to add a new dimension to the due process concept. Suppose the state told grain-elevator owners how much they could charge farmers. Might any figure be assessed? What if the rate ceilings were so low that some businesses would be forced into bankruptcy? Was this reasonable regulation or was it confiscation? If confiscation, how could it be *fair?* In other words, how could this taking of property satisfy the *reasonableness* standard that is the essence of due process? And so the Court vested itself with the power to determine what constituted reasonable, fair rates and regulations for all kinds of business activity.[51] If state and federal legislative standards transgressed these judicially determined criteria, they were labeled as taking of property without due process and declared unconstitutional. So the Court was no longer using the due process provision only to ensure *fair procedures* by decision-makers. Rather, the judges were making the decision themselves. The goals, the ends of policy, the *substantive* rules that government might contrive in regulating the relationship between business and the larger community had become the primary concern of the Supreme Court.

Keep in mind that "liberty" cannot be taken without due process of law either. This term was also papered over with a substantive gloss. When New York decided it was unhealthful for bakers to work more than a ten-hour day, the Court expressed great chagrin. Hadn't employers and employees agreed to longer working hours, asked the majority? How dare the state interfere with the *liberty* of private individuals to strike a bargain as to working conditions! So "liberty" in the Constitution now meant "liberty of contract," a palpably substantive notion.[52]

Dissenting in this case was a new appointee to the Supreme Court, Oliver Wendell Holmes. He chastised his brethren for second-guessing the social policies that underlay the thinking of New York's elected officials. Courts, he said, should strike down statutes only when they were totally unreasonable in the light of our political traditions. In this case, the majority had improperly sought to graft its laissez faire ideas onto the Constitution, a document entirely neutral in the area of economic philosophy. Holmes, we should point out, was no shining political liberal. He simply believed that if a majority wanted to experiment with social welfare measures, it should be allowed to have its way. But his theories of judicial self-restraint were far ahead of their time.

For thirty years, the "great dissenter," as he came to be known, stood against the judicial activism that tended to characterize the Court's work. There was even a period before our participation in World War I when the Justices—and the country generally—appeared to move away from the economics of Adam Smith. Theodore Roosevelt's trust-busting and Woodrow Wilson's New Freedom exemplify this trend. The Court's earlier attempt to make a progressive income tax constitutionally impossible[53] was overriden during this era by passage of the Sixteenth Amendment, the first formal addition to the document since Reconstruction. Seemingly becoming responsive to this drift in public opinion, the Justices, in another case, took a leaf from Marshall's nationalism by ruling that a congressional agency could regulate *intrastate* railroad rates when these were found to burden *interstate* rail transportation.[54]

But the "roaring twenties" snapped the nation back smartly. Our Presidents were Harding, Coolidge, and Hoover, and the presiding officer of the Supreme Court was William Howard Taft. No Chief Justice has ever possessed a more sophisticated understanding of judicial decision-making than Taft. He was determined that men sharing his political perspectives should sit with him on the bench, and he was eminently successful in persuading Presidents to appoint such spokesmen.[55] Once more, "liberty of contract" and substantive due process became the watchwords, while Holmes's ideas of judicial modesty were consigned to dissenting appeals.

Prosperity, of course, took a holiday in 1929, and the voters, clamoring for vigorous governmental intervention in the economy, elected Franklin Roosevelt to the White House in 1932. How would the Supreme Court respond to F.D.R.'s innovative programs? That question posed the greatest dilemma the Justices had known since Civil War days and caused a deep division on the bench. A group of four soon showed it would give the new governing majority little flexibility in making its New Deal work. Three others, disciples of

Holmes, were just as evidently on the other side. And in the middle were Owen Roberts, a man of superficial ideological bent, and Chief Justice Charles Evans Hughes, who, as leader of the Court and as student of history, feared more than all else a no-holds-barred confrontation with the "political branches."

Roosevelt's programs became more coercive as he sought to grapple with the seemingly relentless Depression; at the same time, Justice Roberts became increasingly more intransigent in his opposition to the most vigorous display of governmental regulation in American peacetime history. And as Roberts moved closer to the four irreconcilables, Hughes moved with him, if only to avoid the stigma of marginal, 5-4 decisions invalidating key legislation. The National Industrial Recovery Act (N.I.R.A.) was shot down, in part because the regulation of wages paid to and hours worked by chicken slaughterers was found to be an impermissible extension of Congress's control over interstate commerce.[56] The Agricultural Adjustment Act (A.A.A.) could not stand; after all, farming was the business of the states, not of the Congress.[57] The "laissez faire Court" was fighting the battle of its life in naked defense of its Constitution, a set of political rules under attack from every direction. And the more heated the struggle became, the more inflexible the majority became; its rhetoric took on the garb of a John Marshall "natural law" court, which, robot-like, merely reads the Constitution as it is written and strikes down any legislative attempt to inhibit property rights.[58]

But this was no war to be won by the invocation of jurisprudential metaphysics. Marshall had been an ideologue in his day, but he possessed a keen understanding of the power struggle. The nation's constitutional environment had undergone overnight transformation: millions of people were standing in bread lines, and Roosevelt's feel of the political pulse did not mislead him. In the 1936 elections he received the mandate he wanted, carrying every state but Maine and Vermont. Flushed with victory, and with a Congress solidly behind him, he confronted both Court and country with his famous (infamous?) "court-packing" plan. For each Justice over seventy years old, Roosevelt proposed the appointment of an additional member, the total number of the "rejuvenated" Court not to exceed fifteen. (Hence: with six of the nine jurists having reached age seventy, the "new" Supreme Court would have fifteen members.[59]) After all, said F.D.R., the older judges need help in order to keep abreast of their staggering workload!

Naturally, everyone knew the real reason for the proposal, and even some strong New Deal supporters saw the move as a direct challenge to the legitimate exercise of independent judicial conduct. But the Court itself must have been under intense pressure. In what has come to be called the "switch in time that saved nine," the Justices began to find economic-reform legislation constitutional after all. The Social Security Act passed muster.[60] The noxious practice of employing child labor in industry was now subject to severe regulation.[61] Roberts (and Hughes with him) had gone over to the other side, and a new coalition had been formed. One by one, the "four horsemen," as they had been dubbed, went into retirement.[62] *Their* Constitution was dying, and Roosevelt killed it with his first selections to the bench since he had trounced Hoover in

1932: Hugo Black, William O. Douglas, and Felix Frankfurter. With a sigh of relief, Congress quietly buried the "court-packing" plan; F.D.R. had lost that battle, but he certainly had won the war.

In 1939 the Supreme Court occupied very much the same standing in American politics as had the Court of 1865. Having entered the vortex of controversy and chosen the wrong side in a classic struggle for power, the Justices had been virtually stripped of their capacity to render significant policy judgments. The Court had specialized in defending the ground rules of laissez faire, and this function had suddenly become outdated.

If the Court were to exercise a meaningful role in our "Living Constitution," it would have to carve out for itself some new area of expertise and attempt, this time, not to overplay its hand. But this would be more difficult to accomplish than in the past. For one thing, the "switch in time" had bared, for even the unsophisticated to see, the political nature of the Court's work. With its mystique at low tide, the Court would need an extra measure of support to buttress activist inclinations. Furthermore, the Holmesian theory of self-restraint had now become conventional wisdom and would be very hard to overcome.

These constraints help to explain the Court's unassuming profile in the 1940s. Fear of totalitarian forces from inside and out had moved federal officials to take drastic steps to protect the nation against subversion. During World War II, over 100,000 Japanese-Americans on the West Coast were incarcerated in detention camps; and, when the specter of Stalinism made itself visible to the public, the leaders of the American Communist Party were sent to prison for conspiring to advocate the violent overthrow of government. The Court upheld both decisions.[63] The point here is not that these rulings were right or wrong. Rather, the point is that the Justices had already seen the need to become more aggressive in the general realm of personal rights. For instance, this period is dotted with cases in which they protected the Jehovah's Witnesses from such diverse regulatory schemes as the compulsory flag salute imposed on their children in the public schools and taxes imposed on their sales of religious tracts. But when the chips were placed on the table, the Court had few trump cards during these years to make its sentiments effectual.

The first breakthrough of major proportions occurred in 1954, with the school desegregation opinion.[64] For several reasons, the rights of black Americans constituted a prudent lever for opening up the broad area of civil liberties to judicial supervision. First, there was the historical predicate of the Civil War, which had supposedly stamped out involuntary servitude and led to citizenship for former slaves. Second, Hitler's racist ideology had heightened the sensibilities of many Americans to the inferior status of blacks in the United States. Third, the Court could confine its assertiveness to one sector of the country—the South—by knocking down the dual school systems stemming from deliberate state policies of segregation.

This decision coincided with the appointment of a new Chief Justice, Earl Warren. Much has been written about "Warren Court" activism, as the high bench sought to give broad, expansive interpretations to the libertarian and egalitarian language of the Constitution. For example, the fundamental law now prohibits public school teachers from leading their students in prayer;[65] legislative districts throughout the fifty states must now contain approximately equal numbers of people (that is "one person, one vote");[66] the police now have a duty to inform those accused of a crime that they have the right to remain silent and to consult a lawyer;[67] and, during Warren's tenure (1954–68), not one conviction for distributing an allegedly obscene book or movie to the general public was upheld, in cases in which works were placed before the Justices for their interpretation.[68]

Some general comments about the theoretical underpinnings of these decisions are in order. While the Warren Court was never known for articulating profound jurisprudential themes,[69] its decisions do reflect certain concepts developed by earlier constitutional thinkers. Writing in 1938, Mr. Justice Harlan Stone opened the door to modern-day Supreme Court activism when he identified three areas in which judicial supervision might well be intensified.[70] First, the courts could play a special role in protecting specific constitutional rights—for instance, the Fourth Amendment's check against unreasonable searches and seizures. Second, the courts could play a special role in protecting the democratic process from undemocratic forces. For example, if the people wanted the New Deal, Stone's priorities would put the Justices in the business of shielding voter privilege from undue restraint. (Note that while the Constitution guarantees freedom of speech and other freedoms, there is no constitutional "right to vote" for the bench to defend under Stone's first criterion.) Third, the courts could play a special role in protecting minority groups from discriminatory action undermining their access to the political marketplace. Statutes aimed against Jews, blacks, the Amish, or others might be so injurious that by the time the improvident "democratic experiment" was rectified, the damage could be irreversible; Stone's priorities would accord the Justices flexibility in supervising this unique area of *substantive* law.

If one accepts the premise that majority rule must sometimes be saved from itself—the central assumption underlying "pure judicial review," after all—then Stone's thesis should raise few eyebrows. The problem is that his framework does not justify in any way the Warren Court's activist posture. The ban against "establishment of religion" prescribed in the First Amendment may require the Court to strike down *compulsory* prayer in the public schools, but does it mandate a ban on *noncompulsory* prayer? Keeping the political system "open" may require the Court to invalidate legislative districts that have not been reapportioned for a century, but does it mandate "one person, one vote"?

Perhaps what the Warren Court tried to do was take Stone's three criteria and expand them into a full-blown defense of *constitutional equality:* the police and the accused have equal power in the question-and-answer process; children have equal freedom with respect to the dissemination of religious values in public schools; blacks and whites have equal status before the law; speakers and writers have equal access to the market, no matter what the content of their message. And because equality is attained most feasibly by restricting the power of large, vested interests while expanding the power of the "little person," the result was a deep commitment to individual liberties vis-à-vis governmental authority.[71]

But the Constitution looks *first* to the balance between liberty and authority, a balance that tips sometimes one way and sometimes the other, depending on circumstances. What forces determine those circumstances? The struggle among competing factions in the constitutional environment, a process toward which the President, the Congress, and the Court must pay close attention while they keep a careful watch on one another. For the document does not require that *all* factions be given an equal voice in political problem-solving, so we should hardly be surprised when governmental policy rarely treats *all* factions with scrupulous equality.

To take freedom of expression as an example: those who say that some speech is so filthy it should neither be plastered up on public billboards nor sold on street corners, and those who think some speech is libelous or incites to violence and consequently should be suppressed—those people constitute a long-term majority faction, for they hold a point of view that has left its mark on our mores and laws, a point of view shared by the Founders themselves. On the other hand, there are forms of speech that become subject to regulation only during wartime, while yet other forms of speech can *never* be regulated. Clearly, freedom of expression is no all-or-nothing proposition; there are *freedoms* of expression whose content depends upon what power center does the regulating and what values the power center is protecting.

So the "Living Constitution" is a mix between personal rights and duties, on the one hand, and governmental powers and duties on the other hand, but the ingedients in this mix vary with the particular blend of checks and balances established by custom, law, precedent, and public opinion. Perhaps the mix should be egalitarian in some circumstances (as I shall argue with vigor when I discuss race relations), but far more often the mix should not yield an egalitarian connection. In theory, then, one might have anticipated considerable tension between the Warren Court Constitution emphasizing *equality* of rights and duties, and the "Living Constitution," emphasizing *correlative* rights and duties. At times that tension was more than considerable.

Some general comments about the politics of the Warren Court decisions we have discussed are also in order. By and large the holdings did not challenge either the President or Congress as they sought to attain certain political objectives. It is state and local officials who make most of the arrests and who round up the "porno house" owners. As a matter of fact, New Deal economic egalitarianism dovetails rather well with Warren Court constitutional egalitarianism. Cries of protest against the "new judicial activism" came largely from: (1) the South, (2) "conservatives" (generally Republicans) who felt the Justices were too concerned with the rights of the individual and not enough concerned with society's rights, (3) a few prestigious intellectuals (mostly law professors) who continued to advocate judicial modesty in the interests of propriety and political horsesense, and (4) bread-and-butter Democrats living in the crime-infested urban centers, who perceived the Justices as ivory-tower atheists advocating a "kid gloves" approach to lawbreaking.

Clearly, this substantial opposition was too diffuse and, consequently, too lacking in political clout, to launch a serious counterattack. But the Warren Court, as so often has happened to Courts of the past, fell victim to circumstances beyond its control. The Vietnam War, stretching on and on, was the principal cause of a cleavage in Democratic Party ranks, severe enough to propel Richard Nixon to the White House. And while he proved flexible in such matters as China policy, Nixon proved unrelenting in his opposition to Warren Court activism. He was fortunate in having the opportunity to name four nominees to the high bench. And he took full advantage of the situation by selecting men—Warren Burger as Chief Justice, Harry Blackmun, Lewis Powell, and William Rehnquist—who he believed shared his overview of Supreme Court policy-making. The evidence shows him to have been a reasonably good prophet.

The Supreme Court today

The middle years of the 1970s find the Supreme Court in a period of transition. It is possible to delineate, at the risk of oversimplification, three postures the Justices assume in interpreting the fundamental law. The four Nixon appointees do not support the broad conception of constitutional equality that the Warren Court found so appealing. On the other hand, Thurgood Marshall, William Brennan, and William O. Douglas (when he sat on the bench),[72] holdovers from the activist majority of the 1960s, continue to endorse this approach; typically, then, they have squared off in opposition to the "Nixon four." Marching to their own drumbeats are Potter Stewart, a Republican named to the Court by Dwight Eisenhower, and Byron ("Whizzer") White, a Democrat selected by John F. Kennedy. Complicating matters even further is the fact that there appears to be no such thing as a Stewart-White "middle-of-the-road" bloc, roughly analogous to the Roberts-Hughes alignment of the 1930s. A glance at the short history of the Burger Court shows there are issues that find White gravitating toward a centrist position;[73] there are issues that find Stewart playing this role;[74] and there are issues that find the two combining with either of the more visible factions.[75] Of course, one can point to significant rulings where only a single Justice has dissented (the odds would favor either Douglas or Rehnquist assuming the role of loner); in fact, one can even find a unanimous opinion or two in the judicial haystack.

Naturally, these diverse approaches to constitutional values have taken their toll on Warren Court consensus. The Burger Court has expanded on some of the new doctrines, held the line with regard to others, and reacted adversely to yet others. States now possess some discretion in defining what is obscene in literature, movies, and so forth, and judicial interpretation of these statutes will be considerably less stringent.[76] The controversial *Miranda* decision, under which the police are required to inform defendants of their legal rights, has not been overruled, but its scope has surely been narrowed.[77] On the other side, the school desegregation decision of 1954 has been enforced with much rigor in the South,[78] while the Court's perception of church-state separation has become even more pronounced.[79]

The question is commonly asked: Where should the Court be going? To address the inquiry requires one to ask two further questions: (1) Where has the Court been? and (2) What are the Justices fighting about?

History demonstrates that the power to read and interpret the Constitution is not promoted by invoking some simple, straightforward calculus. The Court was a powerful force in policy-making with activists like Marshall and Warren at the helm, yet the exploits of Taney and the "four horsemen" of the New Deal period left only "self-inflicted wounds." Holmes's self-restraint of the 1920s might have spared our politics many shock waves had it been adopted, but judicial modesty does not right any of the wrongs done to an author whose book is censored, to a voter who lives in a gerrymandered district, or to a child who attends only "separate but equal" schools. It is also alleged that Justices should be either "strict" or "broad" constructionists. In other words, they should either interpret the Constitution in a literalistic way, sticking closely to the letter of the document, or they should infuse the document with some of their own notions, ostensibly so that our charter of government can be kept abreast of the times. But Marshall made his name by broad construction of the commerce and contract clauses, while Holmes made his by a strict interpretation of the due process clauses; and Warren Court innovation spawned extraordinary disputation by supporting a very literal interpretation of free expression, strictly limiting the power of elected officials to regulate speech. Finally, it is surely not helpful to evaluate Supreme Court Justices as political liberals or conservatives. Was Marshall pronouncing conservative doctrine when he said the states were bound by a national Constitution? Was Holmes a liberal because he thought his colleagues were talking too much? When the Warren Court said *it* would decide whether a book was obscene rather than letting juries do the job, was this liberalism or conservatism?

There is a school of thought which teaches that the Constitution is forever in the process of unfolding, like some great peacock's tail, that its language and meaning have become richer and deeper with each Supreme Court reading of the scripture. The theory is misleading. What the Court has done is to apply a variety of tools to an ever-changing set of circumstances, all for the purpose of achieving meaningful ideological influence without endangering its power base. On occasion it has gotten too far out in front of the dominant political forces, and on other occasions it has lagged too far behind. When the Justices lose step in this fashion, they often speed up or slow down through sudden shifts in doctrinal consistency until a better accommodation has been achieved. So the Constitution as a two-hundred-year old dynamic corpus is actually a somewhat untidy set of rules and norms, containing its share of threads and patches, as Gilbert and Sullivan might have phrased it.

The tough questions facing the Burger Court would also seem to resist solution by applying one straightforward mathematical formula. Not that either Justice White or Justice Stewart has found the right combination, but they may well be on the right track. The issues—society's power to regulate the traffic in pornography, the ghetto black child's right to attend suburban schools in the Detroit and Denver areas, Congress's authority to provide millions to the financially unstable parochial schools—are much too disparate. And lurking underneath the issues themselves are questions of judicial activism versus judicial restraint and constitutional stability versus constitutional change. In short, our politics is trying to wrestle with the very tenacious substantive question of how to reconcile the correlative freedoms and obligations which the individual and the ever-expanding tentacles of the state have to one another; furthermore, our politics is trying to agree on what procedural tools of coercion should be used to effect this reconciliation. No pat formula we can find buried in the Constitution or elsewhere—including both political egalitarianism and knee-jerk opposition to egalitarian values—will serve as a guiding light. But will the Justices have the temperament, the craftsmanship, and the resiliency to establish the necessary priorities and policies?

The Court as political mechanism: the appointment process

For the past several pages, I have talked about the doctrines and policies the Supreme Court has advanced. Now let us look at the Justices themselves and how they are appointed. The typical Justice, who is between 50 and 55 when nominated for service on the high bench, was brought up in affluent surroundings and educated in the best schools and has enjoyed a distinguished career in the public sector.[80] We are talking about mature professionals—many of whom have traveled in the most prestigious circles and have been "movers and shakers" in our society. It is fanciful to believe that these people shed a lifetime of acculturation, experience, and conviction when they report for Supreme Court duty. In fact, the great questions of public concern they will confront on the bench may intensify their devotion to these principles. Moreover, we should not be surprised to learn that those who have a considerable stake in what the Justices do, try their best to influence the process by which they are selected. Is it any wonder that the selection process, the criteria used in choosing nominees, and the underlying political factors motivating these appointments are all part of the "Living Constitution"? To these issues I now turn.

What are the qualifications for the job? The Constitution mentions none, but the implicit rules spotlight at least two. A prospective nominee must be a lawyer; of the hundred-odd individuals who have sat on our highest judicial panel, all have been members of the bar. That is because we expect our Justices to have formal training in the quasi-mystical symbols of constitutional law. Another criterion is practical political experience. Every Supreme Court member—save one—had at least some training in the political arena before he made it to the top, and one-third of this group came from families with a tradition of prior judicial service.[81] So the Justices form a kind of inbred social elite, but in their younger days they were exposed to the political rough-and-tumble. Clearly, this apprenticeship period helps identify ideological views, party preference, and other elements of leadership that the President, sifting through the list of probables, needs to be apprised of. And, of course, participation in political life can provide the visibility—and maybe the "inside track"—that every candidate must have.

But what criteria are used to whittle down the list of aspirants? Henry Abraham cites five (and not in any particular order of importance): political availability; ideological affinities; geographic, religious, and other demographic factors; objective merit; personal considerations.[82]

The most reliable gauge for predictive purposes is political party ties. Approximately 90 percent of all selections are from the President's own party. And why not? Sometimes it is a cut-and-dried matter of paying off political debts; Dwight Eisenhower's choice of Earl Warren has often been labeled a reward for delivering the California delegation at the 1952 Republican National Convention. But more often, it is simply a matter of general patronage considerations.

The second criterion, ideology, is another implicit norm. Presidents, of course, want judges who will vote on the big issues the way they themselves would vote, since they know judicial decision-making is part of a larger political decision-making network. Court-watchers disagree on the chief executive's predictive powers. Skeptics[83] note that the liberal Woodrow Wilson nominated the conservative James McReynolds, while James Madison, a late-in-life convert to Jeffersonianism, named Joseph Story in the hope that he would counterbalance John Marshall, only to see Story out-Marshall the Chief Justice in nationalist fervor. But the most careful empirical study of judicial selection finds these vivid illustrations running counter to the general trend.[84] For instance, President Taft, a conservative Republican, picked three Democrats to fill vacancies on the Court and later, as Chief Justice, advised President Harding to name another Democrat.[85] For a judge to think as he did was more important to Taft than party affiliation. In each instance, the appointee later made Taft look like a seer.[86]

Every now and then, sectional or socioeconomic criteria prevail. Early in our history, state citizenship was significant; a chief executive could not afford to overrepresent Massachusetts or Virginia. More recently, it has been less a matter of state than region, though one New Yorker almost always can be found among the nine. The geographical element affords Republicans an opportunity to invoke their oft-used "Southern strategy." In Taft's day, the elevation of Louisiana's Edward White to the Chief Justiceship meant a possible pick-up of crucial votes in the Senate for Taft's legislative program. In Nixon's day, the selection of Clement Haynsworth (South Carolina) and G. Harrold Carswell (Florida), though both failed of Senate confirmation, fulfilled his pledge to provide Southern representation on the Court, and certainly he hoped to collect a few extra electoral votes for his efforts. With respect to religion and race, knowledgeable observers assume there is a "Catholic seat" and a "Jewish seat" on the bench. William J. Brennan currently holds the former, while the latter, filled in succession by Benjamin Cardozo, Felix Frankfurter, Arthur Goldberg, and Abe Fortas, lies dormant. There may now be a seat for blacks, as Lyndon Johnson made it quite clear Thurgood Marshall was chosen, in part, because of his race. Is a "female seat" far behind?

And what of sheer talent, so-called objective qualifications? Rarely is a person selected entirely for this reason. The pages of history are strewn with brilliant constitutional scholars who were not nominated because they failed to meet the necessary political and/or ideological criteria.[87] On the other hand, Wilson's determination to place Louis Brandeis on the Court is perhaps a fair instance of a President choosing a Justice on the basis of merit, although it is true both were Jeffersonian liberals. Brandeis was considered to be one of the legal giants of the century, and even though Wilson suffered political losses because no Jew had ever before been nominated, the President was determined to have him. There is also evidence that Herbert Hoover named Benjamin Cardozo in part because he was thought to be the best man.[88]

Of all five criteria, the "personal considerations" factor accounts best for why *one* particular person—rather than others of similar bent—ultimately reaps the reward.[89] But not often does a chief executive promote only those who are close friends. Yet this was standard operating procedure for Harry Truman. He filled four vacancies, and it would be fair to label each choice a political crony.

The President, as we know, does not have a free hand in all this. He must persuade a majority of senators to endorse his selection. The process of confirmation for Supreme Court appointees may be divided historically into three periods: (1) In the nineteenth century, more than 25 percent of these choices were vetoed by the Senate, many for partisan reasons. (2) In the twentieth century, prior to 1968, the Senate rejected only *one* selection and that by a single vote. (3) From 1968 to the present, three nominations have failed. Why the switch in recent times?

In 1968, Chief Justice Warren told President Johnson he wanted to retire, but he was willing to stay on until his successor had been approved. Johnson named Abe Fortas, a close personal friend and member of the Court since 1965, to replace him as Chief Justice.[90] Now Fortas's name had been cleared easily enough on the first go-around, so the risks appeared minimal. But times had changed. The Warren Court, as it carved out new frontiers of individual rights, was now front-page copy. And Fortas was in the vanguard of this movement. The debate in the Democratically controlled Senate was loud and interminable. Fortas got the message, and he asked Johnson to withdraw his name. A year later, Fortas resigned from the bench; the news broke that he had agreed to accept a yearly fee from a man later convicted of illegal sales of stock and sent to jail.

Two years later, it was Richard Nixon's turn. He had already promised to name Justices who would be responsive to his "law and order" theme, and when the time came he kept that promise. Warren Burger, selected to replace Earl Warren, sailed through, but when Nixon named Clement Haynsworth, the fur began to fly. There was evidence that the nominee had helped adjudicate cases involving corporations in which he owned stock. In the backwash of the Fortas embarrassment, some senators thought Haynsworth's indiscretions of major proportions. Also, Haynsworth was a Southerner with a voting record on the lower federal bench that bespoke judicial restraint. He was beaten, 55-45.

Nixon then nominated G. Harrold Carswell, another Southern jurist with another nonactivist voting chart. Carswell owned almost no stock in any company! On the other hand, Senate "liberals" argued he was a pedestrian figure, at best. Even Carswell's supporters admitted he was no Holmes or Frankfurter.[91] His name was turned back, 51-45. Eventually, Harry Blackmun of Minneapolis won confirmation, and he has also proved to be no judicial Odysseus.

What can we make of these skirmishes? From the standpoint of constitutional theory and sheer logic, there are powerful arguments supporting a no-holds-barred review by the Senate. The President is not naming someone to sit in the White House circle, but someone to sit in an independent branch of government, an institution possessing equal status with the presidency. Why shouldn't the Senate exercise 50 percent of the voice in selection, and why shouldn't an appointee whose views and policies are considered dangerous to the general welfare be rejected?[92]

But we are not students of theory and logic alone; we are students of politics. In 1900 or 1920 or 1940, Fortas, Haynsworth, and Carswell would have all been confirmed. Fortas was an activist in defense of personal rights, but he wasn't in the same league with several of Roosevelt's appointees who walked in with no Republican opposition. The conflict-of-interest charges against Haynsworth would surely not have caused the Framers themselves to blush. Finally, we have had "mediocre" Justices à la Carswell on the Court since the founding of the Republic. In short, an implicit "rule of the game" had held sway for many decades: if the candidate was respectable, he would be acceptable. What was at issue in the 1960s—and still is at issue—has been the Warren Court. The G.O.P.-Dixiecrat coalition took its frustrations out on Fortas, just as F.D.R.'s senatorial legions would have given the "four horsemen" a vote of no-confidence had they been handed the opportunity. Today the Warren Court lives on through the doctrines it advanced. The Senate liberals love it, while Nixon-style conservatives can't stomach it. Stripping away the varnish, Nixon's *articulated* policy was: "I'll name people who will likely repudiate Warren Court principles I can't abide"; the Senate's *unarticulated* policy has been: "We'll reject any candidate who will likely repudiate Warren Court egalitarianism, if we can find any legitimate excuse for so doing." In the Burger and Blackmun instances, there were no such excuses; there was only ideological disenchantment, and this was not sufficient politically considering the mores of the confirmation process. I repeat: if the Justices are going to slay dragons, they take on great risks. One of the greatest is a potential loss of status when the fount of wisdom they control is dragged through the political muck. That is what has befallen the Court today.[b]

Rather than ending on a note of cynicism, let me go back a bit to larger questions inherent in the appointment process. Speaking to issues of presidential selection, Felix Frankfurter excoriated the nomination of Supreme Court

[b] Gerald Ford aped the Nixon formula successfully when he chose John Paul Stevens, a seemingly nonactivist type who, like Burger and Blackmun, was politically unassailable. Stevens received swift approval in the Senate.

members for ideological or political reasons. The true test, he submitted, was "functional fitness"—that is, "The search should be made among those men . . . who give the best promise of satisfying the intrinsic needs of the Court," and these men are "thinkers, and more particularly legal philosophers."[93]

It is hard to disagree with the contention that Supreme Court Justices should be people of breadth and learning, students of history and philosophy. But I continue to be unimpressed with Frankfurter's formula as a single-variable tool.[94] In our politics, the President tends to head up a dominant coalition of political forces. He is elected to do a job, and he has a right to push hard—within the bounds of constitutional propriety—for the adoption of values he has advocated during the campaign. One of the prizes to be won at the ballot box is control of the Supreme Court (in the contemporary era, a chief executive will get to fill a vacancy once every seventeen months).[95] The Justices' "main contribution," in typical circumstances, is to legitimize the essential policies of popular government by weaving new interpretations from old constitutional cloth.[c] Surely we now realize that in the long-term battles between the "political branches" and the Court, the Court loses.[96] In the short run, when friction between these power centers may be accelerated, the chief executive can surely resort to "value packing" as a legitimate political weapon. The whole problem with Frankfurter's theory is that it does not define judicial policy-making as an integral part of national governmental decision-making, and, therefore, it does not define the Court's labors as struggles over competing constitutional values. Of course, political realities—such as senatorial reaction—will always constrain Presidents, but this is a qualitatively different kind of check from a self-restraint that would inspire a President to name only the "best" people, whether or not they agree with his policies.

The Court as political mechanism: the decisional process

What actually goes on inside the Supreme Court? How are decisions reached? From our study of the appointment process, one might be led to believe—erroneously—that the Justices receive cases and then "vote their consciences." But this assumption takes no account of the Court as a social institution, wherein nine rather different, strong-willed statesmen must work together. Nor is it clear what the political implications of the words "vote" and "conscience" are in this context.

When we think of any decision-making group from a political perspective, we should think at once of *leaders* and *followers.* Who is attempting to exert power? How? Is the leader successful? Why? Or why not? The Supreme Court has a formal leader-follower apparatus—eight Associate Justices and one Chief Justice. The Chief Justice has no greater voting power than the Associates, but the title clearly evinces leadership. Let us examine that leadership role in decision-making.[97]

Litigation is accepted for review, and briefs are filed by lawyers representing the contending parties. The Justices and their staffs of assistants (law clerks)

[c] The cartoon character Mr. Dooley put the matter somewhat more cynically when he said: "The Supreme Court follows the iliction returns."

study these intensively. In controversies of significance, oral argument is heard. Counsel for each side makes a statement and may be questioned either closely or indifferently by the Court. The nine Justices then meet in what is called the "conference," a strictly confidential meeting at which the Chief Justice presides. He will present the cases for disposition, and he might outline what he thinks are the salient points. In short, it is his prerogative to structure the discussion and to oversee the give-and-take. Eventually a vote is taken, and this process is consummated in systematic fashion from junior Justice through senior, with the Chief expressing his conclusion last.

The chairmanship function is the formal seat of the Chief Justice's power. In his management of the conference, he will attempt to play at least one of two roles. Perhaps he will strive to be the Court's intellectual leader, to shine in debate and ideological riposte. Or perhaps he will endeavor to be the Court's social leader, catering to the human needs of his peers, and effecting compromise through his warmth and good fellowship.

Rarely does a Chief Justice have the ability and flexibility to wear both hats, though Charles Evans Hughes (1930-41), with his photographic memory and his emotional maturity, did just that. Under his leadership, personal conflict was minimized, and the Court's decisions were not influenced greatly by friction among the Justices. An equally admirable condition exists, though, if the Chief performs one of the two tasks, and works in concert with a peer who performs the other. This is no mean feat, because the Chief must here understand his own limitations. William Howard Taft (1921-30) was his Court's social leader, and he was sharp enough to leave the thorny intellectual dilemmas to Willis Van Devanter. On the other hand, Chief Justice Harlan Stone (1941-46) was a failure in both areas. He wrangled over issues, was at times inarticulate, and created animosities by being much too formal in discussions. The result was a terrible conflict over intellectual leadership among Hugo Black, Felix Frankfurter, and Stone himself, and a void in social leadership, with no one around to bridge gaps and promote consensus. Is it any wonder that the Stone Court produced ideologically extreme opinions, with opponents sometimes throwing the sharpest of debating "needles" at one another?[98]

After the vote is taken, the task of writing an opinion for the Court majority must be assigned. When the Chief Justice is a member of the prevailing view, the choice is his to make; if he is a dissenter, the senior Justice among the majority performs the function. The opportunities for bargaining at this stage are legion. The person who writes the Court's official statement must please not only himself but those colleagues who share his judgment. He will be anxious especially to stifle *concurring opinions,* separate views by Justices who voted as he did but who feel they must speak their own minds because his presentation does not satisfy them. Perhaps, also, a *dissenting opinion* can be headed off, if the Court's statement soft-pedals certain issues or doctrines. So to assume that Justices do nothing but stand up for the values they think proper and right is to neglect the inevitable drift toward accommodation by all collegial political agencies, which prefer to face a questioning public from a position of strength and unity.[99]

Perhaps the most controversial research of recent years in the Supreme Court decision-making area involves the counting of the Justices' votes. If we can compute Henry Aaron's batting average in a season, why can't we compute a judge's "voting average" with respect to certain variables and thus derive precise data on how members of the Court differ in their approaches to major policy issues?

As we have seen, however, life on the Court is not so simple. When we talk of Aaron's batting average, we are discussing the elementary exercise of dividing times at bat into base hits. But when we talk of a Justice's voting average, we must relate how often X voted with Y and how often they each voted for a particular value, such as free-speech claims. Even if the formidable statistical problems can be resolved, we are still faced with enormous hurdles, of which I shall indicate three. First, two Justices might vote together most of the time on free-speech issues, but very often they approach the problem from completely different vantage points. Some of the more rabid quantifiers have argued that a Justice votes against free-speech allegations because he has a negative attitude toward a broad, expansive view of free speech.[100] Perhaps this assessment does describe accurately a Tom Clark or a Sherman Minton (two of Truman's appointees), but suppose a Frankfurter, in the true spirit of judicial restraint, voted against free-speech allegations because he thought the problem should be handled by another governmental agency? In other words, voting charts may not be valid indexes of either *overt policy preference* or *unconscious predilection.* Second, there is the whole question of how much a *vote* conveys on its own. A comprehensive statement of views figures to be a much better indicator of philosophy than a naked vote. This is especially true of Supreme Court Justices who relate at least as much to ideas as they do to litigants. If we based our counting procedures on doctrines or issues debated in opinions rather than on votes, we would take a step forward.[101] Third, and most basic of all, no quantitative scheme can capture the indecision, the bargaining, the switch-overs, and the eventual lineup of the Justices that often lie beneath the votes *and* opinions in important cases. Though I think the estimate is extreme, perhaps the only thing quantitative analysis of judicial policy-making can ever tell us is what our intuition and insight have grasped already.[102]

The Court as political mechanism: the compliance process

What happens to an important Supreme Court decision after it has been promulgated? The Court's judgment is supposed to be the law of the land, so one naturally assumes these pronouncements are accepted automatically in the larger political context. But no such rule of automatic compliance exists. To understand what actually happens, we should distinguish between two levels of implementation: enforcement by high-level federal officials—that is, President, Congress, and the lower courts[103]—and enforcement by state and local officials.

Our history books are dotted with examples of visible, overt attempts by federal authorities to resist controversial Supreme Court rulings. President Andrew Jackson, in an episode that is perhaps apocryphal, set the standard for self-righteous outrage and confrontation when he bellowed: "Well, John Marshall has made his decision; now let him enforce it." More recently (1968 to be precise), Congress threw down the gauntlet by passing a statute that allowed federal judges to admit into evidence all voluntary confessions, whether the accused had been informed of their rights under the *Miranda* ruling or not. But the most clear-cut instance of noncompliance in this century involved the *Brown* decision, with its drastic negation of dual school systems in the South. However, this must be considered a special circumstance, because the Court itself was largely responsible. Fearing an upheaval of the largest dimension if their decision were enforced to the letter at once, the Justices temporized by delegating to the lower trial courts the power to shape desegregation plans for the public schools. The sole criterion they insisted upon was that the orders be issued "with all deliberate speed."[104] Ten years went by, and only a trickle of "good-faith compliance" decrees had been shaped; the subordinate judges, born and raised in the South and subject to intense pressures from both politicians and the media in their home states, either hemmed and hawed or defied with impunity the *Brown* edict.[105] If the Congress and the Court itself had not stepped into the breach and laid down stricter ground rules, who knows how long full-scale obedience might have waited in the wings.

Still, there is no evidence that federal executive, legislative, or judicial officers flout Court holdings except in unusual cases where reaction against controversial new policies runs high. They know when the Justices have handed down critical opinions, and their staff of legal assistants can explain to them what the Court has in mind. The "fit" between constitutional orders and compliance may not be perfect, but the norm of Supreme Court supremacy is understood and generally accommodated. This is most fortunate, because the Justices would have precious few ways to coerce compliance without the aid of those "purse and sword" attributes the "political branches" wield.

At the level of state and local enforcement the hiatus between word and deed is much greater. A plethora of individual studies designed to measure the impact of Supreme Court judgments at the grassroots level has been published over the past decade,[106] and while it is not easy to frame generalizations based on these, certain broad themes crop up again and again.

One of these themes, or problem areas, has to do with *lack of knowledge.* Suppose the Justices adopt a new definition of obscenity. Will movie censors in Detroit comprehend its nuances? The chances would be far from bright.[107] Sometimes the public servant who administers particular programs does not even realize that the relevant constitutional standards have been reformulated. In part, the breakdown in communication stems from pedestrian training and lack of legal sophistication that so often characterize city and state personnel; on occasion, the breakdown arises from inadequate media coverage of what the Court has said; at still other times, the breakdown is exacerbated by the wide splits among the Justices themselves, which in recent years have tended to blur the message.

Another variable that helps explain noncompliance at this level involves *lack of agreement with the new policy* by the principal enforcing agent. Suppose the Justices tell school boards around the country that they must curtail all devotional services on public property. Who implements the new policy? Obviously, the very boards, superintendents, and teachers who have been running these programs for a substantial period of time. No wonder more than half of Tennessee's school districts paid not the least attention when the Court ordered a stop to Bible-reading unless it was part of secular instruction.[108] After *Miranda* was handed down, a group of Yale law students sat in the New Haven police station on a twenty-four-hour basis for eleven weeks. They found that the prescribed warnings sometimes were not delivered on cue to arrested persons, but even when the proper advice was given, the police often used a tone of voice lacking in enthusiasm or animation; the message frequently got lost in translation. The students summed up their findings succinctly: "Not much has changed after *Miranda*."[109] Of course, many of these state and local officials rationalize their behavior by saying—probably with considerable truth—that they are supporting values generally accepted in their constituencies and communities. But rarely do the voters hold the officials accountable for the manner in which they implement these doctrines,[110] so we are talking mostly about the vested ideological opinions of lower-echelon public bureaucrats.

A final factor in noncompliance is *lack of public sympathy for the Court* today. At long last, political science has invoked Gallup-style survey techniques to measure public reaction to the work of the Supreme Court. We can now verify the deep-seated respect that the average person accords to our highest judicial branch as an institution. However, we also know the Warren Court's activist stance made the Justices rather visible, and that an overwhelming majority of Americans who had some knowledge of their decisions viewed the Court in an *unfavorable* light because of them.[111] And when grassroots officials attempt to evade their compliance responsibilities, we tend to find strong antipathy for the contemporary Court as expert and legitimate Constitution reader.[112] Common sense should tell us there is a high correlation between general public suspicion of the Warren Court's visible rulings, and the rather intense disdain for the Court by these enforcement specialists. It remains to be seen whether the Burger Court's somewhat higher ratings in the popularity polls will help achieve a better compliance track record.[113]

This account should not be overdramatized. It is wrong to think that the typical Supreme Court decision is ignored in the precincts of American law enforcement. It is also wrong to talk of compliance as only a short-term matter; when the Court seeks broad constitutional change, the results take time. As we have seen with regard to overt school segregation, the final proof is in the ultimate effectuation of the announced policy. Had the long-range impact been largely exercises in noncompliance, then a different assessment of the Court's political savvy would undoubtedly be warranted. Finally, when we evaluate general public reaction to the bench, it is wise to remember that some of our more talented and creative leaders were not appreciated even in their lifetimes. In sum, it all comes back to the salient issue: is the new policy sensible, equitable, balanced, and consistent with the most fundamental norms that underlie the "Living Constitution"?

NOTES

1. The term "Justice" is an elevated title given to judges who sit on the Supreme Court. Perhaps it is meant to convey the notion that the Court dispenses the purest form of equity we can muster.

2. Compare the political tirades of candidates for governor, senator, and President when they present their views to the public.

3. The leading spokesman for the school of judicial prophecy was Sir William Blackstone. His *Commentaries on the Laws of England* was considered the fount of wisdom during the last century.

4. Mr. Justice Owen Roberts, speaking for the Court in *United States v. Butler,* 297 U.S. 1 (1936).

5. As any high school American history course teaches, members of the Supreme Court are nominated by the President and confirmed by majority vote of the Senate.

6. Most Justices are reluctant to discuss the matter in their opinions. An exception was Felix Frankfurter, though, it has been argued with some success, he may have been a trifle fixated on the subject. See his dissents in *West Virginia v. Barnette,* 319 U.S. 624 (1943) and *Baker v. Carr,* 369 U.S. 186 (1962).

7. The notion was coined by John P. Frank. See his "Review and Basic Liberties," in Edmond Cahn, ed., *The Supreme Court and Supreme Law* (Bloomington: Indiana Univ. Press, 1954), p. 110. However, his definition is limited to Supreme Court oversight of congressional enactments. I use the concept in broader form to include the review of any action sanctioned by a co-equal branch of government. The power to judge the constitutionality of *state* laws, as Frank says, is of a different species; but it is not logical, given the contemporary power structure, to equate a review of executive acts with a review of state acts, a presumption he seems to accept.

8. Most members of the Constitutional Convention chose to join the Federalist ranks with the rise of the two-party system. As I have noted, the Twentieth Amendment, ratified in the 1930s, abolished these "lame-duck" congressional sessions.

9. Recall the old catch phrase: "Congress passes the laws; the President enforces the laws; the courts interpret the laws."

10. Can Congress abolish lower federal courts, even though *all* federal judges hold life tenure? The Justices have never met this issue head on. Of course, Congress could not abolish the Supreme Court, because the Constitution provides for its existence.

11. A writ is merely a judicial order; mandamus is a command from a judge to a public official telling the official to fulfill some responsibility under the law which he or she has not carried out.

12. John Jay, our first Chief Justice, was so bored with his job that he gladly tendered his resignation following a successful bid for the governorship of New York.

13. In *Chisholm v. Georgia,* 2 Dall. 419 (1793), the Court made a false start by holding that states could be sued in federal court (even against their will) by citizens of other states. The reaction was so adverse the decision was reversed in a few months by the Eleventh Amendment.

14. The official citation for *Marbury v. Madison* is 1 Cr. 137 (1803). Because this book emphasizes constitutional politics, the reader will find the footnotes replete with references to Supreme Court decisions. This is as good a time as any to explain these hieroglyphics. A typical citation might be "15 U.S. 206." That simply means the case can be located in Volume 15 of the *United States Reports,* page 206. These reports are a complete compilation of all Supreme Court rulings; they are published by the federal government and can be found in any respectable library. In the early days, Court decisions appeared under volume titles borrowed from the last name of the chief compiler and editor. Thus, *Marbury v.* (that is versus) *Madison* can be found in Volume 1 of *Cranch's Reports,* page 137.

15. Charles A. Beard, "The Supreme Court—Usurper or Grantee," *Political Science Quarterly* 27 (1912), pp. 1-35.

16. Article No. 78 is his best statement on the subject.

17. The cases are *Pollock v. Farmers' Loan & Trust Co.,* 158 U.S. 601 (1895), leading to the Sixteenth Amendment, and *Oregon v. Mitchell,* 400 U.S. 112 (1970), resulting in passage of the Twenty-sixth Amendment.

18. These comments reflect the provocative insights found in Robert A. Dahl, "Decision-Making in a Democracy: The Supreme Court as a National Policy-Maker," *Journal of Public Law* 6 (1958), pp. 279-95.

19. This is the language of Article III. I have not enumerated all the possibilities suggested by the Founders, but the salient items will suffice. The guiding principles underlying the various elements of jurisdiction—both original and appellate—were (1) to insure that the Court would hear any legal controversy involving a significant exercise of federal power and (2) to allow the Justices to sit as neutral arbiters when states of the Union, or persons from different states, wished to test their legal rights against one another.

20. 7 Wall. 506 (1869).

21. U.S. Supreme Court Rules, Rule 19: Conditions Governing Review on Certiorari.

22. The proposal was known as the Butler-Jenner Bill (S.2646, 85th Cong., 1st Sess., 1957).

23. This link between the Court's jurisdictional mandate and the "cases and controversies" requirement is discussed in *Baker v. Carr,* 369 U.S. 186 (1962).

24. Henry P. Johnston, ed., *The Correspondence and Public Papers of John Jay,* vol. 3 (New York: G. P. Putnam's Sons, 1890-93), pp. 486-89.

25. *Gordon v. United States,* 2 Wall. 561 (1865). The Court will also not accept jurisdiction if it thinks the litigation has been prearranged. Obviously, parties working in collusion are not adversaries. *Chicago & Grand Trunk Ry. Co. v. Wellman,* 143 U.S. 339 (1892).

26. *Frothingham v. Mellon,* 262 U.S. 447 (1923).

27. *Flast v. Cohen,* 392 U.S. 83 (1968).

28. 405 U.S. 727 (1972).

29. *Mora v. McNamara,* 389 U.S. 934 (1967); *Holmes v. United States,* 390 U.S. 936 (1968).

30. *United States v. Curtiss-Wright Corp.,* 299 U.S. 304 (1936); *Martin v. Mott,* 12 Wheat. 19 (1827).

31. The most thorough discussion of the doctrine is found in Charles G. Post, *The Supreme Court and Political Questions* (Baltimore: Johns Hopkins Press, 1936).

32. This line of analysis doesn't explain why the Court refused at least to receive cases on the subject and *then* invoke "political questions." A skeptic of Warren Court priorities might argue that the Justices had made so many enemies because of their boldness elsewhere that they lacked the necessary political maneuverability even to participate in the constitutional dialogue!

33. 7 How. 1 (1849).

34. *Gillian v. Morgan,* 413 U.S. 1 (1973).

35. 408 U.S. 1 (1972).

36. For another recent case perhaps demonstrating the same linkage, see *Sarnoff v. Shultz,* 409 U.S. 929 (1972).

37. I want to express my considerable intellectual debt to the late Robert G. McCloskey, whose book, *The American Supreme Court* (Chicago: Univ. of Chicago Press, 1960), expresses in much more complete form the general historical orientation conveyed in the following section.

38. *McCulloch v. Maryland,* 4 Wheat. 316 (1819).

39. *Gibbons v. Ogden,* 9 Wheat. 1 (1824).

40. *McCulloch v. Maryland.*

41. *Fletcher v. Peck,* 6 Cr. 87 (1810); *Dartmouth College v. Woodward,* 4 Wheat. 518 (1819).

42. The story of "federal judicial review" is told in Chapter 8.

43. *Charles River Bridge v. Warren Bridge,* 11 Pet. 420 (1837).

44. *Dred Scott v. Sanford,* 19 How. 393 (1857).

45. See *Ex Parte Merryman,* Fed. Case 9487 (1861).

46. *Slaughter-House Cases,* 16 Wall. 36 (1873).

47. *Plessey v. Ferguson,* 163 U.S. 537 (1896).

48. *Civil Rights Cases,* 109 U.S. 3 (1883).

49. *Wabash, St.L. & P. Ry. Co. v. Illinois,* 118 U.S. 557 (1886).

50. *United States v. E. C. Knight Co.,* 156 U.S. 1 (1895).

51. *Smyth v. Ames,* 169 U.S. 466 (1898).

52. *Lochner v. New York,* 198 U.S. 45 (1905).

53. *Pollock v. Farmers' Loan & Trust Co.*

54. *The Shreveport Case,* 234 U.S. 342 (1914).

55. Walter F. Murphy, "In His Own Image: Mr. Chief Justice Taft and Supreme Court Appointments," in Phillip Kurland, ed., *The Supreme Court Review* (Chicago: Univ. of Chicago Press, 1961), pp. 159-93.

56. *Schecter Poultry Corp. v. United States,* 295 U.S. 495 (1935).

57. *United States v. Butler* (see note 5 above).

58. And compare the logic of *Butler* with the logic of *Marbury.*

59. The Court has had nine members since before the turn of the century. The Constitution does not specify how many Justices there will be, so Congress decides by statute. Because federal judges sit for life, it is much easier to raise the figure than to lower it. To accomplish the latter, one must await death or resignation and then fail to appoint a successor.

60. *Steward Machine Co. v. Davis,* 301 U.S. 548 (1937).

61. *United States v. Darby,* 312 U.S. 100 (1941).

62. They struck at least as much terror into the hearts of opponents as did Notre Dame's 1924 backfield. And they deserve something more than anonymity for their efforts. Their names were George Sutherland, Pierce Butler, James McReynolds, and Willis Van Devanter.

63. *Korematsu v. United States,* 323 U.S. 214 (1944); *Dennis v. United States,* 341 U.S. 494 (1951).

64. *Brown v. Board of Ed.,* 347 U.S. 483 (1954).

65. *Engel v. Vitale,* 370 U.S. 421 (1962); *Abington School Dist. v. Schempp,* 374 U.S. 203 (1963).

66. *Reynolds v. Sims,* 377 U.S. 533 (1964).

67. *Miranda v. Arizona,* 384 U.S. 436 (1966).

68. *Jacobellis v. Ohio,* 378 U.S. 184 (1964); *Memoirs v. Massachusetts,* 383 U.S. 413 (1966).

69. Robert G. McCloskey, "Deeds Without Doctrines: Civil Rights in the 1960 Term of the Supreme Court," *The American Political Science Review* 56 (1962), pp. 71-89.

70. *United States v. Carolene Products Co.,* 304 U.S. 144 (1938), p. 152, note 4. Compare Alpheus T. Mason, *The Supreme Court From Taft to Warren* (Baton Rouge: Louisiana State Univ. Press, 1958), Chs. 5-6.

71. Compare the discussion in Walter F. Murphy, "Deeds Under a Doctrine: Civil Liberties in the 1963 Term," *The American Political Science Review* 59 (1965), p. 78.

72. Mr. Justice Douglas resigned his seat on the court in 1975, and President Ford replaced him with John Paul Stevens, who appears to be a "swing man," unlike Stewart or White.

73. *Baldwin v. New York,* 399 U.S. 66 (1970); *United States v. Kras,* 409 U.S. 434 (1973).

74. *Baird v. State Bar,* 401 U.S. 1 (1971); *San Antonio School Dist. v. Rodriguez,* 411 U.S. 1 (1973).

75. *United States v. Dionisio,* 410 U.S. 1 (1973); *United States Dept. of Ag. v. Murry,* 413 U.S. 508 (1973).

76. *Miller v. California,* 413 U.S. 15 (1973); *Paris Adult Theatre v. Slaton,* 413 U.S. 49 (1973).

77. *Harris v. New York,* 401 U.S. 222 (1971); *Schneckloth v. Bustamonte,* 412 U.S. 218 (1973).

78. *Alexander v. Holmes Bd. of Ed.,* 396 U.S. 19 (1969); *Swann v. Bd. of Ed.,* 402 U.S. 1 (1971). However, the *Brown* doctrine may have rougher sledding in the North. See the Burger Court's disposition of *Milliken v. Bradley,* 418 U.S. 717 (1974).

79. *Committee for Public Ed. v. Nyquist,* 413 U.S. 756 (1973).

80. John Schmidhauser, "The Justices of the Supreme Court: A Collective Portrait," *Midwest Journal of Political Science* 3 (1959), pp. 1-57.

81. Ibid.

82. Henry J. Abraham, *The Judicial Process,* 2nd ed. (New York: Oxford Univ. Press, 1968), p. 63.

83. See especially the eminent writings of Charles Warren, *The Supreme Court in United States History* (Boston: Little, Brown, 1922), vol. 1, pp. 21-22.

84. Daniel S. McHargue, *Appointments to the Supreme Court of the United States,* unpublished Ph.D. dissertation, U.C.L.A. (1949), p. 633. Concurring in this assertion is Robert K. Carr, *The Supreme Court and Judicial Review* (New York: Rinehart, 1942), p. 243.

85. Taft's influence on Harding's choice of Pierce Butler is traced carefully in David J. Danelski, *A Supreme Court Justice is Appointed* (New York: Random House, 1964).

86. See Murphy, "In His Own Image," in Kurland, ed., *The Supreme Court Review.*

87. Circuit Judge Learned Hand is one famous example. A contemporary illustration would be Professor Paul Freund of the Harvard Law School.

88. See Ira H. Carmen, "The President, Politics and the Power of Appointment: Hoover's Nomination of Mr. Justice Cardozo," *Virginia Law Review* 55 (1969), pp. 616-59.

89. Richard K. Burke, "The Path to the Court," unpublished Ph.D. dissertation, Vanderbilt University (1958), pp. 243-44.

90. Point of order: When a *Chief* Justice resigns, the President can, if he wishes, name one of the Justices to head the Court; the Senate still must confirm the appointment; then another person would be selected to replace the Justice elevated to the Chief Justiceship; the Senate, of course, gets to look over the second nomination, too.

91. Senator Roman Hruska of Nebraska will long be remembered for his ringing endorsement: "Even if he [Carswell] were mediocre, there are a lot of mediocre judges and people and lawyers and they are entitled to a little representation, aren't they?" As quoted in James F. Simon, *In His Own Image* (New York: David McKay, 1973), p. 122.

92. The case for careful Senate review is well presented in Charles L. Black, Jr., "A Note on Senatorial Consideration of Supreme Court Nominees," *The Yale Law Journal* 79 (1970), pp. 657-64.

93. Felix Frankfurter, "The Supreme Court in the Mirror of Justices," *University of Pennsylvania Law Review* 105 (1957), p. 795.

94. The following expands, in slightly different form, my general overview presented in "The President, Politics and the Power of Appointment," pp. 654-59.

95. Samuel Krislov, *The Supreme Court in the Political Process* (New York: Macmillan, 1965), p. 10.

96. Dahl, pp. 293-94.

97. I am relying here on David J. Danelski's fine piece, "The Influence of the Chief Justice in the Decisional Process," in C. Herman Pritchett and Walter F. Murphy, eds., *Courts, Judges, and Politics,* 2nd ed. (New York: Random House, 1974), pp. 525-34.

98. For specific instances, see J. Woodford Howard, Jr., "On the Fluidity of Judicial Choice," *The American Political Science Review* 62 (1968), pp. 43-56.

99. Walter F. Murphy, *Elements of Judicial Strategy* (Chicago: Univ. of Chicago Press, 1964).

100. See, for example, S. Sidney Ulmer, "Supreme Court Behavior and Civil Rights," *Western Political Quarterly* 13 (1960), pp. 288-311; Glendon Schubert, *The Judicial Mind* (Evanston: Northwestern Univ. Press, 1965).

101. Compare C. Herman Pritchett, *Civil Liberties and the Vinson Court* (Chicago: Univ. of Chicago Press, 1954), pp. 177-200, and Ira H. Carmen, "One Civil Libertarian Among Many: The Case of Mr. Justice Goldberg," *Michigan Law Review* 65 (1966), pp. 301-36.

102. This view is expressed in Wallace Mendelson, "The Neo-Behavioral Approach to the Judicial Process," *The American Political Science Review* 57 (1963), pp. 593-603. The seminal work in the "jurimetrics" field is C. Herman Pritchett, *The Roosevelt Court* (New York: Macmillan, 1948), a study which shows that these quantitative materials are useful at least as an aid to careful qualitative reflection.

103. Much less is known about the long-run compliance proclivities of lower-level federal agencies, though I would hypothesize that these bureaucrats are much more knowledgeable and much more respectful of Supreme Court rulings than their state and local counterparts.

104. *Brown v. Bd. of Ed.,* 349 U.S. 294 (1955).

105. The story is told in Jack W. Peltason, *58 Lonely Men* (New York: Harcourt, Brace & World, 1961).

106. These studies are compared and contrasted in Stephen L. Wasby, *The Impact of the United States Supreme Court: Some Perspectives* (Homewood, Ill.: Dorsey Press, 1970).

107. Ira H. Carmen, *Movies, Censorship, and the Law* (Ann Arbor: Univ. of Michigan Press, 1966).

108. Robert H. Birkby, "The Supreme Court and the Bible Belt: Tennessee Reaction to the 'Schempp' Decision," *Midwest Journal of Political Science* 10 (1966), pp. 304-19.

109. Michael Ward et al., "Interrogations in New Haven: The Impact of *Miranda,*" *The Yale Law Journal* 76 (1967), p. 1613.

110. Exception: How a Governor Wallace might have reacted to the *Brown* decision. I discuss in great detail the larger clash between national directives and state response when I describe the workings of the federal system in Chapter 8.

111. The data come from Walter F. Murphy and Joseph Tanenhaus, *The Study of Public Law* (New York: Random House, 1972), pp. 41-43.

112. Birkby, "The Supreme Court and the Bible Belt," and Richard M. Johnson, "Compliance and Supreme Court Decision-Making," *Wisconsin Law Review* 1967 (1967), pp. 170-85.

113. In 1969, 25 percent of a national sample thought the Court was doing a good job, while 23 percent thought the Court was doing a poor job. In 1973, the respective figures had shifted to 31 and 15 percent (*The Gallup Opinion Index,* August 1973, Report No. 98, p. 9). Note: The 1969 data are not comparable to the data cited in Murphy and Tanenhaus (note 111). The former explores public opinion, the latter explores *informed* public opinion.

3
the lower courts: home of equal justice?

For the popular mind and for much of the literature of political science, the Supreme Court holds considerable fascination; the lower federal courts, however, are rarely accorded equal time. How many federal trial court judges are there? What functions do they perform that rise above the mundane? And are the courts of appeal nothing but stepping-stones over which litigants tread before they reach the "big time" in Washington?

The lower courts, both past and present, have frequently adjudicated great cases. But an even more compelling reason for us to understand their essential dynamics is that each year these tribunals make decisions affecting the lives of thousands. Their power is great; indeed, it is their authority—not the weight of Supreme Court majesty—that will touch the average citizen, if any unit of the federal judicial system ever does.

Civil cases

What is the typical dispute that might wind up in a court of law? X, clearly intoxicated, drives his car recklessly and smashes into a storefront. He is sued for damages by the owner. This is *civil* litigation. The government plays no role in the proceeding except to provide judicial machinery for its settlement. A second broad area of trial work involves *criminal* law. Y pushes heroin or starts a brawl in the local tavern. He is arrested by the police and brought into court, accused of violating some specific statute. In this situation, government is anything but neutral; nevertheless, judges and juries are supposed to be just as impartial in criminal litigation as in civil suits.

However, if I sue my neighbor for trespassing on my property, or if I am arrested for murdering my brother, I will rarely be tried in a federal court. Normally, the state or local judicial process will decide my fate. What kinds of cases, then, are serviced at the national level? Three separate classes deserve consideration:

1. *Civil* actions in which a citizen of one state, claiming personal injury, brings suit against a citizen of another state; more than $10,000 must be at stake (example: the intoxicated motorist is an Ohioan traveling across New Mexico, and his crack-up causes great damage).

2. *Criminal* actions in which the F.B.I. or its counterparts enforce federal penal statutes (example: Smith and Jones are arrested for printing money).

3. *Civil* actions in which Congress has enacted legal rules, but in which implementation through noncriminal remedies seems appropriate (example: personal injury suits involving admiralty law).[1]

In sheer poundage, civil cases far outweigh criminal cases initially filed for federal court disposition. More than 70 percent of the 140,000 actions instituted in fiscal 1974 were of the civil variety; furthermore, about 11,000 of the 18,000 actions eventually adjudicated at trial turned out to be civil in nature.[2] Most of these were suits between individuals or corporations, so the U.S. government was neither plaintiff nor defendant. The preponderance of private-law controversies has helped blur the image of the lower courts. Students of American politics are so alert to "public" issues involving the rights and obligations of governmental officials that they have spent little energy examining the process by which civil suits in the private sector are decided. But because federal judges often resolve crucial social and economic questions in such litigation, a typical civil action deserves description.[3]

The prototypical controversy would have to be a category 1 dispute—that is, in which the contestants are citizens of different states. More than a third of the private-law suits begun in fiscal 1972 were of this kind, about 25,000 cases.[4] The following hypothetical situation traces the major steps through which the ensuing litigation would be likely to pass.[5]

After three decades of hard work in the Philadelphia business community, X decides to build a winter home in Florida. He hires construction expert Y to do the job at a cost of $50,000. But about a year after the home is built, severe deficiencies begin to crop up. The roof leaks, and damage to X's furniture is considerable. The windows and doors are not secure, so cold drafts penetrate the house. The back yard seems to have been improperly graded, because there has been soil erosion. X pleads with Y to do something about the problems, but Y says he is not liable because, he maintains, the house was in good shape at the time X took possession. Furthermore, he argues, X must have thought so, too, because he paid Y in full when title to the home changed hands. The $50,000 dream house has become a $50,000 nightmare, and legal action is virtually the sole antidote.

First of all, X should hire a lawyer. In civil action, the government does not provide any legal services for litigants no matter what their financial circumstances. Fortunately, X has some money in the bank; otherwise, he would either have to go into debt or work out an arrangement with counsel, thus increasing substantially whatever attorneys' fees accumulate. The lawyer will doubtless make every reasonable effort to settle the affair out of court, because trials are an extremely protracted business for all concerned. Fortunately, the overwhelming majority of such disputes are resolved through a process of informal give-and-take.

If negotiations at this point prove fruitless, plaintiff's counsel faces a big decision: Should X sue in the state (Florida) courts, or should he rely on diversity of citizenship and go into federal court? Why might he select the latter? Because it is perhaps easier to prove damages under federal negligence standards? No, for even if a federal tribunal is chosen, it will be located in Florida, where defendant lives and where the alleged property damage took place; and the court must apply *Florida's* legal rules. The reason federal courts were given jurisdiction over such controversies in the first place is that local biases against out-of-state parties like X might well be weaker in federal court. Yet the presiding federal court judge will undoubtedly be a citizen of defendant's home state, as will members of a jury, should one be empaneled.

When we dig deeper, however, there still may be important considerations prompting a plaintiff to exercise diversity rights. Federal trial courts use federal *procedural* standards, and the rules of evidence are often more liberal than state rules. Also, it is generally felt that federal judges are better qualified, though this is difficult to verify. Along the same line, some authorities believe that neither state judges nor juries are as responsive to certain allegations as their federal counterparts. Thus, because of the prejudice sometimes shown by state trial judges, civil rights suits lodged in the South have traditionally invoked the national judicial process. Last, we have two objective measures: the length of the respective dockets and the geographical proximity of the respective courtroom facilities.[6]

In any event, we will say a federal forum is selected. X's counsel first files a complaint. It spells out, from plaintiff's point of view, the who, what, why, when, and where of the matter. After the court sends defendant notice of this action, Y has the option of responding, to present facts and allegations as he perceives them. At this point, either side may invoke the important *discovery* procedure, which allows each to inspect evidence the other might possess. Discovery techniques militate against surprise strategies by lawyers once the trial commences. Finally, one last-ditch effort will be made to bring the parties together at a *pre-trial conference* in the judge's chambers. Generally this meeting provides enough impetus to surmount remaining barriers; only about 10 percent of civil cases actually get beyond this stage (11,000 in fiscal 1972).[7]

Our hypothetical litigants, however, are hopelessly stubborn, so a duel to the end is inescapable. As I have indicated, they are both bound to pay for their belligerence, because the informal canons of our civil law reward those who compromise. If confrontation is what people want, delay is what people get.

The chances are 50–50 that these two hardy souls will have to wait in excess of sixteen months before their case is decided, and the chances are one out of ten they will have to wait more than forty-two months![8]

Why does the process uncoil like some sleepy rattler? The question is not so easy to answer. We know the percentage of civil and criminal cases filed has increased far more rapidly over the past thirty-five years than the percentage of new judicial seats. From 1964 to 1974, the former figure increased by 45 percent, while there has been no increase in appellate judgeships since 1968. We also know the federal courts must handle not only these actions but also the almost 200,000 bankruptcy petitions submitted each year.[a] That is not the whole story, though, as will be evident once the *criminal* process is laid bare. But the alarming rise in personal-injury controversies litigated at the federal level exemplifies the fact that the crush of civil business is part of the problem.[9]

When the trial finally looms, the question of jury participation must be faced. The Constitution's Seventh Amendment preserves the right to a hearing before a jury in all civil suits held in federal court where more than $20 is involved and where *legal* rather than *equitable* standards are controlling. Let me explain this last point. When A sues B, A wants something. The standard compensation for alleged wrongs committed, as in our hypothetical case, is money. But sometimes the *legal* remedy of dollars and cents is inapplicable. What A may need is a court order keeping B from doing something that will cause irreparable harm. To accomplish this, A would ask the judge for an *injunction* to stop B's activities. An injunction is not a legal remedy; judges grant such relief only in extraordinary circumstances as a matter of *equity*.[10] I will discuss the use of injunctions later; for now, the important point is that in civil suits held before federal judges, *no* trial by jury is guaranteed unless traditional legal remedies (such as money) are sought. Of course, nothing forces litigants to utilize a jury, but if either X or Y wants one, it is required. In fiscal 1972, one-third of the civil cases heard in federal courts employed juries.[11]

A federal civil court jury decides all questions of fact, and such determinations—unlike questions of *law*—cannot be appealed. Moreover, the jury—whose verdict must be unanimous—decides how much money goes to the litigant who carries the day. And because no one's life or liberty is at stake, it places culpability where the preponderance of evidence lies; neither litigant is protected by the "beyond a reasonable doubt" rule. The jury also has the benefit of the judge's views, for it is the presiding officer's prerogative to comment on the evidence presented and even to set aside what seems to be an arbitrary verdict. And both judge and jury usually obtain access to defendant's testimony, even if defendant would rather remain silent; the self-incrimination shield is rarely applicable to civil proceedings.

Whether Congress should abolish federal jurisdiction over diversity cases is a question that continues to prompt debate among court reformers. As more refined transportation and communication facilities tend to make us ever more nationalist in outlook, the *current* procedure under which a citizen of one state

[a] Congress has the power to enact a national bankruptcy law; the first such statute appeared in 1841.

sues the resident of another might smack of a bygone regionalism. Certainly one might well ponder why such parochial disputes as automobile injury cases, which today comprise the largest chunk of diversity litigation, should be adjudicated in national forums. In any event, increasing inflation will amost surely prompt Congress to raise and reraise the financial stakes necessary to exercise the option.

Criminal cases: pre-trial rights

Procedural due process, right to counsel, and the protection against self-incrimination

I now turn to the typical criminal law action commenced in the federal courts.[b] My hypothetical prosecution concerns narcotics seller Q, because the largest single type of case brought to trial in fiscal 1972 (14 percent; 6,500 defendants) involved illegal drug use.[12] Q has been apprehended by customs authorities when he tried to bring heroin into this country from abroad. Drug smuggling is a serious crime known as a *felony;* felonies should be distinguished from the category of less offensive violations called *misdemeanors.* Under federal statute, felonies are generally crimes that could bring a prison term of more than six months.

Let us assume the police have made their arrest with scrupulous propriety. Immediately, three significant constitutional guarantees come into play. The first of these is *procedural due process of law.* As I indicated in Chapter 2, this entitles every person to a fair hearing. But suppose the customs people want to make things easy on themselves. Or suppose they think Q is ready to talk and implicate "higher-ups" in the smuggling ring. All he needs, they guess, is a little shove! Now, under procedural due process, no confession can be coerced. There was, for example, a famous decision involving three blacks arrested on murder charges in Mississippi. The police simply tortured them until they confessed. What difference, then, if the trial itself was a picture of decorum?—the fairness principle had already been subverted. The Supreme Court struck this procedure down.[13] Psychological pressure is no more acceptable. The Court also threw out a confession obtained by Tennessee police after grilling an accused for thirty-six hours under a battery of electric lights.[14] The traditional criterion under due process is: confessions must be *voluntary.*[c]

[b] The impact of the lower courts on our constitutional politics is very much a study of typical cases, tendencies, and trends. But sometimes "glamour" litigation—the rare controversy involving the visible and the powerful—can have a greater impact on our governmental system than mountains of typical occurrences. The following account attempts to provide balanced coverage, emphasizing the usual but including generous discussion of the unusual.

[c] These two cases dealt with *state* police action, not federal law enforcement. Sometimes the Constitution allows one layer of government to do what the other layer cannot. But remember: *Procedural due process* binds the federal government (see the Fifth Amendment), and it also binds the states (see the Fourteenth Amendment). So any relevant case involving the states would have been decided in the same way had federal officers been implicated. Unless otherwise noted, constitutional freedoms discussed in this chapter are as applicable to one level of government as they are to the other. The specific relationship between federal constitutional rights and state action is taken up in Chapter 8.

A second constitutional right attaching immediately is the *right to counsel,* guaranteed in the Sixth Amendment.[d] The provision is applicable to both felony and misdemeanor proceedings; a convicted party may not be imprisoned for a single day if the opportunity to receive legal assistance has been denied.[15] The reason is obvious. Judicial processes are extraordinarily technical matters, which even an adroit citizen has little chance to master. And attorneys have the resources, know-how, and freedom of action to prepare cases with an objectivity and competence few defendants can ever match. That a citizen should be incarcerated after legal assistance has been sought and denied is now considered constitutionally impermissible. Indeed, if Q is indigent, the federal government must provide legal aid free of charge.

But is an individual obliged to have a lawyer? It is hard to believe anyone would ever choose to be without one. On atypical occasions, though, a defendant might wish to defend himself. In such cases, counsel may be waived, but the judge must be sure the choice has been intelligently exercised. The courts presume against the waiver option and insist that the defendant meet a heavy burden of proof, because they feel that, if he is left to his own initiative, his chances of survival are poor.[16] Still, counsel cannot be jammed down the accused's throat: "The defendant, and not his lawyer . . . , will bear the personal consequences of a conviction."[17]

The third constitutional provision relevant at this early stage is the Fifth Amendment's protection against *self-incrimination.* The federal government may not compel individuals to testify against themselves in criminal cases. Every person, it has been said countless times, must be presumed innocent until proven guilty; the shield against self-incrimination buttresses this concept, because it mandates the police and the prosecution to forage for evidence of wrongdoing without relying on the prospective defendant to help them out.

Let us say Q is brought to a federal police installation for questioning. He does not have to say anything! But suppose he decides to cooperate, at least for the moment. Maybe he thinks a show of responsiveness is the best policy. After a time, though, he becomes nervous. Perhaps the police are getting too close to the truth. Or perhaps he is innocent, and they don't seem to believe him. Suddenly, Q demands a conference with his lawyer. The police must grant this request, for our Constitution "strikes the balance in favor of the right of the accused to be advised by his lawyer of his privilege against self-incrimination."[18]

It is important to appreciate fully the significance of the *Escobedo* doctrine. Defendants in federal court have traditionally been given the right to legal representation at every appearance before a judge—that is, not only at the trial itself but at pre-trial and post-trial confrontations. According to our canons of justice, these are "critical stages" in the criminal process; defendants need counsel's help, or they might fail to assert their rights. But the protection against self-incrimination takes us a step further. Once a suspect becomes, in

[d] But the clause is relevant only to criminal cases; it was clearly not meant to cover either appearances before congressional committees or civil litigation.

effect, the accused, *all* question-and-answer sessions are seen as critical stages. It is precisely at this point, the Court has said, when legal help is most needed; otherwise, the protection against self-incrimination might be overborne. The *Escobedo* holding in essence merges the right to counsel and the self-incrimination privilege, so that the two together will enhance the presumption of innocence principle. The *Escobedo* doctrine has been criticized as not giving the police sufficient latitude. Lawyers will surely tell their clients to keep quiet, opponents contend, thus making reasonable inquiries impossible. Supporters, however, say the police are attempting to take advantage of the suspect's ignorance—a suspect aware of his or her rights would never volunteer information.

As it has turned out, though, *Escobedo* was merely a precursor to the most provocative criminal justice decision of the past quarter-century. In this case—which we have already come to know as *Miranda v. Arizona*—the Supreme Court announced new ground rules for interrogating suspects. Assume the police confront Q on the street, where they present him with an arrest warrant. Immediately, they must issue the following kind of declaration:

> Mr. Q, you are under arrest. You do not have to say anything, but if you do, your comments may be used against you in a court of law. You have a right to see an attorney, and he may be present at any questioning you might wish to undergo. If you cannot afford a lawyer, one will be appointed to help you.[19]

The *Miranda* warnings need not be articulated every time the police talk to a citizen in the performance of their duties; but the checklist does have to be communicated whenever an investigation has become an *adversary* proceeding and the interviewee is considered the prime suspect. This holds true even when authorities are not ready to arrest anyone. As a matter of fact, federal officials are constrained by law from engaging in extensive interrogation of suspects except during the pre-arrest period. With all the debate over *Miranda,* this much is certain: the decision bans the introduction at trial of all evidence elicited by interrogating the accused if law enforcement officials failed to deliver the prescribed warnings at the proper time. The age-old "voluntary confession" principle now applies only to situations in which the *Miranda* format has been observed.

What prompted the *Miranda* ruling? The Court majority saw incommunicado questioning of accused persons as inherently "police-dominated" situations. The individual has been deprived of personal liberty, is obviously at a disadvantage, and might not know his or her rights. The Justices construed this intimidating atmosphere to be potentially destructive of the self-incrimination protection. The dissenters (four out of nine) argued vigorously that the new rules would curb *all* questioning of suspects and, therefore, ring the death knell for confessions themselves. How many people will admit culpability, they asked, if not first interrogated? Yet it is a fact that the F.B.I. had been issuing precisely these warnings for years prior to *Miranda.*

During Q's detention, the police ask him to participate in certain routine procedures. For instance, they fingerprint him; take his photograph; and ask him to appear in a lineup for purposes of witness identification. They might even want to ascertain his blood type or obtain samples of his handwriting. These procedures he cannot resist on the grounds of self-incrimination. The police here are seeking only *physical evidence* as opposed to *testimonial evidence.* What the Fifth Amendment protects is the person's right to keep quiet, and nothing more. But the lineup, in contrast to the other routines, is a critical stage in the criminal process; therefore, Q's lawyer must be allowed to attend. The idea is to prevent the police from unduly influencing witnesses as they identify the accused. None of the other procedures involve either participation by ordinary citizens or the use of technical, legal expertise by the suspect.[20]

Bail and preliminary hearing

After arrest, Q should be brought before a magistrate as expeditiously as possible. The charges can be read and bail set. The Constitution says, "Excessive bail shall not be required," and the use of the sweeping term "excessive" appears to presuppose freewheeling judicial oversight. The Supreme Court itself has said practically nothing about what "excessive bail" means. Authorities seem to agree that the purpose of bail is to ensure defendant's presence at further judicial proceedings, since failure to appear will mean forfeiture of the amount paid. Certainly bail was never meant to be a kind of punishment; indeed, federal statute classifies it as a *right,* and this surely is consistent with the constitutional language cited above.[21]

In our hypothetical litigation, Q submits he has always lived in the community and has two children in school—clear signs of local attachment. Prior to the late 1960s, such assertions would probably have done a defendant little good, for the magistrate had no time to investigate these claims. Therefore, bail was usually pegged only to the seriousness of the offense. Obviously, that criterion worked against low-income suspects, because it is this class which is generally accused of heinous crimes such as peddling narcotics. Q would likely have been unable to meet the steep figure assigned and would thus have been faced with an unpalatable choice: either get a loan at very high interest rates from a bail-bonding company, or sit in jail until the case is terminated. One study showed that as many as 50 percent of those indicted on felony charges in one particular city could not obtain bail and so remained incarcerated.[22]

These inequities prompted Congress to pass the Bail Reform Act in 1966. This statute provides for the pre-trial release of all suspects charged with noncapital crimes who demonstrate meaningful community ties—that is, an overall background indicating they will appear at trial. What the law has done is eliminate bail-bonding and its exorbitant fees; more important, the law eliminates the policy whereby "dangerous" suspects were saddled automatically with the steepest bail payments, a norm that discriminated against poor people and was clearly inconsistent with the purposes of the constitutional right. Of course, the law also eliminates *entirely* the bail requirement for those who satisfy the courts' criteria of prospective personal accountability. In any event, Q will now be *released on his own recognizance*—that is, set free because he is, prima facie, reputable.

Next on the agenda, Q is brought before another magistrate, this time for a *preliminary hearing.* While not specified in the Constitution, this step has a certain practical significance. There the prosecution must show that a crime has been committed and demonstrate that there is *probable cause* to believe Q is the culprit. The presiding official tries objectively to evaluate whether there are grounds to hold Q for trial. If so, the case will go forward. The chances are about 9 out of 10 that the prosecution can clear this hurdle.[23]

The grand jury

With probable cause established, Q's case goes before a *grand jury.* The Constitution prescribes this step for all persons outside the military who are accused of a "capital" or "otherwise infamous" criminal offense. "Infamous crimes" have been defined as those that could lead to imprisonment.[24] Grand juries have a history steeped in common-law tradition. They consist of from twelve to twenty-three citizens, who sit behind closed doors and listen to the prosecution's case. If a majority believes the evidence has satisfied the probable-cause test, an *indictment* will be issued, binding defendant over for trial. The Framers considered the grand jury an important check on federal authorities. A panel of one's peers, they thought, would throw out any arbitrary, capricious, or flimsy allegations presented by overbearing government officials.

In our time, however, the grand jury receives mixed reviews at best. For one thing, it is much more unwieldy than the preliminary hearing, which helps explain the rise of that procedure in our "Living Constitution." Furthermore, the Supreme Court has never held the device binding on state criminal processes, which contributes to both its somewhat tarnished reputation and its irregular use at the grassroots level. Then there is the charge that the prosecutor controls grand jury deliberations, because members see only evidence he chooses to submit about people he wishes to indict. Approximately 95 percent of all requests for indictments are reported favorably.[25] Finally, empirical data indicate the typical grand jury is *not* the cross-section of a community that constitutional theory anticipates. Whereas most serious crimes are committed by blue-collar, working-class men, grand jury selection overrepresents greatly three entirely different segments: (1) the elderly, who are no longer gainfully employed; (2) "professional jurors," who make more money at this "job" than they would at any other; and (3) middle-aged housewives, who have no children to look after.[26] If this discrepancy were intentional, the typical grand jury could be labeled constitutionally deficient. But it is simply not possible to obtain a satisfactory random sample, because of (1) the low value most people place on grand jury participation and (2) the low wages paid to grand jurors, which means many people cannot afford to take time off from work to serve.

During the past few years, grand jury procedures have given critics something new to talk about. The traditional protective functions performed by these bodies quite often take a back seat today to a new kind of grand jury function, so the argument runs, one that emphasizes freewheeling investigatory probes. Not that the "Sherlock Holmes grand jury" affects the Q's of this country and not that it indicts many people either. Rather, the alleged scenario goes this way: Justice Department officials in Washington decide to look into the activities of various radical groups around the country; soon, underling prosecutors appear in court, asking judges to convene grand juries; these units are then charged with investigating supposedly illegal acts, and their research *might* lead to the issuance of indictments. The unique feature of this operation is the jury's role as police investigator. It does not stand by, passively waiting for the prosecutor to present evidence. Instead, it actively subpoenas witnesses, pursues leads, builds cases, and then (maybe) indicts individuals. Of course, the entire process is performed in concert with—or even under the direction of—governmental legal personnel. In the early 1970s, thirteen such inquests, all attaining national attention, were held. More than two hundred witnesses were forced to testify upon threat of contempt citation. These unwilling participants have been characterized as "young New Left radicals, anti-war intellectuals and Catholic leftists."[27] Later, in 1974, the other end of the political spectrum came in for its share of attention as a special grand jury zeroed in on the Watergate cover-up. In any event, the specific objections lodged against such investigations include:

1. Grand juries have the power to look into alleged criminal conduct ("Sherlock Holmes" inquiries have been convened in the past to investigate organized crime), but the particular searches carried out are fishing expeditions and arise out of political controversy.

2. Witnesses called before these groups have no protection against unrestrained prosecutors, whose tactics are inquisitorial.

3. Grand juries that emphasize investigations compromise their role as protectors of the innocent; the two functions are essentially incompatible.

By way of evaluating these claims, if we grant that grand juries should have an investigative role, then the subject matter of these inquiries was appropriate for their consideration. For instance, two of the hearings looked into the publication of the Pentagon Papers, secret intelligence information whose contents were taken without authorization by antiwar advocates. Another inquest dealt with an alleged plot to kidnap Henry Kissinger and to sabotage the heating system of the nation's capital. Obviously, these several acts are, or would have been, illegal and had to be investigated by somebody.

But if the substance of the hearings was within a grand jury's proper jurisdiction, what about the procedures invoked? First, there is ample evidence that many of the questions submitted were vague, open-ended, irrelevant, and constituted intrusions into the zone of free speech and expression protected by the Constitution.[28] Second, because witnesses were invariably forbidden to be represented by counsel during testimony, a possible deterrent to the excessive enthusiasm of interviewers was removed. Third, the Supreme Court has not delineated *any* constitutional checks necessary to cure the inequities in grand jury performance that these complaints exemplify.

There is this question to consider: Does the prosecutor manipulate the investigating grand jury, as some contend, or does the grand jury attempt to carry the prosecutor along on the backwash of its zeal? For instance, an oft-cited rumor was that the Watergate grand jurors voted to indict Richard Nixon while he was still President of the United States, a step Special Prosecutor Leon Jaworski considered of dubious constitutional propriety. Ultimately, he succeeded in restraining them; Nixon was named an unindicted co-conspirator.[29]

So we come to the nagging question central to all others. If the Supreme Court is not going to bring grand jury forums into the checks-and-balances mainstream, should we not let the police do the spade work, and let grand juries stick to the tasks of either indicting or correcting prosecutors' mistakes by refusing to indict?

Plea bargaining and arraignment

Throughout the pre-trial period, negotiations commonly occur between prosecution and defense lawyers. These negotiations are called "plea bargaining," and this process usually begins to gather momentum once the grand jury has handed up an indictment.

What is plea bargaining? We must recognize that it is usually in the interest of *both* sides to avoid a full-dress confrontation in court. The federal attorneys want to win; but their calendars are overloaded with suits requiring prosecution, and they may lack the proof necessary to press home full enforcement of the law. As for defendants, trials take time and money and, of course, are risky. Moreover, sentences for guilty parties following trials are invariably higher—sometimes much higher—than those handed down after guilty pleas are entered.[30] Clearly, the context for serious bargaining exists, and this effort takes two forms: either the accused pleads guilty to a lesser offense, or pleads guilty knowing that the admission will pave the way for leniency in sentencing. There can be no doubt, then, that the extraconstitutional transaction known as plea bargaining is the most critical stage in the entire criminal enforcement process.[31]

An excellent example of plea bargaining involved one-time presidential assistant Charles Colson. Faced with the prospect of innumerable indictments relating to the Watergate cover-up and the covert operations of the notorious "Plumbers" group, he undertook negotiations with Special Prosecutor Leon Jaworski. The agreement between them was as follows: Colson pleaded guilty to a charge of concocting and carrying out a conspiracy aimed at defaming

Daniel Ellsberg's reputation in the public press before his (Ellsberg's) trial for stealing the Pentagon Papers; in return for dropping all other indictments filed and pending, Colson was to cooperate fully with Jaworski on other relevant inquiries.

As might be anticipated, plea bargaining arrangements have come in for their share of criticism. The Constitution, it is said, looks to open trials, not to secret agreements, for the determination of guilt or innocence. Those who tend to sympathize with defendants feel that federal authorities have an inherent advantage in the negotiations because of the pressure they can exert. On the other hand, those who tend to take a "law and order" posture believe that the guilty rarely get what they deserve. A blue-ribbon commission—convened by the Nixon Administration and reflecting the latter concern—has called for the abolition of plea bargaining.[32]

Once again, the key question appears to be the extent to which the courts will supervise plea bargaining. The Supreme Court has ruled these negotiations constitutional if the defendant's cooperation is both voluntary and intelligently exercised.[33] It will be hard, in any event, to do away with this kind of negotiating unless Congress allocates far greater financial resources to sustain the criminal justice operation.

Our friend Q, however, has been indicted for committing an odious crime, and the federal prosecuting attorney has sufficient evidence to believe he can get a conviction. Q will now be brought before a magistrate in an *arraignment* proceeding. Here, the grand jury's allegations are read, and defendant will plead guilty or not guilty. It is at this stage that plea bargains are consummated officially. Prearranged guilty declarations are announced, and sentence is then passed.[e] Even after arraignment, not-guilty declarations may be reversed through subsequent plea negotiations. Interestingly enough, guilty pleas have fallen from 79 percent (1964) to 62 percent (1973), undoubtedly the result of Warren Court decisions tightening up the police interrogation process and therefore making it more difficult to obtain confessions.[34] As for Q, he pleads innocent and hopes for the best.

Just how long is the entire pre-trial process likely to take? If Q's case is being handled in one of the more congested, high-crime urban communities, the answer as late as 1975 was about one year. I have described part of the "delay in court" problem already. I must stress here that the "political branches" have formulated an ever-expanding federal criminal code but have refused to spend more than a paltry $100-200 million per year to fund the national judicial system. Needless to say, the result has been to make a mockery of the Sixth Amendment, which guarantees the accused a speedy trial.

To meet this problem, which has been with us for at least two decades, Congress enacted the Speedy Trial Act of 1974. It requires that suspects be charged within thirty days after arrest, that arraignment follow within another

[e] The most famous plea of recent times was Vice President Spiro Agnew's *nolo contendere* admission in 1973. This unusual option has the effect of saying: "I throw myself on the mercy of the court, but I do not admit guilt per se."

ten days, and that the trial commence within sixty days thereafter; this one-hundred-day maximum is to become effective in stages by 1980. If in any trial the prosecution ignores the deadlines, charges must be dropped. The Speedy Trial Act is an important *beginning*. We shall have to see what legislation is provided to avoid the pitfalls of assembly-line justice.

Criminal cases: rights at trial

The jury

With courtroom confrontation unavoidable, Q's attorney must decide whether a jury should determine Q's fate. Trial before a *jury of one's peers* has been considered among the overriding civil liberties guaranteed by Anglo-American jurisprudence going back as far as Magna Carta, which bound the sovereign to respect the common-law jury's verdict. The Constitution actually mandates the right in no less than two places. The original document says: "The trial of all crimes . . . shall be by jury"; and, as if to ensure absolutely its vitality, the Sixth Amendment says: "In all criminal prosecutions, the accused shall enjoy [a] public trial by an impartial jury. . . ."

Federal trial juries were carbon copies of their common-law antecedents until very recently. They always consisted of twelve members, and their decisions had to be unanimous. Yet even though relevant constitutional language is unambiguous, trial by jury was never guaranteed in *all* criminal court actions. Historically, the crime had to be *serious*—one for which the accused might be imprisoned for six months or longer.

While the Court has never retreated from this last reservation, it has nonetheless rethought both the functions of the trial jury once it is convened and the way in which it should be constituted. In a severe departure from precedent, the Justices ruled in 1970 that juries might consist of as few as six members. To sustain its updating of the constitutional privilege, the Court explained the jury's essential contributions to our criminal justice system: (1) it places the commonsense judgment of lay citizens between accuser and accused and (2) it places verdicts of culpability in the hands of the general community. But, the majority believed, these tasks were not a function of any particular number of panelists. So long as the figure was large enough to provide a good chance for cross-sectional representation of the larger social environment, it would meet the constitutional standard.[35]

Two years later, in a corollary decision, the Justices nearly threw out the unanimity requirement for conviction. Actually, a majority found that unanimity was not a material aid to the commonsense judgment lying at the heart of jury duty. The rule would be defunct today but for a curious split among the Justices; five of them voted to uphold it for entirely different reasons.[36]

These holdings evince a less than wholehearted endorsement by the Court of the traditional jury system. Surely it is far easier to obtain convictions with a six-person body than a twelve-person body, assuming the unanimity criterion applies. And no debate is necessary to demonstrate that a split verdict offers far less protection than complete agreement. This suspicion of the jury trial norm as an effective canon of justice is not reflected in practice, however. During 1960, about 70 percent of all federal criminal cases were heard before juries, and this figure includes minor prosecutions, where the invocation of juries has never been accepted as a matter of right.[37] Corresponding data for the subsequent fifteen years show little drop-off. Everything else being equal, Q's lawyer, then, will opt for jury consideration.

Theoretically, the participants ultimately selected are supposed to represent reasonably the defendant's peers. In the days when English common law was controlling, the term "peers" referred to members of one's social class. Q, being the typical accused party in a narcotics case, comes from the lower end of the socioeconomic totem pole. What are the chances that his trial will be held before a tribunal of his peers? None. Under federal law, jurors are chosen at random, and this comports with our egalitarian premises; when Americans think of trial before one's peers, they undoubtedly have in mind a cross-section of the larger citizenry. The prevailing statute (enacted in 1968) also militates against the original concept. Under the 1968 law's criteria, lists of eligible participants are drawn randomly from voter registration tables, and a disproportionate number of lower-class people do not register. More important are the same factors that affect the makeup of grand juries: working-class individuals generally cannot afford to spend day after day in court at the salary this service commands. So, once more, white-collar representation is maximized.[38]

Trial juries, the Constitution tells us, are also supposed to be "impartial." Here, Q's attorney has some influence. The law allows a specific number of *peremptory challenges* by which the defendant's lawyer can dismiss a prospective juror for no reason at all. Perhaps after questioning a candidate, our lawyer's experience says the person is unsympathetic or appears to be too inflexible. Here is a good spot for peremptory dismissal. Virtually unlimited challenges can also be made on the basis of *cause.* If, under interrogation, the prospective juror shows prejudice, he or she will be turned down.

Juries, if they are conscientious, have a tough job. They cannot participate in the examination of witnesses, and they cannot take notes during testimony. Yet they are charged with evaluating all of the *facts* presented; from this information, it is their task to determine if Q is guilty *beyond a reasonable doubt.*

But what really goes on when jurors deliberate? There is the hypothetical "twelve average citizens" model, which envisions rational discussion and lengthy deliberation, resulting in truth winning out over error. Then there is the hypothetical "twelve hostile citizens" model, which envisions bickering between jurors and irrational exchange.[39] Research performed by the Chicago Jury Project does not support either stereotype;[40] but, because juries make decisions in strict privacy, the relevant data, though often gleaned from acceptable interviewing techniques, must be treated with care. Evidently, most juries take a vote as soon as they retire. This ballot is usually not decisive, but in 90 percent of the instances the majority eventually wins out. The deliberative process is rarely protracted; most of the discussion involves procedural matters and reflections on the trial. The myth of one lone juror standing against eleven opponents, forcing a "hung jury," is just that.[f] The research also indicates that judges would have agreed with juries' decisions 81 percent of the time, probably the most noteworthy finding among the data.[41]

Most objections by legal experts to jury trial concern questions of time, money, duplication of effort, and elitism. It is said that empaneling a jury drags out the criminal process unduly; that paying jurors higher salaries to induce participation is not worth the price; that trial by judge is as fair as trial by jury; and that judges are professionals, whereas juries are amateurs attempting to cope with the technical issues of modern-day problem-solving.

But none of these factors will likely persuade Q to change his mind. The average person does not trust a single robed figure to decide whether he must serve a term in prison. Judges are perceived to be too well educated and too hardened by constant contact with the world of disrepute. And they are seen as creatures of the "system." In fact, of the 19 percent of cases in which the Chicago Project noted disagreement between judge and jury, the former did show a marked propensity to convict.

There are larger issues of policy as well. The jury can help break down the walls that often separate the judiciary from public influence. Prosecutions under unpopular laws soon stop when juries do not support them with convictions. It is true that this check runs counter to the notion that juries only find *facts* and do not make decisions of *law*. But theory used to tell us judges never made law either! In their elaboration of the "common touch," citizens cannot be coerced into ignoring such equitable considerations. And, of course, most statutes are *not* unpopular. In the typical case, then, jury participation performs the avowedly political function of legitimizing the court's dispensations. The average American needs to feel his case has been heard by the "people" and not by some insensitive bureaucrat. Who can blame him!

The lawyers

Q will now come to trial. The leading actors in this process—make no mistake about it!—are the lawyers for both sides: the prosecuting attorney, who represents the interests of the United States, and the defense attorney, who represents Q. I have already touched upon the constitutional "right to counsel" guarantee. But what impact does the lawyer-client relationship have on the federal criminal justice process in the courtroom?

I should first make some general comments on the training of lawyers and the workways of the legal profession. The typical member of the bar is educated at an extraordinarily competitive, relatively prestigious school, where learning centers on the mastery of legal principles distilled from important court decisions. Hypothetical sets of facts are devised in the classroom, and the various rules are tested against the "facts" of the case. This training instills in

[f] When jurors cannot reconcile their differences, a new trial will be ordered.

the lawyer a high regard for the law's formalities and uniformities. Furthermore, the practitioner develops a self-image as the guardian and custodian of these principles. And the public at large fortifies this self-image, because it also perceives the advocate as belonging to some inner circle whose members understand the mysterious symbols of legal rhetoric. It is no surprise, then, that lawyers are ordinarily a fairly conservative lot.[42]

The federal courts, of course, decide real controversies, and the hallmark of a controversy is an adversary relationship. But one must probe the lawyer's role in our juridical system to understand what, in fact, this adversary relationship is all about. Q's attorney has a single objective: to get Q acquitted without breaking the law. The prosecuting attorney also has a single objective, once a decision to try the accused has been finalized: to get Q convicted without breaking the law. So criminal advocacy entails neither a "social worker" role, which would give due consideration to paternalistic values, nor a "social science" role, which would give due consideration to the dispassionate search for truth. Rather, it entails what Jerome Frank has called a "fight" role[43] but what might be better termed a "professional gunfighter" role, because the objective of each attorney, acting as the client's "hired sharpshooter," is to outdraw the opponent—the other "hired sharpshooter." This can be accomplished by the salutary skills of outthinking, outarguing, and outreasoning opposing counsel, but it can also include such tactics as surprise motions in court, designed to catch the opposition off guard; obscure precedents, dredged up to get the client off on a technicality; and Oscar-winning performances delivered to an entranced jury.

The bar's Canons of Ethics give sustenance to even the more unvarnished exercises in adversary justice. Attorneys may do anything within the law to help their clients and are prohibited from divulging *all* confidences shared with clients unless necessary to prevent crimes.[44] One famous lawyer said it is even permissible for advocates to tell lies occasionally if the need for a proper defense dictates. He also argued that attorneys are *ethically neutral* in their duties; therefore, counselors need have no compunction about taking any case they wish, regardless of the merits.[45]

To those who would question this sort of standard, one might rejoin, "Attorneys are supposed to protect their clients; justice is the job of the court." Such sentiments state the conventional wisdom very well. Political scientists, however, might put the matter this way: lawyers are political actors; the adversary system is one of many political relationships that might be contrived between advocate and client, between advocate and court of law; we accept the principle of adversativeness because it comports with various attributes of our constitutional environment, most notably an emphasis on the individual's capacities and values; we fail to redress the more antisocial attributes of adversary justice probably because of a reflex reliance on the "survival of the fittest," capitalist ethic; hence the adversary system unbalanced by countervailing public interests is an essential norm embedded in the "Living Constitution."

How might the "professional gunfighter" model affect strategies employed by Q's lawyer in this litigation? Two instances drawn from contemporary politics will demonstrate the possibilities available to dedicated, single-minded counsel.

In 1971, a federal grand jury indicted the Reverend Philip Berrigan and Sister Elizabeth McAlister for conspiring to kidnap Henry Kissinger. The government selected Harrisburg, Pennsylvania, as trial site, evidently hoping that the jury's makeup would reflect the low percentage of Catholics and the high percentage of both fundamentalist sects and military personnel in the area. The defense countered by conducting intensive personal interviews with registered voters, the universe from which jurors would be chosen. A list of "no-no" criteria was developed: no Episcopalians, no Presbyterians, no college-educated people, no business people, no person who had an abiding trust in government. Through the use of peremptory challenges, a panel fairly supportive of antiwar dissent (1968-style) was obtained.[46] This jury, incidentally, could not reach a verdict when it eventually received the case.

Now let's turn to a completely different kind of trial. In 1973, John Mitchell and Maurice Stans were indicted for allegedly impeding an investigation of financier Robert Vesco's dealings in the stock market; as a reward for the supposed intervention, Vesco had contributed $250,000 to Richard Nixon's reelection campaign. The trial was the first involving former Cabinet officials since Warren Harding's day. Again, the defense worked up a profile of prospective jurors, this time based upon modern marketing research techniques. The criteria were: no Jews, no "limousine liberals," no *New York Times* readers, no white-collar workers. A clear majority of "desirables" was once more obtained by prudent use of the peremptory challenge. In this case, both men were acquitted on all fifteen counts brought against them. Yet, as matters evolved, their most forceful spokesman during jury deliberations turned out to be the one member of the panel whose background did not conform to expectations![47]

Some might argue that such machinations demonstrate the impracticality of trial by jury in our time. Others might simply ogle before the shrewd, informed "game plans" of counsel and conclude, "To the winner belong the spoils." But a third observer might summarize the results this way: "From a shoot-out, only rational justice is shot down."

A complete picture of Frank's "fight" theory of trial advocacy comes to the fore only after the judge has commenced proceedings. Its most glaring attribute concerns the questioning of witnesses. Lawyers do everything legal to intimidate those who testify for the opposition. It is almost an accident when either judge or jury is confronted with witnesses' normal demeanor. Counsel also specialize in surprise testimony difficult for their "learned adversaries" to bone up on in advance.[48] The "discovery" mechanisms I discussed earlier as an important part of the civil process have traditionally been absent from the criminal courtroom chess game.[g] Frank himself described the legal and constitutional issues raised in litigation as "implements of persuasion"—that is, intellectual symbols brandished to gain support for the client.[49]

[g] Under rules passed by Congress in 1975, there now exists a defense-triggered discovery process for witness lists. If the defense wants to divulge its roster, then the government can be made to do likewise.

Of course, there have always been attorneys, small in number but impressive in expertise and zeal, who are primarily committed to advancing social causes through judicial activism rather than advancing the cause of particular clients. One immediately thinks of advocates who toil for the N.A.A.C.P. and the American Civil Liberties Union.[50] But the overall impression among much of the current student generation is that this country is saddled with lawyers who are primarily motivated by the dollar; one writer has, perhaps intemperately, called our system one of "whorehouse justice."[51] The trend is reflected in the new "public-interest" practitioners who have emerged of late from the law school womb.[52] After graduation, they specialize in defending three somewhat similar sets of legal interests: poor people; political and cultural dissidents such as protest marchers and the Symbionese Liberation Army; and environmental, consumer protection, and similar less-articulated policy concerns of increasing relevance to citizens in general. The demands of these students while in law school already have had their impact; there has been a considerable revamping of curricula so as to provide new courses of study. And certainly no one can accuse the new breed of selling its soul for the dollar at this early stage.

But what real consequences this kind of advocacy will work upon our political processes and institutions is still an open question. First, public-interest law received great impetus from deep-seated dissatisfaction with the Vietnam War, the upsurge in civil rights protest, and governmental efforts to resist militant forms of dissent in both areas during the 1960s. Can the movement prosper without highly visible political stress? The jury is still out. Second, to what extent will "radicalized" lawyers move on to the plush offices of the Establishment once they think they have paid their dues to society? The jury has not decided this question, either. Third, "Young Turk" lawyers would likely term the "fight" notion an antisocial extension of an antisocial doctrine, laissez faire. But have they defended their clients in any significantly different way? Indeed, *are* there other options? Just how the new wave can combat (1) the inherent advantage which affluent litigants possess in civil cases because they hire "top guns" and (2) the inherent advantage the state possesses in criminal cases, with its superior resources, remains a mystery. Last, there is a matter of mislabeling. The poor have legal interests, and these must be represented. But to argue that either the rights of the poverty-stricken or the rights of the wealthy are wrapped up in the *public interest* is dubious. It may be a step forward for one's heart to be with one's client, but the correlation between either and what is "good for everyone" could very easily be zero.

With all these reservations, the defendant who places trust in a public-interest lawyer will likely not be sacrificed on the altar of either assembly-line production or self-serving compromise. Q, of course, will not be so fortunate, because, unless he is indigent, he probably won't qualify for this type of assistance. The chances are that his attorney will be a practitioner who handles a multitude of cases bearing sharp resemblance to his own. The lawyer will spend little time and energy preparing Q's defense, will plea bargain if at all possible, and will be more concerned with a place in the political hierarchy of the courthouse than with any single client's fate. For the court is a modern, large-scale bureaucracy, and there is greater professional, economic, and intellectual community of interest among its chief affiliates—judges, prosecutors, defense attorneys—than exists between any of them and the outside world. It follows that building a practice is much easier when one's ties to the organization are secure. But most important, crushing caseloads coupled with limited resources and personnel require the bureaucracy and all its parts to "play ball" or see the whole system break down. Thus are links in the organization drawn ever closer, while the accused's rights fail to achieve full flower.[53]

Serious crimes, in any case, are least amenable to compromise. As I have indicated, the prosecutor is most confident of winning a conviction. Furthermore, public support can be counted on, because selling drugs is regarded as a particularly heinous offense. If probabilities govern, Q will plead not guilty, but his resistance will be to no avail. Less than one-fourth of the criminal cases fought to the bitter end in federal court terminate with an acquittal.[54]

The trial judge as peacekeeper

What about the official who supervises the proceedings? The trial judge's first responsibility is to preserve order in court. Procedural due process means little if the hearing is not conducted with a spirit of calmness, detachment, and scrupulous objectivity. Moreover, tempers easily can become ruffled because so much is on the line for a defendant. The judge must be constantly on the alert to anticipate breaches of decorum and must avoid, if at all possible, confrontations with either counsel or the accused that might jeopardize the image of judicial impartiality.

During the past decade, it has been increasingly difficult to maintain tranquillity in potentially emotional circumstances. For instance, suppose Q is black and feels the government is "railroading" him because of racial bias. He may see the judge and the various courtroom formalisms as oppressive instruments of authoritarianism. The judicial process can degenerate rapidly when a defendant's resentment erupts into explosive tantrums. In such circumstances, how can the judge preserve order and at the same time honor the Constitution's Sixth Amendment guarantee affording all accused parties the right to confront any witness testifying against them?

The Supreme Court has ruled that defendants can *waive* their right of confrontation through improper conduct. If after a warning from the judge, the accused continues to harass the court, the presiding officer has three alternatives: (1) to order the defendant from the trial room until he or she promises to be cooperative; (2) to have the defendant bound and gagged; (3) to find the defendant in contempt. The first remedy has the advantage of preventing further outburst and the disadvantage of stifling entirely the confrontation privilege. An example of the second remedy occurred during the famous Chicago Seven conspiracy trial of 1969, in which seven self-styled radicals had been indicted for allegedly having crossed state lines with an intent to incite a riot at the Democratic National Convention in 1968. One of the defendants was Black Panther leader Bobby Seale, who became so enraged at Judge Julius Hoffman for not allowing him to defend himself that he went on a shouting spree during the trial. Hoffman ordered Seale to be gagged and physically restrained. This, at least, kept him in the courtroom, so he could see and hear what was going on. But how can a jury concentrate on testimony when the defendant is wiggling in anguish, unable to move around or speak? Eventually the judge gave up and ordered Seale to stand trial on a later occasion. The third remedy, contempt, seems fairest on its face but can be subject to abuse; where the accused is charged with a serious offense, it may pay to sit in court piling up contempt citations, if such conduct will prevent the completion of *any* trial.[55]

Further complicating this dilemma has been the proliferation of "political trials"—that is, criminal hearings at which "public opinion and public attitudes on one or more social questions will inevitably have an effect on the decision."[56] Over the years, such confrontations have tended to involve "radicals of the left," largely for two related reasons: (1) when the United States has perceived clear and present dangers from abroad, the activists have generally opposed a militant stand against those threats; (2) Americans believe that Communist activities are designed to overthrow, not to reinforce, the constitutional order. However, the trial of a John Ehrlichman or a Gordon Liddy on Watergate-related matters is every bit the political confrontation that the trial of draft-card burners was a few years ago.

Actually, it is virtually impossible to keep political elements from intruding upon the judicial process at certain times. When a crime has been committed, our constitutional system of criminal justice demands that the accused be tried, regardless of his or the government's political motivations. However, with all the publicity and argumentation by press and politicians that occur over such cases, can public opinion on the accused's political ideology always be fenced out of the courtroom? The jury-selection process must make us doubtful; if we are to have free speech, we must anticipate that some people will judge others by what they themselves think and believe.

Obviously this political dimension can exacerbate tensions during the trial, especially when defendants and/or their attorneys intentionally use the hearing process as a forum for ventilating their ideologies. And strife reaches a climax when disorderly antics are used not to dramatize the defendant's "just cause" but to destroy the court itself as a legitimate decision-making instrument. The hearing then may become a tragi-comedy, with the accused's hatred of the system assuming overriding importance.[57]

For example, in the Chicago Seven trial, two of the defendants, Jerry Rubin and Abbie Hoffman, came to court one day dressed in judicial robes; the garments were eventually removed and trampled upon. On an earlier occasion, David Dellinger, a third defendant, stood up and began reading the names of soldiers who had died in Vietnam. Dellinger also called Judge Hoffman, to his face, "a liar" and "the assistant prosecutor." Clearly, these men were not attempting to convey a sense of political helplessness to what they hoped would be a responsive jury, but were emoting against the idea that they should be brought to trial by *anyone* for what they considered political dissent in the Tom Paine tradition. But if accused parties are allowed to decide for themselves when they can be charged with criminal offenses, due process under the Constitution becomes a nullity.[58]

I have mentioned the contempt process as perhaps the most suitable antidote to counteract such excesses. In the usual situation, a judge first issues standard warnings to the person treading in dangerous waters and then, if these do not suffice, slams down the gavel and says, "That will cost you $10," or "That's three days in jail." But if the sentence imposed is longer than six months, it is treated as though it were a *serious* crime, and a trial by jury is required in federal court.[59] This is an important check against a judge who, wounded by contumacious behavior, lashes back in dictatorial style. In the Chicago Seven litigation, Judge Hoffman manipulated his contempt authority so that each *separate* offense amounted to less than a six-month penalty, but the *total* time of imprisonment for most of the defendants ran far beyond that time. The appellate courts promptly ordered a new trial to rectify these punishments.

The trial judge as referee

If the judge is fortunate, all courtroom participants will be on their best behavior, and full attention can be devoted to the main judicial task: umpiring the confrontation between opposing counsel. The job is essentially one of ruling on all legal points that arise, and, for the sake of convenience, this responsibility can be divided into two categories.

First, the hearing must meet minimal standards of fairness before it ever gets off the ground. Suppose Q's house had been ransacked without a warrant, and a diary itemizing heroin sales unearthed. Q's lawyer will undoubtedly ask the judge to render the diary inadmissible on the ground that the search was unconstitutional. Or suppose the media have so blanketed the marketplace with details about the youthful clients Q has allegedly recruited and "hooked" that an impartial trial seems impossible. Again, Q's lawyer should ask the judge for a *change of venue*—that is, to move the hearing to a place where passions are less heated. The presiding officer must ascertain whether the search was indeed contrary to law, or whether the geographical vicinity is in fact so saturated with unfavorable opinion that a fair hearing appears out of the question.

After Daniel Ellsberg had been brought to trial for copying and distributing the Pentagon Papers, the defense learned that President Nixon's team of agents (the "Plumbers") had illegally broken into Ellsberg's psychiatrist's office in hopes of finding out more about the alleged theft. Prosecutorial officials themselves had clearly done nothing wrong; nor, indeed, was there proof that the trespassers had taken damaging evidence. But the judge dismissed the case against Ellsberg because the *federal government's misconduct* had made a fair trial impossible.

Second, once the hearing gets going, the presiding judge must ordinarily decide a whole raft of technical legal issues. Rarely do these entail broad questions of constitutional relevance; rather, they concern the rules of procedure lawyers must observe. Possibly the judge's single most important duty at this point is to rule hearsay evidence out of order. Suppose the star prosecution witness submits testimony against Q based on conversations with a third party who is afraid to step forward or who is an undercover agent trying to remain anonymous. This is hearsay, and the judge should be asked to disallow it. People are not to be found guilty by rumor, conjecture, or violations of courtroom rules and regulations.

One of the main criticisms lodged against the trial court mechanism is that judges do not aggressively search out the truth on their *own* behalf. Think of the social utility of a criminal process in which judges not only referee a contest but become independent advocates for justice. They might insist, for example, that attorneys share information with one another through discovery procedures. They might also summon their own witnesses or interrogate in depth those whom counsel have called. Invocation of these tools could help narrow appreciably the gap in skill and resources between lawyers and would, perhaps, diminish the number of jury verdicts predicated largely on such factors.[60] To repeat, the adversary system has always been part of the "Living Constitution," but we have not learned to balance its more combative tendencies with corollary devices geared to benefit the public interest.

I have noted the rise of plea bargaining as an informal adjudicative substitute for the trial process. But judges do not have to sit idly by and authorize any and all such agreements if these fail to meet their sense of social propriety. Judge John Sirica's handling of the Watergate break-in cases serves as the classic model. One of the co-defendants, former C.I.A. operative Howard Hunt, offered to plead guilty to three of the six charges brought against him. But Sirica rejected this proposal out of hand. In his opinion, the government's case was so compelling that Hunt should plead guilty to all charges or be tried on all. In short, he permitted no "deals" that might obscure a search for answers to the two nagging questions of highest policy significance: (1) Who authorized the Watergate wiretap operation? (2) Who supplied the seven break-in participants with the thousands of dollars used to fund the operation? I want to stress that this kind of scrutiny is even more vital at the pre-trial pleading stage than during the actual trial; without dogged judicial oversight early on, there might not be a trial! Yet, like the other freewheeling weapons cited above, its use is very much within the discretion of judges; being creatures of both "fight" theory mores and "court as bureaucracy" mores, they just don't employ such tools very often.

The trial judge and the jury

After each side has rested its case, a verdict must be handed down. Obviously, where defendant has waived the right to a jury, it is up to the judge to sift through the facts, determine who is telling the truth, apply the law with great care, and keep in mind the "beyond a reasonable doubt" standard. As I have said, judges are likely to reach much the same verdicts as juries would; where there is disagreement, judges are apt to be tougher on the accused. Beyond this, scholars know as little about a judge's fact-finding propensities as they know about a jury's methods.

Q, though, has had a trial before a panel of his peers. This body must ascertain the facts, but the presiding officer has a duty to *charge* these jurors before they retire—that is, to explain the relevant law in everyday language for the jury's consideration. The charge comprises the legal standards the panel will apply to the facts of Q's case as the members construe those facts, and only then can a verdict be reached. A judge must tread carefully here, for many a trial has been voided on appeal because the charge either was too vague or constituted an incorrect rendition of the applicable statutory guidelines. The jurors may take notes while being charged, but they cannot have a copy of the judge's statement during their deliberations.

Sometimes a charge to the jury can involve great issues of constitutional politics. In 1948, the leaders of the American Communist Party were indicted under the Smith Act. This statute makes it illegal for anyone knowingly to advocate the overthrow of the United States government by force or to organize any group or distribute any literature advocating such overthrow. It also outlaws conspiracies to so advocate or organize. In his charge to the jury, Judge Harold Medina interpreted the Smith Act in two significant ways. First, he said, the law does *not* suppress the teaching of the propriety of revolution as worthwhile doctrine. So if Thomas Jefferson had delivered a speech or published a pamphlet saying, "A revolution every twenty years is good for the soul of the country," he would have been exempt from prosecution. But, Medina found, if defendants had put the Communist Party together and spread the gospel of insurrection because they were conspiring to incite revolution at some propitious moment, then they were acting contrary to the law. Second, said Medina, if you, the jury, find these defendants did act in this fashion and for these reasons, a verdict of guilty is mandated. In so ruling Medina was exercising the power that all federal judges have to interpret the Constitution and uphold (or knock down) legislative enactments; Congress, he said, had not violated defendant's free speech rights by passing the Smith Act.[61] The Communists were convicted.

If we want to evaluate the judge's charge as a political measure, we must at the outset assess its impact. Jerome Frank has argued that the typical jury cannot understand the "mumbo-jumbo" of the charge and therefore ignores everything the judge has said. The result is unstructured and irrational decision-making.[62] Jon Van Dyke, however, cites evidence showing that juries do try to follow instructions; he thinks they are intimidated by the judge's constant claim that the law stands higher than their own moral preconceptions. For this reason, Van Dyke feels defendants often have two strikes against them.[63] But even if two juries deciding the same kind of case hewed carefully to instructions, we could scarcely predict their verdicts. Whereas such a panel found Dr. Benjamin Spock guilty of conspiring to violate the draft laws, a jury equally concerned with the substance of the judge's charge found John Mitchell and Maurice Stans not guilty of conspiring to obstruct justice.[64] Charges, after all, come in different sizes, shapes, and descriptions, as do juries. Whatever impact a particular charge may have, there are few data showing that charges per se constitute bias favorable either to the state or to the accused. The tough question, which Van Dyke fudges, is this: If juries followed the "moral conscience of the community" rather than the law, would they be more or less merciful toward defendants?

But what about the charge's political function from a normative perspective? Judges cannot be robot-like in interpreting the Constitution; juries cannot be robot-like in interpreting instructions. However, shrewd judges know their craft; we make no effort to educate juries with regard to *their* craft. Perhaps what the courts must do is to expand upon the charge so that it includes guidelines to help jurors temper the law with the human touch in a systematic way, considering retribution and mercy both. The meaning of intent under the law seems especially relevant here. But I doubt if there is wisdom to the contention that a jury should *disregard* instructions when these rules are contrary to the moral sensibilities of the group. Legal norms written by elected officials may be subject to reasonable and equitable interpretation but not purposeful obliteration.

The trial judge as punisher

Assuming a verdict of guilty has been returned, as is likely in Q's case, it is the judge's responsibility to impose sentence. Here, the statutes provide for considerable flexibility, specifying only minimum and maximum sentences for most crimes. The judge will take into account such factors as defendant's cooperation, any feelings of remorse Q may have conveyed at his final appearance in court, and the health of immediate family members. Considerable disparities therefore appear in sentences for similar crimes, depending upon the circumstances, the judge, and the theory of sentencing being applied. For example, should the judge stress rehabilitation factors in prescribing penalties or emphasize punitive aspects? There are many theories on the subject and no hard-and-fast rules, mostly because social scientists really can't say what consequences will ensue when penalty x is meted out to culprit Y.

Recently, some well-publicized trials have yielded striking examples of these differing theories. Judge Gerhard Gesell, noting that "morality is a higher force than expediency," gave former Nixon aide Charles Colson very nearly the strongest permissible sentence, despite both Colson's bargain with Special Prosecutor Leon Jaworski and his well-publicized repentence and conversion to Christianity.[65] A different attitude was shown by Judge Edward Gignoux, brought all the way from Maine for the rehearing of contempt charges against six of the Chicago Seven and their lawyer, William Kunstler. While Gignoux found that David Dellinger had committed seven offenses, and he convicted Kunstler for having launched a vicious tirade against Judge Hoffman, he meted out *no* punishment. Four years had elapsed, and Gignoux decided that no good purpose could be accomplished by imprisoning the defendants at that point. Judge John Sirica's theory, as exemplified in the sentences he gave to the convicted Watergate burglars, is yet another approach. Sirica's aim was to expose the entire range of Watergate culpability. All sentences, he announced, would be framed to assist in this effort. At times excoriating defendants because he thought they knew more than they were saying, he threatened to throw the book at them unless they cooperated to the hilt with both Senator Sam Ervin's Watergate committee and the Watergate grand jury. If the defendants were forthright, however, he promised to take their candor into account when final sentences were prescribed. The medicine worked its intended wonders. One of the lawbreakers, James McCord, "spilled the beans" about both John Mitchell's authorization of the break-in and "hush money" payments made in order to buy defendants' silence, while Howard Hunt's testimony regarding the entire gamut of White House "horrors" was seen by millions on television.

And yet Sirica's tactics raise some serious questions. One of the rights the defendants possessed under our Constitution was the protection against self-incrimination. And confessions *coerced in any* fashion are not admissible in court. Didn't Sirica compromise their rights by holding incredibly harsh sentences over their heads? Some experts think so. Again, the salient issue cannot be escaped: What is sentencing supposed to accomplish? Sirica disbelieved the defendants' claims of sole personal responsibility. So he took radical steps which were, without doubt, inherently coercive. But is it more defensible to find someone guilty of contemptuous conduct and then let the defendant walk away unscathed, as Judge Gignoux did? It comes back to the *politics* of sentencing, and the following test may be as good as any: Which dispensation of judicial power better conveys to defendants that the courts will meet them 50 percent of the way but no more, once their guilt has been ascertained? Judge Sirica demanded a heavy price because the stakes were so high, but the suspended sentences he eventually handed out to cooperative defendants show he came close to the 50–50 rule of thumb. Judge Gesell didn't give a cooperative Charles Colson an inch and probably overreacted against the accused's misuse of power. Judge Gignoux gave an unrepentent William Kunstler a slap on the wrist and probably underreacted to society's need for responsible conduct from the bar.

Returning to Q, we ask, "What kind of penalty can he expect?" With no major political issues to complicate his case, he will likely get a stiff sentence, though not the stiffest permissible. We know he pleaded not guilty and so forced the prosecution to the limit. But we also know he qualified for pre-trial release under the Bail Reform Act. Empirical research shows a significant relationship between fruitless not-guilty pleas and tough sentencing, on the one hand, but also a significant relationship between pre-trial release and lenient sentencing on the other hand.[66] When evaluated against the "50 percent of the way but no more" test described above, there is little question that Q's punishment will be an exercise in irrationality. Why? Because the positive and negative factors taken into account have little bearing on either society's legitimate interests in punishing people or the individual's legitimate need to be treated as something other than a number.

A final accounting

How long did the trial last? Q received a faster hearing than he would have gotten in a diversity case. In fiscal 1974, those who opted for jury trial had a 50-50 chance of knowing the outcome within six months of the time their case was filed, while a judge's ruling would have been issued approximately sixty days earlier.[67] Yet Q's trial probably took twice as long as it would have taken in 1960. Just as Warren Court decisions expanding the accused's rights have lowered the number of guilty pleas and hence increased the number of trials, so these rulings require judges to spend much more time deciding whether federal officers seized evidence properly and questioned suspects properly.[68]

We all agree that efficiency cannot be weighted more heavily than individual freedoms; but to enlarge personal rights also imposes a duty to make these rights meaningful within a context of social responsibility. In present circumstances, this duty must be assumed by the "political branches," and the means must include more money; more personnel; more limitations on the "fight" theory of legal presentation; more regulation of the cases that can be brought into federal court (diversity litigation is certainly the most expendable); and more stringent penalties to discourage serious crimes, whether they be perpetrated by Watergaters, self-styled radicals, or people like Q.

To sum up, the Constitution guarantees many procedural rights that civilize our federal criminal justice system. As implemented over time, these norms, though sometimes subject to criticism, are undoubtedly part of the "Living Constitution." Yet the system as a whole does not function with a coherence, a smoothness, and a sense of fairness we associate with that "living" document. It is devoutly to be wished that the powers of national government and the rights of the individual within the criminal justice environment will achieve the kind of balance—and therewith the kind of legitimacy—we consider fundamental to those organic rules.

The federal district courts

"The judicial Power," says the Constitution, shall be placed in the hands of a Supreme Court "and in such inferior Courts as the Congress may . . . establish." This provision is another instance of compromise between the nationalists and the states' righters at Philadelphia. The former group wanted a strong *federal* court system to process cases of *federal* concern, while the latter group thought the *state* court hierarchy could handle *federal* business along with its own, with the Supreme Court sitting as final arbiter. Unable to bridge this gap, Madison proposed the agreed-upon language, which passed the buck to Congress.

The Judiciary Act of 1789 established our first set of federal judicial tribunals.[h] It consisted of a Supreme Court and district courts, one in each state. Suppose a person were arrested for committing treason in violation of federal statute. That individual would be tried in a district court and could appeal on matters of law to the Supreme Court. But suppose the states' rights bloc had won out in Congress, and the 1789 statute had *not* created an inferior federal judicial level. The accused traitor would then have been prosecuted in the *state* trial courts and could have appealed to the state supreme court and, as a last resort, to the U.S. Supreme Court. To those who believed in Articles of Confederation philosophy, this arrangement made perfect sense.

District court powers

The federal district courts, then and now, are *trial* courts; they also possess only *original jurisdiction*—that is, they receive no cases on appeal.

None of this is mentioned in the Constitution. The Congress organized these courts, and the Congress assigns them business. And what Congress can give, Congress can probably take away. There is a question of constitutional propriety here, but if Congress is able to terminate a district court's existence, it is rather obvious that Congress is able to take the lesser step of revising a district court's business.

This point emerges graphically from a review of labor-management strife before the federal courts. It used to be common practice for the "laissez faire" judiciary to issue injunctions forbidding strikes by disgruntled workers. An employer would somehow find a way to make a federal case out of what could possibly be regarded as "pending irreparable damage" on the part of the employees. But Congress, in 1932, passed the Norris-LaGuardia Act, largely prohibiting district courts from providing such injunctive relief; and the Supreme Court said this withdrawal of lower court authority was permissible.[69] In 1947, however, a Congress with a different view *returned* some of this power in the Taft-Hartley Act. Few now would question the constitutionality of these maneuvers.[70]

District courts, like all judicial tribunals, rely mostly on the contempt process to bring about compliance with their orders. I am not now referring to *direct contempt,* such as the in-court behavior of some of the Chicago Seven; the usual confrontation concerns behavior outside the courtroom. A typical instance of *indirect contempt* involved a white racist named John Kasper. After a federal district court in Tennessee had ordered the desegregation of Clinton High School in 1956, Kasper made national headlines by leading a campaign

[h] Remember this law? A small portion of it, vesting in the Supreme Court the power to issue writs of mandamus, was later voided in *Marbury v. Madison* (see pp. 32-33).

to resist the directive. Aroused by his exhortations, crowds of irate citizens congregated around the school threatening any black student who dared to show up. Kasper's only response to an injunction demanding that he "cease and desist" was to urge further obstruction. The school board asked the district court to find Kasper in contempt. Acting on this request, the judge ordered his arrest. A full-dress trial was then held, with rights to counsel, cross-examination, and due process strictly observed. Kasper was found guilty of criminal contempt.

To what extent can Congress regulate these contempt procedures? This is a "twilight zone" area. It is one thing to say Congress may abolish a district court; but it is quite another thing to say a court can be stripped of enforcement weapons that are the very essence of its judicial function. Thus, separation of powers precludes Congress from turning a court into a legislative organ. The Supreme Court Justices have never approved congressional regulation of the *direct contempt* mechanism, ostensibly because keeping order in the courtroom is fundamental to judicial autonomy. But the *indirect contempt* process is not as integral, and minimal legislative standards can be ordained. Where an alleged contempt of court constitutes an alleged violation of federal statute, Congress has found that trial before a jury should be afforded. If, then, John Kasper's harangues had included threats against some federal official—an illegal act—he could have had a jury trial for the asking. This provision is considered a permissible limitation on the district court's *jurisdiction* rather than an unconstitutional abridgment of some essential judicial attribute.[71]

Organization and appointments

There are ninety-one federal district courts in the United States and almost four hundred sitting judges. Naturally, these courts hear only "cases and controversics."[i] When criminal or civil litigation is initiated, it generally comes before one judge, who will supervise the subsequent proceedings. District court judges rarely act as a team; when we talk of a district court we are really referring to a particular federal judge making decisions.

If this lone judge is *the* court, it becomes crucial to understand how he or she got there. The Constitution says that all federal judges are to be appointed by the President and ratified by majority vote in the Senate. The "Living Constitution," however, reverses these roles. Richardson and Vines sum up the "core process" through which district court judges are selected: "Senator(s) of presidential party, and/or local presidential party and president and his advisors interact to produce a nominee who is then affirmed by the acquiescence of Senate Judiciary Committee and majority of Senate."[72]

The Senate sits in a dominant position. Federal judgeships are the most desirable of political plums because the pay is good and tenure is for life. Since

[i] This is another basic judicial feature Congress cannot amend.

earliest times, then, these appointments have been governed by patronage considerations. The President must play ball with senators from his own party or, if there are none, had better listen to noises from the grassroots faithful. President Truman found this out when he tried to ram his choices down the throat of a fellow Democrat, Senator Paul Douglas of Illinois. The Senate stuck with Douglas and rejected Truman's appointments. This sort of "log-rolling"—in which senators tend to support the choice of a colleague for a position occurring in the senator's state over the nominee of a President who shares the senator's political party label—is known as "senatorial courtesy." Still, one can exaggerate the vitality of this convention. Senators can suggest names and they can even veto names; but they do not own the selection process, at least not in modern times.[73]

The President himself does not ordinarily soil his hands during the screening stage. He delegates supervision of this process to his Attorney General, who, in turn, assigns the responsibility to the Deputy Attorney General. The deputy is no bureaucrat, but an important policy-maker. John Kennedy's Deputy Attorney General was Byron White (now Mr. Justice White). Ever since the 1950s Justice Department officials have taken a strong initiative in exercising the President's power by making independent searches for candidates and evaluating senatorial choices. Differences of opinion will ultimately be adjusted through the usual executive-legislative negotiations, with the President taking "one good, hard look" at the final selection.[74]

Complicating matters since 1947 has been a Special Committee on the Federal Judiciary, an arm of the American Bar Association, which rates all potential nominees on a scale from 1 (not qualified) to 4 (well qualified) with respect to legal talent. These data are supplied to the Justice Department and must be given due weight because politicians generally cannot afford to alienate the most prestigious of American legal organizations.

Many constitutional scholars do not like the idea of a private group dictating the makeup of the federal court system to elected officials. Furthermore, the A.B.A. has a long history of supporting "right-wing" political values, and so it is not considered truly representative of the legal community.[75] Yet one must not overrate its influence. Almost 10 percent of the nominees chosen by Eisenhower and Kennedy did not meet A.B.A. criteria.[76] While the organization does have a say, it certainly does not have a veto.

Once a particular candidate receives the nod, senatorial confirmation is usually a formality. Nominations accomplished through the "core process" described above are ratified more than 99 percent of the time.[77]

If the recruitment effort is avowedly political, district court judges should present an overtly political profile. Indeed they do. More than 90 percent of the appointees designated by every President since Franklin Roosevelt have come from the same political party as the chief executive.[78] Furthermore, about half of Johnson's and Nixon's choices "had records of *prominent* partisan activism."[79] But does the political variable really make a difference in the way federal district judges decide cases? The meager data show that on *some* issues there is a *slight* tendency for judges to vote the way their party usually stands on those issues.[80] However, in attempting to gauge how trial court judges respond to cases in which urban social issues were at stake, Kenneth Dolbeare concludes: "Political party is apparently not an important factor. . . ."[81]

How can we summarize the role of the federal district courts in our national governmental apparatus? The judges whom Dolbeare studied supported the policies of the cities against attack by dissatisfied individuals 81 percent of the time, and he suggests that *localism* is the prime factor in explaining why district court judges vote the way they do.[82] This is easily understood. To the best of our knowledge, trial court officials usually are born in the general geographical area they serve, go to law school in the state where their district is located, and tend to have held governmental positions in that state.[83] Moreover, district court jurisdictions are often drawn along state lines; no district includes portions of more than one state; the judges must live in the district they represent; and "senatorial courtesy" by its very nature is a decentralizing force. In other words, the district court judge performs the function of applying federal judicial policies to the local level, but does so gently, as essentially a creature of the region.[84]

The federal circuit courts of appeal

The circuit courts of appeal stand between the district courts and the Supreme Court on the federal judicial hierarchy. Comparisons between these intermediate forums and their trial court associates are instructive. Gross figures can be deceiving, but well over 90 percent of all cases filed for consideration never reach the appellate stage. Moreover, it is in the context of district court responsibility that most constitutional values relevant to the judicial process are put into practice. Finally, because trial court policy-making is very much open to public scrutiny, we know far more about what these bodies do.

The circuit courts of appeal, as we now recognize them, did not take shape until 1891. In large measure, Congress created them to meet the significant rise in litigation that accompanied the increase in population in the late nineteenth century. But beneath the surface lay the same federal-state friction that had influenced the politics of district court organization. Nationalists wanted circuit courts established to relieve the Supreme Court of some of its appellate workload; states' righters agreed the Justices were overburdened, but they recommended placing some Court authority in the hands of *state* appellate tribunals. The federalists won this war because, after the demise of the Confederacy, the trend toward national unity was irresistible. The 1891 statute afforded a right of appeal from district to circuit courts, and there most cases would stop. At this writing, there are eleven intermediate appellate courts serviced by approximately one hundred judges. Only about 5 percent of all federal controversies ever get beyond this layer of adjudication.[85]

The federal appellate courts attract some outstanding people. Many circuit court judges have been superior to the general run of Supreme Court appointees; they lacked only the political qualifications—or, more likely, they weren't in the right place at the right time—to move higher. Probably the most famous judge to sit on the courts of appeal in this century was Learned Hand, who was surely the intellectual superior of 90 percent of Supreme Court personnel.

Judge Hand wrote the most widely cited and debated opinion handed down by a circuit court in the present generation. This decision stemmed from the previously mentioned trial, in 1949, of Communist Party leaders; they had appealed their conviction, saying the Smith Act was unconstitutional. Freedom of expression, they argued, could be limited only if it posed a "clear and present danger" of illegal activity, and they denied any immediate plan to incite law-breaking. Judge Hand ruled against them. In his view, the gravity of the "evil" presented by the Communist Party in the context of Russian-American cold war antipathy was extreme. Furthermore, the *probability* that this revolutionary cadre would strike when ready seemed clear to him. Free speech, he concluded, could be regulated in a manner sufficient to avoid the danger. Government need not wait until the signal was given and hostilities commenced.[86]

The Supreme Court decision upholding Hand's argument was an anticlimax, because it was based largely on his theories. A plurality of the Court even admitted its intellectual debt: "We adopt this statement of the rule. As articulated by Chief Judge Hand, it is as succinct and inclusive as any other we might devise at this time. . . . More we cannot expect from words."[87] In all likelihood, Hand's opinion will far outlive the final disposition entered by his superiors.

With the exception of the Court of Appeals for the District of Columbia, each circuit tribunal supervises a particular geographical region comprising at least three states. This fact alters drastically the effects of "senatorial courtesy" in filling vacancies.[88] Without doubt, the President's assistants in the Attorney General's office now have the upper hand, and they engage in a far-ranging search for good prospects. Of course, senators from states in a particular circuit, if they belong to the President's party, will push their candidates, but there is often real competition among them. However, an understanding exists that the nod will ordinarily go to someone from the state of the judge being replaced; about 70 percent of the appointments consummated in the early 1960s satisfied this norm. In such cases, the senator(s) from that state "clear" the President's final choice; this show of patronage is an important check on executive branch freedom. Finally, the A.B.A., with its set of ratings, once again stands ready to inspect all serious aspirants; the Justice Department, then, is constrained to choose those who possess first-class professional credentials. By and large, though, the usual political attributes weigh most heavily. More than 90 percent of the nominees are members of the President's political party, and about 80 percent of them were at one time partisan activists. With respect to more subtle ideological factors, both Kennedy's and Eisenhower's assistants made every effort to steer clear of candidates who were not "our kind." Nor does the less pointed imprint of "senatorial courtesy" lead to a breakdown in the appointees' community ties; there is often a strong flavor of regionalism in their backgrounds. To sum up, the differences between the sociopolitical characteristics one might ascribe to district and circuit court judges are not great;

but by any objective test the latter are better qualified to tackle tough legal problems.

What does a typical circuit court do? It will have nine judges, and one of these—the senior person on that particular bench—will carry the title Chief Judge. Circuit courts are collegial bodies in the fashion of the Supreme Court, but rarely does an entire appellate membership get together to hear a particular case. Rather, the Chief Judge's important and unique power comes into play. He or she assigns panels of three jurists to each appeal. The Chief Judge thus could influence greatly the decision-making process by juggling opportunities, though obviously panel-stacking is not considered "according to Hoyle."

The circuit courts are much busier than they used to be. In 1960, they received less than 4,000 appeals from the trial courts; by 1972, the figure had risen sharply, to about 12,000.[89] Of this total, *civil* cases outnumbered criminal cases approximately two to one; however, in the 1964–74 period, the rate of criminal convictions appealed jumped from 33 percent to 75 percent! Counsel for contending parties present arguments in the same fashion as they do before the Supreme Court, but, as we found in studying the district tribunals, judges have a way of not allowing their dockets to become bloated. Approximately 40 percent of the appeals are dispensed with even before a formal hearing.[90] However, the chances for obtaining a full-dress inquiry are much better here than before a district court.

What do we know about decision-making in the circuit courts? Voting studies of circuit court behavior are more prolific than comparable trial court analyses, in part because the universe of judges on the higher bench is far smaller. In the important civil liberties realm, the courts of appeal seem to play the role of reversing district tribunals that had initially denied libertarian claims. Evidently, when an allegation of individual rights is upheld in the first hearing, there is no appeal; most of the relevant cases involve persons who think they have been deprived of libertarian privileges in the district court.[91] There are also data showing that appellate judges can be separated on a liberalism criterion—that is, two rather distinct camps tend to form on matters concerning civil liberties, criminal law, labor cases, private economic questions, and so on. Hence, a judge who normally votes in favor of free speech issues also tends to vote for the rights of the accused, of labor, and of debtors and tenants.[92] Moreover, Republicanism correlates extremely well with economic conservatism and fairly well with political conservatism. In plain English, G.O.P. judges seem to favor business, while Democrats appear to favor labor and government against business; however, with respect to free speech and due process, the judges' party background provides less satisfactory clues to voting behavior over time. There is evidence, though, that reactions to these "political" issues have become, in the past decade, a function of partisan polarization, probably because President Johnson named to the courts of appeal Democrats who construed Warren Court egalitarian values broadly, while President Nixon named Republicans who construed those values narrowly.[93] Of course, the voting-study figures cannot capture the negotiations, persuasion, and other nuances of compromise that are a feature of political groups, including circuit courts.[94]

If anything, these computations, taken together, may overemphasize differences between district and intermediate courts. The fact is that 75 percent of all decisions reached at the trial level and subsequently brought up on appellate review are affirmed, and in the controversial criminal litigation category the concurrence ratio climbs to 83 percent.[95] Furthermore, the data showing the existence of liberal and conservative blocs are based mostly on *split* decisions (where the vote was 2-1), and the overwhelming number of judgments are unanimous (there is much less dissent in the courts of appeal than in the Supreme Court). This overriding ideological consensus gets lost in the figures, and most of that consensus is supportive of the district courts and the governmental policies these courts initially endorsed.[96]

On the other side, however, are those special instances where circuit judges zero in on local policies that are completely out of phase with federal policies. Thus, race relations decisions adjudicated in the Southern district courts favorable to state government get rough treatment when reviewed above.[97] And the fact that economic liberalism does emerge as a cutting edge between Republicans and Democrats shows that the circuit courts are responsive to this dimension of *national* partisan debate.

The federal court "system"

To what extent can we compare and contrast the roles and functions of the district, circuit, and Supreme courts? These structures are commonly thought of, after all, as knit together into some larger unit called the federal judicial system. But what does "system" mean in this context? In general usage, the term may be defined as a combination or arrangement of parts which form some larger whole, a whole that, in turn, is governed by ordering principles susceptible to rational statement and understanding. Applying this definition to the federal judiciary, we discover easily what the parts are and what the whole is; we also realize this package forms a portion of the constitutional framework. Much less clear, however, are the *rational principles* governing the total. Whatever they are, these norms must be considered salient facets of the "Living Constitution."

One theory of federal judicial coherence[98] is the *hierarchical,* which sees litigation moving from trial courts to courts of appeal and, finally, to the Supreme Court. It envisions the federal judicial system as a vertical pecking order, with the highest court gravely handing down a body of decisions labeled "constitutional law." Another explanation is the *bureaucratic.* Here again, the Court makes key policy, but its underlings do the "dirty work" by filling in gaps. Thus, the lower courts possess a measure of independence with respect to implementation, which allows them to make marginal policy contributions.

When we trace the movement of cases up and down the federal judicial ladder, though, both theories fall short. First, the overwhelming proportion of litigation filed simply never gets beyond the district court stage. Second, cases are appealed on questions of *law,* not on findings of *fact* at trial. Reversals are sought in order to rectify the introduction of spurious evidence, improper charges to juries, and the like. So when the two layers do wind up examining the same controversy, they usually are looking at a dispute that has assumed a radically different form in the interim. However, the hiatus separating the Supreme Court from the courts of appeal is much greater. In 1971, 2,800 requests for relief from intermediate court action were docketed with the Supreme Court, but only 5 percent were reviewed. The rest of the Justices' workload comes either from the state supreme courts or directly from the district tribunals—these cases have skipped the circuit courts because of special circumstances. The latter two categories combined constitute a majority of the Supreme Court's calendar. In sum, the Justices decide somewhat less than 10 percent of all controversies placed before them per year; the total number would be about 350.[99]

It is important to take a close look at the universe of decisions reaching the Justices through regular federal appellate channels. First, 60 percent of such cases are criminal rather than civil in nature, a marked contrast from the workload of the lower courts.[100] Second, 70 percent involve litigation in which the district and circuit courts *agreed,* and, of that group, the Justices overruled the lower courts' consensus 70 percent of the time. These findings show the Supreme Court tends to concentrate on a different class of policy issues from the lower courts; they show the Justices tend not to involve themselves in resolving district-circuit disagreements; and they show the high bench introduces conflict into the system rather than stabilizing the patterns established by its lower court assistants. Finally, where there is disagreement between trial court and intermediate appellate court, the Justices side with the *former* two-thirds of the time.[101]

Taken as a whole, the data demonstrate graphically that the Supreme Court is performing a unique judicial role, a responsibility that cannot be articulated through hierarchical or bureaucratic schemes. This conclusion is reinforced by the politics of recruitment. About 50 percent of all Supreme Court Justices had no previous judicial service. Presidents have realized such qualifications convey little information to help them predict desired performance on the high bench; indeed, Felix Frankfurter has written, "The correlation between prior judicial experience and fitness for the Supreme Court is zero."[102]

The Court, then, does not make any systematic appellate review of what lower court officials deem appropriate. Furthermore, the Justices spend little time either slapping their wrists if they stray too far from preexisting standards or holding their hands in the wake of challenge from disaffected litigants. What the Court does, briefly stated, is to perform the role of independent policy formulator with respect to constitutional norms. The Justices sift through cases, take the very few that present consequential issues of federal dimension, and use them as platforms for updating the deep, abiding rules of our political system as they affect the contemporary power struggle.

What, then, *is* the ordering principle underlying the federal judicial system? Perhaps an *administrative* model is appropriate. If so, the courts are bound together not by either case flow or policy but by sheer organizational and bookkeeping arrangements.

To test this hypothesis, we can look for a moment at two institutions, the Judicial Conference of the United States and the Administrative Office of the United States Courts.[103] The Judicial Conference was created in 1922 and includes representatives from the entire federal court system. This body adopts procedural guidelines for all constituent panels; while Congress has the final say, it rarely exercises a veto. The Conference can promulgate canons of ethics for federal judges. Following the forced resignation of Mr. Justice Fortas in 1969, it attempted to clarify exactly what income-generating outside activities would not be considered unseemly or inappropriate. The Administrative Office, founded in 1939, is really an arm of the Conference. This agency controls the hiring and supervision of the thousands of support personnel employed by the courts, and it accumulates piles of statistics on docket conditions and budgetary matters.

There is no question that the administrative oversight model has some applicability, yet we must also understand what these bodies do *not* do. The Judicial Conference has never developed a rational plan for governing the federal judicial apparatus.[104] For example, the trial courts exhibit great differences in population per district and show graphic discrepancies in the number of districts allotted per state. When Congress creates new judgeships, it merely jams them into preconceived, historically ordained trial court units. Naturally, *localism* is maximized. And the population disparities among the intermediate courts are gross; in fact, their boundaries are drawn intentionally to preserve their regional political integrity. Such patterns of control undoubtedly have a deleterious impact on the availability of judicial services to *people;* yet the Judicial Conference has never addressed any of these compelling issues. Even the collection of data on docket conditions stored at Administrative Office headquarters is executed by the local courts themselves. If there is no *centralized* policy with respect to either national judicial organization or the accumulation of information indispensable for drafting such a blueprint, one must conclude that a coherent body of national law manages to emerge from this local-regional hodge-podge only in spite of itself.

Atop the great entrance into the resplendent Supreme Court building, the following words are engraved: "Equal Justice Under Law." I suggest that this motto is the adhesive—the transcendent ordering principle—that cements the federal court system. Federal judges know they are entrusted with the responsibility of enforcing the Constitution and all federal law consistent with the Constitution. The maxim expresses the "rules of the game" as we think they should be applied to judicial relief. The "balance" undergirding the Constitution itself sets as a goal the norm that when people go to court in search of a fair hearing, the law will be administered without regard to their economic and social status—just as the law itself is presumed to be objective. Throughout this discussion, we have noted instances where the system does not live up to the implications of our guiding motto. To the extent that these inequities are systematic, widespread, durable, fundamental, and condoned as ethically responsible, they are part of the "Living Constitution." But the larger norm, the generally accepted standard, the ultimate end by which we measure human behavior in this context—Equal Justice Under Law—is an even more integral part of the "Living Constitution." It remains to be seen if the principle can outlive its exceptions.

NOTES

1. Where do the federal courts derive jurisdiction over these categories? Just as Congress spells out the *appellate* litigation which the Supreme Court may hear, so Congress enumerates both the *original* jurisdiction of the trial courts and the *appellate* jurisdiction of the courts of appeal. For instance, the $10,000 figure in "diversity" litigation mentioned above may be raised or lowered any time appropriate legislation is enacted. See p. 94.

2. Sheldon Goldman and Thomas P. Jahnige, *The Federal Courts as a Political System*, 2nd ed. (New York: Harper & Row, 1976), p. 25.

3. For criticism of political science scholarship for tending to ignore the private-law area, see Martin Shapiro, "From Public Law to Public Policy, or the 'Public' in 'Public Law'," *P.S.* 5, no. 4, (1972), pp. 410-18.

4. Glendon Schubert, *Judicial Policy Making*, rev. ed. (Glenview, Ill.: Scott, Foresman, 1974), pp. 84, 89-90.

5. The following commentary is based in great measure on Chapter 5 of Delmar Karlen, *The Citizen in Court* (New York: Holt, Rinehart and Winston, 1965).

6. Herbert Jacob, *Justice in America*, 2nd ed. (Boston: Little, Brown, 1972), pp. 181-82.

7. Schubert, p. 85.

8. Goldman and Jahnige, p. 25.

9. See Chief Justice Warren Burger's ringing indictment of the "delay in court" problem, reprinted in Howard James, *Crisis in the Courts*, rev. ed. (New York: David McKay, 1971), pp. iii-xii.

10. Historical note: The English jurists of old who dispensed common-law writs were forbidden to provide equitable relief. Only the king's agent could bestow these unusual benefits. American judges issue injunctions, but the time-honored standard of proof obtains. Now, as then, courts were expected to stay their hand until all other remedies had been exhausted.

11. Schubert, p. 85.

12. Ibid., p. 92.

13. *Brown v. Mississippi*, 297 U.S. 278 (1936).

14. *Ashcraft v. Tennessee*, 322 U.S. 143 (1944).

15. *Argersinger v. Hamlin*, 407 U.S. 25 (1972).

16. *Johnson v. Zerbst*, 304 U.S. 458 (1938); *Von Moltke v. Gillies*, 332 U.S. 708 (1948).

17. *Faretta v. California*, 95 S. Ct. 2525 at p. 2541 (1975).

18. *Escobedo v. Illinois*, 378 U.S. 478 (1964).

19. *Miranda v. Arizona*, 384 U.S. 436 (1966).

20. *United States v. Wade*, 388 U.S. 218 (1967); *Gilbert v. California*, 388 U.S. 263 (1967); *Schmerber v. California*, 384 U.S. 757 (1966).

21. David Fellman's comments on the use and abuse of bail are very much relevant here. See *The Defendant's Rights* (New York: Rinehart, 1958), pp. 19-25.

22. Caleb Foote, "Compelling Appearance in Court: Administration of Bail in Philadelphia," *Univ. of Pennsylvania Law Review* 102 (1954), pp. 1032-33. These data were probably extreme, but the general proposition is surely valid.

23. Henry J. Abraham, *The Judicial Process,* 2nd ed. (New York: Oxford Univ. Press, 1968), p. 136.

24. *Ex Parte Wilson,* 114 U.S. 417 (1885).

25. Abraham, p. 106. For a much more positive assessment of the grand jury's independence, see Robert Scigliano, "The Grand Jury, the Information, and the Judicial Inquiry," *Oregon Law Review* 38 (1959), p. 310.

26. See the citations gathered together by Schubert, p. 105, note 3.

27. David J. Fine, "Federal Grand Jury Investigation of Political Dissidents," *Harvard Civil Rights—Civil Liberties Review* 7 (1972), p. 433.

28. The following interrogation was submitted to one witness: "I want you to describe for the grand jury every occasion during the year 1970 when you have been in contact with, attended meetings which were conducted by, or attended by, or been any place when any individual spoke, whom you knew to be associated with or affiliated with Students for a Democratic Society, the Weathermen, the Communist Party, or any other organization advocating revolutionary overthrow of the United States, describing for the grand jury when these incidents occurred, where they occurred, who was present and what was said by all persons there and what you did at the time that you were in these meetings, groups, associations, or conversations." Fine, p. 435, note 10.

29. Nor was this action without its difficulties. The prevailing constitutional view seems to give grand juries three options: indict, dismiss, or shut up. *Wood v. Hughes,* 212 N.Y. 2d 33 (1961). These strict limitations are designed to keep grand juries from engaging in mud-slinging exercises—of accusing people without giving them a chance to have their day in court. The minority view is based on the argument that grand jury investigations are kept strictly secret for everyone's protection, and so the only way a panel can inform a watchful public of its findings is to issue prima facie conclusions of culpability where indictments are impossible.

30. Goldman and Jahnige, pp. 127-28.

31. David W. Neubauer, *Criminal Justice in Middle America* (Morristown, N.J.: General Learning Press, 1974), p. 195.

32. Ibid., p. 196. Good reading on this and related issues is Abraham Blumberg, *Criminal Justice* (New York: Quadrangle Books, 1967).

33. *Brady v. United States,* 397 U.S. 742 (1970).

34. Goldman and Jahnige, p. 129.

35. *Williams v. Florida,* 399 U.S. 78 (1970).

36. *Apodaca v. Oregon,* 406 U.S. 404 (1972). This cleavage did not save the unanimity feature at the *state* level, where it need not be honored. With this single exception, the constitutional right of trial by jury amounts to the same thing in federal and state jurisdictions.

37. Richard J. Richardson and Kenneth N. Vines, *The Politics of Federal Courts* (Boston: Little, Brown, 1970), p. 88.

38. Jacob, pp. 123-24.

39. The great film *Twelve Angry Men* exemplifies this conception. I have testified in cases involving alleged violations of obscenity statutes and have deliberately tried to read the jurors' faces as I spoke. I can report no success. Their eyes stare back with impenetrable opaqueness, and one wonders if there is any wisdom in it all.

40. The work of the Project is discussed in Harry S. Kalven and Hans Zeisel, *The American Jury* (Boston: Little, Brown, 1966).

41. The results are summarized nicely in Jacob, pp. 127-28.

42. Alexis de Tocqueville, *Democracy in America* (London: Saunders and Otley, 1835), Ch. 16.

43. Jerome Frank, *Courts on Trial* (Princeton: Princeton Univ. Press, 1950).

44. These are Canons 15 and 37, respectively.

45. Charles P. Curtis, "The Ethics of Advocacy," *Stanford Law Review* 4 (1951), pp. 3-23.

46. Jay Schulman et al., "Recipe for a Jury," *Psychology Today* (May 1973), pp. 37-44, 77-84.

47. Martin Arnold, "How Mitchell-Stans Jury Reached Acquittal Verdict," *The New York Times* (May 5, 1974), pp. 1, 41. The informal leader of the group was a bank official who managed to play (as Danelski would call it) the dual role of "task" and "social" leader to the hilt. Is it surprising that a body of twelve jurors should operate according to the same social stimuli as nine Supreme Court Justices?

48. Frank, *Courts on Trial.*

49. Jerome Frank to Felix Frankfurter, December 9, 1935, reprinted in C. Herman Pritchett and Walter F. Murphy, eds., *Courts, Judges, and Politics,* 2nd ed. (New York: Random House, 1974), p. 137.

50. The practitioner as "interest group representative" is studied in Jonathan D. Casper, *Lawyers before the Warren Court* (Urbana: Univ. of Illinois Press, 1972).

51. The term is drawn from Florynce Kennedy, "The Whorehouse Theory of Law," in Robert Lefcourt, ed., *Law Against the People* (New York: Random House, 1971), pp. 81-89.

52. Robert Borosage et al., "The New Public Interest Lawyers," *The Yale Law Journal* 79 (1970), pp. 1069-1152.

53. Abraham S. Blumberg, "The Practice of Law as a Confidence Game: Organizational Cooptation of a Profession," *Law and Society Review* 1 (1967), pp. 15-39.

54. Goldman and Jahnige, p. 129.

55. *Illinois v. Allen,* 397 U.S. 337 (1970).

56. Borosage, p. 1095.

57. Ibid., pp. 1095-96.

58. For a political scientist's view of these events, see David J. Danelski, "The Chicago Conspiracy Trial," in Theodore L. Becker, ed., *Political Trials* (Indianapolis: Bobbs-Merrill, 1971), pp. 134-80. While defendants' motives and actions speak for themselves, Judge Hoffman's turgidity throughout the proceedings served only to inspire disrespect for the bench. The trouble is that the average federal judge rarely walks around a college campus to learn the symbols of the latest radical gospel.

59. *Cheff v. Schnackenberg,* 384 U.S. 373 (1966).

60. These are Jerome Frank's suggestions. See *Courts on Trial,* p. 93. Some scholars disagree with this activist approach. They feel "dignity and forebearance" are the watchwords of proper trial judge behavior, at least when a jury is present to be influenced. If I believed the hearing were as much a ceremony as an investigation, I might be persuaded, but where "life, liberty and property" are at stake, I think a more vigorous tack is required. For the contrary view, see Charles E. Wyzanski, Jr., "A Trial Judge's Freedom and Responsibility," *Harvard Law Review* 65 (1952), pp. 1281-1304.

61. The charge is found in *The New York Times* (October 14, 1949), p. 15.

62. Jerome Frank, *Law and the Modern Mind* (New York: Coward-McCann, 1930), Ch. 16.

63. Jon M. Van Dyke, "The Jury as a Political Institution," *The Center Magazine* (March 1970). Naturally he thinks the charge system is open to criticism for precisely this reason.

64. Compare Van Dyke's comments in "The Jury as a Political Institution" with Arnold's journalistic investigations (note 47).

65. *Time* (July 1, 1974), p. 12.

66. Goldman and Jahnige, pp. 127-28; Jacob, p. 73.

67. Goldman and Jahnige, p. 25.

68. See Chief Justice Burger's remarks in James (note 9).

69. *Lauf v. Shinner and Co.,* 303 U.S. 323 (1938).

70. During his presidency, Richard Nixon proposed that lower federal courts be stripped of their authority to order busing of pupils for the purpose of eradicating school segregation. But his recommendation to Congress was based on the latter's legislative power under the Fourteenth Amendment, *not* exclusively on whatever general authority the lawmakers have to expand and contract a district court's jurisdiction. This facet of the busing question is discussed in Chapter 11.

71. *Michaelson v. United States,* 266 U.S. 42 (1924).

72. Richardson and Vines, p. 60.

73. Harold W. Chase, "Federal Judges: The Appointing Process," *Minnesota Law Review* 51 (1966), p. 191.

74. Ibid., p. 196.

75. Joel B. Grossman, *Lawyers and Judges* (New York: John Wiley, 1965). But there is evidence the A.B.A. leadership is becoming less predictable. For instance, Chesterfield Smith, president of the organization during the Watergate blow-up, stated Richard Nixon should not be given immunity from possible prosecution, and he also said those who refused to serve in the armed forces during the Vietnam War should receive unconditional amnesty.

76. Richardson and Vines, p. 66.

77. Ibid., p. 62.

78. Schubert, p. 24.

79. Sheldon Goldman, "Johnson and Nixon Appointees to the Lower Federal Courts: Some Socio-Political Perspectives," *The Journal of Politics* 34 (1972), p. 939.

80. Richardson and Vines, p. 105.

81. Kenneth M. Dolbeare, "The Federal District Court and Urban Public Policy," in Joel B. Grossman and Joseph Tanenhaus, eds., *Frontiers of Judicial Research* (New York: John Wiley, 1969), p. 388.

82. Ibid., pp. 384-85, 395.

83. Ibid., pp. 386, 394; K. N. Vines, "Federal District Judges and Race Relations Cases in the South," *The Journal of Politics* 26 (1964), p. 343; Richardson and Vines, pp. 71-73.

84. Dolbeare, p. 391; Richardson and Vines, p. 169.

85. Richardson and Vines, pp. 26-35.

86. *United States v. Dennis,* 183 F. 2d 201 (1950).

87. *Dennis v. United States,* 341 U.S. 494 at p. 510 (1951).

88. The following remarks are based on Chase, pp. 218-20, and Sheldon Goldman, "Judicial Appointments to the United States Courts of Appeals," *Wisconsin Law Review* 1967 (1967), pp. 186-214.

89. Compare Richardson and Vines, p. 116, with Schubert, pp. 84-85.

90. These various data are from Schubert, p. 85.

91. Richardson and Vines, p. 133.

92. Query: Should this pattern be labeled "liberalism" or "egalitarianism"?

93. The data are taken from Sheldon Goldman, "Voting Behavior on the United States Courts of Appeals Revisited," *The American Political Science Review* 69 (1975), pp. 491-506. But note this: Demographic characteristics—for example, age, religion, and party preference—do not seem to play an important role in *explaining* the judges' voting disparities (Goldman, p. 504). It is one thing to say Democrats and Republicans approach problems somewhat differently, but quite another thing to say these differences stem from party ties.

94. A study describing some of the qualitative dimensions of a circuit tribunal is Marvin Schick, *Learned Hand's Court* (Baltimore: Johns Hopkins Press, 1970).

95. Schubert, p. 85.

96. Dolbeare, p. 391; Goldman and Jahnige, p. 203.

97. Dolbeare, p. 394.

98. The views of Richardson and Vines, pp. 143-45, 149-50, 161, support some of the arguments made here.

99. Schubert, pp. 23, 46-47, 79.

100. Ibid., p. 78.

101. Richardson and Vines, pp. 153-54.

102. Felix Frankfurter, "The Supreme Court in the Mirror of Justices," *Univ. of Pennsylvania Law Review* 105 (1957), p. 781.

103. The most complete study of these agencies is Peter G. Fish, *The Politics of Federal Judicial Administration* (Princeton: Princeton Univ. Press, 1973).

104. Again, I acknowledge an intellectual debt to Richardson and Vines for their observations on these matters. See pp. 38-45, 49-53, 173-74 of *The Politics of Federal Courts.*

4
the congress: paper tiger?

The Congress of the United States is a study in contrasts. Nowhere more than here are the Constitution and the "Living Constitution" so often worlds apart. The Constitution vests the legislative branch with vast powers, but many of these powers have assumed forms in the "Living Constitution" undreamed of by the Framers. The foremost question for our concern is. Has Congress merely adapted its charge in the light of changing conditions, or has Congress abdicated its constitutional responsibilities?

Theory informs us that the federal government is divided into three co-equal branches, but "separation of powers," I have shown, cannot be taken literally. Correspondingly, these power centers were not created as exact equals. The very first article delineates *legislative* power and comprises more than half the original Constitution. Remember, the colonists' prime political objective during those revolutionary years was to limit the king's executive authority by establishing popularly responsive lawmaking organs. Although the Articles of Confederation went too far in that direction and the Constitution was intended to redress this imbalance, a close inspection of Articles I through III is highly revealing. The Framers, evidently, had only a vague notion of the power that presidents and judges would wield; their functions are couched in general terms. Not so the Congress, for its authority is highly specific and detailed. The Founding Fathers undoubtedly saw the legislative branch as the leader in governmental initiatives. The Congress could not control executive or judicial branches, but it would be *primus inter pares*—first among equals.

No observer of our present-day national politics would label the Congress a leader in action, though recent developments have made it a leader in *reaction.* News reports abound with presidential feats in foreign affairs and with presidential efforts in the economic sphere. The Supreme Court remains highly visible, with new policy salvos in the civil liberties-civil rights domain. Were it not for Watergate and the drive to impeach Richard Nixon, however, Congress would have been almost without a profile throughout much of the present and previous decade. From 1974 to 1976, to be sure, the curious mix of a nonelected minority-party chief executive flailing away at national travails and an extraordinarily large majority-party margin in Congress enhanced almost overnight the influence of legislative power. During that period, the House and Senate had the votes to counter, with considerable success, executive policy thrusts regarding the most sensitive domestic problem areas. Congress even possessed more legitimacy than the White House, until a series of sex scandals eroded whatever advantage in political purity came its way as a result of Watergate.

In this chapter, I shall examine what our national legislature is empowered to do, what it has done of consequence in the past, how it does things today, and why it has seemed to do so little over the past several years. Finally, I shall place in this much larger context the attempts Congress has made lately to recapture a place in the sun.

The essentials of legislative power

In the popular eye, members of Congress are perceived as lawmakers. An image comes to mind of bills being brought to the floor and voted for or against. The opening sentence in Article I accords with this impression: "All legislative powers herein granted shall be vested in a Congress. . . ." This simple declaration is replete with meanings. First, the "legislative" authority referred to is obviously the power to pass laws; so, if the Constitution means what it says, the entire arsenal of congressional lawmaking is enumerated there for all to see. Second, the entire legislative function evidently belongs to Congress and nobody else.

But, of course, almost everything in the Constitution is open to interpretation, elaboration, and argument, so perhaps some legislative powers aren't listed specifically in the fundamental law. Still, John Marshall said: "This government is acknowledged by all, to be one of enumerated powers."[1] And ninety years later the Justices reiterated the premise: "But the proposition that there are legislative powers affecting the Nation as a whole which belong to [Congress—even though they are not mentioned in the Constitution], is in direct conflict with the doctrine that this is a government of enumerated powers."[2] The theory has been stated unequivocally because the Court echoes our traditional commitment to *limited government,* to a national regime whose lawmakers cannot do anything and everything just because they feel it is consistent with the public interest.

But we must dig deeper than these generalized assertions. In my discussion of the *McCulloch* decision,[3] I noted how the Jeffersonians challenged Congress's power to create a national bank. They invoked the litmus test of "specific mention": Where does the Constitution say Congress can establish a banking system? The fact is there are seventeen delegated legislative powers delineated in the first article. They authorize Congress to lay and collect taxes, go into debt, regulate foreign and interstate commerce, coin money, establish post offices, constitute inferior federal courts, declare war, govern the nation's capital and so on. Nowhere are the words "create banks." But there is an eighteenth provision, and it sets out Congress's *implied* power. The legislature may do anything "necessary and proper" to make its delegated authority effective.

Now, Jefferson thought "necessary and proper" had a *restrictive* meaning: Congress had the power to do only what was absolutely necessary to perform delegated functions. Marshall met Jefferson's argument with some of the most memorable prose ever penned by a Supreme Court Justice:

> A constitution, to contain an accurate detail of all the sub-divisions of which its great powers will admit, and of all the means by which they may be carried into execution, would partake of the prolixity of a legal code, and could scarcely be embraced by the human mind. It would, probably, never be understood by the public. Its nature, therefore, requires, that only its great outlines should be marked. . . . It must have been the intention of those who gave these powers, to insure . . . their beneficial execution. This could not be done, by confiding the choice of means to such narrow limits as not to leave it in the power of congress to adopt any which might be appropriate, and which were conducive to the end. [The necessary and proper clause] is made in a constitution, intended to endure for ages to come, and consequently to be adapted to the various *crises* of human affairs. . . . To have declared, that the best means shall not be used, but those alone, without which the power given would be nugatory, would have been to deprive the legislature of the capacity to avail itself of experience, to exercise its reason, and to accommodate its legislation to circumstances.[4]

We have here the very essence of legislative responsibility. Congress's authority is limited, but Congress possesses a generous measure of discretionary, *necessarily implied* power, which is the mainspring of enlightened policy-making. If a national banking system appears to be the best method for managing the dollar, then so be it. There is little question that Marshall's ideas comported entirely with the Framers' conception of the magnitude and breadth of congressional rulemaking; and for us today, this mix of *specific, delegated* authority and *general, implied* authority forms the cornerstone of appropriate legislative action.

But what of the inference that lawmaking is the sole prerogative of Congress? Here again the clear imperatives of the Constitution can be taken just so far. The art (science?) of legislating, especially in an industrialized age, can involve extraordinarily intricate calculations based on masses of ever-changing data. For example, determining precisely what duties should be levied on thousands of incoming commodities from all over the globe presents technical questions that would occupy all of Congress's time if common sense were not controlling. In addition, fee schedules often must be adjusted quickly to meet rapidly changing market conditions. And if five-hundred-odd members of Congress are not students of the tariff, they are certainly not noted for overnight action either. What the legislative does is to give to professional experts, sitting at the President's right hand, power to decide what tariffs should be imposed.

Now if this grant were a blank check, there is no doubt the courts would find it unconstitutional. If "separation of powers" means anything, the three branches cannot go around giving their rights and duties away with no strings attached. In the case of the tariffs, however, Congress had set up certain criteria—such as prevailing costs of production—to keep the technicians on the right path. Said the Justices: "If Congress shall lay down by legislative act an *intelligible principle* to which the person or body authorized to fix such rates is directed to conform, such legislative action is not a forbidden delegation of legislative power."[5] That the legislature can delegate fact finding is clear enough; but it can also delegate a considerable portion of its decision-making prerogatives. However, this grant must be hedged about by a plan, a principle, a set of standards conveying a reasonable sense of what the parent body has in mind. Once again, a balance between rational goals and prudent implementation is the constitutional format. Federal governance today is in great measure an outgrowth of this device, as I shall later detail.

When we move from the area of domestic affairs to the area of foreign policy, though, the "rules of the game" suddenly become very different with regard to both the enumerated powers doctrine and the delegation of power doctrine. The Congress is endowed with certain definite constitutional powers here—the authority to declare war and control foreign commerce, for instance—but its flexibility transcends these specifics. Indeed, one should substitute the phrase "inherent powers" for "enumerated powers" at this level, because the legislature possesses whatever authority is necessary to place the United States on an equal footing with every other sovereign nation. In this role it has regulated the discovery of new lands by American citizens and provided for the exclusion as well as the deportation of aliens. The Supreme Court did not assess the constitutionality of these statutes by invoking the delegated-and-implied power mix. Rather, it affirmed the measures in the light of inherent legislative authority to protect the nation's welfare and independence, authority residing in the sovereign's hands.[6] Actually, the Justices are so defensive in this area, that they have hinted that the "political questions" concept does not allow for judicial review of relevant enactments.[7]

What about the delegation of lawmaking responsibilities in the realm of external affairs? In the 1930s Congress told President Roosevelt he could cut off all arms shipments by private citizens to war-torn South American countries if he believed an embargo might promote peace. The underlying plan or principle present in the *Hampton* tariff case was clearly absent here. But, the Justices said, "Congressional legislation which is to be made effective through negotiation and inquiry within the international field must often accord to the President a degree of discretion and freedom from statutory restriction which would not be admissible were domestic affairs alone involved."[8] So, at this level, the prevailing constitutional standard is carte blanche.

Congress as dominant branch: compromise and coercion in Civil War days[9]

Constitutional responsibility takes many forms, depending on the prevailing political conditions. All the branches have had their moments of weakness. Whereas the national legislature may not be our strongest and most vital power center today, it surely was 110 years ago. What sort of climate could produce an era of congressional dominance, and how might Congress's constitutional prerogatives be adjusted to meet such contingencies?

At root, lawmaking responsibilities can fulfill two completely different roles in policy formation: Congress can be either chief political *bargainer* or chief political *authority figure.* In the first instance, it strikes a balance among competing interests and drafts rules agreeable to all. In the second, it enacts whatever regulations it considers appropriate and lets the chips fall where they may. Almost never will the political contours of the day permit the legislature to maximize its options and play both roles; but if Congress is meeting its obligations, it ought to be able to perform one. These models for action should be kept in mind as we examine the constitutional politics of congressional action during the Civil War period.

The slavery question proved to be more than the usual sectional conflict, for it split the country into two clear-cut, virtually irreconcilable regions comprising the same number of states. Given the Senate's representational scheme, Congress's ability to perform accustomed constitutional chores was tested as never before or since. But it tried, and that is more credit than either the executive or the judicial branch deserves.

The great congressional figures of the period—Henry Clay, John C. Calhoun, Daniel Webster, and Stephen A. Douglas—have become almost as legendary as the Founding Fathers, and their major legislative achievements bear familiar titles: the Missouri Compromise, the Compromise of 1850, the Kansas-Nebraska Act. Basically, these statutes attempted to resolve a single pressing problem—namely, the extent to which slaves would be allowed to reside in the federal territories west of the Mississippi. The Free-Soilers, led by Webster, thought Congress should ban involuntary servitude outright in these lands. The South, led by Calhoun, opposed all such efforts, fearing new states formed from the territories would eventually side with the North to upset slavery and the entire plantation way of life. The architects of compromise, led by Clay and Douglas, tried to skirt this stalemate with a variety of devices. First, there was the line-drawing technique, the division of disputed lands between settlers from North and South; second, there was the "Noah's ark" approach, whereby free and slave states were admitted to the Union only two-by-two; third, there was "popular sovereignty," meaning each territorial unit would decide for itself whether to allow slavery.

These efforts were doomed, largely because the central issues were not amenable to prudent legislation that could balance successfully the needs of diverse interests. On the contrary, the slavery issue involved unbridgeable differences of opinion between relatively equal political factions over the meaning of fundamental constitutional norms. Property, the Constitution tells us, cannot be taken unless "just compensation" is provided and "due process" afforded, but could the ownership of people be regulated without regard to such limitations? Moreover, if slavery as an institution was threatened in a manner considered unconstitutional, could disgruntled states exercise the option of secession if pushed to the wall? And once both sides forgot the nature of constitutionalism and came to define slavery and states' rights from a *moral* perspective, it was just a matter of time before they fractured the "rules of the game" and brought the nation to war.

During Lincoln's time, the presidency dominated policy-making in unprecedented fashion; but with Confederate dreams in ruins, the pendulum of national authority swung dramatically toward Congress. The "Great Emancipator" had been killed, and his replacement was the intransigent, undiplomatic Andrew Johnson, a Southern Democrat. The Supreme Court, meanwhile, was at its nadir, pulled down by the weight of *Dred Scott.* And even Lincoln's political genius and common touch would have been greatly challenged by the tempest of revenge sweeping through the North and its representatives in Congress. Ten years earlier the legislative branch had been the leader in compromise; now it would be the leader in authoritarianism.

Congressional policy was built around several specific, not entirely compatible goals. These included absolute political equality for former slaves; severe punishment of Southern "traitors"; a strong and viable Republican Party, benefiting immeasurably from both black enfranchisement and ex-Confederate disfranchisement; and last, legislative branch preeminence so that executive and judicial authority could not stifle these grandiose plans. The program, then, was in one sense extraordinarily humanitarian, in another sense very pragmatic, and in yet another sense frighteningly inquisitorial. Furthermore, in the House's Thaddeus Stevens and the Senate's Charles Sumner, this strategy had all the shrewd and zealous leadership needed to overcome any obstacle.

But constitutional justification was necessary to provide symbolic reinforcement of the ends in view. Congress could not simply proceed as it wished; it would be accused of violating the implicit "checks-and-balances" constraint.[10] Stevens and Sumner were equal to the task. For Stevens, the Confederacy had made war against the United States and should be likened to a foreign nation; the former states were now "conquered provinces" whose status resembled federal territories. For Sumner, secession was akin to "state suicide"; the rebellious South had forfeited all its political rights under the Constitution. But the two approaches ended at the same point: Congress could do whatever it thought appropriate to reconstitute these "territories" into law-abiding states.

Presidents Lincoln and Johnson, meanwhile, had developed constitutional doctrines of their own, and they too possessed tactical tools of substance. In their view, secession was null and void from the start; therefore the states retained their essential political identities. Of course, rehabilitation mandated assistance, but the chief executive possessed the requisite tools. He was commander in chief of the armies; hence, he could control Reconstruction policy in the field. Furthermore, because moderation seemed desirable, his pardoning power would be most useful in paving the way toward reconciliation.

But Congress would brook no interference, and it possessed one weapon in its constitutional arsenal that the President lacked. "Each House," says the document, "shall be the Judge of the Elections, Returns and Qualifications of its own members. . . ." The rejuvenated governments in the seceded states could hardly get off the ground if Congress rejected the credentials of their newly elected legislators. This discretion was used to the hilt. Representatives chosen according to Andrew Johnson's lenient specifications were never seated; until these "states" satisfied specific, tougher guidelines, Congress said, they could just languish on the sidelines. Stevens and Sumner were now in the saddle.

The first major step the new majority took was to pass the Civil Rights Act of 1866, conferring national citizenship on all blacks born in the United States and giving them the same rights to own and transact real and personal property that whites possessed under the law. The former provision was clearly contrary to *Dred Scott;* however, the latter provision seemed constitutional because Congress has power to enforce through legislation the Thirteenth Amendment ban on slavery and its many aspects.

Sharper Radicals like Stevens knew the Congress had gone too far, so they tried to cover their tracks by drafting the Fourteenth Amendment. Frankly, this amendment, had it ever been implemented as intended, would have changed the entire shape of American constitutional government. Of course, it overruled Chief Justice Taney's dictum that emancipated blacks could never be United States citizens. But, of even greater significance, it also included a battery of individual rights *immune from state action* and *enforceable by appropriate act of Congress.*

This is not quite so complicated as it sounds. For instance, the amendment says a state cannot deprive any person of the "privileges and immunities" possessed by American citizens.[11] There is evidence the Radicals wanted to use this clause as a weapon against future state abrogation of basic individual rights. That objective could have been accomplished in two ways, evidently. Either the Supreme Court would be brought into the picture via traditional channels, or *Congress itself might do the job.* And the legislative role possessed boundless potential, for, armed with the necessary and proper clause, Congress could perhaps impose upon the states *its* definitions of "privileges and immunities." However, not only has the Supreme Court never accorded a broad meaning to this phrase, but the legislative branch itself has shied away from making the language more meaningful.

The Republicans refused to seat any outlaw state's congressional delegation until that state ratified the Fourteenth Amendment.[a] Only Tennessee went along, and the recalcitrance of the rest merely bolstered the Radicals at the

[a] Query: How could a state participate in ratifying a constitutional amendment when it had forfeited its constitutional position as a state? No scholar has squared this circle yet!

polls; in the off-year elections of 1866, their number swelled to veto-proof proportions.

And now the floodgates burst. The Reconstruction Acts were enacted turning Dixie into five military districts governed by generals of the army exercising martial law. In blatantly unconstitutional style, trials of civilians were held under the supervision of armed forces personnel; [12] and when this statute was challenged in the courts, the Congress stripped the Justices of their right to hear the case, as I have recounted elsewhere. Under the protective wing of military control, carpetbaggers and scalawags framed new state constitutions consistent with Radical aims, and the states were then returned to full partnership following their forced acceptance of the Fourteenth Amendment.

As for President Johnson, the Congress moved to emasculate him entirely. When vacancies opened on the Supreme Court, the Senate refused to consider his nominees. Furthermore, General Grant was empowered to issue all army orders and to appoint and remove all army officers. With passage of the Tenure of Office Act (1867), the chief executive's authority to remove his *own* subordinates became subject to senatorial concurrence. And when Johnson ignored this last restriction, he was impeached and very nearly ejected.

The Radical movement unleashed only a few more policy thunderbolts, and these were eminently defendable in theory if unenforceable in practice. The Fifteenth Amendment was ratified, insulating black suffrage rights from state manipulation; and the Civil Rights Act of 1875 gave to persons, regardless of race, the right to use all public accommodations (for example, hotels, theaters, and other businesses open to people generally) on an equal basis. But eventually, Republicans saw they could build a winning coalition without "waving the bloody shirt"; the country turned to prosperity and laissez faire; and the former Confederates were reinstated, thus beginning a long chapter in "separate but equal" racism. The Supreme Court chipped in with legitimizing constitutional ideology, holding the Civil Rights Act of 1875 null and void on the ground that Congress could use its Fourteenth Amendment power to ban only *state* discrimination, not racist acts by private individuals and businesses. [13]

For students of the federal legislative process, these events provide invaluable instruction. During the antebellum period, the primary political issues were domestic rather than international. Congress was the most effective seat of power because it possessed tools for achieving internal compromises that the other two branches lacked. Of course, controversial policy questions invariably bring to the fore competing conceptions of constitutional government; but when disagreement centers almost exclusively on the legitimacy of such constitutional concepts, and when the debate breaks down in moralistic diatribe, then the Constitution has ceased to fill its acknowledged role. That is exactly what happened here.

During the postbellum period, the political problems were just as domestic and just as intense, and, once again, debate over the constitutional rules eventually obscured all else. But on this occasion, Congress could impose its will virtually without restraint, because public opinion had swung dramatically toward a completely uncompromising posture. The result was government by "terrible swift sword," with President, Supreme Court, and half the states rendered impotent. That the Radicals should have invoked the amending process to give black people citizenship plus all rights commensurate with citizenship can only merit applause; but that they should have tinkered with the amending process in hopes of uprooting the entire balance between state and national officialdom can only be considered overkill. In our time, there has been much talk of "White House horrors." But the Civil War aftermath shows Congress also has the capacity to turn its face toward extremist constitutional politics. Now we must understand how the legislative branch could have evolved from the authoritarian monolith of 1867 to what it is today.

Congress in the era of "sleeping nationalism"

From the constitutional politics standpoint, Congress's record as lawmaker during the 1870–1933 period exhibited certain unifying themes. National legislative power tended to be more assertive than executive power and was certainly more progressive than judicial power; still, Washington scarcely stood in the forefront of policy initiatives. The period also showed some diversity. From 1870 to 1901, Congress was surely the most adventurous of the three branches. The overriding issue was probably currency control, with farmers in the western states demanding easy money to help them take out loans and meet their mortgage payments and shipping fees. In response to these protests, laws were enacted making silver (a less precious metal than the standard medium of exchange, gold) a base for the dollar. Thus an important precedent was established: Congress could mobilize its control over the monetary system to ward off financial privations. Also relevant in this context were the first income tax laws, an egalitarian gambit that the courts managed to refute for a time.

During those infrequent moments when a relatively vigorous President came on the scene, the legislature was moved to even stronger action. The Civil Service Commission was established with Rutherford Hayes in the White House, and the Tenure of Office Act was repealed under proddings from Grover Cleveland. At this time, Congress also moved against exorbitant railroad rates by creating the Interstate Commerce Commission; while the groundbreaking Sherman Act, designed to outlaw all interstate monopolies in restraint of trade, followed soon after. As I have noted, though, the Supreme Court, infatuated with substantive due process and states' rights, very much emasculated these efforts, a position not entirely unpopular at that time.

The decades from 1901 to 1920 were a time of strong executive leadership and, once more, illustrate Congress's heightened ambition when the right push is provided. With Theodore Roosevelt in office, the Pure Food and Drug Act became law, while under Woodrow Wilson's energetic hand, both the modern-day Federal Reserve System and the Federal Trade Commission were authorized.

Generally speaking, the legislature was greatly influenced by two rapidly developing notions of constitutional law. First, the channels of interstate relations could be closed to noxious goods like unclean foodstuffs[14] and noxious practices like the white slave trade.[15] Second, the taxing power could be used not only to raise money but to regulate antisocial behavior such as deceptive business manipulations.[16] For a short time, then, Congress was determined to check the growth of unbridled corporate power and to frame a centralized monetary system, all for the purpose of *preserving* the implicit constitutional norm of free enterprise. But the prospect of global entanglements saw the Senate revolt against President Wilson by killing our participation in the League of Nations, and isolation became the dominant theme.

From 1921 to 1933, Congress again surpassed the President in assertiveness, and the result was a decline in its own accomplishments. During the early 1920s, attempts were made to help out farmers, who, as usual, were up to their ears in debts and falling prices; later, with the Depression truly upon us, agencies such as the Reconstruction Finance Corporation were created. But while Herbert Hoover was an activist compared to Coolidge, his remedies remained consistent with established "rules of the game." But now the great debates in Congress over whether the Constitution permitted regulation of monopoly capitalism in the name of free market capitalism were no longer relevant. The emerging question was: Did Congress have the power to save the nation from economic ruin?

Congress and the New Deal

As the *McCulloch* decision makes manifestly clear, the legislative branch is given ample power to ameliorate widespread national adversities. John Marshall's language is unforgettable:

> Let the end be legitimate, let it be within the scope of the constitution, and all means which are appropriate, which are plainly adapted to that end, which are not prohibited, but consist with the letter and spirit of the constitution, are constitutional.[17]

Only once before, during Reconstruction, had emergency conditions moved the Congress to assert these prerogatives in full measure. But if sheer, unadulterated fear is the criterion, then the Depression's impact was even more traumatic than that of the Civil War. And, whereas 1867 had found the "political branches" in mortal combat, the lawmakers of 1933 were not at all inhibited by executive action. In fact, they were driven to expend every ounce of their remedial authority by a President who had a very aggressive legislative "game plan" and in whom they placed the greatest confidence.

It will not be my purpose to review the mass of legislation spawned by New Deal politics. Rather, I want to examine the extraordinary changes in constitutional theory that occurred, emphasizing how these new ideas pertained to Congress's responsibilities.

Franklin Roosevelt's initial assault on the Depression was embodied in the National Industrial Recovery Act (N.I.R.A.). Here, Congress mandated the creation of "codes of fair competition" in the basic industries. These codes were to be drafted by businesses themselves in cooperation with governmental representatives; final approval was placed in the chief executive's hands. In a year and a half, codes (constitutions?) were promulgated for more than seven hundred industries, and these were binding on *all* producers, whether or not they had participated in the negotiations.

To understand the controversy surrounding the N.I.R.A., one must appreciate the scope of the new rules it established. They dealt with every facet of management: how much pay workers should receive; how old employees must be; how many laborers could be hired; what business practices were unfair; to what extent various natural resources could be utilized; and so on. Roosevelt's theory was that a national economic crisis could be met only by tight administrative control of the marketplace, but he opposed steadfastly the nationalization of industries.

The Supreme Court declared the N.I.R.A. unconstitutional by a vote of 9–0. The Justices said Congress had delegated wholesale its lawmaking capacity both to private business and to the President, without setting up appropriate guidelines. What, the Court asked, did "fair competition" mean? Nowhere was this term defined. "Would it be seriously contended that Congress could delegate its legislative authority to . . . industrial associations . . . so as to empower them to enact the laws they deem to be wise and beneficent for their rehabilitation . . .?" [18] So the first broad attempt at federal intervention failed; Congress had not taken the time to develop a policy or plan that would confine administrators—public and private—in their quasi-legislative rule-making. In fact, it is the virtually unanimous view of historians that the N.I.R.A. was a failure from the start. New Dealers had simply deluded themselves into thinking that these fiercely independent, highly competitive economic units could govern themselves in the name of some larger public interest.

A second important weapon in F.D.R.'s legislative arsenal was the Agricultural Adjustment Act (A.A.A.). It offered financial subsidies for beleaguered farmers if they would withdraw some of their land from cultivation—the funds to be collected via a tax on middlemen who purchased the farmers' produce. The obvious purpose of the measure was to raise prices, but how could the law be justified constitutionally? New Deal advocates believed Congress's authority to levy taxes to provide for the general welfare was more than sufficient justification.

The ensuing litigation proved to be more important for its explication of the general welfare clause than for its subsequent burial of the A.A.A. That is because this constitutional language had never before received meaningful interpretation, and, in the hands of an activist Congress, it sat as a potential launching pad for resolving any and all public issues. This prospect troubled the Court, for if the legislature could enact statutes to advance the general welfare, then the Constitution would no longer be a charter of enumerated powers. Congress, the Justices said, can *tax and spend* to promote the general welfare but not do anything else solely for that purpose.

But could Congress tax and spend for the general welfare in a manner not included in other delegated powers? Was the general welfare provision (like the

Constitution's Preamble) merely rhetorical, or was it an independent grant of lawmaking discretion? The Justices—in the tradition of Marshall—went the way of generous interpretation—"The power of Congress to authorize expenditure of public moneys for public purposes is not limited by the direct grants of legislative power found in the Constitution."[19] While the A.A.A. was subsequently knocked down as an interference with states' rights, the Court's opinion vests the legislative branch with tremendous discretion in meeting social crises by manipulating the nation's purse strings.

The "general welfare spending power" was later used successfully to sustain the New Deal's unemployment compensation system. The tactics of implementation were altered somewhat, however. Under federal law, employers were required to pay a tax to fund unemployment compensation; but should the *states* institute their own unemployment insurance programs, subsidized by their own tax on employers, then businesses would have to make only *one* payment, to the *state.* These monies could then be distributed to the unemployed as spelled out in the state program. This gimmick is known as a "tax offset," and it is a neat device for cajoling states to meet certain social-policy standards.

The Supreme Court, by now the recipient of more than its share of excoriation from the "political branches," approved the law. To the majority, monies accumulated and spent to alleviate massive unemployment were, without doubt, a valid expenditure for general welfare purposes.[20]

Finally, we must confront the whole raft of essential New Deal enactments predicated on the *commerce power.* The Justices of Franklin Roosevelt's first term—being anticentralist—generally accepted the old adage of the 1890s and 1920s that Congress could regulate commerce but not production (see pp. 46–47). It took the "Court-packing" sword of Damocles to convince them that the legislature could both abolish child labor and set up employee-management bargaining mechanisms for all firms sending merchandise through interstate channels. Chief Justice Hughes summed up Congress's prerogatives in no uncertain terms: "When industries organize themselves on a national scale, making their relation to interstate commerce the dominant factor in their activities, how can it be maintained that their industrial labor relations constitute a forbidden field into which Congress may not enter. . . ."[21]

Clearly, New Dealers had succeeded finally in framing a constitutional consensus: the national economy was now susceptible to *centralized regulation,* but the doctrine of *enumerated powers* and the integrity of Congress's mission as *dominant legislative rule-maker* had been maintained.

Congressional legislation in the modern era[22]

World War II brought an end to Roosevelt's constitutional revolution. If I am correct, Congress's major legislative accomplishments over the last thirty years have followed certain fairly definite patterns with respect to constitutional philosophy, and I would divide these into three quite separate units of analysis.[23]

Civil liberties and civil rights legislation

First, Congress has responded to pressing civil liberties–civil rights issues in clear-cut, authoritative style. Notice, however, that the enactments have been aimed at two completely different objectives. With respect to *civil liberties*, the idea has been to protect the Constitution and the "peace of the United States" against speech that allegedly poses threats of internal subversion, a legislative role that had been established long ago with the Alien and Sedition Acts of 1798. I would place the Smith Act of 1940,[24] the McCarran Act of 1950, the Communist Control Act of 1954, and the antiriot statute, invoked against the Chicago Seven, in this group. With regard to *civil rights*, the primary purpose has been to integrate black Americans into the mainstream of political participation and to guarantee them constitutional equality. The Civil Rights Acts of 1957, 1964, and 1965 are of this genre.

The casual observer will note other differences between these two clusters of legislation. By and large, Congress has enacted "antiradical" statutes over the opposition of Presidents, while it has enacted civil rights statutes with the help of very strong initiatives from the executive branch. Furthermore, the former create a danger of curtailing individual freedoms, while the latter were passed in order to expand individual freedoms. But they are bound together by their mutual involvement with the politics of *moral* choice. The consensus sees racial discrimination as an unconstitutional outrage, and it sees revolutionary conspiracies the same way. The result has been two sets of laws that can be implemented to the hilt because the standards enunciated are clear and punitive.[25]

For example, the McCarran Act of 1950 called for all "Communist-action" organizations to register with a federal agency. If a suspected group did not come forward, hearings were to be held. Should sufficient evidence of Communist domination be presented, the agency was to promulgate a compulsory registration order. At that point, certain definite rules and regulations binding on the group's activities would come into play: the names of members were to be divulged; organization literature distributed through the mails would have to be labeled "Communist propaganda"; no member could travel abroad or work in a defense plant; and so forth. On the other hand, the Civil Rights Act of 1964 makes it illegal for any "public accommodation" that "affects commerce" to deprive a person of service on racial grounds. The term "public accommodation" is clearly defined as almost all places of business open to the public generally. And a business "affects commerce," specifically, when it serves an interstate clientele or when the goods it sells have moved in interstate commerce. And the penalty is straightforward: racial discrimination is a violation of the federal criminal code. So as regards both statutes, traditional congressional legislative functions have been preserved, and certain implicit, "Living Constitutional" norms have been enforced unequivocally.

Social legislation

The second area of legislative accomplishment contains a host of important statutes consistent with traditional New Deal ideology, the bulk of which were passed during Lyndon Johnson's White House tenure. Having assumed executive power in the wake of the Kennedy assassination, Johnson charged the lawmakers to help him create the "Great Society" by enacting sweeping reform befitting even his hero, F.D.R. Congress, in a burst of sentiment, responded eagerly; and after Barry Goldwater's presidential obliteration, a legislative branch swollen with liberal Democrats opened the floodgates. Typical Johnson programs were the Economic Opportunity Act of 1964 and the Appalachian Regional Commission. President Kennedy's innovative farm and trade expansion measures also illustrate Congress's efforts on the economic front, which dominated the news before Vietnam. With the more conservative Richard Nixon and Gerald Ford in the White House, the legislative branch was not nearly so active; but, as I hope to make clear, the essential constitutional problem posed by the policy thrusts of the 1960s remains the same.

The legislature entered the post-World War II era armed with immense power to tax and spend for the general welfare, to control interstate and foreign commerce, and to place prohibitive taxes on noxious merchandise to drive it off the market. Obviously, Congress could work its will by establishing forthright regulations, as was common practice in the 1930s. However, these avenues have not really been exploited. Rather, the legislature has chosen to *delegate* the necessary rule-making prerogatives to others. Typically, Congress writes a broad, undefined set of conditions whose meaning is subject to limitless interpretation; it then hands the power to interpret these criteria either to the President and his countless assistants or to some other administrative body.

This is a rather significant critique, so instances must be specifically cited. The Congress of President Kennedy's tenure passed a far-reaching tariff law (the Trade Expansion Act of 1962), which is the basis for *all current negotiations* relating to trade barriers. Before 1962 the chief executive could negotiate agreements with other countries only on *named items;* since this enactment, he has been able to bargain over entire *categories* of goods. His discretion in expanding and contracting the content of each category is unprecedented.

This same Congress also tried a new approach to agricultural subsidies. Instead of encouraging farmers to withdraw land from cultivation, it paid them to grow less. This new policy could be enforced only by sending federal inspectors to the farms for verification purposes. The farmers, reacting against what they perceived as "police statism," rejected the entire program in a special referendum, the statute having *delegated to them* the final right of approval. In this situation, then, it was the very group to be regulated that determined the applicable rules!

What about Congress's record during the Johnson Administration? In 1965, the Appalachian Regional Commission was inaugurated. Monies were appropriated for such needs as road construction and sewage improvement, all in order to attack the economic privation that exemplifies life in this area. But the commission, which formulates policy, is made up of the governors of the states in the region and one federal expert. It takes a majority vote of the governors to authorize anything; hence, Congress has delegated to the *states* all power to uplift Appalachia's economic status!

One year earlier, the Economic Opportunity Act, with its various community action programs (Job Corps, VISTA, and others), had been enacted, a law often cited as indicative of what government can do by way of "progressive" legislation. The grant of power enunciated in this statute brings back memories of the N.I.R.A. The director of the O.E.O. (Office of Economic Opportunity) is allowed to set up programs of "useful work experience"; VISTA (the "domestic Peace Corps") employees are supposed to "combat poverty," if the governor of a state goes along; a community action program must satisfy "only one basic criterion"—"It must be broadly representative of the interests of the community."[26] In other words, anything goes.[b]

Nor did President Nixon's incumbency make any discernible difference. The most provocative piece of domestic legislation enacted between 1969 and 1974 instituted wage and price controls over an inflation-ridden economy. What criteria were formulated?

> The President is authorized to issue such orders and regulations as he may deem appropriate to stabilize prices, rents, wages, and salaries *at levels not less than those prevailing on May 25, 1970.* Such orders and regulations may provide for the making of such adjustment as may be necessary to prevent *gross* inequities [italics added].[27]

These regulations were eventually abandoned—but not because Congress took bold action of some other kind.

To summarize: The general area of domestic lawmaking in the *economic* sphere is now governed largely by the *delegation of power* principle. The legislative branch today does not build a consensus by promoting bargains among power groups. Nor does the legislative branch, riding the wave of an overwhelming mandate, make its own pace by authoritarian fiat. Congress simply gives up the ghost in advance, and, in so doing, it ignores the message of *Schecter,* which warned against "delegation run riot." However, the Supreme Court has done nothing lately to resurrect the *Schecter* argument. In fact, we

[b] Even the very popular and visible Head Start program has suffered from this malady. That O.E.O. offshoot gives preschool children from poverty-stricken homes a crash course in basics so they can be "competitive" in kindergarten. However, Head Start's missions are either formulated and implemented by the virtually autonomous public schools, or they are developed by the virtually autonomous community action groups, where the poverty-stricken themselves are entitled to hold places on the policy-making boards. There are, then, in effect, no meaningful *legislative* standards to be met by these programs.

have become so inured to "delegation run riot" that the Justices have never been asked to declare these statutes unconstitutional.[c]

International affairs legislation

As its third major legislative accomplishment, Congress has passed a considerable number of significant laws, treaties, and resolutions[28] relevant to foreign policy. After the Second World War, it became reasonably clear that isolationism was no longer a viable option; in the atomic age we had to either exercise leadership or create a void that others might fill to our everlasting discomfort.

The struggle against the Axis enemies appeared to justify an extraordinary delegation of decision-making from Congress to President. Thus, the Lend-Lease Act of 1941 gave President Roosevelt discretion to supply military resources to the Allies without any inhibitory guidelines. A statute passed in 1942 allowed an executive agency the right to renegotiate all government contracts with manufacturers so as to avert the accumulation of "excessive profits." But no meaningful definition of what constituted an excessive increment was included! Considering the President's wartime constitutional weapons and the *Curtiss-Wright* precedent (see footnote 8 above), these authorizations were probably permissible.[29] Yet, in hindsight, they established an unfortunate trend, because modern-day legislative policy-making seems to have a penchant for overdelegation unless the politics of moral choice is at stake.

Congress's role in foreign affairs during the crucial postwar years can at best be described as a mixed bag, if jurisdiction and responsibility under the Constitution serve as our guide. On one side, the Senate engaged in a so-called great debate over the executive's power to send troops unilaterally to Europe in support of this country's N.A.T.O. obligations. Eventually, proponents carried the day, but only after senatorial participation in the entire process was assured. On the other hand, Congress enacted the Marshall Plan, which, for all its humanitarian attributes, constituted a massive delegation of policy-making initiative to the American business community. Marshall aid helped revitalize the shattered Western European economy. But, while public monies were parceled out, the blueprints for program implementation were drafted by the *private* sector.

Finally, there were the roles Congress *never* played: the Senate failed to pass upon the Yalta and Potsdam agreements because these were never submit-

[c] Just so I do not leave myself open to charges of oversimplification, I readily admit that Congress's appetite for drafting tough regulatory standards does occasionally spill over into the social-legislation domain. An excellent example is the Taft-Hartley labor-relations statute, which subjects trade unions to a whole series of constraints; for instance, it bans "secondary boycotts," the practice of picketing third parties. The Taft-Hartley Act was the brainchild of the "Mr. Republican" of the 1940s, Ohio Senator Robert A. Taft, who was convinced organized labor had gained too much power, a leverage that could paralyze the nation's economy if exploited to the full. But this statute is strictly an exception, if only because it was enacted by the exception among modern-day governmental exceptions, a *Republican Congress.*

ted in treaty form. The Congress failed to vote on a declaration of war with respect to the Korean "police action." And the Congress failed to certify our participation in the Nuremberg war crimes trials. My point is that in none of these instances did the legislative branch seek to formulate constitutional theory that would justify either its participation in or its abstinence from the policy-making terrain at issue. Congress thus robbed many of these efforts of the *legitimacy* they needed to gain whatever acceptance they may have deserved, and it placed itself at a terrible disadvantage in implementing meaningful checks against arbitrary presidential behavior.

The 1960s, as we saw, were a period of delegation gone wild in the domestic sphere. Should anyone have been surprised, then, when President Johnson extracted from Congress a blank check with regard to Vietnamese military intervention? Here is the crucial language of the Gulf of Tonkin Resolution: "The Congress approves and supports the determination of the President . . . to take all necessary measures to repel any armed attack against the forces of the United States and to prevent further aggression."[30] Eventually a national debate was held on the constitutionality of the "war"—but it was held in the streets, on the campuses and, after the fact, in the Congress. By that time, after all, our intervention had become pregnant with *moral* overtones, and it was too late.

The dominant norm: self-government through log-rolling

Congress's legislative record provides the best clue to its potency in the American governmental scheme. In order to be effective, the legislative branch must play one of two roles: either it will be chief political *bargainer* among competing interests, or it will be chief political *authority figure*, where its function is not coercion through compromise but coercion, period. Which hat it chooses to wear depends greatly on the issues involved, for Congress's constitutional authority does not extend equally to all facets of decision-making. And very often Congress has no choice in the matter because of the existing political balance.

During the past quarter-century, there has been "Living Constitutional" consensus regarding most of the traditionally significant concerns facing the "political branches"—that is, the underlying purposes and uses of domestic and foreign policy. Our elected officials are supposed to provide for both economic stability at home and protection against totalitarian aggression. In theory, Congress seems capable of making crucial policy choices with respect to the former need, while it imposes meaningful checks on the executive as he supervises the latter task. In short, present-day political life is akin not to the antebellum years, when compromise was a necessary consequence of the constitutional friction dividing the land, but to the postbellum era, in the sense that a clear majority is massed behind the basic goals of statecraft.

So what has Congress done? It has reverted to N.I.R.A.-style politics by very often delegating the heart of its authoritative capacity to others—to bureaucratic underlings who possess maximum flexibility to negotiate appropriate rules and regulations in the light of claims advanced by relevant interest groups.

But if there is so much agreement on strategic policy considerations, why has Congress placed so much reliance on compromise and consensus-building in the first place?

During the peak years of congressional activity—when a strong ideological ally sat in the chief executive's chair—the legislative branch was under the influence of twentieth-century liberal philosophy—which traditionally extols social change, and which, in recent times, surely has envisioned government's playing a major role in working such change. But liberalism is of two minds with respect to law, because *law is the embodiment of coercion.* Recall Jefferson's fear of national authority, which he believed boded ill for individual rights. So legislative power, to the liberal, is largely a tool for encouraging *self-government through log-rolling.* That is, when economic and social interests petition Congress for a redress of grievances through the sympathetic efforts of their chosen representatives, the lawmakers ordinarily give them the power they need to solve their own problems in consultation with administrative functionaries. Congressional conflict is consequently minimized because each interest or faction gets a piece of the action. Use of legislative power to enforce norms via majority rule is reserved for "state occasions." The watchword is delegation of power, not regulation by either persuasion or power. Here, then, is one reason—but by no means the *only* reason—why Congress might well be labeled the paper tiger of our constitutional universe.

The House of Representatives

The face of Congress is much more than a checklist of its legislative record, however. And the constitutional politics of congressional action encompasses much more than the doctrines underlying such legislation. We must now consider both the internal processes and the internal power structures that animate congressional behavior. These decision-making routines and pecking orders appear nowhere in the Constitution but without doubt have become integral segments of our "Living Constitution."

Apportionment

The Founding Fathers thought the House of Representatives would represent people, not territory. This conviction is disclosed in two pertinent provisions: (1) "The House . . . shall be composed of Members chosen every second Year by the People. . . ." (2) "Representatives . . . shall be apportioned among the several states . . . according to their respective numbers. . . ." Regarding the first item, although the Framers were greatly divided as to which "people" should share in the selection process, they definitely thought the "people's representatives" must be subject to frequent "popular" checks. The second item, the *apportionment* provision says, almost literally, "The more people the state has, the more seats it gets."[31] The House itself, however, was left to construct a precise mathematical formula for apportionment, including, of course, the specific requirement in the Constitution that each state have *one* seat no matter how few people live there. The nub of the problem is this: How much larger does state X have to be before it merits one more seat than state Y? Experts have developed various computational systems, but naturally, these can result in dissimilar allotments of representatives. No matter what scheme is adopted, however, maximum as well as minimum constraints obtain because since 1913, the total number in the chamber has been set, by act of Congress, at 435. In the meantime, our population has grown from 98 to 210 million, so the number 435 might seem outmoded. As we shall see, though, if the House gets much larger, it could very well be incapable of democratic governance.

Congress has certain tools it can invoke in aid of apportionment obligations. First, the Constitution says a census shall be taken every ten years in order to ascertain how many people reside in each state. It also says, "The times, places and manner of holding elections for Senators and Representatives, shall be prescribed in each state by the legislature thereof; but the Congress may at any time by law make or alter such regulations. . . ." As a rule, the states do take the initiative, but, every now and again, Congress uses this provision to implement apportionment responsibilities. Thus in 1842 it said representatives must be chosen according to the *single-member district* plan: every state with more than one seat would henceforward be divided up into distinct geographical areas, each with its own representative. No longer could House members be elected *at large* (in statewide contests),[32] and no longer could there be *multimember* constituencies (more than one representative per district). In 1872, Congress became even bolder, mandating equal numbers of people for each district, while in 1901, it decided these subdivisions should be "compact."

The principles of population equality and compactness were crucial. If Congress refused to confront the tough political task of drawing the actual *district lines,* nevertheless the state legislatures could no longer indulge in *gerrymandering*—that is, manipulate boundaries to maximize the strength of, say, a particular party or region.

However, in 1929, Congress reverted to laissez faire. It dropped requirements for both equality and compactness and merely decided, every ten years in the light of fresh census figures, how many representatives the several states deserved. That is, it delegated to the states themselves power to do the rest, with only the single-member-district string attached. And sometimes the states would do nothing, even in the face of massive population shifts! The most noteworthy example was the migration of people from the countryside into urban communities. But rural interests controlled most state legislatures, and they refused to accept a reapportionment which would have deprived them of that control as well as their accustomed national representation. In Illinois, for example, the legislature rejected every attempt to redraw House district lines from 1901 to 1948; Chicago, with more than 50 percent of the state's population, was given only ten of Illinois's twenty-five seats. And not even the Supreme Court was willing to redress this imbalance. In 1946, such cases were found to be nonjusticiable; they were considered "political questions." Said Felix Frankfurter, "The remedy for unfairness in districting is to secure State legislatures that will apportion properly, or to invoke the ample powers of Congress. . . . It is hostile to a democratic system to involve the judiciary in the politics of the people."[33] But "the people" did nothing, and neither did the Congress or the legislatures. Finally, a more activist Supreme Court stepped into the breach.

The *Wesberry* decision,[34] handed down in 1964, was one of the earliest attempts by the Warren Court to interpret broadly whatever egalitarian principles are expressed in the Constitution; it was also one of the most significant decisions ever handed down regarding the power of Congress. The majority opinion argued that when the Framers vested "the people" with the right to select House members, it was also the Framers' intent to establish intrastate population equality among districts. In other words, if New York State has thirty representatives, each one must represent an equal number of people. But how equal? The new guideline is: "As nearly as practicable, one man's vote in a congressional election is to be worth as much as another's."[35] Mathematical exactness is certainly impossible, but a good-faith effort is required; the Court has yet to accept any congressional apportionment scheme that included as much as 10 percent differential from smallest to largest district.

The weight of scholarly judgment on this subject is that the Warren Court "mangled constitutional history."[36] It is difficult to believe the genteel pragmatists who wrote the Constitution were wedded ideologically to egalitarianism in a manner suggested by the *Wesberry* majority. For the Founders, it was enough that one legislative branch would express state parity, while the other branch would allow more populous states greater influence. On the other hand, if the document reflects a concern for population as the key attribute of House representation, the Court, given its duty to update constitutional themes, is hardly guilty of judicial caprice when it says that equal districts are now required.[37]

But this argument assumes the matter is justiciable! It assumes the Court can tell members of Congress what guidelines they must use to apportion seats. Prevailing constitutional theory, we know, tells us a great deal about the prevailing balance of power in our government. No clearer picture of Congress's standing today can be found than in the Court's asserting: "For years you have ignored the rights of citizens in determining how *your* membership is to be formulated; now you will do things our way."

While reapportionment *within* states has always been a political hot potato, it is of considerably less significance than the colorless process of reapportionment *among* states, which occurs at the beginning of each decade. That script discloses how geographical regions stand in relation to one another quantitatively, in terms of voting power. Here are some raw figures:

The twelve North Central states constitute the largest bloc, though they are losing ground; indeed, the South (loosely construed) has slightly greater representation and also seems to be holding its own. Actually, however, most of the South is *losing;* it is Texas and Florida that are gaining, and these are hardly typical Southern communities. Meanwhile, New York and Pennsylvania are falling off as California grows by leaps and bounds. It will not be long before the Western states outstrip the Middle Atlantic region.

REGION	1950	1960	1970
New England	28	25	25
Middle Atlantic	87	83	79
North Central	129	125	121
South Atlantic	60	63	65
South Central	74	70	69
Mountain	16	17	19
Pacific	43	52	57

Membership

Who is entitled to sit in the House? The Constitution merely says that representatives must be twenty-five years old, a citizen for seven years, and a resident of the state from which they were chosen. However, "Each House shall be the Judge of the Elections, Returns and Qualifications of its own Members. . . ."; and, "Each House may . . . with the concurrence of two-thirds, expel a Member." Traditionally, both chambers construed widely their authority to weigh the "qualifications" of potential peers. On one occasion, the House refused to seat an elected member from Utah because he was a convicted polygamist; on another occasion, it rejected the papers of a Milwaukee congressman who had been found guilty of sedition. And, of course, Reconstruction policy hinged on the ability to bar alleged Confederate sympathizers from taking their seats. Evidently, the "Living Constitution" accorded Congress the power to exclude duly elected representatives who failed to meet perceived standards of morality, deportment, or good citizenship. It is not an exaggeration to term these criteria the very essence of the "blackball" system traditionally invoked by Greek-letter societies.

Then in 1967, the long-entrenched practice creaked and crumbled with the Supreme Court's ruling in the Adam Clayton Powell case.[38] Powell, Harlem's congressman of many years' standing, was *excluded* from the House on grounds that he had (1) taken public money for his own private use, (2) filed misleading accounts to "cover up" these financial dealings, and (3) improperly refused to pay damages after being found guilty of libeling a private citizen. Following the House vote, Powell went to court seeking payment of his back salary, compensation he would have received had his election been honored, and the Justices were led irresistibly into the thorny "qualifications" thicket.

Powell asserted he could not be excluded if he satisfied age, citizenship, and residence requirements; the House asserted the entire dispute was an internal congressional matter, a "political question" if ever there was one. The Justices ruled in Powell's favor, again invoking the "intent of the Framers" technique. After rummaging through available historical documentation, a majority said the Founders had intended the exclusionary check to weigh only the three "qualifications" specified in the document. If the House wanted to enforce more general norms of conduct, it would have to seat the elected official, *then* oust him.

The Court emphasized that the power to expel was stated in sweeping language, whereas the power to exclude was applicable only to "Elections, Returns and Qualifications." Moreover, *expulsion* requires a *two-thirds* majority vote, another clue that this provision was a substantively different kind of control mechanism. The House then, had emasculated its own expulsion authority by beefing up its exclusionary authority, an unconstitutional shortcut that may have cost Powell his seat.

As in the *Wesberry* apportionment decision, the Justices again left themselves open to the objective criticism of constitutional historians, who did not agree with the Court's assessment of the Framers' intention.[39] A second common denominator with *Wesberry* is that the two cases cut through the "political questions" doctrine in order to redress internal House procedures. Such intervention might well have been justified had Powell been either excluded *or* expelled in violation of some prohibition in the Constitution. But there is no evidence Powell was excluded because he was black; there is evidence Powell was excluded because his colleagues considered him a crook. But instead of calling this a matter of legislative discretion and invoking the "political questions" rubric, the Court demolished one hundred years of congressional precedent and, somewhat after the fact, ruled the Radical Reconstructionist seating policy of Civil War days unconstitutional (see p. 113). From the standpoint of democratic values, the decision maximizes the right of voters to choose whom they will for House membership; but it minimizes respect due a branch of Congress in one of the most "personal" functions it can perform, deciding who will participate in its business. The judgment is merely another example of legislative impotence, for better or worse.[40]

The power structure: centripetal forces[41]

The House of Representatives has an intricate organizational scheme. In describing and assessing this network, we must consider the historical record of its actual workings, as well as the way the network accommodates the legislative struggles and the clashes of personalities and interests that are endemic to a body such as this.

Underlying the entire structure are two basic, irreconcilable tensions. *First,* the House is a big place. It has 435 members, and most of them are strong-willed, ambitious people who have worked their way up the power hierarchy. They have not only their ambitions but also their constituents' needs to serve. Left entirely to fend for themselves, they would soon produce chaos. So a rather stringent power structure has been conceived to keep things running smoothly. Yet such authority sometimes suffocates individual prerogatives, and this has led to occasional rebellion. The tension between libertarian principle and ordered responsibility is very much present today. *Second,* there are antagonistic forces in the House that battle constantly over whether the power structure should be *centralized* or *decentralized.* Some representatives want authority to emanate from the top; others want it to sit in the committees. But note this: *The two* sources of tension overlap considerably. Hence, a member of libertarian bent is *not* necessarily a decentralizer; and a member committed to tight controls may *not* want these regulations flowing from a single apex. In this section, we will look at those power centers which promote overall, *centralized* decision-making.

I begin with the Speaker, almost always the most powerful person in the House and one of the most powerful in the entire government. As presiding officer of the chamber, he supervises debate and parliamentary procedure with a velvet fist. He has considerable leeway in controlling access to the floor, and he rules on all points of order. The prototype of the successful Speaker was Sam Rayburn of Texas, who held this post throughout the 1940s and 1950s. Rayburn possessed several of the qualities necessary for success: he was a strong, forceful leader, most effective at working out compromises in the "cloakrooms"; [d] he was an experienced, senior man, who understood the traditions of the chamber to a T; and he did not paint himself as an ideologue, so his leverage was rarely impaired by overcommitment to doctrine. Today, Thomas O'Neill of Massachusetts serves in this position.

The most meaningful check on a Speaker's ultimate authority is the political party mechanism. He is selected, technically, by a majority vote of his peers. But the Speaker is always a member of the majority party in the chamber and is chosen by the *party caucus* (that is, he is nominated via majority vote of his partisan colleagues convening as a group). This is a major source of his political leverage. The Speaker is forever huddling with committee chairmen, presidential staff, and high-ranking leaders of both parties to plan strategies for the days and weeks ahead. If he mobilizes his partisan and parliamentary resources properly, then, all important proceedings on the floor will clear through him.

While it is evident the Speaker benefits tremendously from the unwieldy makeup of the House, historically his authority has ebbed and flowed in reaction to the larger power struggle between centralizing and decentralizing forces. By the turn of the century, it had become traditional for him to name *all* members of *standing* (permanent) *committees* and to designate the chairmen of these committees. He himself held sway over the Rules Committee, which, as we will see, dictates precisely what bills should be considered. Armed with the power to control debate, the Speaker directed the workings of the House both on and off the floor.

The Speaker as one-man ruler fell by the wayside with the Progressive tidal wave of 1910. Throughout the country, people were clamoring to excise "invisible government" and demanding a return to "popular democracy." It was the era of Teddy Roosevelt, Bob LaFollette, and George Norris, and it was a coalition of Democrats and Norris Republicans that toppled Speaker Joe

[d] This is congressional parlance for "behind the scenes."

Cannon of Missouri. Demanding "equal rights," they removed the Speaker from the Rules Committee and abolished his right both to staff standing committees and to hand-pick their chairmen. To these mavericks, party discipline did not justify quasi-dictatorialism; but they also saw Cannon as a reactionary who opposed their legislative program. This was not the first time—nor would it be the last—that a new majority in the House moved to change the rules so as to push through its own policy preferences. To this day, though, the Speaker still appoints all *select* (special) *committees* and *conference committees* (ad hoc groups that bargain with senatorial counterparts). In sum, the leadership of the House is now a study in diffusion, but the Speaker is numero uno.

Somewhat lower down on the totem pole are the *majority* and *minority leaders.* The former heads the political party with the most votes in the House; the latter fulfills this function for the "loyal opposition." The roles they play depend on whether the President's party commands a majority in the chamber. If so, the majority leader is responsible for guiding the chief executive's legislative program through the House. Since Franklin Roosevelt's day, Democratic Presidents have almost always been in the enviable position of having a party ally as majority leader,[42] while Republican Presidents have almost never been so fortunate.[43] Where the two parties divide executive and legislative control, pressures for compromise are maximized. The minority leader must have help from the majority, or the President's recommendations will gather moss. Nor can the majority leader and his party overplay their advantage, or they risk a White House veto. Such division has been infrequent, however; the typical situation finds Speaker and majority leader in constant contact as they seek to keep their party together and make the President's legislative record a source of pride. Meantime, the minority leader will try, under obviously difficult circumstances, to build up more than token opposition; and, if the power mix is appropriate, perhaps can even put together a coalition of majority party dissidents and minority party forces. As is well known, Southern Democrats and Republicans commonly band together in this fashion.

The position of majority leader has had a checkered history. Until the present century, there was no such official post; the Speaker usually tapped somebody to take on its functions. After the insurrection of 1910, however, the majority leader actually surpassed the Speaker in power, because he was also chairman of the Ways and Means (tax-writing) Committee. Under his direction, this body took over the selection of all standing committee members. But such power did not last, and today, the majority leader plays no meaningful role with respect to committee responsibilities. From 1910 until the present, though, the majority leader has been chosen by a vote of his party's caucus.

The minority leader's job has also had its ups and downs, though generally because of personal rather than institutional reasons—there is nothing more demoralizing in politics than defeat. While no majority leader has ever been demoted by his party, two minority chiefs have lost their jobs in recent history. Gerald Ford rose to power in the House by ousting Indiana's Charles Halleck in a 73–67 showdown vote of the Republican caucus.

Also deserving of mention are the party caucuses. At one time, the Democratic caucus had real teeth. Oscar Underwood of Alabama, the majority leader, was the most powerful person in the House. Elected by his fellow Democrats, he ran the caucus and led the membership in debate. Formal, binding votes on key issues were taken at caucus meetings; and anyone who "bolted" was punished, perhaps through denial of a first committee preference. The upshot was one legislative triumph after another for Woodrow Wilson and the Democratic Party. Over the past several years, though, such party discipline has been viewed as incompatible with members' rights to vote their consciences (and their constituents' interests). Generally, the Democrats as a group have done little more than choose their top leaders, though the rivalry with President Ford, combined with an unusually large party majority and a spirit of reformism generated by young "liberals," has led recently to some important votes instructing party committee members to send legislation to the floor for action. The Republican caucus also has run the gamut from true policy formulator to legislative vestigial organ, but the paucity of G.O.P. members in the House during the 1970s has made their caucus of little practical concern.

An interesting development of modern vintage has been the steady growth of the Democratic Study Group. Founded in 1957, it usually numbers about 150 self-styled liberal Democrats, who perform joint research missions, meet together over coffee and highballs to "brainstorm" legislative approaches, and issue reports. Obviously, the organization was formed as a counterweight in policy development to the conservative power structure, and its success as a home for ideologues can be measured by the fact that over the past ten years it has been able to disburse an increasing amount of campaign money to like-minded partisans.

The power structure: centrifugal forces

We now turn to those power centers that serve as *decentralizing* forces in House decision-making. Actually, there is only one example, but one of enormous influence—the *committee system.*

Committee organization, too, has undergone great change over the years. In the eighteenth century, when the House had sixty-five members, it was a true debating society. There were no permanent committees. Select committees were created when the need arose to put a set of general policy views into definitive form, and they went out of existence as soon as their drafting tasks were concluded. The Speaker named committee personnel, but he acted mostly as an agent of the executive branch, because Hamilton (as Treasury Secretary)—and Jefferson after him—used their party leadership to influence the entire gamut of policy-making in the House. The fulcrum of legislative influence was the party caucus, for there the leadership asserted its will.

The man most responsible for changing this system was Henry Clay, who, as Speaker, made committee selections independent of presidential designs.

Armed with this authority, Clay encouraged the development of standing committees, which he perceived as bastions of strength insulated against executive branch influence. Bills would be referred automatically by the Speaker to the committee that had jurisdiction of the subject matter, and if a committee decided to pigeon-hole (bury) a bill, this was deemed appropriate. By 1825, the standing committees had attained predominant status in the legislative process.

As the decades went by, this trend proceeded apace. When Woodrow Wilson came to write his great study of the Congress in 1885, he found fifty-odd standing committees in the House and a Speakership much weakened by feuding, self-protecting committee chairmen. Said Wilson in exasperation:

> The leaders of the House are the chairmen of the principal Standing Committees. Indeed, to be exactly accurate, the House has as many leaders as there are subjects of legislation; for there are as many Standing Committees as there are leading classes of legislation.[44]

If the committee chairmen and their islands of influence are not quite so powerful today as they were one hundred years ago, they are still of tremendous importance. It is clearly very hard to undermine their institutional base of support, for they are chosen in large measure by the automatic, neutral criterion of *seniority.*

Let us assume there are more Democrats in the House than Republicans. The chairmen of *all* committees—standing or select—must then be Democrats. Why? Not because of seniority, but because ultimately it is the House itself that approves committee lists, and such votes are strictly party-line affairs. Now suppose a chairman dies, or retires, or is defeated in an election. Who takes his place? Answer: Almost always, the senior person on the committee who belongs to the majority party. By "senior," I mean not the oldest person but the person who has been on the committee the longest. The seniority principle is by no means as old as the Republic; however, from the 1940s until 1975 the system was administered without deviation.[45] The "almost always" qualification is a strictly contemporary reservation.

Why are the chairmen so powerful? A quick recitation of their discretionary latitude will make the point graphically. The typical committee head determines the agenda for every meeting, decides if hearings should be held, creates all subcommittees and appoints their members, designates the committee's staff, and shepherds chosen legislation through the various turnstiles of House supervision.

There are now twenty-two standing committees in the House, and most of them have numerous subcommittees. Naturally, these minigroups have chairmen, too. In the overwhelming majority of cases, seniority determines who will succeed to chairmanship vacancies; but it is considered legitimate for the committee boss, occasionally for personal reasons, to skirt the rule and tap somebody else. Subcommittee heads generally exercise the same measure of freedom in their domain as chairmen do in their larger spheres, so when one talks of "government by chairmen" one should include subcommittee leaders as well.

What impact does seniority have as a "Living Constitutional" precept? Again, let us assume the Democrats are in control, as was the case in 1964. In that year, 63 percent of their representatives were from the North. However, the South held more than 50 percent of both committee and subcommittee chairmanships. Because seniority is the key criterion, committee leaders tend to be older people who have been reelected countless times. And the South has traditionally gotten the lion's share, because, as 1964 figures show, most safe (one-party) seats are located there. With regard to subcommittee leadership, Southerners are even more overrepresented. When committee heads from the South violate the seniority principle in choosing these officials, there is some evidence they pick junior Southern allies over veteran Northern foes.

In the long run, though, Northern Democrats should fare better in their quest for chairmanships. For one thing, redistricting in the wake of new census data is hurting the rural areas and, when combined with "Republican flight" to the suburbs, is producing a significant increase in safe urban seats.[46] For another, the Democrats elected as a result of the 1964 Johnson landslide have solidified their incumbencies and have become entrenched in the House power structure.[47] Indeed, the trend is already in high gear; only ten of the twenty-two chairmanships are now held by representatives from states commonly considered Southern.

How does a congressman get on a committee? Ever since the Speaker lost the power of appointment, each party has used a *Committee on Committees* to piece together its share of the puzzle. For more than sixty years, the Democrats' Committee on Committees consisted largely of the Democratic membership in the very important Ways and Means Committee, obviously an entrenched bureaucracy of senior personnel. Late in 1974, however, the long-standing power of the Ways and Means Committee was scrapped, and the right to choose panel members fell to the party's *Steering and Policy Committee.* In effect the executive arm of the party caucus, this forum is a potpourri of middle-range and upper-level senior people, most of whom are either appointed by the Speaker or elected by the caucus itself. Why the change? Probably because it enhances the influence of the caucus and therefore is part of the same new-found egalitarian mood that has curbed the Democrats' use of the seniority system. The Republicans' Committee on Committees is made up of the senior G.O.P. representatives from each state; and this unwieldy body assigns decision-making authority to a nine-person subcommittee of especially senior people who come from the big, populous states where most Republican voters live. The Republican committee selection process, then, more accurately reflects electoral results; the Democrats' committee selection process more accurately reflects rank-and-file party opinion in the House itself. Both nominating devices mirror essentially the wishes of established, proven members. Key personnel decisions are rarely made by newcomers, no matter what the organizational setting.

The most important committees in the House are (1) Ways and Means (the money collector), (2) Appropriations (the money spender), and (3) Rules (the committee that funnels most important bills to the House floor).[48] Indeed, no member can serve on more than one of these; they are known as "exclusive" committees. These spots are so desirable, that party leaders make a special effort to instruct their respective committees-on-committees as to whom they should appoint. And the chamber's leaders generally have their way. Making it to the inner sanctum of these legislative havens requires candidates to satisfy certain conditions: (1) they must demonstrate willingness to play the game according to the rules of good fellowship, so that the dignity of the House is never jeopardized; (2) they must represent a district whose demands will not interfere with this norm-playing role; (3) they must come from the same state as the previous incumbent, if possible. With respect to the "nonexclusive" standing committees, however, the party nominating groups have a much freer hand. The significant factor in filling these slots is the extent to which the final choices strengthen reelection prospects for particular aspirants.

All representatives have three essential goals: to be reelected, to maximize personal influence, and to promote what each sees as wise public policy.[49] Certain committees, such as the three at the apex of prestige, emphasize *power* per se; some members will strive without end for these coveted spots. A representative from a highly competitive farm district, though, may simply want to sit on the Agriculture Committee and cater to the constituents' needs. Still other members—ideologues—will gravitate toward Foreign Relations or, perhaps, Education and Labor, where policy orientation and partisan strife are highlighted.[50] The total membership figure for each committee is set down in the rules of the House, and the ratio of Democrats to Republicans is supposed to reflect the overall split in the parent body. Because these parameters are pretty well fixed, applicants are numerous, but openings are few. However, there is some indication most first-term congressmen do pretty well in the light of their preferences; the more seniority members pile up, though, the less able they are to attain their committee choices.[51] Evidently, the intense competition among senior people takes its toll.

In this discussion of the recruitment process, we have seen the overriding importance of seniority in the selection of committee chairmen and its influence on even general committee membership. But the fact is that over the past several years the seniority question has been the most burning "constitutional" issue on the House agenda. What are the arguments pro and con? Seniority's advantages are fairly obvious: it puts power into the hands of experienced people, who can hold their own in the jungle of Washington politics; furthermore, the very objectivity of the system precludes the incessant intraparty warfare that would undoubtedly arise under a less determinate formula. Seniority's disadvantages are also not hard to fathom: it sometimes rewards congressmen who are old and not much else; furthermore, the system heightens the influence of geographical regions—especially, it seems, the rural areas—where the two-party system is weak. With regard to the last item, which is a *representational* question, seniority really does no more than embody the very nature of the House itself. That is, the way in which the chamber recruits both its members and its leaders fosters an innately conservative posture; therefore, the House is a rather conservative place. The district system (1) creates little pockets of safety, one decade behind current population distributions; (2) is organized by state legislatures, which have no interest in encouraging House responsiveness to public opinion; and (3) maximizes the power of parochial interests and their problems to the detriment of national party and ideological concerns. These factors produce a House membership more infatuated with continuity and established norms than one might anticipate, and the emphasis on seniority, with its bias toward age and predictability, is a natural outgrowth of all this.[52]

Now I must fold another ingredient into the mix. The art of legislation is far more complicated today than it used to be. The cause is specialization. Our social system has supposedly become so complicated that a representative is required more and more to be a master of some small area rather than a jack-of-all-trades. The proposition holds, it is alleged, even when the congressman's primary goal is simply "helping my friends back home."

The drive for greater specialization has led to the establishment of a raft of subcommittees—139 at this writing—which concentrate on the most esoteric of legislative details. Exacerbating this process is the large size of the House. Few members hold committee chairmanships, so there are dozens of others striving for exposure and hoping to make a name for themselves—to get their hands on a budget and a cause. Also, both the executive branch and the pressure groups like the subcommittee culture; it provides them with a ready entree in the form of a staff of specialists with whom they can work at close quarters (*dominate*?). There is even a name for this tripartite alliance among legislative enclaves, executive branch bureaucrats, and interest group advocates: "government by whirlpools." This phenomenon is simply another example of what I earlier termed "self-government by log-rolling." And, to repeat, subcommittee make-up and function are generally the prerogatives of the committee chairmen, never of the House as a whole.

The relationships among subcommittee specialization, the congressman's drive to achieve reelection by catering to salient interests in the home district, and seniority can be summed up this way:

> Whatever else it may be, the quest for specialization in Congress is a quest for credit. Every member can aspire to occupy a part of at least one piece of policy turf small enough so that he can claim personal responsibility for some of the things that happen on it. . . . What the congressional seniority system does . . . is to convert turf into property. . . . This property automatically appreciates in value over time.[53]

Now let us total up the scorecard and see where we stand from the perspective of "Living Constitutional" norms. The proliferation of subcommittees is surely the crowning achievement of decentralized House governance.[54] It also makes clear the purpose of this decentralization—to achieve ever more internalized delegation of power. Is not this cleavage in House self-management a fitting companion to the chamber's exercises in externalized delegation of power, the enactment of vague statutory rules that are the cornerstone of interest-group "self-government by log-rolling" (see pp. 120–24)? A fair characterization of these two norms is that they are wrapped up in some kind of symbiotic Gordian knot.

It is against this backdrop that the seniority system has come under serious challenge of late, has become, as I said earlier, the most burning "constitutional" issue on the House agenda. At first, the impetus for reform was mostly provided by liberals in both parties; they pushed the leadership to expand the powers of their respective caucuses; then, in the early 1970s both caucuses finally instructed their committees on committees to ignore seniority if they found other criteria for either panel participation or chairmanship more equitable. The caucuses also reserved the right to reject nominations made by the committees on committees. Also of importance, though it received little publicity at the time, was a move by the Democratic caucus to limit each member to a single subcommittee chairmanship; this reform should spread responsibility around a bit more evenly.

To the surprise of few, no marked deviations from the seniority rule in naming panel members occurred overnight.[55] In the 1974 off-year elections, however, the Democrats gained approximately fifty seats, and another twenty-five freshmen Democrats succeeded to seats already in the party fold. These "Young Turks," most of them less committed to chamber traditions than their elders, were not content to sit around slowly accumulating tenure, and they had more than sufficient numbers to capitalize on the drift toward centralization already building up. The upshot was that twenty first-term Democrats were placed immediately on major committees over the claims of senior party members. But the sparks really flew when the Democratic caucus ousted the chairmen of three important committees.

Hypotheses abound as to what prompted this drastic reshuffling. One explanation is that many first-term Democrats ran on a "post-Watergate morality" platform, pledging "openness" in government if elected. Another theory is predicated on long-standing liberal grievances over Southern conservative domination. The most plausible explanation would seem to incorporate a number of givens working in combination: lackluster party leadership incapable of controlling the volatile caucus; the feeling of some first-term liberals that any vulnerable conservative should be purged; the inability of some chairmen to bargain and "communicate."[56] Evidently, the reaction against decentralization was not motivated by a desire to promote aggressive legislative initiatives. Rather, the caucus is being used to balance decentralization, because diffusion of power stifles the libertarian drives of a Democratic membership more individualistic (egalitarian?) than in years gone by.[57] But these are unusual, extremely changeable times, so it would be presumptuous to predict the death knell of seniority, much less of the delegation of power principle it helps sustain.

Without question, House politics have tended toward decentralization since the Cannon revolt of 1910. And House politics have also become more and more circumscribed by objective, neutral rules such as seniority. Yet organizational formality usually goes hand-in-hand with concentration of power, not diffusion of power.[58] Assuming the membership does not reverse field drastically, why should the House be an exception?

Perhaps the anomaly can be explained in the light of what may be the truly fundamental norm that has conditioned internal House affairs in recent years: delegation of power. It is no accident the House has stressed objective rules; and this choice may well have stemmed from the desire to promote logrolling and to defeat planning. In this context, purposeful moves toward centralization involve either majority rule or some kind of arbitrary, dictatorial power. These steps would make the House a partisan, ideological force in the power struggle. That is a role which the membership, given its constituency, traditions, and ambivalence toward law as a coercive instrument of policy, has shown no inclination to play.

The legislative flow[59]

Now that we have discussed the organizational features of the House, it is time to see how these patterns function with respect to the ostensible purpose of the House—legislation.

More than 15,000 bills and resolutions are introduced into the lower chamber each year, and every one must be turned over to a committee. This task is usually pro forma, but where there is doubt as to jurisdiction the Speaker decides. Only 11 percent of these items ever get out of committee; indeed, only a small proportion will even receive careful consideration. Moreover, bills that do not run successfully the entire legislative gamut and become *law* during the length of Congress's tenure (the two-year period between elections) will have to *start all over again* with reintroduction.

Committee reflection centers on proposals sponsored by the President, an influential House colleague, or a prominent lobbying organization. However, in this era of super-delegation, the chairman invariably sends these items along with all the others down the line to a subcommittee. Deep in the inner recesses of these units, "government by whirlpools" works its will. Perhaps Congressman Smith, representing a strong tobacco-planting constituency, has introduced legislation to help the local growers; the bill filters down to a subcommittee on tobacco, which Smith happens to chair and where his friends are accorded the red-carpet treatment. A civil servant from the Agriculture Department is also on station, ready to chip in with administrative and technical expertise.[60]

If the bill is taken seriously it will usually create its share of public concern; thus, hearings must be held. Congressmen pro and con will ask to be heard. Pressure groups pro and con and executive officials pro *or* con (the White House always puts on a united front) will also send representatives to testify. These sessions are open to everyone, and they may serve any number of needs: to ascertain public opinion, to gather information, to build a record of endorsements, to make the proposal more visible, to make the chairman more visible, to allow opponents of the measure a chance to blow off steam, to slow down the chances of adoption and so on. Most of the melodrama takes place at the subcommittee level, but if the bill is crucial and well publicized, the parent committee may also invite witnesses. However, the actual preparation of the legislation, motions to amend, and debates on the merits take place in *executive session,* traditionally not accessible to public scrutiny.[e]

Should the proposed measure get past this most difficult screening process, it is placed on one of three calendars. There is the Union Calendar for money bills, the House Calendar for all other legislation of a public nature, and the Private Calendar for nonpublic proposals. The ordinary course of events would find the House taking up each item as listed on the calendars; but to put the matter this way would be to oversimplify.

Private bills do not affect citizens generally; rather, each proposal is drafted to help a particular individual, such as someone to whom the government owes money. About 350 are adopted. Their impact on the political universe is minimal; yet, 35 percent of all laws enacted are of this type. Once a month, bills lying on the Private Calendar become *privileged.* In other words, the Speaker *must* bring them forward in chronological order to be voted upon. This is a handy way to expedite their disposition.

Turning now to "public" business, we find a great many noncontroversial propositions and a small number of provocative items. The Consent Calendar provides a mechanism for cleaning up the less inflammatory business. Any member can have a bill placed on this list, and *twice* a month the Speaker is required to call proposals off the docket. However, if objection is heard, a particular measure must be held back for future consideration. More laws ultimately emerge in this fashion than via any other route save the Private Calendar.

On two days of each month, motions to suspend the rules may be placed before the House. Should such a request carry, any bill can be taken up no matter what its current status. However, two-thirds of those voting must approve, and, even before there is a tally, the Speaker may choose not to recognize the proponent! In other words, the Speaker can simply deny the floor to anyone who wants to make such a motion. Clearly, then, business of real consequence can seldom be handled by rule suspension, so this is just another way of clearing up the leftovers.

[e] But as a result of 1970 legislation, meetings can now be thrown open if a majority concurs—another triumph for the "politics of openness" which the liberal reform movement has championed.

Some committees are empowered to bring up so-called *privileged bills.* The most important are money bills. Since government cannot function without funds, special provisions are formulated for ensuring the smooth passage of money bills. Public works measures—"pork barrel" legislation—are also privileged. Behind public works bills an exchange, spoken or unspoken, takes place: "You take this pet project for your district, and I'll take that pet project for my district." "Pork barrelism" means jobs, money, and constituency happiness. If we know what bills are privileged, we gain insight into what members perceive to be top-priority legislation.

The overwhelming percentage of important items sit on their respective calendars until the *Rules Committee* acts. This important group receives about 150 bills per Congress. If the membership thinks a measure is frivolous or, more likely, bad policy, it may never see the light of day. This occurs in about thirty instances. But the major authority Rules possesses is to control the way a piece of legislation will be treated on the House floor. Very often, if the Committee does not care for a bill but is not in a position to kill it outright because of potential political liabilities, it provides what is called an *open rule.* This allows the opposition to offer amendments during floor debate. The panel might also set a maximum time for discussion. Conversely, if Rules either likes a proposal or merely wants to "play ball" with the bill's sponsors, it can provide a *closed rule;* no amendments can then be proposed, and the time for debate can be shortened as well as lengthened. Clearly, the chances to "water down" a bill or persuade colleagues of its improprieties would then be poor.

The Rules Committee invariably attracts highly senior members, and its orientation has historically been conservative. By this I mean the panel has constituted a major stumbling block for reformist legislation carrying a high price tag. Franklin Roosevelt's domestic programs ground to a halt when a coalition of Republicans and Southern Democrats sitting in the Rules Committee thought enough was enough. Of course, when the pressure is really on, Rules must go along. This would ordinarily occur under two circumstances: (1) when the majority party decides to take a united stance, or (2) when liberals from both parties decide to take a united stance and election results have given them the necessary votes. With all the talk of "obstructionism," though, it is fair to say the Rules Committee has only reflected the traditional bipartisan conservatism of the parent body in bouts with executive policy innovation.[61] And that explains the unusual turn of events whereby the committee now does little to block the House's spending proclivities. The "anti-Goldwater" class of 1964 supplies the seniority; the "anti-Watergate" class of 1974 supplies the votes; the result is a more liberal than usual House and a more liberal than usual Rules Committee.

Is there any way to dig a bill out of a committee that keeps it locked up? The major recourse is the *discharge petition.* First, 218 House members (a bare majority of the entire chamber) must affix their names to a list for all to see. Should that occur, a motion to bring the particular provision before the House becomes privileged on the second and fourth Mondays of each month. As one might expect, it is not easy to muster this large a group, for signing the petition constitutes a direct challenge to key leaders. From 1937 to 1960, only twenty-two of two hundred attempts were successful, and in only fourteen instances did the proposal eventually get beyond the House.

At long last, a measure wends its way to the House floor for a vote. The debating and amending format will almost always have been worked out by the Rules panel, but one more point on this score needs to be made: the House rarely allows *nongermane amendments*—in other words, additions that have nothing to do with the substance of a bill. The Speaker—with aid from the parliamentarian—ascertains the relevancy of prospective changes.

Over the past forty years, bills coming to the floor have tended to be more conservative than Administrations would have liked. As I indicated above, one typically finds a liberal Democrat in the White House jousting with a less-than-innovative House, also controlled by Democrats. During the Nixon-Ford years, though, the converse was usually the case. The House has been fairly liberal and was decidedly more so than either President. In these situations, the lower chamber serves as catalyst for policy change rather than as a force for governmental restraint. An example would be the $2 billion Public Works Acceleration Act, designed to create 170,000 new jobs by putting people to work on water and sewer projects. Nixon vetoed the House-initiated proposal.[62]

What can be said about the voting patterns of House members? Political party affiliation seems to be the best single predictor of whether congressmen as a group will say "Yes" or "No" to pending legislation.[63] But the explanatory value of partisanship varies as we move from issue to issue. On the question of *government management,* there is a tremendous gulf between the two parties, with Democrats strongly favorable and Republicans strongly against; on the question of *social welfare,* there is a considerable gulf between the two parties, with Democrats again favorable and Republicans opposed; on the questions of *international affairs* and *civil liberties,* political party information is practically meaningless. In foreign policy matters, House voting patterns depend heavily on the President's party affiliation. This area of expertise is his domain, and he has a way of persuading party colleagues to go along. Historically, this has usually been in the direction of greater American involvement. On the matter of civil liberties, the crucial cutting edge is geography; North and South are deeply divided over the entire spectrum of rights legislation but especially so when civil rights are at stake.[64] A caveat on partisanship, though: as a determinant of roll-call voting in both House and Senate, its influence has been on the downgrade since 1900 and now stands at an all-time low[65]—to some extent, perhaps, a reflection of decreased voter concern with party labels.

But what exactly is the relationship between House decision-making on the floor and constituency opinion? Generally speaking, House members think they know their districts through the mail they receive, the meetings they attend in their local bailiwicks, the straw polls they conduct, and what they learn from their own subcommittee labors. But this information base is far short of perfect. So while they are creatures of their districts and while they live in fear of electoral rebuff, House members sometimes miscalculate grassroots opinion.

More specifically, the "fit" between constituency notions of good public policy and House voting patterns varies with the issues. Hence, they dovetail nicely on civil rights, are fairly proximate on social welfare questions, and in different worlds with respect to foreign relations.[66]

Summing up "legislative flow" in the House, we see that the process certainly becomes more *centralized* as bills get closer to a House vote. The committees and subcommittees are studies in diffusion; but, in fairness, they do serve to weed out minor matters and thus focus the attention of the House on important legislation. The Rules Committee is decentralized in that it can march to its own tune; Rules members usually are amenable to bargaining with the floor leaders and other committee chairmen, however. Once legislation arrives on the floor, the arbitrary manipulation of calendars, the privileged status accorded both to motions offered on certain specific days and to important legislation on any day, and the virtual impossibility of the average representative either to take the floor or to move a suspension of the rules bespeak centralized authority of dramatic proportions.

The contributions of the House of Representatives to the "Living Constitution" can be summarized as follows: with respect to performing its policy-making chores, the House very much tends toward the *delegation of power* principle. With respect to enforcing established internal rules of governance, the House is *conservative* in orientation, though the winds of reform are gathering momentum. With respect to the manner in which power centers are organized, the House is highly *decentralized*. Finally, with respect to the flow of legislation—no matter what programs are embodied in the proposals—the House, once it decides to move, is *centralized* almost to the point of authoritarianism.

The Senate

In many respects, the Senate is a less complex body to describe than the House. That is mainly because its decision-making network is much less intricate. Moreover, the upper chamber presents far fewer problems with regard to constitutional standing. Whereas apportionment questions keep the House hopping, they affect the Senate not at all. The Constitution allots two seats to every state in the Union, and that provision cannot be altered without the agreement of those states losing their equality of representation. The Framers intended senators to represent their states' interests and to stand as a check against the "popularly controlled" House. In order to shield the Senate from the short-run winds of political opinion and caprice, they gave members six-year terms, only one-third of their number to stand for reelection at each two-year interval.

With respect to membership, the explicit qualifications are slightly higher than those demanded of House members: senators must be at least thirty years old; have been a citizen for nine years; and, again, an inhabitant of the state they represent. Until the past decade, though, the Senate utilized the same sort of "blackball" criteria in judging the qualifications of participants that the House imposed prior to the Adam Clayton Powell ruling (see pp. 127–28). This decision, of course, was binding only on the lower chamber; however the principle expressed there has been followed ever since in the Senate. This response was perfectly appropriate, for surely one branch has no greater power than the other to establish membership standards.

The "formal" power structure[67]

The Senate differs drastically from the House in that it lacks the tensions created by irreconcilable forces. There is no dramatic struggle between centrifugal and centripetal pulls, and there is no great debate between libertarians and authority-oriented leaders.[68] After all, the Senate has "only" one hundred members, and many have achieved national exposure. At the least, they know one another well, and they have gone a lot further in politics than their House colleagues. The Senate is really a kind of paradox: it is *egalitarian* in that the members treat one another as equals; but the egalitarianism seems to encourage *diversity* rather than conformity. The tone of the upper chamber, then, is largely one of *individualism* very much tempered by implicit social norms of right conduct. This mix produces a relaxed, leisurely atmosphere where bargaining among "clubmates" is highlighted. These characteristics should be borne in mind as I describe the official Senatorial power structure.

The Senate has no Speaker. Its presiding officer is the Vice President, and, other than his rarely invoked power to break a tie vote, he possesses only the tools we normally associate with a town-meeting moderator. He recognizes members when they seek the floor, and his rulings on points of order can be appealed to the larger forum. When he vacates the chair (which is almost always the case, for the modern "Veep" is the President's personal good-will ambassador), the presiding officer is the *president pro tempore.* By convention, this position is given to the senior person in the majority party. In spite of the pretentious title, though, his powers extend only to supervising floor debate in undramatic fashion.[f]

With no Speakership, the posts of majority and minority leader are more important here than in the House. The leader of the party in power is responsible for scheduling the Senate's business, but, as a matter of courtesy, he consults freely with his opposite number "across the aisle." The idea is to accommodate all members who have an interest in pending business; senators are very busy people, and the norms are loose enough that the calendar need

[f] The position receives more attention than it deserves because the president pro tempore stands third in the line of succession to the White House, behind the Vice President and the Speaker of the House. Congress has the delegated authority to decide who follows the "Veep" in this order, a function it has exercised none too wisely by entrusting the potential responsibility of the presidency in the hands of two venerable, inbred, party wheelhorses.

not become an oppressive instrument. The role of both floor managers vis-à-vis the Administration's program is, naturally, quite similar to what we found in the House.

Lyndon Johnson is generally considered the model majority spokesman. He knew everything going on in the chamber and worked hard to place each party member in a satisfying position of responsibility. With his knowledge of the legislative process and his mastery of the quid pro quo, he exacted great loyalty for Democratic Party needs as he saw them. Once, when Johnson made a rare mistake and miscounted the outcome of an important tally, he yelled across the floor to Delaware's Senator Frear: "Change your vote!" Frear, who must have owed the Texan a favor, complied. Johnson's "team" won, 41-40.[69] In short, he was the "master persuader."[70] His successor, Mike Mansfield of Montana, who served from 1961 to 1976, was not considered tough enough, and he failed to rival Johnson's record or level of prestige.

Throughout the 1960s, Illinois's Everett Dirksen served as minority head, and he also was thought to be a leader of the first rank. Dirksen earned the trust of his fellow partisans, and he respected their individual notions of good policy. He became a master of compromise in dealing with the majority, because he could count on solid support from his own outnumbered forces.

Both Johnson and Dirksen were criticized on occasion for being ideologically elusive, but positions of partisan responsibility in an individualistic, egalitarian body like the Senate cannot be held by substantively oriented legislators. These leaders—by definition—must be students of *procedure* (that is, experts in getting things done), and they cannot afford to be much else.

In the Senate, rather than a party caucus, there is a Democratic Conference and a Republican Conference; and these titles convey more accurately the advisory, purely conditional influence such assemblies hold. Their only meaningful role is to select the floor leadership; they have yet to dump their first committee chairman.

The Senate, as one might anticipate, has a full-blown committee system, with seniority as the binding standard for allocating chairmanships among majority party personnel. But seniority developed much earlier in this body than in the House; it was utilized almost without exception even before 1900. While the lower chamber adopted the rule as a check against the arbitrary conduct of the Speaker and, later, the majority leader, in the Senate, seniority *antedates* the evolution of a centralized officialdom. When, around 1912, the upper chamber moved toward greater concentration of power individual members did *not* resist the trend, for they were already protected by the seniority tradition. So this difference in "Living Constitutional" norms helps explain why the Senate has been a more peaceful place over the years.

In the 1950s and much of the 1960s, Senate committees were controlled by Southerners. For instance, in 1961, 34 percent of all Democrats came from the South, but 56 percent of the chairmanships were held by this group. And, over the same period, the prestigious committees had an overwhelming proportion of conservative Democrats.[71] Among Republicans, Midwestern conservatives were also overrepresented in the senior committee positions, but they have *not* been overrepresented on the more prestigious committees. Why?

The answer lies in the rules employed by each party's Committee on Committees. The floor leader (majority or minority) heads the Democratic version and names most of the other members. Of course, he turns by and large to influential colleagues. As usual, the South is traditionally overrepresented on this panel (seniority = influence). And, because senators' "top choice" committee assignments have always been governed by give-and-take, *not seniority,* the senators from Dixie could name many of their own. But the Republican Committee on Committees has always applied the seniority standard in passing out committee leadership jobs. In other words, senators who were around the longest had first claim on vacancies. In this context, then, the "reactionary" seniority rule has *prevented* G.O.P. Midwestern factionalism from dominating party representation on the key committees.

Generally speaking, Southerners have been losing power over the past ten years, even though the Democrats continue in the vanguard. At this time, liberals hold a majority on the more prestigious committees; the South is now underrepresented on the party's Committee on Committees; and this committee allows no more than a single good committee assignment per member until everyone gets one premium slot (the "Johnson rule"). One must keep in mind that the G.O.P. is becoming a force to be reckoned with in Dixie, and the liberal Democrats elected in the Goldwater slaughter of 1964 are moving to the fore. There has been no more important political development for understanding the Senate as it is today. Nevertheless, even though only 31 percent of Democrats are Southerners, 53 percent of the committee chairmen are still Southerners.[72]

Consistent with the new trends has been a new flexing of muscles by each party's Conference, and, as in the House, seniority has been the target. From now on, every Republican who is slated to assume the top post on a committee must be certified by party peers on that panel. If they reject him, the Conference itself must decide if he will be allowed to move up. And Democratic senators instructed their Committee on Committees to ignore seniority in choosing members to the new Budget Committee. Geographical and ideological balance alone were taken into account.

These tendencies toward democratization are also consistent with the explosion in committee work for all senators. Not that the problem is a new one. There are seventeen parent committees in the upper chamber and only one hundred senators. Every member, then, has approximately three committee seats. But over the past twenty years, the number of subcommittees has increased enormously. There are now 103 of them, so each senator has about *nine* such assignments. Obviously, the typical member does not have time to keep up with all these chores. Yet he will rarely complain, since he will almost certainly get to work in the legislative area he covets most. The strategy, then, is to expend most of his energy tilling his field of choice, while deferring to colleagues as he carries out other assignments. The present-day Senate is full of experts on narrow subjects: Senator Stennis is "Mr. Armed Services"; Senator Muskie is "Mr. Pollution"; Senator Ervin was "Mr. Constitution" (though, to be sure, these are very broad categories compared to House specialization, where there is a "Mr. Cotton" and a "Mr. Sugar"). But the chamber is woefully short of generalists, lawmakers who have a broad, coherent, well-thought-out grasp of political processes in the grand Webster-Clay-Calhoun manner. And so bargaining and negotiating are magnified accordingly, as specialization triumphs again. Still, the trend is entirely consistent with the overriding individualist-egalitarianism described earlier.

Incidentally, the growth of subcommittees has diminished the influence of parent committees. Committee chairmen in the Senate have the same general powers as their House counterparts, but they must contend with the greater equality among members that these autonomous subcommittees reflect. Thus, a mere 28 percent of subcommittee chairmen are from states below the Mason-Dixon line. So House committees and their leaders have greater influence, and this is consistent with the decentralization theme so prevalent there. The proliferation of upper chamber subcommittees, I must emphasize, is *not* a force for decentralization; it simply gives members platforms from which to maximize specialization by launching their own pet legislative salvos. Under the informal rules of comity that prevail, they usually have their way.

The "informal" power structure[73]

If ever a government agency could *not* be understood properly by mastering an explicit authority ladder, that organization is the Senate. Evidently, there exists a set of "folkways"—normative standards of behavior—which members are expected to observe. When senators fail to measure up, their effectiveness is very much lessened. These implicit norms have been controlling ever since the early 1800s, although, like all viable "rules of the game," they have received occasional doses of modernization. There is some dispute as to who enforces discipline when the standards are breached, but there is surprisingly little disagreement on what the standards are. They can be listed almost as a constitutional "Canon of Duties":

1. Thou shalt serve a quiet apprenticeship, being especially careful to show respect for seniors and to seek out advice from "those who know."

2. Thou shalt work hard at the politically unrewarding legislative details and shun undue publicity.

3. Thou shalt master a few specific areas of skill and not attempt to be a "know-it-all."

4. Thou shalt be courteous to colleagues and never insert personal invective into debate.

5. Thou shalt "give a little to get a little." The name of the game is log-rolling.

6. Thou shalt love the Senate and its traditions above all else.

These rules exist because they perform useful functions in institutional harmony. Hence: Keeping one's mouth closed upon arrival allows a person to learn the ropes without making a fool of oneself; reaping rewards for uninspiring work keeps the drudgery under control; developing specialized skills allows the Senate to have every nook-and-cranny of the legislative spectrum covered by somebody; courtesy constrains heated debate over tough policy items from degenerating into "mudslinging"; reciprocity promotes teamwork and keeps any one person from manipulating the highly flexible rules to serve his own purposes; "love of Senate" inhibits members from spending too much time contemplating "love of presidency."

But the senatorial folkways also contain inherent biases. When a fledgling senator from a highly competitive two-party state comes to Washington, he feels a need to make a name for himself quickly. This prompts him to sponsor bills and make speeches. Already he has violated Canon 1. Next, all members are burdened by demanding favor-seeking constituents; but if the noise from Georgia is noticeable, the noise from California is unbearable. So senators from larger states try to spread-eagle the legislative field. Now Canon 3 has been violated.

The most obvious bias, however, is political ideology. The folkways help to maintain the status quo and frustrate reform—and thus to play right into the hands of the rural Southern Democrat-Midwestern Republican governing vortex. And the brash young senators from big two-party states certainly tend to be liberals. Very often, it is this bloc that has had the most difficulty adjusting to the givens.

Who enforces these norms, and what are the tools of coercion? W. S. White, writing in 1956, said the Senate was governed by a clique, an "Inner Club." It included members who, over a long period of time, had developed noteworthy records of fealty to the six "Living Constitutional" commandments. To work with these leaders and their rules was to court success; to work against them was to court ignominy. Not surprisingly, this inner circle comprised mostly a bipartisan conservative coalition, though liberals like Hubert Humphrey had also managed to earn their way in.

The depth of the "Club's" sanctions can be seen in the rise and fall of Wisconsin's Joseph McCarthy. As a freshman senator, he launched a "crusade against communism" by hurling accusations at many notables from the safety of the Senate floor.[74] Because of their high regard for individual prerogatives, many of McCarthy's colleagues winced but did nothing. Only when he took after fellow senators did recriminatory action begin to develop. For example, his calling New Jersey's Robert Hendrickson "a living miracle . . . with neither brains nor guts,"[75] was an important factor in the membership's decision to organize a select committee to investigate his tactics. Sitting on this panel were such "Club" members as Republican Arthur Watkins of Utah and Democrat Sam Ervin of North Carolina. Cornered on the sinking ship, the Wisconsin firebrand challenged his colleagues' patriotism by terming the committee an "unwitting handmaiden" of the Communist Party.[76] That sealed it. The Senate voted to condemn McCarthy for his name-calling, thus pulverizing his status and reputation. When he would rise thereafter to deliver a speech, he could rely on either stony silence or a walkout. He had insulted the "Club" stalwarts—Virginia's Harry Byrd, Mississippi's John Stennis, and Georgia's Richard Russell, among others—and he was never to recover.

This "insider" thesis has not gone without challenge. A somewhat contradictory view[77] stresses the acceptance of these duties among a vast majority of the body, not merely a few old-timers. Furthermore, if there ever was a "Club," it certainly does not have the vigor of twenty years ago. The tremendous dispersion of power among individual members via the subcommittee explosion—along with the attenuation of Southern numbers—has heightened personal influence greatly. Surely no clique can dictate terms today with respect to the flow of legislation. Still, the norms abide, and seniority abides! No senator could help himself more than to have Mississippi's John Stennis or West Virginia's Robert Byrd in his corner.

The legislative flow

With both the explicit and implicit senatorial power structures on the table, I return to the progress of our hypothetical piece of legislation.

Senators introduce many fewer bills than their House counterparts, approximately 3,000 items per Congress. Again, however, it is the Administration, the prominent interest groups, and the few important lawmakers who account for the bulk of important business. I should note that legislative proposals can originate in either chamber; but most important bills are introduced *concurrently* in the two chambers by House and Senate co-sponsors, for time is of the essence. The recommendations will be assigned to committees by the presiding officer, and the substantive jurisdictions of these groups are again fairly straightforward. Generally, measures are processed first by the plethora of subcommittees, which have become the key legislative organs.

After a bill is reported out of the committee, it goes onto the Senate Calendar. There is no Private Calendar, no Union Calendar, and no traffic-cop Rules Committee. As in the House, though, a device has been provided for clearing away noncontroversial pieces. Each Monday a call of this calendar is in order, and if bills are provocative they will be passed over. Others can be dispensed with quickly.

Floor debate in the Senate is as freewheeling and flexible as House debate is turgid and truncated. First, *unlimited* discussion is permissible here. If Senator X receives recognition, he can talk, and talk, and *talk*. And he can talk on anything. Extensive discussion of legislation is a prized perquisite; senators love to call their chamber the "greatest deliberative body in the world."

But there must be some restraint, or nothing would ever be accomplished. The two floor leaders are charged with devising a schedule that meets the needs of concerned participants. The arrangements are then ratified by *unanimous-consent agreements.* For instance, the majority leader might take the floor and make the following announcement: "I ask unanimous consent to begin debate at two o'clock today on Senate Bill 2936, the Defense Appropriation Act; each side will have five hours to state its case; a vote is scheduled for four o'clock tomorrow." From a chronological standpoint such agreements could overlap very easily, because while some bills require only minimal debate, others involve a far larger segment of the membership. But, whereas the House can deal with only one proposal at a time, the Senate has ample capacity to juggle several simultaneously. Obviously, unanimous-consent motions can be shelved by just one objection, and this occasionally occurs when a member feels his prerogatives have received short shrift. But usually all arrangements have been worked out in the "cloakrooms"; and the majority leader realizes he must cater somewhat to every person. From the standpoint of power politics, one can say that each bargain represents a culmination in coalition-building by advocates and dissenters. Until one side or the other feels the time for action is ripe and has the votes to work its will, senators will keep talking. And very few of these coalitions extend beyond the particular question involved.

On rare occasions, bargains simply cannot be struck. And if a minority feels seriously threatened by the proposed legislation, it may decide on the extreme tactic of talking a measure to death. Almost everyone is familiar with the *filibuster* technique. Wayne Morse of Oregon holds the all-time record, speaking against the tidelands oil bill for more than twenty-four consecutive hours. Senators have been known to read from the Bible and even to quote Grandma's recipes while holding the floor.[78] The only way to stop a filibuster is to impose *cloture,* which requires a three-fifths vote of the entire body (sixty members). Even then, each senator is allowed half an hour to talk on the merits of the pending measure.

Invoking cloture is very difficult—the feat has been accomplished only about twenty times. Therefore, a far more practical way to stop the endless discourse is for the majority to water down its proposal. This is what filibusterers are waiting for. Indeed, a compromise can be so antiseptic that initial proponents of the bill may wind up voting *against* their own creation.

After almost every election, liberal Democrats and Republicans try to change the rule by lowering the cloture requirement to majority vote. They claim that any other margin of victory allows a minority to control the legislative process. Special attention is drawn to the Southern contingent's use of nonstop debate to veto civil rights bills. But Northerners, and liberals generally, are not above talking endlessly when it suits their purposes! Perhaps the pros and cons boil down to this: if one thinks a legislative branch should express majority will, then one would disdain unlimited discussion and look to the courts for protection of minority rights; however, if one thinks the Senate has a special—indeed unique—legislative responsibility to check the popular will as expressed in House action, unlimited debate might well seem appropriate.

Aside from the right to talk without abridgment, the most important parliamentary rule in the Senate relates to the amending process. In the lower chamber, all additions to a bill must be *germane* (that is, relevant). But in the upper chamber amendments can be completely unrelated to the bill at hand. The principle of nongermaneness is significant for two reasons. First, it is an excellent means of shortcutting a committee. If a bloc of senators wants to debate a measure on the floor, it can skirt the entire legislative circuit by offering the proposal as an amendment to any pending bill—which is yet another reason why committees are more responsive to colleague opinion in this chamber. Second, the procedure is a great way to fend off executive branch disapproval, for if the proposition is attached to an item the President cannot afford to veto (like a special appropriation statute), it becomes law. Such nongermane amendments are called "riders," and, of course, they can always be filibustered.

Suppose the House and Senate pass the same bill but in somewhat different forms? Normally, one branch will accede to the wishes of the other. However, where controversy exists, a *conference committee* must convene. This is an ad hoc group of senior congressmen from both branches, and its task is to iron out all disagreements. House conferees are named by the Speaker; Senate conferees are named by either the Vice President or the president pro tempore. To nobody's surprise, the dominant party in a chamber is given majority representation on each and every conference deputation. Only 10 percent of all enactments go to conference, but they are among the most far-reaching. On the other hand, Senate leaders have been known to place "riders" on bills solely for the purpose of having "trading chips" they can "cash in," in order to preserve what they really want.

Conference committees command considerable power, for they can even write completely new provisions into legislation if needed to achieve compromise. By tradition the bargains have been struck behind closed doors; however, in 1975, both Democratic caucuses voted to throw committee deliberations open to public scrutiny unless one of the conference delegations lodged objection. Naturally, the House and Senate went along, since the majority party had spoken. Here is another victory for openness, a further reaction against Watergate; but it remains to be seen whether any meetings dealing with sensitive subjects will reach a larger audience. A conference report is almost always accepted by both chambers, after which it finally arrives on the President's desk.

Senate-House comparisons

It will be useful, at this point, to compare the Senate, with its *individualist-egalitarianism,* and the House, with its penchant for *decentralization,* from the standpoint of legislation approved. Political party affiliation, we now know, has much the same effects in the Senate as in the House. If Democrats and Republicans divide significantly on government management issues in the House, they will divide significantly in the Senate. And if party membership means nothing in the House with respect to civil liberties, the generalization holds in the Senate. Evidently, their electoral processes embrace the same "political community."[79]

Yet the upper chamber is demonstrably more liberal than the lower chamber. John Kennedy and Lyndon Johnson found it much tougher to "get things done" in the House than in the Senate. This political fact of life seems at odds with constitutional theory: the House was designed to be more responsive to the "people's" desires; the Senate was designed to keep majorities honest.

There appear to be three interrelated reasons for this paradox. The salient factor is representation. The typical state has a more ideologically liberal constituency than the typical House district in that state, *as these districts are contrived.* Ethnicity, urbanism, percentages of blacks and Jews—all the parameters normally associated with political liberalism—make much more of a dent in the *state* of New York than in the average *district* found in New York State. It is a question of how House district lines are drawn and of keeping up with population movements. Moreover, racial and religious minorities live in concentrated areas; hence their representational opportunities are minimized.

A second factor, dependent on the first, is the internal structuring of the House. With conservative ideology overrepresented there, liberal legislation gets lost in the decentralized committee woodwork. Not only are votes on the House floor less responsive to liberal presidential pleas, then, but also reformist proposals have a much tougher time getting to the floor at all.

Finally, the larger the constituency represented, the more heterogeneous is the constituency and the more visible is the representative. In the more heterogeneous constituencies—the states themselves—*vox populi* is less apt to be parochial in orientation and more apt to be heard above the demands of one or two well-organized, well-funded parochial groups. Should senators cater disproportionately to a few special-interest demands, they can much more easily be seen and held accountable. Also, both diversity of constituency and visibility of the public servant enhance that official's opportunity to exercise independent judgment on policy matters, to lead rather than only to follow.

With respect to larger "Living Constitutional" values, the fact that the Senate is less decentralized than the House does *not* mean the upper chamber is less smitten with *delegation of power.* The awesome, unwieldy subcommittee system used there makes this point graphically. The subcommittees may be important vehicles for legislative activism through individual initiative, an important centralizing tendency. *But what the delegatory principle does is constrain policy coordination, overall planning—in short, any systematic ideological program development.* The House may be fairly conservative, and the Senate may be fairly liberal. Yet, from the standpoint of constitutional politics, they are both deeply committed to delegation of authority.

One final point on interchamber "Living Constitutionalism." Nelson Polsby posits a direct relationship between the growth of "structural institutionalization" in a legislative body and the growth of implicit norms that its members honor.[80] By increased "structural institutionalization" is meant more formal rules, greater division of labor—in other words, a proliferation of explicit roles and functions. As these patterns expand and prosper, so informal, unwritten codes of proper conduct among legislators expand and prosper.

I doubt the validity of the proposition as a general theory. Where explicit rules are adopted and achieve a degree of permanence, the results can run the gamut from much greater comity to revolution. Where implicit norms have taken hold, explicit norms are often superfluous. The House of Representatives has a much more intricate, formalized set of rules and division of labor than one finds in the Senate; yet an implicit code of rights and duties is the lifeblood of the upper chamber, not of its volatile opposite number.

Polsby further notes the increased "institutionalization" in *both* houses, and he naturally links this trend with the proliferation of such "tame virtues" as "reciprocity, courtesy and predictability."[81] In 1851 Representative Brooks stormed into the Senate and pummeled Charles Sumner with his cane until Sumner collapsed. Today such conduct would be undreamed of. Yes, indeed, we are more civil in the 1970s. But let me put forward my own hypothesis: *A legislature, or any other political forum, becomes more and more genteel to the extent that it sloughs off the challenging policy questions and parcels them out to others.* Responsibility breeds tension; congressional politics of 1851 had plenty of both. Challenging, forceful political leaders never promise their colleagues or their constituents a rose garden. I agree that increased institutionalization in Congress is rooted in the much more complicated political organism that is the United States today. But the triumph of collegial tranquillity in the Congress, I suspect, is *not* rooted in this increased institutionalization; it is another corollary to the delegation of power theorem.

I think this thesis receives vindication when we bring our analysis well into the 1970s. During the Nixon-Ford era, the Democratic Congress became a much more potent force for independent initiative than in the immediately preceding years, when Democratic Presidents called all the shots. The legislature marched against Nixonian abuses of power and Fordian passivity in the face of a faltering economy, launching Watergate investigations to overcome the former and enacting public works programs galore to overcome the latter. Should we be surprised, then, to see committee chairmen suddenly lose their jobs, committee procedures suddenly undergo revision, and party meetings suddenly become forums for heated debate? Thus do power and responsibility breed friction and innovation with respect to the prevailing rules.

The power to investigate

The House and Senate do much more than pass laws. They also exercise *nonlegislative* responsibilities, and, with respect to these, Congress's record is far more forceful than the lawmaking exploits it has generated. Indeed, as the legislative branch seeks to cope with the problems of an increasingly complex social order, and as it seeks to check an ever-proliferating executive branch, it turns more and more toward nonlegislative weapons for positive results.

I begin with Congress's power of investigation. Theoretically, legislative hearings are a tactic invoked to further statute-making authority; and, truth to tell, the vast majority of significant laws *are* predicated upon detailed findings of fact which could have come only via the investigatory process. Nonetheless, most of the politically volatile and therefore highly controversial congressional inquiries over the years have led to little or no legislation. They have obviously served other needs. What are these needs, and to what extent do they bear upon American constitutional processes?

Potentially sensitive investigations can be broken down into four convenient subdivisions:

	FEDERAL GOVERNMENT	OTHER
CIVIL LIBERTIES	Ervin Committee (Nixon tapes as incriminating evidence)	H.U.A.C. (Communist subversion)
OTHER	Walsh Committee ("Teapot Dome")	Investigations of business and labor practices

Committee inquiries can either focus on a facet of the federal government or can involve some other segment of the political system, usually private action. This distinction between power centers investigated seems basic. Also of importance is whether the search for information implicates protected individual rights.

With regard to investigations of national governmental agencies, our concern is with those bureaus housed in the executive branch.[82] Virtually the entire range of White House authority lies in departments established by law, from the highest Cabinet posts down to the local fish and game preservation offices. A Senate Finance subcommittee, then, has no qualms about calling in the Secretary of the Treasury and asking him why he has not done X, Y, and Z to fight inflation. Nor will some Armed Services subcommittee be bashful about inviting the Secretary of Defense to drop by and explain why the Russians have more ICBMs than we do. In fact, some congressional committees are specifically designed to keep an eye on administrators rather than to develop new legislation. For example, each chamber has a Government Operations Committee. The operations panels are readily distinguishable from so-called lawmaking committees, for the latter have been allotted particular subject-matter jurisdictions (for example, the Agriculture committees). It is standard procedure for a Government Operations panel to insist that department heads file reports describing how their agencies spend the funds they receive from Congress and why. Or perhaps some lower echelon officer was dismissed by a Cabinet Secretary, and the disgruntled party issues statements to the press alleging malfeasance. Again, it is usual to find a Government Operations committee or subcommittee jumping in and demanding a complete explanation. These many processes have been called Congress's *supervisory* power; they have also been called Congress's *oversight* function. But whatever the name, these "watchdog" actions are qualitatively different from lawmaking per se, and they possess many more teeth.

What limitations confine these investigations? The Senate's inquiry into the "Teapot Dome" scandals of the Harding Administration points up one noteworthy check. A select committee under the chairmanship of Montana's Thomas Walsh had been authorized to examine the whole sordid mess. One party subpoenaed by the committee refused to cooperate. The Walsh Committee, he said, was not considering any legislative proposals and was merely meddling in his private affairs by asking him questions. But the Supreme Court decided otherwise, ruling that the Committee had been charged with inquiring into the functions of a government agency created and subsidized by the legislature. Congress has a right to gather facts regarding any issue, if the subject matter is one on which legislation *could be passed.* In this case, a thorough examination of the Department of Justice might have prompted the enactment of laws restructuring the Attorney General's office. Obviously, though, the Court was laying down an important limitation on the power of Congressional oversight as well. The investigative function cannot extend to issues within the exclusive jurisdiction of either the executive or judicial branches. Such actions would intrude upon *separation of powers.* [83]

What public questions are the sole concern of the other two branches? Could a Congressional committee launch an inquiry into the Supreme Court's use of pure judicial review, call the Justices as witnesses, and ask them about their private conversations in conference? No. Recently, a House subcommittee looked into President Ford's pardon of Richard Nixon. The power to issue declarations of clemency is an executive prerogative pure and simple. What possible legislation could be passed regarding the Nixon pardon? None. And of course the President could not be compelled to present evidence in such proceedings. [84]

The relationship between the Bill of Rights and congressional oversight of executive departments is an untapped area. The political repercussions could only be deleterious, should a member of the President's official family refuse to cooperate, citing some constitutionally protected freedom. Suppose, however, Senator Ervin's investigations into the Watergate break-in had led to a court order upholding his committee's subpoena of Nixon's tapes? Could the then-President have utilized the self-incrimination rule ("I refuse to surrender the tapes on the ground they might tend to incriminate me")? Considering that the typical witness may invoke this privilege when appearing before a congressional committee, the answer would seem to be affirmative.

One might also think close ties with the chief executive's policy orbit—remember, the "political branches" are generally controlled by the same political party—would extract a degree of congressional solicitude perhaps not accorded the usual witness. Yet, there are startling exceptions which probably demonstrate the rule. I recall Senator Joseph McCarthy denouncing General Ralph Zwicker as being unfit to wear the uniform of the United States Army.[85] I also recall Senator Lowell Weicker and former presidential advisor H. R. Haldeman leering at one another with steely, unblinking eyes, as Weicker accused the entire Nixon Administration—including the witness—of corroding our constitutional order.[86] These are the incidents indelibly etched in my memory, at least when congressional investigations of alleged executive branch misdeeds make headlines or earn television coverage. That these senators had the power to investigate foreign subversion in the armed forces and illegal campaign contributions is incontestable as well as beside the point. Whether one saw Zwicker as a "Communist dupe" or Haldeman and his associates as "right-wing extremists," this sort of invective disparages the individual's personal rights, because it is entirely insensitive to his good name, reputation, and standing in the community.

Congressional inquests into the private sector very often evince sensationalist qualities as well. Again, I am not discussing the ordinary and necessary searches for data. My subject is the investigation loaded with political rhetoric and implication. A typical liberal thrust is to launch an inquiry that "shows" Wall Street or General Motors has manipulated the public. The conservatives' pet move, on the other hand, is an investigation of organized labor and an exploration of alleged "boss exploitation" of the rank-and-file member. These routines constitute what amounts to an informal "watchdog" supervision of private power influence. Congress seems to think it should keep an eye on vast centers of private economic control to ensure that the public is not damaged. Such investigations are constitutional; again, legislation *could* be passed to meet whatever noxious practices are disclosed.

The most sensitive of all investigations are those that touch on the civil liberties of private individuals. The President and his assistants have ample clout to defend their interests, while labor and management are blessed with, respectively, the votes and the money to make their desires effective. But Congress has a long-standing tradition of inquiring into the affairs of unpopular political movements, and sometimes the Bill of Rights is put to a severe test. The most ambitious (notorious?) task force specializing in these matters has been the House Un-American Activities Committee (H.U.A.C.), abolished only as recently as 1975. Whether controlled by Democrats or Republicans, this group concentrated on ferreting out alleged subversive activities by subpoenaing Communists, ex-Communists, and "Communist sympathizers" and eliciting their testimony. But the committee was no more a legislative tribunal than the Government Operations committees have been; it almost never wrote new laws.

What, then, was H.U.A.C.'s function? Foes would argue the panel specialized in character assassination; any cause considered "far left" was made the subject of investigation. Friends would argue its metier was *exposure,* to put the glare of publicity on people who use their constitutional freedoms to unhinge the Constitution. This much appears incontestable: H.U.A.C.'s machinations have been more responsible for judicial oversight of *legislative* inquiries than any other single source.

The most prominent instance has been the *Watkins* decision.[87] A former Communist Party member was willing to tell the committee everything about his connection with the organization, but he refused to detail the beliefs and actions of past associates. H.U.A.C., he said, had no sweeping authority to rummage through the private affairs of other people.

The Supreme Court agreed. The Justices said congressional committees can only ask questions *pertinent* to the particular inquiry. They also indicated that the subject matter of the investigation must be within the unit's jurisdiction as authorized by Congress. In other words, no *fishing expeditions!* If a witness thinks the interrogations have strayed off course, he can ask for an explanation of their relevance; the committee then has a responsibility to make this clear. But H.U.A.C. had done nothing of the sort. Its attitude toward the witness had been: we can ask any questions we think appropriate. Its attitude toward the witness should have been: we are studying so-and-so, which we have been given the power to do, and we are asking such-and-such questions because without that information so-and-so will remain elusive. Watkins, then, had been denied due process of law. This is *procedural* due process which requires every law to have a clear meaning. The *Watkins* case tells us every congressional inquest and the questions asked therein must also have a clear meaning and not be either vague or unstructured.

The Court has also said the First Amendment's free speech guarantee is applicable to congressional inquiries. That is, Congress not only is forbidden to pass laws which unduly limit political expression but also is forbidden to ask questions which unduly inhibit political expression. Does this mean a witness could successfully invoke the protection whenever he thought investigators were intruding into that domain? Hardly, for Congress possesses broad authority to pass laws regulating Communist activities. As the Justices have said: "The ultimate value of any society" is "the right of self-preservation," and there is considerable evidence showing Communists advocate the destruction of our polity.[88]

But the impact of free speech protection should not be undervalued here.

These probes are justified only when the investigating unit can "convincingly show a substantial relation between the information sought and a subject of . . . compelling [governmental] interest."[89] Now "Communist activities" (as opposed to speech by Communists) *are* a matter of compelling governmental concern.[90] So if an agency like H.U.A.C. can link up a witness's or an organization's behavior with these activities *in advance,* it is entitled to pose leading questions. H.U.A.C., for instance, was allowed to ask a teaching assistant at the University of Michigan if he had ever belonged to a given Communist organization. The witness had already been identified as a former member of the group, and the committee was clearly looking into Communist infiltration of educational facilities.[91] But the presumption is that free speech values are a successful bar against this sort of interrogation.

These cases are crucial because they bring legislative branch inquests within the purview of the checks and balances scheme. Congressional oversight of alleged domestic subversion, like its other "watchdog" endeavors must be seen essentially as a nonlegislative function, a vehicle for mobilizing public opinion so that the rights of the majority are not sacrificed on the altar of some insatiable, power-hungry minority. Nonetheless these boards of inquiry can also become smitten with a lust for power; they too must be supervised and constrained by rules.

The power of impeachment

Traditional studies of the American political system used to include a section on impeachment for strictly academic reasons. Everyone "knew" you could never impeach a President or a Supreme Court Justice; but thoroughness and scholarship required that something be said about the process.

Obviously, impeachment must now be taken seriously as a nonlegislative congressional weapon carrying the gravest implications for constitutional politics. To be sure, it is unlikely that another chief executive in this century will be forced from office. Rather, the Nixon impeachment inquiry must be seen as part of Congress's larger effort to reassert itself in the never-ending struggle for power among federal agencies. Like its blood brother, the "oversight" function, impeachment has done more to make Congress a viable force in that power struggle than any legislative effort it has undertaken of late.

The key question raised by this extraordinary weapon is the toughest to answer: What is an impeachable offense? Anyone who followed the Nixon debacle knows the constitutional standard: the House of Representatives impeaches and the Senate (by two-thirds vote) removes a federal official from office when "Treason, Bribery, or other high Crimes and Misdemeanors" are shown.[g] To the extent that *criminal* misbehavior is at issue, the controlling terms are "treason" and "bribery," because they are specific examples of what

[g] We have to watch out for the word "misdemeanor" in this context. Under modern legal guidelines, running a red light is a misdemeanor, but no thoughtful person thinks a President can be impeached for anything so trivial.

the Framers had in mind. In that context, the allegations clearly must involve serious breaches of the law.

The first article of impeachment that the House committee chaired by Peter Rodino approved was based on this standard. President Nixon, the panel unanimously concluded, had been involved in *obstruction of justice* by being a party to the Watergate cover-up. Entanglement in such a conspiracy surely constitutes an impeachable offense; moreover, clear and convincing evidence surely pointed to Nixon's culpability, once relevant portions of the President's tapes were publicized.

A second article concurred in by a majority of committee members is much more sticky. President Nixon, it found, should be impeached on an *abuse of power* charge. The chief executive (1) takes an oath to uphold the Constitution and (2) is charged with enforcing the law. The Rodino panel alleged Nixon had violated both strictures by attempting to obtain confidential tax information on "political enemies" from the Internal Revenue Service; authorizing the F.B.I. to conduct electronic surveillance of individuals, where no lawful purpose was at stake; establishing an extralegal unit (the "Plumbers") which performed illegal covert operations; responding dilatorily when he discovered close subordinates were involved in the Watergate break-in and cover-up; dismissing Special Prosecutor Archibald Cox. In the committee's judgment, these actions constituted repeated violations of the constitutional rights of citizens, repeated interference with the proper administration of justice, and repeated compromising of duly authorized government agencies.

Now this article did not accuse Nixon of breaking the law. It did accuse him of intruding on citizens' rights and of misusing the powers of his office. Under normal circumstances, when a person is threatened by arbitrary government authority he goes to court and demands a redress of grievances. And there are certainly ways to hale a chief executive into court; Nixon was hardly the first White House occupant to be accused of violating the Constitution and twisting the powers of his office beyond recognition.[h] Yet the House Judiciary Committee was alleging something more, a *continuous pattern of unconstitutional, unethical conduct.* The moral element in the "abuse of power" charge is fundamental.

I will illustrate. During the 1930s, the Supreme Court handed down a battery of decisions that Franklin Roosevelt and his friends considered constitutionally indefensible. But not even F.D.R. argued the Justices should be impeached, even though they had promulgated a continuous pattern of (in his eyes) unconstitutional rulings. In the opinion of the Rodino majority, Nixon had done the same thing, but unlike the Hughes Court of the 1930s, his actions were allegedly not taken in good faith. He knew (or should have known) he was doing what he had no right to do.

[h] Practically all the evidence needed to press appropriate litigation had been flushed out through pressure applied by Judge Sirica, the investigations of the Watergate grand jury, and the Supreme Court's ruling requiring the President to hand over relevant tapes.

In sum, the "abuse of power" notion appears to be grounded in a definition of misdemeanors that includes moral turpitude. The Founding Fathers may well have intended impeachment as a check against such conduct,[92] but the matter is open to great debate, and I wonder about the wisdom of presidential removal based on some vague moral standard.[93] If the chief executive is accused of unethical conduct, why not leave it up to the voters?

These inquiries into the nuances of constitutional *law,* however, must not divert us from our primary concern—constitutional *politics.* The fact is that the impeachment process is almost never activated, because the "Living Constitution" does assume public opinion—not constitutional confrontation—will determine who sits in the White House. The Rodino committee rejected articles of impeachment alleging President Nixon had improperly ordered American troops to invade Cambodia and had improperly spent public monies to enrich the worth of his real estate holdings. It considered the first accusation too partisan and too much a matter of constitutional interpretation, while it considered the second accusation too petty for such deliberations. Moreover, Nixon did resign. In a bygone era, the Stevens-Sumner Congress came within one vote of ousting Andrew Johnson, not on moral or legal grounds but solely on political grounds. We may regret that the contemporary Congress lacks the legislative commitment of those days, but at least it honors the convention shared by virtually all our leaders to refrain from pushing their destinies and theories into an abyss of constitutional psychosis, a significant implicit norm worth remembering.

The power of the purse

We must now address Congress's most potent weapon, control over taxing and spending. The intake and outflow of funds is here considered *nonlegislative* authority, even though accomplished via lawmaking. At least in theory, *control* over the purse strings is separate from and neutral of policy; no matter what substantive considerations weigh uppermost, the legislature must still find and expend dollars. In practice, policy and money are handled differently as well. When Congress passes laws, it always *authorizes* funds to foot the bill, but these measures aren't actually paid for until the particular appropriations are provided through legislation, which may or may not occur. Moreover, Congress can allocate money, but that doesn't mean it has levied the necessary taxes to avoid deficits.

Budgetary matters are central to democratic government. Madison made this point succinctly:

> This power of the purse may, in fact, be regarded as the most complete and effectual weapon with which any country can arm the *immediate representatives of the people* for obtaining a redress of every grievance and for carrying into effect every just and salutary measure [italics added].[94]

But if fiscal management is Congress's greatest instrument of power, then fiscal management also constitutes Congress's greatest failure. As such, it is a fitting anticlimax to this chapter.

Compared with the House and Senate, everyone's Aunt Minnie runs her financial affairs with a maximum of decorum and rationality. She must choose her purchases in relation to all the things she needs and in the context of the income she has available. If she miscalculates, she will have to pinch pennies until she pays for the miscalculation.

Traditionally, Congress has not worked with a master plan of fiscal policy, no *legislative budget.* Each revenue-producing measure and appropriations measure is taken up separately. Some move through the legislative process rapidly; others move at a snail's pace. Before the fiscal year runs out, all will be enacted, *maybe.* But the proposals are not geared to any overall dollar figure. There is no cooperation between relevant House and Senate committees except in the inevitable conference get-togethers. What happens is that the President, armed with facts and numbers prepared by his experts, submits *his* budget, and the Congress carves it up in its ad hoc, pragmatic, incremental way. The end product, usually, is a hope that everyone will get a just piece of the pie and the vain expectation that the taxpayers, the treasury, and the dollar itself will survive the roughhousing.

The dynamics of congressional organization have contributed to this malaise. Special attention should be focused on the House. The lower chamber has unique constitutional prerogatives in this sphere, and it guards them jealously. As a reaction against Parliament's "taxation without representation," the Founders decided that all revenue proposals must originate in the House, and upon this provision has arisen a corollary assumption entitling the more popular branch to initiate appropriations bills as well.[95] The result is that House decentralization promotes fragmented fiscal management, for the two committees involved in financial decision-making, the Appropriations Committee and the Ways and Means Committee, are totally different bodies that rarely interact.

One fact holds true for both groups: they are staffed with senior safe-seat holders who are motivated less by public policy views than by the prospect of *wielding power.*[96] Their first concern, then, is influence, not ideology. And the House wants these committees to be influential enough to stand up against presidential budgetary priorities. The larger membership also wants them to be *responsive* to the chamber as a whole, which explains why the top party leaders play important roles in selecting their personnel.[i]

But beyond this, the two committees differ greatly. The Appropriations (that is, spending) group is nothing but a holding company for twelve virtually autonomous subcommittees. These dozen preserves have honed to a fine art the emasculation of executive branch recommendations. Evidently, this strategy

[i] Remember that appointment to "exclusive" House committees is determined by much more than a pat seniority test.

predominates because (1) it is consistent with the fiscal conservatism that has traditionally pervaded the House, and (2) it epitomizes independence from presidential intimidation. The proof that the parent committee is a tight little social system lies in the customs surrounding subcommittee preeminence: each member sticks to his own subcommittee, all subcommittee recommendations are accepted by the parent committee, and so on. Finally, partisanship is deescalated because dollar amounts are too easily compromised and too hard to translate into policy choices.

The Ways and Means (that is, fund-raising) Committee, though, fights over tax shelters for the rich and tax rebates for the poor, inherently partisan issues.[j] Party orthodoxy is expected and even encouraged. Furthermore, the committee is not subordinated to an institutional apparatus; rather, personalities tend to predominate. Its chairman for many years, Wilbur Mills, was one of Capitol Hill's most powerful leaders. But Mills was no despot, and partisanship did not run amok. The committee cultivated high standards of technical competence and determined to write bills that satisfied the majority House leadership.

Under Mills's direction, this body had no subcommittees; members prided themselves on being *policy generalists,* not figure jugglers. But as all Washington-watchers realize, the venerable Arkansas legislator ran afoul of both stripper Fanne Foxe and a drinking problem; he resigned his chairmanship under fire in 1975. Ways and Means is now smitten with the bug of decentralization; it has created a batch of subcommittees for more efficient (egalitarian?) management. On the other hand, the Democratic caucus "packed" the panel with twelve new members, most of them liberals, following the 1974 elections. This should make the group more responsive to current House sentiment, which we know is atypically left of center.

If these two creatures of the House are miles apart, they are close together when contrasted with their opposite numbers in the Senate. Such gross disparities are explained by everything we know about the two chambers. Senators represent states, not districts. Because their constituencies are much more diffuse, they are under much greater pressure to perform "errand boy" service. Senators are also individualists who see one another as relative equals. This means that upper chamber Appropriations and Finance Committees[k] cannot possibly wield the influence of their House counterparts; it also means that

[j] What with delegation of legislative power being the prevailing rule, tax battles constitute Congress's bravest long-term effort to achieve meaningful policy goals. So-called tax expenditures—taxes the government chooses not to levy on income—are really indirect subsidies, and in 1975 they cost the federal treasury $88 billion. Important examples are the investment tax credit accorded to businesses purchasing new equipment, the deduction accorded to homeowners on their mortgage interest payments, and the exemption accorded to the retired for Social Security income. Note these subsidies are usually authorized on a case-by-case basis; they rarely embody a *comprehensive* package of legislative priorities.

[k] The Senate's *Finance* Committee performs the same functions as the House *Ways and Means* Committee.

these units are more accessible to the entire membership than are those counterparts.[1]

So both panels are responsive to the clientele needs of individual senators across the country. Every economic interest imaginable descends upon these upper chamber units, demanding a redress of grievances from contrary House treatment. (Does not the process dovetail with the Senate's more liberal posture?) Their pleas often receive a kindly reception, which only heightens House-Senate tensions; the Ways and Means Committee looks with disdain upon the nonprofessionalism of the Senate Finance Committee. Clearly, *inter-chamber rivalries* resulting from both differing constitutional prerogatives and differing internal folkways have made rational financial policy-making only a dream.

Congress is now trying to do something about this sorry state of its fiscal powers. In 1974 it enacted a comprehensive budget reform law, restructuring (as of 1977) the entire taxing and spending process.[97] Chiefly responsible for making the statute work are new Senate and House Budget committees. The law gives these units something the legislative branch has never before had, a *fiscal analysis capacity.* A new Congressional Budget Office equipped with top-quality staff personnel will, it is hoped, provide these committees with some countervailing power in their inevitable jousts with the executive.

In brief, the new scheme will follow these steps each fiscal year:

1. The President submits his budget to the Congress.
2. Each committee submits its budget to its chamber's Budget Committee.
3. The Congressional Budget Office sends its report to the two Budget committees.
4. These two panels formulate a *budget resolution.* The statement will contain overall target figures for revenue intake, money outflow, and debt levels. Furthermore, the resolution is supposed to designate how much money will go to defense, health, and so forth, and how much money will go to each committee of the Congress. These new bodies, then, not only deal with aggregate figures but also map out *priorities* among competing interests in both the larger political universe and in Congress itself. Naturally, this resolution must be approved by both chambers; but the policy statement does not bind the legislature, it merely *guides* the legislature.
5. All "authorization" (that is, all laws requiring the spending of money) bills are wound up.

[1] Remember, no "exclusive" committees exist in the Senate; with only a hundred members, the workload of each participant is very great; a recent headcount shows *seven* Appropriations Committee members were *chairmen* of other standing committees.

6. All appropriation bills are wound up.

7. A *budget reconciliation measure* is approved. Suppose the Congress has disregarded central features of the initial overall plan. The reconciliation process is for the purpose of ironing out differences between what Congress planned to do and what Congress actually did.

It would be hopelessly naive to think the old routines and patterns of congressional fiscal management will now wither away. The law explicitly recognizes specific waivers Congress can invoke to slow things down. Furthermore, the entire machinery is subject to the usual House and Senate maneuverings—for instance, "gag" orders from the Rules Committee and filibustering. It is anyone's guess whether the new format will stand up against the very real threat of quarrelsome committees vying for preferential financial treatment.

What prompted the legislature to rise above both its own inertia and internecine conflict to pass this law? The broad, sweeping force at work here has been the seemingly irresistible power of the President. This authority has been expanding for the past half-century, but never faster than under Lyndon Johnson and Richard Nixon, as the Vietnam War seemed to exemplify. And it was Vietnam that awoke the legislature to new possibilities for counterattack centered on its age-old control of the purse strings. When President Nixon persisted in bombing Cambodia as late as May 1973, both chambers passed a bill forbidding his use of funds for that purpose. Nixon rejected the proposal, but Congress had made its point; two days after his veto, the President announced a deadline for halting the bombing, and he kept his promise. Given the legislature's power to manage money, there is little doubt the fund cut-off was entirely constitutional, and, in the hands of a veto-proof Congress, this authority would have far more than propaganda value. The larger significance of this feud doubtless was not lost on a majority of members, who may well have seen the vast potential of fiscal responsibility as a tool for seizing at least some of the executive's policy-making initiative.

A more specific reason prompting budget reform lies at Nixon's doorstep. The Democratic-controlled Congress was outraged by his use of the *impoundment* procedure. Congress, we know, appropriates money, but is the chief executive mandated to spend it? Suppose he finds such expenditures unnecessary. Or perhaps a quick change in circumstances has made the spending fruitless. Thomas Jefferson once refused to use $50,000 appropriated by Congress for new gunboats because a "peaceful turn of events," he thought, negated their utility.[98] In fact, presidential impoundment of public monies has been employed innumerable times by many chief executives.

But Nixon used his discretion largely as a means to flout congressional authority. His impoundments were often not based on anything having to do with the particular program financed, nor were they usually based on foreign policy or defense considerations within his special realm of constitutional responsibility. For instance, Nixon refused to spend $6 billion earmarked for water pollution abatement, because he thought such appropriations were inflationary. The legislature, however, thinks it is as competent as the President to fight economic adversity. So Congress decided to strike back. And it reacted within the context of the new budget reform spirit, for how could questionable executive branch practices be restrained with full legitimacy unless the legislative branch disciplined its own inflationary tendencies?

The President's impoundment authority is now limited by precise guidelines found in the budget reform law. Should he cut total spending for fiscal policy reasons or terminate programs by refusing to spend money, his orders will be revoked automatically unless Congress affirms such steps within forty-five days of his decision. These regulations illustrate how the legislature can assert its will effectively and well within proper constitutional confines.

Conclusion

Calls to reform Congress are legion. In this section, I will compare and contrast two oft-mentioned, quite different proposals for reform and assess the implications of each.

It was Woodrow Wilson who argued most forcefully that Congress should be akin to the British Parliament and the President should be a Prime Minister. Assuming his party had a majority in both chambers, the chief executive would push his program through the legislature, relying upon the votes of an ideologically homogeneous partisan following. The party in power would be both *responsible* and *accountable;* if the people became disillusioned with its program, they could throw out its proponents.

Wilson's scheme entails revolutionary changes. Our two parties would have to undergo monumental realignment; the committee system would have to be shackled, and the seniority rule, which emphasizes longevity and predictability rather than ideological accountability, would have to go; finally, the Congress would be forced to take a back seat to the President in policy-making.

The Wilsonian notion maximizes unity of governmental purpose and effort at a time when Americans are becoming more and more tied to one another's destinies. Without doubt, the nation is getting smaller, sectional and ethnic heterogeneity are attenuating. Political problems tend to be national in scope and to require swift national action, else the entire system flounders. Wilson's approach stresses, as well, a meaningful vote by intelligent citizens on visible and comprehensible policy alternatives. Certainly the electorate is informed today as never before.

But how do you force Congress to become a rubber stamp? How do you uproot decentralization in the House? How do you turn a chamber of 435 members representing relatively homogeneous interests into a forum for ideological debate? How do you prod senators to give up their wedded bliss as individualist-equals? The seniority system, to be sure, is creaking at the hinges; but even today Congress is not ready to plunge into the internal squabbles which the selection of chairmanships on the basis of *merit* and *ideology* would involve.

A second scheme worthy of attention does not involve changing our two-party system, or even abolishing the seniority principle. Rather, it emphasizes Congress, in its role as the "friendly-enemy" of its sister "political branch," the executive, keeping that branch honest through a variety of checking devices. Congress would use its *nonlegislative* power to oversee administrative action from top to bottom. The constituent constitutional elements would be the power of the purse, the power of investigation, and the power to reshape offices and responsibilities within the executive branch when necessary. The scheme also entails a renewal of Congress's proper *legislative* role. It emphasizes policy formation; therefore, it would necessitate scrapping *rampant* delegation of power. The idea would not be to propose a comprehensive legislative package; only the chief executive, with his national constituency, need entertain such ambitions. Nor would the idea be to take "pork barrel" away from the average congressman, who feels it is his trump electoral card. The idea would be to promulgate authoritative standards where *national* legislative concerns are at stake.

At the moment, Congress is fired up against a presidency it thinks has wandered from the straight and narrow. This passion must be translated into programs which define terms, set standards, and regulate conduct.[99] If Congress thinks poverty is a *national* problem, then Congress can define poverty and select the strategic weapons for combatting it. And if Congress thinks high prices, welfare, and the power of corporations are national problems, then Congress can do likewise with them.[m] It is a question of dissolving "government by whirlpools," where interest group self-government is destructive of national community and where bureaucratic controls suffocate legislative independence. Congressmen as diverse in their militancy as Henry Clay, Robert A. Taft, and Fred Harris would have settled for no less.

Congress is to some extent a paper tiger. The question is: Which attributes of its "Living Constitution" must be reworked to meet these criticisms? If the overarching goal is speed, or unity, or efficiency, or maximizing through law the opinions of a majority, then the first of these schemes would suffice. If the overarching goal is to reestablish a reciprocal check and balance of power between the legislative and executive branches, then the second of these schemes would suffice.

[m] A "great debate" over proposed national air pollution standards, for instance, might prove enlightening. The Clean Air Act takes the daring step of delegating to the Environmental Protection Agency the power to publish a list of pollutants it thinks have an "adverse effect on public health and welfare." The E.P.A. can also institute national air quality standards based on whatever criteria are necessary to protect the public health (Public Law 91-604 [1970]). Again and again, such terms as "public welfare" and "public health" are bandied about without accompanying definitions, and then congressmen want to know why citizens don't take greater interest and pride in what they do.

NOTES

1. *McCulloch v. Maryland,* 4 Wheat. 316 at p. 405 (1819).

2. *Kansas v. Colorado,* 206 U.S. 46 at p. 89 (1907).

3. See Chapter 2, p. 42.

4. *McCulloch,* pp. 407, 415.

5. *J. W. Hampton, Jr. & Co. v. United States,* 276 U.S. 394 at p. 409 (1928).

6. *United States v. Jones,* 109 U.S. 513 (1883); *Fong Yue Ting v. United States,* 149 U.S. 698 (1893).

7. Ibid. But suppose Congress used its inherent powers in the international field to undermine the President's delegated functions—for example, the commander in chief role? Could the Supreme Court referee such disputes? Again, we shall see.

8. *United States v. Curtiss-Wright Export Corp.,* 299 U.S. 304 at p. 320 (1936).

9. The political science literature evaluating Congress's legislative exploits from a constitutional politics standpoint during these years is woefully meager. The best one can do is rummage through the good work done by historians. I have found the following to be of use: Carl B. Swisher, *American Constitutional Development* (Boston: Houghton Mifflin, 1943) is excellent for its clarity, though I think it lacks subtlety; Alfred H. Kelly and Winfred A. Harbison, *The American Constitution,* rev. ed. (New York: W. W. Norton, 1955) discusses the constitutional law nuances in a more complete fashion than does Swisher; and Eric L. McKitrick, *Andrew Johnson and Reconstruction* (Chicago: Univ. of Chicago Press, 1960), analyzes the constitutional politics of the 1866-67 period in truly outstanding fashion. Unfortunately, the McKitrick study appears to have no antebellum analogue. In any event, my approach and conclusions differ from all of these.

10. But I do not contend that the Radicals used the Constitution *only* as an instrument for rationalization. They must have *believed*—as I am sure Calhoun, Clay, Hamilton, et al. also believed—that the document sustained their basic values. But they all used their powers of reasoning to build constitutional arguments to give their deep-seated ideas about the nature of our polity added respectability.

11. I hope these comments ring a familiar note. See my remarks on this same subject in Chapter 2, p. 45.

12. This practice had been denounced by the Supreme Court even before these episodes. See *Ex Parte Milligan,* 4 Wall. 2 (1866).

13. *The Civil Rights Cases,* 109 U.S. 3 (1883).

14. *Hippolite Egg Co. v. United States,* 220 U.S. 45 (1911).

15. *Hoke v. United States,* 227 U.S. 308 (1913).

16. For example, in *McCray v. United States,* 195 U.S. 27 (1904), the Court upheld a very high tax on oleomargarine colored to resemble butter. The Justices refused to look behind the law at the rather obvious intent of Congress, restricting their inquiry to whether the tax as a tax was permissible. Most of the statutes and administrative bodies mentioned here are still alive and well. I shall discuss each in greater detail as the occasion arises.

17. *McCulloch,* at p. 421.

18. *Schechter Poultry Corp. v. United States,* 295 U.S. 495 at p. 537 (1935).

19. *United States v. Butler,* 297 U.S. 1 at p. 66 (1936).

20. *Steward Machine Co. v. Davis,* 301 U.S. 548 (1937).

21. *N.L.R.B. v. Jones and Laughlin Steel Corp.,* 301 U.S. 1 at p. 41 (1937). The great case of *United States v. Darby,* 312 U.S. 100 (1941), makes the very same point. The New Deal eventually had its way on the question of federal control over agriculture, too; in *Mulford v. Smith,* 307 U.S. 38 (1939), a new A.A.A. based on the impact of farm production upon interstate trade was upheld.

22. The following remarks owe an intellectual debt to the thesis presented in Theodore J. Lowi, *The End of Liberalism* (Chicago: W. W. Norton, 1969). For the record, I do not share Lowi's contention that contemporary liberalism is *incapable* of formulating tough

policy guidelines; see, as an example, my Chapter 6 for a discussion of the Warren Court's lucid, coercive (doctrinaire?) rules. And I certainly do not agree with Lowi that this country needs more administration from the top rather than less. But his grasp of the "delegation of power" principle as a modern-day congressional panacea is an extremely important contribution to constitutional politics.

23. Obviously, not every piece of legislation fits neatly into these categories. For example, statutes covering the internal workings of the Congress itself are hardly applicable.

24. The Smith Act was passed before we entered World War II, but the Roosevelt constitutional era had already ended. The war was at that time uppermost in our thoughts.

25. Of course, I do not mean to endorse or disendorse any of these particular statutes. The normative question is here beside the point.

26. Lowi, pp. 235-36.

27. Public Law 91-379, Title II (1970).

28. A *law* is enacted by majority vote of House and Senate, but if the President exercises the veto privilege, then a two-thirds majority in each chamber is needed to override; a *treaty* is ratified by a two-thirds vote of the Senate, with the House playing no role whatsoever; a *resolution* is merely an expression of opinion by the House, the Senate, or both. While resolutions normally do not carry the force of law, a President can be much more aggressive if he has the force of congressional opinion behind him.

29. The Supreme Court upheld the "excessive profits" criterion in *Lichter v. United States,* 334 U.S. 742 (1948).

30. Public Law 88-408 (1964).

31. And three-fifths of all the slaves in each state were also to count. Naturally, the Thirteenth Amendment, abolishing involuntary servitude, terminated this proviso.

32. Sometimes the House ignores the rule prohibiting at-large seats, though at this writing only states with a single House delegate utilize their entire jurisdictions as districts.

33. *Colegrove v. Green,* 328 U.S. 549 at pp. 553-54, 556 (1946). Actually Frankfurter's sentiments did not represent the majority position on the Court, though at the time his views were widely understood to do so. *Colegrove* is one of those strange decisions in which the Court's message was lost in translation because the Justices split into so many subgroups.

34. *Wesberry v. Sanders,* 376 U.S. 1 (1964).

35. Ibid., pp. 7-8.

36. Alfred H. Kelly, "Clio and the Court: An Illicit Love Affair," in Phillip B. Kurland, ed., *The Supreme Court Review* (Chicago: Univ. of Chicago Press, 1965), pp. 135-36.

37. Robert G. Dixon, Jr., *Democratic Representation* (New York: Oxford Univ. Press, 1968), pp. 190-92.

38. *Powell v. McCormack,* 395 U.S. 486 (1969). For a detailed account of the Powell turmoil in Congress, see P. Allen Dionisopoulos, *Rebellion, Racism, and Representation* (DeKalb: Northern Illinois Univ. Press, 1970).

39. Leonard Levy, "The Right Against Self-Incrimination: History and Judicial History," *Political Science Quarterly* 84 (1969), p. 1.

40. It boggles the mind to imagine how Thaddeus Stevens would have reacted to an analogous Supreme Court decision rendered in his day. Have we gone from an era of legislative domination to an era of judicial domination on the domestic front in one century?

41. General source materials I found helpful in preparing the following two sections are George B. Galloway, *History of the House of Representatives* (New York: Thomas Y. Crowell, 1962); Randall B. Ripley, *Party Leaders in the House of Representatives* (Washington, D.C.: Brookings Institution, 1967); and Nelson W. Polsby, "The Institutionalization of the U.S. House of Representatives," *The American Political Science Review* 62 (1968), pp. 144-68; and the many references cited in these works.

42. Exception: Harry Truman's tenure from 1947 to 1948.

43. Exception: Dwight Eisenhower's tenure from 1953 to 1954.

44. Woodrow Wilson, *Congressional Government* (Cleveland: World Publishing, 1963), p. 58.

45. N. W. Polsby, M. Gallaher, and B. S. Rundquist, "The Growth of the Seniority System in the U.S. House of Representatives," *The American Political Science Review* 63 (1969), pp. 787-807.

46. The data and analysis here given come from Raymond E. Wolfinger and Joan Heifetz, "Safe Seats, Seniority, and Power in Congress," *The American Political Science Review* 59 (1965), pp. 337-59. A note on the Republican situation. The Midwest—and especially the rural Midwest—is overrepresented among *senior* G.O.P. House leaders. However, the suburbs, where most Republicans live, are gaining as reapportionment proceeds.

47. Robert S. Erikson, "Malapportionment, Gerrymandering, and Party Fortunes in Congressional Elections," *The American Political Science Review* 66 (1972), pp. 1234-45.

48. The following remarks are based on data found in Nicholas A. Masters, "House Committee Assignments," *The American Political Science Review* 55 (1961), pp. 345-57. It remains to be seen if the Democrats' new committee recruitment procedure will work changes in these patterns.

49. Richard F. Fenno, Jr., *Congressmen in Committees* (Boston: Little, Brown, 1973), p. 1. The view that congressmen are interested essentially in obtaining reelection and that their machinations can best be understood as rational steps toward achieving this goal is set forth in David R. Mayhew, *Congress: The Electoral Connection* (New Haven: Yale Univ. Press, 1974).

50. Ibid., Ch. 1.

51. D. W. Rohde and K. A. Shepsle, "Democratic Committee Assignments in the House of Representatives: Strategic Aspects of a Social Choice Process," *The American Political Science Review* 67 (1973), pp. 889-905.

52. The "fit" between chairmanship and larger House conservatism is developed somewhat differently in Barbara Hinckley, *The Seniority System in Congress* (Bloomington: Indiana Univ. Press, 1971).

53. Mayhew, pp. 95-96.

54. See George Goodwin, Jr., "Subcommittees: The Miniature Legislatures of Congress," *The American Political Science Review* 56 (1962), pp. 596-604, and Thomas R. Wolanin, "Committee Seniority and the Choice of House Subcommittee Chairmen: 80th-91st Congresses," *The Journal of Politics* 36 (1974), pp. 687-702.

55. An exception involves the recently created House Budget Committee. It is much easier to sidestep tradition when a completely new policy is being implemented.

56. These are the shrewd observations of Rowland Evans and Robert Novak, "Something Worse Than Seniority?" *Washington Post* (January 25, 1975), p. A19.

57. But one cannot ignore the ever-increasing number of careerists in the House, for, without question, the average district is becoming *less* competitive. In other words, more and more congressmen are putting together longer and longer seniority strings. The above changes, then, may be an attempt by some frustrated old-timers to get to the pinnacles of power faster. The result could be greater *decentralization.* See Charles S. Bullock III, "House Careerists: Changing Patterns of Longevity and Attrition," *The American Political Science Review* 66 (1972), pp. 1299-1300.

58. Polsby, Gallaher, and Rundquist, p. 807.

59. For an in-depth description of the procedures and data discussed below, see Lewis A. Froman, Jr., *The Congressional Process* (Boston: Little, Brown, 1967).

60. I take up the bureaucracy's contribution to this three-cornered exercise in Chapter 7, and I discuss pressure group participation as well as pressure group influence on Congress through the electoral process, lobbying, and so on, in Chapter 9.

61. James Robinson, *The House Rules Committee* (Indianapolis: Bobbs-Merrill, 1963).

62. See Gary Orfield, *Congressional Power: Congress and Social Change* (New York: Harcourt Brace Jovanovich, 1975), pp. 233-35.

63. Julius Turner, *Party and Constituency* (Baltimore: Johns Hopkins Press, 1951);

Duncan MacRae, Jr., *Dimensions of Congressional Voting* (Berkeley: Univ. of California Press, 1958).

64. Aage R. Clausen, *How Congressmen Decide* (New York: St. Martin's Press, 1973). It is worth noting, however, that the opinions of fellow House members to whom congressmen feel kinship are probably the best barometers of how they will vote in particular cases. John W. Kingdon, *Congressmen's Voting Decisions* (New York: Harper & Row, 1973), p. 22. As in most human situations, the social factor tells much of the story; but one cannot base predictions on personal networks not yet formed.

65. Mayhew, p. 103.

66. Warren E. Miller and Donald E. Stokes, "Constituency Influence in Congress," *The American Political Science Review* 57 (1963), pp. 45-56.

67. General source books used in preparing this segment are Lewis A. Froman, Jr., *The Congressional Process* (Boston: Little, Brown, 1967) and Randall B. Ripley, *Power in the Senate* (New York: St. Martin's Press, 1969).

68. Of course, the Senate has had its share of power struggles, reform movements, and reorganizational schemes, but these conflicts have lacked the hills and valleys characterizing comparable shifts in the House. To that extent, I think it unnecessary to keep as sharp a lookout for historical development and precedent in discussing upper chamber politics.

69. David J. Vogler, *The Politics of Congress* (Boston: Allyn and Bacon, 1974), pp. 105-06.

70. Ralph K. Huitt, "Democratic Party Leadership in the Senate," *The American Political Science Review* 55 (1961), pp. 333-44.

71. These data are in Ripley, *Power in the Senate,* pp. 61-62.

72. Ripley, *Power in the Senate,* pp. 62-66; Ripley, *Congress: Process and Policy* (New York: W. W. Norton, 1975), p. 100.

73. This section is based on my understanding of Donald R. Mathews, "The Folkways of the United States Senate: Conformity to Group Norms and Legislative Effectiveness," *The American Political Science Review* 53 (1959), pp. 1064-89, and William S. White, *Citadel* (New York: Harper, 1956). Compare R. K. Huitt, "The Outsider in the Senate: An Alternative Role," *The American Political Science Review* 55 (1961), pp. 566-75.

74. The Constitution gives congressmen an absolute defense against libel suits for anything they say in floor debates or speeches. This privilege accords them a chance to probe and argue without hesitation, but in the hands of an unscrupulous person it is a license to commit character assassination.

75. *Congressional Record,* vol. 100, part 12 (1954), p. 15857.

76. Ibid., p. 15953.

77. Nelson W. Polsby, *Congress and the Presidency,* 3rd ed. (Englewood Cliffs, N.J.: Prentice-Hall, 1976), pp. 75-92.

78. The most famous filibuster may be Bob Hope's performance in a movie called "The Louisiana Purchase." I seem to recall him down on his knees, praying for divine assistance. The Huey Longs and Strom Thurmonds were not far behind him for melodramatic impact.

79. Clausen, p. 94.

80. Polsby, "The Institutionalization of the U.S. House," pp. 166-67.

81. Ibid., p. 167.

82. Investigations of the "independent regulatory agencies" are discussed in Chapter 7. The constitutional questions raised by such inquiries have not been so compelling, and these inquests rarely bristle with controversy.

83. *McGrain v. Daugherty,* 273 U.S. 135 (1927).

84. These remarks do not extend to Congress's impeachment responsibilities, which I will discuss presently.

85. *Congressional Record,* vol. 100, part 12 (1954), p. 15869.

86. *Hearings before the Select Committee on Presidential Campaign Activities,* 93rd Cong., 1st Sess., pp. 3128-32. And see also a tape of that telecast, for which there is no substitute. One must remember that Haldeman had not yet been tried for, much less convicted of, any crime.

87. *Watkins v. United States,* 354 U.S. 178 (1957).

88. *Barenblatt v. United States,* 360 U.S. 109 at pp. 127–28 (1959). See also *Dennis v. United States,* 341 U.S. 494 at p. 507 (1951).

89. *Gibson v. Florida Investigation Committee,* 372 U.S. 539 at p. 546 (1963).

90. Ibid., at p. 551. The *Gibson* decision involved an inquest by Florida officials, not federal personnel, but from the standpoint of free speech protection this can hardly make a difference.

91. *Barenblatt v. United States.*

92. The most thorough investigation of the impeachment process is Raoul Berger, *Impeachment: The Constitutional Problems* (Cambridge, Mass.: Harvard Univ. Press, 1973). He thinks the Framers would have approved the impeachment and conviction of a President on grounds broader than whether the incumbent had breached criminal legal standards. The evidence tends to support his conclusion.

93. After President Ford pardoned Nixon, there was talk that Ford would go on and give clemency to all other Watergate suspects yet untried. I recall Carl Albert, then Speaker of the House, remarking that such an action might be construed as an abuse of power. (*Congressional Quarterly Weekly Report* [September 14, 1974], p. 2457.) Meaning what? That Ford would then have committed immoral deeds? That Ford would then have violated repeatedly his constitutional oath? That Ford would then be subject to impeachment? New constitutional theories certainly have their place, so long as we know what they involve when we create them.

94. James Madison, *The Federalist,* No. 58.

95. Madison thought that this power to commence tax measures would accomplish nothing. His prediction was not a good one, for relevant House committees are far more powerful than their senatorial counterparts, in part because of this constitutional entering wedge.

96. Comments in this section concerning the two Appropriations committees are based on Richard F. Fenno, Jr., *The Power of the Purse* (Boston: Little, Brown, 1966). Observations concerning congressional revenue committees are based on John Manley, *The Politics of Finance* (Boston: Little, Brown, 1970). Also of great help to me in integrating these materials was Fenno's *Congressmen in Committees* (Boston: Little, Brown, 1973).

97. Public Law 93-344 (1974).

98. As quoted in *Congressional Quarterly Almanac* (1973), p. 253.

99. Of course, the Supreme Court might disagree with the legislative branch's interpretations of its own constitutional prerogatives. That is a different question. And, certainly, the voters might disagree with Congress as to both the nature of national action and the prudence of the rules prescribed. But what we have now is national concern, national power, and precious few norms or guidelines that express meaningful, comprehensible national policy.

5
the president: constitutional superstar?

Each power center and each procedural norm in the federal government's machinery possesses unique features, characteristics conveying the distinctive role of that institution or rule both in theory and practice. What are the peculiar traits of structure and function that distinguish the American presidency and its responsibilities? To what extent does the White House's contemporary posture in the constitutional system strengthen or weaken the dispensation of executive power?

The more one reviews both relevant history and relevant theory, the more one must be struck by two constants pervading any analysis of the presidential role. They are so basic that it is easy to underplay them. The first is that the American chief executive is *a person alone.* Certainly the President is surrounded by an official family of advisors, Secretaries, briefcase carriers, and even "court jesters." But when it comes to the big decisions that pass over his desk, he must take full responsibility, for he has no peers. Sociological theory may be an essential element in studying House, Senate, and Supreme Court policy-making, but psychological theory and historical analysis emphasizing the impact of "great men" are the proper staples for describing and evaluating the leader who must stand apart.

The second constant is that the President possesses enormous *power*—he is armed with the terrible weapons of brute force. The Constitution entrusts chief executives with the power to *command,* to *execute,* to *veto.* The "Living Constitution," we shall see, entrusts them with the power to protect both *law and order* and *national security.* Moreover, it vests them with more subtle species of power: a capacity to propose far-reaching policy initiatives; a capacity to sell these initiatives to an entire nation of constituents waiting to be led by "their President"; a capacity to influence, cajole, sometimes even twist the arms of lawmakers in order to achieve success for their objectives. Finally, both the Constitution and the "Living Constitution" give them extraordinary power to deal with crisis situations of all shapes and descriptions.

Those Presidents who have excelled in the dynamics of coercion and persuasion have withstood the test of history. But there are constraints on this power. In great measure, the following presentation attempts to describe the prerogatives of our "constitutional superstar," analyze the many checks contrived to hold him in balance, and evaluate the sufficiency of those checks.

The "war power": Lincoln style

If ever the President is given a free hand to conduct his business, that situation arises when the nation is plunged into war. In one of its infrequent commentaries on the relevance of constitutional standards to battlefield conditions, the Supreme Court has said: "The war power . . . is a power to wage war successfully. . . ."[1] As usual, however, this kind of flat assertion raises more questions than it resolves. Who wages war, the President or Congress? During wartime, are there *no* limits to what the "political branches" can demand from an obedient citizenry? Finally, and most basic of all, when is a war really a war?

To begin with, the Constitution does *not* give the chief executive any "war power" per se. It is Congress that has authority to "declare War," "raise and support Armies," "provide and maintain a Navy," and call out the militia in order to "suppress Insurrections and repel Invasions." But the Constitution does say the President is *commander in chief,* and this power ranges over the entire spectrum of strategic and tactical military operations.

President Truman's embroilment with General Douglas MacArthur is a classic case in point. World War II hero MacArthur had held a series of news conferences while serving as supreme commander of American forces fighting in Korea, at which he advocated a far more vigorous prosecution of the conflict than Truman endorsed. The chief executive finally was forced to dismiss him, in part because of their irreconcilable differences and in part because of these public displays, thus emphasizing once again that civilian control over military affairs is a salient constitutional norm and that it is the President's job to implement this concept in the field.

To illustrate further the scope of the President's authority: the legislature, as long ago as 1795, delegated him power to mobilize the militia whenever an invasion had occurred or constituted an imminent threat.[2] The chief executive, after all, is the one person who can move swiftly when emergency conditions arise: Congress is too unwieldy a body to make decisions rapidly. But suppose his assessment of the circumstances is ill-advised? Suppose he mobilizes an army and there is no crisis? Will the courts interfere? No, this incendiary power lies in his hands exclusively. Congress has reposed its trust in the commander in chief; an abuse of such discretion can be met only by legislative oversight and voter reaction.[3]

In contemporary times the President's role as chief military officer has gone far beyond battlefield command. This broad conception gained respectability with Abraham Lincoln and his reaction to Confederate secession.[4] Lincoln, as we all know, is considered one of the great Presidents, but it is our task to examine his sweeping notion of executive power with objectivity and not yield an inch to the forces of mythology.

Shortly after the Confederate bombardment of Fort Sumter, Lincoln ordered a blockade of all Southern ports, and to this end the Union navy began capturing neutral ships and cargoes. A blockade is an act of war, a step taken by one sovereign nation against another. We must therefore ask: (1) How could the President commit the United States to war when Congress had not declared war? (2) How could the President take warlike action, while at the same time alleging the Confederacy was merely a group of rebels and not a nation-state?

The Supreme Court tried hard to justify Lincoln's initiative.[5] The chief executive, it said, possessed inherent power to meet military might with military might. Full-scale hostilities had broken out, and Congress was not required to formalize the conflict with a name. While the legislature lacked authority to declare war against a group of states, the South had become so strong that Lincoln was compelled to employ all the techniques of international combat. However, the sharp dissent submitted by four Justices is difficult to discredit. They thought the chief executive can meet insurrections by using only traditional commander in chief powers; he cannot take Congress's authority for his own, thus turning a rebellion into a war with all of the ensuing policy consequences of such action.

History's verdict has been to look with sympathy upon Lincoln's plight: he was faced with an almost impossible dilemma; moreover, the Framers were hard-nosed pragmatists who would have endorsed his efforts to keep the nation together.[6] But this view accords enormous powers of peacekeeping and warmaking to *one* official. A thousand years may go by before a state again tries to secede, but buried beneath the above litigation is that largest of questions I framed earlier: When is a war really a war? Some notable commentators have criticized the Court's judgment with just this thought in mind. They think a decision to "go all the way" should be made by a collegial political chamber, the Congress,[7] indulging in whatever debate time permits.

Actually, Lincoln's conception of his "war power" went well beyond the commander in chief provision. He also relied heavily upon the oath Presidents must take under the Constitution when inaugurated: "I do solemnly swear [or affirm] that I will faithfully execute the Office of President of the United States, and . . . preserve, protect and defend the Constitution. . . ." How, Lincoln reflected, can I honor this commitment unless every remedy to save the nation is exhausted? And so: "I felt that measures, otherwise unconstitutional, might become lawful" when national integrity lay in the balance, for without a country there could be no constitution.[8] Hence, Lincoln issued the Emancipation

Proclamation, an executive order freeing all slaves in the border states. The male segment, 130,000 strong, could then be added to the Union military machine. Under normal conditions, a presidential (or congressional) taking of private property without compensation was constitutionally indefensible;[9] but, in time of civil strife, Lincoln thought it an entirely appropriate aid to extinguishing Confederate hopes.

Most readers are familiar with the expression: "You can't break the law to enforce the law." Lincoln could hardly be accused of such antics here. His actions were not intended to implement any law, whether statutory, constitutional, or moral. They were justified only as an indispensable means to preserve the United States.

Lincoln also instituted *martial law* in those Union-dominated areas where Confederate sympathies were running high, using his commander in chief prerogative as a building block. Martial law is the displacement of civilian rule by military authority. Arrests are made by armed forces personnel; trials are held in court-martial proceedings. There is no indictment by grand jury and no hearing before a jury of one's peers. Furthermore, Lincoln suspended the *writ of habeas corpus,* an action never before taken by federal officials. Under the Constitution, judges must grant such a writ and release an accused person unless proper legal grounds for detention are set forward. A habeas corpus remedy, then, forbids the state from holding citizens incommunicado. However, the document, pragmatic instrument that it is, allows this "Great Writ" to be set aside should the "public safety" warrant. Congress clearly could issue the necessary directive. But that the chief executive could institute a massive system for the detention of suspected Confederates took this country to the brink of a police state.

These extraordinary acts were reviewed by the Supreme Court in the *Milligan* controversy.[10] Plaintiff was a civilian arrested by military personnel in Indiana, on charges of treason and sedition. A commission of army officers pronounced him guilty and sentenced him to death. By unanimous vote, the Justices found this entire process unconstitutional. The judicial power lies in courts created by the Congress, their opinion began, and the legislative had never created these military tribunals. The President had unceremoniously and arbitrarily wiped out the civilian court system and replaced it with courts of his own making. If Indiana were a battlefield, where judges and juries could not serve in detached decorum, then the commander in chief's discretion would necessarily predominate. But "martial law cannot arise from a *threatened* invasion. The necessity must be actual and present; the invasion real. . . ."[11] In the Justices' view, Lincoln had abolished due process of law in one clean stroke—indeed, breaking the law to enforce the law.

Had the Court stopped here, *Milligan* would be hailed as a monument to the libertarian credo. A five-man majority went much further, however. Answering a question that had never been asked, they said Congress itself could not have done what Lincoln had done. Supplanting the judicial process and substituting military rule was *absolutely* impermissible no matter how serious the threat! Of course, the Justices could afford to indulge such sentiments because the Civil War had ended, and the nation was no longer teetering on the ropes. However, we have already seen that when the question finally was asked, in the *McCardle* case (see p. 35), the Court pulled in its horns and refused to apply the full thrust of *Milligan* absolutism to a real live military regime bristling with political and emotional intensity—that is, to the Radical Republicans' exercise in constitutional authoritarianism.

With respect to Lincoln's habeas corpus suspension, the Court really never tendered a definitive ruling. Writing on his own, Chief Justice Taney felt the order invalid without question. I have already recounted how he demanded the release of one Merryman, only to see his opinion ignored by the commanding general of Fort McHenry (see p. 44). Two great constitutional scholars—Corwin and Randall—think the legitimacy of Lincoln's blanket policy an "open question,"[12] but a suspension of the writ where military hostilities pervade the scene seems to me to be a "necessary and proper" means of implementing executive control over the armed services.

Lincoln came to office with the nation split, his predecessors in the White House having been largely responsible for allowing insurrectionist ideology to assume the gigantic proportions of nation-state identity. He met the greatest crisis in our history by constructing—in theory and action—the most fearsome conception of executive authority yet seen. That he achieved success for his aims is beyond doubt; and these aims can hardly be challenged even in retrospect.

But there is a line of thought and behavior in Lincoln's approach that remains open, at the least, to great debate. Yes, the Emancipation Proclamation was probably constitutional. Yes, the blanket suspension of the habeas corpus guarantee was administered with reasonableness, because Lincoln was a man of real compassion and understanding.[13] Still, Lincoln seemed oblivious to the checks and balances spirit ingrained in the Constitution. For him, Congress had no useful role to play in adjusting the document to the unique conditions of wartime, although, without doubt, there was ample time to debate and adopt legislation imposing both martial law and habeas corpus suspension upon communities well removed from the fray. In short, my feeling is that he overreacted. Lincoln, though he cannot be blamed for Radical Reconstruction, created a mood—an air of legitimacy—for the use of unilateral political power, which was seized upon and distorted by men far less visionary than he. And it is precisely when the chips are down that power must be shared and the spirit of balance in the Constitution lived up to, else one might wonder if the political apparatus really were a living organism!

The "war power": Roosevelt style

On December 7, 1941, "a date which will live in infamy,"[14] the Japanese air force launched a sneak attack on Pearl Harbor, Hawaii, destroying virtually the entire Pacific fleet. The United States has never stood closer to the brink of destruction than at that moment. Within a week, Congress had declared war against all the Axis powers—Japan, Germany, and Italy. The man who would lead the ensuing great effort in national unity had already attained unprecedented popularity as a chief executive in this century; on three occasions the voters had sent Franklin Delano Roosevelt to the White House by overwhelming majorities. For making war on the Depression he was revered by millions. But now, with the nation under attack from both Japan and Germany, he was given carte blanche.

In the days following Pearl Harbor, many people believed the Hawaiian Islands would shortly be invaded. Undoubtedly the governor of the territory must have thought so too, for one day later he imposed martial law and suspended the writ of habeas corpus. In fact, the entire governmental structure—legislative, executive, and judicial—was turned over to the commanding general of the armed forces stationed on the islands.

Under what authority were such drastic measures taken? Hawaii, at that time, was federal property, and Congress, remember, has the power to pass laws regulating territorial possessions. In this instance, there actually was a statute giving the governor discretion to promulgate martial-law orders when he considered the danger of invasion to be real and when the public safety required such action. Now the governor of a territory is a *presidential* appointee, and, of course, the commanding general owed his allegiance to the chief executive. As a matter of fact, Roosevelt himself approved the gubernatorial proclamation. These details demonstrate that what transpired constituted official policy by the executive branch—backed up by legislative direction—to bring about military rule in the Lincoln manner.

In 1946, the Supreme Court found these regulations illegal as applied to a man convicted for disorderly conduct in public. The incident occurred early in 1944, two years after Pearl Harbor; yet the criminal trial was a court-martial proceeding, and defendant's right to habeas corpus relief was disallowed as well. A majority on the bench could not believe that Congress had vested executive officials with power to close the civilian courts for days—not to mention years—on end. Constitutional rule, it said, was the very antithesis of military rule; martial law, as the executive branch had employed the term, could be adopted only in battlefield conditions. Until a time when the courts were unable to fulfill their obligations, the "public safety" was not so endangered as to sustain the uprooting of civil justice.[15] This decision, then, jibes with the Civil War *Milligan* case (see p. 173). Once again, the Court denounced executive attempts to close down federal judicial tribunals fully capable of conducting business as usual. And the Justices also intimated that if *Congress had given such authority to the commander in chief in so many words,* such a law would have been unconstitutional.

The stage is now set for a discussion of President Roosevelt's most controversial wartime policy, the ostracizing of Japanese-Americans. Although no military hostilities had touched the continental United States, in California the sound of alarm quickly reached high intensity, as long-standing prejudice against Oriental ethnics was ready-made fuel for the fire. To military officials, the situation also seemed volatile: thousands of Japanese were living in little enclaves; some were aliens, some were American citizens, and some held dual citizenship (were citizens of both Japan and the United States); there was simply no time to distinguish those whose sympathies lay with the emperor of Japan from those whose devotion to the United States was unimpeachable.

Responding to these grave conditions, the President issued an order in February 1942 giving generals of the army power to establish military districts where necessary and to exclude security risks therefrom. Shortly afterward, the generals classified the entire West Coast—from the ocean to forty miles inland—as a defense area, and they ordered all persons of Japanese extraction living in the area to be in their homes every evening from 8 P.M. to 6 A.M. With full knowledge of this proclamation, Congress passed a law making it illegal for anyone to violate military orders issued in the light of F.D.R.'s policy declaration.

The Supreme Court upheld this curfew unanimously. No one doubted that the "political branches," acting together, could keep civilians away from so-called sensitive areas in time of war. But could an exclusion order be made binding only upon one single group identified strictly on the basis of national origin? Given the threat of invasion, the Justices said, those responsible for the nation's security could reasonably take account of the danger posed by people whose first loyalties might belong with the enemy. These residents—even if citizens of the United States—stood apart, because the United States was at war with Japan, not some hypothetical foe.[16]

Provocative as the Court's curfew holding may have been, it merely prepares us for the harshest, most naked use of the "war power" ever seen in this country. In May 1942, the commanding general for the West Coast military zone ordered all 112,000 residents of Japanese ethnic stock out of the area. These people, 70,000 of whom held American citizenship, were moved to "war relocation centers" in the Rocky Mountain states. Applicants were permitted to leave these compounds only when they had obtained both a job and a place to live in an area certified by the supervising government officials. Naturally, violation of the expulsion and detention orders was subject to the criminal penalties Congress had earlier devised.

Korematsu, an American citizen of Japanese heritage, was arrested for refusing to leave his home. He was found guilty and appealed to the Supreme Court. The Justices split 6-3, but the majority upheld the rules under challenge.[17] In an opinion by Mr. Justice Hugo Black, the Court agreed that the exclusion order in question was a much more serious interference with individual rights than a curfew. Yet the military had ample reason to believe the public safety posed an imminent threat, and the ejection remedy bore a definite relationship to preventing sabotage and other illegal activity. As for Korematsu's claim that the threat of invasion had passed, Justice Black thought all doubts should be resolved in favor of the military and civilian officials, authorities who felt there was no adequate way to ascertain the loyalties of such a large group with any degree of efficiency and speed. To sum up, I can only quote Black himself:

> Korematsu was not excluded from the Military Area because of . . . his race. He *was* excluded because we are at war with the Japanese Empire, because the properly constituted military authorities feared an invasion of our West Coast and felt constrained to take proper security measures, because they decided that the military urgency of the situation demanded that all citizens of Japanese ancestry be segregated from the West Coast temporarily, and finally, because Congress, reposing its confidence in this time of war in our military leaders—as inevitably it must—determined that they should have the power to do just this.[18]

The issue of confinement in detention camps was never faced directly. Still, one cannot doubt the Court's response. Incarceration with the intent of isolating loyal from disloyal Japanese-Americans would almost surely have been validated. However, the Justices did strike down the custody of admittedly patriotic citizens who were unable to meet the criteria of job, home, and satisfactory geographic location required under the regulations. Once loyalty had been ascertained the Court said, these citizens could no longer be detained.[19]

What sense can be made of all this? In the Hawaiian episode, Congress had given the governor of a federal territory the right to impose martial law under emergency conditions. Yet, as the Court saw things, this only allowed him to mobilize military resources "for the maintenance of an orderly civil government and for the defense of the Islands against actual or threatened . . . invasion [and] was not intended to authorize the supplanting of courts by military tribunals."[20] In the *Milligan* situation, moreover, the Court had castigated any curtailment of the judicial process by President or Congress unless violence required such action. But there was no violence in California in 1942. Furthermore, neither martial law nor habeas corpus suspension—both of which would have affected the *entire* public—was considered necessary to maintain order in California in 1942. "All" it had taken to handle the problem in that state was the forced curfew, evacuation, and segregated detention of *every* member of *one* ethnic group and nobody else. To be sure, these "suspects" were given due process of law in trials before civilian judges and juries when the occasion arose. But where was individual freedom more constricted: Indiana in 1861? Hawaii in 1942? California in 1942? And if the answer is the Japanese cases, how can one explain the paradox in judicial response?

We know that the President has his "war power" and the Congress has its "war power." In the litigation involving the rights of Japanese-Americans, the Supreme Court was confronted with the two *together,* conjoined in policy affirmation. The President was pushing his commander in chief role to the fullest, while Congress was pushing its power over the declaration of war to the fullest. The Supreme Court simply could not stand against this kind of juggernaut, so, in effect, it adopted a kind of implied "political questions" posture. On the other hand, Lincoln's and Roosevelt's court-closing policies had not received congressional approval; they were much more susceptible, then, to judicial rebuff. And one final difference—pragmatic in nature—must be emphasized. When the Japanese cases were decided, the war was still going on; when the other decisions were rendered, the guns had long since been holstered.[21]

A fair assessment of Roosevelt the commander in chief is as difficult to frame as is one of Lincoln the commander in chief. For instance, his exclusion and detention of Japanese-American citizens is roundly condemned by scholars generally.[22] If only the constitutional politics of international warfare were so nice and neat. Unfortunately, people die in wars, and property is demolished. And Pearl Harbor, taken in conjunction with the Nazi onslaught, certainly looked like the brink of absolute disaster. I personally feel very uncomfortable defending the policy of forced evacuation, but I feel even more uncomfortable with post hoc textbook recriminations. If Roosevelt—whom many consider a great President—blundered here, it may well have been because, like Lincoln and other "greats," he overreacted to events and consequently failed to share meaningful power with Congress. Remember, the legislative branch's sole contribution was to make illegal acts done in violation of an executive edict. Congress's obsequious reponse may have been constitutional, given the emergency conditions, but presidential power need not transcend measured legislative checks even in wartime.

The "war power": President versus Congress

Throughout my presentation of the President's role as commander in chief, the shadow of Congress has lurked in the background. It is surely naive to pursue a discussion of contemporary presidential war power until countervailing legislative weapons are demarcated. When we talk about the authority to declare war and to provide for armies and navies, we are only scratching the surface of Congress's war power. The legislative branch can do—and has done—much more.

The classic instance, which will forever spark controversy, is the authority to provide for conscription. The traditional argument is that if Congress can create an army, it can coerce citizens to fight in the trenches and barricades. To allegations that conscription is a form of involuntary servitude, the standard and prevailing answer has always been: one owes a duty to the state to take up arms when the need arises, and "need" in a democracy is a matter for legislative determination.[23]

During World War II Congress enacted a whole battery of laws regulating the national economy in drastic, unprecedented ways. Food was rationed so that an individual could buy only a given portion of meat per month, while prices and rents were fixed across the board. The war power rationale underlying these statutes was never contested seriously; if soldiers are dying in combat, surely those on the home front can be compelled to make lesser sacrifices.

Furthermore, Congress's war power is a proper basis for broadening the authority delegated to administrative officials; thus, giving the Office of Price Administration power to fix prices under a set of standards approaching N.I.R.A. open-endedness was upheld, in part because of the ongoing emergency.[24]

When war ends, does the war power abate? Could Congress have said in 1948: "The war may be over, but the strife caused by war is still with us; therefore, emergency legislation must be enacted"? This is no hypothetical situation, for the Supreme Court upheld a rent control law passed in that very year as a response to the housing shortage caused by demobilization. Congress's war power extends to alleviating social problems caused by war and includes returning the nation to peacetime equilibrium.[25] So this war power may last well beyond a cessation of hostilities. But how far beyond? The courts have never hazarded an answer; it would be no mean feat for judges to speculate successfully on when the problems of war lie behind us. The point is that Congress has almost unlimited range in implementing its war power capacity, and this discretion should be sufficient to shackle any overzealous chief executive.

This principle is displayed graphically by a study of the famous *Steel Seizure Case.*[26] With American troops fighting by the thousands in Korea, negotiations for higher pay between steel manufacturers and their employees ground to a stalemate. And the workers faced with the decision to give up or strike, chose the latter.

Consider President Truman's plight at that moment. North Korea had attacked South Korea, a country where American soldiers were then stationed. Truman, as commander in chief, had decided to stand and fight. He had received full backing from the United Nations, and, under his leadership, this country was converted to quasi-wartime status. Congress had not declared war, but it had made no effort to stand in the President's way either. And now a nationwide steel strike threatened to cut off the flow of munitions and weapons to the troops.

Essentially two courses of action presented themselves to Truman. The first was to invoke the Taft-Hartley Act, passed by Congress in 1947. This statute gives the courts power to issue injunctions against strikes when the President can show that irreparable damage to the national health or safety is threatened. Under the law, an injunction triggers an eighty-day "cooling off" period, during which labor-management negotiation must be resumed. A second possibility was for the President to act on his own constitutional authority. That is, as commander in chief, charged with supervising American military commitments, perhaps he could order a halt to the strike.

Truman, acting with the requisite dispatch, resolved to take the second road; he issued an order *seizing the steel mills.* Until such time as employers and employees could work out an agreement, the United States would in effect operate these plants. But Truman went one step further; he immediately reported his action to Congress, saying, in essence: "You have supported my actions in Korea by passing various laws (the draft, a price stabilization program) and my order keeping the flow of steel unobstructed is an attempt to implement the policy we have formulated."[a]

Truman's interpretation of legislative-executive responsibilities was not without its problems, however. In deliberating the Taft-Hartley proposal, Congress had considered giving the President a property-seizure option, but, in the end, had expressly rejected that alternative. To this extent, Truman was doing precisely what the legislature said he could not do. Why, then, did the chief executive ignore the Taft-Hartley approach? Here is where constitutional law becomes constitutional *politics* with a vengeance. Organized labor had fought the Taft-Hartley measure with all its might, fearing the law would impede unduly its right to strike. Consequently Truman, a liberal Democrat, had vetoed the bill, though a Republican Congress had overridden his action. So the President ignored Taft-Hartley because he did not feel its method for handling these disputes was in the public interest. But the chief executive had already lost that battle in the marketplace of the legislative process, so, in effect he was carrying the strife of partisanship over into the realm of law enforcement.

Needless to say, the steel manufacturers were incensed at the President's action. They brought suit against the Secretary of Commerce, the official Truman had designated to carry out his order.[b]

In a notable decision, the Supreme Court eventually upheld the steel owners. Unfortunately, the majority opinion prepared by Hugo Black hardly does justice to the constitutional nuances of this litigation.[27] His approach is shot through with "either-or," black or white statements in an area full of gray shadings. Black found that the President's commander in chief role gave him no authority to seize these mills, because the chief executive's formidable policy weapons in the "theater of war" do not extend to the domestic manufacture of war materials. Only Congress, not the military establishment, could approve a temporary confiscation of private property. Nor could Truman's action be justified as a faithful execution of the laws. The President had made his own policy, for Congress never expressly approved—in fact, it had rejected—the steps taken here. So Truman was *making law,* a clear violation of separation of powers doctrine, for under our system, Black said, *all* legislative authority belongs to Congress.

Several other Justices, in concurring opinions,[28] did a better job of probing the intricacies presented in this case. They avoided neat, artificial distinctions between "theater of war" and "theater of peace" or between "legislative power" and "executive power." The President, in time of armed conflict, does have inherent power to protect the nation from military embarrassment. *Had*

[a] He also welcomed additional legislation from Congress, which, he conceded, would supersede his order, but Congress never took any action as a result of the President's communique.

[b] This step is worth more than passing attention. In my discussion of impeachment (p. 157), I said allegedly unconstitutional acts by the executive could be challenged in court, generally by suing the President's aides. Here is a good example of the technique.

Congress remained silent, the chief executive, though he does not have a blank check, could have employed reasonable, prudent weapons of coercion (such as seizing these factories) to protect the nation's integrity. The fatal flaw in Truman's response, then, was that he acted *contrary to established law.*

The *Steel Seizure Case* has many lessons to teach. A majority on the Court agreed there is a residual executive war power, which may extend *even to the home front* when the occasion warrants. That doctrine is far more flexible than the Court's dicta in the Civil War and Hawaii martial-law cases, where the Justices even talked about *congressional* power as helpless unless actual conflagration engulfed the affected precincts. But, the Justices also agreed, the legislative war power has greater scope than the executive war power. When Congress applies that power to subjects properly within its "delegated or implied" jurisdiction, the President must yield. Even in the present controversy, in which Congress took no initiative whatsoever, constitutional forces were at work to keep the presidency within lawfully prescribed bounds. Obviously, legislative capacity in this delicate area would be much greater if Congress itself became involved rather than letting the Court fight its battles.

This lesson in constitutional politics—like so many other lessons worth remembering—finally came home to roost with the Vietnam War. Unlike the legislative vacuum surrounding our participation in the Korean conflict, Congress at least had enacted the Gulf of Tonkin Resolution to sustain presidential intervention in Southeast Asia.[29] I have already described how Congress's uneasiness over the unending struggle led it to attempt pursestring constrains on executive management of the conflict. Antiwar sentiment moved the legislators to repeal the Gulf of Tonkin declaration itself in 1970. But, of course, this reversal did not end our involvement in the fray, and from the results of the Nixon-McGovern election, it seems clear the voters were rejecting a "cut-and-run" strategy. Indeed, the Administration made no effort to resist the legislative challenge; it contended the President—as commander in chief—had full authority in any case to protect the lives of American forces already committed to battle. And why not? If Truman could send our troops to Korea *without* legislative approval, couldn't Nixon keep them in Vietnam without legislative approval? As a matter of fact, the harsh reality is that the chief executive has ordered our armed forces to do battle in about 125 separate instances lacking meaningful congressional support.

So the larger question was: Couldn't Congress have invoked constitutional power to keep us out of Vietnam in the first place? A few critics condemned virtually all unilateral presidential initiatives committing the nation to warfare; but this view has little credence, because there are too many obvious exceptions. Suppose the country is suddenly confronted with a clear and present danger of attack. Suppose American lives and property abroad are threatened by violence. Besides, the President's war power has become too much a part of the "Living Constitution" for such drastic revamping. More modest revisionists were concerned primarily with building constitutional theory that would give

Congress a check on the executive so he could not indiscriminately make war on his own. The upshot of their efforts was passage—over President Nixon's veto—of the 1973 War Powers Act. It prescribes the following:

1. The President may send troops into battle or into a "zone of danger," only if (a) Congress has declared war, (b) Congress has passed other enabling legislation, or (c) there is a national emergency caused by enemy attack.

2. A presidential commitment of armed forces overseas, without congressional endorsement, must terminate ordinarily within sixty days. However, such commitments can be extended another thirty days where necessary to *disengage* our troops from their responsibilities.

3. Congress may now order the chief executive (via resolution not subject to his veto) to cease and desist from making war, where he has unilaterally committed troops to combat.

The 1973 statute is predicated upon certain theoretical assumptions. The President's war power maximizes speed, efficiency, and decisive action. The Congress's war power emphasizes debate, compromise, and consensus-building. As a rule, we expect the latter virtues to prevail; if the Framers had desired the former virtues to be prime constitutional pillars, they wouldn't have created an elaborate checks-and-balances scheme. So the War Powers Act presumes in favor of congressional authority and judgments; it gives the executive only as much elbowroom as emergency conditions necessitate, for it is in times of crisis that he is best suited to act.[30]

The War Powers Act is no doubt constitutional. If Congress possesses the delegated power to declare war, it possesses the implied power both to define "war" and spell out the "whens" and "wheres" of an entrance into "war." A tougher question is whether the new law really changes anything. Would it, for example, have kept a chief executive from indulging in some international adventure had it been enacted years earlier? Here are a few educated guesses: The statute would not have forbidden Woodrow Wilson to send troops across the Mexican border in search of Pancho Villa's renegades, because these marauders had again and again "invaded" our soil and devastated the property of citizens. The statute might have given James Polk pause before he dispatched troops to territory claimed jointly by the United States and Mexico, but Congress actually did take a vote after the fact and wound up declaring war. The statute would not have deterred John F. Kennedy from blockading Cuban ports in the wake of evidence that the Russians had installed highly provocative missiles on that island; and, indeed, Congress did approve his response shortly thereafter. The statute would have forced Congress to take some kind of vote on our Korean involvement. The statute would not have changed the nature of executive action toward Vietnam *one little bit,* because Congress did approve the Gulf of Tonkin Resolution.

The War Powers Act has received only one test. That occurred after Cambodian naval forces seized an American vessel, the *Mayagüez,* in international waters and took the ship and its crew to Koh Tang Island. Fearing they would be moved to the mainland, vastly complicating any rescue efforts, President Ford at once directed that the ship and crew be retaken. As a result, the marines stormed Koh Tang and recaptured the vessel; in the meantime, three Cambodian gunboats were sunk by U.S. warplanes.

Some members of Congress protested vainly, claiming the President had introduced troops into battlefield conditions without receiving legislative approval. But I do not think the statute requires the President to stay his hand where Americans have been attacked. Moreover, time was clearly of the essence; and Ford's actions were entirely defensive. The operation was terminated in two days when the American sailors were surrendered voluntarily.

The law's chief accomplishment is to vest Congress with a legitimacy in war-power policy-making hitherto lacking. It limits the danger that one person sitting in the White House could do irremediable harm through military adventurism. The statute has a "we sink or swim together" air about it that is surely consistent with implicit constitutional norms. From the standpoint of public confidence as well as the need for broad representative participation in the life and death political decisions facing the Republic, the law is hard to fault.

"Mr. Foreign Affairs"

The Framers, we now understand, saw the legislative branch as "first among equals." Whereas congressional prerogatives and responsibilities needed to be spelled out with great care and precision, the other two departments could be accorded powers of very broad description. Actually, though, these generalizations are applicable only to matters of domestic concern. In the field of international relations, the rules of the game are turned upside down, for here "the President alone has the power to speak or listen as a representative of the nation."[31]

More than one hundred years before this was penned, Congress recognized the truth of the matter by making it illegal for private citizens not certified by the President to enter into discussions with foreign emissaries regarding matters of international diplomacy. No citizen has ever been convicted under the Logan Act, but there is a question whether former Attorney General Ramsey Clark and other peace advocates actually violated the statute when they made their way to Hanoi during the Vietnam War and exchanged views with Ho Chi Minh's deputies.

What constitutional language anoints the chief executive "Mr. Foreign Affairs"? He selects our ambassadors with the concurrence of a Senate majority and has *sole authority* to receive the credentials of ambassadors sent here from abroad; the entire question of whether we will accord diplomatic relations to a particular regime lies in his hands. The Senate almost always accepts the chief executive's choices for posts overseas, but when Gerald Ford tapped Peter Flanigan to be ambassador to Spain, allegations that the nominee had "sold ambassadorships" during the Nixon years led to a speedy withdrawal of the nomination. Harry Truman invoked the President's unilateral power of national recognition with powerful domestic political effect when, in 1948, he granted our prestigious mantle of legitimacy to Israel. The foreign policy implications of this move—like the repercussions that would arise should a contemporary President recognize the People's Republic of China—can hardly be overstated.

The President also negotiates treaties with foreign dignitaries; but the upper chamber can reject these agreements if two-thirds of their number so decide. That this check can carry real sting was demonstrated in no uncertain terms when the Senate killed Woodrow Wilson's League of Nations proposal. But the President normally reserves all power to negotiate treaties. Finally, in his commander in chief role he might wish to sit down and consult with other commanders in chief regarding questions of mutual security. Taken together, these explicit functions have generated complicated communications and intelligence networks tying our chief executive to capitals of the world. The "Living Constitution" assumes that a President should collect and maintain "confidential sources of information" so that his "very delicate, plenary and *exclusive* power"[32] in the international arena may be exercised prudently and realistically.

The treaty mechanism was undoubtedly intended to be the formal instrument through which the United States would consummate international arrangements. Certainly this is the traditional procedure employed by heads of state, and it was to keep Presidents within the confines of constitutional balance that the Framers provided a senatorial check. But are there matters of constitutional dimension *not* negotiable at the international bargaining table? The debate over what inherent substantive limitations—if any—bind the chief executive's treaty power is an old one, and it is worth careful analysis.

Wanton slaughter of birds had captured public attention even before the turn into this century. In 1913, the superaggressive Congress working with President Woodrow Wilson enacted legislation regulating closely the killing of migratory fowl. The federal judiciary frowned on these laws, however, claiming there were no delegated powers upon which they could be predicated. In response to this setback,[33] Wilson set about framing a treaty to solve the problem. As a result, the United States and Canada formally agreed upon a joint effort to protect the countless species of birds that fly back and forth over the countries' common boundaries. Specifically, the treaty called for each nation's legislature to formulate whatever code of wildlife protection seemed appropriate. And so Congress—once the agreement received senatorial endorsement—repassed the very regulations that had earlier been shot down by the courts!

This stratagem provoked considerable anxiety. "Congress and President are using the treaty weapon as a means to expand their authority beyond constitutional recognition" was the war cry emanating from detractors. Especially intransigent were state officials who saw the fowl as an important foodstuff for their citizens and who felt the treaty impinged upon their rights under the Tenth Amendment to enact hunting regulations in *their* interest.

The Supreme Court spoke to these issues in 1920 and has not discussed the topic since.[34] It sustained the migratory birds pact, ruling that, while congressional statutes must conform to "delegated or implied" guidelines, treaties need only deal with subject matter of international scope and magnitude. How can we consider ourselves a sovereign state, Mr. Justice Holmes asked, if the country's diplomats cannot negotiate on matters of common concern among nations? Moreover, the treaty constituted no subversion of specific individual liberties guaranteed in the Constitution; it contravened only some strained expansion of states' rights. The interests of a Wyoming or a Pennsylvania could not cripple the nation's capacity to work out contracts with the representatives of other peoples.

I wish to emphasize the point that treaties rank as part of the supreme law of the land. That message is pronounced in so many words by the Constitution. And the wild fowl case shows Congress can use treaties as a basis for enacting legislation, under authority from the necessary and proper clause: "The Congress shall have power . . . to make all laws which shall be necessary and proper for carrying into execution [all the] powers vested . . . in the Government of the United States. . . ." In other words, not only can Congress legislate to implement its own power, but wherever the document distributes responsibilities to a federal agency or official, the Congress is authorized to step in and pass laws facilitating the exercise of these responsibilities. And one such responsibility is the treaty-making provision.

I stress these fundamentals because some reputable people harbor deep concerns over the far-ranging scope of treaty-making. If the instrument can be used to expand the horizons of congressional jurisdiction, as in the migratory birds case, have we not created a monster that could some day be used to subvert the entire constitutional balance? Is this sheer fantasy? In 1945 we joined the United Nations, the Senate having ratified the United Nations Charter in the form of a treaty. Could not Congress now enact legislation by way of implementing our commitment to the Charter, proposals heretofore beyond the jurisdiction of its delegated and implied authority? Indeed, could not the Supreme Court declare a state law null and void because it violated the Charter itself, a treaty that is part of our supreme law?

For instance, Article 55 of the United Nations treaty pledges nations to foster "universal respect for, and observance of, human rights and fundamental freedoms for all without distinction as to race, sex, language, or religion." Suppose the National Organization for Women went before the Court and demanded an end to all sexist standards contained in local, state, and federal law on the ground that such laws run afoul of treaty obligations. Or suppose Congress enacted the Equal Rights Amendment in *statutory* form, using Article 55 as its constitutional foundation.

The Vietnam War provides a real-life example. In the late 1950s, the U.S. Senate ratified our participation in the S.E.A.T.O. (Southeast Asia Treaty Organization) arrangement. One of the stipulations was that we would defend

South Vietnam from armed aggression. Did this mean Congress's power to declare war had evaporated totally with respect to S.E.A.T.O. obligations? Did this mean the President could send troops on his own authority to Vietnam if he thought aggression had taken place? The whole business is really open to conjecture, though the S.E.A.T.O. pact allowed a signatory nation the "out" of meeting (or not meeting) treaty responsibilities in accordance with its own constitutional processes. In short, we didn't have to send any troops there, unless *we* felt our own rules had been preserved.

But what are these rules? Lyndon Johnson thought the Gulf of Tonkin Resolution was sufficient; Harry Truman thought *no* congressional action was needed; George McGovern thought the S.E.A.T.O. arrangement undermined the entire fabric of legislative competence in warmaking because it gave the Trumans and the Johnsons the leeway they needed to implement their theories of executive preeminence. Clearly, the search for constitutional limitations on what treaties may prescribe is not the hallmark of constitutional extremism.

One suggestion dating back to the 1940s is the so-called Bricker Amendment. It would throw out the migratory birds decision by making treaties ineffective as internal law unless they were first implemented by an act of Congress "which would be valid in the absence of a treaty." So if the legislative branch moved first—*and had the delegated power to move first*—a treaty could then be invoked as a legal basis for limiting the rights of both states and individuals. This proposed constitutional amendment has been debated many times in Congress but has never passed either chamber. I feel it goes too far; international problems amenable to the treaty power often cannot be solved in the context of a constitutional scheme acceptable only to members of *one potential signatory nation.* But treaties, like every other coercive political weapon, are subject to abuse. At some time in the future, we will face these basic questions: (1) What fundamentals of our politics must remain inviolate from international negotiation? (2) Should these fundamentals be spelled out by judges in the courts, by voters at the ballot box, or by codification in some constitutional amendment?

The search for answers to these questions is complicated by a fairly recent development: there are almost *no more treaties made.* Wars have changed, and so has the way they are resolved. The decline of formalized troop confrontations stems from logistical refinements in the way people go about killing their fellows; the decline of formalized international covenants is strictly a matter of political expediency, which, with respect to American government, raises serious questions for the "Living Constitution."

Our three most recent wars—the Second World War, the Korean War, and the Vietnam War—all involved high-level meetings and agreements with our allies, and all led ultimately to pacts between this nation and its enemies, spelling out the details of disengagement, if not peace. But the great political decisions agreed to during and after these wars were *never* formalized by treaty. I do not mean to suggest the treaty device is a dead letter. This nation belongs to various alliances with countries of common cause: N.A.T.O. (North Atlantic Treaty Organization) is one example. And quite often our top-level arms agreements with the U.S.S.R. are laid before the Senate as treaties, for example the ban on nuclear testing in the atmosphere. But treaties just aren't what they used to be. Still, consequential agreements among nation-states are just as plentiful. What form of arrangement has taken their place?

I will explore two substitute mechanisms, both of which involve *unilateral* presidential action. Each was developed to a fine art by Franklin Roosevelt, who, without doubt, was the all-time champion of the international commitment *sans* treaty.

Throughout the joint effort to demolish Nazism, the leaders of Great Britain, the Soviet Union, and the United States—Churchill, Stalin, Roosevelt—met for consultation at such exotic places as Teheran and Yalta. As commanders in chief of their respective military machines, they knew they had to pool their resources to obtain victory. But their agreements also involved high political stakes. Instance 1: As a price for obtaining Russian participation in our struggle against Japan, we promised her all rights to the Kurile Islands. Instance 2: By agreeing to let Russian troops reach the Elbe River in Germany ahead of our own, we practically guaranteed the U.S.S.R. total hegemony over what is now East Germany.[35] The constitutional principle exemplified by these presidential maneuvers is this: the commander in chief has power to negotiate *executive agreements* with his international counterparts, and these transactions may involve relevant political as well as military understandings. Moreover, such agreements need not be submitted to the Senate for its ratification because they are not treaties. The President is acting under his supervisory control of our military destinies in the field, and not under his formal treaty-negotiating authority.

Roosevelt also worked out another quite different application of the executive agreement. After the 1917 Russian Revolution, the United States steadfastly refused to recognize the Bolshevik regime because of widespread distaste for its ideology and its actions. F.D.R. thought the Soviets were here to stay and that we might as well work together on mutual problems. Therefore, in his unabridged capacity to receive ambassadors, he accepted the credentials of Soviet diplomat Maxim Litvinov as official representative of the Soviet government. But Roosevelt did so only as part of a quid pro quo: the U.S.S.R. would renounce their claim to the millions deposited in United States banks by Russian businesses before those firms were nationalized following Lenin's triumph. These monies would now be transferred to Uncle Sam's coffers.

The Supreme Court accepted this use of the executive agreement procedure. The President has every right to base formal recognition upon whatever criteria he thinks appropriate to the national interest. And the conditions entered into via executive agreements have the same legal standing as congressional statutes and treaty obligations: they are part of the supreme law of the land; thus they are binding in the courts of this country if challenged by private citizens or states.[36]

The Supreme Court has never declared an executive agreement—or a treaty—unconstitutional, so presidential power in this area has never been hedged about by explicit constitutional standards. What is more, whereas the

Senate can reject treaties for any reasons that appear persuasive, there is no check whatsoever on executive agreements except the force of public opinion. In fact, an irresponsible though popular President can use the device as a means to skirt senatorial consideration, thus striking a severe blow against the cardinal check-and-balance norm of our governmental system.

It would be helpful if one could differentiate clearly the subject matter or policies appropriate to each of these two instruments. Unfortunately, the terms resist such compartmentalization. I would suggest only a starting point or theoretical overview: treaties should be the *rule* because their implementation requires a joint effort by public officials with different constituencies; executive agreements should be the *exception* because their implementation is the work of a single person, an official who might be marching only to the tune of self-aggrandizement. I think the test is faithful to the Framers' intentions, because they provided for treaty-making and said nothing about executive agreement-making. If I am right, it is time to readjust this portion of the "Living Constitution."

We have come face to face again with the larger question of executive-legislative relations. If Congress must reassert itself with respect to the war power, should Congress not also flex its muscles along the larger frontier of international relations—that is, increase its participation in international give-and-take and thereby reduce the President's status as "Mr. Foreign Affairs"?

Some have suggested that both branches repose a little confidence in each other. Instead of Presidents drafting treaties and calling them executive agreements, and instead of Congress striking back by telling the President under what conditions he can send troops overseas, these observers recommend mutual trust in the form of meaningful collaboration.[37] For example, Woodrow Wilson should have cooperated with Senator Henry Cabot Lodge in 1917 to get the League ratified, just as Truman cooperated with Senator Arthur Vandenberg in 1947 to get N.A.T.O. approved; and the argument has been advanced that congressional-presidential estrangement over Vietnam could have been avoided had Johnson and Nixon exercised better consultative channels with the Senate Foreign Relations Committee, whose senior Democratic members, J. William Fulbright and Frank Church, later became militant "doves" almost out of sheer desperation.

Obviously, prior discussion with legislative leaders should be part of any chief executive's master plan to recruit allies and build a dominant consensus. But real collaboration implies a sharing of the power necessary to achieve policy initiative. And it is hard to envision a President voluntarily surrendering prerogatives practically enunciated in the Constitution.

There is also a serious question as to whether either Congress or the nation would benefit from "political branch" partnership in foreign affairs. It is one thing to bridge the separation of powers with a vigilant checks-and-balances scrutiny; it is another thing to paper over this separation with collaborative devices that may dampen potential oversight. Where the President controls the levers of collaboration, may not the confidence that results be only a myth?[38]

High officials in the Nixon Administration told congressional leaders of the necessity to bomb neutral Cambodia and to keep the whole business secret. The leaders nodded their heads in *confidential* assent, and from that day on, Congress's capacity to criticize this issue of high policy was thoroughly compromised. Probably, the checks and balances inherent in a system of presidential policy-making and congressional oversight are more valuable than any benefits accruing from Congress's increased participation in policy formulation.

"Executive privilege": the "Nixon tapes" controversy

When we move from presidential activities in foreign relations to presidential activities at home, the very nature of executive authority undergoes drastic transformation. The fundamental "balance of power" notion embedded in our constitutional fabric suddenly comes alive, as the Watergate cover-up and its aftermath make abundantly clear.

In the most general terms, the President of the United States is vested with two quite different kinds of constitutional authority. First, he possesses *ministerial* responsibility—a responsibility to fulfill highly specific obligations imposed upon him (or his aides) by law. In this he has no discretion and no policy-making role; these are duties he *must* perform. If he fails to implement such rituals, he can be sued through his deputies. The classic example, of course, involves President Jefferson, who violated a ministerial trust when he told his Secretary of State, James Madison, not to deliver the official "seal of approval" due Judge Marbury, as had been provided through statute. John Marshall, remember, specifically found against Jefferson on that point (see pp. 32–33). So, with respect to clear-cut obligations imposed on them by Congress, executive personnel must follow the law, *anything their boss says to the contrary notwithstanding.*[39]

The second kind of power the President possesses is *discretionary:* it encompasses all of the *political* and *executive* punch inherent in the office. When the President acts as commander in chief, he is exercising discretionary authority. He is assessing a situation and bringing into play the tools best suited to meet particular exigencies. The same usually goes for his most fundamental power on the domestic scene, *to make sure the laws are faithfully executed.* Of course, this clause embraces all ministerial tasks, but his role typically entails a choice of weapons: "Do I enforce them this way or that way?" "Which is the most feasible?" "Which is the most politically rewarding?" So long as the President neither violates the Constitution in executing the law[40] nor "breaks the law to enforce the law,"[41] the decisions are for him to make. Moreover, *members of the executive branch cannot be sued either to be made to enforce discretionary power or be kept from enforcing discretionary power.* The courts will not entertain jurisdiction in these disputes, holding that political functions can be challenged only when they have been employed to abridge personal or property rights.[42]

This background information is indispensable if we are to understand the "Living Constitution" surrounding the modern presidency. The Roosevelts, the

Eisenhowers, and the Nixons would have had no chance to make rational choices if they failed to acquaint themselves with a wide variety of alternatives. These men needed information and they needed staff dedicated to a search for that information. Hence, a President writes letters, dictates memos, and, in this technologically sophisticated age, may make tape recordings of important conversations dealing with every issue under the sun. All chief executives have considered candor from their advisors mandatory for effective consultation, and they have seen confidentiality as the cornerstone of candor.

No one questions the constitutionality of either rounding up confidential information or storing it away until some later time, even for posterity. In fact, the same "rules of the game" apply to legislative and judicial decision-making as well. Candor and confidentiality are as necessary in the senatorial cloakrooms and in the Supreme Court Conference as they are in the President's Oval Office. And most scholars believe the permanent records kept of these communications are owned by the individuals who authorized them.[c]

Although protection of these records has never been given a specific constitutional justification, separation of powers theory has generally had a constraining effect, as some historical examples make clear. When a treaty is submitted to the Senate, that body cannot leaf through presidential discussions with foreign diplomats leading up to the agreement—unless, of course, the chief executive consents. Actually it was the House that made the boldest attempt to obtain such information; however, in the nation's first confrontation between President and Congress over what later became known as "executive privilege," George Washington refused to honor this request. Furthermore, few scholars contend that congressional committees can subpoena Presidents and Supreme Court Justices[43] or that the courts can subpoena executive or legislative officers regarding the performance of their public responsibilities.[44] During a H.U.A.C. inquest into the appointment of suspected Communist Harry Dexter White to a government post, this now defunct committee subpoenaed former President Truman and his Attorney General, Tom Clark, who had since been named to the Supreme Court. Justice Clark refused to honor the directive, and Truman also declined, saying separation of powers meant little if a President knew his official acts would be subjected to scrutiny by a co-equal branch once his term of service expired.

The implicit norm that all three branches can protect the essence of their constitutional functions in the face of pressure from the other branches received a severe test in the Nixon tapes incident. As is well known, Nixon had placed an automatic recording system in many rooms of the White House, ostensibly to obtain a complete record of his conversations. That these tapes were Nixon's personal property follows logically from the above remarks; that they could have been an invaluable aid to him in the management of his office

[c] Mountains of these data are housed in libraries across the country, established by the dignitaries themselves or their heirs. John F. Kennedy's correspondence with various people is housed in Cambridge, Massachusetts, and Lyndon Johnson's taped conversations are at the L.B.J. Library, the recipient of Johnson's bequest.

seems evident.[45] However, in testimony before several investigative units, John Dean, former counsel to the President, related conversations he allegedly had had with Nixon during which much of the Watergate cover-up was contrived. Later, the existence of the White House taping system held promise of verifying either Dean's contentions or Nixon's denials. The issue was: Did any branch of government have power to take custody of these materials and use them as a means for establishing the truth?

Two candidates at once stepped forward. The first was Senator Sam Ervin's select committee investigating illegal election activities, with special emphasis on the machinations of the Committee to Re-Elect the President.[d] How can we get the full story of Watergate, Ervin wanted to know, without hearing the President's tapes? The second was the grand jury convened at the request of Special Prosecutor Archibald Cox to look into, and hand down indictments relative to, alleged Watergate wrongdoing. How can the criminal process go forward, Cox wanted to know, without grand jury inspection of relevant tapes?

Needless to say, Nixon opposed any of the possible moves. John Marshall, he recalled, had commanded Thomas Jefferson to turn over relevant correspondence for use in the Aaron Burr trial, but President Jefferson had declined to do so. This course of action, Nixon asserted, was entirely justified under "executive privilege,"[46] the doctrine that shields the internal decision-making process of the presidency from co-equal branch scrutiny. In other words, "executive privilege," like its counterparts "legislative privilege" and "judicial privilege," is a facet of the larger separation of powers idea, subject entirely to the discretion of that department's leadership.

The Ervin committee took the initiative. Marching into Judge John Sirica's court, it brought suit against Nixon, demanding he turn over the various tapes. Here was a predicament to give any judge nightmares. On one side was the Senate clamoring for subpoenas. On the other side was the President of the United States brandishing "executive privilege." But Sirica was equal to the task. Congress, he said, had not given the district courts *jurisdiction* to referee civil suits between the "political branches." Unless the entire legislative authority jumped on the Ervin bandwagon, the case could not proceed. This was a political riposte worthy of the great Marshall.[47]

But the Senate committee was tenacious beyond all expectation. It rounded up the necessary congressional endorsement and once more beat a path to the courtroom—on this occasion, Judge Gerhard Gesell's bench. However, the panel's luck had not improved. Pushed to the wall by this exercise in legislative-executive intransigence, Gesell—like Sirica before him—found a way out, this time invoking the rights of now indicted Watergate cover-up suspects. If Ervin's committee were victorious, the dissemination of the tapes might jeopardize defendants' rights; if "executive privilege" triumphed, at least no adverse publicity need by feared.[48] Gesell's opinion obviously does not represent any far-reaching judgment on the scope of checks-and-balances doc-

[d] Ervin's team had, by that time, much evidence establishing C.R.P.'s involvement in the Watergate break-in.

trine in this difficult area, but his argument does build nicely on Sirica's earlier wisdom: when the courts are trapped by "political branch" crossfire, they are extraordinarily adept at finding a good foxhole!

A few months later, it was the special prosecutor's turn. By this time, Leon Jaworski had replaced the deposed Archibald Cox. Whereas Cox wanted these records given to the *grand jury,* Jaworski was much more judicious: he waited until indictments were returned against John Mitchell, H. R. Haldeman, and their associates and he was perfectly willing for Judge Sirica to act as a censor in screening the relevancy of materials at their trial. These are very significant differences. Cox believed "executive privilege" was subservient to the grand jury function; this "Sherlock Holmes body" even had power to examine the most confidential, sensitive material imaginable in its search for wrongdoing. His attempt to put this theory into practice cost him his job. Jaworski's far more modest claims were, in effect: "The investigation is over; the men have been indicted; a fair trial is impossible unless the President's records can be treated as evidence where appropriate; without a fair trial, of course, there can be *no* trial; to be sure, some of the information found on the tapes has nothing to do with Watergate; all *irrelevant* information can be excised by Sirica, monitoring the recordings in private."

This far-reaching controversy was brought before the Supreme Court in the spring of 1974. By that time, lawyers representing some of the indicted parties were also screaming for access to the tapes. Undoubtedly they felt that if Nixon could be implicated, it would aid their clients' chances appreciably. This development made life a little easier for the Justices; neither prosecution nor defense was claiming the introduction of taped materials would jeopardize legal or constitutional rights.

The Court's opinion—representing the unanimous views of men who seldom agree on anything substantial—was a masterful *political* document, showing once again that the Justices can roll with the punches as well as the most sophisticated elected partisans. Virtually everyone came away with something. The President does possess broad, inherent "executive privilege," said the Court, thus slaying the theory put forward by a small band of academicians that this doctrine was spurious and should be buried forthwith.[49] But "executive privilege" has its limitations. Nixon had called Jaworski's litigation a "political question," but the Justices recounted how they had looked into Adam Clayton Powell's suit against the House of Representatives. In that case, the Court sought to *balance* what amounted to "congressional privilege" in seating elected members against Powell's claim of constitutional deprivation. Why, the Court asked, can't allegations of "executive privilege" also be balanced against other needs? A healthy respect for the principle of "pure judicial review" dating back to *Marbury* required no less (see pp. 32–34). Had the President cited a claim of privilege based on the need to protect military or diplomatic secrets, the Justices warned, maybe a "political question" would have been raised. But all we have here, the opinion reminded, is a President saying, "My conversations are private," on the one hand, and courtroom adversaries asking, "How can our claims receive a fair hearing without this information?" on the other hand. The Court could balance these claims, and it did so by ruling that the tapes must be delivered to Sirica for his perusal and censorship.[50]

More than one commentator summed up this ruling as: "The President is not above the law." But there is much more to the decision than that. First, what does this holding *not* tell us?

1. It resolves nothing about the right of a grand jury to subpoena presidential communications.
2. It resolves nothing about Congress's power to subpoena presidential communications. In 1954 Senator Joseph McCarthy told all executive officials to turn over to his Government Operations Committee any evidence of Communist subversion. Neither Senator McCarthy's theory of "executive privilege" nor Senator Ervin's theory of "executive privilege" is addressed in the Court's opinion.
3. It resolves nothing about the chief executive's authority to shield highly volatile information involving matters of either foreign affairs or national security.

What, then, is the importance of this opinion? What *does* it tell us? For the first time, the Supreme Court ruled that a President's *discretionary*, political deeds involving the internal management of his department can be challenged through the judicial process.[e] Scholars always believed the impeachment check could reach into the Oval Office and bring such documentation forward. But now the notion of fair trial, of due process, also commands that the discretionary function of "executive privilege" be forced to yield. With respect to the details of actual enforcement, the *Supreme Court* has declared itself open to judge whether a President improperly invokes his shield, while it has charged *trial court judges* with sifting through a President's communications to ascertain whether they are relevant in specific criminal litigation.[51]

When the Court says "executive privilege" is a viable constitutional doctrine, it is surely enforcing the "Living Constitution." But when the Court says this privilege must give way to one of the basic rights contained in the letter of the Constitution—due process—it is most certainly carving out a new constitutional balance between the President and the federal court system.

The power to hire and fire

The President's ability to run his department wisely and to achieve maximum results from his decision-making endeavors depends greatly on those who surround him. The Framers understood this, and they realized the chief executive could hardly be comfortable in his job if he were not blessed with top-level

[e] Recall the distinction made earlier between the President's *ministerial* and *discretionary* powers (see p. 189). Ministerial functions, if not performed, can be compelled via the judicial process. Therefore, if the Court's opinion instructed President Nixon to exercise ministerial duties, it would have political relevance but would hardly have been a constitutional milestone. But the power of a chief executive to engage in private discussions with his advisors and to record them for his own private use or for posterity can in no way be labeled ministerial; they are clearly discretionary.

assistants of his own choosing. As a result, they gave him the power to appoint "Officers of the United States" with the concurrence of a Senate majority. This term embraces ambassadors, department heads, and other important policy personnel, such as Cabinet Secretaries, directors of the F.B.I. and the C.I.A., and commissioners who sit on the various important regulatory agencies.

The Framers also discussed the nomination of "inferior officers"—that is, lower-level appointments. Perhaps because of the diversity of these underlings, Congress was empowered to determine whether they would be selected by one of three available means, the choice to be dictated by the nature of the particular position: (1) by the President himself, (2) by the heads of the various agencies involved, (3) by the courts. "Inferior officers" would include federal marshals (who are really sheriffs charged with enforcing judicial decrees), collectors in the internal revenue and customs bureaus, and U.S. district attorneys. If Congress decides these lower-echelon people should be chosen by the President, then the Senate retains its ratification check; but when Congress decides, for instance, to create a civil service system so that these people should be chosen via objective standards of competence, then the power of ratification is, in effect, waived.[f]

The power to hire top policy leaders, then, may be likened to the treaty-making authority; senators have an after-the-fact say, but the President initiates the choice. But who *fires* these people? It seems that the Framers, in their "infinite wisdom," forgot to say anything about the power of dismissal.

The Supreme Court first spoke to this question in 1926.[52] President Wilson had fired a postmaster named Myers. In so doing, he failed to consult the Senate, though there was a statute on the books saying nobody in Myers's position could be removed unless the upper chamber affirmed. Myers had challenged his ouster, claiming Wilson could not sack him unilaterally. The Court's opinion was written by Chief Justice Taft, the only former President ever to reach our highest judicial panel. His statement construed as broadly as conceivable the chief executive's sole authority to fire federal personnel. At root, the Taft thesis, obviously a product of his experience in the White House, stems from the discretionary, political nature of the President's power to implement faithfully the laws of this country:

> The vesting of the executive power in the President was essentially a grant of the power to execute the laws. But the President . . . must execute them by the assistance of subordinates. . . . As he is charged specifically to take care that they be faithfully executed, the reasonable implication . . . was that . . . he should select those who were to act for him. . . . The further implication must be . . . that as his selection of administrative officers is essential to the execution of the laws by him, so must be his power of removing those for whom he cannot continue to be responsible.[53]

[f] There is a third set of federal employees, intimate members of the chief executive's family who are attached to him rather than to a department or bureau. I refer to his staff aides, personal advisors, and the like. The President chooses these assistants, and Congress plays no role whatsoever in their selection or retention. I will discuss this last cadre at some length in Chapter 7.

So the statute inhibiting this "power of removal" was an unconstitutional breach of the separation of powers maxim.

Taft's opinion marched undeterred over a whole raft of difficulties:

1. Hadn't the Reconstructionist Congress hamstrung Andrew Johnson's dismissal prerogatives by enacting the 1867 Tenure of Office Act? Taft dismissed that precedent flippantly, calling Thaddeus Stevens's brainchild "invalid."
2. Myers was an inconspicuous postmaster, obviously an "inferior officer." Wasn't it spurious to build a case for the proper presidential dismissal of *everyone* he appoints[54] around this one instance? Indeed, what does a postal official have in common with, say, a Secretary of State?
3. Congress could have vested Myers's *appointment* in either the judicial branch or in the head of the postal service. Had it done so, Congress would then have been able to give these officials dismissal authority as well. Why, then, couldn't the legislative branch take the lesser step of allowing the chief executive to nominate postmasters while limiting his power to remove them?

In a biting dissent, Justice Holmes relied mostly on this third point. Congress, he said, has created the office of postmaster, so Congress can abolish the office of postmaster; Congress has allowed the President to appoint "inferior officer" Myers, so Congress can limit the power to remove "inferior officer" Myers. Where the legislative branch has enacted policy within its rightful jurisdiction, Holmes concluded, the President's power to execute the law cannot override that policy, an opinion that would be echoed by several Justices in the later *Steel Seizure* decision.

But there was no restraining the Chief Justice. He even asserted that a President could fire *superior officers sitting on important federal regulatory agencies.* Now these bureaus perform not only executive tasks but also legislative and judicial tasks. For example, the Federal Trade Commission makes rules forbidding assorted unfair advertising practices and holds hearings to determine if these rules have been violated. Congress, well aware of that fact, sought to insulate this agency from presidential interference, from the chief executive's *discretionary, political preferences.* He would exercise the power of appointment, but board members *were given set terms of office and could be dismissed only for specific reasons such as neglect of duty.* To this, Taft was now saying: The President cannot interfere with F.T.C. decision-making, but if he thinks board members are exercising authority in a misguided or inefficient manner, he can fire them; otherwise, he is not faithfully executing the laws. Without doubt, Taft's approach could allow a President to gain control of all these "independent," "nonpartisan" tribunals in direct violation of legislative intent.

In the *Humphrey* decision of 1935,[55] the Supreme Court disagreed with Taft. This case stemmed from F.D.R.'s dismissal of F.T.C. member William

Humphrey, Roosevelt's decision to remove having been based entirely on the incumbent's conservative views. Roosevelt had relied on the *Myers* opinion, but the Justices were now prepared to draw more subtle kinds of distinctions. Myers's public responsibilities had nothing in common with those entrusted to Humphrey, they found; a postmaster was an executive official pure and simple, while the F.T.C., because of its hybrid functions, was not really housed in the executive branch at all. The President's discretionary power to enforce the law gave him no authority to dismiss anyone outside his department unless the dismissal was consistent with congressional wishes.

The hiring and firing issue is important because, to the extent that officials hold tenure at the whim of a coercive agent, they must submit to his every desire. The line between Myers-type and Humphrey-type federal employees continues to distinguish legislative from executive control over the removal power; but that line has become a bit uncertain as the tasks of government grow larger and more innovative. Sometimes trying to ascertain whether X works for the executive branch is an exercise in hairsplitting.

One such problem played a significant part in the Watergate drama. Following the conviction of several Nixon campaign workers for perpetrating the Watergate break-in, the Senate passed a resolution requesting the President to name an independent special prosecutor to investigate all charges of wrongdoing in this sensitive area. Ordinarily, the Justice Department would have been expected to pursue such matters, but, given prima facie evidence of White House involvement, this unprecedented step commanded widespread support. The resolution—like all such resolutions—carried no legal power, but the Senate at that time was considering Nixon's nomination of Elliot Richardson to be his new Attorney General. It became clear that confirmation would hinge on whether the Watergate investigation were turned over to an independent investigator.

As part of an informal agreement between the nominee and the Senate, Richardson, with the President's full backing, settled on Harvard law professor Archibald Cox to be the special prosecutor. Cox was to serve directly under the Attorney General, but Richardson promised that, if confirmed, he would not remove Cox from office "except for extraordinary improprieties." Richardson also said Cox's tenure and service would have to be "consistent with [my] statutory accountability for all matters falling within the Department of Justice."[56] For his part, the special prosecutor assured senators he would follow up on all leads even should they take him to the President's doorstep. Richardson was subsequently approved, and Cox began his intensive search for Watergate culpability.

It was not long before John Dean's testimony, coupled with the revelation of the President's taping system, gave promise of ventilating the whole cover-up. Cox, having failed to secure the tapes he considered relevant, filed suit against the chief executive. A full-fledged confrontation before the Supreme Court seemed imminent. At this point, Nixon offered a compromise. John Stennis, Mississippi's elder statesman in the Senate, would listen to the tapes and hand over all relevant information in summary form to Cox's Watergate grand jury. If the special prosecutor refused this offer, he would be out of a job. And that is exactly what happened. Cox rejected Nixon's arrangement, claiming he could not use Stennis's summaries as evidence in court. The President then ordered his Attorney General to dismiss him, and when Richardson failed to act, Nixon had them both fired in what came to be known as the "Saturday night massacre."

The constitutional politics question presented here is straightforward: Did the chief executive have power to remove the special prosecutor? Nixon's brief might have been written this way: "Cox sits under Richardson, who sits under me; Cox has no right to bring his superior officer—the President—into court for the purpose of running through his private papers; I had to show him who was boss, so I had him fired, as is my right in managing my department." Cox's brief might have been written this way: "I was appointed as a special investigating officer; I could only be fired for 'extraordinary improprieties,' and going into court is not improper at all; the Senate confirmed the Attorney General because he agreed to honor my independence; the President's action has violated the intent of Congress and the built-in neutrality of my post."

Both sides have a case; but the tragedy lies in the avoidability of it all. If only Congress had passed a law setting forth the constitutional status of the special prosecutor's position. This statute could have vested appointment power in the Attorney General (Cox was obviously an "inferior officer"), vested removal power in the Attorney General, and set out with indisputable clarity what standards would control dismissal.[g] Even Taft's *Myers* opinion condoned that kind of check on presidential authority.[57] Instead, the legislature left the whole thing up in the air through the medium of a "gentleman's agreement." As we know from our study of informal Senate norms, "government by handshake" can be a cohesive element in the "Living Constitution," but not when the two "political branches" are locked in the most torrid of constitutional crises.

Protector of "law and order"

The President's power to "take Care that the Laws be faithfully executed" clearly extends to all statutes passed by Congress and all decisions handed down by the federal judiciary. Most of this work is done without fanfare and borders on the humdrum, since usually compliance is automatic or at most requires the gentle nudge of a federal marshal armed with the necessary subpoena. However, when Congress lays down a vast new program of legal constraints—a civil rights statute, for instance—enforcement problems are myriad. Executive officials face the same difficulties they encounter when the Supreme Court suddenly compels the state legislatures to reapportion. The critical problem in this regard is: How does the chief executive meet what he considers a particular threat of noncompliance?[58]

[g] Armed with these legal weapons, Cox could then have brought suit claiming he had been ousted unconstitutionally (as Humphrey did); and should Nixon have refused to reappoint him following Cox's successful appeal, Congress would have had ample ground for commencing impeachment proceedings.

Excellent examples are provided by the struggle to eradicate racial segregation in Southern schools. In the late 1950s a federal court order had required the admission of black students to Central High School in Little Rock, Arkansas. Governor Orval Faubus, determined to fight "forced integration" at every turn, called out the Arkansas National Guard and directed it to restrain black students from entering Central High. Such action, he claimed, was necessary to prevent mob violence. After an injunction had been issued enjoining the governor from further obstructionist tactics, he withdrew all troops under his command from the scene and thereby turned loose that portion of the white citizenry he had helped to inflame. This faction proceeded to harass all desegregation attempts.

President Eisenhower now entered the picture. First, he sent federal troops to Little Rock. On what authority? Ever since 1795, Congress has empowered the chief executive to deploy the armed forces wherever the laws of the United States are being subverted by illegal combinations or assemblies. Second, he issued a proclamation calling the Arkansas National Guard into federal service. This power is also given the President by legislative enactment, and he invokes it where mob rule has become the order of the day. But from what source does Congress get the authority to mobilize a state's militia? *From the Constitution.* So Eisenhower, vested with that discretion, stripped Faubus of any further potential to inhibit federal law enforcement.

President Kennedy utilized the same arsenal of weapons in 1963, after the federal courts admitted James Meredith to the University of Mississippi, a previously segregated institution. It took 300 federal marshals, 3,000 federal troops, and a presidential order federalizing Mississippi's National Guard to restore order.

In 1975, a highly incendiary situation developed in South Boston, where angry whites raged against a federal court-ordered cross-busing scheme. President Ford eschewed the remedies used by Eisenhower and Kennedy, though considerable violence occurred. The options lie entirely in the President's hands, for the power to execute the laws is essentially discretionary. Ford's conclusion that the crisis did not warrant such a drastic response was a value judgment within his range of competence.

In implementing desegregation orders, Presidents Eisenhower and Kennedy were relying largely on statutory authority. But if the power to prevent breakdowns in law enforcement is a constitutional grant, then the chief executive must also possess *constitutional* means to effectuate it. This idea, really, was the crux of Chief Justice Taft's opinion in the postmaster case; and his contention, though it has been refined, has never been refuted. Outside of his ability to root out wrongdoing in the executive branch, what steps, then, can the President take under the Constitution to prevent illegal action? When can these steps be activated? What limitations—other than the checks-and-balances restraint spelled out in such cases as the *Steel Seizure* decision and the *Humphrey*-F.T.C. decision—prevent this executory power from reaching arbitrary and dangerous proportions?

Just prior to the turn of the century, Supreme Court Justice Stephen J. Field, while serving on special assignment in California, was asked to resolve litigation over ownership of $1 million. As Field saw things, one claimant, a Mrs. Terry, had no basis for her demands. She proceeded to provoke bedlam in the courtroom, screaming that if Field ever showed up in California again he could expect to be killed on sight! This threat received considerable publicity, and the President placed a federal marshal, Neagle, at the Justice's disposal. When Field again passed through the state, Mrs.—and Mr.—Terry were waiting for him, armed to the teeth. The husband made the first move by drawing a knife, but Neagle had the last word by shooting down the assailant—and the California police arrested him on a charge of murder!

In his appeal to the Supreme Court, Neagle claimed he had struck down Mr. Terry in the performance of his official duty. California's argument was that the President lacked authority to make Neagle a bodyguard and clothe him with law enforcement responsibilities. Congress had not enacted legislation allowing the chief executive to take such action, so there was no "law" for him to implement faithfully.

Mr. Justice Miller's opinion is a monument to the President's extensive power in this area. The authority to "take Care that the Laws be faithfully executed" includes protecting "the rights, duties and obligations growing out of the Constitution itself . . . and all the protection implied by the nature of [our] government."[59] Among these rights and duties is a federal government capable of performing the functions assigned to it. How could Supreme Court Justices dispense legal remedies in a fair and objective fashion if they stood unprotected against the threat of bodily harm? Obviously, all government officials are entitled to this sort of minimal aid, and the President, as "Mr. Law and Order," has the constitutional authority to assess the danger and provide the necessary protection.

Speaking directly to the point at issue, the Court said: "There is a peace of the United States"; the performance of federal judicial proprieties free from violence or intimidation is a small part of the national peace; these measures are—like statutes, treaties, and court decisions—part of the *supreme law of the land;* and Neagle was exercising duties properly delegated to him.[60]

What is this peace of our national constitutional polity that the President may protect with orders that have the force of law? Suppose riots broke out in Illinois making mail delivery impossible, and suppose judicial decrees enjoining the combatants were ignored? The President has "dormant power"—that is, inherent executive authority—to call out the troops, stop the fighting, unclog the channels of communication and transportation and arrest the participants for contempt of court.[61] So the "peace of the United States" entails the proper functioning of federal governmental instrumentalities and the proper administration of rules and regulations promulgated by them; threats against those federal interests can be met with force of arms if necessary, *so long as Congress has not decided otherwise.* The President cannot break statutes either to enforce other statutes or, as in this case, to enforce the "peace" of the nation.

Today, we don't debate the chief executive's "dormant power" or his capacity to protect the "peace of the United States." Rather, politicians talk about maintaining the "national security" against those who would subvert our political system. There is no difference; the terms simply have been changed. People very often think they are facing entirely new problems, but for as long as people have employed governmental institutions, there have been threats to "national peace" or "national security." What constitutional protection do we have against a President whose reaction to such dangers is more damaging than the dangers themselves?

Every President from Franklin Roosevelt to Richard Nixon conducted wiretap programs against domestic organizations allegedly threatening our national security. Perhaps the most notorious instance involved bugs placed on Martin Luther King's telephone by the F.B.I. during the Kennedy years. Still, some argued that certain groups (such as the Weathermen and the Black Panthers) were plotting to subvert the constitutional order. The executive branch needed intelligence information to combat this grave danger, and the data could be obtained only via clandestine avenues. Indeed, they said, these threats against internal security were so different from the usual brand of lawlessness that search warrants permitting the wiretaps need not be obtained; feasible tracking of these conspiracies was too complex and intricate for proper judicial cognizance.

A Supreme Court, ranging in conviction from the rights-oriented William O. Douglas to the duties-oriented Warren Burger, unanimously rejected this position. The phrase "domestic security" was necessarily imprecise; all the more reason, then, why the courts should stand ready to check the chief executive's wiretap authority. A search warrant was an important shield against arbitrary governmental intrusions into the home. From now on, all domestic intelligence wiretaps would require prior judicial approval.[62]

The courts have had other opportunities over the past few years to curb executive officials who have gone far afield in their defense of national security. By secret presidential order, Nixon, in 1969, established an intelligence-gathering unit called the "Plumbers" to plug security leaks in the executive branch. The head of this group was Egil Krogh, and his assistants were Howard Hunt and Gordon Liddy, who later took part in the Watergate burglary and cover-up. Krogh himself was responsible to White House domestic advisor John Ehrlichman. These men concentrated their attention on Daniel Ellsberg, a suspect in the theft of the Pentagon Papers. Determined to prove that Ellsberg had violated the law, they gathered as much evidence as they could about his activities. In the process, they decided to burglarize the office of Dr. Lewis Fielding, Ellsberg's psychiatrist, in hopes of corralling new information.

Ehrlichman, Krogh, and the others were eventually indicted and brought to trial, charged with violating a federal statute protecting the civil rights of citizens. The "civil right" involved was the Fourth Amendment protection against unreasonable searches and seizures; the "citizen" involved was Dr. Fielding. This, after all, wasn't even a case of wiretapping; it was an old-fashioned attempted burglary. There was no search warrant and no prior consultation with any judge. Besides, Dr. Fielding hadn't been accused of stealing confidential government documents, nor was the covert operation aimed at reclaiming those documents. To this, the "Plumbers" relied on the defense that Ellsberg had *probably* taken secret papers relating to Vietnam War strategy, and *future* leaks had to be prevented, or else the national security would be jeopardized.

One can hardly believe this thesis merits serious deliberation. Perhaps Nixon had inherent authority to create a special task force to probe for security leaks in the executive branch. But that these men would unilaterally sneak into the homes or offices of patently innocent citizens and rummage through their private papers seems totally unacceptable. Certainly the legal justification presented by the ringleaders at trial persuaded neither judge nor jury, and all were convicted.[63]

Is there any threat to the national security that would allow the President the kind of "search and seizure" discretion I have been discussing? We need only return to the constitutional politics of Vietnam participation for a good test. Once again highly classified information—this time involving American bombings of neutralist Cambodia—was leaked to *The New York Times.* Enraged and frustrated by this breakdown in security, President Nixon ordered the F.B.I. to wiretap the phones of both government employees and newspaper reporters who might have been responsible. The fruits of these machinations were the "Kissinger taps," so named because the then chief of national security affairs had designated those in the best position to feed the information.

The Court has never told us whether the President can invoke unilateral authority to wiretap the phones of persons who have allegedly publicized top secret troop movements during wartime.[64] This doubtless is a much closer case. But why couldn't a judge have been asked to issue wiretap search warrants? The damage had already been done; twenty-four hours spent in presenting evidence to a magistrate could hardly have made a difference. The answer must lie in the Nixon Administration's "Living Constitution." There, "national security" took on such sweeping proportions that the objective observer could hardly differentiate it from the usual "law and order" problems without a scorecard. The fear of omnipresent threats left no room for the sharing of responsibility with judicial officers. But in the end the courts had their day, punishing through the criminal process and checking through the medium of constitutional interpretation those whose theory of law enforcement made them a law unto themselves.

Architect of policy[65]

The debate over constitutional face

The foregoing has described what the chief executive can and cannot accomplish under the Constitution. Now the questions arise: (1) What does the President do? (2) How does he do it?

Each President must approach his work from some set of premises, biases, convictions, goals. Surely a crucial mainspring is his *conception of the office.* The writings of our more reflective chief executives seem to indicate two quite distinct and irreconcilable notions of the President's constitutional-political role.

Theodore Roosevelt propounded the "stewardship theory" of executive responsibility: the President should serve the public interest or, as he put it, "the common well-being of all our people." Whatever Roosevelt thought needed to be done he was prepared to do, unless the action violated constitutional or statutory law.[66] Roosevelt's hand-picked successor, William Howard Taft, took a far different view. The President, he felt, could perform only those functions specifically given him by the Constitution, along with whatever else was necessary and proper to the implementation of those delegated grants.[67] Not that Taft viewed presidential power as tame and indecisive; his opinion for the Supreme Court in the postmaster case belies that idea. But Taft believed all three co-equal branches must hew to the same constitutional criteria in dispensing their powers. Should some political issue fall outside the scope allotted them, the matter resides with the people, unless they amend the document. Roosevelt's thesis, on the other hand, seems to place the chief executive on a somewhat higher pedestal; whereas the other two branches need an excuse to act, he can move right in unless his way is blocked.

Generally speaking, those Presidents who have advocated the Roosevelt "steward of the people" approach are classified by historians as "strong," while those who have adhered to the Taft "self-restraint" model are termed "weak." Most chief executives who served prior to the Depression can be placed in the latter group—with a list of exceptions including Washington, Jefferson, Jackson, Lincoln, T.R., and Wilson. Since the 1930s, however, only Eisenhower and Ford remotely approach the passivity of a Buchanan or a Coolidge.

Yet this classification has its ambiguities. Jefferson and Jackson, for instance, were "strict constructionists," strongly opposed to Hamilton's "big government" philosophy. So "strength" must imply an ingredient beyond juridical notions of constitutional role. A strong President seems to make the most of his opportunities, attempts to influence public opinion, pushes hard for the values he thinks worthy of support, and molds the presidential office so that it is responsive to his personal needs and style. Again: I am still talking about constitutional role, but the orientation has shifted to *basic patterns of behavior employed by assertive individuals for the purpose of getting the job done.* When we combine these two features—conception of the office and the vigor with which that conception is manifested—we have isolated the "Living Constitution"—that is, the basic behavioral norms—underlying any President's constitutional face.

However, being "strong" has nothing to do with being "great"[68] or "liberal," for power can be galvanized by any manner of person standing for any kind of political credo. Nor does "weak" signify "inept" or "conservative."

Pre-Depression "strong" Presidents

Most White House occupants prior to the modern era[69] made only marginal additions to presidential influence. They had their pet programs and their unique methods of operation, but they made no deliberate, systematic effort to upstage Congress and Court in key areas of policy development or to alter significantly the division of labor among the three departments. *They were simply not extraordinarily assertive in their manipulation of power.* Clearly, the most efficient way to characterize the growth of presidential power during the pre-Depression years is to emphasize the motives, efforts, and achievements of the select "strong" group. The "Living Constitution" now accords the President seven important responsibilities to use for better or worse.[70] These are (1) Chief of State, (2) Party Chief, (3) Chief Legislator, (4) Chief of Administration, (5) Chief of the Public Peace, (6) Chief of Foreign Affairs, and (7) Commander-in-Chief. We will see how the various "strong" executives manipulated these roles in order to promote the particular values and policies they endorsed.

First on our list, naturally, is George Washington, who was elected in 1788 and served through 1796. He played a significant part in developing six of the seven constitutional roles enumerated, the only exception being Chief of Party. (There were no political parties in his day, and he was opposed to them in any event on the ground that they were divisive.)

Washington instituted many important precedents we take for granted today; indeed, we take his presidency a bit for granted, too. We seem to assume that because he was our first chief executive, he was able to do more than most incumbents to influence the office. There is truth in this, but our first President could just as easily have been pliable, acquiescent, or even docile in his exercise of power.[h] Here is how he, *more than any other President,* forged the office we know today:

1. *Chief of State*—that is, head of government. There is a bit of royal bearing in the chief executive's image, and Washington helped put it there with his "war hero" credentials and his nonpartisan stance. He chose to be inaugurated in a public ceremony much like a monarch's coronation. He also proclaimed Thanksgiving Day a national holiday. The chief executive is our moral leader and our symbol of national unity. Today he has his own theme music—"Hail to the Chief"—and he lights a national Christmas tree, whether he goes to church or not. It was Washington's sense of style and mood that gave these trappings legitimacy. But he also refused to serve more than two terms, when he could have had the position for life. In so doing, he short-circuited any attempt to place the presidency per se above the checks-and-balances system.

[h] James David Barber, in his notable study of presidential decision-making, labels Washington "passive."[71] By this Barber means the Squire of Mount Vernon did not invest great energy in fulfilling his responsibilities, for an "active" chief executive is defined as a veritable whirlwind, which he quite clearly was not. But while aloofness and austerity—traits Washington possessed in spades—may be indicative of passivity, they certainly are not indicative of weakness.

2. *Chief Legislator.* The Constitution instructs the President to report to Congress on the nation's health and empowers him to propose legislative alternatives. Washington went directly before joint meetings of House and Senate for the purpose of delivering State of the Union messages. Furthermore, Hamilton, sitting at his right hand, constantly met with legislative leaders to press home the chief executive's sentiments. So the President as "lawmaking catalyst" was launched by Washington as well.

3. *Chief of Administration.* Washington disallowed senatorial participation in the nomination process for "Officers of the United States"; he invoked "executive privilege" for the first time; and he molded his chief departmental advisors into a Cabinet. The whole notion of an independent executive branch, with the President as head, got off the ground successfully during Washington's tenure because he quickly saw the alternative—subservience to Congress.

4. *Chief of the Public Peace.* When Hamilton's program for raising revenues through a tax on liquor met with armed resistance, Washington mobilized state militias and restored order. However, he quashed the Whiskey Rebellion only after all possibility for negotiation had been exhausted. Washington believed in a strong, viable central government, but he recognized that "law and order" imposed blindly was counterproductive.

5. *Chief of Foreign Affairs.* Washington's greatest substantive accomplishments lay in international relations. He barred the Senate from participating in the treaty-negotiation process. He also issued a proclamation of neutrality with respect to the 1793 war between France and a coalition of European rivals; and when "citizen" Genêt, the ambassador sent here by the French revolutionary movement, threatened to undermine that policy, Washington sent him packing. The United States, he believed, should steer clear of all "foreign entanglements" and develop self-sufficiency; from the larger perspective, he thought the President should speak for the nation in matters of external relations. International diplomacy has been in executive hands ever since.

6. *Commander-in-Chief.* Washington personally took command of the armed forces during the Whiskey Rebellion, an action never since repeated. But who can forget Eisenhower's campaign promise of 1952: If elected, I will go to Korea and see what can be done to get us out of that morass. Only a chief executive who has an impeccable military reputation could play these roles; yet civilian control over the military is implicit here, and that norm received a big boost from Washington's precedent.

Washington may not have been a born innovator; his prime concern may well have been to build stability. But through his understanding of the balance of power principle in a constitutional republic, the President's chair was given virtually all the authority any assertive leader would need in the agrarian, nontechnological world of those times.

Our next subject is Thomas Jefferson (1800–08). The man who penned the Declaration of Independence brought to the White House a brilliant mind of catholic bent. Men must free themselves from the confinements of a rigid social class system, he had taught, so they could use their God-given natural rights to achieve happiness. Government was the enemy of the individual, who could best exercise reason free from political constraint.

Advocate of the French Revolution and the cause of the "little person," Jefferson organized the Republican Party (now the Democratic Party) as a counterbalance to Hamilton and his Federalist legions. Jefferson's unique contribution, then, was as *Party Chief.* He was the first President elected on a party platform, and he was committed to pushing his program through Congress. As promised, the Alien and Sedition Acts were allowed to lapse, and the Adams "midnight judge" statute, which had spawned *Marbury v. Madison,* was repealed. Through his proddings, Republicans in the legislature developed highly centralizing caucus machinery. Binding votes were taken, as party members pledged themselves to support the President's policies. His role as *Chief Legislator* was so successful that he did not veto a single bill during his eight-year tenure. On the other hand, Jefferson did not allow these roles to undermine the *Chief of State* function. "Every difference of opinion is not a difference of principle," he argued,[72] thus leading the way in maintaining those fundamental principles that transcend party policies.

Andrew Jackson (1828–36) was a poor boy from Tennessee who knew nothing of philosophy and had made his name as a general; yet he was a Democrat in the egalitarian spirit of Jefferson, and a "strong" President in the path-breaking tradition of Jefferson. Whereas Adams had sought to ape Washington's "man above strife" presidency and had failed, Jefferson had won the reins of power for the avowed purpose of rooting out the dying patricianism championed by Hamilton. Whereas both Madison and Monroe allowed themselves to be controlled by their party faithful in the Congress, Jackson revolted against that trend and plowed it under.

Jackson has been called the first modern President. When he came to power, the two-party system had already faded away: the Federalists were no more, and Jefferson's party had become a claque of feuding individuals and blocs. As *Chief Legislator,* Jackson developed the practice of vetoing bills because he thought them unwise; theretofore, the President had intervened only when he thought a proposal unconstitutional. As *Chief of Administration,* Jackson removed executive personnel without hesitation and substituted his own people, thus giving birth to the notion of the President as patronage dispenser. Finally, as *Party Chief,* he instituted the national convention, an instrumentality the chief executive could control; no longer would presidential nominees be selected via congressional party caucus. His opponents soon were flocking to the newly formed Whig Party, and its campaign theme was: Get rid of King Andrew!

Jackson was the first President elected under the rules of universal manhood suffrage and the first "commoner" to sit in the White House. His supporters were the national rank and file, and he fought relentlessly to maintain national integrity in their name. When South Carolina said it would "nullify" the Tariff Act, Jackson threatened to send in the armed forces if that state did not recognize the primacy of federal law. He made war on the "capitalists' paradise," the Bank of the United States, by withdrawing all federal monies deposited there, and, when the Secretary of the Treasury resisted his maneuvers, Jackson fired him. This bold endeavor altered profoundly executive-legislative relations, because up to that time Congress's control of the pursestrings was understood to bind the Secretary's discretion. From then on, fiscal management drifted toward White House domination. Is it any wonder that Kallenbach concludes: *"In his hands the office became a major instrument for achieving popular control over governmental policy"?*[73]

I have said much about Abraham Lincoln (1860–65) already. Quite obviously, he construed his *Commander-in-Chief* and *Chief of the Public Peace* functions in ground-breaking fashion. But Lincoln was assertive not merely in promulgating a blockade of Confederate ports and suspending the writ of habeas corpus. Lincoln was also the *Party Chief* who backed Stephen A. Douglas into a corner in their debates and who, unlike the Pierces and the Buchanans before him, refused to temporize over the expansion of slavery. And this Lincoln knew that in wartime his Republican Party needed to absorb anti-Confederate Democrats in order to maintain consensus. In a sense, then, I am also talking about Lincoln the *Chief of State.* He detested slavery, but he would not place abolition ahead of national unity. So he set up a coalition Cabinet, and when the war was over, he issued liberal amnesty terms for the defeated South in order to bring the rebels back into the fold with as little stress as possible. It was this deft combination of pragmatism, statesmanship, and humanitarianism, all merging in the most awesome declarations of executive power ever mobilized in this country, that made Lincoln unique.

It took another forty years for our politics to produce a chief executive in the Lincoln tradition of leadership. Theodore Roosevelt's "stewardship" (1901–08) relied on a personal magnetism that made his family life and habits a model for Americans everywhere. Born to the purple, the Roosevelts were, in a sense, just plain folks, too; indeed, the notion of the President's kin as "First Family" dates from them. As *Chief of State,* Roosevelt must have been a political security blanket for millions.

How did he accomplish this? He was educated at Harvard; he was an outdoorsman and a big-game hunter, who made much of his top physical condition and athletic prowess; he commanded the "Rough Riders" in their famous charge up San Juan Hill in Cuba during the Spanish-American War. When collegiate football came under the gun for excessive violence, T.R. threatened to abolish the sport if rule changes were not forthcoming. Shortly thereafter, the forward pass, with all its finesse, was introduced, and the allegations of mayhem subsided. Richard Nixon's dialogues with National Football League dignitaries never made such a dent!

Roosevelt tried to set moral standards in politics as well as in the popular arts. As *Chief Legislator,* he pushed Congress to adopt his Square Deal, being the first President to give his program a Madison Avenue nickname exemplifying the higher virtues. He fought for conservation, becoming our first prominent environmentalist. Finally, he launched a major effort against the "malefactors of great wealth" by using the *Chief of Administration* hat to "bust the trusts." Unlike his predecessors, he did not allow business interests a free hand; if they chopped up forests indiscriminately, or put adulterated foods on the market, or controlled a sector of the economy, he felt the President had a duty to respond.

T.R. was a man of unbridled resourcefulness. He made himself the grand mediator of turbulent labor-management disputes, for his conception of the President's *Chief of Public Peace* hat dictated no less a responsibility. As *Commander-in-Chief* and *Chief of Foreign Affairs* he set many a precedent by dispatching the marines to settle disputes in Central America, and the Panama Canal was one of the fruits of these interventions. On the home front, then, Roosevelt believed in the noblesse oblige of the presidency as protector of manners, morals, and the public welfare; on the foreign scene, these attitudes found expression in a sanctimony and bellicosity that every now and again manifest themselves in our dealings with others.

The last "strong" pre-Depression chief executive was certainly Woodrow Wilson (1912–20). Andrew Jackson may be labeled the "first modern President," but Wilson must be given credit for bringing the office itself into the political context of the twentieth century. Wilson—like Jackson—was a Democrat in the Jeffersonian mold, but he realized that the territorial growth of the United States, coupled with universal manhood suffrage, had created a tremendous mass base capable of harnessing governmental power for its own purposes. No longer need the "little person" fear the state, for he could control the state with his vote. And the capstone of this control was the presidency, because the chief executive alone had the entire nation as his constituency. Flushed with electoral triumph, the new President could lead his party and the Congress in drafting coherent policies to help that majority. Wilson had grasped a basic attribute of contemporary American politics: *egalitarian participation carried with it the seeds of executive domination over legislative decision-making.*

Wilson saw the President as a kind of prime minister. Jefferson had scrapped Washington's practice of appearing before the Congress to present recommendations because he saw the ritual as too formalistic. But Wilson resurrected the procedure, because it was dramatic and gave the chief executive's plan of attack increased visibility. His State of the Union speeches were aimed at Congress, but they were also aimed at the people. He was a master orator and rhetorician; he used his skills to cajole legislators and manipulate public opinion. Having set the stage with his prose, he would follow through by sending detailed messages to Capitol Hill outlining his major policy thrusts. The practice—now commonplace—whereby bills would be drafted by executive officials and introduced by legislative allies established itself under Wilson.

His record in Congress was absolutely remarkable, the most impressive prior to F.D.R.; and his New Freedom was really the first complete and systematic roster of proposals ever submitted by a President to the legislature. Whereas T.R.'s "stewardship" envisioned the chief executive as a leader apart, more particularly as an ombudsman bargaining and knocking heads for his notion of the general welfare on his own authority, Wilson advocated sweeping institutional policy changes through the law. His goal was to reorder the economic system by again placing it in the hands of competitive small units owned and managed by the individual entrepreneur. The tariff was lowered; the banking system was given new direction; and antitrust policy was toughened. And Wilson orchestrated the entire production through the medium of binding votes taken in congressional majority-party caucuses. Theodore Roosevelt had been Hamilton brought up to date; Woodrow Wilson was Jefferson in contemporary dress.

On the domestic scene, then, Wilson made tremendous changes—as *Chief of State,* by rallying popular support for his program; as *Chief Legislator,* by driving home a thoroughgoing set of recommendations; and as *Chief of Party,* by commanding consensus from partisans in the Congress.

Almost as innovative was Wilson the wartime President. Never before had this country participated in a worldwide military effort. As *Chief of Administration* and as *Commander-in-Chief,* Wilson claimed authority to establish by executive proclamation the War Industries Board, which supervised industrial production in dictatorial fashion, and the Committee on Public Information, which exercised a sort of informal censorship over the media. Equally important was Wilson's conception of his *Chief of Foreign Affairs* hat. He appointed himself our prime negotiator at Versailles, thus introducing the whole notion of "summitry," and he invoked the *Chief of State* function as an auxiliary device by making speeches all over the country to drum up support for League of Nations ratification.

With regard to the First World War and its aftermath, Wilson's innovative policies were a blend of the effective and the ineffective. He showed that constitutional democracy could muster all the power necessary to fight a world war, even at the risk of approaching the monolithic structure of the "garrison state." And he brought the nation to the doorstep of a world organization which was to be dedicated to peaceful cooperation. Here Wilson ran out of gas, because he had forgotten that sometimes the *Chief of State* must compromise and not be the slave of his own rhetoric. Returning from Versailles, the League of Nations treaty in hand, he found a Republican Congress waiting for him. Middle-of-the-roaders stood ready, anticipating his assent to mild amendments that would assure safe passage. But for the President, the League as written was "the only hope for mankind," a consummation authorized "by the hand of God who led us into this way."[74] He would not compromise. To nobody's surprise, the Senate killed "his" League; "hellfire and brimstone" gospel employed without regard to political realities is hardly the stuff of policy-making under a system of checks and balances. Wilson was the first—but not the last—"strong" President to find this out.

The modern President: chief of crisis

What factors distinguish the executive power of today from the executive power of yesteryear? As so often happens, the answer lies in a cliché: this is an age of crisis. When Woodrow Wilson passed from the scene, Americans could forget all about the League of Nations and the New Freedom. They could retreat into the make-believe world of Babe Ruth, bootleg "hootch," and a stock market with no ceiling. Only when this fantasy existence collapsed did Wilson's conception of the presidency become reality. Voters demanded a chief executive who would cope forcefully with an economy that refused to function as billed; later, they demanded a chief executive who would treat the spread of aggression with equal vigor—a "strong" President.[75]

The F.D.R. years were surely a time of crisis, and an argument can be made that the ensuing Truman years saw many a time of crisis as well. Perhaps in part as a result of that lengthy experience, presidential power today is predicated upon the *assumption of crisis.* Whether this assumption is justified is highly debatable. It is difficult to liken our present circumstances to economic collapse and world war. Sometimes events do pose a clear and present danger to the nation's well-being; such events are crises. Sometimes, however, unappetizing consequences are merely part of life's ups and downs, political rhetoric notwithstanding; and these developments must simply be taken in stride.

If I am right and we have been overreacting to any possible threat to our peace, luxury, and security, we have put the President in a bind. To the public eye, he is now "Mr. President, Superstar," and he is supposed to smite the dragons of adversity, danger, and crisis with his rhetoric, his drive, and perhaps most important of all, his image. Actually, this bind has two dimensions: (1) the President often lacks the precise constitutional or political weaponry to solve an alleged crisis; (2) the President, frustrated because he cannot do what is expected of him and what he has come to expect of himself, often wields his authority imprudently and winds up doing more harm than good. These two fundamental aspects of executive power in modern dress surely deserve elaboration, and the records of our contemporary "strong" Presidents furnish the best data.

Franklin Delano Roosevelt (1932–45) was the most charismatic President in this century. He also faced the two greatest political crises in this century: worldwide economic catastrophe and worldwide military hostilities between implacable foes. As *Chief of State* he was both the master of rhetoric ("We have nothing to fear but fear itself") and the master of innovative communication, with his radio "fireside chats" to the nation.

As *Party Chief* he forged a coalition that is still the backbone of the Democratic Party consensus: organized labor, small farmers, blacks, Jews, and the South (at that time, "solid"). As *Chief of Administration* he gathered around him a "Brain Trust" of informal advisors—lawyers, economists, academicians in order to breathe the fresh air of robust dialogue and disagreement. Finally, as *Chief Legislator* he spurred a Congress in his vest-pocket to enact the New Deal with its three R's: relief, reform, and recovery.

F.D.R. had problems too. His popularity was manifest, but he could not control a Supreme Court committed to the values of an earlier day. And so he hatched his infamous "Court-packing" plan, only to see Congress and public opinion reject the F.D.R. "sell" for the first time. Undaunted, he pressed ahead by attempting to "purge" key congressional Democrats who had refused to support his program to the hilt. The plan was to recruit "friendly" party activists, anoint them with F.D.R.'s personal blessing, and put them up against incumbent conservatives in primaries. It backfired miserably. Roosevelt was accused of tampering with local politics and was handed a new Congress controlled by Republicans and Southern Democrats. The New Deal ground to a halt.

Storm clouds were now gathering over Europe, and Roosevelt, convinced that only he could lead the country, broke the two-term tradition and ran for the presidency in 1940. He won reelection then, and, as a physical shadow of his halcyon days, he also ran successfully in 1944. As *Chief of Foreign Affairs* and as *Commander-in-Chief* he institutionalized the summit conference through his meetings with Churchill and Stalin. And in his zeal to forge *personally* for this country a winning partnership in war and in peace, he signed executive agreements that challenged directly the advise and consent, power-balancing procedure we use for consummating treaties. When F.D.R. died, in 1945, his many commitments and accords were left to be executed by Vice President Truman, a man he had not even bothered to train in the fundamentals of diplomacy.

Harry Truman (1945–52) faced a bona fide crisis when he entered the White House: absolute ignorance of what his predecessor had been doing. He learned quickly. As *Commander-in-Chief* he broke Japanese resistance by unleashing our atomic capability against Hiroshima and Nagasaki. As *Chief of Foreign Affairs* he met with Stalin, decided the Soviet leader was more like Hitler than like Churchill, and proceeded to go all out to save Western Europe from the Kremlin's clutches. As *Chief Legislator* he contrived a bipartisan international policy with Republican Senator Arthur Vandenberg; such programs as the Marshall Plan and N.A.T.O. followed shortly. Under Truman the nation's first permanent alliance system was born, and foreign aid became an obligation of national conscience. As *Chief of Party,* he pulled off the electoral upset of the century, touring "mainstream America" in a railroad whistle-stop campaign that saw him denounce the G.O.P. with unrivaled "populist" rhetoric. The phrase "Give 'em hell, Harry" became part of American political folklore.

The Harry Truman of 1949 was perhaps the most popular President in the modern era: as *Chief of State,* he was "just plain Harry," everybody's backfence neighbor. But the Harry Truman of 1952 was the most unpopular President in the modern era, surpassing even Richard Nixon in the last days of his tenure. What went wrong? When the Korean War broke out, Truman had decided to meet force with force. But while he saw the Pacific theater threatened by Communist aggression, he thought General MacArthur's recommendations were too dangerous. The result was a deadlock with Red China and its surrogates on one side and with the U.S. and its surrogates on the other. At home the nation demanded prompt action to meet two alleged crises befalling the chief executive, hard evidence that a few Soviet agents had infiltrated the bureaucracy and that a few members of his White House staff had misused their positions for personal gain. As *Chief of Administration* Truman faltered on the crime issue out of loyalty to his friends; and he took an ambivalent position on McCarthyism, rebuking the senator from Wisconsin mildly while building up a complicated security program for federal employees complete with hearsay-laden personal dossiers. As *Chief Legislator* his Fair Deal went nowhere fast; he, like F.D.R. before him, ran afoul of the conservative coalition.

Frustrated by these various impediments and his impotence in the face of crises he did not really believe existed, Truman lashed out at his enemies: to General MacArthur's many followers, he called Korea a "police action" and a "conflict," not a war; to Senator McCarthy's followers, he called the Alger Hiss case[i] a "red herring"; to his opponents in Congress, he called the Taft-Hartley Act a "slave-labor law." As *Chief of State,* he had become "Harry, the small-town, loud-mouthed incompetent."

John F. Kennedy (1960–63) had one strike against him when he squeaked into the White House with less than 50 percent of the popular vote: he was a Roman Catholic. Kennedy rebutted that threat to his role as *Chief of State* by opening up new vistas for the charismatic political personality with his youth, his good looks, his Harvard education, his skill at turning a phrase, his money, and his magnetic television personality.

But when we take a closer look at the Kennedy rhetoric, we see the urgency of the moment—the *politics of crisis*—implicit in his every message: "We've got to get this country moving again"; "Ask not what your country can do for you, ask what you can do for your country." The message was especially effective in promoting his *Chief of Party* hat, for he capitalized on Republican war hero Eisenhower's low-key, almost soporific presidential tenure (1952–60) by prodding Americans to pay more attention to their social responsibilities. Reawakening F.D.R.'s national coalition, Kennedy's call to arms, combined with his seemingly irresistible personal appeal, spelled defeat for Richard Nixon in their celebrated TV debates and at the polls as well.

And how was that rhetoric converted into public policy-making? Here is a sprinkling of New Frontiersmanship: if the Viet Cong threatens American hegemony over South Vietnam, send in military advisors; if U.S. Steel raises prices, jaw-bone those prices down; if Castro is consolidating his power, mobilize the C.I.A. and invade Cuba; if the people of West Virginia are hungry, feed them; if the Russians are ahead of us in the "space race," beat them to the moon![j] Khrushchev's aborted attempt to place ground-to-ground missiles in

[i] Hiss was a White House advisor, sent to jail for lying about espionage activities. The prime mover in investigating his machinations was a young congressman from California, Richard Nixon.

[j] It was during the Kennedy era that professional football became a national religion and Green Bay Packers coach Vince Lombardi coined the immortal phrase "Winning isn't everything; it's the only thing." I see Kennedy and Lombardi as soul brothers.

Cuba and the dramatic test of strength at Oxford, Mississippi, over James Meredith's academic future were serious business. Nor do I mean the other cases were unimportant. The thrust of my commentary is that J.F.K. saw the presidency as a crisis center; to watch him, one would think the United States had become an Israel surrounded by Arabs. For Kennedy, the New Deal was "old-time religion" entitled to resurrection. But the Congress did not buy it; as *Chief Legislator,* he barely made a dent. Whether Kennedy would have eventually succeeded in convincing the nation that his notion of crisis was reality we shall never know, for Lee Harvey Oswald changed the course of history.

Lyndon Johnson (1963-69) also saw the New Deal as "holy writ," but, unlike Kennedy, he was the master of legislative processes. The civil rights movement, with Martin Luther King at its head, had now attained full flower. This *was* a crisis, for the country's very fabric as protector of human values was being sorely tested. In the wake of the J.F.K. assassination trauma, Johnson shuffled the cards, Republican Senator Everett Dirksen gave them a cut, and the path-breaking 1964 Civil Rights Act was rammed through the Congress, much to the dismay and mortification of the conservative coalition. And when the G.O.P. essayed its "Goldwater Gambit," the President found himself with a majority of liberals in Congress that would have gladdened even Franklin Roosevelt's heart.

Here was the time for "Mr. President, Superstar" to harness his skills as *Chief Legislator,* and Lyndon Johnson was ready and willing to act. So the Great Society was born. Like the New Deal, it was an attempt to help the economically disadvantaged, and like the New Frontier it was presented to the public as an attempt to wipe out social evils that had allegedly reached *crisis* proportions. The Johnson consensus launched a "war on poverty" by passing the Economic Opportunity Act, with its community action programs and its "maximum feasible participation." And the consensus launched a war on inferior schooling in poor neighborhoods by passing the Elementary and Secondary Education Act. As Johnson put it: We will provide "full educational opportunity."[76]

The Great Society was built upon an innovative theory of constitutional politics, which can be stated as follows: the American people have a right to *equality of opportunity,* and the "crisis President" as *Chief Legislator* has a duty to guarantee that right. Underlying this theory was the prevailing "liberal Constitution" (see Chapter 4), with its central tenet, group self-regulation sustained by vague statutory guidelines. If there is a pattern of "Living Constitutional" values which today sums up how the "liberal consensus" addresses the social issues that spawned it in the 1930s, it is Johnson's one-two-three punch: "equality of opportunity"; "maximum feasible participation"; presidential power to guarantee both in the face of abiding crisis. If, indeed, these were crisis conditions, few voters would have argued that L.B.J. had failed to meet them.

But confrontation in Southeast Asia was boiling over. As *Commander-in-*

Chief, Johnson sent a massive fighting force across the Pacific. But Ho Chi Minh was not Everett Dirksen; he would not bargain. The President's domestic political savvy was unavailing on the international front; and in the Mekong Delta 500,000 well-trained American soldiers couldn't deliver. Meanwhile, on the home front, students "trashed" the campuses, resisted the draft, closed schools, and sometimes even fire-bombed buildings. Johnson—like Truman before him—retired from the lists under a barrage of criticism.

Richard Nixon (1969-74) is the one "strong" President of modern times who could not be characterized as a liberal. For him, there was no domestic crisis inherent in Appalachian poverty or in rising unemployment figures. For him, there was a "law and order" crisis. I promise to appoint a new, tough-minded Attorney General, he told a cheering Republican National Convention in 1968; the jungle warfare of city life and the anarchic displays of the antiwar protesters must be cleaned up. Indeed, for those who recoiled from the ever-increasing frequency of muggings and rapes, the madness of the Columbia University riots, and the specter of Black Panther members sniping at police, there certainly appeared to be a crisis in the streets. And on the international scene, Vietnam loomed as crisis-laden as ever. What to do?

With Henry Kissinger at his side, Nixon went after the Southeast Asia stalemate, simultaneously withdrawing our soldiers by increments and intensively bombing Cambodia and North Vietnam. When nothing much happened, he ordered an invasion of Cambodia, the mining of Haiphong Harbor, and even more bombing. Whether because of these steps or in spite of them, Vietnam slowly faded away. So Nixon could turn his attention to arms agreements with the Soviet Union, to China, to détente—in short, from his role as *Commander-in-Chief* to his role as *Chief of Foreign Affairs.* In that capacity, he would grapple with the "super world crisis" of our time, the compelling need for a grand "balance of power" design among the superpowers.[k]

But law and order could not be achieved by such swift and energetic action. Indeed, so long as "those extremists" were still running amok, all the Attorneys General in the world wouldn't make a difference. But something had to be done! So while an occasional flag or draft card would be burned in the streets, and while an old Lyndon Johnson war-planner named Daniel Ellsberg made walking off with confidential government documents seem an honorable deed, and while a "Chicago Seven"-type demonstration every now and again did threaten the general welfare, the President, as *Chief of the Public Peace,* put together his new look: domestic surveillance in the name of "national security."

When one plays with fire and civil liberties, forests and constitutions can burn down. I do not claim Nixon planned the Watergate break-in; that he saw George McGovern and his followers as an unpatriotic, thoroughly dangerous

[k] Nixon was another avid football fan, who, as *Chief of State,* was always huddling with athletes and coaches over possible strategies. One sometimes got the feeling that through his wheeling and dealing with foreign leaders he had created his own Super Bowl from the welter of international embroilments.

political force seems evident. To put the matter bluntly, the President surrounded himself with his own thoroughly dangerous political force, as any fair rendition of his own tapes or the voluminous testimony at various cover-up trials will bear witness. And so was consummated the crisis of crises: impeachment and resignation of a President. Throughout the preceding paragraphs, I have tried to analyze how contemporary "strong" Presidents invoked their "Living Constitutional" roles to smite the dragons of national crisis as they perceived them.[77] But there is one additional factor to fold into the mix. Early in my remarks, I said the study of presidential behavior was very much a study in psychology. Now it is time to pose this question: What kinds of men held the reins of executive authority during this era?

James David Barber thinks there are two personality attributes that determine how a chief executive will approach his constitutional powers and duties. First is the active-passive dimension. Does the President dominate, or is he dominated? Does he attack or defend? Most modern Presidents have been "active," because people generally choose active leaders to meet crisis conditions; at this level, then, the terms "active" and "strong" are virtually synonymous. Second, we have the "positive-negative affect" dimension. Is the President happy and satisfied with his use of power? Or does wielding influence fill him with feelings of skepticism, irritability, perhaps even acrimony? In other words, is the President a "positive thinker," or does he dwell on his setbacks? Does he enjoy the thrusts and parries that are an inevitable part of his very political business, or does he find them distasteful, even threatening?

These two dimensions can be combined to yield four composite character profiles: active-positive Presidents, active-negatives, passive-positives, and passive-negatives. The first and the last of these personality configurations are symmetrical—that is, they make sense in logic. A President who is active ought to feel good about being active; conversely, a President who is acted upon ought to feel upset because he can't control his public destiny. "Active-positives" revel in the results that the prudent display of power should yield; "passive-negatives" steer clear of political in-fighting, stressing instead general, vague, "good-government" clichés wrapped in the rectitude of civic virtue. Thomas Jefferson was an "active-positive" who took direct, forceful steps to help the "common person" and loved every minute of it. Calvin Coolidge, famous for saying, "When a great many people are unable to find work, unemployment results" and just as famous for saying, "I do not choose to run" (for reelection in 1928), was the "passive-negative" prototype.

And who are the "passive-positives"? They are accommodating, compliant sorts, who seek to avoid tension in the search for love and approval. William Howard Taft fits the mold, a man far more infatuated with the law than with power. And there was Warren Harding, who was so vulnerable that even his friends used and abused him. If we have had a "passive-positive" in the White House during the past several years, his name is Gerald Ford.

And who are the "active-negatives"? These Presidents struggle to achieve, struggle to win, struggle to gain and hold power, yet for some reason they are never fulfilled, perhaps because they possess an inherent flaw that makes it impossible for them ever to be fulfilled. A few have a touch of Oedipus about them, while others have only a touch of Arthur Miller's salesman, Willy Loman.

We know the typical contemporary chief executive has been an activist, so if Barber is on the right track, then the individual personality attribute that best demonstrates how particular chief executives employed power is "positive-negative affect." Have these "strong" Presidents played the "Constitutional Superstar" role with the zest displayed by a Jefferson? Or have they only managed to make their lives more complicated and unrewarding?

In the search for an answer, we can return to the contemporary political forum and see how these men conducted themselves. This review, I think, will lead to the following conclusion: *just as there has been an evolution in our definition of and reaction to crisis, so there has been an evolution in the kinds of leaders we have elected President of the United States.* Moreover, I shall show that these two tendencies have had a deleterious impact on one another.

Franklin Roosevelt was the epitome of "active-positiveness": he loved power; he loved action; he loved to achieve results; he related to people rather than to things or ideas; he had a great sense of humor, which energized everything he did. Roosevelt accurately perceived domestic crisis; he went off the track when he placed the success of his New Deal ahead of the separation of powers principle itself. Roosevelt accurately perceived foreign crisis too; here he went off the track because he considered himself indispensible. In this instance, however, the voters seemed to agree with him, because they were willing to rubber-stamp his violation of the "Living Constitution" with its two-term tradition. But the result was another crisis, for his death left a terrible gap in leadership.

F.D.R.'s presidency illustrates that "active-positives" are good at spotting and responding to crises *if they exist;* but it also illustrates that "active-positives" overrate their place in the scheme of things, for, as even Lincoln's incumbency should have taught us, governance by "benevolent tenure" almost always stimulates a clear and present danger to the constitutional rules.

Harry Truman was another "active-positive." But unlike Jefferson and F.D.R., he came up the hard way. His world was Andrew Jackson's world, a universe that teaches people to overemphasize personal loyalty and personal vindictiveness. He also lacked the intellectual breadth necessary to think in macroscopic (much less theoretical) terms.

Truman gauged correctly the crisis proportions of Stalin's brute-force maneuvers, and he acted to meet them. However, his half-in, half-out policy toward the Korean quasi-crisis only caused confusion among the electorate, which probably would have followed him had he chosen either the MacArthur approach or a "nonentanglement" approach with consistency from the beginning. In domestic affairs, his constituents saw crisis where he did not. His failure again was largely a matter of "fence-straddling"; he failed to seize the initiative from Senator McCarthy or make war on McCarthy. Moreover, his verbal overkill only fanned the flames of confusion and frustration.

Truman's presidency illustrates that provincial "active-positives" have difficulty reacting to another person's sense of crisis. In these situations, they tend to tread water, and this can even help spawn crisis, especially when accompanied by the activist's penchant for provocative rhetoric. Notice, however, that the "crises" of his years had already become markedly less explosive than those which F.D.R. faced.

Clearly, John F. Kennedy was another "active-positive," but more on the Jefferson-F.D.R. axis than the Jackson-Truman line. When J.F.K. reached the White House, no emergency loomed on the horizon that remotely approached Stalinist imperialism. Yet his chief academic advisor on the subject of White House management, Richard Neustadt, bemoaned the fact that in this "era of permanent crisis" the President could only persuade, not command. The legacy of the Roosevelt and Truman years is that everyone wants a "strong" President, Neustadt wrote, but the American chief executive has no authority to implement his programs once they have been formulated. On every side are congressmen, bureaucrats, mayors, and governors whom he cannot control; pressure groups annoyed—even angered—because his policies seem to favor competing groups; and, finally, there is his fragile prestige as chief of state, which can tear irreparably should he push too hard on behalf of one specialized bloc of supporters. Hence, his ace in the hole is to choose a policy and to exercise the arts of persuasion and bargaining to get that policy off the ground. If only the President could rely on F.D.R.'s "crisis consensus," Neustadt concluded, then he could perform his duties effectively.[78]

Kennedy's presidency illustrates what an "active-positive" will do when objective crises are sporadic. He will plead, inveigh, perhaps even inspire, for the checks-and-balances system places a premium on persuasion, absent crisis conditions. But he will do more. He will create crises—"pseudo-crises"—and try to trade them in like poker chips for power enhancement. This involves nothing less than reinterpreting the constitutional environment and, ultimately, the "Living Constitution." And this, I take it, is exactly what Kennedy tried to do with his rhetoric and his "one-on-one" competitions.

The Johnson and Nixon Administrations—nurtured in the "pseudo-crises" of "millions of Americans going to bed hungry every night," Viet Cong militancy, and the "breakdown" of national security—suggest that Kennedy did prepare satisfactorily this "crisis consensus." As a matter of fact, alternative candidacies were wrought in perhaps even greater "crisis-oriented" terms: Barry "Mr. Hawk" Goldwater in 1964; Hubert Humphrey, nominee of a schizophrenic Democratic Party in 1968; George "Mr. Dove" McGovern in 1972. Does not this cast of winners and losers demonstrate that politically active Americans—working through their respective parties—were seeing the problems of the 1960s and 1970s through the same glasses of desperation as they had seen the problems of the 1930s and 1940s?

It does not seem to have occurred to political scientists writing in the 1950s and early 1960s that the executive branch had accumulated too much power by the time J.F.K. took office.[79] And while it may have occurred to a voting majority content with Dwight Eisenhower's passive caretakership, all that was just a memory by 1965.

It also does not seem to have occurred to anyone that overly broad conceptions of crisis might help bring to the fore precisely the kinds of people who should not be charged with fighting crisis. Lyndon Johnson, the man who made Vietnam his own war as Wilson made the League of Nations his own peace plan; Richard Nixon, the congenital "Mr. Up-Tight" radical-chaser who would freeze over his own tapes as Johnson froze over Vietnam[1]—these are the men (essentially "active-negatives," in Barber's terminology) whom we encourage to play "constitutional superstar" when crisis is more a state of mind than a state of being.

Of course, I am not saying that Vietnam did not *eventually* become a crisis; that anarchy on the campus—which was caused almost entirely by Vietnam involvement—did not *eventually* become a crisis; that Watergate did not precipitate a constitutional crisis. But several chapters ago, in discussing how the Framers went about the business of writing a constitution, I said it was fraught with danger for us to interpret their problems as we would interpret our own; each era must, in considerable measure, make its own way. Why then is it so difficult for us to see that while Franklin Roosevelt and even Harry Truman had to cope with clear and present dangers to our polity, each "strong" President since 1953 who was called upon to fend off crises was at war with dangers *he largely brought upon himself?* If these Presidents had the capacity not only to persuade but also to command, one's mind is boggled to think of the crises they might have generated. To sum up, we will always have crises, but the problems of 1935 are not the problems of 1977.

Quo vadis, "Mr. President, Superstar"?

From 1974 through 1976, the White House lay in a state of suspended animation. Gerald Ford, who never dreamed he'd be President and never wanted to be, had had the reins of executive power thrust upon him, and he exhibited the same general approach to the office as our other not so strong contemporary President Dwight Eisenhower. He allowed the dust of Nixonism to settle, as Ike allowed the dust of Trumanism to settle; he allowed the nation to catch its breath; he was a caretaker chief executive. But while Eisenhower did not revel in the power of the President and so accomplished less than he might have, his image as war hero commanded the respect of most Americans and most leaders

[1] For more than a year, the nation waited in agony while Nixon pondered whether to release the tapes or destroy them. And to this day, he cannot bring himself to admit personal culpability in anything relating to Watergate.

of the world. When Ike wanted to move, he could get things done, as our rapid extrication from Korean quicksand illustrates. Gerald Ford had no such reputation to fall back on. Still, some comments are in order with respect to his tenure and the notion of *crisis.*

First, Ford proceeded to expend much of the good will surrounding his inauguration by pardoning Richard Nixon before a grand jury even had a chance to indict (or not indict) him. While the chief executive's pardon power is rarely exercised until guilt has been established, it is within his discretion to do so at any time.[80] Yet Ford's feel for public opinion in this matter betrayed him; the outcry of opposition precipitated a real crisis, because it looked as though "Mr. Nice Guy" had made a backroom deal with the man who appointed him. Even after Ford took the unprecedented step of appearing before a congressional panel (and national television) to justify his decision, it was clear he had lost at the very outset the original glow of purity. He was fair political game from then on.

Second, Ford immediately found himself faced with two instances of what can only be called "pseudo-crises." Curiously enough, both involved the vice presidency, though given the unique manner of his promotion to the White House, there really is nothing curious about the little melodramas that unfolded.

Traditionally, the vice presidency has attracted pedestrian figures because he is the President's alter-ego and an impotent one at that.[m] Of course, we have had our share of chief executives fail to live out their terms. After John Kennedy's assassination, the Twenty-fifth Amendment was passed, in part to meet that contingency; an opening in the Veep's post can now be filled by executive nomination and congressional majority-vote confirmation.[n] In this fashion, Ford named Nelson Rockefeller to succeed him, just as he himself had been named by President Nixon following Agnew's abrupt departure.

Now for Ford's "pseudo-crises." One stemmed from a general discomfort over having for the first time in our history neither President nor Vice President who had been chosen at the ballot box. Something is horribly wrong with a so-called democracy, it was contended, when the top two executive officials come to their jobs without electoral approval. Now really! How many voters ever

[m] Even such political heavyweights as Lyndon Johnson (under J.F.K.) and Hubert Humphrey (under L.B.J.) could not do much with the office, and they were shunted well into the background. Perhaps Spiro Agnew made the most of the position from a power standpoint, dramatizing President Nixon's "law and order" and "silent majority" themes with a stridency that would have tarnished the chief's image had he engaged in such forensics himself.

[n] The Constitution originally had provided no means for replacing a Vice President when he moved up a peg; but "Mr. President, Superstar's" responsibilities have attained such awesome proportions that it was considered prudent that there should always be a Vice President ready to fill the breach. This helps explain why Ronald Reagan risked breaking the "Living Constitution" by selecting his running-mate *before* the 1976 G.O.P. convention had settled on a presidential standard-bearer. In times gone by, the post was often dangled in front of the "losing" faction as a consolation prize. But the vice presidency is almost too important for that now, so Reagan thought he could overtake Gerald Ford's lead by tapping the liberal Richard Schweiker *in advance.* And, of course, several of the Californian's staunch supporters screamed bloody murder at the choice precisely because the office has assumed such significance.

actually cast their ballots for a vice presidential candidate? No previous Vice President who succeeded to office on the death of a President has had any more popular mandate than Ford—and this includes Theodore Roosevelt, Harry Truman, and Lyndon Johnson.

The second "pseudo-crisis" centered on Nelson Rockefeller himself. Many were the congressmen who said they could not confirm him because of his wealth. Weeks dragged into months as both chambers more than meticulously examined every nook and cranny of Rockefeller's public and private financial record. Now really, again! The *use* of money is one thing; the ownership of money surely tells us nothing about a candidate's capacity for public service. Fortunately, Congress eventually saw things that way.

The fact that these questions have now retreated into the public's subconscious does not detract from their "pseudo-crisis" status in 1974-75. Indeed, this is part of the problem, for today's so-called crises no longer even require presidential baptism. Every few months, the television camera grabs onto some issue of moment, affords eminent visibility to those who think the dilemma poses grave dangers to the system, and soon the President is called upon to meet the threat. "Pseudo-crises" used to be reserved for mountains, but now they identify even hills. The result is a good case of jangled nerves for everyone concerned.

What does this tell us about the notion of crisis for the immediate future? As the country moves through the middle 1970s, the biggest issues have been economic. The rate of inflation hit 12 percent in 1975, while the ratio of those unemployed hit 9 percent. But this really *was* a crisis, wasn't it? Certainly when judged in the light of Ford's extraordinarily large recession-coping budget deficits, the answer is yes. And certainly when judged against Democratic complaints that Ford wasn't spending enough, the answer is yes. But our budget is *never* balanced anymore; things never quite look rosy enough to allow for what used to be a "Living Constitutional" norm. And what about average citizens? Is their economic security so uncertain when they can buy a $500 color TV set for $100 down, which is exactly what they do under all but the most pressing conditions? From the standpoint of *general* welfare, then, the notion of crisis is a salient facet of our constitutional environment, but the typical recession is mostly "pseudo-crisis," as was amply demonstrated when the patient's partial recovery from the economic quasi-crisis of 1975 took only a year.

And so President Carter—no matter what his predilections—cannot escape the presidential "Living Constitution" that has obtained since Kennedy's day. When he attends church, the press is there; when he plays softball, the press is there; when his young daughter enrolls in public school, the press is there. And from every indication, the public eats it up. So he must lead; he must come up with "game plans"; he must exert power through persuasion and, where possible, command; he must react to "pseudo-crises" as well as crises; and sometimes he must even create crises. The President has always been a leader apart in our political galaxy; now he is "Mr. Constitutional Superstar." For, as I have said elsewhere, today's public philosophy teaches that every legitimate political interest has a right to believe that the state should annoint it with a maximum of luxury, security, opportunity, and participation. And that philosophy's factotum is our "constitutional superstar": in his finest hour, the President is supposed to transcend the power struggle by administering potions to toxic diseases while impinging on no interest's private preserve—that is, he is supposed to do the impossible.

Is there no way to check and balance the President as superstar? I am reminded of Barber's fourfold classificatory scheme, whose simplifications somehow reflect the simplifications surrounding our perception of what Presidents should be like. His "active-positives" deserve special consideration, because they are certainly the most appealing; Americans would ordinarily put these people in the White House if they could. After all, results + image = crisis reduction. And sometimes "active-positives" are the leaders we need. But, if I understand Barber correctly, their natural bent for manipulating power coupled with their freedom from harmful ego involvement makes them not only the best innovators but also political liberals.[81] I think these propositions cannot be accepted without important qualification, just as I think the popular judgment about their "natural superiority" deserves reconsideration.

First, innovative talent is as much a function of *what* as *who.* If we need to find new ways to help blacks achieve their rights or new ways to deal with energy problems, then why would we necessarily elect the same kind of President who is skilled in fighting economic depressions or in "containing" communism? Some of these tasks may require healthy doses of human compassion and the pragmatic temperament—the "active-positive's" stock-in-trade—but others may require an emphasis on ideology or on consistent planning and follow-through. If the ultimate goals range from a sense of equity, to a sense of intellectual integrity, to a sense of survival, it is quite likely the talents needed to shape divergent strategies will be linked to divergent personality characteristics. But just as these other innovative skills are not the stuff of "active-positivism," so they are not the stuff of superstardom either; the building blocks of charisma simply aren't there. And that is why we do not consider someone like consumer advocate Ralph Nader or banker David Rockefeller presidential timber.

Second, the ability to carve out new political vistas is no liberal monopoly. Abraham Lincoln and Teddy Roosevelt—who must be coded as political conservatives, if one must code them—were as concerned with making things happen as any chief executives we have had, especially when we remember the times in which they lived. Moreover, creativity in giving the Constitution a more coherent, a more rational form in practice[82] need not be the task of austere, compulsive "passive-negatives." The problem is that innovative "constitutionalists" aren't considered presidential timber either, because the accent today is on cultivating candidates who will joust with such post-1960 "pseudo-crises" as "we've seen walls built up around Washington."[o] However, their

[o] That Jimmy Carter's clarion cry—delivered with the outsider's Southern twang and wrapped in the compelling imagery of a "John Boy" Walton evangelical Christianity—was nothing but wolf is amply demonstrated by a look at his Cabinet, which is largely a collection of Washington establishmentarians.

names could well be Sam Ervin, Potter Stewart, or William F. Buckley. Finally, for better or worse, does anyone think Ronald Reagan would be a passive President or that he is less happy in life than Jimmy Carter or Gerald Ford? To sum up, personality configuration and value orientation should remain bifurcated as factors influencing presidential performance.

Ultimately, we cannot check "Mr. President, Superstar" until we check our own propensities to lump all crises together, to magnify quasi-crises into full-blown crises, and to magnify issues into "pseudo-crises." This point is fundamental because the Framers put nothing in the Constitution to check superstardom. That check can only come from a more balanced sense of proportion as to our rights and our obligations, else the "Living Constitution" with regard to presidential magnetism will be a tragic footnote to the grand design of the original commodity.

NOTES

1. The pithy language comes from Chief Justice Charles Evans Hughes, speaking for a majority in *Home Bldg. & Loan Assn. v. Blaisdell,* 290 U.S. 398 at p. 426 (1934).

2. Is this an undue delegation of power? Not under the *Curtiss-Wright* doctrine.

3. *Martin v. Mott,* 12 Wheat. 19 (1827). This is the usual "political questions" line employed by the Justices when confronted with military contingencies.

4. The best analysis of presidential "war powers" during those years is found in James G. Randall, *Constitutional Problems Under Lincoln* (Urbana: Univ. of Illinois Press, 1951).

5. *The Prize Cases,* 2 Black 635 (1863).

6. Clarence A. Berdahl, *War Powers of the Executive in the United States* (Urbana: Univ. of Illinois, 1921), p. 76.

7. W. W. Willoughby, *The Constitutional Law of the United States* (New York: Baker, Voorhis, 1910), vol. 2, p. 797; Edward S. Corwin, *The President: Office and Powers, 1787-1957* (New York: New York Univ. Press, 1957), pp. 141-42.

8. Abraham Lincoln to Albert G. Hodges, in John Nicolay and John Hay, eds., *The Complete Works of Abraham Lincoln* (New York: F. D. Tandy, 1894), vol. 10, pp. 65-68.

9. The authority to take private property for a public purpose, known as the power of *eminent domain,* is exercised traditionally by Congress; but the chief executive, as commander in chief, may also confiscate property for similar purposes. The Fifth Amendment entitles the former owner to receive fair compensation no matter which branch of government does the taking.

10. *Ex parte Milligan,* 4 Wall. 2 (1866).

11. Ibid., p. 127.

12. Randall, pp. 136-37; Corwin, p. 146.

13. The vast majority of citizens detained under his emergency program were released in expeditious fashion.

14. The words are Franklin Roosevelt's own, spoken before a hushed and confused joint meeting of the Congress one day after Pearl Harbor.

15. *Duncan v. Kahanamoku,* 327 U.S. 304 (1946). So this is a case where the Supreme Court *interpreted the statute* in a manner favorable to civil liberties. It claimed Congress did not give F.D.R. power to turn Hawaii into a garrison state. And, of course, it said Roosevelt had no more authority than had Lincoln to do these things on his own or through his aides.

16. *Hirabayashi v. United States,* 320 U.S. 81 (1943).

17. *Korematsu v. United States,* 323 U.S. 214 (1944).

18. Ibid., p. 223.

19. *Ex parte Endo,* 323 U.S. 283 (1944).

20. *Duncan v. Kahanamoku,* p. 324.

21. Corwin (p. 256) sees this factor as the crucial variable.

22. A typical blast is Eugene V. Rostow, "The Japanese American Cases—A Disaster," *The Yale Law Journal* 54 (1945), pp. 489-533.

23. *Selective Draft Law Cases,* 245 U.S. 366 (1918).

24. *Yakus v. United States,* 321 U.S. 414 (1944).

25. *Woods v. Miller,* 333 U.S. 138 (1948).

26. *Youngstown Sheet & Tube Co. v. Sawyer,* 343 U.S. 579 (1952).

27. I very much approve the critical tack taken by Corwin with respect to the Court's disposition of this case. See "The Steel Seizure Case: A Judicial Brick Without Straw," *Columbia Law Review* 53 (1953), pp. 53-66.

28. A concurring opinion is an individual statement of views by a judge who agrees with the *decision* but is not satisfied with the explanation found in the "opinion of the Court."

29. Also applicable was our participation in S.E.A.T.O., an issue I discuss presently under the treaty-making power.

30. I think this is a correct reading of Louis Pollak et al., "The Congressional and Executive Roles in War-Making: An Analytical Framework," *Congressional Record,* vol. 116, S7591-S7593 (May 21, 1970), and I think that document captures the constitutional values implicit in the enactment. See Jacob K. Javits, *Who Makes War* (New York: William Morrow, 1973), especially Ch. 19.

31. This is the Supreme Court talking, in *United States v. Curtiss-Wright,* 299 U.S. 304 at p. 319 (1936).

32. Again, this is judicial interpretation. See *United States v. Curtiss-Wright,* p. 320 (italics mine).

33. Strangely enough, the Supreme Court was never asked to review these decisions handed down by federal district and circuit tribunals.

34. *Missouri v. Holland,* 252 U.S. 416 (1920).

35. Many other crucial political judgments relevant to Germany's future status were decided in this fashion. Did any treaty authorize the Allies to carve the defeated foe up like a turkey? No. Did any treaty formalize the occupation zones which to this day result in a fragmented Berlin? No. For the record, these were President Truman's doings, not Roosevelt's.

36. *United States v. Belmont,* 301 U.S. 324 (1937).

37. Robert A. Dahl, *Congress and Foreign Policy* (New York: W. W. Norton, 1950), Ch. XIII.

38. For a novelist's view of what could be in the offing from such a one-sided relationship, see Herman Melville's *The Confidence-Man.*

39. Naturally, Congress's enactments prescribing these duties had better be constitutional!

40. This is where Mr. Truman got himself into trouble in the *Steel Seizure Case,* according to Justice Black's prevailing opinion.

41. This is where Truman got himself into trouble in the same dispute, according to those Justices who said he flouted the Taft-Hartley Act.

42. *Mississippi v. Johnson,* 4 Wall. 475 (1867); *Georgia v. Stanton,* 6 Wall. 50 (1867).

43. Leaving aside the extraordinary process of impeachment.

44. Obviously, if a congressman or other official is arrested for murder, he can be tried like anybody else.

45. These should be accepted as givens, otherwise the great lesson of this episode may escape us. Such assumptions do not require us to render ethical judgment about the use of taping systems employed without the knowledge of those being taped. But on the general question of ethics and listening devices, see Chapter 7, pp. 287-91.

46. However, the Burr trial in no way involved a President's alleged criminal behavior. Does this fact distinguish the Jeffersonian and Nixonian uses of the privilege?

47. *Sen. Select Comm. v. Nixon,* 366 F. Supp. 51 (1973).

48. *Sen. Select Comm. v. Nixon,* 370 F. Supp. 521 (1974).

49. The best statement of that argument is in Raoul Berger, *Executive Privilege: A Constitutional Myth* (Cambridge, Mass.: Harvard Univ. Press, 1974).

50. *United States v. Nixon,* 94 S. Ct. 3090 (1974).

51. When Nixon said goodby to the White House, he left his tapes behind. Congress promptly passed a law placing them under protective custody but guaranteeing "just compensation" should the courts so mandate. This provision enforces the presumption that Nixon owns the materials.

52. *Myers v. United States,* 272 U.S. 52 (1926).

53. Ibid., p. 117.

54. Except, naturally, judges who have life tenure.

55. *Humphrey's Executor (Rathbun) v. United States,* 295 U.S. 602.

56. *Congressional Quarterly Almanac* (1973) pp. 1018–19.

57. See my point 3, p. 195. The supporting precedent, incidentally, is *United States v. Perkins,* 116 U.S. 483 (1886).

58. More general issues of law enforcement strategy are discussed in Chapter 7, where I take up the Department of Justice.

59. *In re Neagle,* 135 U.S. 1 at p. 64 (1890).

60. Ibid., pp. 67–69, 75–76.

61. *In re Debs,* 158 U.S. 564 (1895).

62. *United States v. District Court,* 407 U.S. 297 (1972).

63. Judge Gesell ruled that the break-in was illegal, and that national security reasons did not make such action suddenly legal, even had the President himself given the go-ahead. *United States v. Ehrlichman,* 376 F. Supp. 29 (1974).

64. The Justices have had their opportunities (see *Katz v. United States,* 389 U.S. 347, 1967), but obviously they are not going to tackle this hot potato unless it becomes absolutely necessary. The courts are currently litigating "invasion of privacy" suits brought by former government officials against both Nixon and Kissinger.

65. A good general overview of the President's role, upon which I base many of the following observations, is Joseph E. Kallenbach, *The American Chief Executive* (New York: Harper & Row, 1966), Ch. 7. Also of value is Louis W. Koenig, *The Chief Executive,* 3rd ed. (New York: Harcourt Brace Jovanovich, 1975).

66. Theodore Roosevelt, *An Autobiography* (New York: Macmillan, 1916), p. 372.

67. W. H. Taft, *Our Chief Magistrate and his Powers* (New York: Columbia Univ. Press, 1925), pp. 139–40.

68. Kallenbach, for one, appears to use the terms "strong" and "effective" synonymously. See pp. 267–69 of *The American Chief Executive.*

69. For present purposes, the modern presidency dates from—and includes—F.D.R.'s tenure.

70. The list of executive functions comes from Kallenbach, p. 255, and it is as serviceable as any. For an alternative classificatory scheme, see Clinton Rossiter, *The American Presidency,* 2nd ed. (New York: Harcourt, Brace & World, 1960), Ch. 1.

71. James David Barber, *The Presidential Character* (Englewood Cliffs, N.J.: Prentice-Hall, 1972), pp. 13–14. I rely considerably on Barber's insights with respect to the personality attributes and consequences of presidential behavior.

72. James D. Richardson, *Messages and Papers of the Presidents* (Washington, D.C.: Government Printing Office, 1896), vol. 1, pp. 218–19.

73. Kallenbach, p. 291.

74. Quoted in Barber, p. 20.

75. This conventional wisdom among academicians is summed up as follows: "We have come to accept a powerful executive as normal because crisis is the normal condition of our time." Robert S. Hirschfield, ed., *The Power of the Presidency,* 2nd ed. (Chicago: Aldine, 1973), p. 10.

76. Quoted in James L. Sundquist, *Politics and Policy* (Washington, D.C.: Brookings Institution, 1968), p. 211. I have found this book very useful in thinking through the Johnson "public philosophy."

77. On the important question of how these chief executives mobilized interests around the country to build a winning "crisis-fighting" consensus, see my discussions of party history and electoral behavior in Chapters 9 and 10.

78. Richard Neustadt, "The Presidency at Mid-Century," *Law and Contemporary Problems* 21 (1956), pp. 609-45.

79. For example, every relevant essay save one appearing in the Hirschfield reader (see note 75) operates from the same assumption: if anything, the presidency is not strong enough. The exception is provided by the greatest of all constitutional scholars in the contemporary era, Edward S. Corwin.

80. See such cases as *United States v. Wilson,* 7 Pet. 150 (1833); *Ex parte Garland,* 4 Wall. 333 (1867); and *Burdick v. United States,* 236 U.S. 79 (1915).

81. Barber, p. 246.

82. Barber would call this "system involvement" rather than "people involvement."

6

civil liberties: inalienable rights or reciprocal relations?

Nothing is more intellectually challenging in the world of American constitutional politics—or more emotionally taxing—than civil liberties issues. Public debate surrounding the right to distribute pornography, the duty to bus children for the sake of school integration, the power to stop and frisk citizens on the street, or the practice of reciting prayers in public facilities is getting, if anything, even hotter and more fascinating. One reason for this is the ongoing, highly visible split on the Supreme Court (which I described in Chapter 2) between community-oriented Justices and liberty-oriented Justices, a cleavage that has been with us since the Warren Court first began to make news. This "split" means different things to different people, of course, but there is no doubt that the Court's battles have polarized most interested observers. Another reason why interest in these issues has proliferated is the Watergate affair, with its "Mission Impossible" escapades, "dirty tricks," cover-up trials, and televised hearings.

Indeed, I think Watergate, the civil rights movement, the antiwar movement, the "law and order" movement, and more, taken together, have had a cumulative effect on our consciousness. It is most of all that impact which makes civil liberties debate rage so hot and heavy at this time. And in great measure these specific developments either have been generated by or are reactions against what is perhaps the most fundamental pattern in contemporary American power relationships: the federal government is getting bigger, more active, and more assertive—a trend people seem to applaud or denounce depending on how it affects their rights as they see them.

I have had much to say already about state expansionism. Now the other side of the coin must be developed. I want to focus on civil liberties themselves, and I define the term to include *all personal and property rights guaranteed by the Constitution.* Some of these rights have been presented adequately already: procedural due process of law, indictment by grand jury, trial by jury, in fact virtually all the freedoms associated with the criminal justice system, which I discussed in Chapter 3. As I did there, I will try here to do more than specify why the Constitution provides for these liberties and how they have been interpreted in the light of changing conditions. I shall emphasize how these freedoms are used and ought to be used by real people in today's constitutional environment. Only in that larger scene does the "Living Constitution" of American civil liberties assume meaningful shape.

My discussion will be ordered on the following basis: *the more emphatic the Framers were in stating the breadth of a privilege, the earlier it will be discussed.* I select this criterion because I assume those who wrote the Constitution felt strongest about the freedoms they expressed in the most unequivocal language. Where there is little difference in the fervor of the rhetoric, I will use a chronological test. Date of adoption is too cold and formalistic a barometer when weighed against the intensity of passion conveyed in the script, but it at least emphasizes historical perspective through the *original* Founders' perceptions.

The fundamental assumption governing my choice of theory is that *civil liberties are not a homogeneous package.* The Framers saw some rights as straightforward and considered these the more precious and less susceptible to interference. They saw other rights as requiring, by their very nature, a greater degree of interpretation and limitation. Naturally, our present-day commitment to a constitutional principle may depart drastically from the tenor of the language expressing that principle. But this evolution is part of the difference between a constitution and a "Living Constitution"; I shall do my best to specify those differences.

Ex post facto laws and bills of attainder

I have recounted how the Patrick Henrys and Thomas Jeffersons objected to the Constitution as originally drafted because it lacked a bill of rights. Alexander Hamilton, however, thought a checklist of liberties would do more harm than good; some were bound to be left out and might then be eroded away. No doubt many delegates at the Convention shared this conviction. But certainly the Jeffersonians by predisposition were far more concerned than Hamilton about individual rights. Clearly, any personal liberties endorsed there must have seemed beyond cavil to virtually all the political thinkers of those days.[1] So I will start with them.

For our purposes, the original text sets forward, unambiguously, two fundamental freedoms: government shall pass neither ex post facto laws nor bills of attainder.[2] These terms are easy to define in the abstract. An *ex post facto law* is a *criminal statute* that operates *retroactively.*[3] If Connecticut makes it illegal in 1975 to own hand guns and arrests me because I owned one in 1970, *both* of the elements of ex post facto regulation are present: (1) the enactment is a criminal law—I will go to jail, if convicted; and (2) its application to me is retroactive—that is, it punishes me because I did something before the statute was passed. Furthermore, if I rob a bank in violation of Connecticut law and the maximum prison sentence is five years, my punishment could not be increased to eight years by legislation passed after I had committed the crime. However, retroactivity in lawmaking is not a sin per se. For instance, a tax cut passed by Congress can be applied to income earned *before* the cut was approved. But to punish people for doing something which was legal when they did it is a cardinal sin; armed with this authority, a legislature could zero in on anyone without providing notice as to what standards of behavior were considered socially unacceptable.

A *bill of attainder* is simply *punishment* meted out to specific parties by *legislative* enactment. The Framers knew their English constitutional history; they remembered the secret gatherings of the Star Chamber and the severe sanctions it authorized. Under our system, punishment is the province of the judiciary. The various legislatures must confine their rule-making to broad, general standards aimed at the larger public; they may not impose penalties on particular groups or individuals. That is the marrow of the attainder principle.

By no means, however, have these provisions been a cut-and-dried matter for the Supreme Court. An ex post facto statute must be criminal in nature, but what is *criminal law?* Suppose a New York court finds Dr. X committed an illegal abortion. He goes to jail. Years later, the state legislature decides that anyone convicted of such an offense should not be allowed to resume medical practice. Dr. X, upon his parole, is angry. He thinks the penalty for committing illegal abortions has been increased *retroactively;* this, he claims, is ex post facto. But the weight of precedent is against him.[4] When state legislators prescribe professional standards for doctors—norms relating to moral turpitude and the like—they are not formulating *criminal law.* Therefore, while the statute possesses a retroactive ingredient, it is not ex post facto.

Again, a bill of attainder must dispense punishment to somebody, but what is *punishment?* Martin Dies, the chairman of the House Un-American Activities Committee during the 1940s, believed strongly that F.D.R. had three advisors whose loyalty was suspect. Dies persuaded Congress to pass a law docking their salaries, thus driving them from government. Dies argued that the legislative branch controls the appropriations process. He also argued that government employment is a privilege, not a right, so dismissal from federal service is not punishment. But the Court would have none of it. The statute was a bill of attainder: Congress had outlawed subversion, found the three men guilty of subversion, and exacted punishment by throwing them out of office.[5]

An especially gray area involves "test-oaths." After the Civil War, passionate Northerners, to keep Confederate sympathizers in cold storage, hit on the device of making citizens swear allegiance to the Union before they were allowed certain perquisites. Congress, for instance, excluded lawyers from practicing in the federal courts until they affirmed by solemn pledge that they had never supported the South. The Court called this both a bill of attainder *and* an ex post facto law.[6] The oath was deemed a legislative instrument aimed at particular individuals, who, if they honored their consciences, would not be able to follow their chosen profession. Congress had, in effect, found these people guilty and punished them. The oath's retroactive element—penalizing accused parties for engaging in conduct *legal* at that particular time—meant it violated the ex post facto clause as well.

"Test-oaths" are very much a part of the "Living Constitution," however. Certainly many legislators think—reasonably or not—that they are a fine way to expose subversive citizens whose true allegiance lies with totalitarian causes. During the McCarthy era, the Court upheld a Los Angeles "test-oath" that obliged all prospective city employees to swear they neither belonged to an organization advocating the violent overthrow of government nor had joined such a group in the previous five-year period. A five-man majority said the city was merely taking reasonable precautions to ensure fitness for public employment; hence, the bill of attainder provision was inapposite.[7]

There really is no way to reconcile these two cases. One theory is that when the state asks people to take an oath that they are not doing, never have done and will not do such-and-such, and it conditions an emolument on whether they take the oath, the requirement is a form of *punishment* directed toward *specific individuals or groups* already *tried* and *convicted* of harmful conduct. The other theory is that if the state does not "punish" people in the bill of attainder sense when it either fires them or refuses to hire them because they have done something, then there is no "punishment" in making them swear they have never done that very thing.

Because the oath procedure seems a fairly foolish way to quarantine Communists, Congress has lately attempted more direct means, and the Supreme Court again has evinced considerable uncertainty. In 1959 a law was passed banning Communist Party members from serving as officers of labor unions. A slim five-man majority called this statute a bill of attainder; the legislature had specifically cited a particular political group and then subjected it to regulation in the form of punishment. The four dissenters, however, disagreed that punishment had been inflicted. To them, this was an old-fashioned prophylactic measure, akin to keeping convicted felons from resuming medical careers. As for the singling out of a particular group—the Communist Party—they noted that the Constitution precludes a particular group—congressmen—from holding the office of President![8]

This ruling represents the Warren Court's conception of the bill of attainder principle. Perhaps we shall see yet another reversal when the Burger Court speaks to this issue.

Censorship of speech

The remaining civil liberties examined in this chapter[9] are products of various amendments to the Constitution, especially the Bill of Rights.[a] In my search for clear-cut, unequivocal statements of individual freedom, I need go no further

[a] By way of a final reiteration, the Bill of Rights consists of the first ten amendments and is, in large measure, part and parcel of the original document.

than the First Amendment's blatant antigovernment rhetoric. Let us begin, then, with the following trenchant guarantee: "Congress[10] shall make no law . . . abridging the freedom of speech, or of the press."[b] There is no mystery as to why these privileges were stated in such forceful tones: to promote a search for truth, to encourage debate and opinion, to get out from under all despotic restraints upon free expression. Mr. Justice Black summed up the matter accurately and succinctly: "The First Amendment is truly the heart of the Bill of Rights."[11]

Literally, the government has *no* power to regulate speech and press, but what was the *intent* of the text? It is generally believed that the Framers, extraordinarily knowledgeable in and committed to common-law precepts, espoused the common-law conception of free expression,[12] a conception defined as follows:

> Liberty of the press consists in laying no *previous* restraints upon publications, and not in freedom from censure for criminal matter when published. Every free-man has an undoubted right to lay what sentiments he pleases before the public . . . but if he publishes what is improper, mischievous, and illegal, he must take the consequences.[13]

The early Americans understood very well what "*previous* restraints" meant. The King's Licensor would not allow any matter to be published without his permission, censoring everything before it hit the streets, according to his private standards. The common law was a strong reaction against the monarch's arbitrary agent; but in no sense did it shield from criminal prosecution under the law a person who published something the legislature said could not be published. So previous restraint, or prior restraint, or censorship—three terms meaning about the same thing—was the real target of the Founders' unambiguous language.

The most important Supreme Court decision regarding previous restraint arose out of the machinations of one Near, who published a sheet called *The Saturday Press.* In one of its editions, he alleged that a "Jewish gangster" was masterminding all governmental and criminal activities in his home city, Minneapolis. These charges created a furor, and prosecuting officials at once looked around for a means of reprisal. At their disposal was a most curious state law, reminiscent of the days of monarchical suppression, which gave the *courts* power to suppress publications considered "malicious, scandalous and defamatory." The purpose of the statute was to protect "public morals," the "general welfare," and the "peace of the community." Even if Near's assertions were true, this would not be a sufficient defense! He also had to show that his magazine was produced "with good motives and for justifiable ends." In other words, *the burden of proof was on him* to demonstrate not only the validity of his contentions but also that they contributed to the morals, welfare, and peace of Minneapolis. If he failed, his newspaper would be closed down, which, needless to say, it was.

[b] Although the amendment mentions religious liberties first, this language is difficult to define unequivocally *even as written.* Therefore, I will pass it by for the moment.

The Justices, however, declared the statute unconstitutional, describing it as the "essence of censorship." [14] As they saw things, the offensive element lay in the state's capacity to enjoin Near's right of free expression because *one* of his editions failed to pass the censor. *The only way he could resume printing was to keep coming before the judge and proving to him that each future issue contained only truthful and justifiable material.* Moreover, the fact that a judicial officer rather than a formal licensing agent had banned *The Saturday Press* was immaterial. To be sure, there were "exceptional cases" where censorship would pass muster, and the Court described these as follows: (1) to protect military operations during wartime; (2) to protect the state against forcible overthrow; (3) to protect citizens against obscene material. [15] Our jurisprudence, then, has never considered censorship absolutely impermissible.

Over the years, the Court has maintained strong antipathy toward previous restraints. If the Justices agree that "speech and press" values alone are at stake, they will not condone even an innocent-looking regulation with overtones of censorship. Thus, both an ordinance forbidding the use of sound trucks without a permit from the chief of police and a state law requiring labor union organizers to secure an official card before soliciting were declared unconstitutional. [16] Although there was no evidence that anyone had been denied a license under these programs, the community's interests in regulating raucous noises or preventing fraudulent representation were insufficient to justify these licensing restrictions. In short, the prior restraint element doomed the regulations on their face.

These rulings provide the background against which the greatest debate over censorship in our history recently took place. Daniel Ellsberg had stolen a classified government study entitled "History of U.S. Decision-Making Process on Viet Nam Policy," the Pentagon Papers, which he had turned over to the *Washington Post* and *The New York Times.* The Nixon Administration sought to prevent publication by obtaining an injunction against those newspapers. Prior restraint, the Justice Department argued, was justifiable in exceptional cases; these documents involved secret government discussions of war-making strategy and policy, a patent responsibility of the executive branch; they had been taken contrary to law, and the newspapers had received them as stolen property, an illegal act; the Supreme Court should play the role of King's Licensor and stop publication in the national interest.

The Justices rejected this contention, [17] but their individual views were so disparate that it is hard to capsulize their common commitment. Evidently, the majority's animus toward censorship was so great that it could not grant the President *inherent power* (dormant power?) to invoke the judicial process under these circumstances. That the newspapers had no legal right to such information was not enough. That the United States was at war, that the President was commander in chief and that the documents dealt with relevant military and foreign policy considerations—all taken together, was also not enough.

Would anything have been enough? If the Pentagon Papers dealt with military operations per se (for example, troop movements), then the hedge expressed in *Near* might have been persuasive; but a majority was not convinced that publication of these "brainstorming sessions" imperiled the *national security.* Or if Congress had authorized the courts to restrain dissemination of such sensitive data in wartime, this could have tipped the balance. But, as Mr. Justice Thurgood Marshall took pains to develop, Congress had *rejected* years earlier precisely the sort of censorship authority at issue here. And just as Harry Truman, in the *Steel Seizure* dispute, could not go against legislative policy and take control of the steel industry (see pp. 179–81), so Richard Nixon could not go against legislative policy and use the Supreme Court to run interference for his censorship efforts.

The term "speech"—like the term "civil liberties"—does not delineate a homogeneous category of rights. Take parades. They are clearly a form of expression. But are they "speech" in the same sense as Near's newspaper was? No, because while a procession can promote a cause, it can also involve masses of people marching and tying up traffic for miles around. In effect, then, parades are "quasi-speech"; they merit First Amendment protection, but less protection than newspapers. And so the Court upheld a city ordinance requiring marchers both to obtain a permit and to pay a license fee *before* parading. Of course, the levy could not be discriminatory, and the police had no discretion to withhold a license unless traffic exigencies necessitated. But the unique impact of parades upon citizens' normal activities was sufficient to warrant prior restraint.[18]

So a parade is part speech and part conduct. But obscene publications are not even speech at all! As I will describe later, the Court thinks these items should receive no First Amendment coverage because they are not meaningful attempts to convey ideas. This premise gives life to the "exceptional case" dictum in *Near;* the state has a special interest and prerogative in censoring what the Justices consider verbal pollution.

Let us say a police officer thinks Mr. X, book dealer, is selling pornography. The state undoubtedly has a law making such a transaction a criminal offense. This enactment is not a previous restraint, of course, because (1) the items have already hit the marketplace, and (2) the statute would be enforced via the usual criminal process in a manner entirely consistent with common-law practice. But our state has another statute, too, which enables a police officer to go into court with whatever books he or she thinks are obscene and get a "quickie" hearing before a judge on whether the materials fall outside the ambit of free expression. If they do, the books will be banned. New York State has such a law, and the Supreme Court approved it.[19] The statute is certainly a prior restraint. There is no arrest and no criminal procedure; this is a *civil procedure* lodged against books, not people. How can this decision be distinguished from *Near?* First, this case deals with alleged obscenity, and if obscenity is not speech, then previous restraint becomes a reasonable regulatory option; second, this case allows judges to ban only specific items before the court, not items published at some future time.

A last "exceptional case" worth citing is the motion picture medium. Movies are a kind of free speech "stepchild"; indeed, in 1915 the Court went so far as to label films sheer entertainment, not included within First Amendment coverage.[20] The result was a proliferation of censorship boards around the country, with city and state officials previewing every movie, deleting scenes considered "antisocial," and banning highly provocative pictures outright—not to mention clipping away with greatest dispatch any hint of obscenity. In 1952, finally, the Justices realized a movie might contribute as much to the "marketplace of ideas" as a book or a play, and films graduated from "nonspeech" status to the level of "expression."[21]

This promotion might have slayed the dragon of the censorship board were it not for the obscenity issue. I noted a bit earlier that even suspect books can be subjected to a minimum form of previous restraint. If movies were subjected *only* to similar regulation, at least the First Amendment would apply equally across the "free speech" board. But the Justices have not been persuaded: "Motion pictures are [not] necessarily subject to the precise rules governing any other particular method of expression. Each method tends to present its own peculiar problems."[22] Curiously, the Court has never enlightened us as to what these "peculiar problems" might be. Of course, we can guess: it is one thing to write about sexual relations in Henry Miller style and another thing to show two bodies writhing around on film! This, I take it, is more like "conduct" than "speech"; in other words, while the Court has never said as much, films are still a sort of "quasi-speech."

What all this means is that if New York State were to pass a law requiring *every movie* to undergo a preview by licensing officials, requiring each distributor to pay a permit fee for the purpose of covering all expenses incurred by the state, including the salaries of censors, and requiring all obscene movies to be withheld from exhibition (or spliced so as to render them "nonobscene"), that statute would be constitutional under prevailing standards.[23] The censorship boards must make their decisions quickly, it is true; and they must also go, without undue delay, to court, where the burden of proof is on *them* to demonstrate that a film should be permanently suppressed.[24] These are significant checks upon the state, entirely consistent with *procedural due process.* Indeed, for that reason several of these boards have fallen by the wayside; to my knowledge, only one or two still remain functional. But if various decisions have weakened film censorship as a practical alternative, then other, more recent holdings expanding greatly the power of communities to regulate obscenity could easily prompt new censorship efforts.[c] Yet the typical movie

[c] Somewhat surprisingly, the most important attempt to revitalize film censorship has not resulted from an "antiporn" crusade. Rather, the Chicago City Council, with Mayor Richard Daley's strong endorsement, vested power in the Police Department to review all movies and withhold licenses for items not only devoted to brutality or violence but lacking in literary merit, unless audience membership is restricted to eighteen-year-olds and above. What with violent crimes on the increase, some have argued "blood and guts" magazines and motion pictures are the "new obscenity"; however, the Supreme Court years ago voided a New York State *criminal law* aimed at keeping this sort of *written matter* away from adults as well as the underaged (*Winters v. New York,* 333 U.S. 507 [1948]). Obviously, an antiviolence *censorship* statute applicable to everyone would have even less chance of surviving judicial scrutiny. But the state has a substantial interest in regulating the health, safety, and morals of young people even where "speech and press" are concerned, and Chicago's regulatory scheme inhibits only the dissemination of bestial *movies,* a medium with allegedly greater potential for excess, according to Supreme Court doctrine.

house is not a public, open-air forum; and films are not parades, for they hardly constitute an inherent interference with the rights of others. Why films like *Deep Throat* should justify a second-class First Amendment status for movies generally—a status that leaves them open to the caprice, inconvenience, and financial burden of censorship review—remains an unresolved and important question.

Free speech and subversive speech

Prior restraint is not, of course, typical of the possible legal restraints upon "speech and press." Much more prevalent is the ordinary criminal statute, which, according to the common-law view, can be employed to punish all manner of antisocial expression. But that notion was never accepted in the New World as the manifest unpopularity of the Sedition Act (1798) exemplified. This notorious statute was a Federalist Party creation designed to stop untruthful criticism of national government officials if it was published with the intent to stir up popular discontent. The law remained on the books for only two years, after which the Jeffersonians allowed it to expire unceremoniously. The common-law doctrine of "seditious libel," on which it had been predicated, has not been resurrected since. As I will show, however, those few writers—notably Justices Black and Douglas from the Warren Court activist majority—who have advocated the *absolute, unqualified sweep of free speech rights* have gotten no further than their common-law opposites. In this section, I will discuss how the balance has been struck with respect to the nation's internal security.

Picture the following situation: the United States has recently declared war; troops are leaving for overseas duty every day; the country is gearing up both abroad and at home for a head-on confrontation with the enemy. A solitary, innocuous man appears at a point of embarkation for our military personnel and starts to hand out pamphlets which say, "Stop fighting. You are hurting yourselves. Don't follow orders. Resist the government." Can this protester be convicted of violating a law that forbids anyone to cause insubordination in the armed forces?

These facts are a reasonable facsimile of the famous *Schenck* litigation, which confronted the Supreme Court in 1919.[25] Speaking for a unanimous bench, Mr. Justice Holmes at once dismissed the notion of free expression as an absolute. Nobody, he said, has a right to shout fire in a crowded theater (when there is no fire) and create a panic. But Schenck had not shouted anything, nor had he caused a modicum of confusion. Still, said Holmes, the First Amendment did *not* shield him from prosecution:

> The question in every case is whether the words used are used in such circumstances . . . as to create a *clear and present danger* that they will bring about the *substantive evils* that Congress has a right to prevent. It is a question of proximity and degree. When a nation is at war many things that might be said in time

> of peace are such a hindrance to its effort that their utterance will not be endured so long as men fight [italics mine].[26]

If I may recapitulate: Congress has certain delegated and implied authority; this authority includes the legislative war power; the power to make war includes the power to send troops overseas; the power to transport military forces carries with it the power to stop anyone from intruding upon that transportation; when interference takes the form of "speech," then such speech may be silenced if it poses an obvious and direct threat to the war effort as defined by Congress.

Now the war is over; the troops have come home; peace and tranquillity prevail. Still another pathetic figure appears bearing leaflets reading: "It is time to rise up against the oppressive capitalists who are running this system. You have nothing to lose but your chains." He distributes these pamphlets on a busy New York City street corner and is promptly arrested for advocating, contrary to law, the violent overthrow of government.

These facts approximate closely those of another famous case, the *Gitlow* ruling.[27] Once again, the Court upheld plaintiff's conviction. Government has a right to protect itself against revolution and subversion, the majority contended. These are "substantive evils," and any action constituting violent overthrow could surely be punished. But Gitlow had only handed out pamphlets to those who would take them. Wasn't this the essence of speech and press? And if the First Amendment were applicable, where was the "clear and present danger" that would justify inhibiting his rights? The majority had an answer:

> [In protecting] the public peace and safety, [the state may] extinguish the spark without waiting until it has enkindled the flame. . . . When the legislative body has determined generally, in the constitutional exercise of its discretion, that utterances of a certain kind involve such danger of substantive evil that they may be punished, the question whether any specific utterance . . . is likely . . . to bring about the substantive evil, is not open to consideration.[28]

These Justices believed, in other words, that the state has power to prevent people from planning insurrection against the system; that when somebody goes into the streets to stir up support for such overthrow, he is violating the law; and that the state does not have to wait until he has convinced a legion of followers—every instance of conduct and speech constituting a *bad tendency* in the direction of achieving the illegal goal may be punished.

Put in crude but accurate terms, we have here the most basic kind of disagreement over what freedom of speech means in our constitutional system. Justice Holmes was saying that all doubts must be resolved in favor of speech and press; only when the danger became immediate would he read statutes to authorize retaliatory governmental action. The *Gitlow* majority, on the other hand, was saying that constitutional government is possible only when people play by the rules. If some people won't accept those rules, and use free speech to build revolutionary movements, then the majority that adheres to government by open debate and ballot box can move expeditiously to root out all manifestations of speech tending toward lawlessness. The presumption in these circumstances must be weighted against the ability of speech alone to meet the threat. So we have two conflicting approaches: the "clear and present danger" test and the "bad tendency" test. I am not exaggerating when I say public debate in this country over the role of free expression has been greatly colored by whether one or the other standard seems more sensible and consistent with our institutions.

This difficult question has become even more complicated in the post-World War II period by a second "hot debate": *Which power center should take the lead in striking a balance between liberty and authority where internal security is at stake, the courts or the "political branches"?* In the 1920s, when the Justices were wrestling over *Schenck* and *Gitlow,* the Court's power to declare statutes unconstitutional remained dormant. The issue was simply a matter of *statutory interpretation:* Should laws be construed to maximize or minimize First Amendment values in regulating the speech of revolutionary zealots? But between these two cases and the cold war, Franklin Roosevelt's ultimate victory over the "activist" Court that had opposed his New Deal program brought about the rise of Holmes's *judicial restraint* theory as the dominant constitutional philosophy (see pp. 47-49). Unless legislation were patently unreasonable, the Justices would no longer buck "political branch" policy preferences. Twentieth century liberals smiled contentedly when Congress's economic reforms eased through the courts unscathed; but when Congress's regulation of speech and press for the purpose of thwarting Communist subversion came before the bench, wrangling over the role of *judicial review* broke out anew.

On the one hand were jurists like Felix Frankfurter and John M. Harlan, who held to the now acceptable self-restraint approach. In a democracy, they said, all doubts should be resolved in favor of legislative consensus, not the views of an oligarchic elite. Of course, free speech is a precious liberty, but if the substantive evil is within the sphere of legislative competence, then that branch's judgment as to the proper balance between the rights of the community and the rights of the individual must ordinarily prevail. On the other hand were jurists like Harlan Stone and Earl Warren, who distinguished regulation of expression from regulation of the economy. Free speech, they felt, is far more basic than property rights, because the First Amendment keeps the whole political system open to rational criticism and informed voter control. Therefore, the burden is on the "political branches" to justify any regulation of speech and press. If this burden is not satisfied, *the law is unconstitutional.* To invoke the proper jargon, the Frankfurterians adhere to the "balancing of interests" school, while the Stoneans adhere to the "preferred position" school. In Frankfurter's view, all interests—the community interest in regulating subversion, the liberty interest in talking up the glories of communism—should be balanced without prejudice.[29] In Stone's view, free expression holds a special, preferred place among interests, and this status can be overcome only in extraordinary circumstances.[30] If the Supreme Court of our time has been preoccupied with "clear and present danger" versus "bad tendency," it has been even more at sea over the broad general question of judicial power versus "political branch" power in matters involving civil liberties.

These perspectives come alive when applied to the politics of the last thirty years. For instance, at the outbreak of the cold war, the American Communist Party no longer resembled a collection of ragamuffins in the style of Gitlow; it resembled a collection of hardheaded, thoroughly indoctrinated, Soviet-controlled conspirators. To the Frankfurterian majority, Congress's legislative palliative, the Smith Act—which forbade both advocating and plotting to advocate the violent overthrow of government—was a reasonable regulation of speech. The law properly prohibited expression as "incitement to action"—that is, recruiting members, holding meetings, and exchanging ideas for the purpose of conspiring to mobilize a revolutionary cadre.[31] This approach came to be called the "clear and probable danger" rule, because the *immediacy* of the substantive evil—so crucial to the Holmesian conception—carries little weight here. Indeed, the difference between "clear and probable" and "bad tendency" is hard to fathom. For those who would say Frankfurter had strayed from Holmes's teachings, it is fair to reemphasize that the threat posed by the party in 1920 was somewhat less serious than the threat posed by the party in 1950.[32] But even the "balancers" refused to interpret the Smith Act as making illegal the utterance of revolutionary rhetoric in the form of abstract doctrine. Where no incitement to action *now or in the future* could be shown, a person had a perfect right to extol the virtues of violent overthrow as a socially acceptable remedy.[33] Jefferson's dictum that a revolution every twenty years is good for our national soul had not become subject to legislative constraint.

The internal security cases that best illumine the Court's drift from "restraint" and "balance" toward the "activism" and "preferred position" highlighting the Warren years center on Communist participation in public service. Two especially nice questions stirred legislative concern: (1) Do Communists have a right to teach children in the public schools? (2) Do Communists have a right to work in defense plants?

In the wake of the *Dennis* conspiracy case, the conviction of the Rosenbergs on espionage charges, and the McCarthy investigations, New York State enacted the Feinberg Law, which authorized dismissal of any public school teacher who "knowingly" belonged to a group advocating the violent overthrow of government. No organization could be blacklisted unless given an opportunity to rebut allegations of subversion, and no teacher could be fired without an opportunity to show that his or her liaison with the organization was "innocent." The law distinguished, then, between members who had *knowledge of the allegedly illegal aims of the group,* and members who had joined without a proper appreciation of the group's activities and purposes. In that way, the evils of "guilt by association" could supposedly be avoided, while disloyal activists would be vulnerable. The Court, in 1952, agreed the law was constitutional.[34] The states have a vital interest, it said, in preserving the integrity of their schools against those bent upon undermining the system; molding youngsters' attitudes toward society is a most delicate and sensitive area of communal concern. Suspected subversives possessed the rights of speech and press but not the right to teach in the taxpayers' educational system.

Fifteen years later, the same statute was voided by a far different Supreme Court.[35] The new five-man majority saw two fundamental flaws in the above reasoning. First, public employment could not be conditioned on the surrender of any freedom protected under the Constitution, so the power to keep Communists out of classrooms was no greater than the power to arrest and convict Communists. Second, the state could not punish a citizen simply for being a "known" Communist. Only members who possessed *specific intent* to further the party's illegal goals could be either prosecuted in court or dismissed from public service. In other words, the state had to prove that a suspect joined for the definite purpose of becoming involved in unlawful action. After all, said the Court, "a statute touching [free speech] rights" must be "narrowly drawn to define and punish specific conduct as constituting a clear and present danger to a substantial interest of the state."[36] So if I join the Communist Party with the "specific intent" to perpetrate illegal doings, I constitute a "clear and present danger" to interests a legislature may protect. Otherwise, my Communist Party affiliation is no ground whatsoever for either arrest or any other kind of constraint. For the Warren Court, the "clear and present danger" test was the means through which the "preferred position" goal became a reality in free speech cases. However, the landmark *Dennis* decision still receives judicial sanction, and there is considerable doubt as to whether the perceived danger must be imminent in the fashion Mr. Justice Holmes considered essential.[37]

"Activist" and "restraining" blocs were even farther apart on the question of employment in defense facilities. The dominant libertarian faction struck down a section of the 1950 McCarran Act that had made it unlawful for members of "Communist-action" organizations to work in defense production plants.[38] The provision, they said, established guilt by association alone as a criterion for hiring and firing; Congress could not assume all Communists were of the same malicious predisposition. This line of argument was too much for the dissenters: "The right of association," they said, "is not mentioned in the Constitution."[39] Furthermore, Congress and the President were in a much better position than the Supreme Court to judge what security dangers might arise from Communists working close to the seat of confidential information. If the Communist Party had a legitimate free speech claim with regard to "political branch" jurisdiction over the defense establishment, then a careful balancing of interests was in order; but if the only issue revolved around some tenuous "right of association," then the matter was hardly more than a political question.

The terms underlying this whole debate are "association" and "conspiracy." If one sees the Communist Party as a potpourri of Marxist ideologues and nothing more, then one will likely brand it an "association," thus deserving of First Amendment protection. But if one sees the Communist Party as a band of schemers controlled by a foreign power, then one will likely brand it a "conspiracy," hardly warranting First Amendment coverage even in the light of "preferred position."

But this distinction, unfortunately, is seldom clear-cut. Consider conspiracy trials held during the past decade. The Chicago Seven were tried, in part, for *conspiring* to cross state lines with the intent of inciting a riot at the 1968 Democratic National Convention; Dr. Benjamin Spock and others were tried, in part, for *conspiring* to aid and counsel draft resisters during the Vietnam War; H. R. Haldeman, John Ehrlichman, and other Nixon aides were tried, in part, for *conspiring* to cover up the Watergate break-in. We can assume these people engaged in relevant discussions that were "protected speech." To say, "I think it would be a good idea if all draftees burned their selective service cards" is surely nothing but talk, or the "advocacy of abstract doctrine." In each of the above cases, however, the applicable law required not only that a conspiracy be shown but that *overt acts* committed to further the plot be demonstrated. This only complicates matters, though, because *some of the overt acts alleged were also in the nature of free expression.* (For instance, Dr. Spock and his allies were found guilty of printing and circulating pamphlets as a means of propagandizing selective service evasion.) Yet government does have a substantial interest in stopping riots, draft card burnings, and cover-ups.

Justice Douglas and other "absolutist" libertarians would put all the chips on the side of "association" and throw out the conspiracy trial as a weapon against political deviants;[40] philosopher Sidney Hook and other community-oriented commentators would allow unpalatable speech ("heresy"), but they would press the Smith Act to the hilt against the machinations of a Dr. Spock ("conspiracy").[41] I would propose two alternative possibilities, both of which are based on the supposition that these various groups engaged in some activities that were constitutionally protected and others that were subject to punishment: (1) If one favors "preferred position," the key ingredient is whether Mr. X joined a group with the "specific intent" of committing illegal acts. (2) If one favors "balancing of interests," the key ingredient is whether Mr. X "knowingly" joined a group committed to some unlawful design.

Throughout the century our society has spawned a whole raft of ideological groups that have employed the conspiratorial plot—from the Symbionese Liberation Army and the Ku Klux Klan to former members of the White House staff. Other such groups will doubtless surface now and again. Conspiracy laws and trials are a facet of the "Living Constitution," and in a heterogeneous society such as ours they seem to have their place, else the larger citizenry may not be protected fully from the outsider who would subvert government by consensus. But I think the legitimate scope of free speech values obligates the law to focus on *individual intent and accountability,* not the mere fact of group participation and group behavior. As I pointed out in Chapter 3, the criminal justice system was meant to weigh personal choice, not the integrity and conviction of organizational maneuverings.

Speech and public order

In theory, the classic right of free expression looks pretty straightforward. Yet, as soon as I enter the "marketplace of ideas," my *right* to talk suddenly becomes hedged about by basic correlative *duties.* I have a right to talk, but not to talk any place and every place; I have a right to talk, but not any time the fancy strikes me; I have a right to talk, but not to interfere with someone else's rights; I have a right to talk, but not to turn the community into a jungle with my speech.

The first limitation on any speaker relates to the *quality* of the message. Civilized society presupposes that minimum standards of courtesy and decorum will be observed in presenting ideas in public. A speaker has no right to aim obscenities or other provocative epithets at specific individuals. Such language would very likely prompt a reasonable listener to respond with fists, not with rhetoric, and is not considered speech at all because it has no worthwhile social value. Therefore, laws are permissible that ban such language outright.[42]

The use of profanity in public on a more general, impersonal basis has given the Burger Court a few uneasy moments, however. During the Vietnam War, the increasing rage of peaceful dissenters over their inability to influence the political process and a drastic shift in generally accepted standards of speech among younger people combined in a sometimes volatile mix. In one noteworthy case, a man was arrested for wearing a jacket with "Fuck the draft" emblazoned for all to see. The Court, in reversing his conviction,[43] pointed out that the expletive was directed not against any particular person who might strike back in retaliation but against forced military service. As such, the rhetoric was surely speech. Then did the state possess authority to keep the level of public discussion within bounds of decency? No, said the majority, because "one man's vulgarity is another's lyric,"[44] and any line that state officials might draw would inevitably be drawn subjectively.

This argument has been criticized by several members of the Court.[45] It surely throws the "marketplace" open to forms of expression that might traumatize older people, confuse nine-year-olds, and cause the average person extraordinary embarrassment. One wonders how the Framers of the Constitution would have reacted to the thesis that free speech protects the impersonal use of as many four-letter words as the public speaker considers necessary. But this portion of the "Living Constitution" is clearly in flux, for we live in an age of "telling it like it is," in a media-oriented society, where the elites are sometimes incapable of laying down objective standards of policy even to the extent of protecting ordinary people as they walk down the streets.

Assume, however, that our hypothetical speaker does not swear like a trooper but is extraordinarily forceful in presenting some unpopular idea. In fact, he so irritates those who have gathered to hear him that there is some jostling in the crowd, then some pushing and shoving. The threat of violence hangs heavy. What are the speaker's rights, and what are the community's powers?

For one thing, nobody has a prerogative to *incite riot.* The Ku Klux Klansman who marches down 173rd Street in Harlem in his white sheet is knowingly fomenting disorder and is subject to arrest should he be physically assaulted. But the speaker in the park who espouses a "whites are superior" opinion deserves much greater protection. In fact, though the Court has been somewhat hazy—if not somewhat antilibertarian—on the subject in the past years,[46] I think the modern conception is as follows: the primary duty of the police is to protect the speaker from intimidation by a hostile audience, absent abusive language or direct incitements on the speaker's part. The speaker or the pamphleteer deserves the benefit of the doubt and, in this era of "preferred position," would undoubtedly receive it from the bench.

The First Amendment also protects the right *to assemble peaceably.* When combined with freedom of speech, this yields a composite privilege to picket, march, and demonstrate—as, for example, in the manner of Martin Luther King's civil rights street movement or the myriad student groups abounding on college campuses during the late 1960s.

I have already said, however, that parades were actually "quasi-speech" because they involved conduct that might easily interfere with the movement and speech of others. The same goes for any march or congregation of people. It is one thing to talk but quite another thing to prevent others from going about their business. Therefore, laws limiting the "nonspeech" or "conduct" aspects of such expression are constitutional if the inhibitions against the "speech" aspects are minimal.

Here are some common examples of such legislation. A city ordinance can spell out hours during the day when street demonstrations are permissible; it can prohibit blocking of passageways into and out of buildings; it can proscribe demonstrations on or near courthouse property, because they pose a clear and present danger to the effective administration of justice; it can forbid sit-in protesters to trespass on university property, ostensibly because such *actions* constitute a clear and present danger to the integrity of the educational process; it can limit congregations to traditional places of grievance, such as the streets or state capitol grounds. In a recent controversial case, the Court affirmed the conviction of civil rights workers who held a meeting on jailhouse property and refused to leave when directed to do so. The Justices gave two grounds: (1) states have a right to keep trespassers off their own property if the need is substantial—here, security considerations at the jail outweighed free speech rights; (2) the law specifically punished only people who trespassed with *malicious intent.* Evidently, willful trespass—like specific intent—is another extension of "clear and present danger" doctrine; that is, the substantive evil of a breakdown in prison routine is overtly and intentionally threatened by this form of speech.[47]

According to this logic, even a solitary speaker could have been convicted on a trespass charge. The fact is that *all* First Amendment expression—even if "pure speech" or "pure press"—is subject to what are called "times, places, and manner" regulations. A lone speaker has no greater right than fifty speakers to disturb classroom decorum during school hours, to yell so loudly that readers cannot concentrate in libraries, or to disseminate ideas on atomic proving grounds and other military installations.[48]

This last restriction on "place" requires greater elaboration. If the government may keep all speechmakers and press distributors off that portion of its property not considered a public forum, then the private individual certainly has the same right. My First Amendment liberties do not give me the freedom to make my opinions known on my neighbor's property. He can eject me or sue me for trespass at his leisure. And if I own a place of business, I do not have to allow anyone to come across my threshold for the purpose, say, of handing out leaflets.

In our ever more complicated constitutional environment, though, the distinction between public and private property is not nearly so precise as heretofore. For example, no authoritative commentator has ever argued that free speech rights could be suspended because one entered a business district; leaflets could always be distributed on the sidewalks, for instance. But what about privately owned shopping centers? Do private property rights allow their owners to ban all speechmakers outright from these commercial lands?

The Burger Court has upheld such regulations in a case where opponents of the Vietnam War attempted to pass out handbills in a Portland, Oregon, shopping area. The majority emphasized that many other means of communication were open to these advocates; therefore, the right of free expression must yield to the right to hold property for one's own use. Constitutional liberties are guaranteed only against *government,* not against *private individuals.*[49]

As the political system becomes more and more complicated in the light of burgeoning governmental responsibility and technological sophistication, the voice of the individual becomes punier and punier. And therefore frustrated minorities develop mechanisms for attracting attention: they march, they sing, they yell, they flaunt signs and symbols, they swear, they stage sit-ins, and a few even act out by hijacking planes, blowing up buildings, and shooting at prominent people. Indeed, a new term in our jurisprudence bears witness to this trend—"symbolic speech"—which refers to conduct pure and simple that is contrived to express a point of view and so is labeled by advocates a form of speech. Some Vietnam War critics, for instance, termed the public burning of draft cards "symbolic speech," because it dramatized opposition to our military intervention. And some student demonstrators justified trashing of property because it symbolized antagonism to various university programs and policies.

The Supreme Court has rejected the contention "that an apparently limitless variety of conduct can be labeled 'speech' whenever the person engaging in the conduct intends thereby to express an idea."[50] Therefore, a law punishing the destruction of one's own draft card has been upheld. On the other hand, when students wear black armbands to class and fly their own flags upside down as protests against American military policy, their "symbolic speech" is constitutionally protected.[51] The ruination of property in which others have a substantial interest is one thing; peaceful objections disseminated through critical acts that do not interfere with the rights of others are quite another thing.

But the fundamental issue for civil liberties posed by the "symbolic speech" argument will not go away, because the most effective form of expression, given the present state of our mores and life style, is the *mass movement,* and, by definition, it involves both "speech" and "nonspeech" facets. Does the "clear and present danger" test afford sufficient protection against antisocial mass movements, as the Warren Court seemed to think? Or should the "bad tendency" test somehow be applied to the "nonspeech" aspects of these movements? Complicating matters further is the growing overlap between big government and big private power. It is not simply a question of *private* shopping malls replacing *public* business districts; it is a question of the Pentagon and Boeing Aircraft, or of the Department of Health, Education, and Welfare and the large universities, joining forces in implementing *public* policy. To the extent that Establishment power acquires ever more capacity to order human relations, mass movements will likely test their strength against such authority in times of stress. And to that extent does the average person become ever more the pawn of special interest in tugs-of-war.

Use of the mass movement device, though somewhat abated today, has become part of our political culture, perhaps even part of the "Living Constitution." Groups using such tactics are protected by the same right of association as any other ideological grouping, such as the N.A.A.C.P. or the Republican Party. Yet they cannot conspire to break the law. But these truisms only serve to confront us again with that most basic of inquiries: Are the rights and duties of these participants to be judged primarily by what *they themselves say and do,* or are they to be judged primarily by what the *particular group may say and do?*

Speech and obscenity

A leading civil libertarian of this century once argued that the First Amendment should apply only to the world of *political* give-and-take. Inevitable controls on other kinds of speech, he feared, would necessarily spill over to that most socially significant species of expression, so these controls should be tested against the less rigorous due process standard.[52] The Supreme Court, however, has never approved any such two-tiered test. Freedoms of speech and press mean not only political freedom but also the right to express one's personality and taste through music, art, literature, and countless other aesthetic pursuits. And just as there are people who would corrupt our politics by fomenting revolution, so there are people who would corrupt the arts by peddling pornography. What authority can government command, if any, to regulate that practice?

In the 1957 *Roth* decision, the Justices ruled that obscenity was *not* speech, because it was "utterly without redeeming social importance."[53] In other words, the purpose of an obscene item was to inflame sexual passions, not to convey ideas. Therefore, the First Amendment accorded these writings and pictures no protection whatsoever.

If nothing else, this holding seemed to presage a direct, definite judicial policy. Of course, there was the problem of identifying obscenity. So, without flinching, the Justices contrived a formula for judges and juries to apply: something is obscene if "to the average person, applying contemporary community standards, the dominant theme of the material taken as a whole appeals to prurient interest."[54] This test would surely protect legitimate writers from the forces of prudery and repression, it was believed, because:

1. Works should be judged by their *dominant* mood or intent as revealed in the *whole* representation; secondary themes and passages could not be ripped out of context to condemn the entire piece.
2. Works would be judged by their impact on the *typical adult;* the responses of children and deviants carried no weight.
3. Works would be judged by *present-day* outlook and convention; Victorian mores were irrelevant.
4. Works would be judged by their appeal to *sexual appetites* pure and simple; any other kind of stimulus militated *against* a finding of obscenity.

It soon became clear the Warren Court had bitten off more than it could chew. Never before or since has the high bench's institutional dignity become so completely unglued.[55] The Justices proceeded to split apart on a whole host of issues:

1. What "community" should be evaluated in defining "contemporary community standards"? Was a national community controlling in federal litigation and a state community in state cases? If there was more than one community, could a book be obscene in Rhode Island but protected speech in Connecticut? If there was some national standard, what was it?
2. Did the Court have to see every movie and read every book brought before it for adjudication? If so, where would the Justices find the time?
3. Did an obscene tract have to be *utterly* without redeeming social value? If so, what about items that contained a smattering of non-obscene material inserted only to get around the "utterly" requirement?
4. Was there a difference between obscenity and hard-core pornography? If so, how could they be distinguished?

When one considers the fact that Justices Black and Douglas stuck by their "absolutist" guns, rejecting outright the entire *Roth* test, it is not surprising that the Court failed to develop any reliable way of ascertaining obscenity. The result was that every item brought up for review received First Amendment coverage from a coalition consisting of two "absolutists," three advocates of the "utterly" test, and one subscriber to the obscenity-pornography distinction.[56]

This logjam was broken only when Nixon's four Court appointees joined with Mr. Justice White in 1973 to posit a new set of rules.[57] They retained the wordy *Roth* formula but expunged the "utterly without redeeming social importance" qualification. Government was not required to prove the "impossible negative": that allegedly obscene materials presented *no* speech-like qualities. The new majority also added two standards. An obscene movie or publication must be "patently offensive" (that is, shocking on its face) to community standards; and, taken as a whole, it must lack *serious* literary, artistic, political, or scientific value. All three of these criteria must be satisfied in order to suppress a particular item. Evidently, if a film not only is shot through with the usual overt sexual nonsense one finds in any "adult" movie house but contains scattered discussions of Plato's metaphysics inserted for the purpose of avoiding either a "hard-core" or an "utterly" tag, then that picture may now be suppressed should a community so desire.

The Burger Court also grappled with the thorny "community" question. When a judge or juror is called upon to determine "prurient interest" or "patent offensiveness" in the light of community standards, he or she may now find it unnecessary to rely upon *any specific geographical community*. Everything will depend on how the law is written. Suppose Phoenix, Arizona, is considering a statute punishing the distribution of obscenity. The city council can use its discretion in picking among relevant community standards. The lawmakers might select national standards, state standards, or city standards; indeed, they might even decide to let the courts apply whichever community customs they themselves considered relevant. So long as factfinders do not rely on their own peculiar tastes and preferences, the constitutional standard has been met.[58]

This new consensus steeped in Frankfurterian judicial self-restraint suddenly pulled the Warren Court holdovers together to face the challenge. Justices Brennan, Marshall, and Stewart joined Justice Douglas in his contention that the state had *no power at all* to ban obscene or pornographic publications sold or distributed in the marketplace to consenting adults.[59] But the real difference between the Warren Court's diversity of opinion and the Burger Court's bipolarity is only that judicial activists bear a much more difficult burden. Unless they take an "absolutist" tack, they have a duty to provide guidance for policy-makers by laying down clear standards. Judicial modesty, on the other hand, requires only that the policy-maker formulate a reasonable judgment.

The major forces at work here, then, are hardly the ebb and flow of judicial response; they involve society's long-term acceptance or rejection of various attitudes toward sex. The recommendations of a special blue-ribbon panel appointed by President Johnson to study this entire matter are revealing. Essentially, the nineteen-member body advocated what Justices Brennan, Marshall, Douglas, and Stewart were to insist upon later in the dissent cited above. All laws inhibiting the dissemination of obscenity among consenting adults should be abolished. The report emphasized not the difficulties in defining obscene material but the lack of scientific data showing that explicit sexual material caused criminal behavior.[60] In short, the panel structured the debate in terms of scientific inquiry and empirical information. President Nixon's response to the proposal was a flat rejection; under no conditions would he support any move to repeal criminal legislation in this area. He did not quarrel with the commission's laboratory tests; he probably considered the results irrelevant. His concern—and the concern of most vocal discussants pro and con—was riveted on the *moral* dimension. If one sees obscenity as verbal pollution contaminating the cultural ethos, one will probably tend to think society has a right to monitor strictly its dissemination. If one's sensibilities toward either obscenity or community are not so intensely heightened, one is far more apt to stress another kind of moral imperative, the right of all adults to do their own thing assuming they do not interfere with the rights of others. Neither the derogation of obscenity nor the glorification of individual autonomy is predicated upon any scientific determination.

What about the short-run political consequences of the recent Court decisions? The Justices are not poised to burn books. The Burger Court has already decided unanimously that the movie *Carnal Knowledge* cannot be branded obscene.[61] Nor do I think the First Amendment will crumble if small towns in Maine and Idaho can apply the prevailing three-fold definition in a manner different from the way Berkeley, California, and Times Square apply it. These *are* different communities, and, assuming the legitimacy of regulation per se, I do not think the Constitution mandates a Gresham's Law in the world of prurient appetites. But I have doubts about the free-floating notion of "community" accepted by the current majority. Here is where social scientists can play a useful role. They can conduct research to ascertain how various classes of people respond to various kinds of sexual matter, and such data would surely inform any judge, jury, or legislative body choosing among competing community norms. Beyond that, I wonder when and if the Supreme Court will consider itself put upon by having to see and characterize the various assorted *Deep Throat*'s, a task that will inevitably be its lot. And I wonder what community standards the individual Justices will find controlling!

As any urban dweller can testify, the politics of obscenity regulation is better understood by walking the streets than by examining courtroom documents. "Adult" movie houses and bookstores flourish alongside massage parlors, burlesque palaces, and pick-up corners. Given the Court's 1973 green light to clean up the smut market, it is not too surprising that police crackdowns should tend to move against these sundry activities as if they were all of a piece. But broad legislative brushstrokes that allow for such vice squad maneuvers can pose considerable problems for speech and press that may be "adult" and yet may not be obscene.

An excellent tool for effectuating such policy is the zoning ordinance. Boston, in 1974, decided that all new "adult entertainment" enterprises must be "quarantined" within a two-block "combat zone." And a Detroit "Anti-Skid

Row" ordinance disallows any "adult" film house or bookshop within 1,000 feet of other similar facilities, including taverns and poolrooms. This "spread-out" regulation clearly limits all movies concerned primarily with overt sexual presentation to specific business establishments. The Supreme Court has decided, however, that Detroit's interest in regulating commercial facilities generally sustains these land-use rules, even though here the discriminating factor was the *content* of the speech sold.[62] So restricting the location of "adult" film houses is akin to restricting the location of pawnshops and barbershops.

Free speech versus fair trial

Everyone regards freedom of expression as a cornerstone in our libertarian tradition. But what rules of thumb dictate when the First Amendment runs headlong into conflict with a civil liberty equally precious yet vulnerable, the right of every person to receive a fair trial through due process of law?

Unfortunately, the Court has handled this dilemma with all the finesse of a Howard Cosell. Take the antics of union leader Harry Bridges in the early 1940s. Bridges sent a letter to the Secretary of Labor warning that if a judicial pronouncement rendered against him were enforced, he would call a strike and paralyze shipping up and down the Pacific Coast. He even took pains to inform the press and, thereby, the general public. But when the courts slapped a contempt citation on him, the Justices intervened.[63] Flushed with the early passion of "preferred position," they said that published criticism of the bench was so vital to democracy that it could be stifled only in highly volatile circumstances. And, they continued, Bridges's intemperate remarks did not create such a clear and present danger to the judicial process. This remained the prevailing judicial philosophy until well into the 1960s.

Needless to say, the Frankfurterians never accepted any such one-sided view of the matter. If free speech could undermine community well-being, they believed, then it must carry devastating potential for disrupting the decorum and objectivity fundamental to a fair trial. Could newspapers, right in the middle of a trial, publish editorials branding a judge hopelessly biased or corrupt? Could the media label a defendant "guilty" or "innocent" before the evidence had been presented? Could reporters question prosecution and defense attorneys at leisure? And what effect would these and other activities—pursued in the name of free speech and free press—have upon jurors? All of this troubled Frankfurter and caused him to formulate his own constitutional test: First Amendment rights, if used in a manner reasonably calculated to disturb the work of the courts, were subject to limitation.[64]

The sensational Sam Sheppard homicide case really awakened both Court and public to the excesses of trial by newspaper. Dr. Sheppard had been indicted for murdering his pregnant wife in a bedroom of their posh Bay Village, Ohio, home. Throughout the trial, the tabloid press of the nation—especially the Hearst newspapers—provided daily front-page coverage, replete with assorted innuendo building up the "sex scandal" dimension. Well-known reporters from around the country flocked to Cleveland, and, not content with reporting the news, some decided to *make* news. Robert Considine, in one of his news broadcasts, practically called Sheppard a liar. Walter Winchell quoted a woman under arrest for robbery as saying she was Sheppard's mistress and that her child was his child. The situation was even more unruly in the courtroom itself. The press, given a special table next to counsel, could eavesdrop on privileged conversations, and the reporters often made so much noise it was difficult to hear testimony. At no time did the judge sequester the jury. His attitude seemed to be that the Fourth Estate is king.

The Supreme Court not only reversed Sheppard's conviction[65] but took pains to spell out ways of preventing repeat performances. Trial judges had the right to limit the number of newspaper people in the courtroom, to insulate witnesses from question-and-answer sessions outside the courtroom, to put limitations on the release of information by counsel, and to warn press representatives about the impropriety of floating evidence not introduced properly. Certainly, the Court concluded, jury sequestration and change of venue are important tactics for mitigating many of these difficulties.

Yet the *Sheppard* decision is not without its problems. For one thing, the Court specifically said *prejudicial pretrial publicity alone* would not have violated due process. Furthermore, locking jurors up for months on end hardly gives the defendant a fair shake. Most prospective panelists naturally resist such inconvenience, so they beg off in droves, making it exceedingly difficult to select any jury, much less a representative one. And, of course, changes of venue offer little assistance to a Sirhan Sirhan or a Charles Manson, defendants of national prominence.

For these reasons, among others, the American Bar Association appointed a special committee to look into the free speech-fair trial conflict. Its Reardon Report[66] advocated even more stringent guidelines on press activity. The most provocative suggestion was that both pre-trial and trial proceedings could be closed completely to press coverage when a real possibility of due process deprivation existed.[67] The report also urged judges to control out-of-court statements by *all* participants in criminal litigation.[68] This last recommendation has received some follow-through; for instance, the judges who supervised the Manson and Bobby Seale murder trials issued blanket directives against extrajudicial commentary. But attempts to bar the press from various stages of the criminal process and to dampen pre-trial publicity have had uneven success[69]—which is to some extent fortunate. Prohibitions against press coverage, I think, are constitutionally deficient because they do not balance participation with responsibility; they preclude participation altogether. As to the nagging pretrial-publicity issue, the Supreme Court in 1976 held that a judge could not "gag" the press from reporting either testimony presented or evidence introduced at a preliminary hearing involving a suspected mass murderer, one Simants.[70] This order was a *prior restraint* and, evidently, could be justified only when a *clear and present danger* of prejudice was ascertainable.

The media have become ever more strident in asserting their constitutional status. Thirty years ago, reporters and newscasters proclaimed the virtues of "freedom of the press," a constitutional right they patently possess. In our time, they proclaim the virtues of "the public's right to know," a privilege not mentioned in the Constitution.

What is this "right to know"? For instance, does it mean television cameras must be allowed in the courtroom? So far, the Justices have turned thumbs down on that thesis.[71] Or does it mean that members of the press can refuse to cooperate with a grand jury because their testimony might undermine First Amendment freedoms? This claim, in fact, was asserted by Earl Caldwell of *The New York Times.* He had written some stories on the Black Panther Party and was subpoenaed by a grand jury convened to look into possible wrongdoing by the organization. Caldwell's contention was that unless there were *no other way* of obtaining information *necessary* for the success of the inquiry and which the grand jury could demonstrate he *actually possessed,* then he could not be made to divulge any knowledge he might have. The "public's right to know" carried with it the press's right to protect private sources essential for accumulating newsworthy information; only a "specific need" for his testimony could override that privilege.[d] The majority not only rejected this thesis but went so far as to say the press was under the same obligations as ordinary citizens with respect to grand jury subpoenas. In other words, given the usual, inevitable conflict between a "Sherlock Holmes grand jury" and the media, the media lose outright![72]

This entire free speech-fair trial debate well illustrates the difficulty of reconciling two conflicting liberties. It also illustrates the political blunders both the Court and important private interests can make in molding a "Living Constitution." First we find the right of free press being preferred and the right of due process being deferred. This helps ignite the flames of journalistic pandering in the name of exercising fundamental freedoms, as the *Sheppard* case exemplifies. The legal profession, whose very legitimacy is tied to due process, then produces a Reardon Report; not surprisingly, it advocates corrective measures so stiff they may even be counterproductive. The media overreact by trumpeting the glories of a "right to know" whose contours are unknown, and the Supreme Court overreacts by not only suddenly preferring due process in the form of grand jury autonomy but also by framing that jury's power of investigation in almost absolutist language.[e] To sum up, the press, the bar, and especially the Supreme Court, which is supposed to accommodate co-equal values through neutral principles, must be held responsible for creating constitutional norms that bespeak much power and little balance.

[d] The phrase "specific need" is surely reminiscent of the phrase "specific intent," which I described earlier (pp. 237-38). Again, I think we have here an attempt to clothe the "clear and present danger" argument in new rhetoric, thus enhancing its tractability.

[e] Several newspeople have been imprisoned for refusing to reveal their sources to state grand juries. Commendably, the Justice Department (under John Mitchell) adopted rules forbidding subpoenas to the media unless the information sought is "essential" and all other avenues have been exhausted.

Religious freedom

As the First Amendment protects freedom of speech and the press, it also protects freedom of religion. But "freedom of religion" is only a euphemism. What the Constitution actually says is that government can neither pass laws "respecting an establishment of religion" nor pass laws "prohibiting the free exercise" of religion. The language of the First Amendment is disarmingly unconditional; but, with respect to church-state relations, absolutes are truly impossible on their face because these two prohibitions inevitably run into each other and so must be balanced. To demonstrate the truth of this assertion, I must describe, first, what these two phrases mean when taken separately.

"Establishment of religion"

The establishment provision was given no meaningful interpretation before 1947. Until then, the clause was viewed in two quite different ways. The first was Jefferson's approach: there must be a complete separation of church and state; government should treat religion with an air of detached neutrality; when the state becomes enmeshed in the affairs of God, it demeans religion and opens the door to discrimination. The second view was endorsed by such eminent constitutional scholars as Joseph Story and Thomas M. Cooley.[73] Religion is an inextricable part of our culture; church and state can work together to promote common goals, but no preference can be given some religions over others; most important, the state cannot dub any one faith the official religion, for the Framers, like their colonial ancestors, correctly saw the Church of England as a threat to freedom of worship.

Why did it take the Supreme Court so long to confront this disagreement? Perhaps largely because the tenacious constitutional questions have arisen over the relationship between government-funded education and religion, in two areas: (1) public aid to parochial schools, and (2) the use of religious instruction in tax-supported schools. A brief historical resume will explain why these programs did not spur litigation sooner.

The drive for free public schooling in the nineteenth century was wholly satisfactory to our homogeneous population. But when a significant Catholic minority came to our shores, a massive system of parochial schools was established, because the Church has always seen religious training as a primary duty of education. If the church-school programs could meet minimal accreditation policies laid down by the states, no conflicts loomed on the horizon. Protestant children went to public school, where they received whatever half-baked religious values a board of education thought appropriate; and Catholic children went to private school, where they received a full dosage of religion at their parents' expense. Had there been no parochial education system, the Protestant-oriented trappings found in the public schools until very recently would have been challenged long ago. But once New Deal spending premises became part of the public philosophy, an avalanche of dollars began to flow into the coffers of education. The Supreme Court has been asked to review various governmental aid programs to parochial schools. At the same time, a growing diversity in religious outlook generally has prompted challenges to sectarian practices in public education.

The Court's initial opportunity to speak on these matters was provided by a New Jersey law reimbursing all parents for certain school transportation expenses. In the *Everson* case, the central question, naturally, was whether these rebates could be tendered for transportation to a parochial school. Speaking first on matters of general theory, the Justices endorsed strongly the Jeffersonian idea of church-state separation:

> Neither a state nor the Federal Government can set up a church. Neither can pass laws which aid one religion, *aid all religions,* or prefer one religion over another. . . . *No tax* in any amount, large or small, *can be levied to support any religious activities or institutions,* whatever they may be called, or whatever form they may adopt to teach or practice religion [italics mine].[74]

Despite this dictum, the New Jersey subsidy was upheld on grounds that the state was only trying to help all parents, regardless of faith, get out from under a difficult financial burden. Religion is not established, for example, when firefighters, whose mandate is to put out flames *everywhere,* find it necessary to protect parochial school property. The Constitution requires only that the state be *neutral* toward religion, not that the state be its *adversary.* Somewhat surprisingly, Mr. Justice Frankfurter dissented, contending that too much leeway had been accorded state action; the New Jersey program was an *indirect* subsidy to religious schools and so ran afoul of the establishment criterion.

As the cleavage in the New Jersey case portended, the libertarian-oriented Warren Court endorsed a broad, vigorous, Jeffersonian conception of this provision. The general issue it faced was how to make the public school system safe for nonsectarianism. I can recall the daily regimen of my grade-school years, as I waited for classes to begin. First, the teacher would appoint a student to recite some favored passage from the Bible. Then we would all dutifully bow our heads and repeat the Lord's Prayer. These practices were routine throughout the nation's public school systems, and for the Court largely to eradicate them, as it did during the 1960s, was no mean feat.

One of the specific cases brought before the Court involved a prayer written by the Regents of the New York State school system. It said: "Almighty God, we acknowledge our dependence upon Thee, and we beg Thy blessings upon us, our parents, our teachers, and our Country." Nobody was forced to say this prayer, and the passage invokes no particular faith. But, said the Justices, public officials have no power to compose prayers, period. Furthermore, "a union of government and religion tends to destroy government and to degrade religion."[75] This larger principle governed the holding handed down shortly thereafter in favor of claims by atheist Madilyn Murray O'Hare that both the Bible-reading and the Lord's Prayer exercises were also unacceptable.[76] The state must be *neutral* toward religion, the Justices reiterated; no law is permissible whose *primary* effect advances the cause of religion generally.

With the exception of the school desegregation rulings, no decisions adjudicated by the Warren Court were more controversial than the school prayer cases. They spawned "Impeach Earl Warren" signs along midwestern highways, and they led Congress to give serious consideration to a proposed constitutional change (the "Becker Amendment") to permit voluntary prayer in public facilities. Furthermore, the decisions were very hard to enforce, as various empirical studies have shown. Of special concern to those who deplore religion in politics was the split engendered among sectarian groups themselves. Organizations representing the so-called liberal faiths—Unitarianism, Judaism, Christian Science, and Congregationalism—supported the decisions; groups representing the so-called conservative faiths—Roman Catholicism and the Protestantism of Billy Graham—were highly critical.[77] To the liberals, a public school system disseminating religious values was the worst kind of political authoritarianism. To the conservatives, the Court decisions mirrored a breakdown in religious conviction among Americans generally. No doubt the kernel of this last assertion was correct; but parochial schools were available for those who had the money and the will to support them.

And therein lies the current bone of contention. All private schools need money today, and none more than parochial schools. The state legislatures have been fairly receptive audiences, for the Catholic voting bloc is not to be taken lightly. Nor are the arguments easy to resolve. A prosperous church-supported educational system relieves the already overcrowded public schools of what otherwise would be a crushing student load. Besides, Catholic parents are in a "double-tax" bind; obligated to help support public education, from which they receive no direct personal benefit, they also must help support the private school of their choice. Actually, this is the crux of the whole parochial education fiscal problem: approximately 3.3 million youngsters attended church-subsidized elementary and secondary schools in 1976, but ten years earlier the figure was approximately 5.4 million. So why shouldn't government help lighten their load a bit? these parents might reasonably ask. Didn't the Court authorize such schemes in its 1947 *Everson* ruling?

It is the Burger Court that has confronted these contentions—and has generally reacted negatively toward them. For instance, Rhode Island attempted to supplement the salaries of teachers in nonpublic elementary schools, providing they taught only secular subjects (for example, mathematics) and used only materials found in public schools. Pennsylvania authorized payments to private schools themselves for the purchase of secular textbooks and other instructional devices. Both states required these schools to keep detailed records that state personnel could inspect. The primary effect of the subsidies was to enhance the *secular* rather than the *theological* attributes of parochial education, supporters argued, surely a legitimate goal.

The Burger majority, though, found both programs unconstitutional because they fostered "excessive entanglement between government and religion."[78] The statutes would either allot money to teachers, whose handling of course materials could hardly be censored; or require government officials to rummage through records kept by religious schools for the purpose of determining compliance; or give money only to the *parochial school itself.* And both programs would stimulate political animosities geared to religious differences. While across-the-board aid for *all* parents or *all* children—as in school lunch programs or secular textbooks—would undoubtedly pass muster, the establishment clause was designed to *separate* church and state. In a democracy, religion mixed with politics is a toxic cocktail.

In other words, where the *primary effect* of the public policy is to advance theology, or where the public policy promotes undue entanglement between church and state, that policy is forbidden. Then Congress cannot give millions to church-owned colleges to construct buildings for secular educational nonsectarian purposes, right? Wrong! The primary effect here is to support instruction, not religious instruction. Moreover, an excessive commingling of church and state is avoided; such grants are one-shot items, requiring no year-to-year supervision or detailed estimation of secular versus nonsecular financial allotments. Furthermore, a college is qualitatively different from an elementary or secondary school; older students are more mature and reflective, while younger students are ripe for indoctrination. Therefore, political fragmentation along sectarian lines is much more likely with respect to *state* funding of *lower-level* parochial schools than *federal* funding of *higher-level* parochial schools.[79] But when *states* give money to *private colleges* for programs *readily verifiable as secular,* those subsidies are constitutional.[80] So "primary effect" and "entanglement" are still more important than which politicians donate the dollars.

Evidently, the "establishment of religion" formula is no pat answer. Countless overlaps in everyday church-state relations resist easy classification. Is it constitutional to have a Christmas tree on the White House lawn, paid for out of public funds? Is it constitutional for Congress to open each meeting with a prayer delivered by people of the cloth? Is it constitutional for our coins to carry the motto "In God we trust"? These are unresolved questions.

But from the standpoint of public policy, the key issue continues to be legislative funding of parochial school education. As the school prayer decisions exemplify, there is a deep split in this country between those who consider intimate church-state relations a constitutional outrage and those who consider such relations the building block of a civilized constitutional order. Framing the issue in terms of the economic survival of parochial schools only exacerbates this acrimony. Nor will current Supreme Court doctrine solve the problem; it is the federal government that spends the big money, not the states. As the financial crunch worsens, *lower-level* parochial school officials will turn to Congress, and so the great debate will flare anew.

A complicating factor in all this is the question of whether public schools—drab and conformist as they often seem to be—really serve the needs of our pluralistic population.[81] In this context some experts have urged adoption of a "voucher system."[82] Parents would be given a tax rebate equal to the cost of educating a youngster in the public schools and could use this money to fund whatever private educational option they chose. The constitutionality of the voucher approach is an open question. But I think it would be a curious state of affairs for the Court to give communities a free hand in providing property-tax exemptions for various nonprofit groups (including church groups[83]) and yet give communities little flexibility in providing educational subsidies for various nonprofit groups (including church groups) that manage elementary and secondary schools *accredited by the state.* To say that the people's representatives could authorize write-offs for those who attend military schools, progressive schools, traditional schools, and countercultural schools but not for those who attend Catholic, Muslim, and Quaker schools is to make the church and the state adversaries. Voucher statutes violate neither the "primary effect" standard nor the "entanglement" standard; that kind of balance—whether enlightened or myopic policy—is at least compatible with traditional constitutional values.

"Free exercise" of religion

Viewed in the abstract, the proposition that sectarian convictions and practices are unabridgeable is really nothing but the other side of the "freedom of religion" coin: what government cannot upgrade, it cannot downgrade. But, in the real world, I think that accommodating legislation to the "free exercise" command is even more difficult than reconciling the public interest with "establishment of religion" principles. Because the public sector is forever widening, more and more laws impinge on someone's religious principles or practices. Let's see how.

The Court didn't surround polygamy with "free exercise" immunity one hundred years ago, even though Mormons had vested it with a theological gloss;[84] and the Court today would hardly swallow Mr. Jones's alleged right to promenade down Main Street in the nude, even if clothing violated his religious conviction. Government's capacity to lay down reasonable standards of public decorum and behavior supersede the faith of a solitary dissenter or of a thousand true believers.

But knowing the state may proscribe both bigamy and indecent exposure will not take us far toward understanding the tension between the public interest and the free exercise of religion. What other kinds of legislation have stood up under such challenge? First, there are the usual statutes protecting young people. Just as the underaged may be quarantined from exposure to sexually blatant materials,[85] so they may be kept from selling religious tracts under the child labor laws.[86] Second, there are statutes permitting the nation to compete successfully on the battlefield: Congress allows citizens to file for conscientious-objector status if they have deeply held moral reservations about war *in general.*[f] But a citizen cannot pick and choose among wars, invoking religious con-

[f] Such exemptions may even be necessary given the free exercise provision, though the Court has not really faced up to that question in the context of present-day constitutional politics.

viction as a means to separate moral conflicts from immoral conflicts. The necessities of wartime involve substantial governmental concerns, and the intrusion into religious practice is minimal.[87]

What kinds of legislation have failed to clear the "free exercise" hurdle? For one thing, the public school system must not be used to undermine the religious precepts of minorities. The preclass ritual of my grade-school days included a compulsory flag salute. Any pupil who resisted—though nobody did—would have been considered unpatriotic and subject to expulsion. But Jehovah's Witnesses, who construe the Bible as literal gospel, find national flags offensive because they are "graven images." Mandatory flag salutes, the Court told us in 1943, are breaches of the free exercise clause.[88] Along the same lines, students cannot be required to attend public schools if they are enrolled in private sectarian facilities of comparable stature,[89] and a group like the Amish, whose religion teaches that formal education beyond grade school is a flirtation with worldly temptation, cannot be forced to enroll their children in *any kind of school.*[90] But doesn't that rule trench upon the state's extraordinary discretion to protect younger people, in this case to provide them with the benefits of a good education? No, because the very subsistence of Amish society hung in the balance, and the Constitution does not vest power in the state to educate a self-sustaining, communal religion out of existence.

Numerous conflicts arise when religious activity spills over into the business world. For instance, cities and towns usually make all door-to-door vendors procure a license and tender a standard fee for the privilege. But what if the vendors are missionaries selling their pamphlets for profit? The current attitude is that a nondiscriminatory tax is no more applicable to these salespeople than it is applicable to the church collection plate.[91] But don't the clergy pay income taxes on the salaries they earn? Yes. And don't newspapers pay sales taxes on the editions they sell? Yes. Evidently, the free exercise clause accords a "preferred-preferred position" to speech or press when combined with religion.

Compare the rights of the itinerant peddler specializing in religious speech with the rights of businesspeople whose religion precludes them from working on Saturday. Seventh-Day Adventists and Orthodox Jews, among others, often find themselves in a bind: the state sets aside Sunday as an official day of rest, when by law most commercial establishments must be closed, so either they are obliged to surrender their Sabbath observances or they may well go broke. These so-called state blue laws have been held valid because, for one thing, their primary effect is to enforce the valid secular purpose of providing a communitywide rest day. Moreover, what other device could be employed to achieve that purpose? In a nation of some three hundred denominations, somebody would surely be offended no matter which day were chosen. The peddler case was distinguished on the ground that a town could satisfy its fund raising interests by taxing only nonreligious vendors.[92]

This rationale, of course, could never have survived the "preferred-preferred" test, but it didn't have to clear that obstacle because there was no free speech issue at stake. The problem is that it can't survive the plain and simple "preferred position" test for plain and simple "free exercise" values either! Something must be wrong somewhere.

Perhaps what the Constitution truly obligates is a relatively clean separation between the affairs of God and the affairs of Caesar. If that is true, then free exercise of religion retains "preferred" status only so long as it sticks to matters of faith. For instance, all fifty states have traditionally provided property-tax immunity for houses of worship; such exemptions are part of the "Living Constitution," and the norm seems quite consistent with First Amendment values. However, when free exercise of religion becomes converted into free exercise of the profit motive, it would then be no more entitled to receive preferential treatment than any other well-intentioned entrepreneurial endeavor. For instance, Congress has traditionally provided income-tax immunity for religious organizations; such allowances are also part of the "Living Constitution," but this norm seems an unwarranted expansion of First Amendment values. After all, real estate holdings devoted exclusively to religious purposes generate an annual income of at least $22 billion.[93] Who knows how much money accrues from owning apartment houses and office buildings held solely for investment? To return to the cases involving door-to-door missionaries and Saturday sabbatarians, a principle that separated dogma from dollars would apply equally to both the seller of ideas and the seller of merchandise. The state may regulate or choose not to regulate these endeavors through evenhanded laws that satisfy the "primary effect" and "nonentanglement" criteria, but neither is entitled to "free exercise" immunity.

And now for the real challenge in constitutional politics presented by the freedom of religion clauses: How can the two be combined into a meaningful estimate of permissible church-state relations? There has been much talk over the years about the "high wall of separation" between matters of faith and temporalism, and considerable lip service has been paid to the notion that government must treat religion with a spirit of "strict neutrality." In fact, neither catch phrase describes correctly this segment of the "Living Constitution." Rather, religion—for better or worse—is very much enmeshed in the traditions and contemporary culture of this nation. What the First Amendment forbids—and what the Supreme Court has tried to prevent—is government action whose *primary effect* will either *burden* or *benefit* religion. Even given this kind of pragmatic test, walking the policy-making tightrope is sometimes tortuous. When Congress exempts from taxes individual contributions to religion, some might say this *establishes* religion because it confers special treatment. Others might say the exemption is obligatory, else the state inhibits *free exercise.* It would seem, then, that *incidental* political benefits and burdens are inevitable. That is the teaching of the transportation subsidy as applied to Roman Catholic parents and of the Vietnam War as applied to selective conscientious objectors; the first is no "establishment," and the second is no interference with "free exercise." If we can check the state's overt inclinations to help or hurt religion, the Framers' intention of a realistic balance will likely have been struck.

Equal protection for blacks[94]

After the Civil War, the victorious North moved to eradicate all vestiges of slavocracy in this country through four major constitutional changes: (1) involuntary servitude was abolished immediately (Thirteenth Amendment); (2) the former slaves were made citizens of the United States (Fourteenth Amendment); (3) states were forbidden to abridge voting rights on account of race (Fifteenth Amendment); (4) *no state could deprive any person of the equal protection of the laws* (Fourteenth Amendment).

This last item is phrased, in the Constitution, in much more general terms than are the others; yet, from very early days, there was little question of its intent. The Southern states, having lost the war, had passed laws keeping blacks from enjoying equal political and social status. These statutes the Fourteenth Amendment now made unconstitutional. The term "equal protection" was code language, then, for "black-white equality," which no state legislation could compromise.[95] The Constitution uses neither the term "civil liberties" nor the term "civil rights"; it is the concept of equal protection that provides explicit "rules of the game" sanction for racial uniformity under law.

The struggle to breathe full meaning into "equal protection" has been long and tedious. Until contemporary times, the South was able to devise truly ingenious ways for keeping blacks in an inferior posture. By far the most pervasive was racial segregation. The states did not say, "The white person gets this, and the black person doesn't." Instead, they said, "The white person gets this part, and the black person gets that part." To the Supreme Court, writing in 1896, the only question was whether the parts were equal. Blacks could be made to ride in the back of the bus if the seats were of the same quality as those in the front. And if the state could provide "separate but equal" transportation, it could provide segregated schools, recreational facilities, and lavatories. After all, said the Justices in *Plessy v. Ferguson,* "enforced separation of the two races [in no way] stamps the colored race with a badge of inferiority."[96] The states were only trying to work up reasonable regulations for promoting peace and tranquillity within their jurisdictions, consistent with established mores. Involuntary commingling of the races was not necessary for equality; it would probably serve only as an incitement to riot.

The *Plessy* decision—indeed, "separate but equal" per se—is based on certain definite assumptions about the nature of law. Legislation could work *political change but not social change,* because neither law nor politics could transform people's natural instincts. Only through voluntary consent could social equality or any other form of social action be accommodated. In the last analysis, the Court was saying that individuals, social classes, and races were inherently immune from legal constraint whenever their "naturally dominant position in the scheme of things" was allegedly challenged. For, as I described in Chapter 2, this was the era of *substantive due process,* where state-imposed business regulation in the name of larger community values forever came a cropper of judicial veto. And so was born its analogue, *substantive equal protection.*

As the nation moved slowly away from "racial laissez faire," the Court began to chip away at "separate but equal." The most important transitional step was to transcend equal protection as theory by looking at the realities. For instance, criminal defendant X, a black living in Bessemer, Alabama, is charged with raping a white woman in 1934. He finds no blacks on his jury; probably no black has *ever* been chosen for state jury duty in his county. Alabama insists that blacks are excluded, as are many whites, only because they don't meet standards of competence or of eligibility or because of the luck of the draw. But the Justices stopped paying much attention to what the state averred, and relying on their common sense, ruled that where no black juror had ever served and where qualified black jurors were shown to exist, equal protection had been disregarded.[97] If this empirical approach could be used to judge the constitutionality of all-white juries, it could be used to judge the constitutionality of second-class black schools. When the University of Texas law school declined to admit a qualified black student solely on account of race, arguing that the state maintained a separate facility for nonwhites, the Justices examined the two institutions and found the comparison odious. The school for whites had 65,000 volumes in its library and substantial scholarship funds. The school for nonwhites didn't even have accreditation. But *physical* facilities were not all. The school for whites "possesses to a far greater degree those qualities which are incapable of objective measurement but which make for greatness in a law school" (for example, faculty reputation, influential alumni, "traditions and prestige").[98] The Court's empirical view of equal protection as a political mechanism had taken it from the world of tangible rights to the equally significant world of status relationships and community influence—in short, to the guts of *social power.*

The coup de grâce for "separate but equal" came in the *Brown* decision of 1954.[99] At issue was the constitutionality of dual public school systems in states as different as South Carolina, Delaware, and Kansas. It was not disputed that the physical facilities afforded whites and blacks were comparable. What was in dispute were the intangibles. The Court found that government-supported school segregation "generates a feeling of inferiority as to [the status of black children] in the community that may affect their hearts and minds in a way unlikely ever to be undone."[100] Here, in the training ground for citizenship, the black youngster learns through the official arm of state law that he or she is a second-class member of the society, unfit to mix with white boys and girls. This indoctrination could only impede a child's ability to learn and mature normally. Such consequences rendered racial segregation inherently unequal.

By federal statute, the public schools in the District of Columbia were also racially segregated at that time. This posed a special problem, because the

Constitution mandates equal protection only at the state level and says nothing about the federal government. The Court was equal to this constitutional anomaly, finding such segregation a deprivation of *liberty* without *due process.* Both clauses were derived from "our American ideal of fairness," and racial categories imposed by any level of government were *suspect on their face.*[g] Since school segregation did not further any legitimate public objective, there was no way to rebut the prima facie evidence of unconstitutionality. In other words, a dual public school system for the two races was as arbitrary and capricious as an unfair trial.[101]

The *Brown* decision also rested on certain definite assumptions about law. Constitutional standards are not imprisoned by mores; the political system has enough energy to make them responsive to larger needs. One such need was the eradication of segregation furthered by overt public action; the Justices drew upon research by sociologists and social psychologists purporting to show that enforced separation fostered feelings of discrimination which in turn fostered feelings of inferiority.[102] The concept of equality, then, contained political, social, and psychological ramifications, which could be verified scientifically and imposed by judicial policy-making.

The *Brown* holding was unanimous. The consensus held together for almost twenty years, as the Court went to war against *de jure segregation*—that is, racial separation ordained by law. Virtually all species of the de jure policy were found in the South, which offered firm resistance. There was Governor Faubus's intervention at Little Rock, Governor Wallace's standing at the schoolhouse door in symbolic protest, Senator Byrd's "massive resistance" program in Virginia (an attempt to close down the public schools and then reopen them as "private" facilities funded by tuition grants given to parents by the state legislature). All such defiance failed eventually, but it delayed matters considerably—as did the Justices' unusual procedure of allowing lower courts to frame individual decrees for school districts within their jurisdictions. Finally, the Court threw up its hands in 1969 and announced that "all motions for additional time" are denied; "the obligation of every school district is to terminate dual school systems at once and to operate now and hereafter only unitary schools."[103] Nonetheless, in the end, full compliance required even more drastic steps than had been contemplated initially.

The Supreme Court faced those "drastic steps" in the *Swann* case of 1971. The issue was how to bring the public schools of Charlotte, North Carolina, within the purview of *Brown,* and the key variable was student assignment. Seizing the bull by the horns, the Justices spelled out the extent to which

[g] What other legislative guidelines are suspect under the equal protection standard? One is *national origin.* The Japanese exclusion cases notwithstanding, the Court has said that any such statutory distinction requires rigid scrutiny and can be justified only in "overriding" or "compelling" circumstances. Another suspect classification is *alienage.* Most aliens are citizens of other countries who live here. A state cannot simply bar aliens from welfare benefits or civil service positions. Under "preferred position" theory, the suspect criterion affords protection for readily identifiable, relatively powerless minorities. The Justices have been called on to find sex a suspect standard under equal protection, but thus far they have rejected that invitation.

federal courts could revamp prevailing patterns in order to eradicate de jure racism. With respect to *racial quotas,* the Constitution did not require that schools service a certain percentage of whites and a certain percentage of blacks on a permanent basis; but the imposition of mathematical ratios was a permissible starting point in redressing past inequities. An integrated educational district might have a small number of *one-race schools* (all-white or all-black facilities); but the burden of proof was on state officials to show that discriminatory policies had not created them. With respect to *altering attendance* zones, students could be placed in schools not necessarily closest to their homes, if breaking up de jure patterns required as much. And *busing* was a crucial tool in effecting good-faith implementation; the health of schoolchildren, especially the very young, must be given great consideration, but a seven-mile trip taking about thirty minutes was not unjustified.[104] The Court's solidarity and persistence never seemed more demonstrable. Today racial integration in the South leads the nation; at last report, almost 50 percent of black students attended white *majority* schools.[105]

But deep cleavage was just around the corner. Flushed with success in the South, civil rights advocates were now ready to launch an assault against the more subtle types of school segregation found in the North. There, the enemy was not de jure segregation, in the form of officially sanctioned dual educational systems; the enemy was *de facto segregation,* all-black schools caused largely by disparate income standards and uniracial residential patterns. Evidently, the only way for the courts to get at the de facto racism of the urban ghetto was to posit new constitutional theory certifying the necessity of massive busing programs. And as whites in the North reacted adversely to that gambit, Justices on the Supreme Court started jumping off the boat. Nor was the Court's membership in 1972 what it had been ten years earlier. Richard Nixon's four appointees, I think it is fair to say, were far more skeptical of "desegregation at any cost" than the Hugo Blacks and Arthur Goldbergs who preceded them.

The break-up began when the constitutionality of the Denver school program came up for review.[106] A lower court had found that the board of education used racial criteria in juggling various student attendance zones; but the inner-city schools, made up almost entirely of blacks and Chicanos, were segregated only in the de facto sense and therefore could not be changed under the prevailing doctrine of *Brown* and *Swann.* The Supreme Court disagreed, saying that where some meaningful portion of an educational system had been tampered with unconstitutionally, a prima facie case was established that the *whole* system was contrived in bad faith. School board officials tried to rebut this presumption by saying their ghetto districting was motivated solely by a commitment to *neighborhood schools.* The majority did not attack "neighborhoodism." But, it said, since in this case de jure manipulation had already entered the picture, the educational officers would have to prove either that inner-city segregation was unintentional or that their past de jure policies had not contributed to the current all-minority student profile. Of the Nixon appointees,

Justice Blackmun approved; Chief Justice Burger concurred only in the result, not in the Court's justification; Justice Powell said that ascertaining school board intentions to determine de jure segregation was an exercise in judicial crystal-gazing, and this could not stand up; Justice Rehnquist dissented, arguing de jure errors in one segment of educational programming did not infect the entire policy.

Clearly, the Justices were repositioning themselves, and the Detroit school case formalized the new alignment.[107] The lower court had found clear evidence of de jure segregation on the part of that city's education board. The judge could well have ordered the officials to undo their wrongs. But he rejected that goal; even if the racial mix in all Detroit's schools was in keeping with the city's overall black-white student makeup, the system itself would still be identifiable as a black school system because the Motor City had become Black City. De jure separatism could not be uprooted consistent with the Constitution unless racial identifiableness were eradicated. So the judge ordered large-scale cross-busing of black students from Detroit and white students from fifty-three suburban school districts. Thousands of blacks would be transported to the suburbs; thousands of whites would be transported to the inner city.

The four Nixon appointees, joined by Mr. Justice Potter Stewart, rejected these findings. Since there was no evidence that the suburban schools were unconstitutionally segregated, the lower court judge could not involve those schools. The only way to impose sanctions on suburban education, Stewart stressed in a concurring opinion, was to show that "segregative acts within the city alone . . . [caused] an increase in the number of Negro students *in the city as a whole*,"[108] for it was the existence of a predominantly black population in Detroit—ringed by a predominantly white population outside Detroit—that was truly responsible for racially identifiable schools. In his view, no such de jure racism had been proven.

Justices Marshall, Brennan, Douglas, and White disagreed. Essentially their arguments were: (1) Both the Detroit and the suburban school boards were agencies of the state, and the state was responsible indirectly for all school districting. Thus, Michigan must be held accountable for any violations of equal protection, and its local appendages could be restructured to cure unconstitutional state action. (2) Racially identifiable schools caused by governmental action must be removed. As had been held in the Charlotte decision, no particular white-black ratio was compulsory; but confining desegregation to Detroit simply would not undo segregation. (3) The majority's decision was now giving states a green light to stimulate an inevitable exodus of whites from city to suburb. Soon the most naive observer would see metropolitan areas split by race into two distinct social worlds.

The most important point emerging from these rulings is that the Justices have refused to move against de facto segregation per se. Indeed, in the Detroit case, they did not even get so far as to involve suburban de facto racism through the device of inner-city de jure racism. Some might argue the courts already have bitten off more than they can digest. For instance, the Boston school system is now under orders to eradicate de jure segregation via an intracity busing scheme. That the judiciary can alter pupil attendance zones and impose transportation schemes to attain this goal we have already noted. But the upshot has been a series of demonstrations, physical assaults, and school closings. Yet, time is on the side of interracial education: if desegregation can work in Little Rock and Charlotte, why can't it work in Detroit and Boston?

But none of this is going to stop "white flight" to the suburbs. And so the guarantee of the "Living Constitution" of equal protection with respect to race relations and public school attendance is—as Mr. Justice Stewart implies—a function of where people live: Chicago, Boston, and Washington are becoming black America; Skokie, Newton, and Silver Springs white America. Ten or twenty years from now the Court may be forced to revise its current either-or, de jure-de facto dichotomy. But if the Fourteenth Amendment guarantees interracialism in the use of state facilities, then political sagacity, if nothing else, would seem to inspire earlier action.

The weapons laid down in *Swann* are waiting and ready for use. As we have seen, *a hypothetical racial balance for each school or even for each district is not a constitutional requirement.* It does not necessarily follow that impressive numbers of white parents would respond to busing orders by sending their children to private school. I suspect it would depend on the extent to which they felt threatened by the change-over; for example, they might react far more favorably to a flexible scheme whereby the children of consenting blacks were brought out to meet their children than they would to an inflexible scheme whereby the computer says *x* blacks go here and *y* whites go there. However, whites just might be tempted to go their own way no matter how genuine the threat, if the state were to allow voucher-system options. And so the true complexity of the constitutional question emerges. If we want the "Living Constitution" to satisfy the equal protection standard of public interraciality, can this be accomplished by invoking the most politically volatile of all solutions, coercing middle-class whites to send their children into the ghetto? I doubt it. And can that standard be met if both black and white separatism receive subsidies from the state? I doubt it.

In Chapter 11, I shall propose a comprehensive approach for handling the larger race relations dilemmas, but our educational system must assume some of the burden, especially in the short run. There is no substitute at this time for the pragmatic, judicious use of busing preferably by state legislators who can take the *Swann* remedies and use them to cut across district lines and de facto-de jure distinctions. The prevailing conception is that the courts must somehow make equal protection work, since elected officials can't respond to contemporary racial questions. If that is true, then the "Living Constitution" may well subdivide into a white charter and a black charter.

"Searches and seizures"

In accordance with my overall scheme, the foregoing discussion has dwelt upon individual rights about which the Framers had very firm convictions and which they set forth in no uncertain terms. The remainder of this chapter, however, takes up freedoms not accorded such unambiguous status. Essentially, the Founders recognized government must resort to certain steps, but they were afraid of excesses. Some liberties, then, are couched in rhetoric presumptive of state intervention but seeking also to prevent flagrant departures from respectable conduct.

I begin with the Fourth Amendment, which proscribes "*unreasonable* searches and seizures" (my italics). No provision of the common law has been given greater lip-service than the expression "a man's home is his castle." The Framers knew that the police must have authority to get at both evidence and fruits of crime. But the Redcoats of Revolutionary days used to obtain "writs of assistance" from judges entitling them to rummage at will through the possessions of suspected smugglers, and the Framers made such antics clearly unconstitutional. The Fourth Amendment says that "no [search] Warrants shall issue, but upon probable cause . . . particularly describing the place to be searched, and the persons or things to be seized."

The most important statement of "search and seizure" values was put forward by the Supreme Court almost one hundred years ago.[109] Litigation between the U.S. government and private individuals often involves import duties, the amount of which varies directly with the worth of merchandise brought into the country. To help federal officers collect such fees, Congress passed a law allowing judges to issue subpoenas for records kept by importers, which might prove that customs had been shortchanged. Exercise of this subpoena power rested solely within the magistrate's discretion. If he were to exercise his option, failure to hand over the evidence could be treated as a confession, and the importer not only would have to pay up but might also have to pay a fine.[110]

If one looks with considerable care, the statute's patent unconstitutionality emerges. The Court reasoned as follows: (1) These subpoenas come within the scope of the Fourth Amendment; when the long arm of the law enters one's house and looks through one's papers via the subpoena process, it is consummating a search and a seizure. (2) Many such judicial orders are entirely permissible, but this particular mechanism constituted an *unreasonable* search and seizure device, because the citizen was being whipsawed. If he turned over the evidence, he might well be documenting his own culpability; if he didn't come forward, he *was* admitting culpability. In this respect, the Court said, the search and seizure safeguard and the self-incrimination safeguard overlapped, because compulsory extortion of a suspected person's private belongings could not be used to convict him.

The statute also ignored the "probable cause" requirement governing the issuance of search warrants. As the Court explained years later, justification for authorizing these orders must be based on something more substantial than a magistrate's unfettered suspicions. "Probable cause" is not intended to mean "evidence to convict," however. The correct test is whether a reasonable person, given enough information to render an independent, neutral evaluation, would reach the commonsense conclusion that a warrant should be forthcoming.[111]

Surely, the Fourth Amendment presumes in favor of the warrant procedure. However, the overwhelming percentage of searches are made *without* judicial acquiescence, so from the crude, quantitative standpoint "exceptional" cases have come to govern how the rule is enforced.[112] Almost all warrantless explorations are countenanced because they are *incident to a valid arrest.* For example, if the police are able to show there was probable cause at the time they took someone legally into custody, they can conduct searches of automobiles, boats, and the like, items which might be long gone by the time a warrant was procured. Similarly, the police may take a blood sample from an arrested party to show he was driving while intoxicated. Search warrants are not obligatory, because medical evidence shows the percentage of alcohol diminishes beyond the point of detection within a relatively short period.[113]

Suppose, however, a police officer sees somebody pick up a rock, smash a store window, and stash jewelry away under his coat. There is no threat the detained culprit will run away, but the officer could still reclaim the merchandise as soon as he corralled the man. The law is not inane; it does not require the patrolman to bother a judge before he ferrets out the stolen property. But now suppose the F.B.I. decides to apprehend Z, a suspected counterfeiter. Agents arrive at his house, flash a warrant for his arrest, and proceed to tear his home apart looking for bogus currency. They have gone too far, because a search that is incident to a proper arrest cannot be turned into a fishing expedition. The difficult task, of course, is to draw lines between "limited" (reasonable) quests and "unlimited" (unreasonable) quests, and the Court has not found this easy. The prevailing standard might be put as follows: when a valid arrest is made, law-enforcement officials may search the detained individual and seize both weapons and evidence of wrongdoing; furthermore, they can search the area "within his immediate control" so as to prevent him from resisting detention or destroying evidence.[114]

But what is a "valid arrest"? An arrest made on a warrant issued by a magistrate, of course, is conclusive. But courts allow felony arrests, even when made in the homes of the accused, to be consummated without warrants where probable cause of culpability can be shown later. Yet, as I have said, warrantless searches of buildings are not permissible; therefore, present constitutional policy seems to give greater protection to tangible items than to individuals themselves. Moreover, there is evidence that arrest on grounds of suspicion alone is a widespread excess. The Court itself admits that more than 200,000 such detentions took place between 1968 and 1970.[115]

The typical face-to-face interaction between officer of the law and private citizen does not occur in the context of overt criminal conduct. We are all familiar with the police officer who watches us, who follows us in his car for a short distance, or who stops us on the sidewalk to find out why we are loitering. Such surveillance is not prima facie wrong; the police have an extraordinarily difficult job keeping the peace, especially in the crime-infested cities. But the question is to what extent it constitutes "unreasonable searches and seizures."

Take hypothetical cop-on-the-beat Smith, patroling his beat in a high-crime district in the Chicago Loop. He spots a lone figure walking back and forth, seemingly eyeing a storefront. After thirty years on the force, Smith thinks he knows a "casing" job when he sees one. Keeping his distance, he notes that the suspect's behavior is becoming more and more questionable. To his trained senses, the storeowner is in imminent danger of being held up. Smith confronts the man and asks him for identification and explanation. The suspect mumbles a reply and, suddenly, Smith grabs him by the arm and pats him down for weapons, the well-known "stop-and-frisk" technique. He finds a revolver and subsequently arrests the party for carrying a concealed weapon.

This sort of detective work and law-enforcement procedure is commonplace, and the Court has accepted its constitutionality. To be sure, Officer Smith had "seized" the suspect and had also "searched" him without first obtaining a warrant. On top of that, the Court admitted, there was no probable cause for either the search or the seizure. In spite of these imponderables, an eight-man majority, in an opinion by Chief Justice Warren, said the entire investigative process was *reasonable* and met Fourth Amendment standards. Where the police officer could point to specific facts that, together with rational inferences, would lead him to believe his physical safety was in jeopardy, a search *for weapons* lay within his range of choices. Because American criminals are known for their violence, and given both Smith's experience and the suspect's peculiar behavior, a magistrate could well find the policeman's conduct reasonable and prudent. As for the search warrant criterion, Warren said: "We deal here with an entire rubric of police conduct—necessarily swift action predicated upon the on-the-spot observations of the officer on a beat—which historically has not been, and as a practical matter could not be, subjected to the warrant procedure." [116] So a search for weapons is permissible upon suspicion if the suspicion is based on "tangibles." Those "tangibles" really entail nothing but police know-how and intuition as conveyed after the fact, when the data, for all practical purposes, are impossible to verify. Of course, the Court was moved by the great dangers of contemporary law enforcement, and it sought to balance those dangers against the limited intrusion essayed. But when various minority groups, especially blacks, remonstrate against police harassment and "shake-downs," this is the constitutional doctrine underlying much of the coercion complained of.

Today's most intriguing search and seizure cases involve wiretapping and other forms of electronic eavesdropping. At the outset, however, the Supreme Court felt these tools did not lie within the purview of the Fourth Amendment at all unless physical trespass could be shown. If an F.B.I. agent came inside my house and sprinkled bugging devices around, this was unconstitutional; not so, however, if he tapped my phone conversations from beyond my property, or if he pressed a listening probe against my hotel room wall while standing in an adjoining room. The Court's theory, literalistic to the point of both myopia and sterility, was justified in the *Olmstead* case: "There was no searching. There was no seizure. The evidence was secured by the use of the sense of hearing and that only. There was no entry of the houses or offices of the defendants." [117] In one of his great dissents, Justice Brandeis cut through these superficialities and pointed the way to the gut issues of forty years later:

> Subtler and more far-reaching means of invading privacy have become available to the Government. Discovery and invention have made it possible for the Government, by means far more effective than stretching upon the rack, to obtain disclosure in court of what is whispered in the closet. . . . Advances in the psychic and related sciences may bring means of exploring unexpressed beliefs, thoughts and emotions. . . . Can it be that the Constitution affords no protection against such invasions of individual security?[118]

The doctrine advanced in *Olmstead* was "good law" until the late 1960s, and the only protection against such rampant invasions of privacy by the state was through statute. The best-known legislation on the subject was a portion of the 1934 Federal Communications Act, in which Congress said individuals could not intercept interstate communications and divulge their contents without the permission of the sender. But this provision was shot through with loopholes. For one thing, it obviously restrained the use of wiretaps alone; deployment of more sophisticated electronic gadgets remained unregulated. For another, as I discussed earlier with regard to executive surveillance in the internal security field, the F.B.I. began circumventing the requirement as early as the 1940s. This policy stemmed from an opinion by Franklin Roosevelt's Attorney General, Robert H. Jackson, that the statute banned not wiretapping but only the disclosure of the contents of conversations recorded. And so a wholesale program of electronic espionage was developed to combat domestic subversion, organized crime, and the like. None of the evidence accumulated could be introduced in court against the parties bugged, but such information could be employed against others whose voices were recorded.

It finally dawned on the Court that, with growing technological sophistication, the use of surveillance gadgetry was running amok in government circles and required control. In the *Katz* decision, a majority discarded the physical trespass standard and replaced it with the individual's *right of privacy.* In short:

> The Fourth Amendment protects people, not places. What a person knowingly exposes to the public, even in his own home or office, is not a subject of Fourth Amendment protection. . . . But what he seeks to preserve as private, even in an area accessible to the public, may be constitutionally protected.[119]

In the instant case then, the fact that petitioner had placed his call from a public telephone booth was beside the point; he had expected privacy, and that expectation could not be subverted by a clandestine listening device.

This decision places all such contrivances under the umbrella of conventional "search and seizure" precedent. Theoretically, if a policeman goes before a judge and demonstrates probable cause that certain conversations would reveal criminal wrongdoing, then a warrant authorizing the use of a particular electronic instrument can be obtained. But the 1934 statute still constituted a barrier against the use of wiretapping, even when consistent with the "reasonable search and seizure" test. In the wake of spiraling crime rates, however, Congress seemed to rely upon this decision as an excuse for repealing that ban. Hence, in 1968, substitute legislation was enacted covering the use of all these paraphernalia. The Omnibus Crime Control and Safe Streets Act gives the Attorney General power to obtain eavesdropping warrants for thirty days (renewable for thirty-day extensions) from a federal judge. His search for evidence might extend not only to heinous crimes such as murder and treason but to offenses such as extortion in credit transactions and the bribing of athletes. State judges were empowered to issue similar warrants to their chief law enforcement officials. Furthermore, the law allows both state and federal attorneys to tap phones or bug houses for forty-eight hours without any judicial controls if they have *reasonable* grounds for thinking national security is in danger or organized crime is involved. Is this constitutional? Could F.B.I. agents storm into a meeting of Cosa Nostra officials without a warrant and search the premises looking for incriminating evidence on the rationale that some tipster had told them a narcotics smuggling operation was being planned and the meeting would break up in thirty hours? Of course not. Then why does the F.B.I. have this sort of leeway in utilizing eavesdropping techniques?

I have commented elsewhere on the Court's rejection of inherent executive power to eavesdrop for the purpose of combating domestic subversion.[120] Yet the Omnibus Crime Control Act lies unscathed on the statute books; indeed, the clauses approving electronic surveillance without judicial endorsement have fared very well in the lower federal courts, though they have never been tested before the Supreme Court. I have no doubt—after listening to testimony by the various Watergate and Plumber eavesdropping technicians and watching the assorted TV melodramas that glamorize cloak-and-dagger spying—that a Dr. Mabuse[h] mentality really has crept into the communal ethos of this country. If the taint of *1984* is to be avoided, the Court had better intensify its checking and balancing.

Finally, suppose the police conduct an *unreasonable* exploration into my personal effects and stumble across evidence of the most damaging proportions. Can that information be used in court against me? This question has proved extraordinarily difficult because it is so hard to balance the considerations at stake. I will frame the problem as baldly as possible: if incriminating information, taken unconstitutionally, can be used against me, what will deter the police from flouting the Fourth Amendment at will in order to recruit damaging evidence? Obversely, if police error or malfeasance puts an absolute damper on presenting tainted evidence, will not the successful prosecution of accused felons very often be defeated?

In 1914 the Justices said the Fourth Amendment would be "of no value" if materials taken in an unconstitutional manner could be submitted at trial.[121] And so was born the so-called *exclusionary rule,* which simply freezes the use of tainted information if proper objection is entered by defense counsel. That principle has obtained to this day in the federal courts.

But did the exclusionary rule apply to the states? If it were part of the Fourth Amendment, why shouldn't it? After all, the many freedoms I have

[h] This diabolical fictional character owned a hotel in which every room was equipped with a secret camera. From his central headquarters, he could flick switches and see what all his guests were doing.

discussed in this chapter are as applicable to state action as to federal action. But one of the root problems in gauging "search and seizure" application to state affairs is the question of whether the exclusionary principle really *is* part of the Fourth Amendment. The Court in 1914 seemed to think it was; the Court in 1949 said it wasn't. Mr. Justice Frankfurter called the device "a matter of judicial implication"—a sound means for implementing a particular end, a means that must be honored by the federal judiciary but that states might bypass in their quest for better tools of enforcement.[122] For instance, instead of a blanket condemnation of unconstitutionally seized evidence, perhaps a better way to deter police indiscretions would be civil suits brought against trespassers by private individuals whose papers had been improperly taken. Or perhaps the state might pass a law handing out stiff jail sentences to police who disparaged the Fourth Amendment but preserving the state's right to use the incriminating evidence. In any event, as of 1949, the states were not bound by the exclusionary rule.

Twelve years later, the Warren Court overturned that holding. The Fourth Amendment, it said in the *Mapp* case, would amount to little without the exclusionary principle. Since other possible preventive measures had failed to curb police lawlessness, the rule was more than a means to an end; it was an integral part of the constitutional "search and seizure" guarantee. Clearly a ban on evidence illegally taken was applicable to state as well as federal action.[123]

The *Mapp* decision stands with *Miranda v. Arizona* as the Warren Court's most significant and hotly disputed milestone in the general area of police conduct. Both have been criticized for tilting the scales of the criminal justice system too far in favor of the accused. "Would Lizzie Borden go free if the police failed to warn her of her right to keep silent?" the cynics query. "And would Lizzie also go free if the only evidence against her was obtained through an unreasonable search and seizure?" the same doubters ask derisively.

The Burger Court has not overturned *Mapp,* but the rumblings are beginning to be heard. In a recent decision, the majority specifically said the exclusionary rule is not an inherent part of the Fourth Amendment package.[124] And the Chief Justice himself has denounced *Mapp* in rhetoric deserving of careful study:

> Inadvertent errors of judgement that do not work any grave injustice will inevitably occur under the pressure of police work. These honest mistakes have been treated in the same way as deliberate and flagrant . . . violations. . . . Freeing either a tiger or a mouse in a schoolroom is an illegal act, but no rational person would suggest that these two acts should be punished in the same way. . . . I submit that society has at least as much right to expect rationally graded responses from judges in place of the universal "capital punishment" we inflict on all evidence when police error is shown in its acquisition.[125]

This opinion is important because it elevates pragmatism and common sense above rigid doctrine. Under the common law, evidence could be introduced at trial no matter how it was procured. That approach is no longer viable, because in this era of the "superstate" the police would have too much rope with which to hang dissidents and loners. In fact, research shows that even the exclusionary rule is not much of a deterrent; since *Mapp,* state and local law enforcement personnel have gone about their business pretty much as usual.[126] But if tough new laws are needed so the courts can watch the police, must any and every doubt be resolved against the force? Does that solution jibe with the empirical data of present-day lawlessness civilized people must abide? Of course, we would want to ask the Chief Justice some tough questions, such as, "If a policeman fails to procure a warrant through negligence, has he unleashed a mouse or a tiger?" However, the seeds of balance are there to sprout.

"Cruel and unusual punishments"

The criminal process means nothing if guilty parties cannot be punished. Traditionally, penalties have taken three forms: deprivation of money, deprivation of personal liberty, and deprivation of life itself. By making cruel and bizarre punishments unconstitutional, the Framers were attempting to prevent the crassest spirit of revenge or irrationality from weighing more heavily than the disciplined, well-ordered human need to preserve a civilized polity through reason and law.

Just how do judges decide whether a penalty is either "cruel" or "unusual"? Should they be guided by their own private sensibilities? Such subjectivity seems hard to justify. Our commitment to constitutionalism requires that courts articulate their reasons according to objective standards rationally contrived and, therefore, comprehensible to attentive publics. Should judges base their conclusions on public opinion? Hardly. The tides of emotion and irrationality can engulf 55 percent of the population just as they can engulf a Supreme Court mired in its own predilections. Besides, the logistical problems would be insurmountable.

Take the case of convicted murderer Willie Francis. He was sentenced to die in the electric chair, but when the switch was thrown, nothing happened! There had been an electrical malfunction. Francis was returned to his cell while the contraption was repaired. Meanwhile, the Justices were asked to intervene. Surely it was cruel and unusual punishment, they were told, to make anyone endure a second trip to the executioner. There obviously was no reasonable way for members of the Court to determine how a cross-section of the public would respond to this issue. On the one hand was Francis's dignity and integrity as an individual; on the other hand was a cold-blooded killer, who might avoid society's retribution by a fluke among flukes. Mr. Justice Frankfurter spoke to the quandary in this fashion:

> I cannot rid myself of the conviction that were I to hold that Louisiana would transgress [the Constitution by carrying out] the death sentence, I would be enforcing my private view rather than that consensus of society's opinion which . . . is the standard enjoined by the Constitution.[127]

But how do judges unearth this "consensus"? They must somehow fathom the fundamental aspirations and moods of our constitutional consciousness, isolate the great "rules of the game" as the Framers did years ago, and ask themselves: Is the penalty so objectionable as to "shock the conscience" of Americans? Frankfurter's test comes down almost to matters of philosophy—even aesthetics—as one attempts to grasp the core of traditions underlying our political culture.[128] He simply could not believe the implicit norms of this society—the "Living Constitution"—would be violated if Willie Francis were forced once again to enter the death house. So he put his personal squeamishness aside and supplied the fifth vote needed to uphold the "double electrocution" order.

No doubt the Frankfurterian approach is difficult to apply, but aside from the polar positions of private sensibility and gross majoritarianism it is the best overview yet articulated. I shall now apply his test—and competing tests as well—to the great question of the day in this field: Under what conditions does capital punishment constitute a cruel and unusual punishment?

As this country moved into the 1970s, both Congress and an overwhelming majority of states had laws on the books imposing the death penalty. Treason, first-degree murder, and rape were the three offenses most often inspiring the ultimate sanction. However, beginning in 1960, exaction of capital punishment attenuated drastically. Indeed, not one person was executed after 1967; so the lives of approximately six hundred inmates hung in the balance when the Supreme Court agreed to review relevant cases.

In its momentous 1972 decision, the Justices did not strike down capital punishment per se, but they did find (by a vote of five to four) that the death penalty *as applied* in the cases before them was a cruel and unusual punishment.[129] Under these statutes, the trier of fact—a judge or a jury—determined whether life should be taken once defendant's guilt had been established. But no specified standards governed their deliberations. The laws at issue gave them unfettered discretion to apply whatever criteria seemed appropriate in each case. It was this *wholesale delegation of legislative authority* to judges and juries that the Supreme Court struck down in the *Furman* ruling.

But the Justices were even more divided than the crude tally indicates. Three members confined themselves to finding unacceptable the statutory schemes presented; two members said the death penalty was unconstitutional under any circumstance; four members felt capital punishment was permissible in the cases under review. Here are the salient features of the statements I think best represent each bloc:

Justice Potter Stewart: Retribution is ingrained in human nature; therefore, it may serve as a proper basis for framing punishment through law. But the death sentences at issue here "are cruel and unusual in the same way that being struck by lightning is cruel and unusual."[130] Because such punishments appear freakish, random, and arbitrary, they are void.

Justice Thurgood Marshall: First: Punishment for revenge is impermissible. Second: Public opinion polls show people evenly divided on whether capital punishment is cruel and unusual, but if those questioned had access to the information we have—for instance, that death was no better deterrent than life imprisonment and that the sentencing process is not structured to separate likely recidivists from others—they would find the "ultimate" penalty offensive to conscience.

Chief Justice Warren Burger: The purpose of the "cruel and unusual punishment" clause is to bar certain sanctions generally considered abhorrent, not to second-guess the findings of lay jurors, whose competence in assessing facts and deciding what penalties are suitable in what cases is at least the equal of our own.

These opinions provide the necessary foundation for gauging the Court's evaluation of capital punishment per se. Any inference that the death penalty was now contrary to national community standards because there had been no executions since 1967 was rebutted by the legislative reaction to *Furman.* More than thirty states passed laws authorizing capital punishment in certain situations in which the defendant was convicted of murder, and Congress enacted a capital punishment law to cover cases in which aircraft hijacking led to the loss of life. These statutes took two very different forms: (1) such states as Georgia and Texas not only defined specific circumstances of criminal conduct in which triers of fact could impose death sentences but also allowed them to consider mitigating factors in framing suitable penalties; (2) such states as North Carolina and Louisiana defined various crimes that carried mandatory death sentences. As of March 1976, almost 500 persons, convicted under these laws, were sitting in various death rows. Could these (or any) enactments survive Eighth Amendment scrutiny?

In the *Gregg* decision,[131] the Stewart argument merged with the Burger argument to uphold the Georgia-Texas format. Here, defendant had been found guilty of murder, and the jury had found capital punishment appropriate because the homicide had been committed for financial gain, *one of several aggravating circumstances set out in the law itself.* Moreover, the jury could have waived the death penalty had it found such factors as the accused's youth or lack of criminal record controlling. However, in the *Woodson* decision,[132] the Stewart argument merged with the Marshall argument to void the North Carolina-Louisiana format. Here, defendant had been found guilty of first-degree murder and sentenced automatically to death. Justice Stewart noted that the mandatory taking of life had been frowned on in the United States for well over one hundred years and had been resurrected only because some states thought it the one permissible means of retaining capital punishment after *Furman.* But the crux of his opinion was this ringing declaration: "The fundamental respect for humanity underlying the Eighth Amendment . . . requires consideration of the character and record of the individual offender and the circumstances of the particular offense as a constitutionally indispensable part of the [death penalty process]."[133] To this, the Chief Justice merely said that a state could reasonably find some crimes so heinous as to require mandatory death sentences for the purpose of deterring such crimes.

Now we can apply our earlier tests for "cruel and unusual" to the Justices' core assumptions in these cases. Remember the three models at our disposal: (1) subjective tests, (2) majoritarian tests, (3) community conscience tests. And keep in mind that the first two are hardly defensible conceptions of what the Eighth Amendment forbids.

Mr. Justice Stewart says retribution is a permissible motive for contriving criminal sentencing procedures, and Mr. Justice Marshall disagrees vigorously. But neither tells us what guidelines they have applied to reach these conclusions beyond their subjective, personal viewpoints. Actually, Justice Stewart's entire argument skips back and forth between personal opinion and public opinion. Thus, he says that the death penalty is constitutional on principle because legislatures have responded to *Furman* by reimposing it under different conditions, and he also says mandatory executions are unconstitutional in part because they were rejected by legislative opinion for one hundred years. But we had jury determinations of capital punishment without statutory criteria for one hundred years, too! On the validity of this practice, however, majority rule through elected officialdom yields to Stewart's "lightning bolt" thesis. And legislative imposition of mandatory death sentences following *Furman* yields to his belief that "individualized" sentencing is required where life hangs in the balance. So capital punishment must be personalized, but not too personalized. Based on what implicit norms underlying the "Living Constitution"? I see none, and I consider these to be purely subjective estimates of what is "cruel and unusual."

Chief Justice Burger attempts to transcend superficial belief systems by invoking Oliver Wendell Holmes's "reasonable man" test. He argues that capital punishment is a reasonable legislative response in the same fashion that Holmes argued that regulation of the economic system was a reasonable legislative response. But Holmes showed that the Constitution is largely neutral with regard to economic policy; hence the people's representatives can exercise broad discretion in this area. Burger formulates no tests for determining whether capital punishment is analogous to laissez faire capitalism, that it is a norm which should stand or fall as democratic processes dictate.

And what of Mr. Justice Marshall's essential critique? It is the most ambitious effort of all, because it does specify an objective, nonmajoritarian solution. To be sure, Marshall has no concern for what Americans have prized highly over the years; rather, he seeks to determine what Americans would prize highly if they knew what judges knew! The result is that, unlike Justice Frankfurter's probes for "Living Constitutionalism," he can never grapple with the real, empirical world. He is doomed to invoke *a priori* notions of what people think and do if they weren't real people, living in a real culture, hewing to real correlative rights and duties. But the "cruel and unusual punishments" clause, like all constitutional clauses, was not meant to govern hypothetical people; it was meant to govern flesh and blood people.[i]

[i] The reader may wonder why I have belabored these criteria for judging what is "cruel and unusual." In Chapter 8 I shall explain how these very same considerations are fundamental to understanding the due process clause of the Fourteenth Amendment. And, in our discussion of obscenity, was it not of critical importance to determine "contemporary community standards"? All these questions round out our understanding of how to view the "Living Constitution."

The Justices failed to produce an "opinion of the court" in any of the above decisions. They have legitimized capital punishment, but their reasons remain obscure because they can't agree on how to interpret the Eighth Amendment, much less on what it means. I think that buried in the "Living Constitution" is the following prescription: those who kill in cold blood can themselves be killed in cold blood, if the state so decides by law and by fair hearing. Indeed, this theme is so pervasive that it runs throughout Western civilization and beyond. The standard satisfies humankind's traditional concern for uniformity, predictability, equity, and personal accountability under the law. If our politics cannot reasonably decide to exterminate the Adolf Hitlers and the Charles Mansons, then we can honestly say that the Supreme Court has power to uproot our legal mores with the stroke of a pen.[134]

"Penumbra" rights

Activist Supreme Courts make their reputation by breathing new life into specific constitutional liberties, and therefore, checking the policy initiatives of the "people's representatives." But quite often the Justices find the document's specifically listed freedoms insufficient to express the values of personal choice they consider fundamental. The Framers, of course, couldn't enumerate *every* right that might someday be abridged or even contemplate all the myriad ways the state might divest citizens of their freedoms. Their hedge was the Ninth Amendment: "The enumeration in the Constitution, of certain rights, shall not be construed to deny or disparage others retained by the people." But the Justices have never employed this clause to protect specific liberties, for they fear opening a Pandora's box. Then where has the Court found these other precepts? And what are they?

Our constitutional history provides some curious though revealing examples. In 1796, Georgia repealed a law conveying certain lands to private individuals. Chief Justice Marshall could not believe the state had power to rip up its agreement; however, he was hard pressed to rationalize his instincts. Almost in desperation he said, "Georgia was restrained in part by general principles which are common to our free institutions. . . ."[135] More than one hundred years later, the Court faced a Nebraska statute making it illegal to teach a foreign language in the elementary schools of that state. Parents of German extraction were furious; they wanted the *private* schools they subsidized to transmit their mother tongue. By this time, however, the craft of judicial review was sophisticated enough for the Justices to need more than just "general principles." They found the term "liberty" in the due process clause sufficient for their purposes:

> Without doubt, it denotes not merely freedom from bodily restraint but also the right of the individual to contract, to engage in any of the common occupations of life, to acquire useful knowledge, to marry . . . and generally to enjoy those privileges long recognized at common law *as essential to the orderly pursuit of happiness by free men* [italics mine].[136]

We have here the rhetoric of substantive due process, a doctrine commonplace in the 1920s.[137] This provision was construed not only to protect the individual against unfair *procedures,* especially in the courtroom, but also to preserve certain *substantive freedoms,* such as liberty of contract.

The Warren Court did not invoke overtly any such notion of due process. The typical Justice of the 1960s—a twentieth-century "liberal"—undoubtedly remembered with horror the confrontation between judiciary and executive in the 1930s, when the Court, flushed with delusions of substantive property rights not spelled out in the Constitution, had gotten its fingers burned. Yet a consensus among them believed there were liberties worthy of shelter that were nowhere demarcated with precision. For instance, as I shall describe in detail elsewhere,[138] the Warren Court developed to unprecedented proportions an individual freedom called the "right to travel." But the example most suitable for analysis here is the "right of privacy." Where did that privilege come from, why was it deemed necessary, and what does it mean today?

The landmark case[139] involved a Connecticut law banning the use of contraceptive devices, and the question at issue was whether the statute could be applied to married persons. The majority, in ruling the enactment invalid, said it had a direct impact on the personal, private relationship between husband and wife. Now the Constitution certainly says nothing about wedded bliss being sacrosanct in the face of appropriate state legislation. But the Court felt there was a right of privacy inherent in several discrete clauses. Examples: The First Amendment protects the political association of like-minded people; the Fourth Amendment bans "unreasonable searches and seizures"; the Fifth Amendment ensures that an individual need not incriminate himself. Taken together, these provisions have *penumbras* ("gray areas"), one of which comprises a zone of personal privacy. The state can no more enter that domain than it can abridge freedom of speech:

> Would we allow the police to search the sacred precincts of marital bedrooms for telltale signs of the use of contraceptives? The very idea is repulsive to the notions of privacy surrounding the marriage relationship.
>
> We deal with a right of privacy older than the Bill of Rights—older than our political parties, older than our school system.[140]

I want to emphasize that the Court was not elaborating here upon the notion of privacy which Mr. Justice Brandeis had called the cornerstone of Fourth Amendment protection in the *Olmstead* wiretap case. This is an *independent* right of privacy arising full-blown from the effluence of several clauses seen as a totality. And I also want to emphasize that the Court applied this "right of privacy" to knock down the Connecticut law on contraceptives in the same way it applied the "cruel and unusual punishment" standard to knock down "arbitrary" and "inflexible" impositions of the death penalty. In all these cases the Justices characterized governmental policy as contrary to their notion of basic community standards; *but here the decision was based on a constitutional right never before specified.*

The Burger Court has, in its turn, given the doctrine tremendous impetus, not least by its very controversial 1973 rulings with respect to abortion.[141] The Justices decided that the right of privacy is broad enough to cover a potential mother's decision to terminate pregnancy. However, Mr. Justice Blackmun wrote, this freedom is not absolute; the state may pass laws regulating abortion if necessary to promote a *compelling* governmental interest. What such interest exists in these circumstances? There are two: protection of the mother's health and protection of unborn children. In the instant litigation, the state of Texas had decided by law that life commenced with conception; therefore, abortions were illegal except to save the mother's life. This accommodation of conflicting values, the Justices said, was unconstitutional. The state had used its power to protect the fetus in a fashion destructive of the mother's private decision-making prerogatives. So what balance could be struck? Blackmun laid it out in the form of three separate, neat stages:

1. In the first trimester, a pregnant woman may determine for herself whether to abort, and the state has *no compelling interest* in regulating that personal choice.
2. In the second trimester, the state's interest in preserving the pregnant woman's health becomes so important that reasonable rules governing the abortion procedure may be enacted—the attending surgeon's professional qualifications, the conditions of facilities where such operations are performed, and the like. These criteria suddenly become valid because there is overwhelming medical evidence that after the third month mortality in abortion occurs more frequently than mortality in normal childbirth.
3. In the third trimester, the state's interest in protecting the fetus becomes compelling because by that time it can probably survive outside the mother's womb. Hence, the state can proscribe termination after the point of viability unless necessary to save the mother's life.

Perhaps the reader is surprised to see "strict constructionists" like Warren Burger, Lewis Powell, and Harry Blackmun joining hands with William O. Douglas, William Brennan, and Thurgood Marshall to support judicial activism for the protection of women's rights. That alliance gives us a clue to the role of this new privacy notion in our "Living Constitution."

I have already argued that the modern-day liberal generally presumes *against* government action in the domain of civil liberties. Once the rights of women became classified in his mind as a civil liberty, it was relatively easy for him to frame theories about personal control over one's own body and apply them to the abortion controversy. I see no difference whatsoever between the "clear and present danger" test in free speech cases and the "compelling state interest" test in privacy cases. Both the right to talk and the right to have an abortion now occupy a "preferred position" and, according to conventional liberal ideology, can be regulated only when a precise and immediate threat to society is identified. Meanwhile, the modern-day conservative, generally suspicious of statism, is no more infatuated with invasions of privacy than with "social welfarism." How else does one explain former Senator James Buckley's legislative brainchild, the right of students over seventeen to peruse and challenge for accuracy the contents of dossiers held in their name by the schools they attend, including letters of recommendation?

As the state becomes more powerful, people become disenchanted when they find interests precious to them coming under attack. Is it any wonder that libertarians both liberal and conservative search laboriously for political weapons—including judicial activism—to protect private interests?

But, of course, there is always another side. The Georgia lands dispute arose from revelations that members of the state legislature had been bribed and, consequently, had sold those properties for a song. Why could not a Supreme Court Justice have ruled that states held sovereign power to revoke contracts consummated under fraudulent circumstances? Now take the Court's upholding of a right to teach German in private schools. There, the Nebraska legislature had decided that instructing children in the English language—and only the English language—would promote a sense of community in the state and break down insular ethnic barriers. Mr. Justice Holmes, dissenting, supported the constitutionality of that determination, finding it a matter on which reasonable people might disagree. And, for the sake of argument, take the Connecticut contraception law, which the Justices found shocking. Doesn't the Roman Catholic Church teach that the use of contraceptive devices is immoral? Are the thousands of faithful who follow that precept aping an irrational theological doctrine? No? Then why is the state irrational, arbitrary, and repulsive when it also adopts (for better or worse) that policy as its own?

All this brings me to our "Living Constitution," which includes the privacy rationale underlying both the Court's abortion decision and the Congress's policy with respect to student files. One of the terrible dilemmas inherent in the abortion debate is balancing the rights of the pregnant woman against the rights of an unborn child. Things would be much easier if only scientists could tell us when life begins. But they cannot. Why, then, is a Supreme Court Justice precluded from arguing that we have legislative debate and majority vote in order to resolve precisely this kind of question? The Justices, of course, did not decide the issue either, but their 3-3-3 test in the name of the *potential mother's privacy* surely preempts meaningful participation by elected officials in resolving this social problem through law.

As for FERPA,[142] Congress obviously feared that the private files of students might be compromised by either (1) unauthorized persons such as policemen obtaining access to data held therein or (2) authorized persons carelessly or maliciously placing unfounded, derogatory information therein. Congress's initial response was to let the eighteen-and-overs see *everything*, including letters already received in confidence. When universities set up an immediate howl, the law was changed so that it would have no retroactive effect and so that a student could waive the right of access to specific letters. This means no confidential evaluations received prior to 1975 may be inspected; it also means faculty members will receive assurances of confidentiality for what they write in the future if they choose to have candidates sign release forms.

The basic point is that Congress had to balance students' right of privacy against a referee's right of privacy. The original statutory accommodation proved crude and one-sided and so was revised. But if the initial rules had been contrived by judges, how much longer would it have taken to refine away defects?

This ever-present debate over "political branch" competence versus judicial competence helps structure the role of penumbra rights in the constitutional scheme of things. The freedoms we enjoy—or should enjoy—as citizens cannot be encapsulated in any document; they are too broad and too diffuse. No doubt there has always been a right of privacy inherent in our "Living Constitution," if not in the formal charter itself. It is only in these days of the state as octopus that we have had need to define the privilege with some precision. But there is great dispute as to how these penumbra liberties should be specified. One tradition leans on judicial activism generated by vigilant publics through litigation; the other tradition leans on "political branch" activism generated by vigilant publics through lobbying and voting. The former carries greater legitimacy and symbolic force; the latter has greater flexibility in effecting accommodation. If history is our guide, American politics seems to require both. The heavy question, which is a matter of both constitutional philosophy and empirical evidence, is: What mix between them maximizes the "Living Constitution's" faithfulness to the genuine article?

Conclusion

The Declaration of Independence and the Constitution of the United States, our two major political documents, are predicated on different conceptions of individual freedom. Jefferson—like John Locke before him—saw these liberties as inalienable, natural, and in the spirit of divine purpose. To say Jefferson and Locke were optimists about human reason and intuition is somewhat of an understatement. The Framers of the Constitution, however, were much more concerned with the dispersion of power enforced by checking devices. Civil liberties were essential, but they, too, must be balanced, else freedom would become license and license breed anarchy. To say *The Federalist* contains a germ of pessimism about human reason and intuition is also somewhat of an understatement.

Both these traditions are alive today, reflected in the clashes between moral philosophy and pragmatic adjustment, between inalienable rights and reciprocal relations. But I think nothing would be less prudent than viewing civil liberties from that perspective alone. Amid the masses of data presented in this chapter, one harsh reality stands out: neither the public consensus nor the Supreme Court, which so often articulates that consensus, accepts the notion of individual freedoms as absolutely unabridgeable. And so, in the context of the

"Living Constitution," the dialogue involves a weighing of relative merits, with personal rights and community powers in constant ebb and flow as circumstances shift.

Of course, the issues hardly become less controversial. They may have hounded our polity for decades, as with "bad tendency" versus "clear and present danger" in the free speech domain. Or they may be as contemporary as yesterday's headline: "Woman's Right to Abortion Outweighs Fetus' Right to Life; Burden of Proof on State to Intercede." And they may also be in a state of flux while the Court (and the country?) moves from Warren to Burger, as the conflict over obscenity regulation exemplifies.

And the issues are so disparate! Is the de facto–de jure test the best way to balance the rights of black inner-city Americans against the rights of white suburban Americans? Is a ban on "entanglement" the best way to balance permissible against impermissible state aid to church functions? Is the "specific intent" rule the best way to balance the right of individuals to join groups against the threat of domestic subversion by those groups? What overarching libertarian or societal preconception can crank out the answers in slot-machine fashion? I see none. And what great theory of moral persuasion will help us identify the "goods" and "bads" so we can choose the higher road? I see none.

If the world of civil liberties is governed by the doctrine of reciprocal relations between power centers and human beings, then is there no moral content in that world? Surely, that is a non sequitur. In my opening chapter, I said that the common law contained an ethical quantum; that there was a "higher law" implicit in the Constitution itself; and, finally, that the document has acquired the gloss of a totem through years of good service. History teaches that to wage the struggle for civil liberties as a struggle for some ethereal pursuit of happiness is mostly an exercise in futility. That is why judicial quests for the Holy Grail of substantive due process tend to come a cropper of political reality. But the notion of a Bill of Rights, of an impartial legal order, of a constitutionalism that balances competing social and individual "goods"—these must have moral content or the system cannot abide. I see no indication our "Living Constitution" lacks this moral dimension.

NOTES

1. But the same does not hold for property rights. The charter, as it came out of the Convention, forbade the states to impair contractual obligations (see pp. 15, 42). The contract clause is one civil liberty the Jeffersonians might not have approved because of its property-conscious bias.
2. Also included in the Philadelphia version was the ban against habeas corpus suspension unless the public safety so required (see pp. 173–74).
3. *Calder v. Bull,* 3 Dall. 386 (1798).
4. *Hawker v. New York,* 170 U.S. 189 (1898).
5. *United States v. Lovett,* 328 U.S. 303 (1946). Query: Why didn't the statute violate separation of powers doctrine as laid down in the *Myers* case (see pp. 194–95)? Since when can Congress dismiss executive branch personnel either directly or indirectly?
6. *Ex parte Garland,* 4 Wall. 333 (1867).
7. *Garner v. Los Angeles Bd.,* 341 U.S. 716 (1951).
8. *United States v. Brown,* 381 U.S. 437 (1965).

9. Out of deference to logistical considerations such as contextual clarity, I reserve discussion of a few important items until a later time. For a checklist, see note 94.

10. In spite of the word "Congress," we may assume the First Amendment and all other civil liberties described herein apply equally to states, cities, and every other stratum of government, unless indicated otherwise. This assumption, please recall, also governed my description of such privileges as right to counsel and the protection against self-incrimination, in Chapter 3. I shall explain, in Chapter 8, how "Congress" came to mean "government."

11. Hugo L. Black, "The Bill of Rights," *New York University Law Review* 35 (1960), p. 881.

12. *Robertson v. Baldwin,* 165 U.S. 275 at p. 281 (1897); *Dennis v. United States,* 341 U.S. 494 at pp. 521-25, opinion of Mr. Justice Frankfurter.

13. Sir William Blackstone, *Commentaries on the Laws of England,* William Carey Jones, ed., vol. 4 (San Francisco: Bancroft-Whitney, 1916), p. 151.

14. *Near v. Minnesota,* 283 U.S. 697 at p. 713 (1931).

15. Ibid., p. 716.

16. *Saia v. New York,* 334 U.S. 558 (1948); *Thomas v. Collins,* 323 U.S. 516 (1945).

17. *New York Times Co. v. United States,* 403 U.S. 713 (1971).

18. *Cox v. New Hampshire,* 312 U.S. 569 (1941).

19. *Kingsley Books v. Brown,* 354 U.S. 436 (1957).

20. *Mutual Film Corp. v. Ind. Comm. of Ohio,* 236 U.S. 230 (1915).

21. *Burstyn v. Wilson,* 343 U.S. 495 (1952).

22. Ibid., p. 503.

23. *Times Film Corp. v. Chicago,* 365 U.S. 43 (1961).

24. *Freedman v. Maryland,* 380 U.S. 51 (1965).

25. *Schenck v. United States,* 249 U.S. 47 (1919).

26. Ibid., p. 52.

27. *Gitlow v. New York,* 268 U.S. 652 (1925).

28. Ibid., pp. 669-70.

29. Except, said Frankfurter, "political branch" evaluation of how that balance should be struck must be given preferred treatment. See his opinion in *Dennis,* pp. 217-56, especially note 12.

30. Stone's view is presented in *United States v. Carolene Products Co.,* 304 U.S. 144 (1938).

31. This is the *Dennis* case I have discussed so often already.

32. Mr. Justice Jackson stressed this theme in his *Dennis* concurrence. See 341 U.S. 494 at pp. 561-79 (1951).

33. *Yates v. United States,* 354 U.S. 298 (1957); *Communist Party v. Whitcomb,* 414 U.S. 441 (1974).

34. *Adler v. Bd. of Ed.,* 342 U.S. 485 (1952).

35. *Keyishian v. Bd. of Regents,* 385 U.S. 589 (1967).

36. Quoting *Elfbrandt v. Russell,* 384 U.S. 11 at p. 18 (1966). This language was originally expressed in *Cantwell v. Connecticut,* 310 U.S. 296 at p. 311 (1940).

37. Compare *Brandenburg v. Ohio,* 399 U.S. 444 (1969) with *Law Student Civil Rights Research Council v. Wadmond,* 401 U.S. 154 (1971).

38. *United States v. Robel,* 389 U.S. 258 (1967).

39. Ibid., p. 282.

40. See his dissent in *Dennis,* pp. 581-91.

41. Sidney Hook, *Heresy, Yes—Conspiracy, No!* (New York: J. Day, 1953).

42. *Chaplinski v. New Hampshire,* 315 U.S. 568 (1942).

43. *Cohen v. California,* 403 U.S. 15 (1971).

44. Ibid., p. 25.

45. See the dissents in *Rosenfeld v. New Jersey,* 408 U.S. 901 (1972).

46. *Feiner v. New York,* 340 U.S. 315 (1951). And see also *Terminiello v. Chicago,* 337 U.S. 1 (1949) which, if I am right, would today be

decided *on its merits* in favor of the speech-maker.

47. The "jailhouse case" is *Adderley v. Florida,* 385 U.S. 39 (1966). The other decisions which, taken together, develop the "quasi-speech" principle with respect to marches and assemblies are *Edwards v. South Carolina,* 372 U.S. 229 (1963); *Cox v. Louisiana,* 379 U.S. 536 (1965); *Cox v. Louisiana,* 379 U.S. 559 (1965); *Cameron v. Johnson,* 390 U.S. 611 (1968); *Zwicker v. Boll,* 391 U.S. 353 (1968).

48. *Grayned v. Rockford,* 408 U.S. 104 (1972); *Greer v. Spock,* 96 S. Ct. 1211 (1976).

49. *Lloyd Corp. v. Tanner,* 407 U.S. 551 (1972). And see also *Hudgens v. N.L.R.B.,* 96 S. Ct. 1029 (1976).

50. *United States v. O'Brien,* 391 U.S. 367 at p. 376 (1968).

51. Compare the *O'Brien* decision with *Tinker v. Des Moines School Dist.,* 393 U.S. 503 (1969) and *Spence v. Washington,* 418 U.S. 405 (1974).

52. Alexander Meiklejohn, *Free Speech and Its Relation to Self-Government* (New York: Harper & Brothers, 1948).

53. *Roth v. United States,* 354 U.S. 476 at p. 484 (1957).

54. Ibid., p. 489.

55. C. Peter Magrath, "The Obscenity Cases: Grapes of *Roth,*" in Philip B. Kurland, ed., *The Supreme Court Review* (Chicago: Univ. of Chicago Press, 1966), pp. 7-77.

56. *Memoirs v. Massachusetts,* 383 U.S. 413 (1966); *Redrup v. New York,* 386 U.S. 767 (1967).

57. *Miller v. California,* 413 U.S. 15 (1973); *Paris Adult Theatre v. Slaton,* 413 U.S. 49 (1973).

58. *Jenkins v. Georgia,* 418 U.S. 153 (1974).

59. This assessment may seem contrary to my earlier description of Potter Stewart as a pragmatic, nondoctrinaire jurist. But on the obscenity issue, he had moved into uncharted waters years earlier with his now legendary (comical?) remark: "I have reached the conclusion . . . that . . . criminal laws in this area are limited to hard-core pornography. . . . (I am not sure I will ever be able to define that term), but I know it when I see it, and [the film in dispute] is not that." *Jacobellis v. Ohio,* 378 U.S. 184 at p. 197 (1964).

60. *The Report of the Commission on Obscenity and Pornography* (New York: Bantam Books, 1970), p. 32.

61. *Jenkins v. Georgia* (see note 58).

62. *Young v. Amer. Mini Theatres,* 96 S. Ct. 2440 (1976).

63. *Bridges v. California,* 314 U.S. 252 (1941).

64. Dissenting in *Pennekamp v. Florida,* 328 U.S. 331 (1946).

65. *Sheppard v. Maxwell,* 384 U.S. 333 (1966). The facts presented in my commentary are drawn entirely from the Court's opinion.

66. A.B.A. Project on Minimal Standards for Criminal Justice, *Fair Trial and Free Press* (1966).

67. Ibid., p. 8.

68. Ibid., pp. 5-7.

69. John E. Stanga, Jr., "Judicial Protection of the Criminal Defendant Against Adverse Press Coverage," *William and Mary Law Review* 13 (1971), p. 61.

70. *Nebraska Press Ass'n. v. Stuart,* 96 S. Ct. 2791 (1976).

71. *Estes v. Texas,* 381 U.S. 532 (1965).

72. *Branzburg v. Hayes,* 408 U.S. 665 (1972).

73. Joseph Story, *Commentaries on the Constitution* (Cambridge, Mass.: Brown, Shattuck, 1833), vol. 2, sect. 1870-1879; and Thomas M. Cooley, *Principles of Constitutional Law,* 3rd ed. (Boston: Little, Brown, 1898), pp. 224-25.

74. *Everson v. Bd. of Ed.,* 330 U.S. 1 at pp. 15-16 (1947).

75. *Engel v. Vitale,* 370 U.S. 421 at p. 431 (1962).

76. *Abington School Dist. v. Schempp,* 374 U.S. 203 (1963).

77. These comments are based on William M. Beaney and Edward N. Beiser, "Prayer and Politics: The Impact of *Engel* and *Schempp* on the Political Process," *Journal of Public Law* 13 (1964), pp. 475-503.

78. *Lemon v. Kurtzman,* 403 U.S. 602 at p. 614 (1971).

79. *Tilton v. Richardson,* 403 U.S. 672 (1971).

80. *Roemer v. Bd. of Pub. Works,* 96 S. Ct. 2337 (1976).

81. See, for example, such different critiques as Ivan D. Illich, *Deschooling Society* (New York: Harper & Row, 1971); John C. Holt, *Freedom and Beyond* (New York: E. P. Dutton, 1973); and Jonathan Kozol, *The Night Is Dark and I Am Far From Home* (Boston: Houghton Mifflin, 1976).

82. For a short but helpful discussion of the voucher scheme, see Alice M. Rivlin, *Systematic Thinking for Social Action* (Washington D.C.: Brookings Institution, 1971), pp. 135-40.

83. *Walz v. Tax Commission,* 397 U.S. 664 (1970).

84. *Reynolds v. United States,* 98 U.S. 145 (1879).

85. *Ginsberg v. New York,* 390 U.S. 629 (1968).

86. *Prince v. Massachusetts,* 321 U.S. 158 (1944).

87. *Gillette v. United States,* 401 U.S. 437 (1971).

88. *West Virginia Bd. of Ed. v. Barnette,* 319 U.S. 624 (1943).

89. *Pierce v. Society of Sisters,* 268 U.S. 510 (1925).

90. *Wisconsin v. Yoder,* 406 U.S. 205 (1972).

91. *Murdock v. Pennsylvania,* 319 U.S. 105 (1943).

92. *Braunfeld v. Brown,* 366 U.S. 599 (1961).

93. *Walz* dissent of Mr. Justice Douglas (see note 83).

94. In this section, I do not discuss the politics of the civil rights movement, affirmative action, quota systems, or congressional policy in the civil rights field. These issues are presented in Chapter 11. The contemporary interpretation of equal protection as a weapon for molding economic policy is also reserved for Chapter 11. Finally, commentary on equal protection with respect to voting rights is taken up in Chapter 10.

95. *The Slaughter-House Cases,* 16 Wall. 36 (1873).

96. *Plessy v. Ferguson,* 163 U.S. 537 at p. 551 (1896).

97. *Norris v. Alabama,* 294 U.S. 587 (1935).

98. *Sweatt v. Painter,* 339 U.S. 629 at p. 634 (1950).

99. *Brown v. Bd. of Ed.,* 347 U.S. 483 (1954).

100. Ibid., p. 494.

101. *Bolling v. Sharpe,* 347 U.S. 497 (1954).

102. See the various sources cited with approval in *Brown,* p. 494, note 11, especially the writings of Kenneth B. Clark. This research was criticized not only by the foes of public school desegregation but its friends. Edmond Cahn, for instance, argued that while some behavioral scientists might "prove" blacks suffer incalculable harm at the hands of white racism, other behavioral scientists might some day "prove" that blacks are inherently inferior to whites. His point was that constitutional rules should not be built around the transient, faddish reports of allegedly objective empirical research. Edmond Cahn, "Jurisprudence," *N.Y.U. Law Review* 30 (1955), pp. 150-69. The theories and data currently offered by Stanford's William Shockley have made Cahn a pretty good prophet with respect to how the scientific temperament can be misused.

103. *Alexander v. Holmes,* 396 U.S. 19 (1969).

104. *Swann v. Charlotte-Mecklenburg Bd. of Ed.,* 402 U.S. 1 (1971).

105. *Statistical Abstract of the United States,* p. 124 (1974).

106. *Keyes v. School Dist.,* 413 U.S. 189 (1973).

107. *Milliken v. Bradley,* 418 U.S. 717 (1974).

108. Ibid., p. 756, note 2.

109. *Boyd v. United States,* 116 U.S. 616 (1886).

110. There are laws on the books making illegal the importation of goods with intent to defraud customs inspectors.

111. *Brinegar v. United States,* 338 U.S. 160 (1949); *Draper v. United States,* 358 U.S. 307 (1959).

112. See Lawrence P. Tiffany et al., *Detection of Crime* (Boston: Little, Brown, 1967), pp. 100–05.

113. The cases are *Carroll v. United States,* 267 U.S. 132 (1925) and *Schmerber v. California,* 384 U.S. 757 (1966).

114. *Chimel v. California,* 395 U.S. 752 (1969).

115. *Papachristou v. Jacksonville,* 405 U.S. 156 at p. 169 (1972).

116. *Terry v. Ohio,* 392 U.S. 1 at p. 20 (1968).

117. *Olmstead v. United States,* 277 U.S. 438 at p. 464 (1928); compare *Goldman v. United States,* 316 U.S. 129 (1942).

118. *Olmstead v. United States,* pp. 473–74.

119. *Katz v. United States,* 389 U.S. 347 at pp. 351–52 (1968).

120. See Chapter 5, pp. 200–01.

121. *Weeks v. United States,* 232 U.S. 383 (1914).

122. *Wolf v. Colorado,* 338 U.S. 25 (1949).

123. *Mapp v. Ohio,* 367 U.S. 643 (1961).

124. *United States v. Calandra,* 414 U.S. 338 (1974).

125. *Bivens v. Six Unknown Named Agents,* 403 U.S. 388 at pp. 418–19 (1971), dissenting opinion of Chief Justice Burger.

126. See the findings presented in Note, "Trends in Legal Commentary on the Exclusionary Rule," *Journal of Criminal Law and Criminology* 65 (1974), pp. 373–84.

127. *Louisiana ex rel. Francis v. Resweber,* 329 U.S. 459 at p. 471 (1947).

128. I think this is a fair reading of Frankfurter's opinion in *Rochin v. California,* 342 U.S. 165 (1952). For a criticism of his approach on the ground that it attempts to separate Frankfurter the man from Frankfurter the judge in an artificial, almost nonhuman fashion, one should read C. Herman Pritchett, *Civil Liberties and the Vinson Court* (Chicago: Univ. of Chicago Press, 1954), pp. 245–46.

129. *Furman v. Georgia,* 408 U.S. 238 (1972).

130. Ibid., p. 309.

131. *Gregg v. Georgia,* 96 S. Ct. 2621 (1976).

132. *Woodson v. North Carolina,* 96 S. Ct. 2978 (1976).

133. Ibid., p. 2991.

134. The literature on the capital punishment debate is endless. For a recent work critical of the penalty, I recommend Charles L. Black, Jr., *Capital Punishment: The Inevitability of Caprice and Mistake* (New York: W. W. Norton, 1974).

135. *Fletcher v. Peck,* 6 Cranch 87 at p. 139 (1810).

136. *Meyer v. Nebraska,* 262 U.S. 390 at p. 399 (1923).

137. See p. 46.

138. See Chapters 8 and 11.

139. *Griswold v. Connecticut,* 381 U.S. 479 (1965).

140. Ibid., pp. 485–86.

141. *Roe v. Wade,* 410 U.S. 113 (1973).

142. Official title: The Family Educational Rights and Privacy Act, 1974; official citation: Public Law 93-380 (1974), as amended by Sen. J. Res. 40 (1974).

7

the bureaucracy: organizational maze?

As our narrative moves from the juicy value items on the civil liberties agenda to the drab, colorless, cost-accounting items on the bureaucrat's agenda, the reader may be pardoned if a natural, and negative, reaction has set in. The study of bureaucracy is generally a tedious affair—but for reasons that stem only from the *way* it is studied; the subject matter per se is not, in fact, tedious at all. One of my tasks in this chapter will be to specify those reasons and then avoid the attendant pitfalls.

Definitions and theories: a constitutional politics overview

The first difficulty is the sheer size of the federal administrative apparatus. It looms like some impenetrable jungle, overgrown with white-collar workers and file cabinets. The literature certainly contributes to that image. For example, one well-known study lumps the whole bundle together as "executive agencies," and, without ever defining that term, proceeds to look for their general traits and tendencies.[1] Another writer sets as his goal the analysis of "federal bureaucracy," yet barely mentions the critically important independent regulatory commissions.[2] This omission flows directly from the faulty premise that institutions in the "federal bureaucracy" are essentially alike, and that premise, in turn, stems from a failure to define the term "federal bureaucracy." The fundamental problem is that these studies do not penetrate the jungle.[3] It is necessary not only to define who the bureaucrats are but to compare and contrast their policy-making roles in the constitutional system.

A second difficulty inducing torpor is much more serious. There is a long and distinguished tradition of scholarship in this country that treats bureaucratic management as *apolitical,* that says those who make administrative decisions are *not* making political decisions. Surely, the vast majority of today's specialists no longer believe this, but many well-known figures among them would like to believe that it is a desirable goal. Remember, commentators on the judicial process used to consider judges master technicians, not political animals. But whereas Supreme Court Justices can still capture the public imagination even when viewed as dispassionate experts, the bureaucrat, assessed from that vantage point, comes off as a faceless link in some great chain. After all, judges wear robes, and even the lowliest may be called upon to tackle the "big issues"; administrators lack mystique and are perceived by the average citizen as tackling only "how to do it" questions. I have spent much time humanizing the judiciary, and I hope to do the same with respect to the bureaucracy. But first, a few words on how the administrator came to be considered the epitome of both efficiency and red tape.

Sociologist Max Weber had the greatest impact in this area of analysis. He defined the bureaucrat as an official who holds an impersonal position and makes impersonal decisions. That is, the powers and duties of the post have been laid down by others, as have the rules and regulations to be employed in problem-solving. What distinguishes administrators from other decision-makers is their specialized mode of expertise. Bureaucratic control then, maximizes *rationality* and *competence,* and these values are so significant that any complicated social order (for example, the church, the army, the corporation) would benefit from a heavy dose of managerial governance. To enhance those characteristics, bureaucrats are placed in hierarchical arrangement; each is clearly superior to some and inferior to others. They are also given tenure so that the politician's whims cannot interfere with the free flow of rational and competent choices.[4] Taken at face value, Weber's theories replaced the jungle with the organizational chart.

Many American scholars *have* tended to take these comments at face value. For example, Chester Barnard wrote that the same kinds of people who manage government successfully also manage universities and military establishments successfully. Recipes optimizing decision-making in one could optimize decision-making in another.[5] Indeed, as far back as the turn of the century, social scientists were advocating a simple, neat separation between politics and administration. They saw how, historically, commingling the two had meant wholesale patronage, with widespread mismanagement at best and widespread corruption at worst. In a democracy, they said, the politicians must make the key policy judgments but the application of these judgments must be left to experts chosen via objective standards.[6]

However, Weberian speculation did not fully achieve its American embodiment until after World War II. The thesis that politics could be studied scientifically was sweeping through the academic community. Surely, then, the less volatile field of administration might also be tamed. Leading the way, scholar Herbert Simon said politics was the world of *values;* administration was the world of *facts.* Values are preferences (for example, socialism is better than capitalism, or capitalism is better than socialism); facts are data that can be described as a biologist describes plant life. The idea was to develop sophisticated models and techniques for gathering, systematizing, and processing data.[7] And so the study of administration became the study of computers, budgetary schemes, and cost-benefit analyses. Weber's seeming infatuation with "value-neutral" bureaucracy was no longer the dream of American social scientists in search simply of reform; it had become the dream of social scientists in search of the truth.

As is so often the case, one must go back to the "founding father" and excavate both original meanings and original mistakes in judgment. For one thing, Weber understood that bureaucratic arrangements varied from political system to political system; their form was influenced greatly by a nation-state's constitutional processes. Great Britain, for example, had developed a highly professionalized administrative stratum, which could service either Tory government or Labor government with consummate agility. The "fit" was and is comfortable because British politics maximizes unified authority through the supremacy of Parliament. In American politics, that "fit" would be inherently frictional, because national authority is divided between competing legislative and executive forces. This teaches an important lesson: if we want to aim for a truly scientific bureaucracy, we must consider scrapping separation of powers. For another thing, Weber conceptualized affairs of state as a struggle over means, procedures, and *techniques* alone. He made no attempt to classify governments in terms of their substantive ends.[8] So he is open to misrepresentation by social planners, social scientists, or students of bureaucracy who are concerned only with how to achieve results, not with the results themselves. But procedure—while an important part of our Constitution—is only *one* part of our Constitution. If we forced Jews into concentration camps or confined blacks to the inner cities, what difference would it make if we invoked the proper procedures in so doing! The "higher law" ingredient underlying our commitment to the Constitution could not survive such excesses. And so for us, the study of bureaucracies must include the study of politics, of values, of preferences. And the agencies will then come alive in the same way as an executive, a legislative, or judicial institution.

But how does one delimit the federal bureaucratic machinery? If this machinery is essentially a study in constitutional politics, perhaps I should formulate a test based on *constitutional mention:* where the position lacks specification in the document, the incumbent is a bureaucrat. Under that definition, everyone who works for the federal government would be so classified except the President, the Vice President, members of Congress, and the Supreme Court Justices.[9] But doesn't the Constitution discuss ambassadors, the heads of the various executive departments, and other "Officers of the United States"? Yes, but their powers and responsibilities are never defined, and they are generally subject to the orders of their superiors.[10]

The constitutional-specification criterion, as refined, squares quite well with another possible standard, *degree of visibility.* If opinion polls were conducted, the public doubtless would identify federal bureaucrats as "all those faceless people who work in Washington." The typical respondent would not include members of Congress or Supreme Court Justices; the average citizen, while perhaps not knowing the identity of his or her two senators, at least knows that the *office* exists.[11] The element of invisibility is important. If the federal administrative superstructure is part of the "Living Constitution" (and it is), if the "Living Constitution" includes deep-seated attitudes about the institutions of national authority (and it does), then public appraisal of who the bureaucrats are must be given considerable weight.

Still, the visibility principle is too subjective and too arbitrary. Henry Kissinger was extraordinarily recognizable even before he became Secretary of State, when he served only as a confidential White House functionary. Yet, by the objective criterion of power politics in the American constitutional setting, Kissinger was always responsible for important bureaucratic chores and he was always every inch the President's man. If he had deviated from prescribed paths, his public position could have been cut out from under him forthwith.

My test of constitutional specification and my definition of bureaucracy—all federal employees, except the few above mentioned founts of specific independent power—which flows from that test, are not above criticism. Such definitions and tests depend on one's appraisal of power relationships and political functions. Their sufficiency is an empirical question, really, so it is time to make an investigation.

The White House staff

When describing the presidency in Chapter 5, I deliberately emphasized the personal features of the job. But the contemporary chief executive is surrounded by assistants and advisors, who, as Watergate graphically demonstrated, can wield important political influence. These intimates, known collectively as the White House staff, are part of the federal bureaucracy as I have defined the term. They are also part of the "Living Constitution."

Once upon a time, the chief executive's office did consist of only one person. Not until 1857 did Congress provide money for a White House clerk, while as late as the 1880s Presidents generally wrote out their own correspondence. Five decades ago, Calvin Coolidge had a staff of forty-six, which cost the taxpayers less than $100,000.

The modern notion of a White House staff dates from Franklin Roosevelt, whose personal philosophy of strong executive leadership required an active, aggressive corps of subordinates. One term in office without such aid convinced him of the need for change, so he appointed a blue-ribbon panel to investigate the problem and make recommendations: the President's Committee on *Administrative Management* (my emphasis). True to that appellation, its proposals were couched carefully in "value-neutral" rhetoric; the distinction between "administration" and "politics" was dutifully observed throughout. Not that Roosevelt—the "lion and the fox"—did not know the recommendations were by their very nature political. But both he and committee chairman Louis

Brownlow saw utility in contriving a mantle of legitimacy for the steps they considered necessary and proper.[12] The panel said essentially what F.D.R. wanted it to say:

> The President needs help. His immediate staff assistance is entirely inadequate. He should be given a small number of executive assistants [who] would remain in the background, issue no orders, make no decisions, emit no public statements. . . . They should be possessed of . . . a passion for anonymity.[13]

The staff personnel were to be the President's people. Their salaries would be paid out of the federal treasury, but their titles, duties, and powers were for him to ordain. All this was formalized by executive order, once Congress approved the Brownlow Report through appropriate legislation. Keep in mind: *Under the Constitution, Congress creates all departments, bureaus, and agencies in the executive branch. However, it can also delegate such authority to the President, as was the case here.* From that day on, the legislative branch has kept "hands off" this "inner circle." For instance, the chief executive almost never allows his intimates to testify at congressional hearings, and none has ever been subpoenaed to appear. And he may appoint whomever he wishes; his choices are not subject to senatorial approval.

What did Roosevelt's assistants do? They were intelligence gatherers, checker-uppers, and ad hoc problem-solvers. Most of all, they were *generalists,* who could be moved around like chess pieces to meet any and every contingency. If they were anonymous, F.D.R. felt they could be deployed with maximum effectiveness. But he sensed that if they began to specialize, they might go into business for themselves. When this threat arose, F.D.R. reshuffled their assignments. Nor were personal relationships clouded by the press of numbers. Before the Second World War, he got by with a staff of thirty-seven and the figure rose to only fifty-five when hostilities were in full swing.

Since that time fundamental changes have occurred, and the shifts have mirrored the leadership philosophy of the President. Eisenhower, the former general, was as orderly in his staff arrangements as F.D.R. was disorderly. Ike had a chief of staff—Sherman Adams—who spoke for him and acted as go-between in the ordinary course of events. Under Adams sat a network of support units; and, for the first time, White House personnel served as liaison with congressional leaders, a practice that has continued unabated. Kennedy, on the other hand, scrapped the overt trappings of system as he tried to emulate the F.D.R. model. But J.F.K.'s assistants were tough-minded, upwardly mobile, and visible; they were able to carve out niches for themselves as part of the Kennedy entourage.[14] Even today the names Theodore Sorensen, Arthur Schlesinger, and Lawrence O'Brien ring a bell. Roosevelt never allowed his staff to develop a cult of personality.[15] Finally, Lyndon Johnson employed a style and organizational pattern akin to those of his senatorial days as majority leader. He relied on a closely knit group of "henchmen" who could negotiate for him, keep tabs on the "power mix," and round up votes. In order to play these roles effectively, his staff actually put together the President's legislative package. Task forces were organized everywhere, as Johnson attempted to light a fire under the entrenched bureaucracy. But task forces can themselves become bureaucratic in the "jungle" sense, and there is every evidence that these units did muddy the waters considerably.[16]

In sum, to the generalization that White House staffs closely resemble the organizational philosophy of the chief can be added these observations: as the years went by, the White House staff grew in numbers, grew in power, grew in bureaucratic complexity, grew in formalistic assignment and responsibility, and tended to cut off the President from political give-and-take with other top leaders in government.

Nixon's men: a case study

In the early 1970s, Richard Nixon's staff included about 20 senior officials and 550 permanent aides. His intimate family consisted of, among others, a press secretary (Ron Ziegler), a personal secretary (Rose Mary Woods), a special assistant for consumer affairs (Virginia Knauer), a science advisor (E. E. David), a special consultant (Leonard Garment), two counselors (one of whom was John Dean), and a handful of assistants to the President (four of whom were H. R. Haldeman, John Ehrlichman, Henry Kissinger, and William Timmons). Buried deeper in the woodwork were such people as Charles Colson, Jack Caulfield, Egil Krogh, and E. Howard Hunt. But for Watergate, many of these names would mean nothing to us today. In fact, to a great extent the story of Watergate is the story of the White House staff during those years, and it is a story of political division of labor, political philosophy, and political irresponsibility.

If F.D.R.'s personal corps was a study in the amorphous, Richard Nixon's staff was a study in "organizational chart-itis."[17] Not that his people were bureaucrats in the classic Weberian sense, but there was a rather tight, systematic delegation of authority. Sitting closest to the President was H. R. Haldeman, Nixon's chief of staff. His responsibilities were administrative rather than policy-oriented. Haldeman guarded the President's door, planned his schedule, and was a conduit for information flowing into and out of the chief's office. In all these matters, he took orders directly from the boss. Henry Kissinger and John Ehrlichman were the top staff men with respect to substantive issues. Kissinger was Nixon's assistant for national security affairs, meaning he specialized in matters pertaining to national defense, national security, and foreign affairs. His feats of shuttle diplomacy, opening up avenues of compromise between intransigent parties in both the Middle East and Vietnam, represent dramatic examples of a decision-making role for staff undreamed of during F.D.R.'s day. Ehrlichman was charged with program development for domestic affairs. As Kissinger was liaison between the President and all federal agencies in the security and international fields, so Ehrlichman was liaison between the President and the countless agencies dealing with domestic relations, including the Justice Department. Both worked very hard on budget recommendations and on the ranking of legislative priorities. William Timmons, another presidential assistant, served as link with the Congress; his job was to impress the chief executive's wishes on Capitol Hill.[a] All these men occupied the same general level in the pecking order.

One step below this top echelon was a small group of counselors and special consultants. For our purposes, the key figure is John Dean, the President's legal "eyes and ears." The normal reporting channel was from Dean to Haldeman to Nixon. After the C.R.P. (the Committee to Re-elect the President) was established, Dean began to specialize in the area of election laws and in working up responses to hostile demonstrations and became an important link between the executive branch and the overtly political C.R.P. This position in the power struggle explains why Dean emerged as the pivotal figure in the Watergate episode; he wore the necessary hats to be the closest to the widest range of information.

Watergate, of course, is a tale of charge and countercharge. Many of the charges are still unresolved, and no theory of White House staff responsibility and irresponsibility can be constructed on facts still open to considerable doubt. That Haldeman, Ehrlichman, and Dean were guilty of a cover-up does not appreciably lighten the scholar's burden. The criminal justice system is the best means we have to assess individual culpability, but that system is ill-suited to analysis of the governmental process. It will be necessary, therefore, to construct a record of White House staff involvement based largely on data generally accepted by concerned parties. This record can then be assessed in the light of criteria drawn from constitutional politics, the better to understand what role the "President's men" should play in our "Living Constitution."[b]

We know that Tom Huston of the White House staff was told to develop a plan which would improve the government's capacity to gather intelligence on "domestic radicals."[18] His design called for electronic eavesdropping, burglarizing, and mail openings without judicial approval. The President accepted those recommendations, but they were ultimately "vetoed" by J. Edgar Hoover before they could be set in motion.

We know that Ehrlichman ordered an aide, Jack Caulfield, to tap the phone of newspaper reporter Joseph Kraft.[19] Supposedly, national security reasons were involved, though, again, Hoover refused to participate. Later Ehr-

[a] It is interesting to note that not once during the unraveling of Watergate did Timmons's name seriously enter the picture; he certainly was never accused of wrongdoing.

[b] Some might argue the following is not a fair and complete picture of White House staff activity during the years 1969–73, that I have documented negatives and ignored positives. Others might argue my assertions are only the bare minimum, that reasonable inferences point toward a much more pervasive history of misconduct, especially where conspiracy—usually difficult to substantiate—is involved. But my purpose here is neither to frame an indictment nor to write a detailed history of the White House staff. It is simply to present an unbiased description of an established *pattern* of illegal and unethical behavior so that we may analyze that pattern and discover its implications.

lichman received wiretap information gathered by the F.B.I. in an attempt to ascertain who had leaked to the press information concerning U.S. bombing raids on Cambodia.[20] Ehrlichman stored these materials for safekeeping.

We know that Caulfield was ordered to burglarize the Brookings Institution (a nonprofit, liberal-oriented research center in Washington), to determine if leaked documents were being kept there. We also know Caulfield was told to firebomb Brookings and retrieve the papers in the confusion, if that were necessary. Either Ehrlichman or Charles Colson was responsible for these directives, which, however, were never carried out.

We know that while Caulfield was on Dean's staff he was assigned to develop intelligence reports on Senator Edward Kennedy. In his role as "field researcher" for Caulfield, one Tony Ulasewicz posed as a newspaper reporter and asked deliberately provocative questions at press conferences regarding the Chappaquiddick incident. Caulfield also worked up a plan called "Operation Sandwedge," which he proposed to institute after he left the White House. The strategy involved illegal surveillance of Democrats on behalf of the C.R.P. Attorney General John Mitchell quashed this proposal.

We know that the President established a group called the Plumbers, headed by Egil Krogh, who reported to Nixon through Ehrlichman. The Plumbers were given the job of closing leaks, and to that end somebody dispatched Gordon Liddy and Howard Hunt to burglarize Dr. Lewis Fielding's office. The President was apprised of the break-in, and he either considered it defensible on national security grounds or thought it a mistake unworthy of disciplinary action. Liddy and Hunt remained on the executive branch's payroll.

We know that even after he went to work for the C.R.P., Howard Hunt retained an office in the White House under Charles Colson's wing. Colson was in charge of selling the Nixon program to significant pressure groups. He also dabbled in intelligence-gathering and other clandestine activities. When Hunt was arrested following the Watergate break-in, Dean, at Colson's request, went through the contents of Hunt's safe. He found forged cables designed to implicate President Kennedy in the assassination of South Vietnamese leader Diem. These documents were given to F.B.I. head L. Patrick Gray, with broad hints that Gray destroy them.

We know that John Dean compiled a list of "White House enemies," whose names were to be run through the Internal Revenue Service to see if they could be compromised in any way. Nixon seemed deeply disturbed that the Democrats had been able to get away with such actions, whereas Republicans had been foiled in similar endeavors. The facts are that Presidents Kennedy, Johnson, and Nixon all persuaded the I.R.S. to launch special investigations of tax-exempt foundations and political groups that they saw as political enemies. Moreover, these three Presidents used White House staff members as conduits to mobilize F.B.I. intelligence efforts against political opponents. Such surveillance was clearly unconstitutional because it generally necessitated wiretaps without judicial oversight.

We know that H. R. Haldeman hired Donald Segretti as a "dirty tricks" artist. Segretti was later convicted of writing anonymous letters slandering various Democratic presidential aspirants. We also know Haldeman went to Nixon after the Watergate arrests and told him the F.B.I. had found a check on one of the burglars that could lead back to the C.R.P. He suggested a redirection of the investigation to avoid probable political liabilities, with a cover story that C.I.A. interests were at stake. The President concurred.

We know that Dean supervised payoffs to the Watergate defendants in an attempt to keep them from disclosing who ordered the break-in.

Finally, we know that Colson taped a phone conversation with Hunt without Hunt's knowledge; that Ehrlichman taped a face-to-face conversation with payoff man Herbert Kalmbach without Kalmbach's knowledge; and that Nixon and Haldeman taped *all* conversations in the President's Oval Office without other participants' knowledge.

To understand these machinations from a constitutional politics perspective, we must begin with the President; after all, it was *his* staff. Nixon used Haldeman as a Cerberus guarding the River Styx. The intent was to shield the chief executive from virtually everyone and everything that did not bear on the few overriding questions deemed worthy of attention. Haldeman has said he received advice from Dwight Eisenhower counseling this approach to gatekeeping; clearly, then, it is no accident that both administrations employed the chief of staff principle.[21] In line with his commitment to isolation, Nixon refused to work personally with the C.R.P. He would deal with foreign policy; the C.R.P. would get him reelected.[22]

With the President "above the fray" and his chief of staff an expert in procedural routines alone, the other senior aides had to be specialists, and self-starters at that.[23] And they were. But why did these officials self-start the way they did?

The land was rife with political demonstrations, a small number of which did pose a threat to property and citizen security. There were bombings and leaks of highly sensitive information. Action needed to be taken, most would agree. The President's leadership would surely set a tone, establish a pattern. What did he do? He set up the Plumbers, which he *may* have had the constitutional power to do, and he ordered warrantless wiretaps through his national security officer (Kissinger), which he *may* have had constitutional power to do. He also approved Tom Huston's unconstitutional intelligence-gathering plan, and he refused to discipline the Plumbers after they illegally broke into Dr. Fielding's office. He also talked about "screwing" (John Dean's term) political enemies by subverting I.R.S. files, and he set up a clandestine surveillance system in his own quarters with Haldeman's knowledge. He set the tone, the tone of our old friend, Dr. Mabuse!

Now we can go to the nitty-gritty. What right did Ehrlichman have to order a tap on Joseph Kraft's phone? National security was Kissinger's domain, and supposedly only the F.B.I. performs such tasks. What was Colson doing with forged cables, and how did he get into the leak-plugging business?

His sphere was mobilizing pressure-group support. Certainly if Caulfield thought Colson had the constitutional power to firebomb Brookings and that Ehrlichman could tap Kraft's phone, then there was no reason why he couldn't dream up "Operation Sandwedge." And why weren't the "Kissinger taps" left under F.B.I. auspices? What was domestic affairs boss Ehrlichman doing with them? That turns out to be one question with an answer: Nixon ordered him to take possession![24] Finally, what was master-of-technique Haldeman doing formulating *policy* with respect to "dirty tricks" and full-faith cooperation with the F.B.I.? In short, the White House staff was comprised of specialists, but several of them were generalists in at least one skill: the art of political deceit.

We have come a long way from F.D.R.'s stable of a few checker-uppers, good at moving quickly from problem to problem, while evincing a "passion for anonymity." Executive responsibility is far greater now, and we cannot go back to the 1930s. But if we are going to have White House staff specialization, it must be with direction, under the control of someone who really understands the *substance* of American constitutional politics. Perhaps that role requires a chief of staff, or perhaps it can still be filled by the President himself. In any event, the President's aides should not insulate him from either congressional or administrative leaders. And above all, they must be caught up in the chief executive's conception of wise and proper service, and *that conception must be commensurate with larger constitutional wisdom.* The White House staff is the President's "unofficial family"; if he cannot control it wisely, no amount of bureaucratic legerdemain can.

The "institutionalized presidency"

When Franklin Roosevelt commissioned the Brownlow group to help revamp his own house, he had in mind much more than the expansion of his personal staff. He wanted Congress to create by law a formalized body called the Executive Office of the President, which would consist of agencies dedicated to helping the chief executive formulate policy strategies. I am not talking about the Cabinet and its many departments, already more than a century old. Rather, the Executive Office would develop and coordinate designs of larger scope transcending parochial substantive areas; it would be an "institutionalized presidency." Naturally, the Brownlow Report recommended such action, urging Congress to delegate the chief executive authority to reorganize the executive branch and retain for itself only a veto in case he strayed beyond the bounds of reason. That proposal was accepted, and F.D.R. went to work.

In 1939 the Executive Office employed about eight hundred persons. Some were located on the White House staff, of course. Most of the others sat in the Bureau of the Budget (today known as the Office of Management and Budget). But the Executive Office—approximately three thousand strong in 1976, if we discount the C.I.A.'s far-flung tentacles—did not really take off until after World War II. While F.D.R. wanted expert, institutionalized staff assistance, he did not want the Executive Office to routinize him; his penchant for the ad hoc persisted until his death. Yet, worldwide global conflict had spawned a network of gigantic military bureaucracies, each competing for the chief's ear. And when the hot war of the 1940s lapsed into the cold war of the 1950s, these bureaucracies became more and more entrenched. If they could not tame an F.D.R. dedicated to personalized stewardship, they could and did make certain that Truman would be more responsive. The result was establishment of organizations in the Executive Office, each responsible for formalizing the process by which the President arrived at policy choices in the national security field.[25] The trend toward bureaucratizing this portion of presidential discretion continues unabated, though it generally varies with both the state of world tensions and the state of the arts in war-making.

The most important such agency is the National Security Council (N.S.C.). It was created by statute in 1947 and has four members: the President, the Vice President, the Secretary of State, and the Secretary of Defense. The N.S.C., a sort of "inner Cabinet," is really a legislative attempt to treat the powers of the President as though they could be structured and ordered by committee service. Of course, Congress cannot force the chief executive to use the N.S.C., but the intent is clear enough: the legislature wanted the President to consult with experts in national security matters before he embarked on a significant course of action.

While President Truman was not enthusiastic about the panel, President Eisenhower gave it considerable play, undoubtedly because the machinery jibed with his penchant for organizational formality. A high-level planning board was instituted under the leadership of the President's assistant for national security affairs, and it set the agenda for N.S.C. decision-making. If the council achieved legitimacy under Eisenhower, it became in Kennedy's hands a small, flexible "brainstorming" group, meeting on an informal basis, and the grandiose planning board was replaced by a less imposing unit for research and policy development. In the Nixon–Ford years, the N.S.C. may well have been only a rubber stamp for Henry Kissinger. After all, he sat as *both* its staff overseer and Secretary of State for a considerable period; and he virtually hand-picked his successor to the N.S.C. post. In any case, the N.S.C. is undoubtedly here to stay. While the agency is very much what the President wants it to be, interdepartmental coordination with respect to national security policy has now become bureaucratized.[26]

Some other agencies in the Executive Office of the President may be noted briefly. The Office of Emergency Planning was set up in 1947 on the premise that we had been caught unprepared in 1941 and were not going to let the Russians benefit from a similar lapse. Its stock-in-trade was civil defense and the accumulation of strategic weapons. However, it faded away in the early 1970s, a victim of détente. There was also an Office of Science and Technology created by President Kennedy and charged with sponsoring innovation and research in the national defense area. Its abolition by President Nixon in 1973 was indicative of our occupation with domestic affairs. However, Congress, with Gerald Ford's approval, resurrected the office in 1976, so the executive branch would be better able to formulate long-range scientific and technological policy. Finally, I might note the National Aeronautics and Space Council. Chaired by the Vice President, this group's heyday was the space-race years; however, the panel continues to function, waiting, perhaps, for a political environment more conducive to expenditures in this area.

The Executive Office has also become a preserve for bodies with jurisdiction over domestic problem areas. Again, the trend reflects the ebb and flow of national political concerns. Whereas agencies oriented toward security matters blossomed in the 1950s and 1960s, few agencies handling domestic affairs alone were established during those decades. And while offices of the former description have attenuated during recent times, offices of the latter description have multiplied.

The oldest organization in this category, and one of the most important, is the Council of Economic Advisers. In 1946 Congress passed the Full Employment Act, which committed the federal government to maintain national economic stability. To that end the law sets up a three-member board of professional experts to advise the President on relevant policy. The statute assumes the chief executive must take the lead in preventing excessive deflation, inflation, and unemployment and that to do this he needs scholarly guidance. But, again, the step represents Congress's intention to routinize the President's discretion, to hem in his constitutional authority via bureaucratic consultation. Indeed, institutionalization of the C.E.A. takes this process one step further, because the three specialists require Senate confirmation. The purpose of the law, then, is not merely to provide education for the President; it is to ensure that he will trade ideas with certain kinds of people. This can be interpreted as a backhanded slap at F.D.R.'s practice of consulting with a "kitchen Cabinet"—that is, with his personal coterie of college professors and lawyers. It has been argued that institutionalizing collaboration with experts in some measure beholden to the legislative branch is totally inconsistent with the executive function.[27] However, this objection may be largely theoretical, because Presidents have nominated only experts who look at things as they do (naturally), and the Senate has never rejected such appointees.

When Richard Nixon reached the White House, he recommended sweeping changes in the Executive Office. Congress, he claimed, had made it impossible for Presidents to restructure their own shops in accordance with their own needs. In short, the legislative department had breached the separation of powers. The White House staff, therefore, had become even bigger and more specialized, because if the chief cannot control his "official family," he will create other channels of influence and counsel. The clear split F.D.R. had envisioned between a staff serving *his* needs and an institutionalized network serving the needs of the *presidency* had become blurred, to the detriment of executive branch initiative and independence. The evidence seems to endorse the essence of these charges.[28]

Nixon's antidote, first of all, called for the creation of several new agencies to meet pressing problems. Congress approved much of what he wanted, so there is now a Special Action Office for Drug Abuse and a Federal Energy

Administration.[c] But most significant of all is the Domestic Council, an N.S.C. for internal affairs. With the President himself as chairman, the eighteen-member council conceives and coordinates broad domestic policy recommendations. The guiding hand behind this new exercise in bureaucratization was John Ehrlichman, whose authority vis-à-vis the Domestic Council was roughly comparable to Henry Kissinger's authority vis-à-vis the National Security Council. A preliminary diagnosis concludes that the council has not proven itself in much-needed long-range policy development but has specialized in short-term fire-fighting proposals.[29]

The executive budget: Office of Management and Budget

Congress, we know, has plenary power over the nation's purse strings. But we also know that throughout the past several decades, the chief executive has orchestrated the taxing and spending tune. Naturally, the President does not formulate expenditure priorities by himself. He gets top-grade staff assistance, which over the years has come from the Office of Management and Budget (O.M.B.). In this section I will try to cut through the facts and figures, stressing instead constitutional norms relevant to the budgetary process, with special emphasis on the O.M.B., traditionally the most important agency in the Executive Office of the President.

It was Woodrow Wilson who sold Congress on the idea that the President should propose a comprehensive legislative program. To institutionalize that initiative, Congress passed the Budgeting and Accounting Act of 1921, which imposed a duty on the President to devise an overall strategy each year for funding the countless operations of government. He was to propose expenditures for each unit and revenue collection strategies to finance the necessary outlays. To make the executive budget a workable mechanism, the law also established the Bureau of the Budget, housed in the Treasury Department. The bureau would be the chief's right arm in budget preparation, and its director would be named by the President on his own authority. As a practical matter, the procedure symbolized congressional acquiescence in presidential formulation of substantive policy, because most programs worth debating cost money and are implemented by some agency of the federal bureaucracy.

In getting executive oversight off the ground, President Harding stripped federal bureaus of their long-standing prerogatives to decide how much money they needed and to champion that estimate in the halls of Congress. These agencies would thenceforward submit budgetary proposals to the bureau which would integrate them into some larger package. Naturally, priorities were established and figures rearranged to effectuate the chief executive's grand fiscal design. Presidents Coolidge and Hoover fully utilized this format, a process that has been called *central financial clearance.*

[c] However, when Nixon tried to close down the Office of Economic Opportunity (O.E.O.) without Congress's permission, the federal courts said *he* had breached the separation of powers. When Congress appropriates funds for an agency in the Executive Office, the President must operate that agency at levels mandated by the legislation.

Franklin Roosevelt greatly expanded the scope of this process: *all legislative proposals* advocated by the various administrative units would first be funneled to the budget bureau for appraisal. This innovative mechanism, whereby an executive agency filters through substantive recommendations in the light of the President's preconceived criteria, has been termed *central policy clearance.* The chief executive is here not merely protecting his budget; he is protecting his program. To smooth this shift in responsibility and to dramatize the bureau's elevated status, F.D.R. took the Bureau of the Budget out of Treasury and placed it in the Executive Office, where the director could sit at his elbow.

If anything, central clearance became even more bureaucratized in the 1950s. The Full Employment Act of 1946 enhanced the need for wholistic programming which enhanced the need for a more elaborate funneling system. During these years the Bureau of the Budget's tasks were to collect and collate budget estimates, to see that programs were implemented with an eye toward fiscal responsibility, to analyze and evaluate legislative proposals in the light of the President's program and budget, to conduct administrative studies as a springboard to necessary changes in organizational arrangement and responsibility.[30] As Joseph Kallenbach has said, "The President's recommendation of measures to Congress has become the final, visible part of a vast and complicated bureaucratic operation involving many minds and reacting to a variety of conflicts. . . ."[31]

But how does the Bureau of the Budget (renamed the O.M.B. by President Nixon) actually function? Keep in mind that the budget is an itemized list of proposed expenditures.[32] When we talk about the federal government, which spends over *$300 billion a year*, the calculations determining the distribution of funds are extraordinarily complicated. If one wants to aid cancer research, does one spend more money on hemopoiesis or lymphomatosis? And what is more important, aid to schools or aid to health services? Much is expected of government today, but O.M.B. personnel and Congress alike lack the expertise necessary to answer really technical questions, while the big, broad policy issues merely provoke the standard arguments and counterarguments.

To reach accommodation in these thorny matters, a set of implicit conventions has gained acceptance. First and foremost, the entire process is *incremental* rather than *comprehensive.* This means a yearly budget review never encompasses the whole range of agency activities. The theory is that to keep going over and over the same old policy terrain is too tedious and too divisive. Besides, many programs, such as long-range defense projects and weapons systems, take years to develop; and there are mandatory commitments such as veterans' benefits and interest on the national debt. So the single most important factor in the budget is the preceding year's budget; no more than 30 percent and often less than 5 percent of that total comprises the agenda for debate and negotiation. This small range of increase or decrease in agency funds constitutes increments added to or subtracted from a given base figure.

A second rule of the game is the "fair share." Over a period of time, an agency establishes a claim on some slice of the pie. The expectation is that this commitment will usually require increased funding, if only because of institutionalized inflation; where decreases are mandated, the department will only be cut by a figure commensurate with "fair share" status. Of course emergencies can alter conceptions of "fair share"—crash programs in research, defense, economic pump priming, and the like—but generally the expectation abides. It has been the product of much negotiating and lobbying; it will take much negotiating and lobbying tilted in another direction to change things.

The roles and strategies invoked by relevant power centers approach the level of "constitutional reciprocity." Agency officials are expected to push for increased funding. O.M.B. officials are expected to cut requests because they must protect the President's program and because they expect agencies to pad estimates. The House Appropriations Committee anticipates fat, so it plays the role of budget trimmer; furthermore, it expects the Senate Appropriations Committee will give in to agency begging and replenish monies, so the slashes are even bigger. And the senators do give in as anticipated! One should not be unduly cynical about these machinations, however, because *they only reflect the relative influence of competing networks in the struggle for power.*

The O.M.B. does not simply rubber-stamp the President's preferences. It has a general idea of what he wants, but the choices inevitably involve discretionary authority. Agency officials see themselves as fulfilling the national interest; and Congress as the champion of local interests. The feeling is decidedly mutual, for the legislature sees the O.M.B. as a bunch of bureaucrats who hinder the free play of democratic responsiveness. No wonder three-fourths of O.M.B. recommendations are *reduced* in the wake of legislative oversight.

Besides executive-legislative conflict, the key issue in constitutional politics raised by the budgetary process involves incrementalism. Critics charge that bargaining over small amounts of money parceled out to such faceless entries on the balance sheet as "supplies," "maintenance," and "personnel" is essentially irrelevant. What we need is *program budgeting,* they argue, allocations based on a consensus as to which programs are more deserving. Obviously, this approach would begin with a debate over what policies should be pushed hardest, and then decision-makers would ascertain which programs are best suited to attaining favored goals. Moreover, the computer can be harnessed to calculate statistically the costs and benefits of competing strategies. Incrementalism would be scrapped in favor of comprehensive review, and a continuous dialogue over policies and programs would replace the drab, colorless fencing over amorphous items in which some participants inevitably argue from a position of "vested toeholds" (that is, advantageous "fair shares").

In 1965, President Johnson ordered all departments and agencies to adopt program budgeting. Taking the initiative was the defense establishment, under the leadership of Secretary Robert McNamara, since, at least in theory, one *can* distinguish, and therefore choose, among such programs as strategic retaliatory forces, airlift and sealift forces, and missile defense forces. But program analysis did not work; there just is no scientific way to choose one complete program over another, much less to choose among the policies that underlie them. So we are back where we started from.[d]

Those who defend the incremental approach emphasize the prevailing dispersion-of-power principle, in which public servants represent different constituencies, interests, and value preferences. The "political branches" must, they say, develop tools of negotiation to maximize conflict resolution. And then there is the far-flung bureaucratic maze itself. In the health field, for instance, jurisdiction resides in more than twelve agencies and six departments within the national governmental apparatus, *outside* of those in the Department of Health, Education, and Welfare (H.E.W.). If both the Constitution and the "Living Constitution" of federal bureaucratic organization are predicated on separation of power, only incrementalism in budget-making can accommodate that norm.

These broad assertions are difficult to refute. That a federal budget based on some "science of constitutional policy" is beyond our grasp should be entirely expected.[33] Yet incrementalism seems weighted too heavily in favor of the status quo, of an equilibrium already established no matter what that balance of forces ("fair shares") mandates or portends. Surely there is no substitute for an intellectually honest liberal or conservative leadership, which will check these sensible criteria by challenging bureaucratic priorities when moved to do so. We simply do not have enough political ideologues—let us say, thirty senators who think as Wisconsin's William Proxmire thinks—to make even a dent. And imagine what one such President could do to unleash the O.M.B. in this endeavor!

There is some truth to the claim that "taken as a whole the federal budget is a representation in monetary terms of governmental activity."[34] Certainly central clearance is of fundamental significance. In fact, President Johnson was so concerned about *policy* clearance that he virtually took it away from the Bureau of the Budget and gave it to the White House staff. Needless to say, this centralizing tendency within the executive branch greatly enhanced the political power of the chief's aides, who became top negotiators with agency heads and congressmen.

President Nixon continued this trend when he transferred the major responsibility for policy clearance to the Domestic Council. And his rechristening of the Bureau of the Budget as the Office of Management and Budget signaled a redirection in energies, for the "new" office henceforward would employ its staff of career civil servants to improve management and organizational functions throughout the bureaucracy. The highly political Domestic Council, then, would concentrate on the "what" of legislation; the O.M.B. would concentrate on the "how" of execution. Congressional critics quickly accused the President

[d] However, Jimmy Carter advocated "zero-based budgeting" during his presidential campaign, whereby an agency's *total* financial standing would become subject to reconsideration each year. Would this provide a meaningful check on bureaucratic entrenchment or merely quadruple the red tape? And is there a real difference between zero-based budgeting and program budgeting?

of undercutting agency independence and aggrandizing White House power, and they soon passed a law obliging senatorial confirmation of the O.M.B. director. But they needn't have worried. Nixon's White House staff came unglued in the wake of Watergate, and the Domestic Council's new-found power along with it. The O.M.B. has much the same authority now that the Bureau of the Budget had fifteen years ago.

The Central Intelligence Agency

If the O.M.B. is the President's "right arm" in legislative planning, the Central Intelligence Agency is the President's "right arm" in protecting the national security. But they share only one bureaucratic attribute: both reside in the Executive Office of the President. All of which shows how organizational charts can be hopelessly misleading unless one is sensitive to constitutional politics.

Congress created the Central Intelligence Agency in 1947 to make sure that a Pearl Harbor–type sneak attack would never happen again, and that our "vital interests" around the globe would receive adequate protection against "Communist imperialism." At the least, this mission carries three responsibilities. First, reliable information must be gathered. Most data come from open sources: public documents, scientific journals, interviews. But as we all know, there are also the James Bond escapades, featuring infiltration and secret payoffs to informants. Second, the information must be processed, collated, and properly commingled with data flowing from other bureaus in the so-called intelligence community. For what the average citizen might not know is that there is a National Security Agency, a Defense Intelligence Agency, and a Bureau of Intelligence and Research; moreover, all these "tight little islands" collect information relevant to the national security. But the C.I.A. is the kingpin: it is the largest, employing approximately fifteen thousand people, and it sorts through and places in larger perspective the pieces picked up by the others. Third, and most important, the C.I.A. is charged with advising the National Security Council and its chairman—the President of the United States—as to what is really going on in Kenya, Brazil, Japan, and so on. The power to make *its definition of the factual situation* overseas *the* definition the chief executive hears and on which he will in most cases base his foreign and military initiatives is the C.I.A.'s most important role in the "Living Constitution."[35]

Of special significance in energizing these tasks has been the supersecret "40 Committee," which plans the C.I.A.'s day-to-day operations. This committee is chaired by the President's national security advisor, who serves as vital link between the C.I.A. and N.S.C.

Very early, however, the C.I.A. became something more than an agency for gathering, processing, and interpreting intelligence; it became a paramilitary action machine. President Kennedy's unsuccessful effort to overthrow the Castro government in 1961 has been but one of many coercive intrusions into the political hurly-burly of other countries. During the Truman years, the C.I.A. apparently gave considerable financial aid to pro-American political parties in Italy so as to prevent a Communist electoral victory; during the Nixon years, the C.I.A. apparently helped undermine the Marxist Allende regime in Chile; during the Ford years, the C.I.A. apparently played a key role in Portuguese politics following dictator Salazar's death, attempting to keep Communist factions from obtaining power, and it apparently became embroiled in Angolan politics as well, where the purpose was to sustain the pro-West faction after Portugal had surrendered her hold on that African territory.

One searches Congress's statutory language in vain for some telltale sign authorizing or forbidding such covert operations. The fact is, however, that everyone realized the C.I.A. was doing these things, though the public cannot know the number of such sub rosa enterprises, much less understand all the common denominators allegedly necessitating their use.[36] One denominator, surely, is the argument "If the Communists are going to subvert, we have to countersubvert." The Angolan situation of 1975 is a good example: Castro sent Cuban forces to help the pro-Soviet side, so we thought it appropriate to prop up the other side. But who checks the C.I.A. should it allege the Russians are moving to overthrow the pro-American regime in Tunisia? And who checks the President should he decide to light a fuse under some pro-Communist government in Central America?

A possible answer, of course, is that the Congress—which created the Central Intelligence Agency in the first place—should do the checking. Indeed, House and Senate subcommittees with such jurisdiction have existed from the beginning. Unfortunately, the senior people running these panels treated the C.I.A. the way they tend to treat all bureaucrats—that is, these legislators became co-opted. To be sure, the President is "Mr. Foreign Affairs," so Congress can probably never control the C.I.A. the way it might control the Agriculture Department. But the National Security Act of 1947 specifically bars the agency from performing police, law enforcement, and any other "internal security" functions; its field of endeavor was to be "national security" alone.[37] Moreover, in those days—unlike the Nixon presidential days—most observers realized that threats against "internal security" meant subversion from within, while threats against "national security" meant assault from outside. Nonetheless, Congress couldn't hold the fort; it couldn't even keep the C.I.A. from violating individual rights.

In late 1974, *The New York Times* reported the Central Intelligence Agency had participated in a "massive, illegal domestic intelligence operation" during Nixon's tenure and had committed other unlawful acts dating back to the 1950s.[38] President Ford immediately announced that he would not tolerate such machinations and had in fact terminated them, but that he would appoint a special committee headed up by Vice President Rockefeller to investigate what had actually occurred and make appropriate recommendations.

The Rockefeller panel carefully documented a pattern of illegal and improper C.I.A. behavior. From 1967 through 1974, the agency, under considerable pressure from Presidents Johnson and Nixon, had conducted Operation Chaos, designed to determine if antiwar demonstrations were being orchestrated by foreign governments. This program led the C.I.A. to infiltrate successfully several peace groups and to work up extensive files on more than seven thousand American activists. Furthermore, the agency had been opening mail to and from Communist countries without approval from anyone for twenty years.

Based on recommendations of the Rockefeller commission, Ford issued an executive order formalizing and centralizing the C.I.A. command structure, as well as providing a clearer set of guidelines to limit C.I.A. action. There is now a three-member Oversight Board named by the President, which monitors what the agency is doing; the "40 Committee" (renamed the Operations Advisory Group) has been elevated to quasi-Cabinet status, and the President is to personally review all recommendations for covert activity abroad; the director of the C.I.A. has assumed overall budgetary supervision of every intelligence body functioning in the international arena. The infiltration of domestic groups by the C.I.A. is taboo unless they are composed of suspect foreign elements, and physical surveillance inside U.S. boundaries is also generally off limits.

Congress, however, had no intention of permitting presidentially sponsored review commissions to preempt the field. Flushed with post-Watergate legitimacy, the two legislative chambers organized their own special investigative units. The Senate committee, chaired by Idaho's Frank Church, was by far the more effective. Avoiding both the temptation to release highly classified information and the tinsel world of TV, the panel found that nine hundred major covert operations had been mounted between 1961 and 1975 and confirmed the much-rumored stories of C.I.A. assassination plots, including the agency's incredible conspiracy with Cosa Nostra figures to murder Fidel Castro.

The Church committee recommended making political assassinations a federal crime, publicizing the traditionally confidential aggregate budget of the intelligence community, and giving Congress power to veto paramilitary operations. This last suggestion, of course, is extraordinarily crucial, for it would vest with the two legislative chambers a co-equal voice in authorizing the clandestine use of force to meet the clandestine use of force.[e]

The committee's theory is that because these operations are really small wars, Congress should supervise them just as it supervises de jure conflicts under the War Powers Act. Thus far, however, all the Senate has done is to create a new permanent oversight committee to monitor the C.I.A., while the House has failed to take even this initial step.

The C.I.A.'s track record is living proof that all the problems besetting the typical bureaucratic maze can also beset a body that has no grassroots constituency and cannot be lobbied by the usual pressure groups. First, we have a legislative grant written in almost offhand prose. Second, we have legislative

[e] As a matter of fact, Congress was not even officially informed about these operations until 1974, when the so-called Hughes-Ryan Amendment provided for such disclosures; it was this mechanism that compelled the Ford Administration to report on U.S. intervention in Angola, an effort Congress subsequently stopped cold by cutting off all funds supporting it.

oversight that can at best be termed undersight. Third, we have no evidence that either the C.I.A. or its executive supervisors on the "40 Committee" and the N.S.C. ever formulated rational guidelines regarding the nature and extent of intelligence-gathering, much less of covert operations. The whole business simply achieved its own unstructured, bureaucratic, dangerous momentum.

Fortunately, most of these problems are eminently soluble. The dilemma resisting pat answers is the precise mix that should obtain between executive and legislative policy-making. Meaningful checking and balancing normally presupposes debate and dialogue; but how can the legislative branch debate and second-guess what our intelligence community claims to know about Soviet subversive activities? That Congress has the inherent power to outlaw paramilitary involvements seems a defensible proposition. That Congress can tell the chief executive how to collect intelligence overseas seems an unconstitutional intrusion into his long-standing prerogatives. But if we are going to have covert operations because we think the wolves are congregating at our doorstep, executive branch control over the scope and dynamics of these operations seems mandatory because meaningful dialogue is a practical impossibility. What Congress can do through oversight is make certain the facts presented really do show the wolves are congregating as advertised. In other words, Congress can check and balance the President's conception of national security—to wit, is such-and-such among our vital interests? If the nature of national security cannot be debated, what is left to discuss?

Executive departments: agencies between

Unlike the faceless "institutionalized presidency," Cabinet-level agencies immediately bring to mind a clear picture: the chief executive is sitting at one end of a rectangular table, and seated on either side are his principal advisors, members of the Cabinet and Secretaries of the key departments. Many of those agencies are themselves well known: the Department of State, the Department of the Treasury, the Department of Defense. And they are usually envisioned as very much a part of the President's family, directly subject to his will through the responsible Cabinet officer. But this is where image runs aground, for the impact of separation of powers theory upon Cabinet-level departments is extraordinary. In fact, the heads of these gigantic agencies turn out to be "people in the middle," and the myriad bureaus they administer turn out to be the very marrow of vested bureaucratic power in the federal governmental system. However, for pedagogical reasons, I shall organize the following sections not on the basis of constitutional reality but on the basis of constitutional image—that is, I will describe these departments and their leadership as if power really did flow largely from top to bottom.

The Cabinet

The "President's Cabinet" (Madison's term) first convened under George Washington's direction, and the practice of bringing together leading department heads on a regular, formalized basis has obtained ever since.[39] Since 1921 the Vice President has been considered a Cabinet member. Washington and Jefferson not only polled the Secretaries on many important questions, but they abided by majority sentiment. Even Lincoln asked for votes now and again, but it is legend how he reacted to one: "Seven Ayes, one Nay," he announced; "the Nays have it." So the Cabinet has no more authority than the chief allows.

Another obvious generalization is that the stronger the President, the *less* power his Cabinet possesses as an institution. Andrew Jackson, Woodrow Wilson, and Franklin Roosevelt, for instance, relied far more on intimates ("kitchen Cabinets"). "Weaker" chief executives have tended to repose greater confidence in traditional means of support and advice, and this perspective enhances Cabinet-level consultation. President Eisenhower actually tried to make the body into a general staff, complete with formal agendas and consensus-building. Most contemporary Presidents have had a much more grandiose view of their own power, and so the Eisenhower precedent failed to catch hold. The Cabinet is not a prime decision-making instrument today. And with the emergence of the National Security Council, the Domestic Council, and the proliferation of White House staff personnel, the prognosis is not good.

But why did F.D.R. and J.F.K. find Cabinet meetings boring?[40] Why can't the Cabinet, as the longest-running, highest-level committee in American politics, be a major contributor to executive branch influence? Because the President's house is no more monolithic than the legislative branch; his principal departments are worlds apart in organizational makeup and substantive responsibility (see Table 1).

TABLE 1

DEPARTMENT	SECRETARY (AS OF 1977)	SUBSTANTIVE AREA	BUDGET AUTHORITY[a] (AS OF 1975)	NUMBER OF EMPLOYEES[b] (AS OF 1974)
State	Cyrus Vance	Foreign policy	$ 1.1 billion	33,000
Treasury	Michael Blumenthal	Financial policy	41.3	116,000
Defense	Harold Brown	Military policy	87.5	1,070,000
Justice	Griffin Bell	Legal policy	2.1	50,000
Interior	Cecil Andrus	Natural resources policy	3.8	77,000
Agriculture	Bob Bergland	Foodstuffs policy	15.2	116,000
Commerce	Juanita Kreps	Business policy	1.7	35,000
Labor	Ray Marshall	Working-people's policy	19.7	14,000
Health, Education, Welfare	Joseph Califano, Jr.	Social services policy	116.7	142,000
Housing and Urban Development	Patricia Roberts Harris	Place-of-residence policy	53.9	17,000
Transportation	Brock Adams	Travel policy	19.1	73,000
Energy[c]	James Schlesinger	Energy policy	10.6	20,000

[a] *Source: Budget of the United States Government,* Fiscal Year 1977, p. 313.
[b] *Source:* U.S. Civil Service Commission, "Personnel Management and Effective Government," 1974 Annual Report, p. 55.
[c] Created in 1977 by act of Congress.

What Fenno has called "the psychology of departmentalism" owes at least its overt manifestations to this format. To say that the Secretary of State and the Secretary of H.U.D. must wrestle with totally different problems and satisfy totally different constituencies using totally different weapons is a gross understatement. The typical department head does not have the background, the interest, or the time to get outside his or her bailiwick and grapple with the problems of other departments. Then again, some agencies are too close. The Secretaries of Agriculture and Interior are always at swords' points over where the Forest Service should reside. A Cabinet head who crosses into another pasture even by mistake risks being accused of meddling. The Secretary, then, is a department person, obliged to meet in-house standards. The Attorney General must be a lawyer; the Secretary of Agriculture must have a working relationship with farmers; the Secretary of the Treasury must be a welcome addition to a David Rockefeller board meeting. Teamwork among these disparate souls is hard to come by; when department chiefs need a boost or a commitment they go directly and privately to the boss himself.

What is the Cabinet as an institution good for? We know the chief executive presides at meetings, we know he controls the flow of conversation, and we know he selected these heads, in part to enhance his own political posture vis-à-vis important interests. Moreover, Cabinet membership confers a high status; a department head seems to enjoy special rank, over and above agency directorship. At the level of political tangibles, then, Cabinet meetings serve as a forum for testing out presidential nostrums on assistants representing a wide spectrum of attitudes. But a sagacious chief executive can also use these get-togethers as symbolic exercises in mustering support for his overall national objectives. Then Cabinet sessions become bridge-building devices, affording the President a welcome opportunity to infuse a dose of common enterprise into the departments. And the Secretaries need all the presidential proximity they can accumulate if they are to resist the centrifugal forces within their own shops.[41]

Political executives

The twelve Cabinet members are much more than departmental ambassadors who sit now and again with the chief executive over coffee. Their big responsibility is to oversee the sprawling bureaucratic jungles that are their domains. To do this effectively, they will receive invaluable aid from assistant secretaries and under-secretaries. Together with the leadership in such Executive Office agencies as the O.M.B. and in such independent agencies as the Veterans Administration, these officials are known as *political executives.* The title signifies the role: they are charged with *policy* responsibilities, and they are not covered by civil service rules. What specific functions do they perform? What agency norms influence them in their roles? I turn first to the department heads themselves.[42]

At the outset, one must distinguish among Cabinet members by the agencies they supervise. The Secretaries of State, Treasury, and perhaps Defense, and the Attorney General, are often called upon to perform staff functions for the President that are entirely separate from their bureaucratic ties. President Eisenhower was known to consult closely with John Foster Dulles of State and George Humphrey of Treasury, for instance. President Kennedy obviously valued the advice of his brother Robert, his Attorney General. These departments do not spawn "ministers without portfolio"; it is simply that State, Treasury, and Justice do not cater to specific clientele groups, so their leaders can wear other hats without being compromised.

But the Secretaries of Agriculture, Transportation, Labor, H.U.D., and H.E.W. are agency heads and nothing else. As such, they are truly impaled on the horns of executive-legislative warfare. All executive agencies are either organized by the chief executive with congressional approval or organized by the Congress on its own initiative. Many legislators feel these organizations and their officialdom have no powers save the authority given them by the Congress. And, of course, what legislation imparts legislation can withdraw.

The two qualifications commonly associated with Cabinet rank are administrative experience and policy expertise. Unfortunately, the *political* tests required for "clientele departments" Secretaries are so considerable that the appointees are often not really knowledgeable. The prestigious agencies, conversely, do attract leaders of substance, but sometimes their administrative abilities are suspect. John Foster Dulles was well versed in the intricacies of foreign relations; however, he lived in his own world, and so State Department morale flagged. It has been conjectured that Henry Kissinger suffered from the same limitation.

But don't these Secretaries at least possess sufficient managerial skills to make their departments effective instruments of White House policy? No! They confront the "jungle" syndrome: a bureaucratic expanse of career personnel who arrived years before they came on the scene and who will be there long after their departure. More than half of all senior civil servants (GS-15 and up) have spent their entire professional careers in one agency.[43] A more formidable obstacle is the "holding-company" status of such agencies as Agriculture, H.E.W., Interior, and Commerce. These departments were created decades *after* many of their constituent bureaus had fought the struggle for political survival and captured enough support to endure. Such bureaus sometimes operate under wholly different statutory grants than their newer parent bodies, thus minimizing the Secretary's ability to remove bureau chiefs and transfer functions from one unit to another.

Then again, we cannot even assume the Cabinet participant is always in the President's corner. Perhaps the Secretary must placate congressional appropriations committees or find the department's budget slashed beyond recognition; or perhaps the Secretary must kowtow to pressure exerted by the agency's clientele. The Secretary of Agriculture is often caught between the chief executive and the American Farm Bureau, while the Secretary of Labor (especially in a Republican administration) and the Secretary of Commerce (especially in a Democratic administration) may well side with client over boss.

Nor should we underestimate the roles played by subordinate political executives. Numbering about one thousand, they are, perhaps the "key group in making representative government work within the executive branch."[44] These deputies must see that the President's program receives effective implementation at the agency level. If they fail, the chief executive's initiatives will be mostly rhetoric.[45]

Because they are a faceless lot, generalization about their skills and biases seems especially tempting. One writer has characterized them as part and parcel of the corporate establishment;[46] another has said they are chosen almost entirely for political reasons.[47] A much more accurate estimate might be as follows: while these lower echelon political executives are selected mainly by their Cabinet superiors and almost always belong to the President's political party, they lack exposure to partisan electoral rough and tumble, have become "professional Washingtonians" in their occupational acculturation, and have even come up through agency ranks; hence, while they possess considerable managerial experience and substantive expertise, they also reflect the viewpoints of those interests and clients their departments service.[48]

However, there are again variations among agencies. The departments of State and Defense stress experience in government service and other objective selection standards. At Treasury the search centers on bankers and lawyers—master technicians in the *private* sector. The Justice Department recruits lawyers deeply enmeshed in public affairs; this is a hospitable environment for partisans. Cabinet Secretaries in these shops have the leverage to select aides who satisfy objective criteria and who share their policy commitments, though they cannot ignore the political context of departmental concern. What better way is there to obtain credentials in foreign affairs than employment in the public sector? And as the layperson well knows, there is a strong link between the legal profession and political activism, so why shouldn't this link inevitably color recruitment for the Department of Justice?

But where clientele groups hold the trump cards, the Secretary's leverage depreciates, and subjective recruitment standards imposed from below are controlling: Agriculture turns to the farm community; Interior turns to the western states; Commerce turns to business; Labor turns to George Meany; H.E.W. turns to the new crop of professional academic administrators. And while the "Eastern Establishment" (C. Wright Mills's "upper class, prep school" elite) has a decided edge in competition for State, Defense, and Treasury posts, most other departments are quite responsive to the norm of Jacksonian democracy.

What is important about all this is that political executives come from the same stock and background as their departmental oversight committees in the Congress. Such congruence facilitates bureaucratic-legislative relations but may hinder presidential efforts to "nationalize" the perspectives of these officials.[49]

But do these administrators perform satisfactorily the "general manager" role usually assigned them? Probably not, because they suffer from "vice presidentialism." That is, they are rarely able to establish sufficient rapport with their Cabinet superiors to afford them status as authoritative alter egos. So political executives generally are pushed onto the field of battle, where they serve as connective tissue between Department head and quasi-independent bureau chief.[50]

But to make a political executive "one of the troops" is also to weaken greatly overall political supervision of the many programs entrusted to a plethora of bureaus.

"Government by whirlpools"

In Chapter 4, I described the phenomenon of "internalized delegation of power," whereby Congress passes authority down to committees, which repass much of that authority to subcommittees. But "internalized delegation of power" has an even larger sweep. When private interests come before the Congress in search of aid and comfort, they appear before subcommittees. And when bureaucrats come before the Congress asking for legislation and money, they appear before subcommittees. Moreover, with respect to highly diffuse departments such as Interior, Agriculture, and Commerce, this bureaucrat very often is not the Cabinet member or a political-executive underling but the *bureau*crat in charge of some lower-level administrative pasture. There is a name given to the tripartite coalition of congressional unit, bureau, and pressure group that frequently emerges from such transactions: "government by whirlpools."[51] These alliances comprise a significant set of informal power centers in the "Living Constitution," a network spelled out in no organizational chart.

How, exactly, does this alliance work? The U.S. Army Corps of Engineers is the classic example of a bureau shaking itself free from departmental moorings and carving out a secure niche in the political system complete with congressional and interest-group symbiotic ties.[52] The corps is lodged in the Department of Defense, and one would hardly expect the military brass to put up with an agency evincing wanderlust. And they do not with respect to matters of national security. But corps responsibilities have—for more than one hundred years—included domestic improvements such as flood control, dam construction, and the dredging of rivers and harbors. By tradition, the Defense Department has never attempted to oversee the engineers' activities in this "nonsensitive" area.

All improvements must be authorized by law; indeed, the legislature considers the engineers *directly* under its wing. But does this mean Congress maps out water policy and then commissions the corps to implement that policy? No! These projects are pork barrel political plums coveted by legislators because they mean jobs, money, and votes. And pork barrel projects are generally allocated by log-rolling: "I'll vote for your pet project if you'll vote for mine" (see p. 139).

The ritual works more or less as follows: the Corps of Engineers cannot move until Congress tells it to make a survey; the initial step is taken under the prodding of the two Public Works committees, which have sifted through proposals entered by colleagues and their own membership; the corps holds hearings in the particular area affected, at which concerned parties are invited to testify; individual congressmen, having gotten the ball rolling, keep it rolling by drumming up support; these legislators may well belong to the National Rivers and Harbors Congress, the self-appointed "natural-water pressure group" which conducts *its own* hearings; other members of this lobby include both "local interests" most often pushing for pork barrel (politicians, contractors, the chamber of commerce community), and Corps of Engineers officers themselves, who are ex-officio participants; if the Rivers and Harbors organization issues a favorable report, the corps will be subjected to highly sophisticated steamroller tactics; should the corps concur in these appraisals—*but not before*—Congress will then vote, and its votes are on packages of pork arranged via log-rolling, not on each item judged objectively. Rarely are such catchalls rejected. That is the way decisions are made to modernize the Santa Monica, California, harbor and construct Blakely Mountain Dam and Reservoir on the Ouachita River in Arkansas.

Running throughout the above account, of course, is *externalized* delegation of power, for there are no statutory guidelines to constrain either the corps as it *makes governmental policy* or the myriad private groups seeking to influence the corps. But the deck is stacked in favor of interests that have forged a liaison with the National Rivers and Harbors Congress. A group like the Sierra Club must fight an uphill battle. Recent legislation requiring the Corps of Engineers to file environmental impact statements certifying that projects will not cause ecological disharmony—though a valuable contribution toward reshuffling the deck—obviously does not eradicate "water policy by whirlpool." The only meaningful governmental supervision of water projects is provided by the Public Works committees, whose members tend to come from states and districts constantly in need of corps intervention (for example, the Mississippi Delta area). These panels see the engineers as their private preserve.

Presidents, of course, need no lectures on their virtual impotence with respect to these goings-on. They can always veto a slice of the pork but such recalcitrance carries dire political consequences. Their party faithful rely as much on these trade-offs as the opposition do. And when the old Bureau of the Budget tried to protect the chief executive's program by turning "thumbs down" on excessive recommendations for pork, the corps merely forwarded its favorable impressions to the Public Works committees. Congress, having the last word, ultimately approved the overwhelming majority of these. Indeed, when F.D.R. was given power in 1939 to reorganize the executive branch, the Corps of Engineers was one of the very few agencies he was specifically told not to touch!

As Maass points out, the President should draft legislation for water policy just as he drafts proposals for every other important program area. And Congress should enact *comprehensive guidelines* for improving aquatic resources in particular sections of the country. The blueprints would take into account manifold needs: irrigation, navigation, ecological balance. Naturally, the corps would have to construe those guidelines; like judicial doctrine, they could rarely be made self-explanatory.

But congressmen adore the status quo because individual members get exactly what they want: pork. The corps adores the status quo because it has a home in the legislative branch catering to its every need. Finally, business, labor, and civic groups adore the status quo because their community interests are nurtured to the full. And what I have said about the Corps of Engineers goes for the Bureau of Public Roads, the Public Health Service, the National Park Service, and the Forest Service in their respective spheres. Truly, "government by whirlpools" is another example of a kind of symbiotic Gordian knot, often impervious to Cabinet Secretaries and, in many cases, seemingly impenetrable. Moreover, from what I have said about the budgetary process, it seems clear that the "whirlpool" concept relies not merely on *internalized* and *externalized* delegation of power but on a particular procedure for accommodating interests, *incrementalism.*

In the area of federal budget preparation, comprehensive, all-encompassing strategies seem illusory because the executive and legislative branches are constantly skirmishing over who controls the bureaucracy. But in the area of domestic water policy—where the implicit norms have made the President an onlooker rather than a participant—incrementalism is chosen instead to enhance rampant delegation of power, where Congress deliberately avoids policy-making in the name of group self-government, group accommodation, and constituency contentment. Of course, Congress's loss is the bureaucrat's gain, and the "jungle" becomes just that much more impenetrable.

The Department of Justice: an in-depth analysis

Important though decentralization in the executive departments may be, we must not overemphasize the trees at the expense of the forest. The President makes Cabinet-level appointments in order to infuse the departments with a shot of broad, general policy direction, and his agents do not sleep on the job. They are capable of formulating important decisions for American constitutional government, and, to that end, much of the bureaucratic maze can be harnessed and manipulated.

To illustrate this contention, I will conduct an in-depth tour of one department, noting how it is constructed, characterizing its responsibilities, and describing the impact of leadership-level policy-making upon not only the agency but the interests serviced by that agency. From the standpoint of "Living Constitutionalism," the choice of a suitable laboratory is simple: among executive offices, the Justice Department plays the greatest role in influencing the rules of our political game.

This agency performs two principal functions: (1) enforcing the laws of the nation and (2) representing the federal government in the courts. Here is a simplified organizational chart of the department (see Table 2).

The Attorney General runs the Justice Department and is not only responsible for overall administrative coordination but has the power to formulate (in

TABLE 2

THE ATTORNEY GENERAL THE DEPUTY ATTORNEY GENERAL						
Tax Division	Civil Division	Land and Natural Resources Division	Antitrust Division	Criminal Division	Civil Rights Division	Internal Security Division
	Community Relations Service	F.B.I.	Bureau of Prisons	United States Marshals	United States Attorneys	

consultation with the President, naturally) legal policy for the executive branch. Furthermore, as a matter of tradition, the Attorney General performs significant *political* functions—and I mean "political" in the crude partisan sense. It is no accident that President Kennedy named his brother to the post or that President Nixon named his campaign manager, John Mitchell, to the post. So the Attorney General is supposed to enforce the law with evenhanded, objective detachment and give the chief executive sage political advice. In theory, these roles are worlds apart; in practice, there is no way for any Justice Department head to separate them. Fifty years ago, when the responsibilities of the federal government were the exception rather than the norm, vesting these two functions in one person presented few problems. But now that the "political branches" enter every nook and cranny of constitutional politics, it poses grave questions.

Below the Attorney General is the Deputy Attorney General. This political executive is the chief administrative officer for the department and recommends appointments of all important agency personnel, playing a significant role in screening the credentials of prospective nominees to the *federal judiciary.*[f]

Each division in the department has a particular substantive jurisdiction, and these can be grasped readily by framing hypothetical issues representing the various classes of litigation:

The Tax Division: Should the United States prosecute Richard Nixon on the ground that he improperly deducted the value of his vice presidential papers?

The Civil Division: Should the United States sue C.B.S. newscaster Daniel Schorr, demanding the return of documents he allegedly received without authorization from someone working for the House Intelligence Committee during its C.I.A. investigations?

The Land and Natural Resources Division: Who owns disputed lands in South Dakota, the federal government or certain Indian tribes?

[f] We saw in Chapters 2 and 3 that overt political factors were paramount in filling judgeships.

The Antitrust Division: How much stock in Ford Motor Company can General Motors own before the Sherman Act is violated?

The Criminal Division: Is *Playgirl* an obscene publication, whose shipment in interstate commerce constitutes a violation of federal statute?

The Civil Rights Division: Are the Chicago public schools racially segregated in violation of constitutional standards?

The Internal Security Division: Should the Communist Party be investigated because it may be an arm of the Soviet intelligence network?

And underneath these divisions on the organizational chart sits a tier of what at first may seem lesser agencies and functionaries: (1) the Community Relations Service, which mediates disputes between local communities and minority groups; (2) the F.B.I., which investigates violations of federal statutes and gathers intelligence to protect national security; (3) the Bureau of Prisons, which manages the federal penitentiary system; (4) the U.S. marshals, who enforce the subpoena power of the federal courts and protect federal life and property; (5) U.S. attorneys, who conduct legal business for the federal government throughout the country. And now, suddenly, we see the limitations of organization charts, because the F.B.I. plays a far more important role in determining how Americans exercise constitutional rights than virtually any of the divisions.

It would hardly be possible to review here the manner in which the Justice Department has dealt with all its widespread concerns. Therefore, I will confine my remarks to crucial policy decisions made by recent Attorneys General regarding four volatile issues in constitutional politics: federal criminal justice, black militancy, antiwar protest, and electronic eavesdropping. My focus will center on the Attorney General, the choices open to him, his supervision of departmental inferiors, and the impact of his decisions on American politics.[53]

The first Attorney General to face these problems was Robert Kennedy, who served from 1961 to 1964. During his tenure neither the Vietnam War nor the question of electronic surveillance gained public attention, but Martin Luther King's marches and sit-ins as well as an escalating crime rate posed challenging questions for law enforcement. R.F.K.'s responses to these questions evinced a curious mix of libertarian and authoritarian predisposition. On the one hand, he pushed hard for legislation guaranteeing counsel to an accused at every stage of the federal criminal process and affording pre-trial release to all federal criminal suspects arrested on noncapital charges, whose records indicated they would likely appear at trial. These efforts bore fruit.[g] On the other hand, Kennedy could be a relentless crime fighter, witness his duels with labor

[g] The Criminal Justice Act of 1964 and the Bail Reform Act of 1966 (discussed in Chapter 3) were important attempts to make procedural due process and the right to counsel more meaningful by reducing the correlation between indigence and both pre-trial incarceration and post-trial conviction.

leader James Hoffa, who was subsequently convicted of jury tampering. But precisely in this area the picture becomes murky. There is no question that Kennedy approved on his own authority F.B.I. wiretapping activities carried out against both Martin Luther King and Black Muslim leader Elijah Muhammad. There is also no doubt that the F.B.I. utilized bugging devices *other than wiretaps* to record the conversations of many suspected organized-crime associates. Such techniques were also employed against King. However, it is likely that Kennedy did not know about those goings-on.

Now at that time, electronic surveillance without judicial approval, if employed through physical trespass, comprised unconstitutional "searches and seizures." But F.B.I. use of surveillance devices without trespassing on private property was considered permissible. As long ago as 1934, when Congress appeared to ban wiretapping, other species of electronic spying without physical trespass were almost unknown. There was a joker even in this deck, though. Attorneys General since F.D.R.'s day believed telephone taps were permissible in national security cases if they themselves provided authorization; the F.B.I. had employed these devices during the Second World War. As the years went by, this loophole was extended to more sophisticated mechanisms, which, because their use was not inhibited by federal law, could be employed even without the Attorney General's approval. Thus, in a 1954 memo from Justice Department head Herbert Brownell to J. Edgar Hoover,[54] microphone surveillance, even in the bedroom, was legitimized, if necessary to understand better "the activities of espionage agents, possible saboteurs, and subversive persons."[h]

Let us assume all the Attorneys General from 1940 to 1964 were right when they said they could approve wiretapping for internal security reasons without consulting a judge. Why did Kennedy think either Martin Luther King or Elijah Muhammad posed a threat to our national integrity? How could either be labeled an "espionage agent," a "saboteur," or a "subversive person"? Indeed, what is a subversive person? Is it subversive to establish a black separatist group? Is it subversive to march down the street demanding equal rights? Ridiculous! Of course, it may well be illegal to stage a sit-in on private property, but the criminal laws exist to punish these acts. The point is that such conduct is irrelevant to national security.

What about other forms of eavesdropping perpetrated by the F.B.I.? Remember, there was no congressional statute limiting their use in those days. Much of this surveillance entailed physical trespass, which immediately brings the Fourth Amendment into play. Maybe one can argue that trespass constitutes a "*reasonable* search and seizure" where national security is involved. This is exactly what John Ehrlichman claimed when the Plumbers were accused of

[h] These techniques were not reserved for uncovering or preventing crime; they were also used to gather information—that is, to conduct intelligence work. And note how the term "national security" was here construed to mean "internal security." That is the sort of phrase-shuffling which brought the C.I.A. into domestic politics, but by the Kennedy years the distinction was getting pretty muddy.

breaking into Dr. Lewis Fielding's office. But what does the Cosa Nostra have to do with internal security? And when a nightclub owner "skims" money from the profits of his Las Vegas casino so as to duck the income tax laws, is he a subversive? Clearly, all these eavesdropping endeavors were unconstitutional.

To be sure, Robert Kennedy did not approve F.B.I. bugging and probably did not even know about the Brownell memo. The F.B.I. went its own way in these matters, and the "Living Constitution" with respect to them was what J. Edgar Hoover wanted it to be. Thus, Hoover bugged Dr. King's hotel room, evidently out of an honest belief that the civil rights leader was a "patsy" for the Communists. But the F.B.I. sat under Justice Department jurisdiction; Hoover was Kennedy's organizational inferior. There is no evidence showing Kennedy ever investigated, much less comprehended, what F.B.I. bugging practices were. Such oversight is not in the libertarian spirit, and it is certainly no way to tame a bureaucracy.

From 1966 to 1969, the Justice Department was under the leadership of Ramsey Clark, and his penchant for controversy far outstripped Kennedy's.[55] Clark's visibility stemmed from his low-key, soft-spoken manner combined with an extremely broad view of civil liberties in the context of proliferating crime in the streets, riots in the ghettos, and antiwar demonstrations that sometimes degenerated into lawlessness.

Clark's view of law enforcement was greatly colored by his sensitivity to the social ills he saw about him. He perceived the crime rate as largely a function of poverty, unemployment, inferior education, and poorly trained, underpaid police; he perceived black militancy ranging from civil disobedience to the wanton destruction of property as a function of all these factors plus white racism. Because Clark did not think such conduct could be eradicated by getting tough, he either played down or dismissed out of hand even symbolic gestures designed to placate the fears of a frightened and angered middle class. Moreover, when the antiwar movement achieved maturity, it was necessary, for the sake of consistency, to follow the same general policies in that area as well. And on his flank was Mr. Law and Order himself—the spokesman for the "silent majority"—calling for crackdowns at every turn. I am not referring to Spiro Agnew; I am referring to Clark's *deputy* on the organizational chart, J. Edgar Hoover.

First, the crime issue. When the Supreme Court handed down its decisions in *Escobedo* and *Miranda*,[i] Hoover and other notable law enforcement officials blasted the rulings as counterproductive. Of course, this was pure emotion; who could judge their impact so early in the game? Clark's response, however, was dogma of an opposite order: "Court rules do not cause crime." Then there was the question of electronic eavesdropping. Even after Congress (in 1968) gave the executive branch power to use this weapon *with proper judicial scrutiny*, both President Johnson and his Attorney General said it would not be

[i] These decisions, recall, tighten significantly the power of police to question suspects—see Chapter 3, where they are discussed.

employed except in national security cases. Clark considered such techniques "a waste of time,"[56] even when the Cosa Nostra was implicated.

What about the issue of racial politics? Here Clark was really saddled with Hoover's grandstand efforts to brand protest groups dangerous. The F.B.I. labeled the Progressive Labor Movement in New York "a Marxist-Leninist group following the more violent Chinese Communist line"; declared that the Black Muslims "actively promote racial hatred"; and described R.A.M., with only fifty members, as "dedicated to the overthrow of the capitalist system in the United States." How did the F.B.I. know all this? Through wiretaps approved by Robert Kennedy? Perhaps. Through wiretaps certified by Ramsey Clark? Probably not, for he correctly viewed racial unrest as irrelevant to national security, and he apparently refused to issue such directives. However, there is evidence the bureau bugged and wiretapped on its *own* throughout Clark's tenure, just as it had done during R.F.K.'s years. By what authority did J. Edgar Hoover get into the business of assessing the ideological principles of particular groups? That is the free speech environment, not the environment of law enforcement.

Clark's inability to restrain the F.B.I. ran much deeper, too. When the Attorney General instructed Hoover's office to organize a maximum investigative and intelligence effort aimed at those who might foment disorder, he undoubtedly had in mind such tactics as group infiltration, crowd surveillance, and informer contacts. He thought he could guard against Hoover's excesses by creating an Interdivisional Intelligence and Information Unit, which would collate and analyze all derogatory information collected by the various federal agencies including the F.B.I. But Clark never articulated a set of guidelines that the F.B.I. would have to follow in gathering these data. Left to his own devices, Hoover infiltrated and spied on groups *he* considered dangerous. During this period, the entire New Left movement—from antiwar demonstrators to black student groups—was covered by a gigantic surveillance blanket, which saw countless names, dates, and activities placed on file for future references.[57] Such practices may be constitutional when used for the *specific purpose of preventing or solving crimes,* but when invoked to consummate a dragnet intelligence strategy, they clearly violate First Amendment rights.

The average citizen knew little of this infighting but certainly was aware that the ghettos were burning and, later, that "those kids" were waving the Viet Cong flag, destroying draft cards, and tying up traffic. How did Ramsey Clark respond overtly to the watchful majority, which, for all its reservations, was still favorable to military intervention abroad and was certainly aghast at the rampant lawlessness at home?

Some particulars will illustrate. When itinerant Black Power evangelist H. Rap Brown told an audience in Cambridge, Maryland, to burn the city down, and the city went up in flames shortly thereafter, several congressmen proposed a statute making it illegal to travel in interstate commerce with the intent of inciting riot. If the legislature can ban obscene films from being shipped from state to state, why can't it ban people from traveling from state to state, shouting "Fire!" in a crowded theater wherever they go? Clark's support of this proposal was lukewarm; and even after the Antiriot Act of 1968 became law, he refused to implement it effectively. When violence erupted at the 1968 Democratic National Convention, Clark told the U.S. attorney in charge of the subsequent inquiry to focus on allegations of police brutality; possible violations of the federal antiriot law need not be pursued.

Two other examples deserve mention. After demonstrators impeded the progress of a troop train bound for the West Coast, hearings were held on legislation making obstructions of this kind a federal crime. Clark opposed the suggestion. Then, when protesters burned American flags in public, Congress approved a law banning such desecration. Clark called this enactment unnecessary. Again, the average citizen might have wondered why statutes aimed at safeguarding troop movements in time of war and protecting the nation's most precious symbol should require apologies from the Attorney General. Without doubt, watchful citizens in the "law and order" vanguard were livid.

Clark also failed to distinguish between responsible and irresponsible demonstrators and between broad-minded and narrow-minded law-enforcement officials, when potentially inflammatory confrontations arose. At the time that Ralph Abernathy led the "Poor People's March" to Washington, he was determined to maintain minimal standards of decorum. Clark was able, therefore, to rely on the department's Community Relations Service as a clearinghouse for information on protest activities. Communications channels remained open, and the city avoided serious problems. But when Clark tried to build bridges between Chicago mayor Richard Daley and Yippie leaders Jerry Rubin and Abbie Hoffman in order to avert hostilities at the Democratic National Convention, he was in way over his head. Daley was a J. Edgar Hoover disciple, while the Yippies were bent on higgledy-piggledy. This was no time and place for community relations; it was the time and place for a hard line. The Illinois National Guard might well have been federalized, a tactic President Eisenhower had used during the Little Rock school integration crisis. Instead, a small armed force was deployed *over Clark's objection.* The protesters wound up setting a record for disruption; the police set an even more notable record for brutality.

In the end, majority sentiment did push the Attorney General to move against illegal antiwar activism. Dr. Benjamin Spock and Yale chaplain William Sloane Coffin were indicted, tried and convicted of conspiring to aid and abet draft resisters. Earlier Clark had said prosecutions would be based only on assisting specific individuals, not on statements made to faceless crowds. But when Coffin collected selective service cards, handed them over to a Justice Department official, and then admitted he had deliberately broken the law, Clark had to do something. But by then, the Attorney General's policies had become a lightning rod for partisan political expectations.

Richard Nixon's victory in 1968 brought John Mitchell to the Justice Department, where he stayed until 1972. Nixon pledged that his Attorney General would be far more responsive to law and order pleas than Ramsey Clark had been; and Mitchell would indeed turn out to be everything Clark had not been. If Ramsey Clark failed to grasp the necessary political attributes of his post and if he badly underestimated the citizen's duties even in the face of legitimate grievances, then John Mitchell's commitment to the President's campaign strategy knew few bounds, and his commitment to civil liberties was skin-deep.

With respect to the law and order issue, Mitchell announced he would use the wiretapping and bugging authority given him by Congress to move against organized crime. Mitchell also said his department would abide by the *Miranda* ruling, but that if Federal agents failed to give suspects the proper warnings because of confusion about the doctrine's application, he would then ask the Supreme Court to refine *Miranda* in properly lodged appeals. Such steps hardly constitute threats to the constitutional order.

However, Mitchell put together a far more controversial set of legislative "reforms." One proposal was to institute what was termed "preventive detention" for arrested parties considered so dangerous that judges should not release them pending trial. The Bail Reform Act of 1966 had been based on the assumption that if a suspect would probably face the charges filed against him, he should not be "punished" through detention just because bail payments were beyond his means. But evidence had since shown that a small percentage of defendants (for example, drug addicts needing to feed their habit) were released and forthwith committed serious offenses. However, even if Mitchell's suggestion had contained rational and fair criteria to sort out the dangerous suspects (which it did not),[58] it was subject to this important caveat: if the purpose of bail is solely to guarantee appearance at trial, how can the bail process be manipulated to detain allegedly dangerous defendants?[59]

A second provocative recommendation would have authorized judges to issue "no-knock" search warrants in cases involving easily disposable contraband. Mitchell contended that a whole slew of narcotics operators had escaped prosecution by destroying their wares as soon as they heard the police call out, "Open up in the name of the law." Though perhaps constitutional, nothing is more hair-raising than an F.B.I. agent sticking his head through a window unannounced, so the privacy infringement is fraught with danger. Congress soon approved a preventive detention plan for the District of Columbia and the use of no-knock warrants on a national basis. However, the latter provision was repealed in 1974 after narcotics agents staged several unannounced entries with great vigor—and perhaps excessive roughness—only to find absolutely nothing.

With respect to black militancy, Mitchell adopted J. Edgar Hoover's argument that some protest groups were inherently subversive and should be brought to heel. The Black Panthers were subjected to special attention. Of course, specific Panther members had participated in guerrilla-style shootouts with police. But this did not justify the head of the department's Civil Rights Division stating that the entire organization was "nothing but hoodlums and we've got to get them"; nor did it justify indicting Panther leader Bobby Seale for violating the antiriot statute during the Chicago convention when not even

Mayor Daley's report had implicated him; nor did it justify a rash of "Sherlock Holmes grand jury" inquiries convened at department initiative, which proceeded to subpoena Panther party membership lists and financial records. If the Black Panthers had conspired to incite violence in the ghettos, the laws were on the books to punish such antisocial speech; but no indictments were ever handed up averring the existence of any such conspiracy.

Mitchell was also eclectic in his responses to antiwar activism. First, he boldly asserted the power to conduct electronic eavesdropping of suspected provocateurs in the name of national security without judicial oversight. This resurrection of Robert Kennedy's old thesis led to wholesale surveillance of Vietnam critics until the Supreme Court declared the entire business unconstitutional.[60] Second, Mitchell tried to thwart requests by peace activists for parade permits in the District of Columbia. In November 1969, when a group 65,000 strong asked for permission to march down Pennsylvania Avenue to dramatize their antiwar feelings, Justice Department officials insisted the number be limited to 100 to forestall major disruptions. Eventually, a compromise was effected, and violence was minimal. Third, Mitchell enforced vigorously the antiriot statute passed in 1968. The Chicago Seven prosecution was carried out with his approval, but again, no conspiracy could be proved. And yet the department failed to retry Chaplain Coffin, even though the Court of Appeals, which had reversed his conviction on technical grounds, practically confirmed his guilt. Such inconsistencies make one wonder whether the paramount consideration is law enforcement or public relations.

Over the past fifteen years, the "Living Constitution" has been influenced almost as much by the Justice Department as by the Supreme Court. Certain general themes appear to predominate and deserve special consideration.

The three Cabinet-level officials—Kennedy, Clark, and Mitchell—I have studied here shared at least one common inadequacy: a failure to restrain J. Edgar Hoover and the organization which he headed for almost half a century. During his tenure Hoover freed the F.B.I. from patronage influence, set high standards of professionalism, and did yeoman service in keeping fascist and Communist espionage under control during a hot war and a cold war. And yet even this yeoman service bespeaks an authoritarian personality only somewhat different from those totalitarians he pursued so relentlessly. We now know that from 1948 to 1966, Hoover's people committed more than two hundred "black-bag jobs"—that is, illegal break-ins—against various domestic groups ranging from the Ku Klux Klan to the peaceful, innocuous Socialist Workers Party. We also know that in the years 1956-71, his people conducted Operation Cointellpro, a series of over two thousand counterintelligence maneuvers against these same aggregations, maneuvers that included informing employers about their employees' party affiliations and spreading malicious rumors about their personal lives. And such was the nature of "political branch" oversight that nobody on Capitol Hill or in the White House knew about these unconstitutional doings.[61]

Obviously, Hoover lacked the balanced outlook to remain aloof from ideological jousts with the Warren Court, protest groups, and his superiors in the Justice Department. But he drew considerable sustenance from the law and order faction in Congress, from both white-collar and blue-collar workers, and even from "limousine liberals," who thought him vastly more palatable than Senator Joseph McCarthy during the 1950s. No President dared investigate him, much less fire him. Not even the Nixons and the Mitchells could control him; they merely agreed with him. His hegemony over the F.B.I., and the bureau's impact on the exercise of civil liberties, are a triumph of bureaucratic decentralization at the expense of the hierarchical executive management one associates with a President who is performing faithfully his constitutional duties.

Kennedy, Clark, and Mitchell also failed to delineate guidelines circumscribing the F.B.I.'s intelligence-gathering mission.[j] Actually, the entire federal intelligence community is a study in bureaucratic decentralization: the U.S. government sponsors an incredible *twenty-seven* such agencies. These include the Internal Revenue Service, the Narcotics Bureau, the Secret Service, the Customs Bureau, H.E.W. and the C.I.A. All these executive branch organizations can put citizens' names into dossiers containing both reliable information that serves a legitimate purpose and unreliable information that is derogatory to boot. Talk about the impenetrable "jungle" as a threat to individual rights! Yet is the alternative a central data bank?

When Ramsey Clark created the Interdivisional Intelligence and Information Unit, he was, in effect, putting together a reasonable facsimile of just such a facility. Each week the resident computer would develop a profile for cities around the country based on the marches, rallies, and meetings scheduled; the groups sponsoring them; and any other material informants considered meaningful.[k] Then the computer would predict the likelihood of disorder.

Naturally, John Mitchell did not destroy this apparatus when he came into office. In fact, he helped initiate an Interagency Evaluation Committee, housed outside the Justice Department, which also stored and distributed data on domestic radicals.[62] This intelligence bank was surely of broader proportions than Clark's model, because it serviced *everyone's* needs, not just the Attorney General's parochial concerns.

[j] Perhaps as a reaction against these highly "political" figures and their policies, Gerald Ford's Attorney General, Edward Levi, could only be described as "apolitical." A brilliant legal scholar, he instituted the first set of guidelines ever imposed on the F.B.I.'s domestic security operations. Full-scale investigations can no longer be conducted against peaceful dissidents, but they can be employed against groups that "will" engage in illegal activity with the intent of overthrowing the U.S. government or are "substantially impairing" (for the purpose of influencing federal governmental action) any public function or the channels of interstate commerce. See Nicholas M. Horrock, "Levi Plans Curbs on F.B.I. Inquiries to Avert Abuses," *The New York Times* (March 9, 1976), pp. 1, 43.

[k] As a matter of fact, the Black Panthers were accorded their own printout sheet, while the biographies, travels, and associations of antiwar figures could be pinpointed at a moment's notice.

Should central data files be banned by law? With more than eight hundred personal-information systems extant, we will have duplication and red tape ad nauseam if unification in some form is not achieved; one arm of the executive branch must know what the others are doing, and somebody must know what they are all doing.

Perhaps, then, citizens should be allowed to examine their own files and to challenge erroneous data. In response to a vigorous and searching scrutiny of information systems by Senator Sam Ervin's Subcommittee on Constitutional Rights, Congress passed the Privacy Act of 1974, under which the government must publicize all its personal filing bureaus. Citizens can then ask the Social Security Administration, the Census Bureau, the Product Safety Commission or the like to let them inspect any records of their activities. If the data seem inaccurate, a hearing can be obtained on the issue; then, if satisfaction is still not forthcoming, the courts are open to resolve conflicts. But this enactment does not solve the problems posed here. As common sense should convey, the new statute does not compel the various law-enforcement bureaus to expose their files for perusal. And these agencies can continue to trade information. Even the Census Bureau is still allowed to disseminate its wares.[1]

If we wish to optimize personal privacy, sound law enforcement, administrative rationality, and popular control of the bureaucratic organizational chart, there is no substitute for *oversight.* The President can coerce through his deputies, but Congress must check through its committees. The information ferreted out and exposed to public scrutiny by Senator Frank Church's intelligence panel makes eminently clear what a vigilant legislative branch can do. The writing of meaningful, precise standards keeping the bureaucrats on an even keel is a task that awaits Congress here, as elsewhere.

One final question, perhaps the most salient of all, is: How should federal law-enforcement authorities respond to dissenters who sometimes ignore the distinction between permissible and impermissible expression?

There are those who would lump people together with convenient groups like "activists" or "radicals" and then subject members to prescribed restraints. There are also those who would be more discriminating, drawing distinctions between the Students for a Democratic Society (S.D.S.) and the Black Panthers, say, on the "bad" side and the Poor People's March, for example, on the "good" side. Then there is the policy of not enforcing the letter of the law against "good" people, because this just gets them angry and encourages extreme reactions. A variant of that theme is not to enforce the letter of the law against "bad" people, because this just prods them to be worse.

[1] Most adults have a faint recollection of census-takers knocking at their doors, armed to the teeth with elaborate questionnaires. Obviously, accurate raw figures must be collected for proper reapportionment. But why must census officials know how much money I make, how big my house is, or whether I am a Christian or a Jew? With commendable candor, census-takers admit they share their data with "businessmen, labor groups, research workers," and others,[63] though why Congress thinks this "clearinghouse" function constitutes proper conduct is a fair question.

These orientations are flawed, because our implicit constitutional norms insist (correctly) that the rules be applied evenhandedly to people who violate those rules. Jerry Rubin, Bobby Seale, Martin Luther King, and J. Edgar Hoover all have the same First Amendment *rights and duties;* they can debate—even inveigh—until doomsday, but when they step over that line they are subject to coercion. The fact is that most dissenters who broke the law in the 1960s knew what they were doing, and much of the contempt they harbored for the system was based on their understanding that they would *not* be punished as they deserved.[m] Dr. King expected to be arrested for acts of civil disobedience; in fact, had he been a policeman and had ideological foes tied up the streets, King would have recognized his constitutional duty and arrested those lawbreakers. It is this great lesson in the law's symbolic neutrality that Gerald Ford underestimated when he pardoned Richard Nixon before the judicial process could unwind. An Attorney General who has not learned this lesson forever faces an uphill road.

The civil servant

The stereotypical federal bureaucrat, of course, is not a department head or even a deputy department head, but a white-collar worker of the white race; is an administrator, not a policy-maker; has passed an examination about twenty-five years ago, certifying expertise in some narrow specialty; is a paper-shuffler who possesses the finesse of a Las Vegas card dealer; is inactive politically, but deep down is a liberal Democrat. In this section, I will analyze the issues in constitutional politics surrounding the more than two million civil servants on the federal payroll to see to what extent this stereotype approximates reality.

The growth of a national administrative structure has been marked by a never-ending struggle between those who think the public service should be politically responsive and those who think it should be professionally competent. The former notion held sway from George Washington's time until the 1880s; the latter view has prevailed since, though not without considerable dissent. Washington, an instinctive Hamiltonian, felt that government posts should be filled by the gentry; however, he was not above selecting those who saw statecraft from his vantage point. Jefferson redressed that trend by choosing Republican brethren. But neither he nor his immediate successors recruited extensively from outside patrician circles; moreover, none of them cleared house after their inauguration. So the federal bureaucracy, to the extent we had one, was a rather stable institution within which elites chosen for partisan reasons could hone their political and managerial skills.[65]

Beginning with Andrew Jackson's Administration, *patronage* became the explicit norm by which bureaucrats were recruited. A new President would

[m] Dr. Spock said: "[The federal government's] bankruptcy in the moral sense is proved by its refusal to move against those of us who have placed ourselves between the young people and the draft."[64] What Spock meant was that the Constitution is manipulated at the whim of law enforcement officials; therefore, the "Living Constitution" is not worthy of respect.

dismiss the "ins" and appoint his own associates. The watchword was: "To the victor belong the spoils." But Jackson also attempted to square patronage with constitutional values:

> I cannot but believe that more is lost by the long continuance of men in office than is generally to be gained by their experience. . . . In a country where offices are created solely for the benefit of the people no one man has any more intrinsic right to official station than another.[66]

Jackson's conception of bureaucratic insecurity was entirely consistent with our emerging commitment to democratization. However, he underestimated the complexities inherent in another process that would also soon unfold, *specialization.* As the nation became more urbanized and industrialized, federal jobs could no longer be held by just "anyone." Furthermore, the spoils system bred both high-pressure job-seeking and just plain corruption. When a disgruntled patronage reject took his frustrations out on President Garfield by shooting him down, the tides of change became irresistible.

The "reformers" achieved their goal through the Pendleton Act of 1883. The statute created a competitive civil service, with job applicants to be evaluated largely on the basis of objective criteria measured by test scores. Because employees had proven their expertise, they were protected against dismissal, except in unusual circumstances; moreover, they were not only insulated from political intimidation but actually forbidden to participate in political activities. A bipartisan Civil Service Commission was empowered to enforce this merit system, which today covers the overwhelming proportion of federal workers."[n] National public employment has become a triumph for Weberian organizational chartism, with each bureaucrat slotted into one of eighteen strata (GS-1 through GS-18) depending upon competence and pay.

Buttressed by such "Living Constitutional" norms as the merit system and job security free from political reprisal, the civil service has become a vested interest forever on guard against threats to its status. And there have been several such threats over the years, posed by advocates who view government service from the standpoint of *duties* as well as *rights.* What are these pressures, and how successful have they been?

One important question centers on grounds for dismissal. The civil service rules say workers can be fired if they take bribes, a sanction no one disputes. But can federal employees be dropped for dubious loyalty or for being security risks? That problem recurs in our constitutional politics because whenever international tensions become oppressive, there seem always to be fears that someone is stealing our secrets. Indeed, during the early cold war years, Soviet agents did commit acts of espionage while working for the federal government. So the relevant inquiries are: Who can establish loyalty programs? What guide-

[n] Because many of the top policy positions are now filled by reasonably competent people, the last bastion of full-blooded federal patronage turns out to be the judiciary, replenished almost entirely through "senatorial courtesy."

lines for loyalty are permissible? What procedures leading to dismissal are above challenge?

The first moves in this direction were contained in the Hatch Act of 1939, prompted by the fear of Nazi spying. The statute forbade recruitment of persons advocating the violent overthrow of our government, as well as persons belonging to any organization that so advocates. Harry Truman expanded these requirements when evidence of Soviet subversion came to light. The President's Loyalty Order of 1947 instituted a gamut of procedures that could be invoked to remove personnel accused of "disloyalty." For instance, any employee who had a "sympathetic affiliation" with an organization listed by the Attorney General as "fascist, communist, or subversive" could be sent packing. There were no less than three hundred groups on the list. President Eisenhower refined the Truman approach, substituting the maintenance of security for the requirement of "loyalty," and enumerating as grounds for dismissal other various actions that might compromise the civil servant: drunkenness, drug addiction, and homosexuality, the last included because it allegedly made the employee susceptible to blackmail. Congress also got into the act with legislation authorizing summary suspension of any alleged security risk employed in a "sensitive" position; thus, the ordinary civil service procedures for removal might be skirted. These programs serve today as the cornerstone of the national government's own loyalty and security requirements.

The Supreme Court has never affirmed or denied "political branch" power to set these guidelines. However, if the legislative branch can institute a civil service system, it can surely institute minimal security standards; and if the President must honor the tenure rules established by Congress for the federal bureaucracy, then he must also follow the security regulations Congress ordains. But where the legislature is silent on the subject, the executive can evidently fill the void with his own programs, given his power as chief administrative officer.

Much more controversial, though, is the *substance* of that effort. For instance, where does the Attorney General derive the power to list political groups as subversive? It is true that under the McCarran Act (see p. 119), a special agency wielded just such discretion and with Supreme Court approval. But the agency could not make derogatory findings until a full-dress hearing had been held, with both sides entitled to present evidence. The Truman-Eisenhower program articulated no such procedural standards, nor has the Supreme Court told us whether that omission is a constitutional deficiency.[67] Then there is the question of dismissal without benefit of facing one's accuser. Perhaps an employee does not belong to any group, suspicious or otherwise; yet F.B.I. investigations unearthing defamatory evidence may well lead to dismissal. Again, however, the Court has never held that federal employees facing the loss of position are entitled to know who is submitting allegations of wrongdoing.[68]

But if the Constitution says life, liberty, and property cannot be taken without due process of law, how is the government able to strip an employee of a job without a fair hearing? The conventional retort, implicit in Supreme Court rulings, is that *public service is not a right; it is a privilege.* Since any number of conditions can be attached to the perquisites offered, applicants who do not care for those limitations are free to work elsewhere. In this context, then, the bureaucrat who has been branded a homosexual or has been seen sipping drinks with a Soviet attaché by some anonymous informer retains little more than the option of resigning before being fired.

These loyalty and security checks are only one part of an entire array of political inhibitions placed on civil servants, and that array is also defended under the so-called privilege doctrine. The basic statute on the subject is the Hatch Act, which bans political management and campaigning by these personnel, leaving intact only the right to voice private opinions and cast a private vote. A violation of this code triggers automatic removal. Congress's animus toward partisan activism by government employees stems from the belief that the civil service should be politically neutral, in keeping with its aura of professional dignity and expertise.

The Supreme Court has twice approved this balance.[69] The legislature, it said, could attach these conditions to government service, given the threat posed by even the appearance of an ideologically militant bureaucracy mobilized in support of various candidates and parties. To be sure, Congress could not ordain dismissal for Jews, Republicans, or blacks per se, because that would be discrimination; indeed, the Hatch Act forbids inquiries into an applicant's political views or religious background. But the statutory restrictions were aimed at all forms of political activism, and so they promoted properly the efficiency of the federal service.

In a sense these decisions do not confront directly the core question: Is public employment a right or a privilege? Mr. Justice Holmes spoke to this point in the last century, upholding a Massachusetts law that proscribed political speeches by the police. A citizen, Holmes said, has a *right* to make speeches, but he has no *right* to be a policeman. Ah, if only judges were models of consistency, for years later Holmes faced the same question in different dress and came to virtually the opposite conclusion. Congress had established a post office system, from which it had banned seditious materials. The Justices upheld this proviso, and their judgment clearly rested on the assumption that the use of the mails was a privilege. Holmes dissented. Congress, he thought, could choose to run a postal service or choose not to run a postal service; but if that choice were made in the affirmative, the operation must conform to traditional First Amendment values, *unless there were extenuating circumstances peculiar to the use of the mails as a medium of communication.*[70] In other words, the option of sending written material through the mails was not a privilege to which all manner of conditions could be attached, but it was also not a right lying on precisely the same plane as ordinary speech.

Seen from this standpoint, the question of privilege versus freedom is a false dilemma. There is no either-or choice between alleged duties inherent in government service and alleged rights inherent in free expression. The real question is one of correlative rights and duties, and that mix will vary with the context of power relations. The maturer Holmes seems to have had a better grasp of the nuances of constitutional politics. Today, the mix probably tends toward a more permissive view of bureaucratic political activism. Congress reversed field in 1975, passing a law that allowed civil servants to get involved during their "off hours" in the usual partisan campaigning; but President Ford vetoed the proposal. Traditional constraints on political activism, then, remain facts of federal bureaucratic life.

Over the past several years, the civil service has encountered two other kinds of pressure. They emanate from two different quarters, but they share a common conviction—namely, that the typical Washington bureaucrat is the product of a biased selection process. On the one hand, some blacks argue that employing standardized tests and other "objective" criteria as the sole basis for recruitment guarantees an overrepresentation of white, middle-class values. Nothing is more self-defeating, they charge, than people administering social services who have no feel for the disadvantaged status of clientele groups. There is some truth to these allegations. Certainly there are not enough blacks in the federal service *where they are needed.* Approximately 11 percent of this work force is black, but two-thirds are located in the five lowest GS classes, serving as clerks, secretaries, and the like. And fewer than 10 percent of all the lawyers in the Civil Rights Division are black.[71] Merit-system advocates sometimes ignore the fact that competence is a function not only of education and formal criteria but of human relations. In other words, intangibles such as rapport, sensitivity, and balanced perspective deserve weight on the calculus. If there is no "science" of bureaucracy, there is no "science" of job selection in the bureaucracy. But the argument that fair representation for blacks, Chicanos, and women cannot be achieved unless we scrap the merit system and go back to the patronage system appears to be an exercise in overkill.

The second derogatory allegation leveled against the federal bureaucracy is that the average civil servant, while masquerading as a detached expert, is really a closet liberal. Certainly political conservatives have acted as though this were the case. When Dwight Eisenhower was elected President, he found himself surrounded by bureaucrats recruited into the federal service during the Roosevelt and Truman years. Under the assumption that many had been attracted to Washington because of the prevailing ideological climate, Eisenhower instituted an entirely new stratum of policy-making offices outside civil service control and stocked these with people of his choosing.[72] Richard Nixon was thoroughly convinced that the Kennedy and Johnson Administrations had "packed" the career service with liberal Democrats.[73] Empirical evidence confirms his worst fears. The typical civil servant with a "supergrade" (GS 16-18) rating who worked in the domestic area during the early 1970s was either an independent (36 percent) or a Democrat (46 percent). Moreover, a clear majority advocated *increased* federal funding for social services, a position contrary to the Nixon viewpoint, while those employed in the three agencies most concerned with these programs—H.E.W., H.U.D., O.E.O.—were overwhelmingly

Democratic and overwhelmingly supportive of increased funding.[74] Clearly, Democrats have found public employment in Washington more attractive than have Republicans; and, clearly, Democrats are attracted especially to those bureaus emphasizing liberal values.[o]

A final word about the public service generally: *The merit system—with its emphasis on objective standards—is one of the root causes of decentralization in the federal bureaucracy.* Because we have accepted a civil service based on job security for competent administrators, executive branch policy-makers have an extraordinarily difficult task exerting their will over them. Moreover, these bureaucrats, flushed with political independence and pride in specialized achievement, have developed a professional *esprit de corps* that places their talents and their agency in the category of "my country right or wrong." No examination of the classic argument between the "patronage school" and the "competence school" would be complete without underlining this point. This means, in the broader separation of powers context, that the former recruitment process is consistent with *hierarchical, executive control,* while the latter recruitment process is consistent with *horizontal, legislative control.* And so the never-ending conflict between the "political branches" remains dominant; however, the Congress—or should I say the congressional committees and subcommittees?—appears to be winning at this time.[75]

Miscellaneous governmental agencies

Hard as it may be to believe, there are many federal bureaucratic nests still awaiting discussion. These organizations pose enormous problems for someone trained in the niceties of constitutional theory and structure, for trying to classify them according to any objective scheme is next to impossible. Nonetheless, a decent respect for the premises of organizational chartism requires that a reasonable effort be made in this direction.

First, there is a whole slew of executive agencies that very much resemble Cabinet-level departments but are not called departments and are not headed by Secretaries. Evidently, their responsibilities are just not broad enough to warrant such heady terminology, labels that would allow them to be represented at Cabinet meetings. These units range in size from the Veterans Administration (170,000 employees) to the Smithsonian Institution (2,500 employees); other examples are the Environmental Protection Agency (E.P.A.) and the National Aeronautics and Space Administration (N.A.S.A.).

Second, there are a small number of government corporations that carry out responsibilities normally associated with business enterprise. These agencies are as much *outside* the executive branch as a N.A.S.A. is *within* the executive branch, because their leadership does not report ultimately to the President. Congress has given these bureaus independence to enhance their

[o] That is why Nixon stripped the Office of Economic Opportunity of several "do-good" programs and placed them in more politically responsive departments. The O.E.O.—now known as the Community Services Administration—continues to abide though, responsible mostly for the various community-action programs.

efficiency and administrative objectivity; in other words, there is a presumption that the tasks they perform are not consonant with politics. Examples are the T.V.A. (Tennessee Valley Authority) and the U.S. Postal Service.

Third, there is an equally small cluster of organizations that simply resist any objective categorization. What do the General Services Administration (G.S.A.), the Federal Reserve Board (the "Fed"), and the Civil Service Commission (C.S.C.) have in common? Practically nothing; yet they have as much in common with one another as they do with any other agency. The G.S.A. supervises the use of government property, so its responsibilities are of an "oversight" nature, like those of the O.M.B. However, it does not sit in the Executive Office of the President. The Fed is a bipartisan, independent agency, which is clearly outside the executive branch but is not even funded by congressional appropriations—a distinction sufficient to make it unique. Finally, the C.S.C. is also bipartisan and independent of executive control; however, it is really another "oversight" agency, managing the personnel system of the federal government. All this reflects the great American penchant for pragmatic, makeshift accommodation. A problem arises, therefore an agency is created to handle it. What form the bureaucratization takes is governed by the play of political forces. Grandiose theories of prudent management and constitutional balance are eschewed.

But what general kinds of policy questions are consigned to this potpourri? The following is a partial list of these bureaucratic havens and the subject matter they handle:

Civil Service Commission: federal personnel policy

Energy Research Development Administration: nuclear research policy

Environmental Protection Agency: pollution-control policy

Farm Credit Agency: agrarian mortgage policy

Federal Reserve Board: banking and currency policy

General Services Administration: government property and records policy

National Aeronautics and Space Administration: outer-space policy

National Science Foundation: science research policy

Smithsonian Institution: federal museum policy

Tennessee Valley Authority: Tennessee River hydroelectric and recreational policy

U.S. Postal Service: mail policy

Veterans Administration: veterans' benefits policy

Independent regulatory commissions: a constitutional dilemma

Not even this "soup to nuts" enumeration provides a complete summary of federal bureaucratic miscellany. I have yet to discuss the *independent regulatory agencies.* Here, at least, we have a neat package from the division-of-labor standpoint: these seven units were all set up in much the same way, they all perform the same general tasks in their respective jurisdiction, and their spheres of action all seem to fall within the ambit of modern governmental responsibility. However, it is by no means easy to grasp their place in the constitutional order, which, moreover, has been—and is today—a subject of great controversy.

The seven boards regulate various segments of the American business community. They were established by the Congress, and their members are appointed by the President with the consent of the Senate. However, as we saw when Franklin Roosevelt attempted unsuccessfully to dismiss Mr. Humphrey (see pp. 195-96), a President can remove commissioners only for *cause,* usually misfeasance or malfeasance.[76] Furthermore, membership must be bipartisan (that is, on a seven-person panel, no more than three appointees can represent the same political party). And the prospects are dim that a President will ever be able to control a majority through nomination; the commissioners serve long and staggered terms,[77] in the fashion of U.S. senators. Congress's underlying rationale for creating the independent agencies may be phrased this way: "Because we don't have the time or the expertise to make detailed rules, we are creating these administrative agencies to carry the ball for us; but we will not allow the President to compromise our responsibilities and interests by letting him 'politicize' the bureaus."

Here is a list of the seven, and what they are supposed to do:

Civil Aeronautics Board: air carrier regulatory policy

Federal Communications Commission: quasi-public media regulatory policy

Federal Power Commission: electric and natural gas regulatory policy

Federal Trade Commission: buying and selling regulatory policy

Interstate Commerce Commission: common carrier regulatory policy

National Labor Relations Board: employer-employee regulatory policy

Securities and Exchange Commission: stock exchange regulatory policy

I have said that these various boards are not part of the executive establishment. Neither are they part of the legislative establishment. Of course, Congress can abolish what it creates, but from the standpoint of everyday power relations, the House and Senate do not command these regulatory bodies. Then what branch of government *do* they reside in? The answer seems to be that they constitute a "headless fourth branch"; their so-called independence means that they report neither to President nor Congress, and they certainly do not report or even consult with one another. The ramifications flowing from this no-man's land constitutional status transcend the pat, self-serving congressional justification set out above and deserve further treatment.[78]

The first of these bodies, the Interstate Commerce Commission (I.C.C.), was established in 1887 in response to agrarian protest over escalating railroad rates. But the idea of an *independent* tribunal was certainly not the brainchild of that protest. In fact, the leading farm lobby advocated straightforward legislation rendering various antisocial business practices illegal. Of course, nobody pushed for an executive department to lay down restrictive railroad policy; in that laissez faire era, the idea of a strong President clearing paths in the name of social reform was not even a pipedream. The independent commission idea gained favor, then, because Congress chose to achieve regulation by the least coercive means feasible. Indeed, the I.C.C. was praised initially as a bulwark against "socialist" inroads, because it would strike at monopolistic tendencies undermining our free enterprise traditions. Later, when Woodrow Wilson achieved creation of the Federal Trade Commission (F.T.C.), the justification was that fair and competitive trade would be enhanced, not contracted.

But there are other reasons as well that explain commission acceptability. Railroad regulation, critics alleged, was too complex for elected officials with no expertise; rule making should be placed in the hands of professionals. Furthermore, politics was perceived by reform elements as a "dirty business" in which the vested interests hold sway. The liberal Progressives who pushed for the F.T.C. wanted regulation to be value-neutral, rational, "clean," and an open book. The commissions should be bipartisan, they insisted, for political parties were as grasping as the politicians they served. So the regulatory agencies owe their birth to a strange alliance of forces: implicit faith in the free market, an infatuation with technical skills stemming from our commitment to pragmatism, and the politics of moral uplift championed by Wilson.

However, commission activity did not commence with a full head of steam. Pushed to the wall, Congress was willing to authorize regulation but not to lay down firm, meaningful regulatory standards. As for the protest groups, they were not going to risk half a loaf by insisting on clear and rigorous statutory guidelines. The upshot was an early reliance on the "delegation run riot" principle I inveighed against in Chapter 4 (see pp. 120–22). For example, the F.T.C. was charged with prohibiting commercial practices "in restraint of trade," and if this term was a bit vague, well, the panelists were being paid to work up definitions. The salient point is that Congress refused to spell out its conception of the public interest for the public to see.

Divorced from both legislative and executive aid, comfort, and direction, these agencies turned to decision-making on a case-by-case basis. The nuances varied depending on the bureau, but the model was, and still is, the same. Let me describe some possibilities. The I.C.C. holds elaborate hearings on whether such-and-such freight increase comports with the public interest, given prevailing economic conditions. Perhaps the government thinks a company's request should be denied. Evidence is presented and a judgment rendered that may be appealed to a judicial forum. The F.T.C., for its part, is informed by an aggrieved pharmaceutical firm that the Carter Company has indulged in misleading advertising. The accused party's product, called Carter's Little Liver Pills, is supposed to stimulate the flow of liver bile; but plaintiff says this allegation is a patent falsehood. The F.T.C. holds a hearing, finds Carter's claims to be without scientific foundation, and issues a *cease and desist order.* That is, if the Carter Company does not comply with F.T.C. findings of fact, it will be hauled into court. Carter, not wishing to risk punishment, changes the name of its product to Carter's Pills.[79]

And so, in both theory and practice, the independent regulatory commissions became quasi-legislative, quasi-executive, and quasi-judicial. They make rules (like Congress), enforce rules (like the President), and settle disputes between parties (like the courts). But, as the above scenarios illustrate, the accent from the beginning has been on judicialization, if only because judges, before the New Deal "switch in time," very often threw out regulatory decisions they considered "unreasonable."[p] And an important test of reasonableness was, naturally, whether the agency had invoked judicial standards of inquiry! This crucial development meant that if the federal government went before the I.C.C., say, to protest against an industry practice, it was treated as *just another litigant,* demonstrating facts, pressing legal claims, and citing precedents in an adversarial context.

Everything I have said about the I.C.C. and the F.T.C. is applicable in greater or lesser degree to the other five commissions, which were all set up under New Deal auspices. Franklin Roosevelt did not try to centralize these regulatory functions under his own wing because his reform efforts were also an amalgam of pragmatic responses to pressing problems. Indeed, F.D.R. today is considered by many the President who "saved capitalism." Besides, even then the Congress was suspicious of presidential power, and these agencies were still perceived as a good way to keep the White House from treating the economic system as its private regulatory preserve. But while the New Deal ushered in an expansion of regulatory agency services, there is little doubt that "commissionism" has lost a great deal of its punch. An era of executive activism in fighting economic calamities has institutionalized national fetters on the private-property system. No longer are independent bureaus a necessary compromise for social reformers.

One thing the New Deal certainly did *not* bring about however, was a diminution of judicial formality in the regulatory process. When F.D.R. finally "convinced" the Supreme Court to put aside substantive due process, corporate interests had to try a different approach. They soon hit on *procedural* due

[p] Remember our old friend substantive due process, the great shield of laissez faire (see pp. 46–47)?

process, a concept both liberals and conservatives revere. "The I.C.C. (or the N.L.R.B. or the F.P.C.) has treated us arbitrarily," they would scream. "If the I.C.C. is going to settle disputes, it should be bound by principles of fair play," they insisted. These arguments were received favorably in Congress, which had always seen rule-making by adversary justice as consistent with agency dignity and professionalism. Indeed, one can make a good case for the proposition that if the I.C.C. is going to formulate decisions through judicialization, then all the basic elements found in courtroom procedure should be provided. So the legislature passed the Administrative Procedure Act in 1946, including the following "reforms": a division between prosecutorial and judicial arms within each agency designed to reduce conflicts of interest; placement of the burden of proof on the party proposing changes in regulatory policy (that is, the status quo would carry a favorable presumption); and the right to be heard in a fair, impartial hearing according to the basics of due process. More generally, the statute legitimizes and institutionalizes a preoccupation with judicial ways and means. The typical commission hearing is not the twin of the typical courtroom hearing, but the two share a common philosophical heritage of governance by experts rather than by political representatives.

What consequences does all this have for larger questions of constitutional politics? I will first state the situation and then provide the necessary evidence: *independent regulatory commissions are dominated largely by the most powerful groups they are charged with regulating; therefore, they emerge as the most extreme example of "government by whirlpools" in the entire federal apparatus.*

Keep in mind that these agencies receive no political support from either White House or Congress. Lacking executive branch standing and operating under vague statutory authority, they are supposed to survive in a jungle infested with insatiable interests bent on maximizing profits. Technical experts may excel in routinizing how-to-do-it questions, but without leverage in the power struggle they are ill-suited for developing broad policy alternatives. Furthermore, the case-by-case approach hedged about with judicial formalisms makes it virtually impossible to frame such policies no matter what the skills of the commissioners. As one critic has said, "taking things out of politics" means "taking things out of popular control" and putting them into the hands of private-power centers.[80] The President may appoint agency personnel, but, because he cannot control what they do after confirmation, he tends to select individuals whose orientation is compatible with influential concerned interests. The Congress may appropriate monies to keep the regulatory units afloat, but decentralization in the legislative branch ensures that it is the relevant subcommittees and their chairmen who will exert whatever pressure can be mustered. And economic interests certainly know how to work hand in glove with these subcommittees. It does not take long for independent regulatory agencies to see their jobs as *managerial* rather than *regulatory.* The betterment of commission destinies becomes wrapped up in the betterment of corporate destinies; after all, where would the I.C.C. be without the railroads? At best, the commissions become adept at responding to the needs of competing group demands. At worst, they surrender to the important groups under their jurisdiction.[81] In truth, these agencies are easier pickings than insular bureaucracies located in the executive branch because their alleged strength, independence, is actually their greatest weakness.

What is to be done? The basic problem is constitutional in dimension. Independent regulatory agencies were once described as "a sort of mixture of several things."[82] Our fundamental law looks to a checks-and-balances system, but that mechanism presupposes a separation of powers model. The "Living Constitution" of American business regulation is not built around separation of powers; it is built around "triple-quasi" institutions which check and balance *themselves* into a state of policy paralysis. What is needed is *regulation by public authority,* not *management* under the same old ideological patchwork of decentralization, "delegation run riot," and technical expertise masking private-interest control. The "political branches" have the constitutional power to abolish "commissionism" in the light of a post-New Deal conception of central governmental responsibility for the larger economic order. Comprehensive supervision of business practices could be achieved via precise, exacting statutory criteria, vigorous enforcement of those criteria by executive branch agencies, and equally vigorous congressional oversight of executive action. That strategy would seem to be much more faithful to underlying constitutional themes.

The Federal Communications Commission: a case study

Like the Cabinet-level departments, independent regulatory agencies suffer from facelessness until we penetrate their inner workings and analyze the substantive issues before them. The unit whose jurisdiction is most intimately related to the world of constitutional rules is the Federal Communications Commission. In this section I will describe the nature of F.C.C. policy-making over time, placing emphasis on television and radio programming; for it is in the area of media *content* that modern-day efforts are pregnant with controversy.

Broadcasting is the only channel of expression subject to intensive supervision by the federal government. Of course, all the media—newspapers, films, magazines—must abide by the usual criminal laws, but whereas many people can produce a movie, only a finite number of slots exist on the electromagnetic spectrum. Thus broadcasters themselves recognize that the federal government must regulate the airways if only to prevent stations from running into one another.

The F.C.C. as we know it today was born in 1934.[83] It has seven members, one of whom serves as chairman under presidential appointment, and there is the usual bipartisan quota system. From the start, the agency has been independent in the "headless fourth branch" sense, since Congress was of the opinion that the power to regulate broadcast communication "should be as free from political interference or arbitrary control as possible."[84] The commission possesses authority to determine whether "the public interest . . . would be served by the granting [of a station's license]." No doubt the legislature envisioned the F.C.C. using its grant to halt the audio chaos then plaguing the radio industry, an objective the agency has fulfilled. Nor was the legislature blind to the possibility that First Amendment preachments might suffer, for it specifically forbade the bureau to exercise "the power of censorship" or to "interfere with the right of free speech." The problem is, however, that someone's right of expression is automatically inhibited when channels are allotted to one applicant over another and when channel-owners show some programs but not others. Already, then, we can see the germ of "commissionism" at hand: the board was given almost a blank check in ascertaining the "public interest"; the board's subsistence depended entirely on congressional goodwill and money; the President was mostly locked out of things.

How has F.C.C. policy-making with respect to technological innovation affected free speech values? When a group of industry mavericks tried to win commission approval for low-frequency FM radio in the 1940s, they ran into a stone wall of opposition from established AM interests, who saw the new facility as a direct threat to their own creation, television. Such fears were translated into F.C.C. policy when FM broadcasting was consigned to an innocuous higher-frequency band, thus rendering obsolete all existing FM equipment. This action, plus the growth of television, postponed for more than fifteen years the development of a competitive radio system. So, the F.C.C. had come down on the side of one form of expression, television—which would be controlled by the dominant forces in radio—over another form of expression, FM—which was sure to experiment with new kinds of programming.

The same sort of confrontation emerged in the early 1960s when a movement got started to create two separate television marketplaces: one portion of the country would have only VHF channels; the other portion would have only UHF channels. Again, the VHF outlets were "establishment" concerns, and they unalterably opposed giving the interloper UHFers their own cut of the pie. Hovering in the background, making the major networks especially nervous, was F.C.C. chairman Newton Minow. A Kennedy appointee committed to New Frontier politics, Minow had delivered the most famous speech on record by a commission spokesman, denouncing "establishment" programming as a "vast wasteland" of game shows, violence, formula comedies, sadism, commercials, and boredom.[85] Prominent television interests quickly went to work in Congress, drumming up opposition to all-UHF systems anywhere. The commission was obliged to compromise: television sets were required to provide complete area UHF and VHF coverage, thus strengthening the concept of program diversity, but the all-UHF concept was buried quietly.

A second set of difficult issues revolves around the esoteric question: Who owns the airwaves? The generally held constitutional doctrine is that the "public"—at least in the form of congressional supervision—has controlling stake in their use. Certainly the frequencies are not owned by the broadcasters; in fact, the 1934 law says a license to operate shall be cancelled if F.C.C. rules are disobeyed. What rules has the Commission passed in the "public interest" that have led to license revocation?

Until 1966, station operators could be challenged by competing economic interests only when their options came up for renewal. And never was a license taken away and given to a challenger if "average" performance standards had been met. In other words, the only way to unseat some wealthy custodian of the airwaves was for another prospective wealthy custodian to show that the incumbent had flopped in some clear-cut, inexcusable way.

This interlocking bond between the F.C.C. and media proprietors began to unravel when the United Church of Christ (U.C.C.) challenged the license-renewal petition submitted by WLBT-TV in Jackson, Mississippi. By far the most important F.C.C. "rule in the public interest" is the *fairness doctrine.* It says that (1) stations and channels shall devote a reasonable amount of coverage to controversial community issues and (2) for the purpose of ensuring fairness, operators must provide differing viewpoints a reasonable opportunity to be heard. The U.C.C. claimed WLBT discriminated blatantly against blacks, who comprised 45 percent of Jackson's population. When the F.C.C. refused to allow the church group to present a challenge because it lacked sufficient economic stake in the outcome, the U.C.C. went to court.

Prospects before the judiciary hardly looked promising, because a legislative criterion such as "public interest" is rarely declared unduly vague in our time. Only if *procedural due process* is violated or if the results are totally unreasonable will judges reverse regulatory commission orders. In this case, though, the court said that important civic, religious, professional, and vocational groups have a significant interest in programming and could contest license renewals. In other words, it is the listening audience that really counts, not who will operate the facility and reap the profits. The court ordered the F.C.C. to consider new applicants.[86]

In 1969, the commission startled the broadcasting world by refusing to renew the license of Boston television station WHDH, even though its operator (one of the city's three leading newspapers) had patently satisfied the "average" performance guideline. Instead, proprietorship was given to an applicant who said he would make channel operation a full-time job and would provide more competitive media coverage for the vicinity. In response to protests from the National Association of Broadcasters, the largest industry lobby, Senator John Pastore, chairman of the Communications Subcommittee, introduced a measure to prevent the F.C.C. from considering applicants until it had *first* decided that a license should be revoked. This bill, in turn, raised the ire of several minority-interest pressure groups, the most notable being B.E.S.T. (Black Efforts for Soul in Television). How, these groups asked, can black, Chicano, and other ethnic challengers ever obtain their "fair share" of media control if competition for licenses were nonexistent except in the extraordinary event of obvious incumbent failure? In rebuttal, the N.A.B. argued that a sword of Damocles should not be held over its members' heads until some showing of irresponsibility had been made out.

Into this thicket stepped Dean Burch, the new chairman of the F.C.C., selected by Richard Nixon. An industry man who was fearful that B.E.S.T. might overwhelm Senator Pastore's efforts, he successfully urged the commission to make concessions: if an operator could show that his programming *substantially* accommodated community needs (in place of the old "average" test), and if there were no other serious deficiencies, then his franchise would be continued. Should he fail on either count, however, an open competition would be held.

Infuriated, B.E.S.T. and its allies went to court, where they received complete vindication. The judges thought the new policy unreasonable, because it was weighted very heavily in favor of the operator. They also believed the commission had violated the Administrative Procedure Act by approving its two-step formula without providing notice and hearing to opponents. Only fully competitive confrontation from beginning to end (with heavy burden of proof resting on the challenger) would satisfy the rightful claims of all concerned.[87]

In spite of such ground-breaking developments, the F.C.C. has not made a steady diet of license revocation. The WLBT (Jackson, Mississippi) case, whereby a TV channel proprietor can be ousted for fairness-doctrine violations, has been emulated on only one other occasion. And the WHDH (Boston) case has spawned no offspring. However, attacks continue on all fronts. In a taped White House conversation, President Nixon discussed using F.C.C. authority to oust the *Washington Post* (which had led the way in Watergate investigative reporting) from its custody over two Florida stations.[88] Eventually, challenges were launched by friendly Republican allies, but they failed. On the other side, the Puerto Rican Media Action and Education Council challenged WNET's license in New York, alleging that the public TV channel was discriminatory because no programs were offered catering to Latino and Hispanic needs. The F.C.C. rejected the claim six to one, the dissenter being the commission's only black member, Benjamin Hooks, who used the occasion to label public television "the Caucasian intellectual's home entertainment game."[89]

The threats to bring challenges before the F.C.C. has, however, allowed aggrieved groups to exert leverage on programming. Citizens' organizations have used the technique in such cities as Rochester, Atlanta, and Fort Worth, with the United Church of Christ, B.E.S.T., and Action for Children's Television (A.C.T.) leading the way. As is so often the case, a little coaxing ("We think there's too much violence in your children's programming, but if you meet us half-way, we'll shut up") is more productive than direct confrontation in an F.C.C. "courtroom."

It is the second prong of the fairness doctrine, however—guaranteeing a "balanced" presentation of views—that has really stirred up the proverbial hornet's nest. Under this theory, individuals who think they have been defamed have a "right of reply." In the famous *Red Lion* decision,[90] the Supreme Court unanimously upheld the doctrine with respect to an inflammatory radio speech by the Reverend Billy James Hargis, who had called a liberal writer, Fred Cook, "a professional mudslinger."[91] Cook had asked station WGCB (Red Lion, Pennsylvania) for an opportunity to rebut Hargis's allegation, but the operator (a strong Hargis supporter) had refused. The proprietor wanted to know how the government could compel him to give *free* time to any person who convinced the F.C.C. or a sympathetic judge that he or she had been slandered. Using a sort of "reasonable man" premise, the Justices said that Congress (through its agent, the F.C.C.) might justifiably require media license-holders to share their facilities with persons who otherwise might be shut out of the airwaves marketplace. In short, the right of the viewers and listeners was controlling, not the right of the broadcaster.

Needless to say, citizens' groups rejoiced at the outcome of *Red Lion,* while the station custodians were more than resentful. Their worst fears seemed vindicated when the F.C.C., with strong backing from its new-found allies on the bench, began to apply the fairness doctrine to commercials. Commission members named by President Kennedy had tried to get the group as a whole to endorse limitations on the number and frequency of advertisements; however, the alliance between broadcasters and key congressional committees had made a shambles of the gambit. But the tables were turning, for why couldn't the fairness doctrine be applied to any biased point of view expressed without counterargument. In one case, the environmental group Friends of the Earth obtained approval to rebut automobile commercials. The courts said that such advertisements constituted one side of a public issue—air pollution—so fairness mandated a reply by environmentalists.[92]

Yet sentiment seems now to be swinging against broad conceptions of the doctrine. The basic fear nowadays is that for every opinion expressed on radio or television, ten voices representing other sides will demand to be heard. In this era of network investigative reporting and white papers (reports on some subject, generally serious), an expansive definition of fairness could indeed suffocate media independence.

Again, the Supreme Court has led the way, finding that political advocates have no right under the First Amendment to *purchase* airwave time, even if these media are "owned" by the public.[93] Then the F.C.C. (dominated by Nixon appointees) ruled that the fairness doctrine was applicable only to *controversial* commercials, not to ordinary advertisements promoting particular products. And recently the news has broken that a whole series of fairness challenges against right-wing radio commentaries in the 1960s were actually contrived and financed by an arm of the Democratic National Committee under the approving eye of the White House. Evidently, the fairness doctrine as a "Living Constitutional" norm has not found its center of gravity.

In sum, the F.C.C., once buffeted only by the winds of media and legislative opinion but recently more and more subject to executive, judicial, and interest-group pressure, has also not found even short-term equilibrium in the

"Living Constitution." This factor distinguishes the commission from any other independent board; radio and television are so new and their impact so immense that every power center worth its salt feels constrained to fight for a piece of the action. That the F.C.C. is mostly a playground and all too infrequently a viable combatant, however, is entirely consistent with the concept of "headless branchism."

Taming the bureaucracy

Bureaucratic arrangements seem to exercise an irresistible influence over our lives—for perhaps two reasons. First, there is an element of inevitability surrounding contemporary federal bureaucracy. The central government grows larger and larger, providing more and more goods and services for citizens; naturally, these tasks require administrative supervision and management.[q] If anything, this trend will probably accelerate, because our ever-widening technology means greater industrialization, greater urbanization, greater international involvement, and greater depersonalization. Second, there is something labyrinthine in contemporary federal bureaucracy. The institutions come in all sizes, shapes, and descriptions; their jurisdictions, powers, and duties twist and turn without discernible pattern. This trend may well accelerate also, because variety in administrative response is the spice of both our pragmatic ethos and our decentralized constitutional order. There is considerable irony, then, in the realization that a proliferating organizational maze may pose the greatest internal threat to our fundamental political values. It is an old aphorism that if the end of business enterprise is profit, the end of bureaucratic enterprise is power. This discussion can only conclude by asking how our constitutional traditions, based on a *formalistic* checks-and-balances arrangement implemented by *power-constrained political units,* can withstand the danger of a new "Living Constitution," based on an ad hoc checks-and-balances arrangement implemented by *power-hungry administrative units.* The list below includes several possible methods for taming the bureaucracy, but they must be tried collectively, not individually, because there is no one way to make a congeries of power centers accountable.

1. Federal agencies must be made more *efficient.* The Weberian stereotype has been badly overdrawn, but the civil service is expanding by leaps and bounds. Bureaucrats who wield power make policy decisions, but the ranks are swollen with administrators who mostly administer, especially at the lower stations. So long as personnel are delegated at least quasi-managerial duties, there is a place for standards of pure efficiency.

Leading the way in emphasizing such reforms were the two Hoover commissions of the post-World War II era. Charged by Congress to investigate the organization of the executive branch, they issued reports spelling out procedures for eliminating duplication and overlapping of services.[95] The remedies

[q] Over the past fifteen years (1961–76), more than two hundred new agencies were created, while approximately twenty were discontinued.[94]

suggested were based on the efforts of investigating task force units, which buzzed into and around the President's honeycomb, pointing out ways to save money and energy.

As a matter of fact, Congress's oversight mission contemplates just this sort of efficiency review. To that end, the legislature established the General Accounting Office (G.A.O.) in 1921, which performs independent audits of federal financial transactions and checks expenditures to make sure that they have been made legally. For instance, it reviewed President Nixon's diversion of revenues to enhance the value of his San Clemente estate. This agency is an arm of the Congress itself; the comptroller general, who heads G.A.O. investigations, can be fired only by the legislative branch.[96]

Of course, the chief executive can also initiate comprehensive efficiency checks. In 1971 President Nixon appointed a special advisory council under Roy Ash's direction, which mapped out Hoover Commission-style blueprints on a smaller scale.

Many of the prescriptions advanced by these panels have been raked over the coals in both scholarly and partisan debate. For instance, the Hoover Commission thought that agencies should be grouped according to major purposes so that related functions might be positioned cheek by jowl. But if Washington is going to solve economic woes in Appalachia and in Harlem, what may well be needed is *integration,* not *compartmentalization* of purposes; otherwise, a massive assault on all fronts cannot be mobilized.[97] And when the Ash council recommended the merger of all volunteer agencies into one larger unit, it incurred the wrath of VISTA (the "domestic Peace Corps") supporters, who thought Nixon was just trying to undercut that agency's good works.

Perhaps the Hoover panels' *a priori*s smacked of "organizational chartism," and perhaps Nixon's blue-ribbon group *was* out to defuse VISTA. However, let us stipulate that the best way to fight poverty in the emerging East Coast megalopolis is to organize a federal department for precisely that purpose, armed with every possible social function and resource. Must the taxpayer put up with an inefficient red tape machine known as the Boston to Washington Megalopolis Spendthrift Association? Surely, students of administration—loyal to the values of duly ordained policy-makers—can be charged with the pruning and even karate-chopping of excessive bureaucratic sloppiness to preserve organizational integrity.

2. Federal agencies must be better *centralized.* The President, reported both Hoover panels, cannot enforce his will unless he controls his department heads, who, in turn, control their subordinates. But, again, how does one impose vertical lines of authority on bureaucratic relationships that have grown out of horizontal executive-legislative tugs-of-war, where Congress has done most of the pulling?

Presidents could help themselves immeasurably in the short term if they simply overruled unpalatable regulations imposed by their underlings. Even the usually placid Gerald Ford showed what could be done. When H.E.W. bureaucrats decided that father-son and mother-daughter programs in the public schools were illegal, sexist exercises and that any educational facility permitting them would lose federal financial aid, Ford demanded that the order be rescinded at once; and H.E.W. Secretary Mathews complied at once. Of course, had the chief executive misread congressional opinion on this issue, he might have had his hands full.

Over the longer term, Presidents must mobilize their national constituency to wangle from Congress the reorganizational authority they need. Congress guards its control of power tightly. As one writer put it: "The alliance . . . between group interests, . . . legislative committees or subcommittees, and operating bureaus or agencies preferring the administrative *status quo,* constitutes the most effective political stumbling block to executive reorganization."[98] But F.D.R., when he used the Brownlow panel to legitimize his need for an institutionalized White House, showed what a politically adept and popular President can do.[r]

Nixon made a daring move in this direction with his plan to abolish seven Cabinet departments (leaving only State, Treasury, Defense, and Justice) and to replace them with four new ones combining their various assignments. His blueprint looked like this: a *Department of Natural Resources* would have jurisdiction over land, water, and energy use; a *Department of Human Resources* would have jurisdiction over health, education, jobs, and other social services; a *Department of Economic Affairs* would have jurisdiction over labor-management relations, food problems, trade, and commerce; a *Department of Community Development* would have jurisdiction over urban and rural life in general, including transportation and housing policy. But he never did convince the legislature to let him adopt this scheme.

Of course, the age-old fear engendered by governmental centralization is that power corrupts, and episodes like Watergate are not going to enhance the President's aspirations to consolidate his shop. We know chief executives Kennedy, Johnson, and Nixon all used the F.B.I. to conduct surveillance of political opponents, but does it follow that the President should have only feeble control over the F.B.I.? Surely, this is nonsense.[s] However, there is no substitute for a Congress that checks and balances and for Presidents who play by Marquess of Queensbury rules.

3. Federal agencies must be made more responsive to *fundamental personal rights.* The Supreme Court has addressed this problem of late, and cer-

[r] The 1976 presidential election gave Jimmy Carter a powerful mandate to affect centralization, for he made bureaucratic reorganization a major campaign issue. And, like Roosevelt before him, Carter is blessed with a solid Democratic majority in Congress. But will the legislative branch permit more than cosmetic changes?

[s] Indeed, the guidelines developed by former Attorney General Edward Levi to curb F.B.I. abuses included a dose of centralization: intelligence-gathering missions involving allegedly subversive groups must now be cleared through the Attorney General's office, and he has a duty to terminate these when perceived threats to internal security have abated.

tain procedural guarantees have been forthcoming. In 1970 the Court ruled that welfare payments could not be cut off without an evidentiary hearing, during which the recipient might make an oral presentation, cross-examine adverse witnesses before an impartial arbiter, and be represented by counsel. But what about the argument that welfare is a *privilege* (not a *right*) and so can be distributed according to whatever conditions seem feasible? The majority distinguished carefully between terminating a government employee and terminating welfare payments. To deny persons on public aid the fundamentals of fair procedure might deprive eligible persons of the very necessities of life while they wait for the courts to vindicate their claims. The bureaucracy cannot be allowed to play so fast and loose with individual survival.[99]

Some administrative departments have now set up their own codes of fair procedure. H.E.W. will not allow A.F.D.C. (Aid to Families with Dependent Children) payments to be terminated, and will not allow public-housing tenants to be evicted, unless all the guidelines specified above are honored. Indeed, H.E.W. even provides counsel free of charge for indigents.

There is still very great dispute as to the sweep of these procedural amenities. For example, are civil servants who can be dismissed only for cause entitled to a full evidentiary hearing before termination? Does civil service employment constitute a meaningful property interest, which, like public aid, cannot be foreclosed unless due process is provided? These questions have not been answered authoritatively.[100] Moreover, when parents go on A.F.D.C., they must allow social workers into their homes to ensure proper implementation, and search warrants need not be obtained in advance. A Court majority said that the purpose of A.F.D.C. is to provide minimal standards of *child* care, and if the parents are miffed by the procedure, their remedy is to leave the program without fear of any reprisal. In short, the children's right to receive aid intended for them must be counted more heavily than the parents' right to resist intrusions where "probable cause" has not been demonstrated.[101]

Perhaps the whole business of courtroom procedure has been ripped out of context. Maybe we should not try to judicialize the process by which minimum living standards are maintained. Is it possible that a proper balance consists in providing *no* adjudicatory rules for welfare mothers threatened with the termination of benefits and *no* adjudicatory rules for the almost three *million* tenants domiciled in low-rent, federally subsidized public housing when they are threatened with eviction? Is this any way to tame bureaucracies? I would apply Mr. Justice Holmes's "Post Office" test: the government can either operate a welfare system and a public housing system or not operate them, but once it chooses the former alternative, the basics of procedural equity are obligatory.

4. Federal agencies must be made more accessible to *public perusal.* Perhaps the major reason bureaucrats can maximize power—indeed, very often misuse power by gratifying the needs of only well-organized clients—is because they are invisible.[102] The public either can't penetrate the "jungle" or can't find a copy of the organizational chart, much less translate the boxes and slots into power realities.

Earlier I said Congress passed the 1974 Privacy Act so that citizens can dig out unverified data about themselves from the bowels of the government's countless filing cabinets. But in 1966 the legislature enacted a much more sweeping statute, the Freedom of Information Act. Under the old 1946 Administrative Procedure Act, federal agencies could keep all their records from public view if "required for good cause to be kept confidential." Talk about vague guidelines and blank checks! However, the Freedom of Information Act says that interested parties must be given access to these data unless the material falls within several fairly specific categories.[t] And an individual who thinks a bureau is covering up can sue in federal court, where *the government must shoulder the burden of proof.*[104]

How does the law work? In 1953, Julius and Ethel Rosenberg were executed for slipping secrets about our atomic energy program to the Soviet Union. Twenty years later, their children asked the F.B.I. to release its investigative reports on their parents, hoping to show that a miscarriage of justice had been perpetrated. At the same time, an historian interested in writing a book on the subject also asked to examine the records. When the F.B.I. rejected both requests, it was hauled into court. Petitioners won both cases. Still, it took three years to consummate the Rosenberg appeal, even longer than it takes to consummate an exceptionally protracted criminal proceeding. Surely, the "time frame" can be slashed to one year without adding substantially to bureaucratic red tape.

5. Federal agencies must be made more receptive to *congressional opinion.* When bureaucrats decided that all automobiles had to be equipped with seat belts whose use was required before the cars would function, constituency hue and cry practically forced Congress to step in and throw out the rule. But remedial legislation takes a lot of effort. Perhaps safety clauses written into each agency's "constitution," allowing a majority vote by *either* House or Senate to reject new regulations within, say, sixty days after they are promulgated would be appropriate (see note r, p. 337).

6. One final measure that can be invoked to tame the federal bureaucracy is as simple as a remedy can be—although our "Living Constitution," I think, frowns on it as a means for conducting public business. I am referring to the *abolition of administrative structures, supports, and constraints.*

Louis Jaffe argues convincingly that public organizations have a bias in favor of regulation, which, after all, is their stock in trade.[105] But I think we must not treat regulation, or planning, or government subsidy as a constitutional necessity simply because that door has once been opened. That, more

[t] Obviously, the Freedom of Information Act cannot be used to ventilate "investigatory files compiled for law enforcement purposes" or confidential data specifically protected by executive order relating to either national defense or foreign policy.[103]

than anything else, is the stuff on which the bureaucratic state breeds. If we think the free marketplace of ideas is good enough for framing First Amendment presumptions, then maybe we are underrating the vitality and dynamism of marketplace initiative and spontaneity, inhibited if not suffocated by bureaucratic priorities.

For example, there is an independent agency in the federal bureaucracy called the National Science Foundation (N.S.F.). One of its tasks is disbursing funds to mathematicians, sociologists, economists, and other scholars so they can pursue "worthwhile" research. But perhaps the federal government is out of its element here, because making inherently political decisions about the nature of "good" scholarship merely rewards the "ins" and penalizes the "outs," merely allows fashionable ideas to proliferate and unfashionable ideas to wither.

Among independent regulatory agencies, some say the Securities and Exchange Commission is the one shining star, because the New York Stock Exchange has been stripped of the many excesses that helped fuel the Great Depression. Does this mean we must have such regulation forever? If Wall Street is now capable of self-government, then why not give it self-government? Perhaps what the Postal Service needs is even *more* free enterprise. Perhaps what academic researchers need is to be thrown back on their own resources.[106]

The federal bureaucracy is a complex web of institutions and processes. The norms that govern those structures and functions are a vastly underrated and understudied segment of the "Living Constitution." We learned long ago not to let the Congress intimidate us, and we have made progress in learning that the President must not be allowed to intimidate us either. But we have failed thus far to develop rational strategies for understanding and checking the national bureaucracy. The question is: Will our public philosophy be equal to this task?

NOTES

1. Francis E. Rourke, ed., *Bureaucratic Power in National Politics* (Boston: Little, Brown, 1967), pp. vii–xviii.

2. Alan A. Altshuler, ed., *The Politics of the Federal Bureaucracy* (New York: Dodd, Mead, 1971), p. v. Out of forty articles included in this reader, *one* deals with the independent agencies (see Louis Jaffe's piece, p. 324). Nor does the editor, in his own remarks, delineate their powers, duties, and processes.

3. A good try is Harold Seidman, *Politics, Position, and Power: The Dynamics of Federal Organization,* 2nd ed. (New York: Oxford Univ. Press, 1975).

4. H. H. Gerth and C. Wright Mills, eds., *From Max Weber: Essays in Sociology* (New York: Oxford Univ. Press, 1946), pp. 196–244.

5. Chester I. Barnard, *The Functions of the Executive* (Cambridge, Mass.: Harvard Univ. Press, 1938). Notice the publication date. The thesis had currency well before anyone had coined the phrase "military-industrial complex." Barnard, it is true, saw executive decision-making as an art; but he also perceived it as an *apolitical* art.

6. Frank Goodnow, *Politics and Administration: A Study in Government* (New York: Macmillan, 1900).

7. Herbert Simon, *Administrative Behavior,* 2nd ed. (New York: Macmillan, 1957). For a critique of his arguments, framed from the "polar position" assumption that *nothing* worth studying about politics can be described scientifically, see Herbert J. Storing, "The Science of Administration: Herbert A. Simon," in H. J. Storing, ed., *Essays on the Scientific Study of Politics* (New York: Holt, Rinehart and Winston, 1962), pp. 63-150.

8. Gerth and Mills, pp. 77-78.

9. Or perhaps I should return to Weber and emphasize such factors as tenure and ideological detachment. However, under that kind of definition, I would be relegating the judiciary to the level of administration. Maybe the shoe fits! Didn't I characterize both bureaucratic and judicial roles as sometimes looking apolitical but always being inherently political? Nonetheless, if the Supreme Court were thrown in with the rest of the administrative state, then the crucial factors of political power and political prestige would have come a cropper of sociological theory.

10. In this respect, lower court judges are *not* bureaucrats, for they are, by and large, masters of their own houses as a matter of right.

11. But I am sure the average person has heard of the Cabinet and the F.B.I., too. Such are the inadequacies of tests based on public opinion.

12. Richard E. Neustadt, "Approaches to Staffing the Presidency: Notes on FDR and JFK," *The American Political Science Review* 57 (1963), p. 855. Further observations with respect to the White House staff during the Roosevelt and Kennedy years come from this article.

13. *Report of the President's Committee on Administrative Management* (1937), p. 5.

14. This message runs through David Halberstam, *The Best and the Brightest* (New York: Random House, 1972).

15. Perhaps Harry Hopkins was the exception that proved the rule; but I think he was more in the Colonel House (Woodrow Wilson's chief brainstormer) tradition.

16. Seidman, pp. 71, 85-87.

17. The following data come from the testimony of H. R. Haldeman, John Ehrlichman, and John Dean before Senator Ervin's Watergate committee. With respect to general questions of staff responsibility, their statements are not in conflict. *Hearings Before the Select Committee on Presidential Campaign Activities of the U.S. Senate,* 93rd Cong., 1st Sess., 1973, pp. 926-27, 2514-18, 2524-26, 2871-72. (Hereinafter referred to as *Hearings.*) For a more complete picture of Nixon's hierarchical precepts in executive branch management, I recommend Seidman, Ch. 4.

18. This and the following facts are taken from testimony submitted to the Ervin committee by Haldeman, Ehrlichman, Dean, and John Mitchell, *Hearings,* Books 3, 4, 6, and 7.

19. Ehrlichman was counsel to the President at that time, and Dean replaced him in this post when Ehrlichman moved up to the Domestic Council.

20. These are the "Kissinger taps," which I discussed in Chapter 5.

21. See Haldeman's testimony, *Hearings,* pp. 2868-69.

22. See Ehrlichman's testimony, *Hearings,* pp. 2518-19.

23. Ibid., pp. 2514-15, 2521.

24. Ibid., p. 2534.

25. Neustadt, p. 860.

26. The above comments are based in some measure on Paul Y. Hammond, "The National Security Council as a Device for Interdepartmental Coordination: An Interpretation and Appraisal," *The American Political Science Review* 54 (1960), pp. 899-910, and Stanley L. Falk, "The National Security Council Under Truman, Eisenhower and Kennedy," *Political Science Quarterly* 79 (1964), pp. 403-34. For the N.S.C.'s role in the Cuban missile crisis, see Graham T. Allison, "Conceptual Models and the Cuban Missile Crisis," *The American Political Science Review* 63 (1969), pp. 689-718.

27. This evaluation and other remarks on the C.E.A. come from Lester G. Seligman, "Presidential Leadership: The Inner Circle and Institutionalization," *Journal of Politics* 18 (1956), pp. 410-26.

28. Seidman, pp. 216, 239-41, 313-15. Compare Message of the President of the United States transmitting Reorganization Plan No. 2, 1970, House Document No. 91-275, 91st Cong., 2nd Sess.

29. Seidman, pp. 217, 315.

30. I have relied here on Richard E. Neustadt, "The Presidency and Legislation: The Growth of Central Clearance," *The American Political Science Review* 48 (1954), pp. 641-71. For an update which traces a diminution in budget bureau control and flexibility, see Robert Gilmour, "Central Legislative Clearance: A Revised Perspective," *Public Administration Review* 31 (March-April, 1971), pp. 150-58.

31. Joseph E. Kallenbach, *The American Chief Executive* (New York: Harper & Row, 1966), p. 342.

32. The following account is distilled from Aaron Wildavsky, *The Politics of the Budgetary Process,* 2nd ed. (Boston: Little, Brown, 1974).

33. See Chapter 11, in which I develop this argument considerably.

34. Wildavsky, p. 5. But how do you put a price tag on a civil rights enactment or a Supreme Court ruling upholding the incarceration of Japanese-Americans?

35. Laurence I. Radway, *Foreign Policy and National Defense* (Glenview, Ill.: Scott, Foresman, 1969), p. 70.

36. Ibid., p. 157.

37. P.L. 253 (1947), Sect. 102; 61 *Stat.* 495 (1947).

38. Seymour M. Hersh, "Huge C.I.A. Operation Reported . . .," *The New York Times* (December 22, 1974), pp. 1, 26.

39. The discussion of the Cabinet as a collegial body is based on Richard Fenno's superb study, *The President's Cabinet* (Cambridge, Mass.: Harvard Univ. Press, 1959).

40. The Kennedy Cabinet is described in Theodore C. Sorensen, *Kennedy* (New York: Harper & Row, 1965), pp. 281-85.

41. See Seidman, pp. 91-92, 236, 313.

42. Again, I acknowledge my debt to Richard Fenno's study of the Cabinet, this time for his description of Secretaries as departmental overseers.

43. U.S. Civil Service Commission, *Characteristics of the Federal Executive* (February 1968).

44. Commission on Organization of the Executive Branch of the Government, Task Force Report, *Personnel and Civil Service* (February 1955), p. 39.

45. Dean Mann, "The Selection of Federal Political Executives," *The American Political Science Review* 58 (1964), p. 81. The data which I present below come mainly from this research.

46. C. Wright Mills, *The Power Elite* (New York: Oxford Univ. Press, 1956), p. 233.

47. Arthur Macmahon and John D. Millett, *Federal Administrators* (New York: Columbia Univ. Press, 1939), p. 302.

48. See also Seidman, p. 127.

49. Ibid., p. 130.

50. Ibid., pp. 309-11.

51. Ernest Griffith coined this expression in *The Impasse of Democracy* (New York: Harrison-Hilton, 1939), p. 182, and the notion is embellished in Ernest Griffith, *Congress: Its Contemporary Role* (New York: New York Univ. Press, 1951), p. 107.

52. The classic study of the Corps of Engineers is Arthur Maass, "Congress and Water Resources," *The American Political Science Review* 44 (1950), pp. 576-93, which I have leaned upon in this segment.

53. Much of the information found in the subsequent discussion is detailed in John T. Elliff, *Crime, Dissent, and the Attorney General* (Beverly Hills, Calif.: Sage Publications, 1971). Other helpful references are Victor S. Navasky, *Kennedy Justice* (New York: Atheneum, 1971) and Richard Harris, *Justice* (New York: E. P. Dutton, 1970). However, the interpretations presented are my own.

54. The communication is reproduced in Navasky, pp. 451-52.

55. Nicholas Katzenbach's one-year hitch as Justice Department head separates the Kennedy years from the Clark years. Katzenbach's impact was minimal and will not be explored here.

56. This is Elliff's characterization of Clark's position (p. 52).

57. These facts, plus my subsequent description of other illegal F.B.I. doings, are based on reports prepared by the Senate Intelligence Committee and published in *The New York Times* (April 29, 1976), pp. 31-33.

58. One guideline specified that narcotics addicts who had twice previously been accused of violent crimes, *but not necessarily convicted of either,* could be held in custody for sixty days. Detention of citizens for alleged misdeeds *never proven* is hard to square with due process, unless the writ of habeas corpus were constitutionally suspended.

59. But then, perhaps the Framers also saw bail as a means to keep dangerous people off the streets. If so, the Bail Reform Act of 1966 defeated that purpose totally. Certainly the Founders did not anticipate a pre-trial release format in which money payments would not be standard operating procedure, as I pointed out in Chapter 3, though they did not anticipate extraordinary delays between arrest and trial either.

60. See my discussion in Chapter 5, p. 200.

61. John M. Crewdson, "Intelligence Panel Finds F.B.I. and Other Agencies Violated Citizens' Rights," *The New York Times* (April 29, 1976), pp. 1, 34.

62. See the testimony of John Dean and John Mitchell, *Hearings,* Book 3, pp. 916-17; Book 4, pp. 1603-04.

63. U.S. Bureau of the Census, *1970 Census Users' Guide* (Washington, D.C.: Government Printing Office, 1970), p. 11.

64. Quoted in Elliff, p. 186.

65. Leonard D. White, *The Jeffersonians* (New York: Macmillan, 1951).

66. Quoted in Leonard D. White, *The Jacksonians* (New York: Macmillan, 1954), p. 318.

67. The most apposite case on the subject is *Joint Anti-Fascist Refugee Committee v. McGrath,* 341 U.S. 123 (1951), a ruling that can be objectively labeled as meaningless.

68. See *Bailey v. Richardson,* 341 U.S. 918 (1951), another example of Supreme Court indecision.

69. *United Public Workers v. Mitchell,* 330 U.S. 75 (1947); *United States Civil Service Commission v. National Ass'n of Letter Carriers,* 413 U.S. 548 (1973).

70. The cases are *McAuliffe v. Mayor of New Bedford,* 155 Mass. 216 (1892), and *Milwaukee Social Democratic Pub. Co. v. Burleson,* 255 U.S. 407 (1921). Holmes never enlightened us on precisely what the extenuating conditions might be; but we know that both movies and books are given First Amendment protection, though in somewhat different proportions. I suspect he had in mind that kind of distinction.

71. "Blacks Seek Tougher Equality Standards for Federal Hiring and Promotion," *The New York Times* (November 15, 1970), p. 72. These data obtain as of 1976.

72. Lewis C. Mainzer, *Political Bureaucracy* (Glenview, Ill.: Scott, Foresman, 1973), p. 107.

73. *Hearings,* Exhibit 35, V. 19, p. 9006.

74. Joel D. Aberbach and Bert A. Rockman, "Clashing Beliefs Within the Executive Branch: The Nixon Administration Bureaucracy," *The American Political Science Review* 70 (1976), pp. 456-68.

75. For a good discussion which speaks to this point, see Herbert Kaufman, "The Growth of the Federal Personnel System," in Wallace Sayre, ed., *The Federal Government Service,* 2nd ed. (Englewood Cliffs, N.J.: Prentice-Hall, 1965), pp. 58-69.

76. Exotic terms meaning neglect of duty, poor performance, illegal conduct, and the like.

77. "Staggered" means that their terms expire in different years.

78. This segment of my presentation owes an intellectual debt to Marver Bernstein, *Regulating Business by Independent Commission* (Princeton: Princeton Univ. Press, 1955). I have also found Louis Jaffe's writings useful, though I feel they are too optimistic about regulation by *independent* commissions generally. An example of his work is "The Effective Limits of the Administrative Process," *Harvard Law Review* 67 (1954), pp. 1105-23, 1127-35.

79. This story is not apocryphal; Carter's Pills are still on the market.

80. Paul Appleby, *Policy and Administration* (University, Ala.: Univ. of Alabama Press, 1949), p. 162.

81. Samuel P. Huntington, "The Marasmus of the I.C.C.: The Commission, the Railroads, and the Public Interest," *The Yale Law Journal* 61 (1952), pp. 467-509.

82. The speaker was Joseph Eastman, quoted in Bernstein, p. 64.

83. For the history of the F.C.C., I have relied on Erwin G. Krasnow and Lawrence D. Longley, *The Politics of Broadcast Regulation* (New York: St. Martin's Press, 1973).

84. So said Senator Clarence C. Dill, a "prime mover" for F.C.C. control. Quoted in Krasnow and Longley, p. 11.

85. "Minow Observes a 'Vast Wasteland,'" *Broadcasting* (May 15, 1960), pp. 58-59.

86. *Office of Communications v. F.C.C.*, 359 F. 2nd 994 (1966); *Office of Communications v. F.C.C.*, 425 F. 2nd 543 (1969).

87. *Citizens Communications Center v. F.C.C.*, 447 F. 2nd 1201 (1971).

88. Thomas Whiteside, "Annals of Television: Shaking the Tree," *The New Yorker* (March 17, 1975), p. 62.

89. *Puerto Rican Media Action and Ed. Council v. Ed. Broadcasting Corp.*, 32 RR 2nd 1423 at p. 1442 (1975).

90. *Red Lion Broadcasting Co. v. F.C.C.*, 395 U.S. 372 (1969).

91. The quote and much of the following data are drawn from Fred A. Friendly, "What's Fair on the Air?" *The New York Times Magazine* (March 30, 1975), pp. 11-12, 37-43, 46-48.

92. *Friends of the Earth v. F.C.C.*, 449 F. 2nd 1164 (1971).

93. *C.B.S. v. Dem. Nat. Comm.*, 412 U.S. 94 (1973). This is a fascinating and complex case, about which more should be said. In a very real sense, the decision is *anti*-fairness doctrine. Why? Suppose I want to spend my money advertising on television a point of view I feel strongly about, an issue that has failed to attain station coverage. My comments might enrich the free speech marketplace. They might even prompt replies under a broadened view of the fairness concept, rebuttals that would convince people that my original argument was dubious. But the Court rejects all this, because the license-holders would very possibly have to surrender so much airwave time to these participants that *its* free speech rights would be deprecated!

94. *The Champaign-Urbana* (Ill.) *News-Gazette* (June 11, 1976), p. 21.

95. Both groups were known as the Commission on Organization of the Executive Branch of the Government, and they were chaired by former President Herbert Hoover. Their probes of executive departments and agencies are the most exhaustive we have had. See *General Management of the Executive Branch, A Report to the Congress* and *Concluding Report, A Report to the Congress* (Washington, D.C.: Government Printing Office, 1949); *Final Report to the Congress* (Washington, D.C.: Government Printing Office, 1955).

96. But I must hasten to add that the G.A.O., by definition, is also part of the federal bureaucracy. Who investigates it?

97. Seidman, p. 29.

98. Avery Leiserson, "Political Limitations on Executive Reorganization," *The American Political Science Review* 41 (1947), p. 79.

99. *Goldberg v. Kelly,* 397 U.S. 254 (1970).

100. *Arnett v. Kennedy,* 416 U.S. 134 (1974).

101. *Wyman v. James,* 400 U.S. 309 (1971).

102. See, for instance, Grant McConnell, *Private Power and American Democracy,* 1st ed. (New York: Knopf, 1966).

103. Congressional Quarterly, *Congress and the Nation,* vol. 3, 1969-1972, p. 490.

104. Congressional Quarterly, *Congress and the Nation,* vol. 2, 1965-1968, p. 643.

105. See note 78 above.

106. Several states are currently considering "sunset" laws, whereby administrative bureaus must receive comprehensive review every five years or so and either demonstrate their right to life or be terminated.

8 federalism: semisovereign nation? semisovereign states?

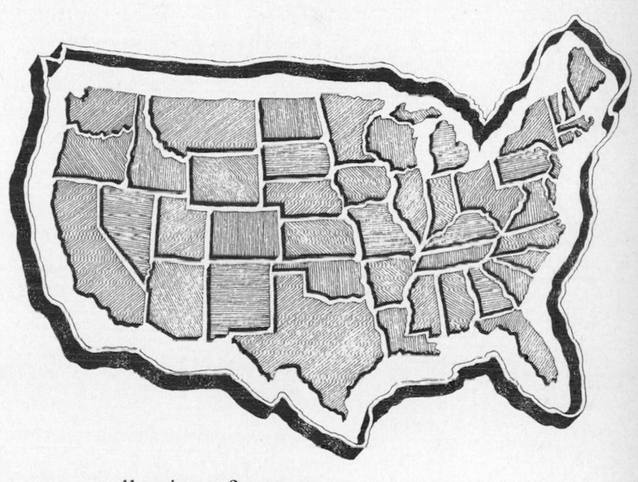

Unlike the many fundamental norms which the Founding Fathers contrived through premeditated act, federalism was and is an American constitutional "given." It received sanction not by dint of any weighing and sifting process, but because our cultural stream of consciousness rejects alternatives. And yet Americans have always been torn by the conflicting state and local versus national claims inherent in the federal principle. These considerations lie at the core of this chapter.

The Articles of Confederation, formalizing power realities following the American Revolution, were based on the assumption that this country was a collection of states. Supreme political authority—*sovereignty*—resided in thirteen discrete units, which had deigned to sign a pact of friendship for ostensible material benefit. But the Framers, before they settled down to reflect, debate, and compromise, voted to dispatch state sovereignty because, as I tried to explain in Chapter 1, people throughout the several states were already deeply committed to a truly national polity. Indeed, the feeling of *community consciousness,* fundamental to viable nation-statehood, had taken hold decades earlier. The Framers, then, were groping toward an idea whose time had come. And if scrapping the notion of confederacy was a "given," the new political relationship between state and national power centers also was beyond deliberation. The only choice was *federalism:* some political authority would be given to each of three branches; the rest would be reserved to the states or to the people (the language of the Tenth Amendment); *but national authority would be supreme in its juris-*

dictional sphere, as Article VI (the so-called supremacy clause) made crystal clear.[a]

What must be especially emphasized is that by definition federalism rests on *divided sovereignty,* where state and nation control some portion of political power independent of the other's authority. But a funny thing happened to federalism on its way from political theory to political reality. The principle, palatable even to New Jersey Plan advocates, became a red flag unfurled before the bull-like passions of sectionalism. Umbilical-cord attachment to mother-state would inspire civil strife and, later, contribute to national governmental emasculation in the face of private economic excess. Today, however, the shoe is on the other foot, the national political apparatus bidding fair to preempt state power at every turn, as its policy-making options swell to mammoth proportions. In our time, states' rights advocates appear the apostles of reaction, just as the rabid nationalists of seventy years ago seemed the missionaries of radicalism.

In this chapter, I shall describe the rise and fall of states' rights as well as the fall and rise of national rights. But—of deeper consequence—I shall examine the whole question of sovereignty in our federal system, for that is the crucial political item dividing people to this day. And it is not primarily a theoretical dispute; the issue centers on the concept of community, and community means real people, real customs, and real social ties. Americans have deep feelings not only for national community but for region, state, town, and neighborhood—communities that oftentimes become synonymous with home. And to the extent that community is linked with such an intensely held social value, it is a mainspring of our constitutional environment.

States' rights as state sovereignty

The basic tenets of American constitutionalism are rarely the private preserve of any one political faction or ideology. Over the course of our two-hundred-year history, the Constitution's virtues have been championed by different sets of interests motivated by different sets of policy preferences. The theory of states' rights is no exception. The "strict constructionists" have endorsed it, but so have the "broad constructionists"; liberals have applauded it, but conservatives have also rhapsodized over it; Democrats and Republicans, the rich and the poor, urban and rural communities, each in turn has at times rallied round and at other times condemned the slogan. What constitutional preconceptions underlie states' rights, and what are the political factors that have sustained it through the years?

The term "states' rights" does not appear in the constitutional text. But the document certainly presupposes healthy, active, *permanent* states. In fact, the Framers' central concern was to keep the states from interfering with *national*

[a] Nobody at the Convention (except Alexander Hamilton) advocated a unitary governmental structure, in which the states, having lost supreme temporal authority, would become appendages of national coercion.

sovereignty; so, while no elaborate checklist of states' rights can be located, an unequivocal checklist of *states' duties* is presented.

What rights, then, does the document ensure? First, boundaries cannot be altered unless the states themselves agree. Second, each state has two senators, and, again, the equal representation formula cannot be manipulated unless the states involved concur. (As we have seen, that formula constitutes the only unamendable provision in the charter.) No state has ever tendered either brand of consent, nor is any likely to. So states are here to stay, and their territorial integrity constitutes the only factor in the Senate's makeup. This fact, when considered in conjunction with the Tenth Amendment's allocation of "reserved" powers to the states, gives us a thumbnail sketch of states' constitutional prerogatives.[1] In other words, the charter nowhere vests states with any *specific* policy-making privileges.

What obligations to national integrity does the Constitution impose on the states? Mainly, these fall into three categories: (1) States cannot coin money or provide for a medium of exchange other than gold and silver. (2) States cannot make treaties or alliances, or levy unnecessary taxes on either imports or exports unless Congress approves. Finally, (3) states cannot keep troops in peacetime unless Congress so authorizes, nor can states engage in war unless either attacked or faced by unavoidable dangers. In other words, the Founders saw *currency policy, foreign policy,* and *military policy* as inherently the business of supreme temporal institutions, national in constituency and scope.

The initial challenge to the Framers' plan for federal-state relations was only to be ten years away. After the Federalist Party had passed the Alien and Sedition Acts, and Federalist judges had refused to rule on their constitutionality, implacable opponents of vigorous national authority, led by Thomas Jefferson, persuaded the Kentucky and Virginia state legislatures to pass resolutions condemning the enactments. Because state assemblies had much more status and influence than they do today, Jefferson's strategy proved an excellent propaganda vehicle.

Virginia's manifesto argued that when the federal government usurped its limited powers in a deliberate and dangerous manner, the states could *interpose* themselves on behalf of aggrieved citizens. The Kentucky Resolution went even further, saying that the institutions of national power lacked ultimate authority to determine the scope of their own jurisdiction. Only the states, *which had created the Constitution,* could protect the sanctity of the Constitution against arbitrary federal encroachment. In the exercise of that responsibility, Kentucky's legislators concluded, the Alien and Sedition Acts must be considered null and void.[2] And when the Federalist-dominated Northern legislatures denounced these expressions, Kentucky drafted a second resolution proclaiming the right of states, given their political and sovereign independence, to nullify unauthorized federal laws.

These statements contain virtually all the ideas necessary to make "revolution by state" a legitimate enterprise. And, of course, that is exactly how the

South would view the Civil War. Jefferson's theory of states' rights, then, owes an intellectual debt to the theory of *state sovereignty.* When judged against the theoretical assumptions of the 1970s, the doctrine of interposition—by which a state could place itself between national government and "the people" so as to protect their precious liberties—and the doctrine of nullification—by which the state could veto national policy deemed unconstitutional—seem nothing but an elaborate rehash of Articles of Confederation power relations.

Were the Jeffersonians, then, already prepared to scrap the grand premise of the Philadelphia undertaking? Undoubtedly not. For one thing, the notion of "pure judicial review" had not even been advanced by the Supreme Court. For another, neither Kentucky nor Virginia attempted to force a confrontation over the Alien and Sedition Acts. Besides, the resolutions countenanced interposition and nullification only in *extreme circumstances;* no general theory of "state judicial review" or "state constitution reading" was advanced. In other words, the Jeffersonians were saying that the national government is supreme within its allotted sphere, but the states may protect those individual rights which are beyond the reach of federal power. Many historians, then, see the Virginia and Kentucky declarations as within the broad spectrum of *divided sovereignty* theory.[3]

The fluidity of constitutional politics during this early period is shown graphically by the fact that many Federalist stalwarts were soon to endorse the same outlook. Having won control of both Congress and the White House, Jefferson's party passed the Embargo Act, severely damaging New England manufacturing and shipping interests. Now the Massachusetts and Connecticut legislatures were moved to draft inflammatory states' rights resolutions. By proscribing trade with Britain and France, Congress had stretched its control over foreign commerce beyond recognizable dimensions, the two states contended; only interposition and nullification could rebuff arbitrary federal power; therefore, the Embargo Act had no binding effect within their jurisdictions. And when the "political branches" tried to federalize the state militia to prosecute the War of 1812, several New England states considered the hostilities nothing but a plot to compel the annexation of Florida; with their British markets hanging in the balance, they actually refused to allow their forces to be nationalized. This overt display of state nullification tactics during wartime was considered extreme and only presaged the demise of the Federalist Party.

As history books tell us, however, it was the South that would make from these doctrinal ingredients a complete thoroughgoing states' rights philosophy. The North, with its more rapid growth in population, technological sophistication, and wealth, was beginning to command a balance of national power. Soon the South would be at the mercy of a presidential-congressional coalition geared to "broad constructionism" in such sensitive policy areas as tariff regulation. The man who saw this trend clearer than most was South Carolina's John C. Calhoun, a distinguished constitutional theorist with a shrewd political instinct. Speaking from his position as Vice President, he fired the sectional loyalties of Southerners by constructing a states' rights thesis that seemed irresistible—if one accepted its basic premises.

Sovereignty, Calhoun argued, was *indivisible* by definition and must be lodged in one specific power center. The locus of sovereignty, for him, was the individual state, which, in its colonial status, had joined hands with like-minded neighboring territories to wage successful revolution against the mother country; had established the Articles of Confederation; and, when those proved unworkable, had dispatched delegates to draw up a more viable compact, subsequently ratified in special conventions they themselves had ordained. But the states had never surrendered their integrity, *their sovereignty.* If *they* held political autonomy, then the institutions of national authority did not. Clearly, a sovereign state could interpret the compact—the Constitution—to which it had affixed its signature; and where state interpretation found national action indefensible, that action could be nullified. Finally, in the most extreme of circumstances, a state might exercise the full panoply of sovereign powers and withdraw from the Union.[4] Here is the triumph of minority rights over majority rule, the triumph of sectional interest over the general interest, the triumph of parochial economic and social folkways over national "Living Constitutionalism," and the retransformation of states' rights into 1780s state sovereignty theory.

The protective tariff of 1832 provided the first substantive test of these ideas. Sentiment throughout the southeastern Atlantic states ran heavily against high trade barriers. American protective tariffs had incited retaliatory protective barriers overseas, and the result was a badly depressed market for the small farmers of this region. When the 1832 rate schedule brought no relief, South Carolina adopted a declaration of nullification, branding the tariff unconstitutional and void. But President Jackson denounced the movement as the essence of revolution and threatened to enforce the tariff by sword and musket. When Congress fell in behind him and other Southern states failed to react, the spirit of nullification quickly crumbled.

Calhoun's theories had failed in their debut because the protective tariff was not perceived by the Southern community as a clear and present danger. But slavery was the backbone of that community, a plantation system complete with landed aristocracy and all the other trappings captured in *Gone with the Wind.* The South began to see a noose slowly tightening around its neck, as the waves of opposition to slavery's extension in the western territories rose ever higher throughout the more powerful North. And the greater the threat seemed to be, the more potent was the lure of Calhoun's states' rights-state sovereignty philosophy, which by the 1850s had become the very marrow of Southern constitutional tradition. In the end, the people of the United States were forced to reconsider, in a forum necessarily more decisive than the Constitutional Convention, the fundamental political attributes of federalism. I daresay it was inevitable that the South would embark on a rendezvous with disaster, once Calhounism and slavery became inextricably linked. James Madison had warned prophetically that the Great Compromise and its guarantee of equal state representation in the Senate would keep the coals of state sovereignty smoldering. But now—finally—the state as supreme political force would meet its Waterloo at Appomattox.

States' rights as "dual federalism"

I described in Chapter 4 Congress's victory over presidential Reconstruction initiatives after the Civil War. Thaddeus Stevens's "conquered province" theory was based upon the assumption that the seceded states had lost their identity as states by making unsuccessful war on the Union. This contention cannot be squared with the major criticism advanced against Calhounism—namely, that secession was revolution because a state could be only a state and nothing more! Civil War confrontation and post-Civil War politics, then, failed to resolve the central constitutional questions: What is a state? What can a state do?

The Supreme Court spoke to this knotty problem in 1869;[5] however, as in other instances relating to Civil War policy,[6] the Justices found themselves attempting to reconcile the irreconcilable. First, they said there could be no Union without healthy, viable, "indestructible" states, wielding their Tenth Amendment powers as the Constitution had intended. This was the Lincoln position beyond doubt, for the Court emphasized that federalism was incompatible with secession. Nonetheless, the Justices continued, the instruments of national authority owed certain constitutional *duties* to the states, and one such obligation was the maintenance of a *republican form of government.* To implement this command, Congress had enacted the several Reconstruction Acts to quash the remnants of disloyalty. Without warning, the Court had gone over to the Stevens position, for the gist of his brief was that any and all states' rights can be suspended should Congress consider that remedy "necessary and proper." To sum up: The "indestructible state" theory is faithful to the federal principle of divided sovereignty advanced by the Framers; the "suspension of states' rights" theory assumes an unequivocal national sovereignty—*unitary government*—where Congress can find that domestic emergencies warrant unbridled legislative intervention.

If I am correct, this decision settled precious little about the extent of states' rights. But as the country repressed the horrors of civil strife, policymaking at the state level resurged significantly. When corporate interests began to spread-eagle the marketplace, it was the states that moved against them. For example, Illinois passed a law setting maximum rates on warehouse owners who stored produce brought to Chicago from farming communities around the Middle West. Suddenly, *states' rights* was no longer code language for *slaveowners' rights.* It had become code language for *consumer rights* in the form of lower prices, and for the farmer's right to escape a classic "rip-off." The Supreme Court upheld the rate regulation, finding these warehouses private property "clothed with a public interest," for they were businesses standing at the very "gateway of commerce," the grain capital of the world. The state's Tenth

Amendment power extended to reasonable control over the manner in which these firms manipulated that gateway.[7]

To what other subjects did this regulatory flexibility obtain? For as long as states have passed laws, their legislatures have employed what is called the *police power,* the authority to lay down rules for the health, safety, morals, and welfare of the general community. A state may insist that citizens be vaccinated to prevent the spread of smallpox, that obscene publications not be sold on street corners, that traffic lights be posted at key intersections, and that a school system with a specified curriculum be established. For similar reasons, a state may ban the manufacture of alcoholic beverages, the sale of marijuana, or the construction of factories in residential neighborhoods.[8] The police power, wrote Mr. Justice Harlan, is "a power which the State did not surrender when becoming a member of the Union"[9] and, therefore, embraces the policy-making discretion that is the kernel of states' rights in a federal system.

Of course, the many decades between Lincoln's tenure and the New Deal are not considered bellwethers of state activism. During those years, when laissez faire was in the economic saddle, the Supreme Court developed substantive due process in order to protect private property from governmental restraint. Nor did the judiciary allow federal regulation to do anything the states were barred from accomplishing; a congressional minimum-wage law applicable to employees in the District of Columbia was as unconstitutional as a New York State minimum-wage law.[10] Indeed, a careful reading of Court decisions during this stretch shows a clear bias in favor of state action over national action. How and why?

One of the social evils reformers railed against during the early twentieth century was child labor. Woodrow Wilson persuaded the House and Senate in 1916 to enact the Keating-Owen law aimed at abolishing the practice. Congress justified its power to set minimum age requirements for boys and girls working in coal mines by saying it could ban from interstate commerce all goods produced by firms employing young children. So an underaged worker need not have handled the particular merchandise sent across state lines; if the child labored for the firm in any capacity, the company's entire interstate output constituted a violation of federal law.

The Supreme Court declared this statute unconstitutional,[11] saying the conditions of production and of manufacture—the criteria for employment imposed by a particular plant in a particular state—were beyond Congress's control over interstate commerce. That a concern transported merchandise beyond state boundaries was beside the point, since this law was intended not to regulate such transportation but to institute a national child labor code, and *child labor practice was solely a matter for state rulemaking.* How did the Court *know* the Tenth Amendment vested minimum age regulations with the states? "The powers not *expressly* delegated to the National Government are reserved" (italics mine).[12] In other words, because the Constitution did not specifically tender Congress control over child labor, the entire matter was entrusted to state supervision.

A second object lesson involves Congress's power to lay and collect taxes. During this period many social reformers saw levies upon individual incomes as the most equitable way to apportion revenue burdens. But could an income tax applicable to citizens generally be made applicable to state officials? Surely the fifty governors are American citizens who can be asked to pay their fair share to the federal treasury, and the countless mayors, state judges, and city council members bear the same taxation responsibilities as John or Jane Q. Public.

Yet the Supreme Court saw things differently:

> The general government, and the States, although both exist within the same territorial limits, are separate and distinct sovereignties, acting separately and independently of each other, within their respective spheres. The former in its appropriate sphere, is supreme; but the States within the limits of their powers not granted, or, in the language of the tenth amendment, "reserved," are as independent of the general government as that government within its sphere is independent of the States.[13]

And if the states and the nation were equals in their respective jurisdictions, then neither could tax the other. The inherent law of political self-preservation required no less, the Court said, because as John Marshall had observed years earlier: The power to tax is the power to destroy.[14]

As things developed, not only were congressional levies against state officials or state instrumentalities prohibited, but congressional levies on subject matter coming within Tenth Amendment scope were forbidden. Again, child labor provided the substantive testing ground. After the Keating-Owen Act had gone by the boards, a law was passed imposing a 10 percent excise tax on the profits of every firm employing the underaged. To this, the Court said that Congress might well transform the United States into a unitary system if it could control through taxation the police powers vested in the states. Thus another legislative enactment bit the dust.[15]

The constitutional philosophy undergirding this line of decisions is "dual federalism," a term coined by Edward S. Corwin.[16] State government and national government coexist, in peace or in competition; each is number 1 in its bailiwick; the former possesses police powers reserved by the Tenth Amendment, while the latter possesses delegated authority only—or, as the "dual federalists" often phrased it, *expressly* delegated authority.

Under "dual federalism," which power layer holds supreme political authority? Are the three great branches of national government the repositories of sovereignty? No, because the states are supreme in *their* jurisdictions. Do the states hold sovereignty in accordance with Calhounian orthodoxy? No, because national government calls the shots within its preserve. "Dual federalism," then, is a theory of *divided sovereignty,* and in that sense it jibes with the Constitution.

But we know that the core principle of federalism is the supremacy clause, which presupposes a national government exercising powers assigned to it no matter what the states think or do. And in all three cases cited above, states' rights controlled national authority; "dual federalism," as I have remarked, contains an antinational bias. The lesson is clear enough: Some conceptions of divided sovereignty are weighted in a manner favorable to central government; others are weighted in a manner favorable to the states.

If the core principle of federalism as perceived by the Framers is the supremacy clause, then the core principle of "dual federalism" is the Tenth Amendment. The advocates of state sovereignty rarely discussed this provision in the 1830s, because they didn't need to. If the states were unhappy with national policy, they could interpose, nullify, and even secede. But the Civil War stilled all these guns, so a second line of defense had to be contrived. Grasping the Tenth Amendment, these advocates now contended that the states had the inside track except where expressly delegated national power was involved. And as in these three decisions, they were able to curtail even Congress's express authority to control interstate commerce and to enact income taxes. That is because the "dual federalist" *reasons backwards:* If the state can do *x,* the national government can't do *x, no matter what!* And, if I may drive a final nail into the coffin of "dual federalism," just where in the Tenth Amendment does the word "expressly" appear?[17]

Who dreamed up "dual federalism"? States' righters? To be sure, but only a particular breed with a particular slant on social values. The typical farmer surely applauded Illinois's efforts to eradicate discriminatory freight rates imposed by one of the all-powerful transcontinental railroads. However, "dual federalism" had little meaning for him, because he wouldn't have cared a tad if Congress, rather than the states, had made the effort. On that issue, though, the Supreme Court suddenly became very nationalistic, saying these constraints interfered with interstate commerce, Congress's domain.[18] The laborer pleading for minimum-wage and maximum-hour legislation was not helped by "dual federalism" either; his bugaboo was substantive due process, which inhibited *both* state and federal action. And what about the small businessman, pleading for a chance to compete? He must have shuddered when the Justices, returning to form, found the Knight Company's vast sugar monopoly immune from the antitrust laws by arguing that such regulation inhibited *production* (a state matter) rather than *commerce* (a federal matter).[19] Because no single state could possibly supervise an enterprise so gigantic, this decision spawned a "twilight zone" private sector that public agencies at all levels were unable to check and balance. Finally, there was the corporate executive, very often basing his charges only on what the traffic would bear: did "dual federalism" redound to his benefit? Surely yes, for while the theory enhances state power, *it does so mostly in a negative sense by undermining national power.* So "dual federalism" is the doctrine of private capital, bending, stretching, manipulating, or just plain prospering, but without government regulation all the same.

Today, "dual federalism" is a dead issue, and I shall presently describe how the homicide took place. But now is the time to look at the other side of the coin, the nationalist tradition.

"Federal judicial review"

Hand-in-hand with states' rights doctrine is countervailing nationalist doctrine; or perhaps it would be more accurate to paint this relationship as contrapuntal, because the two oftentimes mesh in various harmonic patterns depending on the political pressures they must absorb. Either way, nationalism has been every bit as pliable as states' rights from the standpoint of ideological content and factional endorsement. Its advocates have been known to switch sides at the promulgation of a Supreme Court desegregation order, while its adversaries have been known to switch sides with the rapidity of a congressional appropriation.

The grand architects of national supremacy doctrine were Alexander Hamilton, its chief theoretician, and John Marshall, its chief logician. Hamilton played a small role at Philadelphia, but the essays he published during the ratification debates[20] vaulted him to the forefront along with Madison as a prime exponent on the *federal* side. As Washington's Secretary of the Treasury, Hamilton contested Jefferson's states' rights proclivities at every turn, and he authored a paper on the constitutionality of the National Bank, which represents his most systematic and exhaustive treatment of the federal principle.[21]

The national government, he said, is sovereign with respect to its delegated powers; that sovereignty includes a wise choice of the means necessary to carry out legitimate goals, as the necessary and proper clause graphically conveys; the Constitution vests Congress with the great powers of taxation, currency control, and commerce regulation; therefore, Congress can extend credit, establish banks, and promote the general economic health of the nation by encouraging business enterprise; prosperity is power, and power is the aim of every great nation in the family of nations. If Jefferson's states' rights mirrored his infatuation with the simple, noncompetitive, agrarian life style, where each citizen possessed equal property shares, then Hamilton's nationalism mirrored his infatuation with complicated world affairs, where trade, manufacture, money, competence, leadership, and power were the cornerstones of the good life.

Marshall's jurisprudence was largely an effort to make Hamilton's constitutionalism more coherent in the light of specific political embroilments.[22] In the *McCulloch* decision, Congress's implied power to enact legislation "necessary and proper" for the exercise of delegated authority was approved, and when Maryland levied a tax on the Baltimore branch of the National Bank, Marshall invoked the supremacy clause to strike down the tax.[23] In the *Gibbons* decision, Congress's control over interstate commerce received broad and sympathetic interpretation, and a state law conflicting with federal commercial regulations was also voided under supremacy clause doctrine.[24] The pivotal assumption governing both these judgments was not that federal law is superior to state law; the Jeffersonians admitted the primacy of proper national action. The pivotal assumption lay in Marshall's contention that the *federal judiciary* could determine whether federal law and state law are in conflict, plus his corollary assertion that the *federal judiciary* could strike down state law where such conflicts emerge. This concept—"federal judicial review"[b]—was never delineated in so many words by the Framers; yet, *it is the backbone of contemporary federalism.* Under what circumstances did the Marshall Court articulate to the fullest this cardinal tenet of national supremacy?

In 1781 Lord Fairfax, a Virginian, died, leaving an extensive tract of land to his nephew, Denny Martin, an English citizen. States' rights sentiment, of course, has never been more intense than in those early days, and Virginia set about preventing Fairfax's properties from falling into "enemy" hands. By statutory order the estate was confiscated and eventually sold to one David Hunter. Martin sued before the Virginia Supreme Court, which, in what amounted to a hearing by formality, upheld the legislature's action.

Martin now took his case before the United States Supreme Court. On what grounds? The federal government had negotiated and ratified a treaty with England protecting against seizure all lands held in the victorious states by English subjects. The treaty, Martin argued, was part of the "supreme law of the land," Virginia's statute to the contrary notwithstanding. But by what right could he take his case from the state courts to the federal courts? Congress, in the Judiciary Act of 1789, had authorized the Supreme Court to receive cases from the state courts on questions involving interpretation of the Constitution. On that basis Martin pressed his claim, and the Justices reversed the Virginia courts, finding the treaty had indeed preempted contradictory state policy.

A most peculiar series of developments ensued. The state of Virginia went back to its own supreme court to ask: What right did the federal courts have to declare our laws null and void? This was a patent usurpation of states' rights, the argument ran. And Virginia's highest court concurred! The supremacy clause, the tribunal said, mandates only that "the Judges in every State shall be bound" to obey appropriate federal law, but whether federal law *is* appropriate was a question to be answered, as Virginia saw things, by the state court. Federal law was supreme, then, only to the extent that state courts believed the national government had properly construed its own powers. According to this logic, Congress had no authority whatsoever to vest the Supreme Court with supervisory control over state policy; therefore, the Justices' decision in favor of Martin's land claims was unconstitutional! Here was the Kentucky and Virginia Resolutions argument without frills or apologies.

But the United States Supreme Court had the last word. In a memorable opinion by Mr. Justice Story (Marshall's intellectual alter ego), the notion of "federal judicial review" achieved recognition for all time.[25] The Constitution, said Story, was created by *the people* in order to form *a more perfect Union,* as

[b] I use this term in contradistinction to "pure judicial review," where the court declares an act of a co-equal branch unconstitutional.

the language of the Preamble made abundantly evident. The states had not created the Constitution and therefore retained no inherent veto power over federal actions. Owing no debts whatsoever to the states except as certain constitutional language specifically spells out, Congress can expand or contract the Supreme Court's appellate jurisdiction virtually at will. Nothing in the document limited this jurisdiction to cases heard originally in federal tribunals; indeed, had Congress not established lower federal tribunals, courts of first instance would *have had to be* state courts. And then Story enunciated the underlying premise of "federal judicial review":

> If there were no revising authority to control these jarring and discordant [state court] judgments, and harmonize them into uniformity, the laws, the treaties and the constitution of the United States would be different, in different States, and might, perhaps, never have precisely the same construction, obligation or efficiency, in any two states.[26]

Story's logic, though it prevailed, was not inevitable. States' rights enthusiasts had their logic, too. For instance, as Jefferson fought "pure judicial review," so he fought "federal judicial review." Neither the states nor the national "political branches" should be deprived of reading and interpreting the Constitution within their respective spheres, he believed. If all doubts were to be resolved in favor of elected officials over appointed officials, then all doubts were to be resolved in favor of state action over federal action. Calhoun, on the other hand, would presumably have endorsed Virginia's reserved right to secede in the face of hostile national caprice, such as was manifested by the Judiciary Act of 1789. The "dual federalist," a post-Civil War ideologue, approved "federal judicial review," but he might well have said in response to Denny Martin's protestations: both real property policy and inheritance policy are reserved to the states; the treaty between England and the United States violates the Tenth Amendment; it is therefore unconstitutional.[27]

A final comment about Hamilton, Marshall, and nationalist theory. The federal principle they endorsed, which included heavy emphasis on the necessary and proper clause implemented by "federal judicial review," left considerable play for states' rights. Said Hamilton: Congress cannot erect a corporation for governing the police of the city of Philadelphia, because Congress has no delegated authority to regulate the police of Philadelphia.[28] And said Marshall: The national government has only "limited" powers, which are "enumerated" (*McCulloch*), and these do not embrace "commerce which is *completely internal,* which is carried on between man and man *in a state* . . . and which does not *extend to* or *affect* other states" (*Gibbons:* italics mine). Their bugaboo was state power that might interfere with the national integrity, and this integrity, to repeat, hinged upon national policy which would promote and protect private property interests.

National supremacy in full flower

I have suggested many times that the Great Depression changed the course of American constitutional politics. Nowhere is this more apparent than with respect to federal-state relations. The New Deal was not *antistate,* but F.D.R.'s brand of twentieth-century liberalism was certainly *pronational.* How did the Roosevelt Court undermine the "dual federalism" jurisprudence it inherited?

Throughout the early part of the present century, the fight for a states' rights philosophy fertile enough to countenance vast police power experimentation was taken up by Justices Holmes and Brandeis. They opposed the use of judicial review ("pure" and "federal") to foist substantive due process on popularly elected decision-makers grappling with private affairs affecting the public welfare. For example, when New York State authorized a ten-hour maximum work day for bakers, the Court ruled the statute invalid because it deprived employers and employees of their *liberty* to contract mutually acceptable on-the-job conditions. Said Holmes in dissent:

> This case is decided upon an economic theory which a large part of the country does not entertain. . . . [The] Constitution is not intended to embody a particular economic theory, whether of paternalism . . . or of *laissez faire.* . . . I think that the word liberty in the Fourteenth Amendment is perverted when it is held to prevent the natural outcome of a dominant opinion (absent extenuating circumstances).[29]

Years later, the Justices voided a state gasoline tax when applied to the sale of fuel to the United States Coast Guard. A majority thought the levy might compromise the sovereignty of the federal government, just as it had thought applying the federal income tax to state employees might undermine state sovereignty. Said Holmes once more in dissent: "The power to tax is not the power to destroy while this Court sits."[30] In short, John Marshall's epigram must not be blown out of proportion to fetter the reasonable exercise of state police power. And when the Court knocked down an Oklahoma law requiring businesses selling ice to obtain a license, Mr. Justice Brandeis got in his licks:

> To stay experimentation in things social and economic is a grave responsibility. . . . It is one of the happy incidents of the federal system that a single courageous State may, if its citizens choose, serve as a laboratory; and try novel social and economic experiments without risk to the rest of the country. . . . We may strike down the statute . . . on the ground that . . . the measure is . . . unreasonable. . . . [But] if we would guide by the light of reason, we must let our minds be bold.[31]

This celebrated passage embodies a commitment to majority rule, to pragmatism, to the marketplace of ideas, and to a dynamic states' rights capable of articulating rational goals for communal self-interest, absent controlling federal policy.

The Holmes–Brandeis message laid a solid intellectual groundwork for the

Roosevelt Court. Judicial deference to state experimentation outside the civil liberties arena became the watchword. A state minimum wage law for women and minors was upheld, because the use of private property in the form of "sweatshop conditions" might reasonably be considered contrary to the public interest.[32] A state tax levied on citizens generally was found constitutional with respect to federal employees, because no meaningful burden had been placed on *government* per se. In fact, the Court took a very liberal view of both state tax policy impinging upon federal interests and federal tax policy impinging upon state interests. The Justices were more concerned with whether the revenue-raising programs satisfied legitimate social ends (such as generating public monies on an equitable basis) than with whether the ghost of political sovereignty was somehow being undercut.[33] And when South Carolina said motor trucks using state highways could not weigh in excess of 20,000 pounds, the Court approved this regulation as well. Congress, said Mr. Justice Stone, had passed no preemptive legislation in aid of its commerce power, the subject matter was essentially local rather than national, and South Carolina's statute did not discriminate in favor of intrastate over interstate traffic.[c] Minimum state standards for highway use are as defensible as state control over rivers and harbors, state fish and game requirements, and state quarantine laws.[34] The terms "police power" and "health, safety, morals, and welfare" have never received broader definition.

Then why all the fuss today about castrated states? Because there is a genuine fear that since national power now receives virtually unlimited interpretation, the states will serve only as administrative units in the field once Washington swings into high gear. Does the post-Depression Supreme Court's jurisprudence support this perception of federalism's "Living Constitution"?

The commerce power

A fair appraisal must emphasize Congress's control over interstate commerce, because this provision has been a predicate for the most wide-ranging policy thrusts essayed by contemporary liberals and tested in court. In 1938, the Fair Labor Standards Act became national law. A direct challenge to judicial precedent, it banned the employment of children under sixteen in all mining and manufacturing activities carried out by firms whose goods traveled across state boundaries. A totally different Supreme Court overruled that precedent in so many words and upheld these regulations unequivocally.[35]

Mr. Justice Stone's opinion captures the essence of present-day national supremacy. *First:* Regulation of interstate relations extends not only to fostering and protecting commerce but also to prohibiting noxious articles and antisocial activities from that commerce. Stone cited earlier congressional bans on lottery tickets and on impure foods which had been enacted to keep interstate

[c] The modern-day Court will not allow states to disparage out-of-state goods and services in order to satisfy the home folks. State tariffs in any form are now beyond the pale.

channels from being compromised and had been approved by the courts. *Second:* With respect to the argument that Congress was merely using the commerce power as a convenient tool to supervise matters of *state* concern, Stone said the motives and purposes prompting regulation were beyond judicial inquiry, unless a specific constitutional provision had been impinged. Congress's public policy was to proscribe merchandise produced under substandard labor conditions, and this policy could be applied through the commerce power. *Third:* Armed with the necessary and proper clause, Congress can regulate the production of *all* goods manufactured by firms doing business in interstate commerce, whether or not the goods actually leave the state. Legislative power "extends to those activities intrastate which so affect interstate commerce . . . as to make regulation of them appropriate means to the attainment of a legitimate end. . . ."[36] *Fourth:* What about the Tenth Amendment? Said Stone: "The amendment states but a truism that all is retained which has not been surrendered."[37] And the entire spectrum of delegated powers enumerated in the Constitution as well as the vast reservoir of implied power enumerated in shorthand form by the necessary and proper provision had been surrendered! "Dual federalism" was now a memory.

But just how great is Congress's reach if it can manipulate control over commerce among the states to get at commerce within a state? The answer was not long in coming. With an eye to controlling wheat prices, Congress imposed quotas for all wheat producers. If they worked too much land—thus driving supply up and price down—they could be fined. One farmer harvested twenty-three acres solely to feed his own cattle; *none* of the merchandise was shipped interstate. This was double the amount of acreage allotted him, and he was obliged under the law to pay a fine. The Supreme Court confirmed the constitutionality of this scheme, unanimously finding that his twenty-three acre contribution directly affected interstate markets. If each and every wheat grower plowed beyond his quota to provide for his own needs, Congress's price-stabilization policy would be a shambles. And the Court was not about to base constitutional distinctions on the number of acres harvested in violation of reasonable statutory guidelines.[38]

Taken together, these rulings vest Congress with what amounts to a *national police power.* The legislative branch may use the commerce clause to lay down social and economic programs that a consensus believes would promote the public welfare. And in the era of post-Depression liberalism, those programs tend to place limitations on private property so as to provide minimal protection for the financial have-nots. A list of the policy innovations wrought by the sum of "commerce power + implied power + supremacy clause" would be endless. There are national minimum-wage standards and national maximum-hour standards, a national labor-management mediation service, and a national "bill of rights" for the individual union member; and these are a mere indication of legislative control over only one segment of the national buying and selling marketplace, employer-employee relations. To be sure, not all employers have union help, and not all employees fall under minimum-wage-maximum-hour standards. But these circumstances stem almost entirely from national legislative and administrative self-abnegation. Where are the Supreme Court decisions saying that this segment of labor-management affairs is immune from federal control because state jurisdiction would be attenuated? There were none in the contemporary literature—that is, until 1976.[39]

The taxing power

The authority to tax provides Congress with another means to run roughshod over traditional state prerogatives. Though early attempts ran afoul of "dual federalism," today this power has assumed massive proportions, and its potential has hardly been tapped.

As long ago as the turn of the century, the Court tacitly admitted that Congress could levy taxes whose dominant effect was not to raise money but simply to promote a particular policy.[40] The protective tariff constituted an early case in point, its revenue-producing function clearly incidental to keeping away unwanted foreign competition. Today, though, the social goals deemed worthy of cultivation again tend to resemble a modern-day Jeffersonian's platform.

Suppose Congress passed a law taxing all owners of "Saturday night specials" $5,000 per year. Or a law taxing all factories at the rate of $5,000 per *x* amount of noise and air pollution they emitted per year. Would these enactments be approved in the courts? Why not? The taxing power is complete and unequivocal on its own terms, and the fact that Congress was really regulating conduct rather than raising revenue would provide no countervailing constitutional ammunition.[41] But suppose Congress imposed a $5,000 levy on each woman who had an abortion? This would not pass muster because the right to obtain an abortion is now constitutionally protected by the right of privacy. The only check against the taxing authority beyond the Bill of Rights, and the real reason why prohibitive levies such as I have hypothesized above are rarely tried, is the *political* check, the state and local folkways that are so dominant in the electoral schemes by which representatives and senators achieve office.

The spending power

Finally, we come to Congress's power to *spend for the general welfare.* This clause has remained virtually untested in the courtroom, although its impact on the "Living Constitution" has been extraordinary, as I shall demonstrate later. In the present context, however, I am concerned with the provision's jurisprudential standing, and, hence, its potential as a constitutional lever for post-Depression national policy-making in our federal system.

We can agree at the outset that the legislative branch infrequently spreads good will among private citizens by handing them money for their own good.

One rare instance would be Franklin Roosevelt's A.A.A., which tendered farmers financial grants for not producing crops. These subsidies, it was said, enhanced the general welfare. The Supreme Court threw the law out, finding that the money grants were not voluntary—that is, the government cannot exercise coercion in distributing financial gifts. "The power to confer or withhold unlimited benefits is the power to coerce or destroy."[42] Assuming this general proposition has validity, where was the coercion? No farmer had to participate in the "triple A" program. But the Justices thought Congress must either give the money to all concerned with no strings attached or give the money to none.

The A.A.A. decision has never been specifically overruled, but all the blood has been drained from its veins. When New Deal congressmen drafted plans for funding an unemployment-compensation system, the lawmakers tried a new approach, the "tax offset." Congress levied a tax on employers' payrolls, but the employers could avoid contributing if they subsidized an unemployment-compensation kitty established by the state. Ordinarily, an individual state might be reluctant to set up such a program, because businesses would probably gravitate elsewhere. With the Congress snapping up the monies in any event, though, a state would be foolish to sit idly by and not divert the tax revenues for its own use. The term "tax offset," then, makes reference to the federal government's revenue-raising initiatives that entice the states into enacting policies so they can deflect the flow of dollars from national to state treasuries. But was all this constitutional?

The key question was whether the states were being coerced through temptation. The Court thought not—indeed, they were only too happy to take their fair share. Massive unemployment had become a national calamity; Congress could spend money to alleviate that calamity; instead of unilaterally priming the pump, the legislature might enlist state participation by, in effect, holding out the apple of federal dollars. The statute was approved on this basis.[43]

The practical political lessons flowing from this ruling are significant indeed. The first is that Congress almost always spends for the general welfare by giving money to states, cities, and other governmental units. The second is that Congress usually exacts a pound of flesh when disbursing gifts. Today, state and local governments normally are required to keep detailed records, pay out funds only for specific purposes, employ workers who meet minimal standards of competence, and so on. Few critics would argue that the recipients have a valid gripe, since they pant to receive the bounty. The third is that the federal-state financial funnel almost entirely precludes judicial participation in general-welfare policy-making. Under well-known *jurisdictional and standing* criteria, the odds against framing test cases are very great. Should a state argue that its Tenth Amendment powers are being undermined by subsidies so plentiful they cannot be refused, the Court will say: "That purpose may be effectively frustrated by the simple expedient of not yielding."[44] Where there is no controversy, of course, there is no jurisdiction. Should a citizen argue that tax funds are being given away for a purpose unrelated to the general welfare, the Court will say: "His interest . . . is comparatively minute and indeterminable. . . . If one taxpayer may champion and litigate such a cause, then every other taxpayer may also do the same."[45] Where the litigant fails to assert meaningful personal interest, of course, there is no standing.

The dominant inquiry throughout this section has been: Does the post-Depression Supreme Court's jurisprudence support a conception of national power that, if implemented to the full, might well turn the states into administrative lions jumping through the hoops of federal policy formation? Based on our review of commerce power, taxing power, and spending power doctrine, the answer must be a resounding *yes*.

Federalism and due process

In the preceding account of national-state interplay, the word "national" was more often than not synonymous with "congressional." But if we seek a complete constitutional definition of federalism, we must also consider the extent to which individual rights guaranteed by our fundamental law are binding on the states. This subject matter, naturally, is the stuff of judicial politics.

The Bill of Rights was drafted by the Jeffersonians to check potentially oppressive central government, and so Chief Justice Marshall had no trouble limiting the Bill's scope to *federal* action.[46] Arbitrary national power is constrained by the national Constitution, he thought, and arbitrary state power by the state constitutions. Neither Hamiltonians nor Jeffersonians found much fault with that approach.

However, when the Civil War buried state sovereignty, the fundamental nature of citizenship in this country was inevitably changed. The Constitution, for some strange reason, had said nothing about citizenship. Hence the entire matter had been handled at the state level; any individual who met standards set up by state X automatically became a citizen of that state as well as the United States.[d] But with states now relegated to subordinate position, their criteria for citizenship could logically no longer control national citizenship, and the triumphant Unionists well understood this. The prevailing rule now abides in the Fourteenth Amendment: individuals hold national citizenship if they are born in the United States,[e] and they hold state citizenship if they reside there. The former criterion sees an irrevocable bond between person and community; the latter sees a malleable bond easily established and easily broken, clearly the attributes of a secondary relationship. By what strained logic, then, could the states ignore and perhaps trample upon personal liberties inherent in citizenship, freedoms guaranteed by the custodian of that citizenship, the federal Constitution?

In Chapters 2 and 4 I noted the importance of the *Slaughter-House Cases*[47] (see pp. 45, 113 for details). In that ruling, the Justices refused to legitimize the

[d] Exception: Congress had the delegated power to naturalize aliens—that is, to turn them into citizens by appropriate legislation. But those rules were applicable only to immigrants, as is largely the case today.

[e] Exception: Children born in the United States over whom the national government has no jurisdiction—for example, the offspring of foreign diplomats.

constitutional and political changes brought about by the Civil War, for they emasculated the crucial section of the Fourteenth Amendment that said no state shall deprive individuals of the privileges and immunities they held by virtue of their United States citizenship. According to the Court, *the Bill of Rights was not among those privileges and immunities;* the states retained all the inherent power they possessed before the war to hack away at individual liberties guaranteed by the Constitution. That interpretation still stands. However, as I have said many times, by and large the provisions found in the first ten amendments are now binding on the states as well. I will explain how this came about and why the results have had enormous consequences for federalism.

Around the year 1880, a Mr. Hurtado was tried and convicted on a murder charge in the California courts, but neither the state criminal code nor the state constitution contained a guarantee of indictment by grand jury. Hurtado appealed to the Supreme Court, not on grounds that his Fifth Amendment grand jury right was denied, but on grounds that his trial had violated the *due process provision* of the *Fourteenth Amendment.* Hurtado's claim was that (1) the grand jury is ingrained in the English common law, (2) the term "due process of law" contains all of the *procedural* rights guaranteed by the common law, (3) the Fourteenth Amendment has applied due process to state action.

But his argument failed.[48] For one thing, the Justices denied that the grand jury provision could be part of due process because the Framers had prescribed *both* benefits independently in the Bill of Rights. Furthermore, the Justices felt due process was essentially a guarantee of *fairness,* and fairness was an ever-evolving conception varying with the state of the civilized order. To freeze due process in the precise trappings of the common law would "stamp upon our jurisprudence the unchangeableness attributed to the laws of the Medes and Persians."[49] Although the Court admitted there were certain "fundamental principles of liberty and justice which lie at the base of all our civil and political institutions"[50] and which could not be washed away by the tides without abridging due process, evidently, the grand jury failed to meet that test.

Three decades later, the Justices were asked to read the self-incrimination provision into due process and, hence, make it obligatory upon state action. They could have followed *Hurtado,* for protection against self-incrimination is also specifically guaranteed by the Fifth Amendment. But the notion of *substantive* due process had since emerged, and the Court was now much more receptive to claims of individual rights. Said a majority: Due process might well include certain fundamental freedoms enumerated in the Constitution, but only because they are *fundamental,* not because they are so enumerated. This clever maneuver avoided the extreme position taken in *Hurtado* without overruling that position.[f] But was the check against self-incrimination a funda-

[f] I must reemphasize that the Court would have never gotten itself boxed in on this point if another precedent—the *Slaughter-House Cases*—were not lying around inhibiting the use of "privileges and immunities." Remember, the Fifth Amendment may contain a due process clause, *but it does not contain a privileges and immunities clause.*

mental procedural principle inherent in the criminal justice systems common to free societies? No! It, like the grand jury, was merely an artifact of Anglo-American evidentiary proceedings.[51]

The *Twining* doctrine stood until the 1960s, though the Justices were extraordinarily imprecise about how to apply it. For instance, in 1925, the Court said that freedom of speech could not be limited unless due process were afforded;[52] in 1931, freedom of press attained due process status with the famous Minnesota censorship case;[53] in 1934, the free exercise of religion clause was inserted;[54] thus, all three cases became constraints upon state action. Now, without doubt freedom of speech, press, and religion are fundamental but, by definition, cannot be considered part of *procedural due process.* What, after all, does the censorship issue have to do with a fair hearing? Probably the only way to justify including them within the Fourteenth Amendment's due process clause would be via *substantive* due process. And considering the Court's love affair with "liberty of contract," this course seems to have been exactly what the judicial branch had in mind, though that conclusion is strictly a matter of inference.

Meanwhile, the Court even found a situation or two in which state policy had unduly slighted segments of the Bill of Rights designed to shield pristine *procedural* liberties. The best example involved the Scottsboro boys—young, illiterate blacks—who were found guilty of raping two white girls and sentenced to death. The defendants had pleaded not guilty, but they were given no legal advice until the morning of the trial. Hewing closely to *Twining,* the Justices said that the right of counsel had been violated, *not because that right appeared in the Sixth Amendment, but because, given the particular facts of the case, fundamental fairness had been abridged.*

> All that it is necessary to decide . . . is that in a capital case, where the defendant is unable to employ counsel, and is incapable adequately of making his own defense because of ignorance, feeble mindedness, illiteracy, or the like, it is the duty of the court, whether requested or not, to assign counsel.[55]

But when an older, more experienced person was charged with a noncapital felony and made the master of his own defense, the Justices said that due process had *not* been violated.[56] So under some circumstances states could be called on the carpet for abridging the right to counsel, but under other circumstances that right—*always* applicable to federal action under the Sixth Amendment—could be ignored at the state level. And how did the Supreme Court presume to draw the line? The question was whether the states had violated "the very essence of a scheme of ordered liberty . . . 'rooted in the traditions and conscience of our people' . . . [whose absence would be] so acute and shocking that our polity will not endure it."[57] Of course, this was only an elaborate rehash of *Twining* rhetoric.

Why did these developing standards of Fourteenth Amendment due process interpretation hold tremendous consequences for federalism? All the Justices believed that there existed fundamental precepts of personal liberty inherent in the individual's relationship with government. The Congress could not violate these rules, nor could the states. But where were these norms? Evidently, the judge, as student of history, sociology, psychology, philosophy, and constitutionalism, must interpret the signs and symbols of *national community* and cull from them the mainsprings of individual freedom in a social context. Justice Holmes did not think "liberty of contract" measured up, but he certainly thought states were held to "fundamental principles as they have been understood by the traditions of our people and our law."[58] And when California police walked into a Mr. Rochin's house in search of drugs (without a warrant, incidentally), saw him devouring capsules, and rushed him to a hospital where doctors flushed out the incriminating contents via stomach pumping, Mr. Justice Frankfurter wrote for the Court:

> We are compelled to conclude that the proceedings by which this conviction was obtained do more than offend some fastidious squeamishness or private sentimentalism about combatting crime too energetically. This is conduct that shocks the conscience.[59]

Whose conscience was Frankfurter talking about? Not his own, and not the conscience of a transient majority, we may surmise. Again, he must have had in mind the typical reasonable and prudent person of this and other years, people attuned to our customs, our folkways, and the national community standards of fair play we share with other civilized, free societies. Within that framework states might devise *their own community standards,* experimenting as they wished, even omitting from their jurisprudence the grand jury, the protection against self-incrimination, trial by jury, and those attributes of right to counsel not deemed fundamental. But freedom of speech, "liberty of contract," and basic features of right of counsel protection—*in short, the procedural and substantive freedoms a Court majority considered intrinsic to individual liberty*—had attained, at least for a time, immunity from state as well as federal manipulation.

So the central issue comes down to the distinction between national community standards versus state community standards, specifically the extent to which individual rights enumerated in the Constitution carry less weight in *subordinate* political jurisdictions. Does this anomalous phenomenon ring a bell? I believe we have here a subtle variation on the "dual federalism" theme. How else can one define a constitutional politics that had been purged of state sovereignty through civil war, had spawned a Fourteenth Amendment in the war's aftermath, and yet allowed states' rights to override express "rules of the game"?

The New Deal, which, we know, killed off "liberty of contract," also prompted a drive to nationalize the Bill of Rights. Mr. Justice Hugo Black led the fight, developing what has been called the theory of *incorporation.* In brief, Black contended that the Framers of the Fourteenth Amendment had meant to incorporate the Bill of Rights within the privileges and immunities clause.

When this tactic failed,[g] Black turned to a new twist on *substantive due process* as a crutch for incorporation. He argued that the Bill of Rights was part and parcel of due process, *not because these liberties were intrinsically fundamental but because they were enumerated in the Constitution.* (Note: This proposition is the converse of the *Twining* principle.) Once more, Black relied heavily on the intent of those who drafted the Fourteenth Amendment,[60] but the historical record is blurred at best.[61] Thus far, the Court has refused to accept "incorporation," probably for two reasons: (1) The theory rests on substantive due process, which the Frankfurterians have opposed in virtually all its manifestations, (2) The theory has been considered too drastic in the light of our divided sovereignty presuppositions, because one can readily distinguish among these guarantees on grounds of importance, impact, and general acceptance.

So the fundamental issue remained: What is the appropriate balance between federal and state community standards with respect to formulating civil liberties norms? The solution has been a compromise of sorts. The Warren Court espoused what has been called the theory of *absorption:* each segment in the Bill of Rights is judged on its own merits; if the segment is considered primary, it is absorbed by Fourteenth Amendment due process and made applicable in toto to state action; if the segment is considered secondary, it is not absorbed and thus remains totally inapplicable to state action.

There was a pronounced tendency to absorb during the Warren years, as befitted the libertarian (egalitarian?) preferences of the consensus and as befits the larger evolution toward national power since Depression days. For example, in the *Gideon* case,[62] the Justices absorbed the right to counsel in all felony cases no matter what the facts. And in the *Ker* decision,[63] the Justices absorbed the Fourth Amendment lock, stock, and barrel, including the controversial "exclusionary rule." Today, there are few provisions in the Bill of Rights that have failed the absorption test. One is the grand jury requirement, and another is the rule mandating a jury trial in civil cases where more than $20 is at stake, unless the defendant enters a waiver. But the protection against self-incrimination, the double jeopardy rule, and the cruel and unusual punishment clause are now entirely obligatory at the state level.

The Court, naturally, does not label the absorption doctrine a compromise, but it has enunciated theory to justify the shift from *Twining* and similar cases. I quote from Mr. Justice White's opinion absorbing the Sixth Amendment's trial by jury guarantee.

> Earlier the Court . . . asked . . . if a civilized system could be imagined that would not accord the particular protection. . . . [Now the Court asks whether] state criminal processes . . . bearing virtually every characteristic of the common-law system [require] a particular procedure . . . whether, that is, a procedure is necessary to an Anglo-American regime of ordered liberty.[64]

We see here the self-professed pragmatic temperament underlying the larger

[g] Not even the Warren Court would reopen the *Slaughter-House Cases.* The Justices treat the privileges and immunities clause the way they treat the Ninth Amendment—they pretend it doesn't exist—and for the very same reason, the fear of opening a Pandora's box.

movement by twentieth-century liberalism to demolish "dual federalism" and substitute a theory of national supremacy. Specifically, the Justices eschew abstractions and zero in on what will make our particular system of liberty and justice measure up, given our own particular traditions.[h] Just as a national sense of community can now move Congress to pass legislation in the public interest, state opinion to the contrary notwithstanding, so a national sense of community can now move the Court to apply basic liberties across the board, state opinion to the contrary notwithstanding. And if this generalization expresses the temper and mood of contemporary constitutional law, one wonders, again—assuming that states' rights is still a viable doctrine—to what subject matter does it extend?

With all this talk of a modern-day substantive due process, it is important to note that procedural due process is still alive and kicking. An excellent case study involves the rights now accorded minors, traditionally regarded under the law as subject to whatever tender loving care or discipline the state (as surrogate parent) bestowed. Juveniles may no longer be incarcerated unless a fair hearing is provided, including timely notice of charges, representation by counsel, the privilege against self-incrimination, and the right to cross-examine witnesses,[65] but excluding trial by jury.[66] And school authorities, before they suspend juveniles for "more than a trivial period," must spell out the allegations of wrongdoing, present the evidence upon which such allegations are based, and provide the accused an opportunity for rebutting these allegations.[67] Clearly, the hearing rights guaranteed are much more extensive where incarceration may result than where suspension from school hangs in the balance. That is because fundamental fairness—the basic thrust of procedural due process—takes on a different coloration as the alleged deprivations of liberty and property assume different forms.

The grant-in-aid: federalism, post-New Deal style

One can now begin to obtain some feel for the great debate over sovereignty and community around which the constitutional politics of federalism revolves. But a nation-state could not survive two hundred years of such discourse and struggle if incessant hostility were the whole story. In fact, responsible advocates on all sides—pragmatists first and ideologues second, in true American

[h] I must say, however, that I think Mr. Justice White has misread the *Twining* progeny. He is charging both Mr. Justice Cardozo, who wrote the *Palko* "double jeopardy" holding (note 57), and Mr. Justice Frankfurter, who wrote the "stomach-pump" holding, with an excessive concern for "abstractions." That allegation is spurious. These jurists were not concerned with how hypothetical civilized societies conducted their affairs but with how our particular society conducted its affairs when judged against the behavior and traditions of comparable societies as well as our own.

What we really have here is the difference between "old-style" and "new-style" twentieth-century liberalism. Justices Frankfurter and Brandeis approved a meaningful state laboratory system and the general notion of judicial self-restraint. "New style" liberalism, epitomized here by the Warren Court, has no particular interest in the state laboratory concept because it has no particular concern for the state as a meaningful political community (as I shall demonstrate later in this chapter); and certainly "new-style" liberalism has no particular interest in judicial modesty. *The fundamental question* (which I also debate later in this chapter) *is whether one can have a meaningful state laboratory system without resurrecting "dual federalism."*

fashion—realize that a country cannot be run on dogma or without shared responsibility. This very healthy sign of *national community* is, perhaps, what underlies the "Living Constitution" of federalism.

What does shared responsibility mean in macrocosm? Morton Grodzins has remarked:

> The federal system is not accurately symbolized by a neat layer cake of . . . distinct and separate planes. A far more realistic symbol is that of the marble cake. Wherever you slice through it you reveal an inseparable mixture of differently colored ingredients. There is no neat horizontal stratification. Vertical and diagonal lines almost obliterate the horizontal ones, and in some places there are unexpected whirls and an imperceptible merging of colors.[68]

And as Daniel Elazar has shown, "marble cake" politics has a long and distinguished history in this country.[69] Congress began to subsidize free public education as long ago as 1785 by ceding millions of federally owned acres to state and local communities—the term *land grant college* is older than the Constitution! In 1808 Congress appropriated $200,000 to help the states develop their militias. And "marble cakism" cost the federal taxpayer roughly $100 million per year between World War I and the New Deal, with highway construction, vocational education, and agricultural extension services leading the way.[70] Thus a clear pattern was formed years before national supremacy emerged as the conventional wisdom. The embodiment of marble cake was the *grant-in-aid*—"sums of money given by the federal government to lower levels of government in order to finance the performance of specified functions."[71]

Federal gifts to the states proliferated under F.D.R.'s leadership, and *cooperative federalism* was born. The federal government drafts the policy and supplies the cash, while the states provide tactical follow-through in labor and implementation. The Supreme Court in our time is rarely even called upon to rethink the Roosevelt Court's endorsement of such initiatives.

New Deal programs included unemployment compensation, old-age benefits, Aid to Families with Dependent Children (A.F.D.C.), and a public-housing program complete with monies for slum clearance. The big change was not so much the level of funding or even the new policy areas funded; rather, for the first time, national government began to attach significant strings in the form of mandatory state reciprocity. For example, stiff matching requirements were instituted (typically, a state had to provide one dollar for every dollar received). Nor could states participate in the social security apparatus unless their support employees were chosen by merit system guidelines.

Today, grants-in-aid are almost too numerous to itemize (Michael Reagan gives the figure 530 as of 1970),[72] as are the areas of concern. The big items are health, highways, education, and community development (for example, the war on poverty and aid to Appalachia), but welfare ranks first, costing, as of 1970, more than $7 billion—more than the price tag for *all* grants-in-aid in 1961. The total 1971 appropriation for gifts was a cool $30 billion, 25 percent of all federal domestic expenditures, and the ceiling is nowhere in sight. Indeed, demand for the national dollar is now so severe, and state funds lag so far behind national resources, that whatever assumptions about equal partnership may have fueled "cooperative federalism" are no longer meaningful. The 1967 data show that approximately 150 grants were funded entirely by the federal government, while only about 90 grants were supported as much by state and local monies as by gifts from Washington.[73] Let's look closer.

President Lyndon Johnson's "creative federalism," a term coined by Nelson Rockefeller,[74] represented an important departure from the usual central-government activism. Rather than showering the states with gifts, "creative federalism" ignored the states entirely. Not that Johnson suggested scrapping the traditional grant-in-aid, but he did propose going directly to the *cities* and to *private groups,* check in hand.

The general idea was not new, of course. At the turn into the nineteenth century, Congress funneled monies to local communities to establish a public-school system, and by the year 1867 it had bestowed 184 million acres on the burgeoning railroad industry. But against a background of federal-state handholding, Johnson's rhetoric seemed radical even in theory. Why the departure? First, with regard to national-local relationships: the cities were moving inexorably toward financial disaster, as their tax bases became tenuous in the wake of the "white flight" to the suburbs; furthermore, the cities contained seemingly impenetrable pockets of unemployment and poverty; finally, the cities began to go up in smoke. Second, as regards national-private sector relationships: disadvantaged groups were clamoring to control their own communities; moreover, with private industry already under contract to meet the federal government's essential research needs, it seemed logical enough to put corporations into the "good works" arena as well.

If one must distinguish between "cooperative" and "creative" federalism, one must also distinguish between "formula grants" and "project grants." Under formula grants, monies are distributed to all eligible recipients on the basis of predetermined criteria. A typical example is Aid to Families with Dependent Children—and most other welfare programs as well—where Congress automatically matches state allotments according to terms set out in the statutory scheme. In the case of A.F.D.C., the *larger* the state's per capita income, the *greater* must be the state's contribution; therefore, Mississippi receives the most assistance and New York the least. The federal bureaucracy has no discretion to pick and choose among applicants; Washington's influence comes only through whatever strings are attached via the legislative process.

Project grants are far more numerous than the formula variety (Reagan reports that 430 out of 530 grants-in-aid are of this species),[75] although, as of 1970, the federal dollar was divided equally between them. Under the project concept, money is parceled out by federal-government bureaus to those applicants who make the best case for their pet proposals. And the trend favors ever more project grants, because "creative federalism" now holds the apple out to both local governments and private groups, all the subsidies dispersed on a competitive basis.

How did "creative federalism" work in the 1960s? A large chunk of the "project" money went (and still goes) to the biggest metropolitan areas, where the chief aim is urban redevelopment. If a good-size city needed to improve its sewage collection, it went to the Department of Housing and Urban Development. Suppose, on the other hand, the community decided to mount a comprehensive attack on poverty in one particular neighborhood. If it put together a reform program designed to demonstrate what collective action could accomplish, the H.U.D., under the Model Cities Act, would give that program higher priority. "Model Cities" was truly what the architects of "creative federalism" envisioned: saving people by saving cities through research and development. Therefore, it is no accident that waging war on poverty often meant mobilizing quasi-autonomous community-action groups. Even profit-making concerns and universities got into the act as training centers and think tanks.

Now all the subsidies I have described thus far are called *categorical grants.* In other words, the federal government sets up policy categories (for example, housing rehabilitation, mental health), articulates guidelines for implementing each program, and hands out funds to solve particular problems. To a considerable degree, the more precise the category and the stiffer the guidelines, the greater the chance Washington will reap the rewards it seeks. Yet that is true only up to a point. A level of diminishing returns sets in ("hardening of the categories") when a plethora of departments issues a plethora of subsidies in the same general area. Furthermore, the federal bureaucracy takes a heavy toll of many well-charted and well-intentioned plans. It is hard to believe, but the Office of Education has juggled as many as eight separate programs authorized by six different laws aimed at underwriting public libraries.[76] This is excessive incrementalism, preventing the donor from engaging in serious planning and the recipient from engaging in reasonable discretionary implementation. Summing up a common grievance voiced by state and local bodies during the 1960s, former North Carolina Governor Terry Sanford said Congress "enacts too many narrow . . . grant programs with stringent guidelines, unnecessary requirements, and burdensome reporting procedures. These lead to waste motion and ineffective administration."[77]

Such criticisms led the Johnson Administration to experiment with the "block grant." This device merely earmarks expenditures for one particular policy area and allows the cities and states to use the monies in whatever ways seem feasible. A leading example has been the Omnibus Crime Control and Safe Streets Act (1968). Instead of making separate applications for money to help curb criminal conduct piecemeal, the cities now can request a lump sum (which still contains matching requirements and administrative strings, of course) to use on anything from up-to-date computer systems, to police training manuals, to the prevention of civil disorders, to informer payoffs. And in 1974 Congress passed the Community Development Act, consolidating the Model Cities program, urban renewal, and sewage projects into one $3.2 billion block grant. Local officials had objected to money being given to private groups,[78] and they did not enjoy having to clear each segment of their Model Cities blueprints with the particular bureaucratic nest specializing in that grant. The result has been a significant shift in grassroots policy: community development programs, rather than striking out against inner-city blight, now seek to prevent marginal neighborhoods from deteriorating by building parking lots and tennis courts.

The block grant, then, allows the federal government to postulate broad policy preferences by deciding how much money should be spent on mass transportation, as opposed to, say, job retraining. But the block grant relieves state and local government officials of both the categorical straitjacket and the confusion of overlapping bureaucratic preserves, to meet their own particular problems with their own choice of weapons.

Revenue sharing: federalism, Nixon style

Soon after Richard Nixon entered the White House, he took his turn at reorienting our grasp of national-state relations through rhetorical glibness. "Cooperative" and "creative" federalism have failed, he announced; what the country needs is a "new federalism."

Stripped of all its trimmings, "new federalism" constituted a clear reaction against not only Great Society machinations but the whole foundation of post-New Deal federalism, the grant-in-aid. Raw statistics do not convey the full story. In 1965-66, a liberal Democratic Congress passed 136 important domestic measures, including 17 in the educational field and 21 in the health area.[79] Yet in 1969-70 (during Nixon's first two years as President), 143 new grants-in-aid were launched.[80] Simply to abolish cooperative federalism would have been political suicide. But Nixon did have a specific alternative: *revenue sharing.* Congress, bursting at the seams with monies produced from income taxes, would return funds to the state and local grassroots, many of which were financially strapped. Unlike block grants, use of these monies would not be limited even to broad policy categories. In effect, then, *federal revenues would subsidize state and local policy preferences, and that twist on the prevailing balance of power is antithetical to post-New Deal grant-in-aid philosophy.*

In 1972, Congress enacted the State and Local Fiscal Assistance Act. Known as the general revenue sharing law,[81] it commits over $30 billion to approximately 38,000 state, county, city, and town governments for a five-year period. According to the formula approved by Congress, the states get 33⅓ percent, the municipalities 40 percent, and the counties 20 percent, while the residue goes to townships and Indian tribes. Meanwhile, the cost of all grants-in-aid for 1972 alone was $33 billion. So while we are dealing here with a reorientation in "Living Constitutional" theory, the "Living Constitutional" facts with respect to how Washington funnels the lion's share of monies below did not change appreciably.

Looking at the statute's particulars, the student of politics naturally asks: Do certain states or cities gain at the expense of other states or cities? What biases exist in the sharing formula?

In computing revenue shares, the first step is to decide how much money will be channeled to each state. On this point, the Senate and House seemed stalemated. The Senate formula gave equal weight to population, tax effort, and individual income, while the House formula allotted extra points for both *urbanized* population and state *income tax* programs. Clearly, the House plan benefited heavily populated, industrial states; the Senate plan benefited the poorer, more rural states. Perhaps this split stemmed from the age-old difference in legislative branch constituency—the House represents numbers *within states* while the Senate represents *states*.

Enter the American proclivity for bargaining; each state was permitted to use whichever of the two formulas would yield it more money. In the end, thirty-one states opted for the Senate formula, with Mississippi the big gainer at 93.4 percent increase; twenty states used the House format, with the District of Columbia (counted here as a state) the big gainer at a 67.1 percent increase.

The next step in ascertaining who gets what is to decide how much money goes to local governments. The formula allocates one-third of each state's portion to the parent body and two-thirds to the localities. This 1-2 distribution scheme, which does not take into account population, discriminates against the inner cities, whose swollen numbers need the money most. In fiscal 1972, in fact, all categorical grants combined netted the states $27 billion and local governments only $6 billion; thus revenue sharing drastically reordered post-New Deal priorities with respect to which lower-level public officials come away with the most.[82]

Funds are divided among intrastate units in a two-stage process. Revenues are apportioned among all the counties, then townships and municipalities take their cut out of the county pie. At both stages the Senate three-item scheme (population, personal income, tax effort) prevails; so rural interests receive greater consideration within states as well as among states. However, the fiscal inequality between the central cities and their more affluent suburbs is narrowed somewhat.

Nor is Congress simply raking in taxes and returning them whence they came, for a redistribution process has taken place. Twenty-nine states are gainers, with Mississippi and the Dakotas getting back more than double what they put in; twenty-one states (and the District of Columbia) are losers, with Connecticut getting the worst end of the stick, receiving a $.57 return for each $1 expended. All in all, the states showing meager per capita income do very well, and the richer, urbanized states fare less well. This is precisely the phenomenon I described earlier with regard to welfare disbursements. However, states like New York and Massachusetts almost break even under revenue sharing, because their own tax efforts are so great.

How *can* the various public bodies spend their revenue shares—and how *have* they? The states were given a totally free hand; however, the blank check concept became watered down as some congressmen began to worry about according the cities carte blanche to provide social services. So local governments received complete freedom with respect to new capital outlays (facility construction, land purchases, equipment), but maintenance and operating expenses were confined to eight categories, including public safety and transportation. Of course, the various communities could always disburse revenue shares for traditional purposes and thus free other funds for whatever struck their fancy. At first most communities favored capital projects, such as putting up city office buildings or purchasing fire trucks. But when inflation skyrocketed, in the mid-1970s, operating costs received much more attention, with the states concentrating on education and the cities and towns zeroing in on transportation and public safety. Social services stand close to the bottom; only 4 percent of all funds are allocated for those needs. One problem is that the inner cities have so much trouble just making ends meet that they simply cannot open new policy doors. New York City's flirtation with bankruptcy is an extreme example of a national urban malaise.

Revenue sharing: constitutional lightning rod

The politics of revenue sharing constitutes a modern version of age-old battles over federalism. Hence, those interminable debates emerge as a dialogue over "Living Constitutional" rules when we examine revenue sharing in the light of diverse value assumptions.

One way to appraise revenue sharing is to judge it against Nixon's own purposes. We know, first, that the law was intended to decentralize political power. Armed with increased financial resources, state and local governments would do more of the things they considered vital; Congress could only do less. That general aim has surely been fulfilled. Indeed, Congress attached only two important strings to revenue sharing—no monies could be used for construction projects unless prevailing wage rates were observed, and no monies could be used for programs discriminating against persons because of their race, national origin, or sex. The restrictions illustrate an important constitutional fact of life: the national government is held increasingly accountable for every public act that might disparage either the working person or, even more important, commonly accepted civil rights goals.

Second, "new federalism" was supposed to promote systematic planning and better implementation. President Nixon considered grants-in-aid too narrow, because they were imprisoned by inflexible categories, and too much the province of a federal bureaucracy incapable of overseeing their effective administration. On both these counts, the revenue sharing law has been a disappointment. *Revenue sharing does not encourage comprehensive policy-making any more than grants-in-aid do.* Gifts are used either to maintain financial solvency or to make short-term improvements of a nuts and bolts variety. Furthermore, *revenue sharing does not enhance implementation to any meaningful degree.* There is no way in the world to ascertain whether the funds have been employed wisely or efficiently. Usually, the most that can be demonstrated is whether revenues have been spent consistent with the law.[83]

Another way of appraising revenue sharing involves the means Congress selected to accomplish particular ends. For example, the legislature, wanting an indicator of state and local fiscal capacity, chose the incomes of residents.

However, states raise money mostly through sales taxes, while cities and towns rely almost entirely on property taxes. So when revenue sharing rewards governmental tax effort, it is rewarding sales and property-tax initiatives, not levies on income. In other words, it is rewarding *regressive* fund-generating devices, which make only minimal allowance for *ability to pay.* If the way to assist less affluent communities is to place the burden on those communities generating top dollar, then the way to assist self-reliant communities is to place the burden on those communities that decline to tax top dollar. As things stand now, the populous states and cities need money—that is, they need *progressive* tax programs, which emphasize a levy on incomes; yet sales and property taxes have become ingrained to the point of achieving "Living Constitutional" status; and revenue sharing encourages the taxation status quo.

Still another way to appraise revenue sharing is to note carefully who gets what, the gut issue in power relations according to many political scientists. I have shown that funds are not returned to their source communities precisely as they emerged from those communities, though Congress could have readily accomplished a dollar-for-dollar recompense.

Revenue sharing, then, is hardly value-neutral with respect to "who": governments receive the money, not individuals or businesses; poorer communities benefit more than wealthier communities; poor rural communities benefit more than poorer urban communities. However, revenue sharing is supposed to be neutral as to "whats." But does the Chamber of Commerce expect state and local governments to lose any sleep over the needs of the corporations? Does the Urban League expect the state of Mississippi to lose any sleep over the plight of slum-dwelling blacks? Hardly. No wonder, then, that both the Chamber of Commerce and the Urban League opposed the 1972 revenue sharing package. They understood that value neutrality is sometimes an exercise in superficialities.

Finally, revenue sharing must be appraised from the standpoint of American constitutional theory and ideology. A convenient way to proceed is to line up advocates against critics. Conviction then becomes translated into empirically verifiable, far more manageable political reality.

In order to have gotten through a Democratic Congress, revenue sharing must have had considerable bipartisan support. Actually, many modern-day liberals in both parties endorsed the idea. The most articulate among these is probably Walter Heller, Lyndon Johnson's chairman of the Council of Economic Advisers. Writing well before Richard Nixon embraced the notion, Heller said:

> Far from being just a fiscal problem . . . the issue touches on the very essence of federalism, both in a political and in a socioeconomic sense. . . . Indeed, it is from the realm of political philosophy—the renewed interest in making state-local government a vital, effective and reasonably equal partner in a workable federalism—that much of the impetus for . . . new forms of federal assistance have come.[84]

> [The idea is] not simply to make [the states] better "service stations" of federalism but to release their creative and innovative energies. . . . State and local officials . . . need an opportunity to worry . . . about . . . what the world is coming to.[85]

Heller strongly supports the post–New Deal grant-in-aid system, for the usual reasons: Washington must provide basic social-service supplements to bolster the disadvantaged.[86] Yet he sees revenue sharing as an additional feature of today's federalism. Why?

At bottom, Heller's thesis represents a theory of *sovereignty.* The states have a unique role to play in American political life. The "Living Constitution" looks to a balance of power, of sovereignty divided between supreme national authority and an aggressive, healthy state system zealously protecting the public interest. This is the federalism of Louis Brandeis, of Felix Frankfurter, of Franklin Roosevelt. The states, as laboratories for democratic action, experiment, accumulate experience, and pass their findings on for adoption by others.

Of equal significance, Heller's thesis represents a theory of *community.* Regarding issues of war and peace, of employment and unemployment, of inflation and depression, Americans see themselves as Americans, as members of a national community. But regarding issues of public safety and sanitation, of recreation and social deportment, Americans view themselves as members of smaller communities. State and local governments are the smaller communities; they are closer to the people—more visible, more accessible, more comprehensible, and more cognizant of parochial customs, needs and interests.

But, as Heller sees things, in this era of political activism all the sovereign power and rich communal ties amount to nothing without money. K. C. Wheare has argued that federalism is not viable unless the respective governmental units (layers?) are economically secure and adaptive;[87] political independence, then, is predicated on economic independence, an argument bound to influence many twentieth-century liberals who see government's main domestic task as economic redistribution. Revenue sharing thus provides financial sustenance to maintain political and communal integrity and prevent "creeping unitariness."

What is the conservative argument for revenue sharing? Is the Nixon approach a "that government is best which governs least" conservatism? No; the idea is to contract federal authority but to expand state and local authority. What theory of sovereignty lurks here? I think "new federalism" is a modern version of "dual federalism." But "dual federalism" was merely a constitutional contrivance to keep national government on the defensive. The "dual federalists" were essentially laissez faire advocates, equally unresponsive to state power as an innovative policy instrument. Why then can't Nixon's "new federalism" also mask a more basic constitutional commitment, a commitment to some notion of *community?* In the "Nixon Constitution," strong federal authority is needed to protect national security, while strong state and local authority is needed to provide the mainsprings of law and order. Moreover, national government should not sponsor grants-in-aid, while cities and states should not provide legal services for the poor and conduct wars on poverty. But whereas post-New Deal liberalism is a real political threat when mobilized from Washington, economic redistribution and social experimentation run afoul of tighter community mores, private economic power, and "politics as usual" (politics by machine?) at the grassroots level, so Nixonians think they can live with the initiatives commenced there.

Nor did conservatives for revenue sharing suffer any setback from Gerald Ford. Of course, the "Ford Constitution" with respect to federalism is not a carbon copy of the "Nixon Constitution," but Ford, like his predecessor, was very close to the contemporary conservative center of gravity on one point: he wanted to cut away some of the tentacles of the federal grant-in-aid octopus.

Who opposes revenue sharing? Once again, an informal alliance of political liberals and conservatives emerges. The right-of-center critics would accept revenue sharing only if the federal government *cut* taxes so the cities and states could *raise* taxes. They fear that revenue sharing may open the door to national funding—and thus potential control—of *all* public functions at the grassroots level.[88] Consistent with this sentiment is a criticism put forward by Wilbur Mills, who was chairman of the Ways and Means Committee when the revenue sharing law was enacted. "I'm not going to be a tax collector for anyone but the federal government."[89] He contended that public officials tend to be fiscally irresponsible when they know they won't have to raise taxes—that a process wherein someone taxes while someone else spends leads inevitably to unbalanced budgets and an irretrievable cheapening of the dollar. So the chief conservative worries are grassroots fiscal dependency (leading to political dependency) and national fiscal anarchy.

Many political liberals have criticized revenue sharing on general principle.[90] Their common denominator is "new style" liberalism, which is pronational and *antigrassroots* with respect to questions of both sovereign power and communal ties (see my definition in the footnote on p. 367). It embraces the grant-in-aid approach because Washington can lay down categories for social action, which, as the last forty years have demonstrated, will be the "correct" categories from the liberal point of view. In fact, grants-in-aid put forward during the Kennedy and Johnson years were qualitatively different from earlier ones in that the legislation was written specifically to achieve *national* political, social, and economic goals, not merely to aid state action.[91] Why the shift? "New-style" liberal ideology, hostile to grassroots community, had preempted "old-style" liberalism and its concern for the state as laboratory. To the "new-stylers," Congress may be cumbersome and may overrepresent agrarian interests, but it is a paragon of innovation compared with state and local government, which is often long on corruption and racism and short on legislative and technical know-how.

Technical know-how means "bureaucratic expertise." "New-style" liberalism sees federalism very much as an interchange between national and grassroots bureaucrats, all of whom are committed to rewarding their clients.[92]

These bureaucrats have the tools to shape experimentation far beyond the capacities of state laboratories; they need only a few loose legislative guidelines (to avoid the "hardening of the categories" criticism) and a lot of federal money. And the bureaucracy will be managed by the "right" kinds of people, because "new-style" liberalism is committed to helping the "right" clients.

I find all these approaches somewhat wide of the mark; they either underplay, overplay, or totally ignore salient features of sovereignty and community basic to a healthy federalism.

The Heller notion of states and cities as political experiment stations, for instance, sees them as accurate barometers of public need because they are "closer to the people." But are they? Morton Grodzins, after intensive analysis, finds that Jefferson's dictum may have been valid 180 years ago, but not today, largely because of urbanization. Grodzins argues that citizens in *rural* areas are closer to *every* level of government than citizens in urban regions.[93] Life on the farm means neighbor-to-neighbor local politics but also face-to-face contact with the Forest Service officer and the Commodity Credit Corporation agent. These primary relationships are hard to come by in the suburb or the inner city. And today, when television takes us behind the scenes of every Washington melodrama, it is the national leadership and the national political embroilment that receive attention.

The Nixon position, on the other hand, seems to be an updating of "dual federalist" ideology. But can, or should, "dual federalism" be resurrected? Revenue sharing, Nixon-style, does not directly force the issue, because we know it provides sweeteners for less affluent communities, especially agrarian sections. This tells us a great deal about the practical politics inherent in federalism's "Living Constitution." But from the larger standpoint, the "dual federalism" of yesteryear was based on mutual political autonomy; Nixon's "dual federalism" is based on Congress's gravy train. Nixon has called this decentralization. I call it *delegation run riot,* where the supremacy clause is given away without even the recompense of a grassroots trading stamp.

And what of those who disapprove of revenue sharing? The conservative argument that control inevitably follows the purse strings is, like much of today's (and yesterday's) political conservatism, an argument that places too much emphasis on who has money. Some things are more important than money: values, philosophies, norms, rules, *community, sovereignty.* Federalism is a study in differential financial capacities, but it is a study in these other facets as well. If a critique of federalism cannot ignore them, how can a critique of revenue sharing ignore them?

Does the liberal indictment measure up any better? "New-style" liberalism envisions Washington bureaucrats contriving bold, experimental innovations under the purview of flexible legislative guidelines. What does that mouthful mean in the streets? First, the average person may feel closer to the President of the United States than to a county commissioner, but not necessarily feel closer to a federal bureaucrat than to a state or city bureaucrat. Ever-increasing nationalization in our communications and transportation networks does not mean greater citizen affinity toward or legitimacy for the federal organizational chart and its assorted slots.

And what about those creative bursts of energy? In Chapter 4, I talked about the landmark social legislation of the 1960s: the Appalachian Regional Commission, with its gubernatorial veto on federal initiatives; the Office of Economic Opportunity, with its war on poverty to be waged by community action groups, and so on. I referred to the statutes as *externalized delegation run riot,* with Congress handing over the reins of rule-making to the bureaucracy, to state and local government officials, and to private groups. Citing Theodore Lowi,[94] I attributed the entire process to the internal inconsistencies of "interest-group" liberalism, a philosophy that talks about rules and administration and then refuses to draft rules or administer anything lacking moral overtones.[i]

How did the "enlightened" bureaucracy transmit liberal values to the state and local hoi polloi? Looking at program developments in the 1960s as a whole, James Sundquist, who is a staunch supporter of grants-in-aid and Great Society theory if not practice, found that each federal departmental haven developed its own grassroots enclave for statutory enforcement. The result was a veritable tangle of atomistic power centers, often representing different interests and incapable of comprehensive planning. O.E.O. had its community action agencies; H.U.D. had its demonstration units under the Model Cities formula; the Appalachian Regional Commission had its local development projects.

Just as the organizational maze characterizing the federal bureaucracy left its mark in the hinterlands, so too "interest-group" liberalism left its mark. Most of these grassroots enclaves embodied a mishmash of public personnel and representatives of private clientele interests negotiating as equals.[95] The phrase "maximum feasible participation" became a talismanic invocation. But did representatives of the business community, the poverty community, or the black community actually speak for these groups in any formal, legitimate way? Did they "campaign"? Were they "elected"? No. Is it any wonder that those who wound up in the saddle were very often the loudest, the most influential, the best connected, and sometimes the most extreme? And these people were *making public policy.* To the extent that "new-style" liberalism, with its nationalistic fervor, relied upon the conventional grant-in-aid strategies of the 1960s, the credo became mired in the lack of Washington bureaucratic community and a mistaken perception of grassroots community as nothing but selfish power blocs. Both phenomena are the stuff of "interest-group" liberalist decision-making.

[i] A note on semantics. "New-style" liberalism is meant to convey a philosophy with no reverence for any community except *national* community. "Interest-group" liberalism is a different phenomenon. Its advocates would delegate power to the grassroots, *not because the localities represent any kind of meaningful community but because they represent the very opposite of community—that is, warring power blocs.* Either the discrete blocs must be governed (which the "interest-group" liberal is not comfortable doing) or they must be allowed to make their own rules. Obviously, a person can be both a "new-style" and an "interest-group" liberal; on the other hand, a person can just as easily be one or the other or, assuming he is a liberal, neither.

The great debate over revenue sharing has arisen because everyone understands the concept's enormous implications for contemporary federalism. In short, does revenue sharing square with our preeminent constitutional values, with our sense of public responsibility, and with those implicit norms and standards which we have come to feel should control our relations with the state?

I make bold to answer in the negative. We elect members of Congress to do a job: to weigh evidence, to pass meaningful laws with meaningful teeth, to perform their constitutional duties. We elect mayors, city council members, governors, and state legislators for much the same reasons. And when we think the incumbents have not exercised their assigned responsibilities in a manner conducive to good government, out they go. Revenue sharing violates those precepts, precepts I regard as "givens" in the "Living Constitution." Revenue sharing is a textbook example of buck passing; it has no intellectual substance, because the money can wind up God knows where; and, most of all, it nullifies the constitutional balance inherent in federalism, because constitutional balance and the blank check are irreconcilable.

Epilogue: In the waning days of 1976, Congress extended the revenue sharing program through September 1980, authorizing expenditures of $25.6 billion. The only noteworthy change allows local officials to allocate funds for any purpose. It would seem that revenue sharing is moving toward "Living Constitutional" status.

Federalism in the 1980s: what kind of balance?

Despite all the talk about revenue sharing versus grants-in-aid, one cannot build a coherent theory of federalism around either device, because they are too narrow. "Marble cake" means far more than financial give-and-take; it encompasses the multitude of political relationships binding the various levels of American government to one another over the years. If our major task is to understand the "Living Constitution" which federalism exhibits today, then we too must go beyond money.

I begin by returning to the Constitution itself. When we left the Supreme Court, the Justices had laid "dual federalism" to rest, shunted the Tenth Amendment to the sidelines, nationalized much of the Bill of Rights through some dexterous reshuffling of the substantive due process doctrine, and declared grants-in-aid an almost impregnable attribute of the spending power. It might seem that only the contradictions inherent in "interest-group" liberalism plus the Democratic Party split over the Vietnam War have kept us from thoroughgoing national supremacy in domestic policy-making.

But, even judged against standards ingrained in Roosevelt Court doctrine, federalism is no dead letter. The states abide, and their territorial integrity remains protected. They choose their own governors, legislators, and judges; they build their own bureaucracies; their equality regardless of population is recognized overtly in their senatorial representation. As independent power centers, then, they still have some autonomy and some clout. The question is: What meaningful policy-making role can they perform?

I would like to suggest three possibilities. The first is in the mainstream of "new-style" liberalism, the notion of "permissive federalism." This term is as easy to understand as its predecessors—"There is a sharing of power and authority between the national and state governments, but . . . the state's share rests upon the permission and permissiveness of the national government."[96]

To put the argument succinctly: under existing judicial precedents, Congress has power to pass laws regarding any policy question worth citing, grassroots autonomy notwithstanding; our country is fast becoming a national political community, and voters insist more and more upon minimal across-the-board standards in social services; however, the states and the localities they themselves have created stand as bulwarks against unitary government; furthermore, the political-party structure and the representational system used to assign congressional seats reflect this decentralized order; the national "political branches," then, should enact national policy goals as best they can; where the balance of power in Congress makes it impossible to agree on statutory rules, the grant-in-aid device can be invoked, using federal money, federal guidelines, and federal bureaucrats to work with state personnel toward policy implementation; grants-in-aid give grassroots officials the most they can ask for—a voice in deciding which subsidies they need and a voice in the tactics of fulfillment.

The implications of this theory for constitutional politics are staggering. Federalism is perceived as merely an *intergovernmental relationship,* a "process of joint action," a problem-solving arrangement necessitated because Americans are not quite ready intellectually and emotionally to scrap their formalistic grassroots communities. And this relationship bends and flexes with public opinion and interest-group influence, *unbounded by constitutional strictures which hold either party to prescribed roles or standards.* The federal government takes what it can get, and what it can't get, it shares.[97]

The second possibility is in the mainstream of Nixon-Ford conservatism. In 1976, the Burger Court ruled that Congress's minimum-wage and maximum-hours standards were inapplicable to all state and local employees involved in traditional governmental activities.[98] The commerce power upon which the legislation had been based must yield to the Tenth Amendment, Mr. Justice Rehnquist said, for that provision guarantees the integrity of state sovereignty and the essential policies, such as wage rates for state personnel, which keep that integrity intact.

With the pith of an Oliver Wendell Holmes, Mr. Justice Stevens stripped the facade from this pronouncement:

> The Federal Government may, I believe, require the State to act impartially when it hires or fires the [worker], to withhold taxes from his pay check, to observe safety regulations when he is performing his job, to forbid him from

burning too much soft coal in the capitol furnace, . . . from overloading a state-owned garbage truck or from driving either the truck or the governor's limousine over 55 miles an hour. . . . I am persuaded that this statute is valid.[99]

These two approaches, of course, are theories of *divided sovereignty*. Under "permissive federalism," the states retain attributes of supreme temporal power, else Congress would have the clout to abolish them; however, grassroots politics lies subservient to national politics. And what of the Rehnquist formula? It is "dual federalism," in which national politics must give way to the priorities of grassroots politics.

The third possibility emphasizes an ingredient essentially missing from these foci: *community*. To understand the diverse aspects of national community and state community is to understand what the full range of "marble cake" relationships comprising federalism's "Living Constitution" has been and should be. I now turn to some of those aspects and relationships.

The Fourteenth Amendment and the "marble cake"

The central political phenomenon inspiring a sense of national community today lies in the effort to extend fundamental individual liberties. But the cross-currents are far more complicated than congressional civil rights laws and the Supreme Court's "absorption" doctrine, important though those developments have been.

One of the most significant tools of state policy over the years has been the *residency requirement*. States are traditionally cautious about allowing interlopers to utilize public services and public resources. And the Fourteenth Amendment gears state citizenship to residence, as defined by the states themselves. The upshot has been 180 years of domiciliary requirements: out-of-state citizens can't vote, can't run for public office, can't pay the going tuition rate at public colleges and universities, and so on, unless a minimal residency standard is satisfied.

In 1969, however, the Warren Court struck down a one-year residency requirement for collecting welfare payments. Munificent states like New York had instituted this waiting period as an attempt to discourage transients from raiding their financial resources. Ostensibly, if individuals wanted to live in-state for "legitimate" reasons, they would not hesitate to stick it out; however, freeloaders would find the burden formidable. These states also argued that throwing their welfare funds open to newcomers would be unfair to long-time citizens who had helped finance these programs through taxes. The Justices rejected all this in an opinion that, if taken literally, could vastly alter our understanding of federalism.

The Court said, first of all, that the right to travel interstate is constitutionally protected. Under unusual circumstances—when a *compelling state interest* has been shown—this right can be abridged; but the residency requirement under review was intended only to keep the state treasury safe from indigents, not a compelling interest. In fact, this discriminatory policy had resulted in two separate classes: those who could meet the residency standard and so were eligible to receive public assistance, and those who could not meet that standard and so were cut off from the necessities of life. That classification, said the Court, was arbitrary and capricious and therefore violated the equal protection clause in the Fourteenth Amendment.[100]

The logic of this argument is hard to see. For instance, where can one find a right to travel in the Constitution? Furthermore, if a right to move interstate exists and has been violated, why bring in the equal protection clause (and vice versa)? But we must not allow a debate over these niceties to obscure the Court's message. First, there is a liberty of interstate personal movement.[j] Second, under *unusual* circumstances, states can regulate interstate travel.[k] Third, welfare benefits are sufficiently essential to human needs that—once public aid is made available—access cannot be predicated upon state citizenship. To this extent, welfare eligibility is a liberty flowing from national community. If the Warren Court's thesis has any larger relevance, it is as an initial step toward a constitutional policy guaranteeing such basic social services as health, education, and housing standards, no matter what residency conditions the states impose.

But just as grants-in-aid have run into a countervailing trend called "new federalism," so the Fourteenth Amendment as nationalizing agent has been arrested somewhat. We have seen how the Burger Court struck a new balance between national and grassroots community standards in the area of obscenity regulation. The dominant plurality during the Warren years had said: A book is obscene if it violates uniform national standards with respect to patent offensiveness. The Burger Court now says: A book is obscene if it violates national standards as interpreted at the grassroots; each item presents a different set of facts, and the national standard may mean different things *in different communities.* So long as the Court retains a veto power over clearly erroneous findings, the supremacy clause will abide, and First Amendment values (as applied to *state* action by the Fourteenth Amendment) will remain unsullied.

This doctrine is a classic example of balancing a national community standard—free speech—with a grassroots community standard—what the reasonable person living in Seal Harbor, Maine, or Flagstaff, Arizona, or New York, New York, thinks is basically an exploitation of sexual appetites. It is not "permissive federalism" and it is not "dual federalism." But it is "marble cake," for it presupposes political diversity and cooperation under the umbrella of

[j] This right to travel, I suspect, is, like the right of privacy, located in the penumbra of specific individual freedoms.

[k] The "compelling state interest" doctrine, I take it, is Warren Court language for the "preferred position" doctrine; if free speech can be restrained in exceptional cases, the right to move around the country can be similarly restrained.

national supremacy. The Court is telling us—correctly, I think—that not even the Bill of Rights can be applied uncritically across the board to any and every fact situation irrespective of social obligation and context.

Public safety and the "marble cake"

A second, quite different example will also demonstrate the diversity in national-grassroots community values and ties—contemporary federal-state-local relations in controlling crime. Law enforcement was largely a grassroots concern prior to the 1960s. States had their own criminal codes and their own police forces and prosecutorial arms.[101] But all this would change during the Kennedy-Johnson-Nixon-Warren Court-Vietnam-Black Power years.

The Supreme Court led the way, utilizing absorption doctrine to turn the Bill of Rights into something approaching a national code of criminal procedure.[102] The Attorney General's office followed suit, attempting to guide the cities and states out of their "backward" ways (as defined by critical judicial pronouncements), giving them counsel, advice, and technical know-how—hardly a surprising gambit under the Kennedy "new-style" liberal administration. But crime was on the upswing, and self-identified political conservatives made no bones about the correlation they saw between the niceties of Supreme Court intervention (in their eyes, "coddling criminals") and the surge in antisocial behavior. Then, when antiwar protest, civil rights activism, and violence in the ghettos all seemed to ignite at once, the cities and states were naturally placed on the defensive, while conservatives (and the majority of Americans) howled even louder.[103]

Determined to avoid political stigma, the Johnson Administration added to its policy of grassroots *civil liberties* enlightenment a policy of grassroots *law and order* enlightenment. The catchword of the Kerner Commission (a blue-ribbon panel assigned to explain the tumult and the shouting among blacks) was "intelligence gathering," which involved data stored in Washington-housed computers and the rapid-fire dissemination of materials to all law-enforcement officials. Naturally, the F.B.I. was commissioned to gather the intelligence, but information collected by the army and by local police found its way into the computers as well. Shortly thereafter, Attorney General Clark created a Civil Disturbance Group to manage the entire operation, and galvanized into action the Community Relations Service, whose task was to work with local officials and help them establish liaison with black communities in their jurisdictions. The C.R.S. fostered a policy of "creative disorder," whereby militants could protest and mouth the rhetoric of revolution; the hope was that such exercises would wear the dissidents out. To Clark's initiatives John Mitchell added his own pet palliative, electronic surveillance. He openly encouraged state and local police to engage in wiretapping, which, while permissible under the 1968 Omnibus Crime Control Act, was virtually unfettered by legislative guidelines.

No wonder the National Commission on the Causes and Prevention of Violence—yet another blue-ribbon panel, this time under the guiding hand of Professor Jerome Skolnick—saw the local police as a burgeoning political force, a self-appointed minority committed to keeping potential "troublemakers" in line, procedural limitations notwithstanding. Soon the F.B.I. was not only keeping a close watch on the Black Panthers but was also investigating accusations that the police in various cities had harassed, brutalized, and even killed Panther members without justification.

To many civil libertarians, Washington has usually appeared the fount of constitutionalism, and the cities and states the founts of provincialism. They view grassroots folkways as often resembling a veritable closed society, where unorthodox ideas and unorthodox people are jointly frowned upon. Rather than attempting to reform each town council and police department, civil libertarians would, instead, concentrate their attention on one person, the Attorney General; after all, he is the President's legal arm, and the President represents national community and constituency. With all this plus the federal dollar going for the Attorney General, Justice Department control over grassroots law enforcement can look pretty appetizing.

But who would check a national police force—whether it be the handmaiden of "new-style" liberalism or of "new-style" conservatism—should the mix of public opinion and electoral politics incite it to repressive frenzy? A national police force and a national criminal justice system can unleash veritable onslaughts against any deviant group imaginable. And all manner of weapons can be used in such warfare: the President's "dormant power," habeas corpus suspension, searches and seizures in the name of national security, and intelligence files without end. The Civil Disturbance Group, as I discussed fully in my treatment of the Attorney General's office, was uncheckable enough. Incidentally, now that the turbulent years are behind us, the states are fending quite nicely for themselves in the data collection business. The Interstate Organized Crime Index (I.O.C.I.), located in the intelligence division of the California Department of Justice and subscribed to by 200 city and state bureaus, has on file almost 20,000 names of those allegedly connected with big-time criminal endeavor. But at least federal power stands ready to check most abuses this program might involve.

Federal-state-local cooperation in law enforcement during the 1960s and early 1970s was part of the "marble cake." It was also an embryonic police state. And so I would argue that in the world of criminal justice, the clock needs to be turned back toward grassroots community. Of course, *procedural* due process sits in the Fourteenth Amendment as the protector of national supremacy. But that police work is primarily a state and local function seems a lesson well worth remembering. In this most sensitive sphere, the "Living Constitution" can guarantee meaningful balance only when it resembles an upside-down cake.

Federalism as "Living Constitution"

A final challenge awaits us: If our federalism is a rich yet diverse "marble cake," then how does one capsulize its essence in the light of contemporary constitutional politics? Again, I will approach my task from the twin standpoints of sovereignty and community.

First, grassroots communal bonds can be so compelling, even in our age, that state power is sometimes mobilized to challenge directly the doctrine of national supremacy. After the Supreme Court's school desegregation decision, several Southern states passed laws designed to stay the hand of federal authority. The legislatures, by their own admission, were attempting to interpose themselves between national law and the citizens of their states. To them, that law was unconstitutional, therefore they could repudiate it with clean hands and in good conscience. But, of course, the strategy was only a distant replay of the Kentucky and Virginia Resolutions (see pp. 347–48). To all this, the Justices disdainfully mimicked the findings of the lower court: "Interposition is not a *constitutional* doctrine."[104] And when Massachusetts legislators authorized the state Attorney General to bring suit before the United States Supreme Court asserting that the President and Congress could not send citizens of their state to fight in Vietnam without first declaring war, the Justices simply refused to hear the case.[105] Publicly supported racism was once an intensely held value in the South, and antiwar protest was so virulent in Massachusetts that George McGovern carried the state in 1972 against Richard Nixon. Nonetheless, the "Living Constitution" will no longer allow grassroots political institutions to challenge national decision-making where federal officials are asserting their authority against United States citizens. Civil War days are over.

Second, the states can and do still play an important experimental role as policy laboratories.[106] There is New Hampshire's lottery and New York State's Off-Track Betting scheme; there is California's pyramid-shaped system of higher education and Oregon's decriminalization of marijuana possession. Some scholars despair of other states imitating programs that work out, but one need not presume that state stupidity is any more prevalent than federal stupidity. Illinois has followed New Hampshire's lead and established a state lottery, while Alaska has copied Oregon's marijuana decriminalization.

Moreover, the Framers adopted ample tools for interstate cooperation. Under the Constitution, each state *must* give *full faith and credit* to the public acts, records, and proceedings of all other states. This means that when persons or corporations conduct their affairs across state boundaries, all the legal proofs duly accorded them in their home states must be honored elsewhere—for example, Nevada's "quickie" divorce decrees are binding throughout the country.[1] Furthermore, states can make compacts with one another for their mutual

[1] But a state need not enforce another state's criminal code. This matter is covered by a special process, *extradition.* Should a fugitive from state D be apprehended in state F, there is no duty under the law to return the subject. The governor of state D can only negotiate, though usually the request would be honored as a matter of course.

benefit. The New York Port Authority is an excellent example of such an agreement. However, the Framers provided congressional veto power over interstate bargains to prevent states from ganging up contrary to the national interest. To sum up: States are capable of innovation, the word gets around, and both Congress and the Constitution can be invoked to lend a helping hand. It happens all the time.

Third, even though the Supreme Court has given Congress extraordinary authority to preempt virtually the entire spectrum of important policy-making choices, and even though "new-style" liberalism is in a great rush to nationalize whatever the power struggle will allow, something is blocking full implementation of these sovereign powers. Perhaps people simply fear the "federal octopus."[107] But a less superficial answer is that

> Americans have a "federal attitude" towards government which colours their whole approach to governmental problems. . . . This attitude is . . . vague and meandering, and contains contradictory elements.[108]

Moreover,

> the essential nature of federalism is to be sought for . . . in the forces—economic, social, political, cultural—that have made the outward forms of federalism necessary.[109]

These sentiments emphasize the intangible ideas, values, and attachments flowing naturally from our pluralistic cultural matrix. The social embodiment of these intangibles is *community,* by which I mean, as I meant in Chapter 1, people perceiving themselves as bound to some larger corpus. Community involves feelings of kinship, of idea sharing, of personal security and comfort in the company of like-minded people.

What does "grassroots community" mean in this country? It means William Faulkner, sitting alone at his Mississippi homestead, writing about life in Yoktapanawpha County. It means the Cabots and the Lodges, pillars of Massachusetts community, whose center of gravity is not the congressional cocktail circuit but the golf courses and beaches of Boston's North Shore. It means Mayor Daley, who ran Chicago with a passion he could never feel for Washington. It means the farmer, whose family has tilled the soil of Piatt County, Illinois, for three generations. It means the blacks whose forebears have lived and worked in Bessemer, Alabama, since the turn of the century. And it means the Chicanos of Santa Fe. Are not their social standards, their outlook on life, and their personal frame of reference very much wrapped up in the place they call home? No wonder the doctrine of interposition can be resurrected every once in a while by grassroots elites and supported fully by grassroots rank-and-file.

Of course, all these people are Americans, and the Constitution as national symbol is embedded in their consciousness. And Americans have become a more transient people, too.[110] But that devotion to a national Constitution carries with it a devotion to grassroots relationships, because the "Living Constitution" presupposes the legitimacy of those grassroots ties. William Riker has called the national-state political balance contrived by the Founding Fathers a "federal bargain,"[111] as though the emerging consensus were akin to some labor management contract. But the Framers did not represent labor and management, rational and pragmatic though they may have been. Federalism is much more than a formalistic structural mechanism, because not only did the Framers believe we were *one people* and one nation; they believed also we were a *heterogeneous* people who feared putting all our political eggs in a single basket. In truth, federalism was and is an attempt to provide overarching political "rules of the game" based on feelings of national community while allowing grassroots ties, sentiments, and loyalties to prosper consistent with those minimal rules. It is this "Living Constitution" that prevents federal authorities from using all the sovereign power theoretically, but only theoretically, theirs.

As to the future of federalism, compare Presidents Johnson and Eisenhower on the subject. Johnson's "creative federalism" envisioned national government working hand-in-glove with private interests in research undertakings, in effecting social goals, in making this country stronger, more powerful, and more responsive to whatever needs arose. Eisenhower, on the other hand, warned Americans to beware the "military-industrial complex." He feared that an alliance between gigantic economic cartels and the Pentagon might straddle the American landscape, smothering smaller power units while feeding its voracious appetite for profits and influence. Eisenhower was cynical about Washington as a center for social reform because he was a man of the Kansas plains, of the grassroots.

Whatever the merits of this debate, we are de jure citizens of divided sovereignties and de facto citizens of divided communities. This can make for considerable inefficiency, tension, and even conflict, but it also maximizes diversity and balance.

NOTES

1. I might also include the fact that each state, no matter how small, is automatically given one seat in the House of Representatives. I do not include other facets of state representation in the national House nor do I include the role of states in the Electoral College system, for these vary with the population in each unit. I am concerned here with the rights that all states share equally by virtue of their status.

2. These declarations are reprinted in Henry Steele Commager, ed., *Documents of American History,* 5th ed. (New York: Appleton-Century-Crofts, 1959), pp. 178-84.

3. For example, A. H. Kelly and W. A. Harbison, *The American Constitution,* rev. ed. (New York: W. W. Norton, 1955), p. 210.

4. John C. Calhoun, "A Disquisition on Government" and "A Discourse on the Constitution and Government of the United States," in Richard K. Cralle, ed., *The Works of John C. Calhoun,* vol. 1 (Columbia, S.C.: A. S. Johnston, 1851). For insight on what contemporary American leaders lack, these pages are a treasure trove. Politicians really can wrestle with the great issues if they have the talent.

5. *Texas v. White,* 7 Wall. 700.

6. See the *Prize Cases* (Chapter 5), in which the Court upheld Lincoln's blockade of

Southern ports (an act of war) while also ruling that no state of war existed.

7. *Munn v. Illinois,* 94 U.S. 113 (1877).

8. From 1880 through 1930, the Court upheld state police power regulations in such cases as *Mugler v. Kansas,* 123 U.S. 623 (1888), *Euclid v. Amber Realty Co.,* 272 U.S. 365 (1926), and *Buck v. Bell,* 274 U.S. 200 (1927).

9. *Jacobson v. Massachusetts,* 197 U.S. 11 at p. 25 (1905).

10. Compare *Adkins v. Children's Hospital,* 261 U.S. 525 (1923) and *Morehead v. New York ex rel. Tipaldo,* 298 U.S. 587 (1936).

11. *Hammer v. Dagenhart,* 247 U.S. 251 (1918).

12. Ibid., p. 275.

13. *Collector v. Day,* 11 Wall. 113 at p. 124 (1871).

14. *McCulloch v. Maryland,* 4 Wheat. 316 at p. 431 (1819).

15. *Bailey v. Drexel Furniture Co.,* 259 U.S. 20 (1919).

16. His definition and description are found in *The Twilight of the Supreme Court* (New Haven: Yale Univ. Press, 1934), Ch. 1.

17. See Walter Berns's outstanding essay "The Meaning of the Tenth Amendment" in Robert A. Goldwin, ed., *A Nation of States* (Chicago: Rand McNally, 1963), pp. 126-48.

18. *Wabash, St. Louis and Pacific Railway Co. v. Illinois,* 118 U.S. 557 (1886).

19. *United States v. E. C. Knight Co.,* 156 U.S. 1 (1895).

20. *The Federalist,* No. 17 is a fine example.

21. Alexander Hamilton, "Opinion as to the Constitutionality of the Bank of the United States," in Henry Cabot Lodge, ed., *The Works of Alexander Hamilton,* 2nd ed. (New York: G. P. Putnam's Sons, 1903), vol. 3, pp. 445-93.

22. Samuel J. Konefsky, *John Marshall and Alexander Hamilton* (New York: Macmillan, 1964). A more penetrating analysis, which shows that Marshall was no rubber stamp for anyone, including Hamilton, is Robert K. Faulkner, *The Jurisprudence of John Marshall* (Princeton: Princeton Univ. Press, 1968).

23. *McCulloch v. Maryland,* 4 Wheat. 316 (1819).

24. *Gibbons v. Ogden,* 9 Wheat. 1 (1824).

25. *Martin v. Hunter's Lessee,* 1 Wheat. 304 (1816).

26. Ibid., p. 348.

27. Is this far-fetched? Then how come militant states' rights protagonists have for years contended that the "migratory birds treaty" upheld in *Missouri v. Holland* compromises Tenth Amendment interests?

28. Hamilton, note 21.

29. *Lochner v. New York,* 198 U.S. 45 at pp. 75-76 (1905).

30. *Panhandle Oil Co. v. Mississippi,* 277 U.S. 218 at p. 223 (1928).

31. *New State Ice Co. v. Liebmann,* 285 U.S. 262 at p. 311 (1932).

32. *West Coast Hotel Co. v. Parrish,* 300 U.S. 379 (1937).

33. *Helvering v. Gerhardt,* 304 U.S. 405 (1938); *Graves v. New York ex rel. O'Keefe,* 306 U.S. 466 (1939).

34. *South Carolina v. Barnwell Bros.,* 303 U.S. 177 (1938). But this decision has its problems. If you owned a truck line transporting goods from Maine to California, would you enjoy adjusting your vehicles and their contents to meet the regulatory nuances imposed by each and every state along the way, even though intrastate carriers were similarly burdened? In fact, this is a very real problem today, because the truckers respond by either raising their prices (thus sticking the consumer with the tab) or cutting down operations (thus stifling trade and commerce).

35. *United States v. Darby,* 312 U.S. 100 (1941).

36. Ibid., p. 118.

37. Ibid., p. 124.

38. *Wickard v. Filburn,* 317 U.S. 111 (1942).

39. See the *Usery* case (note 98 below).

40. *McCray v. United States,* 195 U.S. 27 (1904).

41. *Sonzinsky v. United States,* 300 U.S. 506 (1937).

42. *United States v. Butler,* 297 U.S. 1 at p. 71 (1936).

43. *Steward Machine Co. v. Davis,* 301 U.S. 548 (1937).

44. *Massachusetts v. Mellon,* 262 U.S. 447 at p. 482 (1923).

45. *Frothingham v. Mellon,* 262 U.S. 447 at p. 487 (1923).

46. *Barron v. Baltimore,* 7 Pet. 243 (1833).

47. 16 Wall. 36 (1873).

48. *Hurtado v. California,* 110 U.S. 516 (1884).

49. Ibid., p. 529.

50. Ibid., p. 535.

51. *Twining v. New Jersey,* 211 U.S. 78 (1908).

52. *Gitlow v. New York,* 268 U.S. 652 (1925).

53. *Near v. Minnesota,* 283 U.S. 697 (1931).

54. *Hamilton v. Regents,* 293 U.S. 245 (1934).

55. *Powell v. Alabama,* 287 U.S. 45 at p. 71 (1932).

56. *Betts v. Brady,* 316 U.S. 455 (1942).

57. *Palko v. Connecticut,* 302 U.S. 319 at pp. 325, 328 (1937). In this case, the Court said that states could deviate from a strict interpretation of the double jeopardy clause but hinted strongly that they could not try people again and again until convictions were obtained.

58. *Lochner v. New York,* 198 U.S. 45 at p. 76 (1905).

59. *Rochin v. California,* 342 U.S. 165 at p. 172 (1952).

60. His thesis is most pointedly stated in *Adamson v. California,* 332 U.S. 46 (1947), dissenting opinion.

61. Charles Fairman and Stanley Morrison, "Does the Fourteenth Amendment Incorporate the Bill of Rights?" *Stanford Law Review* 2 (1949), pp. 5-173, concludes that Black's findings are dubious.

62. *Gideon v. Wainwright,* 372 U.S. 335 (1963). For a valuable human-interest account, see Anthony Lewis, *Gideon's Trumpet* (New York: Random House, 1964).

63. *Ker v. California,* 374 U.S. 23 (1963).

64. *Duncan v. Louisiana,* 391 U.S. 145 at pp. 149-50, note 14 (1968).

65. *In re Gault,* 387 U.S. 1 (1967).

66. *McKiever v. Penn.,* 403 U.S. 528 (1971).

67. *Goss v. Lopez,* 419 U.S. 565 (1975).

68. Morton Grodzins, "Centralization and Decentralization in the American Federal System," in Robert A. Goldwin, ed., *A Nation of States* (Chicago: Rand McNally, 1963), pp. 3-4.

69. Daniel Elazar, *The American Partnership* (Chicago: Univ. of Chicago Press, 1962).

70. See W. Brooks Graves, *Intergovernmental Relations in the United States* (New York: Scribners, 1964), Ch. 14-16.

71. Michael D. Reagan, *The New Federalism* (New York: Oxford Univ. Press, 1972), p. 4.

72. Ibid., p. 55. Much of the data on grants-in-aid found here come from his study.

73. Ibid., pp. 55-57.

74. Nelson A. Rockefeller, *The Future of Federalism* (Cambridge, Mass.: Harvard Univ. Press, 1962).

75. Reagan, p. 65.

76. Advisory Commission on Intergovernmental Relations, *Fiscal Balance in the American Federal System,* vol. 1 (Washington, D.C.: Government Printing Office, 1967), p. 153.

77. Terry Sanford, *Storm Over the States* (New York: McGraw-Hill, 1967), p. 159.

78. Daniel J. Elazar, *American Federalism: A View from the States,* 2nd ed. (New York: Thomas Y. Crowell, 1972), pp. 73, 76.

79. Richard H. Leach, *American Federalism* (New York: W. W. Norton, 1970), p. 168.

80. Reagan, p. 55.

81. For the statute and much of the material cited herein, see Richard P. Nathan et al., *Monitoring Revenue Sharing* (Washington,

D.C.: Brookings Institution, 1975). A helpful update is Ronald G. Shafer, "Divvy-Up Debate," *The Wall Street Journal* (March 27, 1975), pp. 1, 15.

82. Of course, the states send their own monies down the ladder for general support purposes as well, but the figure for fiscal 1972 was less than $4 billion, a paltry sum by federal-bounty standards.

83. Nathan et al., p. 27, as well as Shafer.

84. Walter W. Heller, "Should the Government Share Its Tax Take?" *Saturday Review* (March 22, 1969), pp. 26-29.

85. W. W. Heller, *New Dimensions of Political Economy* (Cambridge, Mass.: Harvard Univ. Press, 1966), pp. 168-69.

86. W. W. Heller, Richard Ruggles, et al., *Revenue Sharing and the City* (Baltimore: Johns Hopkins Univ. Press, 1968), p. 35.

87. K. C. Wheare, *Federalism*, 3rd ed. (New York: Oxford Univ. Press, 1953), p. 53.

88. Harvey L. Lutz, "Tax Sharing," *The Wall Street Journal* (December 12, 1966), p. 18.

89. *Congressional Record*, vol. 117, 92nd Cong., 1st Sess., Jan. 26, 1971, p. H21 off.

90. I am here relying extensively on Reagan's critique and the sources he presents.

91. James L. Sundquist, *Making Federalism Work* (Washington, D.C.: Brookings Institution, 1969), pp. 3-6. For instance, Sundquist notes, the Area Redevelopment Act (aid-to-depressed-areas legislation) begins: "The Congress declares that the maintenance of the national economy at a high level is vital to the best interests of the United States."

92. Charles Adrian, "State and Local Government Participation in the Design and Administration of Intergovernmental Programs," *The Annals* 359 (1965), pp. 35-43.

93. Grodzins, pp. 9-11.

94. Theodore Lowi, *The End of Liberalism* (New York: W. W. Norton, 1969).

95. Sundquist, pp. 19-27.

96. Reagan, p. 163. And in the same spirit is Sundquist, Ch. 1.

97. Reagan, pp. 22, 159, 167.

98. *Nat. League of Cities v. Usery*, 96 S.Ct. 2465 (1976).

99. Ibid., p. 2488.

100. *Shapiro v. Thompson*, 394 U.S. 618 (1969).

101. John T. Elliff, *Crime Dissent, and the Attorney General* (Beverly Hills, Calif.: Sage Publications, 1971), p. 15. The following data are based on Elliff's study, but the conclusions are my own.

102. See Henry J. Friendly's critique in "The Bill of Rights as a Code of Criminal Procedure," *California Law Review* 53 (1965), pp. 929-56.

103. But because alleged wrongdoing by Vietnam War critics generally involved violations of congressional statutes, there was little federal-grassroots interaction with respect to the conduct of these activists.

104. *Bush v. Orleans School Board*, 364 U.S. 500 (1960) at p. 501.

105. *Massachusetts v. Laird*, 400 U.S. 886 (1970).

106. Sanford, Ch. 7.

107. Reagan, p. 22.

108. M. J. C. Vile, *The Structure of American Federalism* (New York: Oxford Univ. Press, 1961), p. 39.

109. William S. Livingston, "A Note on the Nature of Federalism," *Political Science Quarterly* 67 (1952), pp. 83-84.

110. But people also tend to move from certain places to certain places. For example, three out of five families changing residences during the mid-1970s relocated in the same county. More to the point, an area like Orange County, California, may be a community of transients, but its status as meaningful community can hardly be doubted, if overwhelming support for conservative political candidates is any indication.

111. William H. Riker, *Federalism* (Boston: Little, Brown, 1964), pp. 12-25.

9
political parties and pressure groups: irreconcilable forces?

In the context of American constitutional processes, political parties and pressure groups are unalterably linked, yet they seem to have virtually no common characteristics. Pressure groups are highly particularistic; scratch a formal organization lobbying before Congress, and underneath you'll find some homogeneous social interest attempting to enlarge its slice of the pie. Political parties, on the other hand, are highly diffuse; scratch a partisan aggregation in competitive heat, and underneath you'll find the broadest ideological spectrum imaginable among political bedfellows.

Of course the reason one species demands uniformity while the other requires diversity stems from their very different purposes. Pressure groups strive to obtain certain limited objectives shared by the membership: money, jobs, peace and quiet, security, an end to bias, international cooperation, international confrontation, the spread of some compelling idea—the list is endless. But political parties seek only to win public office—that is, to maximize power through the manipulation of coalition rather than increase reward through the triumph of conviction.

Then why do political parties and pressure groups go together? Because they are the major "Living Constitutional" vehicles we rely upon to influence governmental behavior directly. As such, however, they represent two different forces in the American constitutional environment and in our own political personalities: the pressure group represents commonalities of interest binding people together, commonalities that provide necessary quasi-kinship ties; the political party represents mature citizens of affairs, possessing different attitudes and outlooks, yet bartering and competing under mutually acceptable rules, because stability in a constitutional democracy requires no less. The fundamental question is whether the two forces—like the human id and the superego—can live together within one apparatus, or whether they must inevitably tear at each other, making popular influence on American national government an exercise in fragmentation and disorder.

The "group" as constitutional concept

The terms "pressure group" and "political party" are never mentioned in the Constitution. But while the document owes no intellectual debt to notions of party, it owes a heavy debt to notions of group. To understand the "Living Constitutional" world of pressure-group dynamics, we must first understand what a group is from both the constitutional and the political perspective.

James Madison formulated the most complete and most systematic conception of what our fundamental law should contain.[1] His view of politics—like the views of all self-respecting political theorists—was based on a concept of human nature. People, Madison thought, are neither inherently good, as Jefferson preached, nor inherently bad, as Hamilton believed, but a mixture. Furthermore, humans are social animals, aligning themselves with groups not only to attain their selfish goals but because their tastes, appetites, talents, needs, and backgrounds lead them to work, talk, play, and consort with people of their own kind.

If group identification is the human being's natural inclination, for Madison that bond could only be a mixed blessing. If group ties are a civilizing agent, imparting purpose to the human existence, they are also a catalyst to selfish behavior, for people who have banded together in common cause may likely seek aggrandizement at the expense of others. Madison's term for this kind of social grouping was *faction.* The term commonly used today is *interest group.* For Madison, the purpose of government is to check factions.

What are the social forces around which factions organize themselves? Said Madison:

> The most common and durable source of faction has been the various and unequal distribution of property. Those who hold and those who are without property have ever formed distinct interests in society. . . . A landed interest, a manufacturing interest, a moneyed interest . . . grow up of necessity in civilised nations.[2]

But there is more to faction than economics. Division and conflict arise also because people are "members of different religious sects—followers of different political leaders—inhabitants of different districts. . . ."[3]

And how might government constrain faction? By abolishing group interests? Hardly; that would be despotism, not republicanism. The process must be twofold: (1) Expand the scope of national authority and eradicate state sovereignty; a large, pervasive polity would mean a multiplicity of factions and would diminish opportunities for any single interest to dominate. (2) Divide national power into separate units with separate constituencies, then make sure each checks the other. A faction might work its will upon one power cell but hardly on all. The result, Madison hoped, would be a balance of forces, in which "ambition must be made to counteract ambition."[4]

Did Madison succeed? In getting the Convention to put the second goal into operation, absolutely. In getting the Convention to adopt his first prescription without equivocation, no; for, as I said in Chapter 1, the "Great Compromise" guaranteeing the states equal senatorial representation passed despite his vigorous opposition. (The upshot was a checks-and-balances scheme more elaborate than even he had anticipated.) But his understanding of factionalism was penetrating, and his vision of a viable political balance surely became a reality. History shows that around every important public office there clusters a claque of interests and camp followers, attracted by the particular leader or by the powers entrusted to that leader. Centers of power provide a home for politicians "on the make" and for factions jockeying for position. Thus does the Constitution serve as referee in the group struggle; thus does the "Madisonian model" operate.

Madison's insights may have had a striking impact on the Constitutional Convention, but their influence on the scholarly analysis of American politics was at first minimal. Throughout the nineteenth century, teaching and writing emphasized heavily the makeup of formal governmental institutions, the men who directed them, and the programs those leaders advocated; little notice was given to the machinations of factions. Then, in 1908, Arthur Bentley published his ground-breaking work on the nature of politics.[5] Scholarship, he said, must emphasize *the group* and deemphasize both explicit governmental arrangements and political ideology. To comprehend how and why decisions are made, Bentley believed, one must understand which interests or *coalitions of interests* were calling the shots. All else was irrelevant.

Students of politics responded to Bentley by ignoring him. They were turned off by his characterization of theory and values as "mind-stuff" and by his reduction of complicated decision-making processes to the "simplistic" calculus of group pressure. It remained for political scientists writing after the Second World War to show that theory, institutions, and *group interplay* are all salient aspects of the "Living Constitution."

Today's literature on interest groups is staggering, yet the term is constantly misused. David Truman, who extensively updated and systematized Bentley's work, describes it this way:

> "Interest group" refers to any group that, on the basis of one or more shared attitudes, makes certain claims upon other groups in the society for the establishment, maintenance, or enhancement of forms of behavior that are implied by the shared attitudes.[6]

There are two elements in this definition. One is "shared attitudes": some individuals have a common point of view regarding what they do, think, or want. The second is the concept of group expectations in a power context: the shared attitudes prompt an aggregation of individuals to make demands on others. Truman's "interest group" turns out to be a carbon copy of Madison's "faction."[7]

Some scholars confuse the terms "interest group" and "pressure group," employing them interchangeably.[8] However, V. O. Key provides the proper distinction:

> Private associations [may be] formed to influence public policy. These organizations, commonly called pressure groups, promote their interests by attempting to influence government. . . . The political interests of agriculture, for example, may be advanced through . . . pressure groups, such as the American Farm Bureau Federation.[9]

So farmers constitute an *interest group,* as do business executives, laborers, wheat farmers, bankers, auto workers, and plumbers. That members of vocational or professional groups have shared attitudes and that they make various claims on others because of the shared attitudes is self-evident. *But a pressure group evinces formal organization:* it has a constitution, by-laws, and explicit procedures for making decisions; it collects and spends money, and *deliberately attempts to influence public officials.* The A.F.L.-C.I.O. is a pressure group; so are the N.A.A.C.P. and the Anti-Defamation League. And the power of such groups generally depends upon their ability to articulate successfully the claims of the interests they represent.

Interest groups and pressure groups: an analytical enumeration

Writing in the mid-1960s, Key identified four major clusters of interests he thought had made their political mark over time: farmers, workers, business, and "other" groups.[10] He described the shared attitudes animating each group, the felt needs for greater power which have arisen from those attitudes, the formalized pressure aggregations mobilized to satisfy those needs, and the specific maneuvers employed by the aggregations in the field. In this section, I will report Key's basic findings, updating them where I think necessary and stressing their relationship to the "Living Constitution."

Farmers

The public has diverse images of farmers, just as farmers appear to have diverse images of themselves. Only that diversity—a study in uniqueness and a study in inconsistency—can explain the paradoxes of agrarian political activism.

From the founding of the Republic until well into this century, farming was a way of life. The principal economic unit was the family farm; the principal production cost was labor, the farmer's own. Economic ups and downs might affect others, but at least farmers and their kin ate and abided. There are still many family farms in this country, though they have decreased markedly. Yet the homespun image of the crude but gentle agrarian life style remains alive and well, nurtured in the popular consciousness today by the trials, tribulations, and triumphs of the Waltons.[11]

The great change in farming took place when agriculture became a business. Henceforward, land would be tilled not to support a family but to make a profit. The farmer was no longer Jefferson's "noble savage" but a landed capitalist. The life of an agricultural entrepreneur, however, is not an easy one. The farmer plants the fields, then watches untimely rains destroy the crops or perfect weather produce a bumper crop, driving prices into the basement. Shipping charges must always be attended to, and high tariff rates often cut off foreign markets. The typical farmer, then, is a quasi-business executive, quasi-laborer.

The central aim of the agrarian interest bloc is to achieve profit stability, and different segments of the farm community have funded pressure organizations to work toward this end. The oldest such group is the National Grange, famous for leading the fight against laissez faire and exorbitant railroad rates in the 1870s and 1880s. Very much a "moral uplift" aggregation, the Grange has been known to spout a homily or two about the inherent goodness of the family farm while playing its role of leading advocate of the small planter. Far more powerful, however, is the American Farm Bureau Federation (A.F.B.F.), which represents the large, affluent corn and cotton producers. The most militant agrarian pressure group is the National Farm Organization (N.F.O.), which has attracted much notoriety over the past decade by conducting mass slaughter of animals before television cameras, for the purpose, it says, of bringing prices up.

Government's most significant response to the sundry pressures applied by farm groups has been the *parity payment,* a device that works something like this: farmers withdraw portions of their acreage from cultivation; prices will then (it is hoped) rise toward "parity" (that is, the return farmers received in the banner year 1914); should that goal not be realized, the federal government makes up much of the difference in subsidies. At first, the Grange opposed the whole idea of parity because it would "corrupt" the farmer, while the A.F.B.F., taking the "hard-headed" approach, went along. Now the Grange is a strong advocate of government intervention, while the A.F.B.F., in good business rhetoric, talks wistfully about a return to the free market economy.

Overall, agrarian success in the political process has outweighed failure. One must remember that the farm population has decreased steadily in this century; more than 90 percent of Americans do not live in rural areas. One must also remember that overproduction of farm commodities is partially a function of poor management; many farmers have become too efficient for their own good, using the latest equipment to grow more and more crops on less and less land. Finally, farmers, fiercely independent in their interest-group relationships, overwhelmingly refuse to maximize collective action. Their intransigence frustrates political liberals, who have for years dreamed of a farmer–labor coalition; and it also frustrates N.F.O. activists, who maintain that farmers will always be on the defensive until they combine forces to control their end of the market.

Yet, with all these strikes against them, the federal government does rather nicely by most farmers. Rural overrepresentation in Congress, as manifested by the still-vital seniority system, helps quite a bit. And farmers are shrewd voters. Usually thought of as Republicans, they bolted their party and supported "friendly" candidates Harry Truman in 1948 and Lyndon Johnson in 1964. Nor does conservatism prevent farmers from endorsing massive wheat sales to the Soviet Union—a financial boost, indeed.

So the role of farmers in politics is very much like their image to nonfarmers—paradoxical. They are the tillers of soil, who wheel and deal; they can be the wealthy Senator James Eastland or the impoverished tenant farmer; they are the "backbone of the nation" and pragmatists without apology; they are individualists, who have taken *billions* from the government over the years without batting an eyelash. It is this unique amalgam of shared attitudes and felt needs that comprises the agrarian faction's role in the "Living Constitution."

Workers

Key's term "workers" is perhaps too broad. Farmers can be identified readily enough, but as Winston Churchill once remarked to his Labour Party adversaries: We also work![12] If anything, the past ten years have rendered the word even more vague; in this era of the conglomerate, employees can drive Cadillacs and wield enormous power but remain employees because they possess no sense of ownership. For present purposes, I will consider workers to be those employees who do not participate in their company's policy planning or managerial oversight.

James Madison called property the chief source of faction, and it is the contemporary conception of property which has spawned the labor movement. In Madison's day, property meant land, money, precious materials, the fruits of craftsmanship. Today, private ownership of significant proportion means corporate, industrialized power, and this power presupposes a gigantic labor force able to turn the wheels and push the levers. Economically and politically, each worker has little clout; but together, workers have the strength of numbers. They can bring business to a halt by calling strikes; they can control the electoral process with their votes. And they have had to use both remedies where possible, because for them a dysfunctional economic system can mean joblessness, rootlessness, inordinate deprivation.

At first, worker organizers asked only that the state be *neutral* in employer–employee relations, a considerable request given the primacy of substantive due process. Specifically, they called both for the abolition of "government by injunction" (by which judges would order picketing and work stoppages halted because irreparable damage to industry had been shown) and for statutes protecting labor's right to bargain collectively. In the field of partisan politics, the first truly national union, the American Federation of Labor (A.F.L.), refused either to set up its own political party, as its European counterparts had done, or to affiliate with the Republicans *or* the Democrats. Under the extraordinarily adept leadership of Samuel Gompers, the A.F.L. practiced nonalignment and preached the dictum "Reward your friends; punish your enemies." This overall strategy seemed appropriate for an organization representing primarily the skilled crafts; dedicated to keeping communists, socialists, and other radicals from positions of power; and committed to incremental change within the system.

Labor charged to the political front in the 1930s on the heels of the Great Depression, giving an overwhelming endorsement to Franklin Roosevelt's New Deal. With a strong liberal consensus building throughout the nation, the Norris-La Guardia Act outlawed "government by injunction," and, later, the Wagner Act gave labor the collective-bargaining protection it had always sought. Not coincidentally, workers in the heavy industries, under the leadership of United Mine Workers president John L. Lewis, bolted the A.F.L. and founded the Congress of Industrial Organizations (C.I.O.). C.I.O. militants had grown tired of traditional union laissez faire politics; the A.F.L. had not even endorsed F.D.R. in 1936, when he crushed Alf Landon! What labor needed, said Lewis, was a strong legislative program protecting workers against the nation's largest corporations. And so the C.I.O. went to Congress to lobby for action in virtually every substantive area imaginable, from foreign trade to interest rates. Still, the C.I.O. would not tolerate radical infiltration or espouse revolutionary doctrine, any more than the A.F.L. would.

The leadership among labor's pressure-group ranks has had its rocky moments over the past quarter century. One of the problems has been corruption, depicted at its worst in the film *On the Waterfront.* Especially vulnerable have been the Teamsters, two of whose top leaders, Dave Beck and Jimmy Hoffa, were sent to prison. And few observers will forget the 1969 assassination of United Mine Workers maverick "Jock" Yablonski, allegedly ordered by U.M.W. president Tony Boyle. Then there is the related charge of "bossism." Few labor unions can claim to be democracies, or even to have a competitive internal party structure.[13] To meet the worst excesses of organizational oligarchy, Congress passed the Landrum-Griffin Act in 1959. Besides subjecting all union financial affairs to disclosure, the law mandates elections by secret ballot and provides a "bill of rights" for the rank-and-file, including speaking and nominating privileges at union meetings.

Perhaps an even more serious problem has been a certain stodginess, if not conservatism, at the upper levels. This is, in part, an organizational dilemma, for workers constitute no homogeneous body. Yet in 1955 the A.F.L. and the C.I.O. decided to merge once again—perhaps, after passage of the Taft-Hartley law and President Eisenhower's election, to counter a certain loss of momentum. The united front has strengthened ties between labor leaders generally and the Democratic Party leadership generally; labor's governing council has endorsed every Democratic presidential candidate since 1956 save George McGovern. Otherwise, the results have not been earthshaking. The A.F.L.-C.I.O. may have over 13 million members, but it is really only a confederation, incapable of putting together grand strategies above and beyond the usual "bread and butter" grievances. When United Auto Workers chief Walter Reuther, who had built a national reputation by preaching such maxims as "worker solidarity" and "liberal orthodoxy within a united Democratic Party,"[14] saw that the organization lacked ideological mission, he took his forces out of the alliance. And when the Teamsters were expelled for alleged improper doings, Jimmy Hoffa only smiled, as his union organized more and more truckers and became more and more affluent. In more recent years, Reuther's successors backed Jimmy Carter against the more liberal Morris Udall for the Democratic presidential nomination, while A.F.L.-C.I.O. head George Meany made headlines by playing golf with President Nixon, applauding the Vietnam War, and cussing out the "New Left." No wonder labor union activism has acquired an Establishment gloss.

Have these travails affected the political lot of workers? One must keep in mind that labor usually votes Democratic and that (as I will make clear in Chapter 10) cities receive special preference in the Electoral College weighting game. Yet Republicans have fared as well as Democrats in presidential elections since the Second World War; and, while Congress is invariably Democrat-controlled, this often means Southern Democrat-Republican controlled. Labor's overall legislative record, therefore, has been mixed; and, with respect to labor's *most pressing* interests, the past three decades have not been kind. The prime example is the Taft-Hartley Act (1947), which (1) legalized the "union shop," whereby management could hire nonunion people so long as they joined the bargaining agent; (2) outlawed "secondary boycotts"—that is, the picketing of companies doing business with a struck firm; and (3) allowed the states to enact "right to work" laws, which give the individual employee discretion to join or not to join a union. Taft-Hartley has never been seriously amended, much less repealed, though opponents once labeled it the "slave labor law."

On the other hand, in the economic sphere, organized labor has made extraordinary strides; the strike has proved to be the most potent of weapons. Over the past twenty-five years, wages have improved drastically, on-the-job hours have been reduced, pension plans are commonplace, and medical coverage is often fully guaranteed. And when we realize that 47 percent of union members now consider themselves "middle class" rather than "working class," we have better insight into George Meany's political stance, as well as the hard-hat, "law and order" mentality generally.[15]

Labor's freedom to bargain collectively and its pursuit of economic power within the broad contours of the private-property system are now included in the "Living Constitution." Yet the business cycle forever impinges on that Constitution, and unemployment remains a perpetual problem. The

A.F.L.-C.I.O. may have lost some of its impetus as agent for social reform, but the omnipresent threat of joblessness will keep it in the mainstream of political liberalism.

Business

According to conventional wisdom, business is labor's natural antagonist. Indeed, much of what has been said about workers' politics is merely the opposite side of business's politics. And if "worker" is an amorphous term, so also is "business," stretching from the local pub to the multinational corporation. The term "business executive" will be defined here as an *employer or employee* who shares in the firm's policy-making or managerial processes.

We know that the Industrial Revolution transformed economic entrepreneurialism from small, competitive, personalized business power into gigantic, monolithic, corporate power. The names of industrial magnates who owned and operated the early empires are legendary: Carnegie, du Pont, Morgan, Rockefeller. Many of them espoused a "public-be-damned" attitude, summed up by one of their members as follows: "[Labor's rights will be protected] by the Christian men to whom God in His infinite wisdom has given control of the property interests of the country."[16]

The shared attitude energizing business's social philosophy is the preservation of the private-property, profit-oriented economic system. However, just as labor's tactics have run the gamut from laissez faire to strong national intervention, so business has pursued diverse goals throughout our history, depending upon the circumstances. One path has been the search for outright subsidies, such as railroad franchises and high tariffs; another tack has been to talk up the glories of the competitive marketplace, a policy that very often requires strict antitrust laws; a third path has entailed preaching state neutrality, which may well be code language for "let my monopoly alone."

Since the 1930s, business has tended to be even more pragmatic, because the Great Depression tarnished its image badly and sent twentieth-century liberalism's stock booming. That stance is reflected in the evolving images projected by the leading industry pressure groups, the Chamber of Commerce and the National Association of Manufacturers (N.A.M.). The Chamber represents a soup-to-nuts entrepreneurial constituency, so its pronouncements are often general, diplomatic, and given to business jingoism. Chamber literature extols the virtues of free enterprise and evinces fear of "creeping socialism" (for instance, national health insurance). The N.A.M., representing large-factory owners, is far more specific and far more strident. At one time it opposed the New Deal and Fair Deal lock, stock, and barrel, but it now realizes that compromise is inevitable. Still, one would locate it considerably to the right of *The Wall Street Journal.*

Perhaps the most successful business pressure groups are trade associations, which represent almost every set of commercial enterprises imaginable.

Some are fairly visible, such as the National Association of Retail Druggists, but lesser-known organizations speak for furniture manufacturers, paper companies, real estate dealers, and so on. Trade associations take little interest in large public questions, being concerned primarily with protecting themselves against "unfair competition" generated by certain *big* businesses, notably discount houses, department stores, and other price-cutting outfits. Congress is forever considering—and often enacting—"fair trade" laws and "quality stabilization" statutes, whose "public interest" titles serve to disguise the true intent of the laws: to create antitrust exemptions legalizing price-fixing contracts between manufacturer and retailer. Interestingly enough, though such agreements are highly inflationary, there is plenty of cozy handholding between the trade associations and labor groups, because price-fixing helps guarantee *stability* in the market, including the job market.

If the typical worker votes Democratic, the typical business executive votes Republican. But, of course, there are many more laborers than managers; business's political lot would be in a sorry state if its interests relied only on warm bodies. In addition, labor-management negotiations seem to allot workers a bigger and bigger piece of the pie.[a] So to maintain what business regards as its traditional place on the totem pole of economic power, political levers besides those in the voting booth must be pulled.

One such lever is the dollar bill. Business officials know who their friends are in Congress and in the presidential sweepstakes, and they contribute accordingly. Under federal statute, neither corporations nor labor unions can donate funds to candidates for national office; only individuals can do so. The A.F.L.-C.I.O. promotes fund-raising drives among workers, and the proceeds go to the Committee on Political Education (C.O.P.E.), which endorses various aspirants in predictable patterns. But C.O.P.E. cannot begin to match business's financial resources. A typical device is the $100- or $1,000-a-plate dinner, at which candidates "press the flesh" with business executives.

The fund-gathering tactics employed during the 1972 presidential campaign raised serious questions about business's gift-giving activities, however. When Watergate Special Prosecutor Leon Jaworski threatened to initiate criminal proceedings unless public confessions were forthcoming, executive after executive stepped forward, admitting to the illegal donation of corporate funds to Richard Nixon's campaign. The biggest culprit was the Associated Milk Producers, who also broke the law by contributing to Hubert Humphrey's and Wilbur Mills's unsuccessful runs for the White House.

Another such lever is advertising. In concert with its natural allies, the mass media, business launches broadside attempts to convince the public that buying its goods and services is beneficial. To be sure, advertising per se is a form of speech, and some scholars even think it is a necessary cost of production. But advertising, like unverifiably necessary expense account items, is also

[a] Take the so-called escalator clause, affording workers an automatic pay boost when the cost-of-living index goes up. Does anyone guarantee business executives an automatic boost in profits when inflation skyrockets?

tax-deductible. So when Exxon informs us it has devised new drilling procedures to tap hitherto unreachable domestic reserves, and when the quiet, confident voice of actor Burgess Meredith tells us to "fly the friendly skies" in a United Airlines superjet, what we have is a commercial firm and commercial television rounding up clients at the taxpayers' expense. The point is that business realizes that profits and a positive public image go hand in hand.

The role of tax-deductible advertising leads to a final lever, and today it is the most important: the symbiotic relationship between government and business. I am talking about the massive aid which government provides to those corporations that perform government tasks, and I am talking about the massive depreciation allowances given to the states' favorite businesses. When President Eisenhower inveighed against the "military-industrial complex," he could easily have been describing the subsequent billion-dollar effort authorized by Congress to save Lockheed Aircraft from bankruptcy. And data would very likely show that the richest men of our time—Hunt, Getty, Hughes—made at least a *billion* dollars in the oil business. Undoubtedly, their wealth stemmed from the extravagant write-offs for drilling that Congress allowed until 1975, when scandalous oil prices and oil shortages finally persuaded the legislature to curtail such federal largesse.

The "countervailing power"[17] by which big management and big labor check and balance each other is part of the "Living Constitution," though what groups check the myriad trade associations remains a mystery. But President Ford, in moving in federal court to break up the American Telephone and Telegraph Company, and in persuading Congress to tighten up antitrust coverage by banning all state fair-trade laws, may have had in mind another kind of balance as well: good old-fashioned competition supervised under the rule of law.

Other groups

Business, labor, and to some extent agrarian factions arise from the distinct classes of property ownership in this country. But what about the many interests whose common denominators are noneconomic? There are countless such factions, and in this section I will describe some of the more important contemporary ones.[18]

1. *Women.* Until the 1960s, the most prominent post-World War I women's pressure group was the League of Women Voters. Then, as now, the League concentrated on noncontroversial "good government" issues like getting out the vote. Obviously, women's liberation has made a dent in this tradition. A set of public issues exists today uniting women—to the greatest extent since suffragist days. The leading example is the Equal Rights Amendment; other goals include equal pay for equal work, congressional approval of Title IX, which outlaws sex discrimination in schools receiving federal funds, and removal of all sexist distinctions in the law. The most visible feminist pressure group is the National Organization for Women (N.O.W.), which lobbies federal and state officials to attain these ends. Representing many of the women who reject the liberationist tag is Stop E.R.A.

2. *Veterans.* Ex-servicemen have given of themselves to help protect the nation's security, and many feel that this extraordinary sacrifice deserves substantial recompense; hence, their major pressure group, the American Legion, has fought tirelessly for veterans' pensions, bonuses, and preferential treatment in job recruitment. The Legion, while explicitly nonpartisan, is also extremely active in pushing for strong national defense. The organization attempts to be a watchdog of patriotic values, denouncing any "extremist" groups allegedly tinged with pink. The Legion, the Veterans of Foreign Wars, and related groups have been highly successful in their many drives for financial subsidies, because many congressmen are themselves veterans, because an element of national conscience is involved, and because there are no opposing pressure groups to temper excessive demands.

3. *Professional interests.* Doctors, dentists, lawyers, and teachers all constitute factions, and their shared attitudes are prevailing professional standards. The first three generally are politically conservative, because they are economically advantaged and their work requires certain entrepreneurial skills. Teachers tend to be politically liberal, because they are not well paid and cannot maximize profits by rounding up clients. Furthermore, most teachers, unlike their European counterparts, have relatively low social standing.

The most influential pressure groups representing professionals are the American Medical Association (A.M.A.) and the American Bar Association (A.B.A.). A principal concern these groups share is continued quality (exclusivity?) among the membership. This means control of licensing standards, a function they themselves perform with exemplary diligence; nobody gets to practice medicine or law without passing an exam certified and graded by peers-to-be. The state legislatures, then, have delegated to private interests their own police power to determine qualifications. Many are the critics who think such tender loving consideration is in the nature of an outright subsidy that allows the professions to keep supply down and prices up.

On the national front, the A.B.A. is interested primarily in the fitness of judicial nominees, a role I discussed in Chapter 3. The A.M.A., meanwhile, concentrates on legislative attempts to alter the doctor–patient relationship. The group has waged war against "socialized medicine" at every turn, and opposes national health programs as a step in that direction. However, A.M.A. officials have endorsed outright gifts to the poor so long as the recipients are free to choose their own doctors.

4. *Ideological interests.* If the terms "political liberalism" and "political conservatism" are vague in the extreme, millions nevertheless call themselves "liberals" or "conservatives," and such affinities are obviously in the nature of shared attitudes. It is hard to isolate the convictions of the typical liberal or the typical conservative ideologue, but it is not hard to identify the beliefs of self-styled ideological pressure groups.

The best-known conservative, or right-of-center, organizations in recent years have been the John Birch Society and the Young Americans for Freedom. The Birch group was founded by businessman Robert Welch in 1958 and today has something less than 100,000 members. It has advocated, among other things, the impeachment of Chief Justice Earl Warren, and it called President Eisenhower a "lion of the Left."[19] It does not lobby for or against legislation; Welch's pamphlet *American Opinion* simply fulminates against the evils of communism and socialism, decrying this nation's seeming inability to cope with either. The Young Americans for Freedom (Y.A.F.) is the activist campus offshoot of William F. Buckley's *National Review* politics. The Y.A.F. played a leading role in Barry Goldwater's 1964 presidential campaign but maintained a low profile during Richard Nixon's "nonideological" tenure. In 1976 it pulled out all the stops in support of Ronald Reagan's White House candidacy. Broadly speaking, Y.A.F. endorses the free enterprise marketplace and the decentralization of federal power, while it disparages peace accords with the Soviet Union in general and the politics of détente in particular.

The most prominent liberal organizations are the Americans for Democratic Action (A.D.A.) and the Committee for an Effective Congress. The A.D.A. espouses what I have called "old-style" liberalism, and its subtitle might be "bringing the New Deal up to date." It publishes position papers, lobbies extensively, and endorses candidates. The Committee for an Effective Congress is in the same general ideological camp but concentrates on collecting monies to defeat conservative enemies at the polls.

There really is no liberal counterpart to the John Birch Society, perhaps because there is no "conservative sell-out" to weep and wail over. The closest analogue might well be the various offshoots of the now-defunct Students for a Democratic Society (S.D.S.), which was a major aggregation representing radical left interests during the harum-scarum 1960s. Such groups as the October League, the Revolutionary Union, and the Weather Underground continue to publish magazines extolling the virtues of Maoism, the counterculture, and the destruction of public property, as the case may be. The most proximate ideological counterpart to Y.A.F. was probably the S.D.S. itself during its germinal period in the early 1960s; at that time, the group emphasized civil rights confrontation, anti-Pentagonism, and economic egalitarianism. But it broke asunder in 1969 over the use of violence and the reliance to be placed upon communist doctrine.[20]

5. *"Public-interest"* groups. The "new politics" spawned in the 1960s brought to the fore various pressure groups concerned with protecting the public interest. One such organization is Common Cause. The many consumer and government study groups that revolve around the work of Ralph Nader belong in this class. And a third public-interest group is the venerable American Civil Liberties Union (A.C.L.U.).

Common Cause, founded by liberal Republican John Gardner, pursues the "politics of openness." The power of special interests would be diminished, it says, if we could obtain public disclosure of all campaign contributions and of the personal incomes of all officeholders, and if the right of public attendance at virtually all meetings held by government officials were guaranteed. Ralph Nader, on the other hand, has generated a number of well-publicized investigations into many areas: product safety, the workings of the independent regulatory agencies, the efficiency and responsiveness of Congress itself. Whereas Common Cause's specialty is lobbying, and Nader's is the research report, the A.C.L.U. attempts to protect the Bill of Rights by defending the constitutional freedoms of people charged with illegal acts.

Public-interest groups share a commitment to "moral uplift," but their activities have no monopoly on citizen concern. Indeed, there is some question as to what special interests these formal groups represent. One need not belong to the A.C.L.U. to revere the First Amendment; one need not endorse Nader's critique of congressional decision-making to support consumer rights and producer duties. I would hypothesize that these organizations receive most of their support from upper-middle-class, well-educated liberals, who think *their* conceptions of personal freedom, public accountability, and the idea marketplace warrant "Living Constitutional" status.

The universal weapon: lobbying

The public mind often telescopes pressure-group activism into one word: lobbying. And if pressure groups frequently are perceived as self-centered blocs of malcontents, then the lobbyist, as specific agent for this antisocial influence, frequently is typed as an uncommon villain indeed, buttonholing, cajoling, even armtwisting legislators to support tailor-made programs for the powerful at the risk of electoral rebuff. Within these contours, lobbying is evaluated as both pernicious and effective.

To help put matters into proper perspective, one must remember that petitioning government officials for redress of grievances is protected by the First Amendment; lobbying is actually a constitutional right. One must also remember that in our society any federal agency can be approached with the intent of friendly persuasion. When consumer groups testify before the Federal Trade Commission, calling for a ban on aerosol cans because they are believed to threaten the ozone layer, that is lobbying; when the A.C.L.U. comes before the Supreme Court and asks to file a brief as *amicus curiae* (friend of the court) to inform the Justices about special constitutional claims not pressed by plaintiff's lawyer, that too is lobbying. But the significant test of proper perspective centers on the implicit norms of lobbyist participation and lobbyist behavior. I turn now to those dimensions.

By sheer numbers, lobbying in the nation's capital is certainly big business.[21] There are from 5,000 to 10,000 participants, and this small army spends a rock-bottom minimum of $10 million per year, and perhaps as much as $1 billion.

Direct lobbying—that is, face-to-face efforts by professional activists to persuade public officials—is *not* the most powerful tool which pressure groups use on congressmen. Their most effective means is *indirect lobbying,* of which the chief example is grassroots pressure. To this end, the big lobbies have made great use of computers, stuffing them with the names of local faithfuls who figure to be responsive. Grassroots campaigns, which once required weeks to generate, can now be launched in a matter of days.

Congress, of course, realizes that lobbying is protected speech, but it also knows that lobbying, like all other forms of speech, can be constrained where necessary. To that end, the legislature passed the Federal Regulation and Lobbying Act of 1946, which supposedly obligates all groups and individuals in the persuasion business to file reports, spelling out their expenditures and receipts, their employers and employees. This statute, based on the "exposure is the heart of democratic governance" premise, in fact exposes little, and what it does expose is hopelessly misleading.

What are the defects of the lobbying act? First, no organization need register unless its "principal purpose" is legislative persuasion. Obviously, the American Medical Association's raison d'être is not lobbying. The upshot is that many groups which should file statements don't. Second, only congressional lobbying is covered; congressional *staff* lobbying isn't, though everyone knows that the typical pressure-group lobbyist speaks to the senator's aides, not to the difficult-to-reach senator. Third, lobbyists themselves decide what their bona fide lobbying expenses are, and often overlook the thousands spent on "research" and "information distribution" costs. (In 1974, the Chamber of Commerce listed a gross lobbying expenditure of $436!) Fourth, the law ignores the time and money spent lobbying the federal bureaucracy. Who knows the extent to which aerospace firms and other defense interests wine and dine Pentagon officials in an attempt to land juicy contracts? The public was outraged when International Telephone and Telegraph (I.T.T.) lobbyists offered bribes to achieve favorable settlement of an antitrust action. And the public was horrified when I.T.T. employee Dita Beard was hustled out of Washington—by, of all people, President Nixon's private vigilante corps, the Plumbers!—to make sure that no one would ask her any embarrassing questions. Finally, the statute is also inapplicable to indirect, grassroots persuasion. On this count, at least, Congress cannot be faulted. The Supreme Court has given a very narrow interpretation to the law,[22] evidently fearing that to make average citizens accountable for their sundry lobbying excursions would be to impinge on First Amendment rights. Congress's interest in exposing what lobbyists do is apparently broad enough to cover only the pressure-group professional activists and their direct-lobbying machinations.

Most scholars who have studied lobbying's "Living Constitution" consider the practice neither very pernicious nor very effective. Congressmen, it is said, are influenced much more by voting trends than by what the typical pressure-group lobbyist has to say, at least regarding broad policy questions. Moreover, the chief executive usually has ample weapons to protect his program from the sniping of organized interests, the most notable being the power of persuasion, ready access to the media, and, of course, his image as "Mr. President, Superstar." As one writer has argued: "Lobbying as we see it today in Washington presents little or no danger to the system."[23] Yet these conclusions seem rather dated in the backwash of I.T.T., Watergate, and the cacophony of special-interest noise currently emanating from Capitol Hill.

Everyone agrees, to be sure, that a high-status group—the National Rifle Association is an example—with intense feelings about some issue can erect impassable roadblocks to legislative action. Everyone also agrees that even middle-status groups with intense feelings on some issue—for instance, the trade associations—can work their will, provided the policy question is parochial and the opposition diffuse. Indeed, Congress, with its vast legislative and nonlegislative responsibilities, is usually more than happy to give these insular groups a long lead. Finally, most would agree that there is a strong negative correlation between party leadership and lobbying; the weaker the partisan discipline, the more readily lobbyists can penetrate the power structure. There is an important exception to this norm, however: given Congress's conservative bias, an avowedly liberal organization like the A.F.L.-C.I.O. will go nowhere unless the Democratic Party machinery is functioning smoothly.

These last two political facts of life required emphasis when one evaluated lobbying in the early 1970s. During the Nixon-Ford era, we had a Republican President and a Democratic Congress, sometimes an *atypically* overwhelming Democratic Congress. The White House's impact on legislative processes and policy-making was largely negative. Into this vacuum stepped the pressure-group lobbyist, profiting at every turn from Congress's exercise in rudderless decentralization. The average House or Senate member, ordinarily attentive to the organized interests back home—and to the voters—spent a great deal of time listening and serving. This state of affairs abetted the public-interest lobbies as well. Common Cause leaped forward in the power game because the Democrats held an extraordinarily wide margin in Congress and because there was no Democratic President to impose a preemptive legislative blueprint.

The fact is that nobody knows how pernicious lobbies really are, or how effective. I would say, with V. O. Key, that "it all depends."[24] It depends mostly on the degree of ideological consensus in the land; where that consensus exhibits vitality—and it often does—the "political branches" tend to be responsive, and parochial interests must take what they can get. But today, when that consensus—"interest-group" liberalism—is largely "group goodness" as implemented by "group self-government," should we be surprised that lobbying in the 1970s has been more effective and more pernicious than usual?

Pressure groups: democratic stabilizers or divisive elites?

The debate over lobbying is merely part of a larger debate—whether pressure groups are a benign or potentially malignant force in the American governmental system. The conclusion to a discussion of the pressure-group environment must wrestle with that dilemma in the even more encompassing context of "Living Constitutional" values.

Scholars Arthur Bentley and David Truman not only consider interests—that is, shared attitudes—the underlying political phenomenon in the social order but also believe pressure groups to be the backbone of democracy. Their proof runs something like this: interests are good, because they give human existence social dimension and significance; pressure groups are good, because they represent interests and because government by group coalition means government by the majority—and that is democracy[25]; the Constitution is good, because (1) divided power maximizes the number of avenues available for group participation in policy-making and (2) the Bill of Rights gives interests greater freedom to mobilize and express themselves through organized pressure.[26] The notion that groups are essentially good and that government should let groups grow and thrive, regulating them only when necessary, is called *pluralism.* What Bentley, Truman, and many others do is to take the pluralist argument and add that the purpose of statecraft is to formulate those policies which the dominant groups demand.

Now "politics by group action" looks like a pretty dangerous beast. Why can't the "big" groups gang up on the "little" groups and deprive them of their "fair shares"? Indeed, why can't the powerful exterminate the less powerful? Truman speaks to this quandary, arriving at two "solutions." One is the "overlapping membership" notion. Because all of us belong to many interest groups, he says, we are constantly subject to innumerable cross-pressures: one group affiliation might push us in one direction while another group affiliation might pull us in the opposite direction. An individual is not simply a farmer, a conservative, a Jew, a woman, a teacher, or a Chicano. And as our society becomes more heterogeneous as a result of increased specialization, our group ties become more numerous. This merely increases our cross-pressures, and they, in turn, bind us closer together. Hence, James Madison's theory, which posits national unity as an outgrowth of a social system large enough to absorb competing factions, again receives vindication. Most scholars accept the "overlapping" idea.[27]

Yet something is missing—the adhesive binding these interests so they don't wind up in bloody combat. That adhesive, Truman seems to be saying, is the shared attitudes most Americans hold *because they are Americans.* Foremost among these is a belief in the "rules of the game": the correlative rights and duties commonly understood to constrain each individual, each group, and each political office. Now belief in these values rarely leads to pressure-group activism, because rarely are the norms of our system clearly jeopardized. So these interests tend to remain unorganized; they are *potential groups.* But when some individual (say, a Nixon) or some group (say, a subversive organization) comes along and threatens the rules themselves—threatens the "Living Constitution" itself—then these potential groups suddenly swing into action, become intense pressure groups representing whatever implicit liberties or implicit duties are under attack. This "constitutional" check is also generally accepted in the literature (though the translation is my own).[28]

One possible weakness in the Bentley-Truman credo stems from their assumption that government by group coalition means government by majority rule. Bentley and Truman feel that big interests would tend to win out over small interests in the long run. Mancur Olson, on the other hand, believes that individuals will not rationally choose to join large groups as readily as they will join small groups.[29] The reasonable person, Olson says, lacks incentive to affiliate with organizations representing widespread attitudes because (1) the time and money this individual would expend adds little weight to the group's power and (2) the benefits the group would provide if activated—for example, a tax loophole—will be available in any event. Of course, there are some "big" interests with plenty of institutional impetus—among them, labor and its pressure-group satellite, the A.F.L.-C.I.O. To this, Olson contends that large factions *will* coalesce if either of two intervening variables is satisfied. First, those who share the interest may be forced to join. Second, those who share the interest may be tempted to join for reasons other than a prospective joust for power with competing aggregations. But everything else being equal, small "privileged" factions have a big advantage and are likely to reap the harvest of governmental goods and services.[30] Needless to say, that sort of political process hardly squares with democratic politics.

How does Olson's theory mesh with the facts of pressure-group formation and behavior in this country? Why has labor organized effectively? Olson answers: labor's collective political activism is simply a by-product of its chief concern, the struggle against industrial exploitation and the drive to achieve *collective* bargaining as the best defense against such exploitation. Moreover, under the "union shop," workers are now actually compelled to become group participants. In short, if labor tried to form a voluntary pressure organization without a trade union base, it would fail. What about the professions? How can we account for the A.M.A. and A.B.A.? Olson answers: belonging to these groups affords status, connections, and the chance to develop technical know-how by attending national conventions and subscribing to journals. Farm groups? Olson answers: the major agrarian lobby—the A.F.B.F.—was in fact organized on instructions from the state, which decreed that various innovative husbandry methods would best take hold when farmers created their own associations to help implement the new federal programs. And so farm bureaus sprung up, working hand-in-glove with "county agents," funded in part by Congress. Years later, the farm bureaus went into business for themselves, launching their own insurance, marketing, and supply enterprises. Farmers had to join an A.F.B.F. affiliate to take advantage of such services, and the business end is now far more significant to the parent organization than what Congress does or doesn't do. Industry groups? Olson answers: most of these associations are so small that it pays the rational entrepreneur to join. But such large interests as taxpayers, white-collar workers, consumers, or the poor are totally unsuccessful in competing at the pressure-group level, because individuals lack organizational incentive and there are no extrinsic rewards or coercive forces pushing them to collectivize.[31]

The Olson thesis, while highly provocative and compelling, needs some modification. In recent years, many large interests *have* achieved considerable organizational growth. Even though they fall far short of matching business and labor pressure groups, the Nader lobbying efforts and Common Cause represent diffuse consumer and citizen attitudes in a manner Olson's model surely doesn't anticipate. The interesting question is: Why do they exist? Olson makes the point that his notion is applicable in large measure to economic interests. But sometimes, he says, widespread aggregations collectivize for *irrational* reasons best explained by psychological or sociological factors. He might also have added *political* factors, for politics is surely not entirely rational. The leader's drive for power, the interest group's drive to put across some transcendent idea—these charismatic and moralistic attributes are inherent in much political action. Ralph Nader's single-minded dedication and broad appeal, feelings of noblesse oblige, the "higher law" symbolism in the Constitution—such stimuli can coalesce potential groups to challenge perceived "enemies of the people" or "enemies of the system."[b] Only in this sense, however, can latent interests compete with the typical parochial interest and the atypical larger interest (for example, labor), which organize, indeed, for precisely the reasons Olson specifies.

To recapitulate: Interests do not unite under the same strains and stresses; those who share widespread *economic* attitudes are very tough to collectivize. That gives small economic interests a natural advantage, and it shoots a big hole in the Bentley-Truman thesis extolling the "automatic pressure-group coalition" formed in defense of majority sentiment.

There is another reason why the group may be less than a bastion of democratic values. Robert Michels, writing in 1913, coined what has become an aphorism among social scientists: the "iron law of oligarchy."[32] The model, for our purposes, is simple: interests cannot influence unless they form organizations; organizations cannot be successful unless they mobilize a strong leadership corps; leaders labor in a qualitatively different milieu from followers, developing statuses and *interests* of their own; as the organization evolves over time, the leaders inevitably "confuse" their interests with the organization's interests; conflicts of interest between leaders and followers, therefore, are unavoidable; to the extent that democracy is a struggle among competing pressure groups, it is perforce undemocratic.

The pressure-group environment again provides verification. The A.F.B.F. is a "triumph of formal organization," dedicated to rational, bureaucratic self-government.[33] The building-trade unions and most other craft unions are oli-

[b] But numerous members of the dominant, potential groups may not perceive such threats. That is why Nader, the A.C.L.U., and others really speak only for tightly knit *factions within* these diffuse interests, as I argued earlier.

garchical prototypes, and some are even controlled by family dynasties.[34] No wonder that the A.F.L.-C.I.O. lacks democratic virtues. But then the big corporations and the trade associations representing them are hardly paragons of democracy either. Moreover, the "iron law" among pressure groups receives an extraordinary boost when the constitutional polity allows such groups to nestle into the bureaucracy and call their own shots. A few scholars even think our pluralistic roots have lost their spontaneity, because the aggregations they once spawned have ossified. This much is undoubtedly true: if tradition-bound organizations structure the dialogue, siphon off the leadership potential, and hog the influence patterns between private faction and public sector, the result is decadence, not enlightened representation.[35]

But, again, one must beware the pat interpretation. I see little evidence that A.F.B.F. leaders advocate major policies in a manner that displeases A.F.B.F. rank-and-file; nor is there any evidence that the A.F.L.-C.I.O. dues payer is highly critical of George Meany's priorities. And the Teamsters don't complain about all the money Jimmy Hoffa made for them.

Is it possible that interest groups and pressure groups do more harm than good? Nonsense. Pressure organizations are important communications networks. They convey expertise on complicated questions to friends and foes. By informing legislators, they also balance executive branch influence in Congress. (They cannot be blamed if we live in a strange period when the "political branches" spend most of their time bickering.) As a general rule, then, pressure groups play an important role in sharpening debate among formal and informal power centers, serving as data repositories, opinion stations, and idea shapers.[36] Moreover, public officials need to know exactly how significant groups view proposed policy alternatives, and without formal organization to convey such information, smaller interests would often go unheard. The result is a twofold process, which aids the system on both counts: (1) the typical interest group gets an opportunity to vent its spleen and publicize its particular needs and (2) pressure-group activists take this ammunition before the decision-makers, whose political advantage lies in working up alliances necessary to keep contented as many *organized* interests as possible.[37] Here is a kind of "Living Constitutional" representation almost as meaningful as the "official" geographic schemes authorized by the Constitution—in other words, *functional representation.*

As Madison told us, factions are an integral part of our social landscape. As contemporary philosophers have told us, interest groups provide our people with a grassroots, communal sense of belonging which militates against demagogic mass movements and totalitarian tides.[38] These "givens" underlie the American constitutional environment.

But interest groups and their kin, pressure groups, do not guarantee constitutional democracy. Some large economic interests may never organize; some large political interests may organize only when the system is threatened. Day-to-day governmental action, then, may be too highly influenced by insular pressures dominated by a self-perpetuating leadership. Given "interest-group" liberalism and "delegation run riot," they will certainly have too much say. These facts of life have become wrapped up in the "Living Constitution."

However, there is something more to the ways we influence governmental action than group interests and group pressures. Political parties have the potential to check and balance those forces. Whether or not the "Living Constitution" includes such relationships is the next question on the agenda.

Minor parties as pressure groups

In my introductory remarks to this chapter, I said political parties comprise diverse aggregations banded together for one purpose only, to achieve electoral victory. That is why they were created; Jefferson's Republican Party was an unpretentious tactical experiment designed to oust the Adamses and the Hamiltonians from their seats in government.[c] To achieve that end, a party must first nominate candidates. Nomination, of course, requires recruitment—that is, attracting potential winners to the party banner and moving them into advantageous position. It also includes the dramatic act of identifying those whose names will be put forward at election time, and screening out those whose credentials do not measure up. Naturally, the prime criterion is the chance of ultimate victory.

The ingredients in the party recipe are quite simple: candidates, officeholders, sympathetic electorates, and two partly invisible organizations consisting of the "party professionals." Taken together, though, the activists do no more than what I have specified above: they ready the party and its standard bearers for battle; they round up enough interest-group sentiment, pressure-group endorsement, and, most important of all, voter support to win at the ballot box; they assume control of and manage the public sector after victory has been attained.

These remarks, of course, apply only to the *major* parties. Our politics has been dotted with abortive third-party tickets and candidacies: the Abolitionists, the Know-Nothings, the Populists, to name a few. And some third parties have exhibited startling resilience, surviving to this day: the Socialist Laborites, the Prohibitionists, the Communists, the Vegetarians. Obviously, none of these groups has ever entertained genuine hope of winning more than token representation at the national level; they have foregone the urge to broaden their political bases and thereby significantly influence Election Day results.

A solution to the paradox of third parties was suggested by one of my mentors, who told a graduate seminar: Minor parties are pressure groups, not political parties. Does the evidence support his theory? Most third parties in American history have revolved around a single, compelling issue (slavery, liquor, cheap money), and they have gotten into the electoral sweepstakes largely to dramatize their grievances. Sometimes minor parties are co-opted by the major parties, who see their pet proposal as a magnet for their own vote-getting machinations. Actually, this is the highest of compliments, and it may

[c] Unless I note to the contrary, my comments on political parties relate only to organizations which select candidates for *federal* office.

mean ultimate success for the cause. The "minor party as pressure group" thesis seems especially relevant to these "Johnny one-note" movements.

Then we have "ideological parties," most of which evince strong Marxist inclinations. In a real sense, these parties are pressure groups, too, propagandizing proletarian doctrine and undoubtedly hoping that when times get hard, the national parties will pick up some of the minor-party palliatives. Moreover, many aggregations of either stripe—the Socialist parties, the Prohibitionists, and the Vegetarians—smack of religious cults, offering their wares as moral salvation. This also helps explain their subsistence through adversity.

Finally, we have the two most successful minor parties in our history, the Bull Moose of 1912 and the American Independents of 1968. They are distinctive because they tied their fortunes to a charismatic, national figure (Theodore Roosevelt and George Wallace, respectively) and addressed themselves to most of the existing major issues.[39] Yet they were largely pressure groups also, the one campaigning for openness and democracy, the other campaigning against busing, bureaucracy, and welfare. Without T.R., the Bull Moose reverted to the LaFollette-dominated, agrarian-oriented Progressives, and without Wallace, the American Independents are not much more than a curiosity today. To generalize, I would say that third parties are pressure aggregations with a little religion thrown in, though that religion may vary from revealed doctrine to "man on horseback" leadership.[40]

Two parties: why?

Many are the students of Western European democracy who stare in disbelief at American party politics. In countries such as France and Italy, a multitude of groups nominate candidates and strive for victory at the polls; the groups tend to represent fundamental social interests within the polity. Rarely can one party hope to win a parliamentary majority under such conditions, but the public can clearly tell the difference between the competing aggregations. Those who advocate government by partisan coalition find the disadvantages preferable to our bland, faceless electoral politics, where the voters choose between two parties emasculated by constant broadening and compromise. Even the British, who almost always deliver control of the House of Commons to either the Tories or Labour, have a third-party alternative, the Liberals.

Even so, there are certain points of *similarity* between the American electoral process and its Western European counterparts. For one thing, they all employ *competitive party politics.* This tradition is a living reminder that government by mass participation subsists to greater or lesser extent in these societies. In other words, a political-party system presupposes a certain measure of popular involvement. There were no parties as long as the Hapsburgs or the Bourbons were calling the shots in Austria and in France; nor were there parties as long as George Washington held sway here. When governmental power resides in any self-perpetuating aristocracy or superior social class, there is no need for political parties, whether that power is designed to help the few or to help the many by dint of noblesse oblige. And the adjective "competitive" also deserves emphasis, because while the Soviet Union, Egypt, and others may employ party systems, there is no competition among legally recognized formal organizations in these countries. For another thing, just as Western European parties represent social interests, so American parties represent social interests. To understand why we have two parties, then, is to understand the peculiar makeup of social interests in this nation.

I have talked at some length about the heterogeneity of American group life, a pluralism captured by Madison's notion of factionalism. Yet virtually none of these differences rises to the level of divisiveness commonly characterizing Western European social life. Why?

Part of the answer lies in the presence or absence of a revolutionary tradition. The French Revolution was not merely a change in the political guard; it was a social upheaval and a bloodbath. The same can be said for the Russian Revolution. By contrast, the American Revolution, even as perceived by its more militant advocates,[41] was brought on largely because King and Parliament refused to honor their contractual and constitutional obligations, thus depriving the colonists of their rights as Englishmen. The notion that people in this country have some inherent right to revolt has never been generally accepted, in great measure because the Constitution as a legitimate set of rules commands such overwhelming allegiance.

Equally important is the fact that this country has never had a landed aristocracy, save in the old South. The Constitution even forbids state and federal governments to grant titles of nobility, so horrified were the Founding Fathers at privileged-class trappings in the grand continental sense. The stratified class structures European nations exhibit today stem from their feudalist mainsprings. But feudalism never achieved footing here (except, perhaps, via the plantation system); our class structure, then, is much more fluid.[42]

A third major consideration is the very different role sectarian groups play in these countries. Only a few centuries ago, the pope was the principal landholder in what we now call Italy; Cardinal Richelieu was almost as powerful as the king in matters of French political intrigue; and the rivalries between the Protestant Tudors and the Catholic Stuarts are fundamental to an understanding of British politics during the sixteenth century. No wonder Christian Democratic parties abound in Western Europe! But the norm implicit in the First Amendment's separation of church and state bears witness to our belief that when theology enters political discourse, cleavages may become unbridgeable.

If we lack a revolutionary heritage, if we huddle around the Constitution as around a religious totem, if our culture exhibits no great schism between the offspring of privileged and peasant classes, and if religion is muted in our public domain, what major conflicts divide us? Some scholars think that conformity runs so deep here that earthrending disputes over ends and means rarely cause friction. For instance, one writer has said Americans are Lockeans and nothing more, wedded to individualism, free enterprise, and pragmatism.[43] Another writer has argued that American society is nicely held together by both the Judeo-Christian ethic and the governmental institutions and norms handed down to us from the colonial experience.[44] But if the noises which aggrieved pressure groups emit often conceal our overriding consensus, then these writers, while they have tapped important dimensions of the "Living Constitution," have underplayed our heterogeneity.

Over the long sweep of American history, one central bone of contention has usually divided us into hostile camps: the glories of "strong" national government versus the glories of "weaker" national government. This was the leading issue at Philadelphia in the 1780s, and it pervades our politics today. What is more, one party generally huddles around the "nationalist" theme, while the other generally huddles around some "antinationalist" theme.

Yet I think this disagreement as to what national power can or cannot do is really a debate over technique rather than substance. The more important fact is that *certain kinds of people* advocate strong national authority during particular strains and stresses, while *certain other kinds of people* opt for states' rights, or individualism, or a rigorous checks-and-balances scheme, as conditions warrant. The fascinating question is: Who sits on what side?

I contend that those interests which consider themselves the "haves," *the people and the groups who feel advantaged by their position in the system and so attempt to maintain things as they are,* tend to comprise one political coalition; those interests which consider themselves the "have-nots," *the people and the groups who feel disadvantaged and so want to upgrade their position in the system,* tend to comprise another political coalition. I contend further that, generally speaking, the "haves" make up one political party, while the "have-nots" make up the other party. These factional coalitions attempt to use national authority for their own purposes, strengthening it or weakening it according to the power mix and the issues at stake. In essence, this argument owes an intellectual debt to de Tocqueville's dictum:

> The deeper we penetrate into the inmost thoughts of these parties, the more we perceive that the object of the one is to limit and that of the other to extend the authority of the people. . . . I affirm that aristocratic or democratic passions may easily be detected at the bottom of all parties.[45]

To test this thesis, one need only review the genesis and track records of the major parties, paying special attention to their constituencies as well as to their essential principles and political aspirations. But these aggregations are more than simply outgrowths of interest-group cleavage. That explanation would make them social phenomena solely and treat our political institutions as irrelevant, or neutral at best. And when it comes to mobilizing national political power, the Constitution is *never* neutral and *never* irrelevant. The constitutional framework, then, is a factor making for two parties.

The primary element here is that the presidency is the most influential governmental office in the land, and to win that office a party must obtain *268* electoral votes (the minimum majority in the Electoral College). A party accumulating only 20 or 40 percent of the 535 available votes is left with only the forlorn hope that nobody will obtain the necessary majority and that the House of Representatives, voting as states, will be kind and considerate. What party, lusting after victory, would settle for such scraps for the sake of internal ideological consistency, when a coalition here and there could broaden its base and swell its electoral tide ever closer to the magic 268? Clearly, if both major factions play this game, third parties will find it extraordinarily difficult to make more than token efforts to capture the White House.

But let us not forget the Congress. A party aspiring to control the national governmental apparatus cannot be satisfied with executive power alone; both "political branches" must be won. How are congressmen elected? *Through the same two-party process which controls presidential choice.* In other words, each senator represents one state constituency, and victory at the polls requires the party standard bearer to round up more votes than any of the opponents. Although a senatorial candidate needs only a plurality rather than a clear majority, 50.1 percent of the vote wins automatically, so "safety first" prevails, and each party will enlarge its support incrementally to shoot for at least that minimal figure. The same goes for lower-chamber electoral politics. Each House member represents one district, and victory at the polls requires the party standard bearer to round up a plurality. Again, parties form coalitions in quest of a majority vote, preparing themselves to obtain "half a loaf" rather than nothing. The important consequence of all this is that *minor parties will tend to be shut out of Senate and House races just as they are shut out of presidential contests.*

Note, however, two salient points: (1) European legislative-election schemes encourage multipartyism because they usually provide for *proportional representation,* which gives any party legislative seats in accordance with its percentage of the popular vote. In order to make proportional representation work, a political system must use the *multimember district* blueprint. Thus, if party X achieved 25 percent of the vote, it would receive one out of four available seats, four out of sixteen available seats, or the closest number of seats reflecting its electoral popularity. But at the level of national politics, we use the *single-member district* formula up and down the line. House seats are apportioned one to a district; *Senate seats are apportioned one to a district (the state); and the presidency represents a single-member area as well, with the nation serving as a sort of composite district, made up of fifty single-member packages to be captured by plurality vote.* What all this means is that marginal parties get no tangible reward for finishing third, or even second, in any federal election, and this militates strongly against making an initial effort. (2) Our presidential-election formula is responsible for yielding two *national* parties. Suppose we had a parliamentary system in which the prime minister was chosen by legislative vote, and suppose also that Senate and House members were selected as they now are selected. One might find two parties vying for senatorial office in Alabama, and two *other* parties vying for senatorial office in Michigan; one might have two parties waging electoral battle in Texas's 13th congressional district, and two *other* parties jousting for victory in Texas's 9th district. It is the national coalition building aimed at conquering the White House that prevents each discrete single-member district from having its own blend of major-party competition.

The two-party cycle[46]

Let me recapitulate: American voters consider themselves either "haves" or "have-nots," depending upon the interests they share with others, and they gravitate toward the party representing the values and conveying the images of "havism" or "have-notism." Furthermore, American national government can be invoked to help either one cause or the other, depending upon the power factors which obtain; so the battle between these interests and these parties takes the form of a great debate over how much authority national government should wield. Finally, the parties compete on a constitutional and electoral chessboard, whose rules perpetuate the unique two-party conflict. If I am right, each major party in our history should reveal a fairly sharp profile with respect to both social philosophy and constitutional theory, and this profile should be the mirror image of the opposition's profile.

A review of American presidential elections will show three broad, sweeping cycles in party dominance. The first period dates from Jefferson's initial victory, in 1800, until Lincoln's ascendancy, in 1860. During this era, the Democratic Party (initially called the Republicans) held sway: Jefferson, Madison, Monroe, Jackson, Van Buren, Polk, Pierce, and Buchanan were its successful candidates. Only two Whig generals (W. H. Harrison and Taylor) could break the spell, and both died in office and were succeeded by their lackluster running mates, Tyler and Fillmore. The second period, which found the Republicans as much in the majority as the Democrats had been, stretches from 1860 until 1932, when F.D.R. turned things around. The G.O.P. winners were Lincoln, Grant, Hayes, Garfield, Benjamin Harrison, T.R., Taft, Harding, Coolidge, and Hoover. Again, only two Democrats could break through: Grover Cleveland, who was sometimes more Republican than the Republicans, and Wilson, who defeated a divided G.O.P. The third period began with F.D.R. and continues to this day. Again, the minority party could win only when it tapped a military hero (Eisenhower) or profited from divided opposition (Nixon), while the majority had victors in F.D.R., Truman, Kennedy, Johnson, and Carter.

Of course, party fortunes mean more than what happens in the race for the gold ring. Yet when a presidential nominee wins, he generally drags along congressional party candidates on his coattails; and when a partisan coalition dominates the White House decade after decade, congressional domination by that coalition usually follows. In fact, about the only dent the "outs" can make occurs when a Cleveland, a Wilson, or an Eisenhower comes along, captures the public fancy, and pulls congressional candidates in with him.

Now let us examine the dynamics of these cycles. I have pointed out more than once that the Jeffersonians and the Jacksonians advocated a strict interpretation of federal constitutional power, while their archenemies, the Federalists and the Whigs, advocated a broad construction of federal constitutional power. Of course, Jefferson purchased the Louisiana Territory and Jackson held off Calhounism when South Carolina talked secession, but Jefferson's major ideological adversaries were the Hamiltons and the Marshalls, while Jackson's major antagonists were the Marshalls and the Clays.

Why did Jefferson's constituency fear national authority? Because it would mean government by the bankers, the mercantilists, the patricians, and all the other Federalists. Why did Jackson's constituency fear national authority? Because it would mean the same thing, Whig style, because Clay's "American System," complete with high tariffs and internal improvements, was surely locked into the Hamiltonian tradition. And just as Jefferson's troops were the backwoods communities that had fought against ratifying the Constitution in the first place, so Jackson was Mr. Common Man, handing out government jobs to all faithful comers.

The underlying point here is that in those days government as a means to achieve egalitarian purposes was largely unknown; rather, activist government meant organizing state power to help people of privilege—property owners and commercial interests. So the "haves" favored an aggressive federal machinery; the "have-nots" favored a passive machinery. Given the far-reaching social and political trends of that day—western expansion, a proliferating small-farmer class, ever-widening franchise participation—is it any wonder that the "have-nots" generally won out on Election Day?

What happened to the Democrats is that they lost, temporarily, their social center of gravity. Rather than being first and foremost the "people's party," they became first and foremost the "plantation party." But this shift from a primarily western constituency to a primarily Southern constituency was made without sacrificing two cardinal principles: the Democrats could (1) continue to preach limited national government because the slaveowners were as much opposed to federal power as the small agrarian interests were and (2) continue to inveigh against the protective tariff—the single most important issue separating "haves" and "have-nots" until well into the twentieth century—because *all* planters, slaveowners and nonslaveowners alike, needed to sell their produce abroad.

The Republicans, meantime, could get out from under the Federalist-Whig liability of too close an identification with Eastern business interests by becoming antislavery. But Republicanism *was* the natural outgrowth of that tradition nonetheless, for its leaders, *including Lincoln,* were onetime Whigs, who advocated both tariffs and strong national action, though on this occasion that action was geared to stopping the spread of involuntary servitude. Still, the Democrats retained their national majority until the South became so strong it ousted the Stephen A. Douglas-type partisans lock, stock, and barrel. And so for a few short years the Republican Party was the "have-not" party, dedicated to wiping out slavery; the Democrats had become the party of the slaveowner, the purest of "haves," and this flirtation with suicide would make it a perennial challenger for the next seventy years.

If I am correct, though, the slavery question was an intervening variable—of essential significance, to be sure, but an historical quirk, nonetheless—which deflected our two parties from their essential representational and electoral missions. To view the Republican Party as champion of "have-not" interests is to misconceive its very fabric. Thus, it is much more insightful, and much more accurate, to concentrate on Lincoln the apostle of Union rather than on Lincoln the apostle of abolition, which, in fact, he was *not.* And to view the Democratic Party as advocate of the "haves" is also to miss its central purpose in our politics; indeed, as late as 1855 the party's overall stance was better reflected by Douglas's "popular sovereignty" (the right of states to decide for themselves whether they would allow slavery) than by any plantation gospel. Moreover, when the South ultimately turned to secession, it was merely elaborating on the old Jeffersonian-Madisonian states' rights doctrine.

But soon the dust would clear. The Industrial Revolution and subsequent business expansion required governmental protection, and this the Republicans were more than happy to provide. The Democrats retained supremacy in the now-solid South, but gradually their tentacles spread to the West, where farmers were demanding a new kind of politics: *governmental regulation* of private property. We would soon have antitrust laws and an Interstate Commerce Commission, because the United States was no longer the citadel of Jeffersonian democracy, with its conception of limited national authority. By now, popular participation in politics had become so considerable that federal power could be mobilized to harness corporate property. And here is where the Republicans jumped off the Hamilton-Clay-Lincoln bandwagon of strong, activist nationalism and the Democrats jumped on. Suddenly the Republicans were talking about laissez faire and substantive due process, while the Democrats began talking about the notion of federal bureaucracy.

Of course, this process evolved in fits and starts: Woodrow Wilson was much more committed to small competitive units than T.R., but Wilson (a Virginian) was an unreconstructed Jeffersonian, while T.R. was really a Hamiltonian in 1900 dress. And Eastern labor saw little to recommend William Jennings Bryan's plea to cheapen the dollar, for his protest was in the name of western agrarian grievance. So these urbanites supported Mr. Big Business himself, William McKinley. And why not? Immigrants had flocked to our shores and found a prosperity they had never known before. Marxist doctrine would code these legions as "have-nots," but their voting record tells us infinitely more about their state of mind. As long as capitalism performed as advertised, they could give even the Tafts and the Coolidges lukewarm support.

I have argued that slavery was an intervening variable with respect to major-party philosophy and constituency and that the war hero candidate has always been an intervening variable in presidential electoral politics. I would also call Teddy Roosevelt's personality an intervening variable with regard to both party ideology and electoral popularity, and I would put Wilson's reelection because "he kept us out of war" in the same category. To be more precise, I would code those variables accounting for partisan success into three bundles: *primary* factors (where I would place economic questions); *secondary* factors (where I would place the Civil War); and *tertiary* factors (where I would place the vagaries of particular candidacies). Such distinctions, I think, hold the key to a clear understanding of long-term trends and conflicts.

But what about sectionalism? Is that some sort of intervening variable? The question is crucial because when one considers how the several states have voted over time, one sees a clear trend from Jefferson's day even into our own day.

Sectionalism, certainly, is a source of faction: agrarianism versus urbanism; West versus East; South versus North. But my argument is that sections square off against each other in the partisan arena *because of the people who live in those sections.* Do they feel advantaged or disadvantaged? Will national power help them or hurt them? The West voted for Jefferson because it feared Eastern business and the national banks which business would create; the West voted for Bryan because it continued to fear Eastern business and knew only that strong governmental initiatives could shackle that business; Southerners voted against every Republican from 1856 to 1924 because they saw themselves surrounded, put upon, and eventually humiliated by a party of outsiders who had destroyed their hallowed way of life. Prior to contemporary times, only Al Smith's Catholicism in 1928 (another tertiary variable) broke the trend. The East was the birthplace of abolitionism, but it was also the nation's financial and commercial center, and from Hamilton to McKinley to Coolidge it generally voted that way.

The Great Depression accomplished for political-party alignments in the twentieth century what the Civil War had accomplished in the nineteenth: it turned the majority party into the minority party. But there was an important difference. Human bondage may have been a question of economic survival for the plantation owner, but it became a moral dilemma for most everyone else. As such, the issue was atypical for our generally nonideological party debates. Political liability though it had been, the charge of being "soft on slavery" could be shed without disturbing the Democrats' very reason for existence, the defense of "have-not" interests. But party responsibility for prolonged economic adversity was in the mainstream of what these debates are all about; therefore, the Depression would be more difficult for the Republicans per se to overcome.

The Crash of 1929 meant the end of "what's good for business is good for the United States," and it meant the end of both laissez faire and economic substantive due process. Out of the wreckage emerged a new majority, the Roosevelt coalition. This alliance was quite simply a hodgepodge of "have-nots," interests that felt cheated by the system: the long-suffering small farmers; the big-city workers, whose shared experiences now included breadlines and "soup kitchens"; the Catholics and the Jews, who had traditionally voted Democratic in national elections anyway because of their long-standing "underdog" status; the blacks, initially Republican because the G.O.P. was "Lincoln's party," who now saw a friend in F.D.R.; and that strangest of partisan animals, the Southerner, whose revenge against "Lincoln's party" would now be consummated. And lurking beneath this interest-group mix were other salient conditions attesting to the rivalry between the "haves" and the "have-nots." For instance, we now realize that from the 1930s to the present a definite correlation has existed between the status of an individual's occupation and party affiliation.[47] And we know that people who *underrate* their social-class standing line up as Democrats, while those who *overrate* their social-class standing see themselves as Republicans.[48]

The Roosevelt coalition wanted strong governmental action to restrain perceived business excesses, and throughout the 1930s it received such action. Every Democratic presidential candidate since has pledged ever-wider initiatives in that general direction. This grand strategy was extraordinarily successful until 1968, bringing victory after victory for the "founding father" F.D.R. and even allowing Harry Truman to survive a two-way intraparty schism. The Republicans, meantime, fought the usual uphill role of the minority party: when the G.O.P. essayed the (Eisenhower) war hero gambit, and the major issue was military involvement in Korea, it split the Democratic coalition down the middle; and when the Democrats nominated the Catholic Kennedy in 1960, the G.O.P. almost took home the bacon; but it nearly became the "nonparty" when it challenged the coalition head-on by offering up a candidate, Barry Goldwater, who favored abolishing the social security system.

In 1968, however, the Democrats became bogged down over Vietnam policy; their national convention was held amid chaos as Chicago's Mayor Daley, a party stalwart, ordered his police to crack down against "New Left" demonstrators; George Wallace, refusing to support the eventual nominee, Hubert Humphrey, ran his own campaign; "doves" on the war, who had backed Minnesota's Senator Eugene McCarthy, were at best unenthusiastic about Humphrey, Lyndon Johnson's Vice President; and the Republicans nominated a well-known pragmatist, Richard Nixon, who refused to challenge Roosevelt coalition premises. The result was a narrow G.O.P. win. Then, in 1972, the Democrats nominated George McGovern, who said he would crawl to Hanoi if necessary to obtain a peace agreement with Ho Chi Minh. That kind of rhetoric, plus McGovern's visible liaison with student activists and his selection-then-rejection of Senator Thomas Eagleton as running mate, made him appear to be some kind of unpredictable radical. By overcommitting himself on the war issue and soft-pedaling the "bread-and-butter" issues that had kept the "have-nots" on top, he proved that neither party has a monopoly on electioneering wisdom. Things returned to normal in 1976, when Jimmy Carter defeated Gerald Ford by emphasizing public-works programs to remedy nagging unemployment, though Carter's Southern background probably cost him many an ethnic vote in the North and the West.

The congressional picture has been somewhat different because, since the late 1930s, a Republican-Southern Democratic alliance has usually had things its own way. There have been exceptions, of course: the Johnson landslide in 1964 brought to Washington a whole raft of first-term Democrats, while the Watergate scandal, plus an economic downturn in 1974, saw the G.O.P. lose almost fifty House seats. As of 1977, the Roosevelt coalition is less healthy than the liberal Democratic majority controlling Congress would indicate, but healthier than President Carter's wafer-thin victory margin would suggest.

What are G.O.P. prospects for turning things around? The polls show that fewer people call themselves Republicans today than at any time since F.D.R.'s tenure, though some of that must be Watergate backlash. Republicanism cannot succeed over time unless it puts a dent in the Roosevelt coalition. Only one instance of this has occurred: the South has fallen away somewhat from the national Democratic Party. The reason is clear. Democratic Congresses have enacted, and Democratic presidential candidates have endorsed, vigorous, sweeping civil rights legislation that threatens the dominant status of white, rural, Southern political power. Behaving as "haves" whose just desserts are being taken from them, the South has moved toward Republicanism. But until the conservative, patrician electorate represented by Senator Stennis and the "redneck" electorate represented by Governor Wallace join the G.O.P., the South will not have burned its political bridges. The fact is that a highly competitive Republican Party would need more than the South, the usual assortment of business interests, and its traditional share of the farm vote. It would need a sizable chunk of an elusive interest known as the "new middle class." These are the thousands of blue-collar and white-collar workers who earn, perhaps, $13,000 to $20,000 per year as a result of the consistent national economic growth we have enjoyed since World War II, and whose unions are secure (of course, not all members of this faction belong to unions). The "new middle class" also includes the thousands who fear "crime in the streets," who oppose school busing, and who have fled the cities to escape both. Can the Republicans take the preponderance of these voters away from the Democrats?[49] Not if unemployment continues to outweigh the less-partisan issues.

And so we are back to "haves" versus "have-nots." The Democrats' tactics have gone full circle, from Jefferson's passive central government to Hubert Humphrey's aggressive central government, and the Republicans' tactics have gone full circle, too, from Hamilton's aggressive central government to Ford's *quasi*-passive central government. (We can never go back to Jefferson's day!) But the grand alliances and strategies have not changed: the Republicans are geared to interest stratification, with an emphasis on aiding the property owner and business; the Democrats are geared to interest egalitarianism, with an emphasis on property regulation and economic redistribution.

Our decentralized parties: a constitutional overview

Early in this chapter, I argued that Madison's constitutional scheme of balancing factional influence by dividing political power perhaps has worked *too well.* The "Living Constitution," with its decentralized congressional-bureaucratic networks, seems often a perfect setting for small, cohesive interests brandishing intensely held attitudes. In order to achieve broader, more comprehensive policy, coalitions of "have" and "have-not" factions have developed national political parties. But what impact does the Constitution have on the structural makeup and value orientation of those parties?

The relevant determinants are federalism and separation of national powers, the same considerations that influence interest-group potential generally. And they are important in the party and in the group contexts for the same reason: they establish a fragmented representational pecking order of autonomous power centers. Thus, the President represents the nation, senators represent states, House members represent intrastate districts, governors represent states but lack national responsibility, and none of these people can compel the others to do anything. Here, then, are the most powerful elected officials within the party, and the proven vote getters as well, serving totally different constituencies, very often at inevitable cross-purposes.

Yes, presidential nominees can command media attention every four years, and their coattails do transcend, in part, such grassroots attachments.[50] But House members stand for reelection every two years, senators every six years, and governors usually every four years, with their terms often deliberately geared to *non*presidential-year cycles. Furthermore, voter turnout is much smaller in off-year elections—that is, when the White House is not up for grabs—and off-year voters are much older, better educated, more affluent, and more civic-minded than the electors who participate when "Mr. President, Superstar" is being chosen.[51] That is one good reason why the President's party almost always loses congressional seats when White House occupancy is uncontested.

The overall result is that the various candidates must normally run on their own, and they must structure their campaigns to suit whatever blend of interest-group support and issue endorsement will pay off *for them.* Meanwhile, of course, the most ambitious, the most charismatic, and the most successful among this select group will be building their own personal followings as they prepare to run for President. After all, there is no single path to the White House; any significant national or state launching pad will do. Of the sixteen major-party presidential candidates from the onset of the Great Depression until 1976, all but three (Hoover, Willkie, and Eisenhower) were catapulted to the top through gubernatorial or congressional service.

The implications of all this for party structure and ideology become readily apparent when we try to answer these simple questions: Who speaks for the Democrats? Who speaks for the Republicans? During the presidential sweepstakes one might reply, "The presidential nominees." But what about the rest of the time? If party X holds the White House, the reply would be, "The President, almost always"; if party X does not hold the White House, the reply is usually a straightforward "Nobody." Is it any wonder that the two major parties are structurally decentralized and ideologically diffuse?[52]

In fact, one famous political scientist, James MacGregor Burns, claims that we do not even have a two-party system![53] He argues there are really *four* political parties competing in the national power arena: presidential Democrats, congressional Democrats, presidential Republicans, and congressional Republicans. The presidential Democrats are part of the broad, national, liberal coalition that has sent Jefferson, Jackson, Wilson, F.D.R., and Lyndon Johnson to the White House. The congressional Democrats comprise the narrow, local, conservative constituencies that elected the John C. Calhouns of yesterday and elect the Senator James Eastlands of today. The presidential Republicans have their roots in the Lincoln–T.R. tradition; today, they vie with their Democratic, liberal counterparts for national support, and their prominent spokesmen would be the Eisenhowers and the Rockefellers. The congressional Republicans comprise the narrow, local, conservative constituencies that sent Gerald Ford to Congress for over twenty years and send the Barry Goldwaters of today. The presidential parties veer toward liberalism, because they are competing under the Electoral College winner-take-all system, which accords more influence to urban communities. The congressional parties veer toward conservatism, because they are competing under districting formulas—such as the "two senators per state" rule—that accord more power to sparsely populated constituencies.[54] However, the Democratic presidentials are more liberal and activist than Republican presidentials, while the Democratic congressionals are more liberal and activist than Republican congressionals, except with respect to racial politics.

A more conventional critique, however, is that our two parties have all the ideological and structural fortitude of jello and border on impotence. Those who take this view have sounded the clarion call for reform: We must realign the parties! What would our "revitalized" partisan aggregations look like? Very much, it turns out, like blood relatives of Professor Burns's presidential parties. According to one blueprint, endorsed by a select panel of professional political scientists,[55] each party would be governed by a steering committee charged with clearing candidates for office and staking out ideological priorities and issue positions. Presidential candidates, furthermore, would emphasize their philosophical differences rather than their stylistic differences, thus offering voters a "real" choice. The winning candidate, therefore, would possess a mandate from the people to govern; any partisan colleague who bucked the chief could be censured and, ultimately, dismissed from the party. The losers, naturally, would play the constructive roles of critic and "loyal opposition."

Burns himself penetrates more deeply into the substantive nature of renovated party ideology, as well as into the constitutional and statutory changes needed for realignment. The Democrats, upgraded to full maturity, would be the party of "qualitative liberalism," stressing not merely economic issues but large-scale, innovative programs to improve urban life, to make education a more meaningful experience, and to support civil rights as a moral issue rather than as a "bread-and-butter" one.[56] The Republicans, upgraded to full maturity, would be the party of "balance and consolidation," accepting the modern role of national government to formulate broad policy solutions but countering inevitable Democratic mistakes and overoptimism with a more pragmatic, commonsense "qualitative conservatism."[57] As for the political right wing currently housed in both parties, it would slowly gravitate toward the G.O.P., for any attempt to "outpromise" the Democrats on gut economic questions is, as the Goldwaters have correctly claimed, next to impossible.

How can we displace what Burns calls the politics of brokerage, aimed at accommodating disparate interests and pulverized parties? The two presidential aggregations must combine forces temporarily to (1) get rid of the seniority system in Congress, Rules Committee power in the House, and the filibuster in the Senate; (2) strip the states of their time-honored role in drawing House district lines; and (3) develop national dues-paying party memberships, thus preempting loyalties to maverick candidates and officeholders.

Without doubt, these schemes are designed to constitutionalize the presidential activism we enjoyed under Jefferson, Wilson, F.D.R., and Lyndon Johnson—that is, *party government* in the British tradition.[58] Truly national, ideologically identifiable aggregations would make the electoral process more meaningful both by sharpening issues and by transforming the host of individual "one-on-one" competitions we now have into a single partisan "one-on-one," which all the voters could join in. But what protections would the citizenry have against majority tyranny? The parties, it is said, could not slight the forces of moderation, because they would then lose touch with the "middle groups" that hold the keys to electoral success in this country.

Can the so-called Jeffersonian model be constitutionalized in our time? I think not. First, the Madisonian model is not merely a gloss we place on the Constitution; *it is embedded in the Constitution.* That model includes the entire system of checks and balances pervading both separation of national power and federalism. Of course, we could throw out the Constitution. We could raise the terms of House members to four years, or lower the terms of senators to four years, or recast House and Senate district lines so that members of Congress will truly represent equal numbers of people. As a matter of fact, "pure judicial review" can also slow majority sentiment to a snail's pace. The British would never abide a judicial veto of legislative policy-making; why should we?

The problem is that Americans don't want to do these things. They don't even want to take the far more modest step of transforming internal congressional decision-making dynamics into a series of roll-call votes. Why? Because in American politics, tradition, custom, and intuition usually speak more loudly than all the "game plans" critics can muster. Two centuries of experience have conditioned us to beware majorities, beware slogans, beware political leaders who would save us from ourselves, and beware intellectuals bearing gifts. That facet of the "Living Constitution" is also designed to keep our political parties well within the contours of a checks-and-balances perspective imposed by other power centers.

The structure of parties

State party organization

Generally speaking, one might expect our decentralized parties to utilize decentralized structures in managing their affairs. And indeed they do. Hence, my analysis begins not at the national level but at the state and local levels.

Reacting against the "evils" of "invisible government," state legislatures have formulated extraordinarily complicated organizational charts, which parties must ape. A typical scheme would include a state central committee, county committees, district committees, ward committees, and precinct committees. The most important personnel among these are usually the precinct captains, who concentrate on getting out the vote; the district leaders, who preside over precinct activism; the county leaders, who are concerned more with policy than with power; and the state central-committee representatives, who are really ambassadors from the various congressional districts.[59]

Perhaps the best term for political party organization is *stratarchy.* In other words, each stratum within the group wields relatively significant power in relatively independent fashion. One impetus toward stratarchy is that the several districts comprise rather different political universes, and the party is so desperate for votes it must cede enormous authority to the functionaries in charge of these units. The notion of party as a political mechanism run by some homogeneous elite corps—the "iron law of oligarchy"—may well have been applicable to the big-city machines of forty years ago, but today no Tammany Hall calls the shots in New York City. In fact, there is a real question as to how the party leaders can effectively control their subordinates at all. Evidently, the key is *rapport*—that is, working together to achieve a common purpose and thereby developing reciprocal status relationships. The political party, then, is as much a social group as an entity geared to common value considerations.

To verify these generalizations, we can look first at leader-follower interaction within the party. Those who hold top positions of responsibility trip over themselves enticing outsiders into the organization; these networks may have their social centers of gravity, but deviant vocational and ethnic interest groups are sprinkled throughout both hierarchies. Yet most party officeholders are self-starters, attracted to party work because of their own personal needs. However, there is tremendous turnover among the regulars, even at the district committee level. Many precinct leaders feel removed from the decision-making process, so they see no reason to stick things out. Thus, the "top dogs" have been compelled to give them a free hand; in many cases, district supervisors don't know how party affairs are being run below.

A second batch of significant findings relates to party ideology. Although victory seems to be the top concern, a glance at state-organization opinion is all one needs to see where the "haves" and the "have-nots" reside. Democrats are more liberal than Republicans up and down the line;[60] the higher the post, the more liberal is the Democrat; the most conservative Republicans sit in the top echelons. So party leadership, whose role entails articulating issues and plotting grand strategies, is held by the real ideologues. Evidently, it takes such commitment to stay around and move up the hierarchy. Along this line, the typical precinct leader turns out to be no ideologue at all; the rewards of work are friendship, excitement, and status, not the thrill of spreading a gospel—which merely demonstrates again that neither party is painting itself into a doctrinaire box.

Some specifics on the relationship between the state party organization and the general public are also salient. When people are exposed to majority-party doings, they tend to see partisan activism from a more favorable perspective; however, an inverse relationship occurs when the public is exposed to minority-party endeavors. Yet there is no correlation between exposure and caring whether either party wins or loses! This fact shows that neither aggregation was getting its message across to those who were looking and listening, even in a period when party identification was much more stable and frequent than nowadays. These organizations, of course, are concerned primarily with promoting voter participation, and there is a strong link between exposure to party labors and voting; furthermore, people who have contact with partisan activism are much more knowledgeable about politics. But such exposure has a negative impact on college-educated citizens, who probably have trouble relating to both the rough and tumble atmosphere and the busywork. The professional's reception is indeed mixed.

In summing up the roles and accomplishments of the parties, Eldersveld notes how much weaker the state and local party organizations are today than previously. At the turn of the century, they dominated the electoral process through two levers: candidate recruitment and patronage. In our time, the primary system has ousted them, for all practical purposes, from nomination politics, while patronage, once the standard reward for exemplary party service, is now virtually nonexistent. He then concludes in this guardedly optimistic vein:

> The party does perform important tasks in the system. It does recruit leadership which is reasonably realistic, goal-oriented, ideologically distinctive, competitive and oriented to democratic values. It does contribute to citizen interest in public affairs, to party loyalty, to "getting out the vote," and to the confidence of the citizen in the political system. . . . [However], the party is no "master institution" but a minimal efficiency structure . . . performing social and political tasks at a marginal level.[61]

National party organization

If the vigor and responsibility of grassroots party structures have attenuated over the years, have national party structures gained in clout and scope? We can dismiss that possibility almost out of hand.

Whatever permanent national organization exists is housed in the national committees, and theirs are the humdrum functions one might reasonably associate with the apex of decentralized power structure. For example, the committees must decide which cities will host the national conventions; they must manage the national headquarters; they must run their nominees' presidential campaigns. The closest the committees might come to engaging in candidate selection is to ratify the choice of a party candidate if the nominee of a convention dies or resigns—as happened in 1972 when the Democratic National Committee certified George McGovern's designation of Sargent Shriver as his running mate following Thomas Eagleton's forced withdrawal. Nevertheless, while the national committees do not perform life-and-death tasks, they attract both well-to-do influentials and professional activists who like to rub shoulders with the party "superstars." So when Richard Nixon established his own electoral team (the Committee to Re-elect the President) in 1972, he alienated many top people in the G.O.P. Membership in the two committees is technically the business of the conventions, but actually the state delegations propose slates, which are invariably approved. Recently, though, the Democrats have thrown open the doors of committee service in an attempt to provide broader representation. The Democratic National Committee now has about 250 members, while the Republicans have a more modest 150.

Special attention should be given the national chairmen (or chairwomen). By tradition the national committee head for the President's party is quite simply the President's alter ego; however, capturing the "out" party's national leadership often involves a test of strength among competing factions. When George McGovern won the Democrats' nomination, he tapped Jean Westwood to sit in this position, but she fell from power as soon as the election returns rendered McGovern vulnerable. This post carries some punch, because both committees are too large and diffuse to perform executive functions properly. Perhaps the most important role these two officials play lies in the fund-raising area, though Robert Strauss of Texas (the then Democratic national chairman) performed a highly innovative function as consensus builder by organizing, in 1974, his party's first-ever off-year meeting.

Parties and groups: a reprise

In my introductory remarks, I noted the possibility that political parties and pressure groups could disrupt severely one another's representational functions in the constitutional polity. But what, in fact, is their relationship and what does it portend?

Clearly, both vehicles lack the inherent capacity to represent totally our citizenry's diverse political needs. Theoretically, the various factions could invoke the party to handle some public policy grievances, while invoking the group to handle others. If the "Living Constitution" worked this way, then a nice balance might be obtained between the two devices, and any serious friction between them be forestalled.

And sometimes this equilibrium model does appear to characterize political party-pressure group interaction. There is usually a majority party and a minority party. Some groups sit largely under the majority umbrella, others largely under the minority umbrella, and countless others largely on the outside, working both sides of the street. Nor do even the most "inside" pressure aggregations sell their soul to any partisan coalition. For example, when a Democrat resides in the White House, you can bet that the A.F.L.-C.I.O. will maintain a little action on the side, trying to obtain through independent legislative and administrative channels what it cannot obtain through party channels. The same can be said for business's liaison with the G.O.P.

But upon closer inspection, the data show the existence only of a rather tenuous division of labor, not the existence of any such equilibrium. What tends to happen is that as political problems vary, attitudes vary, and so collective action varies in an effort to push government toward favorable response. That means that the nature of the compelling grievances determines whether the system will feature partisan activism or pressure-group go-it-aloneism.

For example, the middle 1930s, with the New Deal riding high, was a season for group coalition and partisan achievement. Twenty years later, the Democratic Party was still the majority party, and the liberal consensus was certainly still around. Yet the overriding variable in national politics was "Ike" Eisenhower; the "political branches" were divided; partisan accomplishment was minimal; group independence flourished. The prevailing shared attitudes had taken a holiday from both parties; the dominant factional alignment was satisfied to work through its own pressure-group machinery, because citizen grievance was mild and interest aggregations didn't have to maximize compromise through party activism to get what they wanted. Indeed, as a general rule, the Constitution is far more conducive to meaningful "group governance" than to meaningful "party governance," given its reliance upon the Madisonian model.

We live in an era when parties are "down" and groups are "up." Whatever one thinks of pressure aggregations, they usually make the most of what they have. But the Democrats and the Republicans are eviscerated, and they themselves, not groups, are the cause. Why?

Citizen grievance, I repeat, is the central pivot controlling party-group interplay. Partisan consensus comes alive when the diverse interests that make up the "haves" (or the "have-nots") relinquish their parochial ways and combine forces to achieve some overriding desire. And just what would that overriding desire be today? The closest is economic egalitarianism, but think of how the Vietnam War, racial politics, and the "law and order" issue have nagged at the Democratic majority since 1964!

So we have been thrown back to our secondary-group resources: those with whom we work and play. In that universe, each interest becomes a bit more feisty, a bit more egocentric.

Citizen grievance, however, is not only a reflection of what organized factions crave; it is a reflection of the reigning public philosophy. In this context, the term "public philosophy" means our political outlook as Americans, as members of a predominant *potential* group who share whatever the prevailing attitude toward constitutional politics may be. That attitude—liberalism—is also group-centered today, for though we covet the security which statism can bring, Americans fear authority as much as they fear anything. Hence the term I have used so often before: "interest-group" liberalism.

Pluralism may be the backbone of our social system, but pluralism cannot provide us with short-term public policy through law, much less long-term constitutional doctrine. Interests must *give* as well as *get;* rights must sometimes yield to duties in the balanced polity. This was essentially Madison's message, and the Constitution is forged in that commitment.

Despite my criticisms, in Chapter 5, of the crisis mentality as a fundamental cause of the "imperial White House," I must say that our uncritical acceptance of the liberal credo approaches crisis proportions. A statecraft that simply pampers interests has no sense of greater good and little sense of self-restraint. The inevitable question is whether this "quasi-crisis" can best be met by centralized party government or decentralized group autonomy. But if the former, then why complain about presidential supremacy? And if the latter, then why complain about the Constitution and the law as pluralist trappings?

The usual state of affairs is for political party and pressure group to provide counterbalance, not through peaceful coexistence but by displacing one another as "top dog" as conditions change. The bottom line is whether the people think parties or groups are the vehicles most deserving of support at a particular stage in our politics. That is one sense in which equilibrium does obtain between the two in the "Living Constitution."

But what happens in the *unusual* state of affairs, one that finds crisis afoot? At that point, the most latent, the most fundamental of potential groups collectivize, defending the "rules of the game" against perceived outrage. A new public philosophy then comes forward, and the party struggle reflects this by giving birth to some new consensus of "haves" or "have-nots." So substantive due process died; so the Roosevelt coalition took hold. That is another sense in which equilibrium obtains between party and group in the "Living Constitution."

History would seem to tell us the "Living Constitution" cannot sustain indefinitely any public philosophy geared exclusively to either rights orientation or duties orientation. To repeat, the existence of such a philosophy portends crisis, and "interest-group" liberalism smacks of unabridged rights orientation. I should think the ideology of checks-and-balances constitutionalism itself would be a sufficient replacement. Still, nobody knows what that emergent philosophy will be, what a new party consensus would look like, or when we can expect either. This I can safely say: The "Living Constitution" will inhibit the new party coalition, even the new public philosophy, from becoming inviolate. That is because *any* group, *any* aggregation, *any* party, is susceptible to excess, is susceptible to stagnation. This also I can safely say: The people decide what the prevailing balance is to be largely with their votes. To the "Living Constitution" and the politics of voting, I turn in Chapter 10.

NOTES

1. I have profited greatly from a reading of James MacGregor Burns's *The Deadlock of Democracy* (Englewood Cliffs, N.J.: Prentice-Hall, 1964), with respect to what he calls the "Madisonian model." But, as will be evident later, I can't buy the normatives in his essay.

2. *The Federalist,* No. 10.

3. Gaillard Hunt, ed., *The Writings of James Madison* (New York: G. P. Putnam's Sons, 1901), vol. II, pp. 366–67.

4. *The Federalist,* No. 51.

5. Arthur Bentley, *The Process of Government* (Chicago: Univ. of Chicago Press, 1908).

6. David B. Truman, *The Governmental Process* (New York: Alfred A. Knopf, 1951), p. 33.

7. Compare Madison, *The Federalist,* No. 10.

8. See, for instance, Bradbury Seasholes, ed., *Voting, Interest Groups, and Parties* (Glenview, Ill.: Scott, Foresman, 1966), pp. 46–47.

9. V. O. Key, Jr., *Politics, Parties, & Pressure Groups,* 5th ed. (New York: Thomas Y. Crowell, 1964), p. 18.

10. Ibid., Chs. 2-5.

11. I am here distinguishing "farm life" from "plantation life."

12. Or words to that effect. I can't recall where I heard him say this, but it was on the campaign trail in the 1950s.

13. An exception is the International Typographical Union. Its governance is well described in Seymour M. Lipset, *Union Democracy* (Glencoe, Ill.: The Free Press, 1956).

14. These aren't direct quotes, but they constitute a fair statement of U.A.W. philosophy to this day.

15. ICPR Codebook for the 1972 SRC Election Study.

16. Quoted in Key, p. 93.

17. The term is from J. K. Galbraith, *American Capitalism* (Boston: Houghton Mifflin, 1952).

18. For blacks as an interest group, see the section on civil rights policy in Chapter 11.

19. Robert Welch, *The Politician* (Belmont, Mass.: Belmont Publishing, 1964), p. ix.

20. What pressure groups do liberal college students join today? Mostly special-interest organizations, I think: groups concerned with civil rights, students' rights, environmental issues, and the like.

21. This section is based on a series of penetrating articles written by Peter C. Stuart for *The Christian Science Monitor.* See the October 8, 9, 10, and 14, 1975, editions.

22. *United States v. Rumely,* 345 U.S. 41 (1953); *United States v. Harriss,* 347 U.S. 612 (1954).

23. Lester W. Milbrath, *The Washington Lobbyists* (Chicago: Rand McNally, 1963), p. 355.

24. Key, p. 138. Though he made this estimate fifteen years ago, I have not seen anyone improve upon it.

25. This is mostly Bentley's contribution. See *The Process of Government,* pp. 226-27, 370-71, 454-55. However, I think Bentley can be interpreted as saying also that democracy is good because it allows for governance by the dominant group coalition!

26. This is David Truman's contribution, though he is much more tentative about the former assertion than the latter. But a compilation of his remarks shows that he considered unitary government totally at odds with our pluralistic makeup. See *The Governmental Process,* pp. 518-19, 526, 528-30, 533.

27. Truman, pp. 506-16.

28. Ibid., pp. 512-14.

29. Mancur Olson, *The Logic of Collective Action* (Cambridge, Mass.: Harvard Univ. Press, 1971).

30. Ibid., p. 134.

31. Ibid., Ch. 6.

32. Robert Michels, *Political Parties* (London: Jarrold & Sons, 1915; reprinted by The Free Press, Glencoe, Ill., 1949).

33. L. Harmon Zeigler, *Interest Groups in American Society* (Englewood Cliffs, N.J.: Prentice-Hall, 1964), p. 174ff.

34. "The Unchecked Power of the Building Trades," *Fortune* (December 1968), p. 105.

35. This thesis is expounded in Theodore J. Lowi, *The Politics of Disorder* (New York: W. W. Norton, 1971), Ch. 1. See also Grant McConnell, *Private Power and American Democracy,* 1st ed. (New York: Alfred A. Knopf, Vintage Books, 1966), Ch. 5.

36. Raymond A. Bauer, Ithiel de Sola Pool, and Lewis A. Dexter, *American Business and Public Policy* (New York: Atherton Press, 1963), pp. 324-25.

37. See Harry Eckstein, *Pressure Group Politics* (Stanford, Calif.: Stanford Univ. Press, 1960), pp. 162-63.

38. William Kornhauser, *The Politics of Mass Society* (Glencoe, Ill.: The Free Press, 1959).

39. Theodore Roosevelt still holds the record for the highest popular vote by a bona fide third-party presidential candidate, 27.4 percent, as well as the record for the highest electoral vote by such a candidate, 88.

40. In a very rare case, a third party might be motivated by the prospect of forcing a deadlock in the Electoral College; the race would then be thrown into the House, where party influence could be bartered for a compromise

on issues. This must have been high on Wallace's agenda in 1968, but the stratagem failed, of course.

41. I suppose I'd have to make an exception for the likes of Tom Paine.

42. This thesis is developed at length in Louis Hartz, *The Liberal Tradition in America* (New York: Harcourt, Brace, 1955).

43. Ibid.

44. Russell Kirk, "The American Political Tradition," *National Review* (February 8, 1958), pp. 133-35.

45. Alexis de Tocqueville, *Democracy in America,* ed. Phillips Bradley (New York: Vintage Books, 1954), vol. I, p. 185ff.

46. An excellent book describing the two-party system over time is Wilfred E. Binkley, *American Political Parties: Their Natural History,* 5th ed. (New York: Alfred A. Knopf, 1965). Also of great help to me were Key, *Politics, Parties, & Pressure Groups* and Burns, *The Deadlock of Democracy.*

47. Norval D. Glenn, "Class and Party Support in the United States: Recent and Emergent Trends," *Public Opinion Quarterly* 37 (1973), pp. 1-20.

48. James A. Barber, Jr., *Social Mobility and Voting Behavior* (Chicago: Rand McNally, 1970), Ch. 6.

49. Some would say that the G.O.P. ought to play down these appeals and launch a major effort to win the black inner-city vote. This could be done within the contours of Republicanism, it is said, by such proposals as tax incentives to encourage the growth of private job-training centers and "black capitalism"—that is, fortifying black businesses with money and expertise to get them off the ground. And this could outflank the Democrats, who place much greater emphasis on public expenditure. Perhaps that is how the Republicans *should* proceed! But the evidence that party leaders or party interests are prepared to move in any such direction is zero; the path of least resistance surely lies in the opposite direction. For a fuller discussion of this question from a policy overview, see Chapter 11.

50. Warren E. Miller, "Presidential Coattails: A Study in Political Myth and Methodology," *Public Opinion Quarterly* 19 (1955-56), pp. 353-68.

51. Angus Campbell, "Surge and Decline: A Study of Electoral Change," in Angus Campbell, Philip E. Converse, Warren E. Miller, and Donald E. Stokes, *Elections and the Political Order* (New York: John Wiley, 1966), pp. 40-62.

52. David B. Truman, "Federalism and the Party System," in Arthur W. Macmahon, ed., *Federalism: Mature and Emergent* (New York: Russell & Russell, 1962), pp. 115-36.

53. Burns, pp. 195-203.

54. For a fuller discussion of these "electoral repercussions," see Chapter 10.

55. "Toward a More Responsible Two-Party System," Report of the Committee on Political Parties of the American Political Science Association, *The American Political Science Review* 44 (1950), Supplement.

56. Burns, p. 321.

57. Ibid., pp. 290-94.

58. Perhaps the best defense of an American-style British partisanship is found in E. E. Schattschneider, *Party Government* (New York: Farrar and Rinehart, 1942).

59. These and other data presented below are taken from Samuel J. Eldersveld, *Political Parties: A Behavioral Analysis* (Chicago: Rand McNally, 1964). This is the most exhaustive account I have seen of party structure and function. But the data base, Michigan's Wayne County, cannot be considered typical, because the Detroit area is so much under the influence of the automobile industry and the enduring struggle for power between the "Big Three" and the United Auto Workers. My presentation emphasizes those findings which would appear to transcend contextual limitation.

60. Compare Herbert McCloskey et al., "Issue Conflict and Consensus Among Party Leaders and Followers," *The American Political Science Review* 54 (1960), pp. 406-27; the writers find G.O.P. grassroots workers to be as liberal as their Democratic counterparts.

61. Eldersveld, p. 526.

10

the electoral process: participatory democracy?

Voter choice, on the face of it, ought to be thoroughly fair and uncomplicated. Politics is very much a study in leader-follower relations, so what could be more equitable or natural than for the followers to get together and select their leaders? To make an electoral process work, one would seem to need only three elements: (1) people willing and able to vote, (2) people willing and able to govern, (3) an agreed-upon mechanism for deciding *who wins.* A constitution that guarantees both decision-making by elected officials and civil liberties to prevent those decision-makers from "going too far" would appear to be the best of all possible worlds: majority rule and minority rights.[1]

Very often we treat elections as though they were just that simple. No matter how cynical we are about politics, "Election Night, U.S.A." is a popular spectator sport. For every candidate who dreams of power, each bid for election is a title fight. And we, the fans—and sometimes we, the voters—want a piece of the action. We want to know whether the public's estimate of a combatant matches the candidate's own—and whether it matches our estimate.[2]

But the "Living Constitution" of our federal electoral system is anything but simple; for it hinges on complex social and political patterns unspecified in our fundamental law and often ignored by the media. We need to know who votes and who does not; who runs for national office and who does not; who pays the election bills and who does not. We also need to understand how candidates are nominated, what issues and ideas they have emphasized in order to win voter endorsement, and whether voters decide the way they're supposed to decide or whether they march to drumbeats politicians often ignore. Finally, we must grapple with the electoral process as constitutional "connective tissue," linking political parties and pressure groups to the power structure; for, in the end, these aggregations will fail dismally if they do not receive some measure of popular support at the polls. Indeed, the more we realize how parties and groups have infiltrated the electoral process, the more we may be inclined to ask: Has voting been converted from the "natural" and "fair" preserve of citizens to some distorted, biased preserve of political elites?

Somewhere between the popular conception of elections as athletic events and the academic conception of elections as variegated social phenomena lies the truth, and the intervening parameter is the Constitution. No voting chart, no party strategy, no pressure-group promise means a thing in this country unless one understands the "rules of the game" found there; they color the entire electoral process, as I shall now try to demonstrate.

The Electoral College

No doubt when one thinks of public elections in this country, one thinks almost automatically of presidential elections. If a person votes only infrequently, it will probably be in presidential years. The chief executive, as we have seen, is the sole representative of all enfranchised Americans.

Alexander Hamilton was enraptured by the presidential office and was equally ecstatic about the election process hammered out at Philadelphia—"If the manner of it be not perfect," he said, "it is at least excellent."[3] The reader is surely familiar with the basics. Each state chooses electors, through whatever process its legislature finds suitable; the number of a state's electors (that is, electoral votes) depends upon the size of its congressional delegation; the electors cast votes for President, with a majority in the entire body needed to secure victory; should no candidate receive a majority after one tally, the election is then thrown into the House of Representatives, which, *voting as state delegations,* must pick from among the top three "nominees"; the House casts as many ballots as necessary until a majority of states settles on one candidate.

Evidently, Hamilton's enthusiasm stemmed from an "electoral college" concept; he believed that such a body could be trusted to weigh carefully the merits of competing aspirants, keeping the public interest clearly in view. Despite general esteem for his political sagacity, Hamilton's judgment on this occasion betrayed him badly. Even had the Electoral College survived as an independent collectivity, it is difficult to believe that the members would have massed behind a single candidate except in the rarest circumstances. And atypical circumstances did obtain in the only two instances when the members' autonomy prevailed—George Washington was victorious by unanimous tallies in 1788 and 1792. (Did Hamilton really think a "man on horseback" would surface every four years?) Given more usual conditions, the College figured to be only a nominating body; the real choice would be made in the House and by vote of state delegations, hardly an appealing morsel for the nationalist Hamiltonians to swallow. Such habitual behavior could easily have made state control over the White House part of the "Living Constitution."[4]

Speculation aside, history has proven Hamilton to be a poor prophet. There is evidence the Founders thought states would eventually adopt the "district system," whereby voters could approve one elector for each intrastate geographic area, precisely as voters today elect one congressman per single-member district.[5] Many did experiment with this device and other methods as well; however, once the practice developed of holding out a state's entire electoral vote *in package form,* that procedure quickly became "constitutionalized."[6] Under this format, which we now take for granted, voters endorse electors on a statewide basis; a plurality for one slate of electors approves that slate. How do potential electors come to be "slated" in the first place? Here the political party, an attribute of Hamilton's "great beast,"[7] has preempted presidential electoral formalisms. The voter who pulled the lever for Jimmy Carter in 1976 was not voting for Carter at all but endorsing a set of electors pledged to Carter who would surely "vote" for him themselves when eventually asked to do so.

The presidency is a national office, but most of the constitutional rules governing the President's election lack national scope. The Electoral College has been virtually a dead letter almost from its inception, but the formula employed to create it lives on, which means that the "semi-sovereign states" live on. Here are some reasons why the presidential electoral scheme nowhere approaches a totally national footing:

1. A candidate can win a majority of the electoral vote even though he has failed to win a majority of the popular vote. Neither John F. Kennedy (1960) nor Richard Nixon (1968) obtained 50 percent of all the votes cast.

2. A candidate can win a majority of the electoral vote even though he has failed to win a *plurality* of the popular vote. This happened in 1888 (Harrison versus Cleveland).

3. Electors every now and again bolt their parties and defy the voters' mandate. For instance, in 1960 Kennedy carried Alabama, but six of the eleven Democratic electors voted for Virginia senator Harry Byrd.

4. It is even possible for the national party to nominate a candidate, then stand by helplessly while the state branch of the party not only taps someone else but puts its slate of electors under the second nominee's name! In 1968, Democratic voters looking to support the party ticket in Alabama would have found George Wallace's electors there, not Hubert Humphrey's.

More subtle factors as well undermine the "nationality" of the presidential election; they stem largely from the fact that we prefer a particular kind of party system, a *two-party system.* In one sense, of course, our distaste for multipartyism abets nationalism, because it is easy to achieve an electoral-vote majority in a "one-on-one" confrontation.[a] *But the combination of state electoral-vote packaging and a two-party system means that presidential campaigns revolve around carrying the big states:* New York, California, Pennsylvania, Ohio, Illinois, and Texas. Nor can one forget that "carrying the state" means obtaining only one vote more than the opposition; all ballots cast for losers count not a smidgeon! Moreover, as any astute politician knows, this sort of scheme benefits greatly the large ethnic-labor vote in the metropolitan communities, because the big cities generally dominate the big states. Hence the maxim: Our presidential electoral machinery featuring a vestigial Electoral College favors liberal Democrats.[b]

Numerous constitutional amendments have been proposed to tinker with the Electoral College machinery. It is senseless to review them all; but the major efforts suggest how various interests might obtain an edge in the presidential sweepstakes.

1. Abolish the Electoral College outright. This would probably help political conservatives and hurt political liberals. John F. Kennedy, as a senator, led the fight to retain the status quo, showing he well understood the dynamics of today's party struggle.

2. Abolish the electors as individuals, but retain the electoral *vote* and divide it in proportion to a candidate's statewide popularity. (That is, a candidate who garnered 45 percent of New York's popular vote would be awarded 45 percent of New York's electoral vote.) As with all such proposals, the big winners would be the big states' inveterate minority voters (for instance, Massachusetts Republicans). But under this device, one-party states would also gain enormously—in effect, their electoral votes would still be awarded by "package"—and most of these are in the quasi-solid South. To that argument, proponents say party competition in these states would flourish overnight.

3. Abolish the electors as individuals, but retain the electoral *vote* and divide it, by and large, according to the old "district" set-up. Thus, Illinois has twenty-six electoral units, twenty-four stemming from its House representation and two from its Senate representation. If a candidate carries seventeen congressional districts and wins a plurality of the state's total vote, award him nineteen out of the twenty-six votes. This recommendation would return us to the in-

[a] As history buffs recall, the House has been called upon to settle only three presidential contests, with Jefferson, John Quincy Adams, and Hayes winning out. The Jefferson-Adams race took place before the Electoral College distinguished between presidential and vice presidential choices, while the Hayes-Tilden mess involved the separate issue of who had carried which states.

[b] As I showed in Chapter 9, both parties tend to nominate liberals, in part because of this machinery.

> tent of the Framers, before states realized they could maximize their power by adopting the "package deal" formula. But under the "Living Constitution," it would be even more beneficial to political conservatives than the proportional scheme outlined in Proposal 2. One reason for this is that congressional district lines need to be redrawn only at ten-year intervals, when new census figures become available, so rural areas, which are losing population, tend to be overrepresented by these legislative units.

Vital though partisan and ideological politics may be in judging the implications of these proposals, larger dimensions must be considered. The greatest dilemma involves the question of *state versus national power.* For one thing, the "smaller" states generally oppose all change, because, everything else being equal, Delaware's (or Wyoming's, or Alaska's) three electoral votes carry greater weight than the wafer-thin popular-vote margins candidates usually obtain there. For another, Proposals 2 and 3, because they are predicated upon a divided electoral vote, would very much enhance the likelihood of elections being decided in the House by state ballot. Indeed, these changes would undoubtedly spur third parties to enter the fray, which could exacerbate greatly the chances of final determination in the House and perhaps give these factional groupings a crucial bargaining position. It seems clear that presidential election by *majority* popular vote (Proposal 1) might well have the same consequences. Minor parties would probably jump in and, once having frozen the decision-making process, offer their support to the highest bidder. Evidently, these schemes do not meet minimal majoritarian or "nationalist" criteria unless a two-stage process is imposed: where no candidate receives 50 percent of the popular or electoral vote (depending upon which proposal were adopted), a run-off between the top two votegetters would be necessitated.

It is fascinating that none of these options has ever come close to adoption. Nonetheless, we have been lucky over the years. A slight change in popular sentiment could easily have yielded a President lacking plurality support; a slight change in the electoral vote could have put the House of Representatives into the driver's seat. But the present system, given the "horrors" of a settlement in the lower chamber, does at least discourage Republicans and Democrats from being ideologically doctrinaire; they must spread their wings or risk minor-party erosion and consequent electoral-vote deadlock. Even so, the Nixon–Humphrey–Wallace race (1968) just missed the House. A third party based less upon regional ties than Wallace's could force the issue. Moreover, there is some danger than a modern-day President lacking a plurality of popular support would be crippled in attempts to govern. The lesson is clear: despite the dangers hidden in the current system, the power struggle between liberals and conservatives is so pervasive, and the role of the states under the current scheme is so manifest, that change will be virtually impossible until the electorate feels cheated by a result.

Congressional and state electors

If the President is seen today as representing all the people, nobody makes such grandiose claims for congressmen. It is hardly surprising, then, that states exert far more control over House and Senate races than over presidential races. What may seem surprising is that states regulate congressional elections almost as carefully as they regulate in-state elections.

Before I talk about the precise qualifications of congressional "electors"—voters—I must reemphasize the constitutional politics of federal legislative constituency, which I described in Chapter 4. Under the charter as originally conceived, senators were chosen by the state legislatures; today, under the Seventeenth Amendment, they are elected by plurality vote in statewide contests. Optimistic advocates of popular sovereignty might argue that senators represent the electors in their respective states; but realists who keep the "two senators per state" rule clearly in view would probably say that upper-chamber members still represent the states, as the Framers intended they should. Both interpretations are correct. The question is which notion of representation better describes the Senate's constitutional role.

House members, on the other hand, are chosen, says Article I, "by the people." But the 435 seats are apportioned *among the states,* so the "people" being represented are *the people of the states.*[8] It does not follow, of course, that the legislatures should determine House members' districts, but such is the clear message in the "Living Constitution." This line-drawing ritual stems from the authority of the state legislatures to prescribe the times, places, and manner for choosing congressmen. We know the House and Senate have ample power to supersede such regulations, but beyond prescribing the "single-member district" scheme, they have let the state legislatures go their own way. Even the Supreme Court decision requiring these constituencies to contain approximately equal numbers of people[9] does not change the fundamental balance of power.

Who, then, does the Constitution vest with the status of congressional elector? Once again the states receive proprietary interest, but here there is no hope of a meaningful congressional check. However, on the question of House selection at least, the Framers wanted to maximize democratic values: the states could determine who might vote for "the most populous branch" of their own legislatures,[10] but once this judgment had been made, these electors automatically qualified to participate in House contests. What kept the legislatures honest in defining House electors throughout the eighteenth and much of the nineteenth century was the people's commitment to mass suffrage at the *state* level. Time has extended this majoritarian premise to the Senate; all it takes to cast a ballot for an upper-chamber seat is the right to cast a ballot for a *lower*-chamber *state* seat.[11]

Today, then, we almost never distinguish between the right to vote for federal lawmakers and the right to vote for state lawmakers. Indeed, the "Living Constitution" now decrees that voters in congressional contests can also vote for presidential electors. No state legislature would dare provide otherwise. Emblematic of this unitary election process is the ballot itself. Applicable state and federal laws have placed presidential, congressional, and countless state-office candidates before us on one sheet of paper to be voted up or down in a single day's work.

Yet the old truism remains: the states decide who can vote. And even in this age of universal suffrage, there are some restrictions: aliens, for example, are fenced out entirely. Only citizens are accorded the franchise privilege, though one hundred years ago as many as twenty-two states allowed aliens to vote.[12] (Have we become more ethnocentric in our liberal majoritarianism?) There are also minimum-age requirements. Although these have varied, no state allows seventeen-year-olds to cast ballots. Then there are a whole raft of "special circumstances," which deny the vote to institutionalized mental incompetents, imprisoned convicts, and ex-felons.

Other restrictions are more controversial. Virtually every state requires voters to register in order to prevent interlopers from "stuffing the ballot box" during the confusion of Election Day. A good hedge against such shenanigans entails preparing advance lists of everyone qualified to participate, then identifying electors and checking off their names as they vote. This is logical enough, but it produces inequities. Many communities provide for periodic registration to clean their lists; however, the dates are often badly publicized. Should a person miss the opportunity to sign up, the chance to vote may have slipped by. Furthermore, many districts insist upon registration via personal appearance, which creates a disadvantage for older people and those who hold odd-hour jobs. Nobody really knows how many people are siphoned off either because of registration red tape or ignorance of the law; but one study concludes that such factors carry appreciable weight.[13] For these reasons, most states now utilize the permanent, one-time registration system, though our individualist tradition has kept us a long way from the European democracies, where *government* assumes responsibility for compiling accurate lists.

Another highly debatable item is the residency requirement, which ten years ago typically meant a one-year waiting period. Again, the rationale was not elusive: states wanted voters to be bona fide members of the political community and thought that some time was needed for newcomers to acquaint themselves with the candidates and the issues. The Supreme Court admitted these considerations were legitimate but called the one-year rule too broad and too crude. Applying the Court's new-fangled one-two punch of "right to travel" and "compelling state interest," the Justices concluded that *durational* residency standards forced a person unconstitutionally to make a choice: travel and don't vote, or don't travel and vote.[14] They intimated, however, that a thirty-day residency period in-state or in-county might be acceptable, and this criterion has been widely adopted.[15]

The states can also prescribe minimal standards of competence for voters, and the traditional device they have employed is the literacy exam. Of course, a "reading" requirement is no test of knowledge, but it has been defended on the ground that intelligent electors must at least be able to determine the names and numbers of the competitors. The same Court that enunciated the "separate but equal" rule in the "gay nineties" found literacy tests entirely appropriate,[16] and even the Warren Court upheld unanimously a novel and ambitious North Carolina law requiring all potential registrants to be able to read and write sections of the state constitution in English.[17] However, the notion of universal suffrage so permeates the "Living Constitution" that Congress approved a recommendation by the Nixon Administration to abolish literacy tests throughout the United States.

Now even if one assumes the legislature has such authority with respect to *federal* elections (under the times, places, and manner provision), how can it ban literacy standards in *state* elections?[18] The Court's argument sustaining this nationwide ban was essentially this: the Fourteenth Amendment forbids states to deny individuals the equal protection of the laws, while the Fifteenth Amendment forbids states to deny individuals the right to vote because of race; Congress may pass laws "necessary and proper" to implement those guarantees; Congress could reasonably conclude that literacy tests discriminate against blacks because of their unequal educational opportunities, since there is palpable evidence showing a decline in voter registration and turnout wherever literacy tests are imposed; *it is not necessary for Congress to show that a particular state exam discriminates against blacks, for such a narrow view of national power smacks too much of "dual federalism."*[19]

Among the political "facts of life" militating against literacy tests is that the right to vote has become the most dramatic, visible symbol of democratic governance in our politics. Against this background I can now present the specific constitutional rules states may *not* abridge in deciding who votes. I have mentioned the Fifteenth Amendment already: race, color, and previous condition of servitude are impermissible criteria. The states of the old Confederacy for years tried to circumvent this provision with a variety of ingenious devices. Perhaps the most familiar was the "grandfather clause." For example, Oklahoma had inserted into its constitution a rule exempting from literacy tests anyone descended from voters legally registered on January 1, 1867, and requiring all others (including, naturally, all blacks) to undergo a stiff (indeed, impassible) exam. Said the Court: "[This provision perpetuates] the very conditions which the Amendment was intended to destroy."[20] Undaunted, Oklahoma's legislature responded with a statute providing that anyone qualified to vote after the Court's ruling but failing to register promptly would be forever barred from the ballot; however, the law also provided a waiver for anyone voting *before* the Court's ruling. Mr. Justice Frankfurter's succinct commentary years later spelled doom for the "grandfather clause": "[The Fifteenth Amendment] nullifies sophisticated as well as simple-minded modes of discrimination."[21]

In addition to the ban against racial bias, the states must honor three other constitutional prohibitions in designating electors. The Nineteenth Amendment proscribes sexist distinctions; the Twenty-fourth proscribes poll taxes as a precondition for voting in *federal* elections; the Twenty-sixth proscribes any age limitation over and including eighteen years. The first of these has led to virtually no conflicts in our constitutional politics, while the last culminated an extraordinarily interesting debate over the very nature of election-process "rules of the game," which I will describe below. The poll tax question fits somewhere in between.

Until the 1950s, most Southern states obligated prospective voters to pay a flat fee before they could cast a ballot—yet another handy way to keep blacks out of voting booths, though, like the literacy test, it screened out many poor whites as well. For years Congress's efforts to do something about the problem had run afoul of the Senate filibuster. One claim was that Congress had no power to outlaw state voting criteria—although, logically, if it can ban literacy tests throughout the land, it can ban poll taxes. Finally, a compromise was reached: a constitutional amendment relevant only to the *federal* electoral process was cleared and quickly ratified.

Supreme Court action ultimately buried poll taxes in state elections too.[22] Writing for the majority, Mr. Justice Douglas said that the equal protection clause forbids states to discriminate against classes of people by formulating arbitrary and irrational categories.

> [Unlike literacy tests] voter qualifications have no relation to wealth nor to paying or not paying this or any other tax. . . . Wealth, like race, creed, or color, is not germane to anyone's ability to participate intelligently in the electoral process.[23]

Dissenting, Justices Black, Harlan, and Stewart suggested, first, that the Court may have indulged in a little modern-day "substantive equal protection,"[24] using this clause to strike down legislative standards not in keeping with its egalitarian biases, just as the laissez faire Court had used "substantive due process" to guillotine legislation it thought "socialist." Second, they said, property qualifications for voting were often used in the colonies and well into the nineteenth century. Third, one might rationally argue that a minimal poll tax helps separate those who really care about civic responsibility from those who would rather put their money elsewhere. Fourth, one might argue (as the Framers would have) that people of means have a larger stake in public affairs than those who lack economic advantage.

This decision again demonstrates the "Living Constitution's" commitment to egalitarianism in voter participation, an orientation entirely different from the Framers' conception of civic duty at the ballot box, but an orientation the Court can implement by redefining explicit guarantees in the fundamental law.

Two case studies in designating electors

The voting rights of eighteen- to twenty-year-olds: the politics of constitutional confusion

As I have said, every state maintains a minimum-age barrier for franchise participation. Throughout most of this century, the "Living Constitutional" criterion was twenty-one years; as late as 1970 only three states (Georgia,

Kentucky, and Alaska) observed a lower limit! However it arose, the standard of age twenty-one was commonly used in a variety of other contexts to differentiate between adults and minors—for instance, in determining who was allowed to drink hard liquor in bars or restaurants. Of course, there have always been reasonable objections to this criterion: many "under twenty-one's" manage to collect college degrees, begin happy marriages, successfully assume responsibility for rearing children, or risk their lives in the armed services. But none of this made an appreciable dent in legislative opinion.

Then came the Vietnam War. Suddenly, college students were in the streets, clamoring, both peacefully and violently, for an end to hostilities and protesting against an Establishment insensitive to morality and justice. Here was the guts of politics: group self-interest in the struggle for power. To put the matter squarely, countless students did not want to be drafted, sent to Southeast Asia, and killed for a purpose at best tangential to their experiences and life styles.

The "political branches" had no intention of terminating the war merely because campus life had become unglued. But in the great game of "demand, then bargain," they knew that something must be done, and they hit upon a tried-and-true palliative: expand the franchise! So the Voting Rights Act of 1970 was pushed by the Nixon Administration and supported with manifest enthusiasm by the Democratic Congress. In one clean sweep, it gave all eighteen- to twenty-year-olds, if otherwise qualified, the right to cast a ballot in federal, state, and local elections.

Why would the "political branches" think that granting college-age citizens voting privileges would mollify them? For two reasons. First, we must recall the political climate of the late 1960s. Liberals, of whatever stripe, tend to be congenital egalitarians who have advocated expanding the franchise ever since the rise of Jacksonian democracy.[25] This value preference had already been lubricated by the Warren Court, which had knocked down state poll taxes and, as we will see, had proclaimed the virtues of "one person, one vote."[26] For those majoritarians, then, nothing seemed more natural than to provide a slice of the majoritarian pie. And what about conservatives like Richard Nixon and his Attorney General, John Mitchell? Traditional conservative philosophy is concerned about the *quality* of voter participation; it supposedly emphasizes an *informed* electorate. But, of course, Nixon and Mitchell were not traditional conservatives, who favor change only when a strong case has been made. They were political activists looking for votes, and they had no intention of alienating the eighteen-to-twenty bloc at the outset by opposing a cause whose time had seemingly arrived.

A second and more profound reason why franchise expansion was deemed admirable was that universal suffrage had long since become part of the "Living Constitution." Its widespread acceptance probably stems from such features in the American constitutional environment as proliferating mass-communication and mass-transportation technologies, a burgeoning middle class, the spread of nationalistic identity, and an optimism about human nature transcending party politics, pressure-group affiliation, and ideological nuance.[27]

When the right "political mix" arose, it was just a matter of time before the potential group advocating universal suffrage collectivized and caused the ban against post-seventeen-year-olds to be lifted.

Did Congress have power to impose such across-the-board relief? The Supreme Court said "yes" for federal elections (by a 5–4 vote) and "no" for state and local elections (by a 5–4 vote).[28] The 1970 decision date tells some of the story, for the factionalism certainly reflects a drift from Warrenism toward Burgerism. The "swing man" was Mr. Justice Black. He thought the times, places, and manner clause, combined with the necessary and proper clause, allowed Congress "to provide a complete code for congressional elections."[29] As for presidential races, Black said the legislature possessed "residual power," inherent in the doctrine of national supremacy, to ensure that federal officers represent their federal constituencies to the greatest extent possible. But Congress had *no* power to set age standards for electors in state and local contests. It could enforce the equal protection mandate, but *equal protection was not applicable to the question of voting age.*

Justices Douglas, Brennan, Marshall, and White believed the measure to be constitutional in toto. Going further than Black, they described the right to vote as a fundamental political freedom, which could be inhibited only through regulations satisfying the "compelling state interest" rule. Perhaps the twenty-one-year cut-off point could survive this test, they speculated, and perhaps not. But Congress had far more authority than the Court to review the states' equal protection guidelines, for the Fourteenth Amendment vested *in the legislature* broad power to weigh and evaluate relevant facts. Indeed, where Congress found the states culpable of equal protection discrimination, the courts must resolve every doubt in its favor, barring only arbitrary and capricious determinations. The legislative judgment that those old enough to fight are old enough to vote was clearly rational and not capricious.

Dissenting, Chief Justice Burger and Justices Blackmun, Stewart, and Harlan disagreed entirely. Their position may be distilled as follows: (1) Congress had *no* authority to lay down age standards for voting under the times, places, and manner clause, since age has nothing whatsoever to do with the time, the place, or the manner of elections; (2) Congress had *no* authority to lay down age standards for choosing presidential electors, since the Constitution vests with the states complete power to decide who sits in the Electoral College; (3) equal protection, said Justice Harlan, is applicable to racial discrimination solely, not voting rights. The other three dissenters disagreed with this last point. If a state drew arbitrary and irrational lines with respect to franchise participation, they felt, Congress could outlaw these under the Fourteenth Amendment; but Congress had *no* power to decide for itself what equal protection means and then overthrow state rules not consistent with that definition; only the Court could interpret the Constitution definitively, and these Justices were prepared to say that age classification per se was beyond equal protection purview.[30]

The Twenty-sixth Amendment, of course, now gives eighteen-to-twenty's voting rights in state and local elections. But the above decision remains crucial because it shows the Court in virtual disarray as the Justices attempted to square constitutional language and constitutional *balance* with the "Living Constitution's" guarantee of unitary electoral qualifications.

Here are some morsels difficult to digest. Mr. Justice Black said Congress has the same power to enact age standards for presidential electors as for its own electors; after all, he emphasized, both executive and legislative chambers are *national* bodies. I think his conception of dormant legislative power comes close to President Nixon's notion of dormant executive authority in the national security field. But ours is a Constitution of *enumerated* powers, and the "times, places, and manner" language shows the Framers were much more willing to provide congressional supervision over congressional races than over presidential races. Thus, the constitutional balance between the states and executive electors is far more favorable to state discretion than the constitutional balance between the states and congressional electors. Meanwhile, Mr. Justice Harlan was so concerned about the *diversity* of electoral qualifications that he would have allowed the states to put an age limit of fifty, sixty, or seventy on congressional electors; for, under his theory, equal protection forbids only racism. But the "Living Constitution" has invested both Court and Congress with power to eradicate irrational state barriers and classifications under the Fourteenth Amendment. This check squares with federalism; Harlan's formula sounds "dual federalish."

The four Justices who lost on the state-local age-limit issue argued in the best tradition of "new-style" liberal nationalism. Their commitment to unitary electoral guidelines was so great that they would permit Congress—*not the Court*—to interpret "equal protection" and wipe out state criteria hither and yon. The only check on Congress would have been "rationality," as though the legislature were here invoking its commerce or taxing power. But the *Slaughter-House Cases* have never been overruled, and semisovereignty in the states does abide. The three Justices who lost on the federal age-limit issue (besides Harlan) refused to accept in any way the "unitary electoral qualification" norm. They interpreted "times, places, and manner" precisely as John Marshall would *not* have interpreted it; and they thought Congress could strike down only those state notions of equal protection which the Court considered arbitrary. Somehow this bloc lost sight of the necessary and proper clause in its deliberations.

Constitutional balance would seem to require a mix between the Framers' notions of electoral diversity and modern notions of electoral congruence. By this standard, Congress clearly has power to allow eighteen-to-twenty's the vote in *its own elections,* but not in presidential contests, much less in state and local elections. Of course, if communities institute *irrational* age barriers for *any* election, then Congress could wipe these out and, under the necessary and proper clause, *impose its own standards.* But the traditional cut-off age of twenty-one would seem to be rational even by today's norms.

An interesting footnote to the Twenty-sixth Amendment was the protest by local townspeople that transient students would register where they went to school and drastically alter voting patterns in the area. Indeed, suppose students united and passed a local bond issue providing for educational benefits or pollution-control programs to be financed, naturally, by levies on local wage earners. States could surely mitigate such dangers by laying down reasonable domiciliary standards for voters who, in effect, have two residences.

"One person, one vote": the politics of constitutional consensus

Now that we have seen *who* may cast a ballot, we come to the equally significant question of *where* ballots may be cast. The right to vote counts for little if electoral districts are drawn fancifully or perniciously.

The term *gerrymandering* has emerged to describe various facts of life about district manipulation in the rough and tumble political world. The typical gerrymander (named, incidentally, for an early practitioner, Massachusetts governor Elbridge Gerry) turns electoral units into odd-shaped grotesqueries to maximize partisan strength. Suppose the Democrats score a smashing victory in Pennsylvania, winning the governorship and a majority in both state legislative chambers. Why can't they pass a law reshaping the various house and senate districts to optimize Democratic chances for years to come? Actually, it happens all the time.

This definition of the gerrymander can be extended to crazy-quilt districts created to water down any minority's voting rights. For instance, in 1957, the Alabama legislature redrew the boundaries of Tuskegee, where a famous black college is located. The result was "an uncouth twenty-eight-sided figure," which had the interesting effect of removing from the city virtually the entire black voting population but absolutely no whites! The Supreme Court found this scheme unconstitutional.[31]

Robert Dixon, who has studied malapportionment extensively, thinks the essence of gerrymandering is not the *shape* of the districts but the *political results.* Thus he says, "Gerrymandering is discriminatory districting. It equally covers squiggles, multimember districting, or simply nonaction, when the result is racial or political malrepresentation" (italics deleted).[32] The point is that electoral units can be drawn with pristine symmetry, while still blatantly demolishing any hope that minorities will obtain meaningful representation.

By far the biggest problem has been legislative *nonaction.* Chapter 4 described the way in which many seats in the national House had remained untouched for decades in spite of radical population shifts, and the way in which these trends discriminated heavily against voters in metropolitan areas. Finally, because Congress refused to rectify state indolence and state bias, the Supreme Court intervened, holding that selection "by the people" requires approximately equal numbers of people to reside in each district.

Much more invidious, however, was nonaction with respect to *state* districting. Take Tennessee during the 1950s. Supposedly, each county was allotted a given number of state legislators depending on the number of voters residing there. But reapportionment had not occurred for more than half a century; the incumbents simply refused to redraw the map to take account of "rural flight." The largest house district had 42,000 people, and the smallest had 2,300; the largest senate district had 132,000 people, and the smallest had 25,000.

Traditionally, the Court had treated these disparities as "political questions." To paraphrase Justice Frankfurter in 1946, the Constitution contained many provisions unenforceable in court. Thus, the document says states shall maintain a republican form of government, but that command could only be implemented by the "political branches" (an example is the Rhode Island Dorr Rebellion case described in Chapter 2). Judges, he concluded, would not know how to draw fair district lines, which, he feared, they would inevitably have to do.[33]

But if the Warren Court was willing to take on "separate but equal," Frankfurterian circumspection would not deter it from taking on "silent gerrymandering." In the famous case of *Baker v. Carr,*[34] a 7-2 majority agreed that the Tennessee districting scheme spawned alleged constitutional deprivations only the courts could heal. The thesis expounded in *Baker* is this: The "political questions" doctrine is a self-restraint device designed to keep the Supreme Court from meddling in policy questions better left to the co-equal, coordinate "political branches"; the doctrine, therefore, is not applicable to *federal-state* relations or, more particularly, relations involving the Supreme Court and states accused of violating civil liberties; the civil liberty at stake here was the *equal protection* clause, because aggrieved Tennessee voters argued that the state districting pattern was arbitrary and irrational; from now on, concluded the majority, federal courts will be open to hear and decide such claims of district irrationality.

Justice Brennan's opinion for the Court was not without its problems. His theory of "political questions," while generally sound, fails to explain satisfactorily why "republican form of government" cases had always been considered nonjusticiable (that is, politically volatile and therefore too hot to handle), even though these cases involved federal-state conflict. Nor did Brennan tell us how the Court would derive standards of arbitrariness in the context of legislative districting. This is an argument Frankfurter stressed in dissent: "What is actually asked of the Court . . . is to choose among competing bases of representation—ultimately, really, among competing theories of political philosophy."[35] And yet this red flag seems entirely inappropriate with respect to the Tennessee litigation, because that state had in fact been guided by *no* theory of politics; therefore its scheme, created through nonaction, expressed *no* policy. Was not "frozen districting" contrary to law the very essence of arbitrariness?

The great question of defining "representational rationality" was largely resolved to the Warren Court's satisfaction in the vital case of *Reynolds v. Sims.*[36] Alabama's legislative districts were as egregiously drawn as those in Tennessee, and for the same reason. By an 8-1 vote, the Justices said this scheme violated equal protection. But Chief Justice Warren's opinion paid scant attention to Alabama's dilatoriness or absence of policy guidelines. His goal was much more ambitious: *to articulate a single, definitive constitutional standard with respect to equitable districting.* That standard would henceforward be called "one person, one vote."

What does "one person, one vote" mean? According to Warren, equal protection obligated both houses of every state legislature to be chosen from electoral units of substantially equal numbers. What was "substantially equal"? The districts must be "as nearly of equal population as is practicable."[37] But most states had never used any such criterion in fashioning their legislative representational maps, by and large following instead the Founders' federal blueprint: their lower chambers were designed generally to reflect population, while their upper chambers (state senates) were designed generally to reflect counties or some other land measure. So, with "one person, one vote," the Supreme Court threw out not only every representational chart that was supposed to mirror population and didn't, but also every districting formula not based on population per se. Said the Chief Justice: "Legislators represent people, not trees or acres. Legislators are elected by voters, not farms or cities or economic interests."[38] Thus *Reynolds* invalidated the constituencies of at least one legislative house in every state and of both houses in most states.

In another case decided the same day,[39] the Court was faced with a Colorado bicameral formula under which one chamber represented numbers and the other represented several ingredients including geography, economic interests, political blocs, *and* population. But *the voters had approved these diverse schemes in a special referendum.* Did that make a difference? *No,* for if a majority of voters could not establish a state church, they could not band together to defeat "one person, one vote."

As Dixon makes clear, the Chief Justice's logic stands or falls on the premise that there is a *right to vote* as compelling and absolute as a black's right to be free of racial segregation.[40] The common denominator for Warren was equality: blacks stand equal with whites; the ballots of all voters must be weighted equally because all voters possess equal rights. But is there a right to vote? Of course, the states cannot disfranchise persons because of sex, race, and the like. But beyond these well-established caveats, the Constitution gives them virtually a free hand to decide who can elect federal and state officers and under what conditions. Furthermore, members of the House represent not people per se, but people *in their respective states.* Even the Constitution was ratified by the people *in their respective states.* As Mr. Justice Stewart said: "Legislators do not represent faceless numbers."[41] People have identities, interests, aspirations, and they do belong to *communities.* The noted political economist John R. Commons thought "functional representation" a much "fairer" scheme than *any* electoral mode based on voter geography.[42] Under these decisions, all state laws giving weight to "functional" factors are *unconstitutional.*

Warren's conception of a homogeneous set of individual liberties, which includes "one person, one vote," plus his conception of a homogeneous national community to which American voters owe their only allegiance, is "new style" liberal jurisprudence in the raw. But the correlation between these two dubious premises and *fair representation* is precisely zero, as the whole history of gerrymandering tells us. I can draw a map for any state in the Union containing *x* numbers per electoral subdivision, and at the same time cancel out the votes of most significant minorities in that state. If by "fair representation" is meant a reasonable opportunity to affect the legislative process by voting (and what else can the term mean?) then the only hope is to provide the various important interests with some chance of getting their candidates elected. When representation is viewed from that perspective, population will always be a factor, but only one factor.

Yet, "one person, one vote" abides even without Earl Warren, despite some uncomfortable moments. The follow-up to *Reynolds,* for instance, was a veritable inundation of lower-court decisions thrusting aside one, and sometimes even two, state legislative reapportionment formulas because the numbers were not equal enough. At times perhaps even the Brennans and the Thurgood Marshalls wondered whether the "numbers game" was worth declaring legislative branch after legislative branch unconstitutional.[43] And some of the doctrine's rough edges have been honed. We have learned that "equal numbers of registered voters per district" may replace "equal numbers of people per district" under certain conditions,[44] and that state judges chosen at the ballot box need not be selected via a "one person, one vote" plan.[45] But the Warren majority never took a backward step and, in 1967, it applied "one person, one vote" to the myriad city and town council district schemes throughout the land.[46]

The great test was certain to be the Burger Court's attitude; thus far, it has managed to make only a slight dent in the Warren formula. When Virginia redrew the map for its house of representatives, population was given very high priority; but the legislature allowed nine of the fifty-two units to vary from the norm by more than 6 percent, thus giving a few counties some chance to obtain minimal representation. The Court said such exceptions were rational, and therefore permissible. But it also said that a "state's policy urged in justification of disparity in district population, however rational, cannot constitutionally be permitted to emasculate the goal of substantial equality."[47] Moreover, the Burger Court has been every bit as zealous as the Warren Court with respect to "one person, one vote" at the national (House of Representatives) level.[48] However, that the Burger consensus uses one standard at the state level and a second, more rigorous standard at the federal level represents a crack in the "unitary electoral qualifications" model.

The big picture in contemporary apportionment politics nevertheless remains the birth and survival of "one person, one vote." Obviously, this is more than liberal ideology flexing its muscles. What seems to be at work is the long sweep toward egalitarianism I discussed earlier, for "one person, one vote," no matter what its theoretical shortcomings, lies smack in the mainstream of twentieth-century consensus politics, just as the Twenty-sixth Amendment is consensus politics. But the majoritarianism implicit in giving eighteen-year-olds the vote can be balanced by educational standards that transmit an appreciation of the "rules of the game." The question is whether "one person, one vote" can be balanced by other juridical formulas to give adequate weight to interest-group affiliation and local community.

The direct primary

The principal object of political-party activism, I said in Chapter 9, is to win elections. Without doubt, partisan politics permeates the voting process outlined in the Constitution, giving root to several "Living Constitutional" norms. I begin my discussion of this relationship by examining how party subgroups nominate candidates for state and congressional office.

In Jefferson's time, political parties were considered private clubs pure and simple, and the membership made its own rules. The nominating power automatically devolved upon the party leadership, which meant a caucus of state house and senate members. But beginning in the 1820s, the legislative "smoke-filled rooms" were gradually replaced by party conventions. This process of "reform" was generated by Jacksonian democracy, which preached popular control over party "machines." Delegates to these state conventions were chosen either through a single-stage direct election by the party faithful or through a two-stage process, involving first a selection by the rank-and-file of delegates to district meetings and second the selection of state delegates by these district caucuses.

The hopes for broad participation in partisan affairs kindled by the convention procedure failed to materialize. Power was merely transferred from elected officials to party professionals. The activists immersed in everyday organizational endeavor were the ones who turned up at precinct meetings, and they naturally selected leaders committed to speak for them at district and state meetings. The entrenched oligarchy used control of party machinery, and sometimes even brute force, to keep dissidents under control. And so was born a new American "Living Constitutional" officer: the political "boss."

At the turn of the present century, the Bob LaFollette midwestern Progressives picked up where the Jacksonians had left off. Their guiding premise was that, just as economic interests became subject to regulation when they entered the public sector, so political parties could be constrained by law when their activities determined which candidates would be presented to the electorate. The device they hit upon to bring party politics under popular control was the *direct primary,* the selection of nominees at the ballot box by the partisan rank-and-file. In 1903, Wisconsin enacted the first statute making party primaries the official nominating procedure. State after state followed suit, typically establishing a uniform primary day, providing electoral machinery (ballots and administrative personnel), and authorizing voter eligibility standards. Today, the party convention as the sole means of choosing state and congressional standard bearers is practically a dead letter.

Most states employ what is called the *closed primary,* which restricts participation to party members, the theory being that only party members should decide what candidates deserve nomination. But, of course, party identification has always been an elusive concept in our politics. As things now stand, states utilize many different formulas to ascertain affiliation and loyalty. They sometimes compel voters either to enroll as party members when they register or forfeit the right of primary participation, and they sometimes ask voters on primary day either to pledge that they are party members or to assert that they supported the party's candidates at the last election. Some schemes are less foolproof than others. In Illinois, for example, electors can change party on primary day, but if someone challenges them, they must swear that the switch is in good conscience. This charade used to be fairly common practice in the rough and tumble of Chicago politics.

A few states employ the *open primary,* allowing electors to participate in whichever party's selection process they wish. The voter simply says, "Give me a Democratic (or Republican) ballot," and if all other qualifications are met, the request will be honored. The open primary is defended by people who want to maximize popular sentiment and minimize the best laid plans of the party professionals. In fact, the scheme has more currency than my definitions indicate, for many closed primaries are selective in name only. When electors can leave one party and enter another with the raise of a hand or the scrawl of a signature on primary day, partisan affiliation is practically meaningless, and nomination contests become magnets for interested onlookers.[49]

As the primary became more generally accepted, the Supreme Court began to pay greater attention to its impact on the electoral process. The issues raised were difficult: if the parties could run primaries without state interference, could they not subvert the right to vote by imposing arbitrary standards of participation upon candidates and electors? If, however, parties were subject to governmental restraint, might not this power be used to stifle minority parties or inhibit new parties?

A classic situation arose out of the post-bellum South. There, with virtually no G.O.P., the Democratic nomination for governor or senator was tantamount to election. Obviously, if blacks could be fenced out of the Democratic primary, their voting impact would be nullified. Texas passed a statute forbidding their participation, but the Supreme Court struck it down as a flagrant violation of equal protection.[50] So the lawmakers tried another tack, making each party the sole judge of who could vote in its primaries; and the Democrats, nicely attuned to the hint, then decreed: whites only. But the Supreme Court remained unpersuaded. The party had acted pursuant to state action, so equal protection was again binding.[51] Finally, the legislature got the message: Just let our party alone to "do its thing." Its hunch was sound. Equal protection forbade only racist *state* action, the Court said; political-party discrimination was *private* action, akin to the racist bars imposed by the Elks Club or the Masons. Thus did the "white primary" receive constitutional vindication.[52]

It is important to understand the precise holding of this case. The Justices did *not* say that primaries in general, or the "white primary" in particular, were exempt from governmental sanction—that Texas could not, for instance, step in and wipe out these racist policies. The Court's decision, then, did not undermine the LaFollette argument that partisan activities must be controlled when they threaten the public welfare. But the Court's ruling did immunize the primary against litigation based upon either the Fourteenth or the Fifteenth Amendment, because these provisions forbid only racist *state* action. And it seemed to nullify Congress's power to abolish such invidious practices. What the Court couldn't do by interpreting the Civil War clauses Congress apparently couldn't do by interpreting them either. This seemed to mean Congress was forbidden to regulate primaries at all.

Now let me approach the problem from another direction. Ballot-box "stuffing" is as old as democracy itself. In 1870, Congress enacted legislation punishing any attempt to deprive citizens of their federal rights. Found constitutional, this statute was held binding against an election official who had tampered with ballots cast in a congressional race. The Supreme Court said the right to vote for House members was constitutionally protected, *once the citizen satisfied all state requirements* (since any elector certified to cast ballots in state lower-chamber races can automatically cast ballots in federal lower-chamber races). And the nation's lawmakers might reasonably choose to protect this right against chicanery, given their power to prescribe times, places, and conditions for conducting congressional elections.[53]

But suppose the culprit had given ballots a fast shuffle at *primary* time? In 1941, the Supreme Court, shifting somewhat, said the right to cast a vote in a congressional primary was every bit as fundamental as the right of franchise in a congressional election. The primary had become an integral component of these elections, so Congress's power under the times, places, and manner clause was equally applicable here. In short, the congressional "elections" the legislative branch could protect through the criminal process included congressional primaries, given the broad scope of the necessary and proper provision.[54]

Thus did the Court undermine the entire "white primary" rationale. If the state silently delegated to private groups (the parties) its constitutional role in managing the congressional electoral process (absent preemptive national rules, of course), and if the constitutional right of franchise at congressional elections had now been extended to congressional primaries, how could the parties running those primaries violate the Constitution any more than the states could? Adopting this argument, the Justices struck down the "white primary" in 1944 as an infringement of Fifteenth Amendment values.[55]

However, this commingling is not without its constitutional dilemmas. Earlier we saw that residency criteria for voting in elections must be narrowly contrived to meet the "compelling state interest" rule. We have also seen that the closed primary often is built around some kind of waiting period. If primaries and elections stand on the same constitutional footing, does not "compelling state interest" doctrine apply to the former as well? And, if so, would that mean only essentially open primaries could meet the constitutional burden of proof?

The Supreme Court spoke to this problem in 1973, finding primaries and elections could *not* be lumped uncritically together. New York State required voters to express their party preference eleven months before the next primary. By a narrow 5–4 margin, the Court sustained this rule, citing the dangers to a stable party system inherent in party raiding.[56] But states cannot bar electors from a primary because they voted last time in the other party's primary, for this would lock participants into preexisting declarations unless they disfranchised themselves by skipping a primary.[57]

This debate bears directly on what constitutes a viable and meaningful electoral process, because some political scientists have voiced considerable doubts about the direct primary in general and the open primary in particular. Primaries per se receive their strongest endorsement when adopted in one-party states. If Mississippi Democrats even today used the state convention rather than the direct primary, voters would be disfranchised. Indeed, uniparty states very often have what amounts to either a two-party system or a multiparty system comprising the various factions within the larger partisan umbrella. But in states in which Republican–Democratic competition prospers, the inherent divisiveness of the primary is frequently overriding. Under the convention scheme, the party professionals knew they had to gear their candidate choices toward the middle-of-the-road electorate. But primaries allow extremists to take their case directly to the rank-and-file, so they became a fertile field for "personalized politics." Popularity with a narrow clique may yield primary victory but irreparably damage the party's chances in the general election. Moreover, one does not have to endorse Professor Burns's Jeffersonian "two-party model" to realize that primaries fought out between transient factions mobilized around ex-movie stars, ex-astronauts, and ex-athletes can make a shambles of party organization. And if all this is valid for closed primaries, it is dogma for open primaries, where electors can move like itinerant peddlers from party to party, often capturing control of a party's apparatus through their votes for such-and-such interloper.[58]

One possible compromise lies in amalgamating the convention and primary tools. A handful of states use a *preprimary convention,* at which the party activists meet and decide on their choices. This process is called "slating." Then, the direct primary is held, with the convention's nominees labeled as such on the ballot. In this way, the voters can take account of what the professionals think, if they care to. Such a balanced approach deserves broader testing, at least, but as things stand now the primary is yet another example of rampant decentralization in party decision-making.

Nominating presidential candidates

The growth of national conventions

Our two major parties come alive when the presidential contest looms. To many Americans, the national convention, which meets every four years to nominate presidential and vice presidential candidates, as well as to write a platform, *is* the political party, so special attention should be devoted to it.

These gatherings are not as old as the parties themselves. The earliest presidential nominating forums were caucuses of all party members in the legislative branch. Their inherent inequity lay in providing no representation for party members in states and districts controlled by the opposition. Naturally, they also tended to reward "insiders."

The national convention was part of the startling impact Jacksonian democracy had on American electoral politics. The popular forces surrounding the Tennessee war hero doomed the property qualifications for voters that most states traditionally had imposed, swept aside all ways of selecting presidential electors except universal manhood suffrage, and brought state nominating conventions to the front. And these forces also moved against King Caucus, who in 1824, had denied their leader the Democratic Party nomination. A national party meeting would allow for rank-and-file voice, it was said, because delegates would be selected in the highly representative state conventions.

The significance of these national assemblies from the standpoint of constitutional politics cannot be understated, because they are clearly consonant with separation of powers theory. Had King Caucus abided and been nourished by contemporary stresses and strains, we might well have a parliamentary system in this country today. And, of course, congressional domination of the executive branch would make far more significant the localist-oriented decentralization Congress exhibits. The convention system, however, goes hand in hand with the Electoral College scheme in maximizing national values far more than would legislative control. Generally speaking, conventions are brokers of parochial party interests, and, as "grand compromisers," they inspire the nomination of noncongressional types (that is, members of what Burns has called the two "presidential parties"), whose broad appeal to the American "great middle" maximizes the chances for ultimate victory at the polls. And yet there are many who think the national assembly is too *decentralized* an operation for selecting contemporary chief executives. They find it anomalous that "Mr. President, Superstar" should be selected by a claque of state delegations.

The preferential primary

When political-party organization is on the agenda, it is best to work from the bottom up, so let me first describe how delegates are chosen to attend the national conventions. From Jackson's time until the turn of the century, state conventions were the exclusive nominating agencies; a typical delegation, then, would undoubtedly include the top party professionals and votegetters, with their trusted aides rounding out the list. This process provoked the same criticism that launched the direct-primary movement: the rank-and-file could express its will only at second or third hand. Florida and Wisconsin were among the first states to try an alternative, *the presidential preference primary,* which caught on so quickly that by 1924 more than twenty states had followed suit, another triumph for Progressive Party ideology. After thirty years of relative quiescence, the presidential primary is again riding the wave of success. In 1968, fifteen states employed it; in 1972, the figure was twenty-two plus the District of Columbia; in 1976, it was thirty-two plus the District, and these contests accounted for about 77 percent of all delegates. The reasons for this resurgence are evident: cynicism about party leadership and "smoke-filled rooms," cynicism caused by Watergate revelations, and an ever-greater deference in our public philosophy to "one person, one vote."

There are really *two* kinds of presidential preference ballots electors might confront. First we have the "beauty contest," in which voters are asked whether they prefer candidate A or candidate B. In a second scheme, slates of delegates are pledged to particular aspirants, and electors can either vote for one slate in toto or skip down the columns designating the names of individual delegate choices. These preference polls, then, are quite a hodgepodge. A state could use the "beauty contest" routine, yet all delegates might be chosen at party conventions. Another state could provide both the "beauty contest" option and delegate selection by ballot, but the "losing" candidate's slate might fare very well if it includes many familiar names. A third state could decide that some delegates should be elected by all the voters and others chosen in districts. Each statute seems to have its own idiosyncracies.

How important have the preferential primaries been? Virtually every competitive race for a major-party nomination since the Second World War has been decided pretty much by a vote in one of these contests. But the states that made the difference have varied with each four-year cycle, so everything depends on the candidates and the visible issues. In 1952, Dwight Eisenhower's reputation as "votegetter supreme" was firmly established when his more than 100,000 write-in tallies in the Minnesota primary put Robert A. Taft's campaign forever on the defensive; in 1960, John F. Kennedy proved that Protestants would support a Catholic, when he trounced Hubert Humphrey in a state almost devoid of Catholics, West Virginia; in 1964, Barry Goldwater carried California against Nelson Rockefeller and showed that a conservative could win a pivotal state; in 1968, Eugene McCarthy's efforts in New Hampshire and Wisconsin may well have shown President Johnson he could not be renominated; in 1972, it was California again, with George McGovern squeaking by Hubert Humphrey, the big issue being Vietnam. And what of Jimmy Carter? Can we put our finger on precisely which primary gave him the permanent initiative among Democratic candidates in 1976? No, but in his case the primary system per se is the key, for he was a complete "outsider," lacking both power base and visibility until he took to the hustings.

But none of this necessarily makes presidential preference primaries a plus on balance. One problem is that candidates can usually pick and choose from among the contests they wish to enter; thus, there is considerable randomness and disorder to the whole business. Another problem is that these contests force candidates to hopscotch around the country, wearing themselves to a frazzle even before they have been nominated. Then there is the problem inherent in all primaries: they debilitate party organization and enhance the impact of the mass media. Estes Kefauver became an overnight presidential primary folk hero during the 1952 campaign (attired in coonskin cap to boot!) because he had presided over senatorial hearings into organized crime that received high TV ratings. Edmund Muskie's publicly shed tears of anguish, occasioned by a vicious newspaper attack on his family during a 1972 primary, made the news everywhere and led to his being labeled "unstable," a tag he could never seem to shake. Moreover, states' tests for party loyalty are becoming less demanding. Traditionally, only Wisconsin (the birthplace of Progressivism) employed the open primary, but in the 1976 Texas G.O.P. "beauty contest" a massive conservative Democratic cross-over enabled Ronald Reagan to hand Gerald Ford a shellacking. On the other hand, primaries provide good testing grounds that can indicate how candidates will fare under fire, especially sectional figures on the prowl for badly needed exposure.

It would help if we had more information about who voted in such contests. Some have argued that the state preferential primary is the best way to gauge rank-and-file sentiment. Yet preliminary data show that those who vote in preferential primaries are *not* representative of grassroots party opinion, just as those who vote in direct primaries are *not* representative of grassroots party opinion.[59] Participants tend to be better educated, more affluent, and much more cognizant of political affairs than party nonparticipants. Evidently, only the activists care enough to vote even in contests with presidential implications, and, of course, the best informed and most concerned are those who have obtained a maximum share of what "the system" has to offer.

Political scientists have tended to praise the mix between state primaries and state conventions displayed by our presidential nominating politics.[60] That mix would seem defensible on grounds of balance. But balance presupposes a rational accommodation between conflicting forces. The problem with the current system is that the mix is strictly ad hoc; only chance and extraneous political factors govern which states use conventions and which use primaries. The tension inherent in the status quo, as reflected by the recent upsurge in primary usage, seems to indicate that this "balance" is not part of the "Living Constitution."

Inside convention halls

To understand how national conventions operate, one must again appreciate fully the built-in conflicts between parties as state organisms and parties as national organisms. From the beginning, the major-party assemblies decreed how many delegates (that is, *votes*) the various states would be accorded, based generally on their strength in the Electoral College. If this choice seems reasonable, it was in fact a triumph of theory over hard realities, because it assumed that party strength was apportioned nationally on an equitable basis. The futility of G.O.P. efforts in the South showed this to be invalid, and all hell broke loose when President Taft's delegate strength in Dixie (where he figured to win zero electoral votes) helped quash Teddy Roosevelt's comeback in 1912. As a result, the Republicans adopted the "bonus rule," giving extra influence at their conventions to states carried by previous G.O.P. congressional and presidential standard bearers. That guideline holds to this day.

The Democrats have had similar problems. For instance, their conventions traditionally honored the "unit rule," which bound *all* delegates from a particular state to support the candidate favored by a majority of that delegation. Therefore, "big" states like New York could control the convention.[61] In part to prevent such dominance, and in part to keep the solid South within the fold, the Democrats for one hundred years required a two-thirds majority for presidential nomination. Hence, some Democratic conventions were endless melodramas; it took 103 ballots to nominate John W. Davis in 1924. Both procedures are gone today. Franklin Roosevelt led the charge against the two-thirds rule in 1936, because he realized that his coalition would continue to flounder in the face of Southern convention veto power. In its place, the Democrats adopted the "bonus rule," which gave Dixie a measure of solace. The "unit rule" survived until 1968. Today, delegates vote as individuals no matter what the state parties think, and potential nominees need obtain only a majority vote. These changes represent victories for a party organization attempting to maximize national power in the face of state and sectional pressures that seem less and less formidable.

Another longstanding source of conflict lies in the interplay between national convention rules and state statutory requirements governing the delegate selection process. That cleavage comes to the fore when rival slates claim they are the "real" representatives of state party opinion, which seems to occur at least once during every divided convention. In 1972 the McGovern forces and the Humphrey forces locked horns over this issue, and the Democratic nomination hung in the balance. McGovern had won the California preferential primary, and under California law he was entitled to that state's entire 271-member delegation. Humphrey's followers protested vehemently, claiming newly adopted party regulations had rejected "winner-take-allism" as discriminatory. The party's Credentials Committee, controlled by anti-McGovernites, proceeded to seat a number of Humphrey's California contingent proportionate to his vote there; in response, the McGovern backers asked the courts for relief.

Pulled into the fray three days before the convention opened, the Justices said that it was impossible to reach a decision on such short notice, and chided one of the courts of appeal for finding that the McGovern delegates had been denied their constitutional rights. However, they added a gratuitous comment seemingly endorsing the conventions' long-established custom of judging the credentials of participants without regard to state law and policy. As we later learned, the Justices thought the "private club" theory of political-party structure and function was steeped in free speech values, and states lacked power to decide which *representational scheme* could be used in selecting *national party* delegates.[62] (I must emphasize that these decisions leave untouched a state's ability to oversee *state party* doings.) The Humphrey forces eventually lost the battle and therewith the war, for the convention as a whole seated the entire McGovern California entourage.

Certainly the most controversial effort by a contemporary national assembly to control state party nomination procedures involved the "quota system" allegedly established by the Democrats following the riots at their Chicago meeting in 1968. With women's liberation, political activism among blacks, and protests by students against the Vietnam War all on the rise, the Democratic convention moved to establish what would eventually be called the McGovern-Fraser Reform Commission. Its task was to broaden participation in nomination politics and to make "the party of the people" look a little less like "the party of middle-class, middle-aged white males."[63] Finding that blacks, women, and young people between eighteen and thirty were underrepresented at the 1968 meeting, the McGovern panel decided that to overcome past discriminatory policies, those groups should be given delegate places "in reasonable relationship to the group's presence in the population of the State." "Mandatory imposition of quotas" was deemed unnecessary,[64] though how this "reasonable relationship" could be attained without them remained unclear. In any event, the changes were startling: black representation rose from 6 percent to 14 percent of convention participants; the eighteen-to-thirty group skyrocketed from 2 percent to 23 percent; women improved their numbers radically, from 14 percent to 36 percent.

When the 1972 convention opened, something happened to the Democratic Party. Instead of the well-oiled, well orchestrated "controlled confusion" of other years, the viewer was confronted with an endless series of speeches advocating such platform proposals as abortion on demand and civil rights for homosexuals; an endless series of nominations for presidential and vice presidential "candidates" unknown to the public; and an endless series of interviews with celebrities like Paul Newman and Shirley MacLaine. When the dust had cleared and George McGovern's victory was recorded for posterity, many of the "old pros" were heard to grumble that the "quota system" had stacked the deck against them. Yet the evidence indicates a somewhat different picture. McGovern's victory was a result not so much of the affirmative action steps taken to aid previously "underrepresented" interests as of accumulating delegates in primaries.[65]

But the "quotas," if that is what they were, could not survive McGovern's poor showing against Richard Nixon. To pick up the pieces of party cleavage, the Democrats embarked on another first, a "miniconvention" of party leaders, convened at Kansas City in 1974. The assembly pledged continued support for affirmative action programs to help previously underrepresented minorities, but it scrapped the "reasonable relation to population" guideline and reaffirmed the McGovern-Fraser condemnation of quotas. Each state party would have to submit an affirmative action plan to a national compliance committee, the meeting decided, but if that plan were acceptable and lived up to in grassroots decision-making, no challenges to the makeup of particular delegations would be entertained at the 1976 assembly.[66] If TV viewers wondered why the 1976 Democratic convention was a study in lassitude, they needed only to keep these facts in mind: (1) Jimmy Carter's people were pretty much calling the shots. (2) The party was tired of maximizing its chances for defeat and so eschewed the "debate at any price" syndrome. (3) The 1974 "miniconvention" had laid a solid foundation for coalition building; there were no delegate challenges in 1976. On the other hand, the casual viewer might have noted a drop-off in black representation.

The fundamental question here, of course, was raised at the beginning of this chapter: What is fair representation? More specifically, which promises greater equity, "one person, one vote" or "demographic apportionment"? A "winner-take-all" vote or "proportional representation"? Is it "fair" that George Wallace, who received more popular support in preferential primaries than any other Democratic candidate, should have had no chance at the 1972 national convention? Is it "fair" that under rules governing the 1976 Democratic convention, each delegation, if chosen by state primary or convention, had to be apportioned according to the candidate preferences of those who participated in the selection process, but no such apportionment was required if delegates were elected on a district-by-district basis? That scheme helped Jimmy Carter enormously, which is why he opposed (unsuccessfully) the repeal of this so-called loophole primary at the 1976 assembly.[67] And yet fairness may simply be the wrong criterion. The Constitution was not intended to be "fair," first and foremost; it was intended to be a viable set of rules that balanced power for the purpose of sustaining consensus and moving the new nation forward. That kind of pragmatic overview has been lacking in recent Democratic Party decision-making, and that is one important reason why the party's electoral track record has not reflected its majority status.

The national conventions have always had their stern critics.[c] The most common alternative proposed is a national preferential primary, which certainly would enhance popular participation. Yet the direct primary system has severely undermined state parties; think what a transcontinental direct primary might do to the inherently weaker federal party organizations. At the least, such a drastic step would be bitterly opposed by the "old guard." And congressional legislation on the subject would be of questionable constitutionality. Congress's inherent power to make federal officials secure from state manipulation may be a sufficient basis for allowing persons under twenty-one to vote for presidential electors,[68] but does Congress possess inherent power to impose presidential-candidate selection processes on *private groups involved in free speech activities?* Indeed, the Court has already said that nominating procedures and elections are not congruent.

Moreover, the convention has certain advantages. It is a fragile institution

[c] One famous foreign observer arrived in this country to see democracy at work, attended our national party assemblies—with their combination O'Hare Airport-Barnum and Bailey atmosphere—and came away muttering: "God takes care of drunkards, of little children, and of the United States!"[69]

because national parties are fragile coalitions; yet, unlike a primary, it provides possibilities for compromise. The candidate who has really shown superior national following usually obtains the nomination, but there are "side payments" that can be parceled out to losers—the vice presidency and platform concessions (although the platforms can be nothing more than high-sounding collections of vague promises, because neither party is ideologically homogeneous). As things stand now, the conventions may overdo the "men's lodge" syndrome because the leadership is determined to stress commonalities rather than animosities, but without the conventions, would we have meaningful political parties at all?

Financing federal elections

A healthy, competitive electoral process costs money, and political parties traditionally have had to raise funds. These efforts provide well-heeled interests with considerable leverage for influencing the political process, which has long been troubling to many observers. Popular participation, they argue, must not be corrupted by the undue effects of largesse emanating from a few affluent sources.

Before the 1970s, Congress tried a variety of tools for attacking such problems. First were the usual criminal statutes designed to punish bribery and similar offenses. Second were laws banning political donations by corporations and labor unions, on the ground that stockholders and the working rank-and-file might not concur in top management's choice of candidates. Third, on the theory that exposure has its own ameliorative effects, were enactments requiring disclosure of the amounts contributed, those who did the contributing, the amounts spent, and the reasons why they were spent. Fourth, to protect the public from excessive propaganda, were laws limiting how much money could be expended in elections. Finally, there were statutes limiting the funds individual donors could contribute, an obvious attack on the "money talks" syndrome.

Most of these efforts, however, packed minimal clout. Thus, the disclosure provision was inapplicable to primaries; the provision mandating expenditure limitations was applicable only to how much money each political committee could spend, so the parties merely created more committees; the provision limiting individual gifts to $5,000 per candidate did not stop wealthy patrons from spreading $5,000 lumps around to help support a variety of candidates and their committees.

The Presidential Election Campaign Fund Act of 1971 was a major breakthrough. It afforded taxpayers an opportunity to endorse and subsidize public funding of presidential campaigns. A person could choose to allocate $1 of his or her income-tax payment to a common election fund to be distributed among eligible parties. Presidential and vice presidential candidates of each major party (one that had obtained 25 percent of the popular vote in the preceding election) were to be allotted an amount equal to 15 cents multiplied by the number of United States residents eighteen years and over. The amount given minor parties (those that had obtained between 5 percent and 25 percent of the previous presidential vote) was to be computed by the same formula, though with account taken of their less-favorable showing. New political parties would be compensated after the election at a rate commensurate with the ballots their candidates received. If the kitty failed to generate funds satisfying a party's entitlement, the difference could be made up by private contributions.

This legislation was not merely a triumph of the public welfare over the forces of private excess. Republicans, being the "have" party, have always been much better fundraisers than the Democrats.[70] Indeed, the Democratic National Committee was $9 million in debt after the 1968 election, whereas the Republicans were solvent. That is why the debates in Congress were so partisan and why Nixon signed the measure *only* when the Democratic Congress postponed implementation until after the 1972 contest. Incidentally, in its first year of operation (1973), a mere 3 percent of the taxpayers used the $1 check-off; however, in 1974, the figure jumped to 15 percent, as compared to a previous high in donation participation by the general public of 9 percent during off-year elections.[71] It is instructive to see how political participation can be promoted when the government provides a gentle shove!

The statute also raises several constitutional problems. Is it appropriate for Congress to tell the two parties that they must spend the same amount of money? If the Democrats have an advantage in bodies because of their inherent majoritarianism, why shouldn't the Republicans be able to use their natural financial advantage? Is a state-imposed equilibrium on spending money for political ends very far from a state-imposed equilibrium on how many speeches a candidate can make? And what about the provisions throwing new parties onto the mercies of private benefactors and locking old minor parties into a funding formula that reflects how they did on the last go-around? In 1912 the Bull Moosers, with Teddy Roosevelt at the helm, wouldn't have gotten a nickel until the election was over, while without T.R. this same party would have reaped a comfortable subsidy in 1916, though it made hardly a ripple at the ballot box. The very nature of the electoral process can be altered significantly by the financial tools the various competitors are able to command. The 1971 law helps the Democrats, hurts the Republicans, and will have various effects on minor parties, depending on what interests they represent.

We can now begin to understand the extraordinarily comprehensive and precedent-shattering Federal Campaign Act of 1974.[72] This statute represents the confluence of many sources: the tremendously high cost of the 1972 presidential campaign (the McGovern team spent $38 million and the Nixon team $56 million, or twice as much as it had spent to defeat Hubert Humphrey); the meager contributions of Americans generally, only 12 percent of whom opted to fund either party in 1972; the persuasive lobbying of Common Cause, which filed a crucial lawsuit compelling complete disclosure of Nixon's campaign war chest; and, of course, Watergate, with its illegal corporate contributions and "laundering" of money to hide contributors' identities.

The clear need for reform, however, hardly produced a well-considered legislative package. In fact, virtually every provision bristled with constitutional doubts. Shortly after the bill became law, a bizarre coalition of Senator James Buckley (Rep.-N.Y.), former Senator Eugene McCarthy (Dem.-Minn.), the conservative magazine *Human Events,* and the New York Civil Liberties Union filed suit in federal court to have the statute thrown out. Stranger still, the two prominent public-interest lobbies were arrayed against each other: the Civil Liberties Union claimed that the rights of free speech and privacy were being abridged, while Common Cause argued that the legislative branch had asserted a "compelling interest" in preventing financial manipulation of the electoral process. The upshot was a Supreme Court decision upholding some parts of the law and voiding others.

These are the salient statutory features as they applied to each phase of the electoral process, and the Supreme Court's assessment of them:

1. *Presidential elections.* Major party nominees were permitted to spend $20 million, and this amount might be drawn either from the check-off kitty established in 1971 or from private sources. Third parties could obtain subsidies under the old formula. All eligible groups figured to (and ultimately did, in 1976) sign up for the "no strings" public gift.

The Supreme Court approved the check-off system as an entirely voluntary mechanism. The Justices said Congress can give major parties more than minor parties in order to prevent raids on the public treasury by inconsequential groups and avoid the pulverization of the two-party system. And they accepted the $20 million limitation because Congress can place restraints on the gifts it bestows.

2. *Presidential primaries.* Major-party aspirants were allowed to spend up to $10 million, if they could raise that much. The check-off pool would fund $5 million, should a candidate be able to attract $5,000 worth of contributions, of $250 or less per donor, in each of twenty states.

Again, the Court accepted the "subsidy by voluntary check-off" principle, as it did Congress's stipulation that candidates demonstrate broad geographic and personal appeal to qualify for federal funds. But the Justices voided the spending ceiling, saying that to limit a candidate's pocketbook was to limit free speech opportunities.

3. *Congressional elections.* Generally speaking, Senate candidates could spend no more than $100,000 in primaries and $150,000 in elections; House candidates $70,000 in each case.

This provision was invalidated. Candidates have a right under the First Amendment to spend as much money as they can legally muster to express their views and to recruit voters.

4. *Across-the-board criteria binding on the individual benefactor.* The law allowed donors to contribute a maximum of $1,000 per year to any candidate running in a primary or an election, and a maximum of $25,000 in toto. All donors giving more than $100 must be identified publicly.

The Justices upheld these regulations. Congress can demonstrate a "compelling interest" in limiting both corruption and the appearance of corruption stemming from large individual contributions. The free speech rights of patrons remained inviolate, the Justices said, because donors could find ways to spend all they wanted, provided that no funds beyond the prescribed ceilings were given to *particular candidates.* And disclosure vindicated the legitimate legislative aim of informing the electorate as to who controls the purse-strings of what candidate.

5. *Enforcement.* The law created a Federal Election Committee (F.E.C.) to interpret the new guidelines, disburse funds, and hear complaints. Of its six members, two were to be appointed by the President, two by the House, and two by the Senate. Nominations were to be confirmed by majority vote in both chambers.

The Supreme Court found that F.E.C. members were "Officers of the United States," who must be appointed by the President subject only to senatorial approval. In the aftermath of Watergate, Congress had been reluctant to give the chief executive such power, but these important administrative-policy functions could not be vested with "inferior officers" (that is, congressional minions) under our separation of powers scheme.

This last ruling had significant political consequences. During the many months it took Congress to rejuvenate the F.E.C., the flow of public monies to candidates ceased. Several Democratic aspirants—among them Birch Bayh and Fred Harris—were forced to terminate their campaigns for this reason.

The balance struck by the Supreme Court, which allows government to set limits on campaign *contributions* but not on campaign *expenditures,* poses a serious problem. Why is my right to give candidates money any less substantial than their right to spend money? Besides, nothing prevents the aspiring officeholder from whispering to "fat cat" contributor Jones: "Don't make out another check in my name, or you'll overstep your limit; just put up a billboard praising my virtues in the 7th District, where I'm running behind."

Adamany and Agree point to other weaknesses in the legislation. For instance, why provide public funds for presidential campaigns and not for congressional campaigns? The preferential treatment accorded the chief executive will strengthen his position in dealing with Congress to the detriment of legislative power and independence. On the other hand, at least half of the House districts are dominated by one party; public funding in those areas might boil down to a free ride for aggregations with little support. And why must presidential aspirants collect money in *twenty* states to obtain federal subsidy when they can win the White House by carrying only *eleven* states? The criterion seems to misconceive the "state equality" theory, and it certainly discriminates against those candidates (usually governors) with only a sectional reputation.

Finally, the law contains a weakness of critical practical importance: the incumbent chief executive enjoys a tremendous advantage over his competitors. President Ford did not spend one nickel from his campaign war chest until 1976, claiming his various trips and speeches around the country before that time were made in his capacity as a "noncandidate." These machinations, of course, were unavailable to all other announced candidates, including his sharpest critic during the preconvention period, G.O.P. rival Ronald Reagan; they had to spend money in the usual way. If we are going to have financial equality in the presidential electoral process, how do we nullify the incumbent's ability to make political hay at taxpayers' expense by claiming to speak as a noncampaigner?

Congress and the Supreme Court are now on record as saying: "Money corrupts; a great deal of money corrupts a great deal." But just as "fair representation" remains elusive, so does "fair financial representation."

Public opinion as constitutional attribute

The subtitle of this chapter links democracy—that is, majority rule—with participation. And surely the most obvious illustration of political participation in this country is casting a vote. I now want to discuss the mainsprings of citizen attitude and value underlying participation in general and franchise participation in particular. Essentially I am concerned here with personal opinion, but because the world of politics is in the public domain, it turns out I am talking about *public opinion* and its conception of relevant political phenomena.

American public opinion, like the political institutions and processes I have discussed already, evinces attributes of "Living Constitutionalism." If long-standing, deeply felt attitudes toward the Constitution are part of the "organic, living document," as I said in Chapter 1, so are fundamental, durable attitudes toward the nature of our political system and what that system should be doing. And like all other such explicit and implicit norms, these opinions are set in a "constitutional environment" that helps to shape them and give them meaning.

The most important point about the constitutional environment in this context is that Americans don't know or care very much about politics.[73] Quiz the electorate on some *specific* question, such as whether Congress should fund the B-1 bomber, and a majority will have scarcely a notion of what the pollster is talking about.[74] The average prospective voter has opinions on broad questions ("Should the United States be more friendly toward Russia?"), but basically the electorate holds intense attitudes only about issues with a *personal* meaning, one it can translate into everyday experience and self-interest. Query the population on civil rights and you'll get nitty-gritty opinions, because civil rights can be interpreted to mean "busing my children" or "violence in the streets" or "I want equality." Query the population on foreign affairs in peacetime, and the responses will be a study in vagueness. To sum up, the only *political* variable Americans consider seriously when assessing their prime hopes and fears is the threat of war. Their chief dreams and worries entail matters of personal situation: health, economic security, family harmony. No wonder the level of political participation in this country is extremely low, except for voting.[d]

There are several ways to conceptualize the "Living Constitution" of

[d] The only other activity in which more than 10 percent participated was to *give political opinions!*[75]

American public opinion. One is to delineate which political values receive the kind of support we associate with the larger system itself. For openers, the citizenry has strongly advocated social legislation (for instance, minimum wages, Medicare) since the Depression.[76] Any attempt by the government to renege on the commitments to economic egalitarianism that are the cornerstone of the Roosevelt coalition would be akin to a violation of norms specifically set out in the Constitution. However, the state cannot simply propose governmental handouts to the poor and expect majority support. Here, the American "work ethic" intrudes; besides, most people don't see themselves as being so badly off that they would benefit from food stamps and a guaranteed income. Americans are also very positively disposed toward the "law and order" theme, which means they favor a get-tough policy against unruly demonstrators, criminals, anyone who allegedly threatens the political or social order by interfering with the rights of others. This issue is much more visible than it used to be because of 1960s turbulence—that is, implicit values have become mobilized by environmental conditions, so they receive articulation today as explicit concerns.

Basic policy values are tougher to pin down in the civil rights and foreign affairs arenas, even with the striking impact of busing and Vietnam. Public opinion is committed to black-white equality in the abstract, but leery of both Washington-enforced equality and what it regards as the "extremist" civil rights movement. Public opinion is committed to international involvement and cooperation in the abstract, but leery of unilateral action that would boomerang. The Vietnam episode has had such culture-boggling effects that a rebirth of isolationist sentiment is readily discernible. It is fair to say that there is no "Living Constitutional" consensus on just what the terms "civil rights" and "foreign relations" should mean as working instruments of national governance.

Now let us focus on political issues of a different sort, not partisan issues but those of constitutional stability. I have said much already about our political "rules of the game," *but do citizens actually accept such rules as valid?* On general principle, popular endorsement is overwhelming. People believe, say, that "the minority should be free to criticize majority decisions." But on concrete questions, adherence to traditional constitutional norms becomes watered down. For example, less than 50 percent of Americans think that Communists should be allowed to run for public office or make speeches to spread their gospel.[77] But then, as the discussion in Chapter 6 showed, there is a wide range of opinion even among constitutional scholars as to how those who would use the system to subvert the system should be treated!

How can one capsulize those basic shared values which promote what political scientists call "system maintenance"? V. O. Key lists the following, gleaned from his research on public opinion: (1) Americanism, (2) suspicion of authority, (3) fairness in playing the political game, (4) individualism, (5) the majority should have its way, (6) pragmatism.[78] What do these sentiments mean exactly? My interpretations are as follows: (1) the average citizen puts country ahead of any other social or political force, (2) the average citizen looks with a jaundiced eye on unchecked power, (3) the average citizen thinks all strata of society should have an equal voice in what government does, (4) the average citizen treasures individual ability and initiative, (5) the average citizen accepts as legitimate the results voting majorities produce, and (6) the average citizen has little interest in political dogma or ideology.

Of course, we live in a pluralistic society; our life styles and our conceptions of the "good" vary enormously. Such diversity could threaten the stability of the above "rules" but for two other abiding norms. One, a key attribute of the American constitutional environment, is that there is no deep-seated polarizing force dividing our people in the grand European manner (see Chapter 9). Second, we possess strong pangs of civic duty, which tell us we *should* participate in politics.[79] This sense of community consciousness, this "we" feeling, is a kind of "cultural superego"; obviously it qualifies as a shared attitude. Yet what difference can a keen sense of obligation to participate make, if people don't in fact participate? I would hypothesize that civic duty is the agent galvanizing potential groups to organize when their adherents see the system coming under siege. As such, it must be ranked as a crucial norm contained in the "Living Constitution," a norm transcending parochial interests and their excesses.

This picture of the popular state of mind is one the Founding Fathers would recognize. For instance, the idea that the typical American was hot and bothered about politics two hundred years ago is—as I specified in Chapter 1—pure myth. And Americans have traditionally been flagwavers, as the discussion in Chapter 11 on foreign policy will demonstrate. About the only changes the Framers would find startling are the recent preoccupation with economic egalitarianism—though the commitment is as old as Jefferson's writings—and the expunging of white supremacy from the Constitution and some of the "Living Constitution."

The voter: roles, identities, influences

Many students of American government—critics and defenders alike—see voting as essentially a manifestation of power politics, an act locked into the struggle for victory between two political parties and the innumerable factions undergirding them. Thus far, I have overrepresented that view, describing voting behavior largely as a function of *party affiliation* and *group affiliation.* Other students, however, see the electoral process as a significantly independent mechanism allowing participants to cut through group ties and allegiances. Voting is a meaningful check on decision-makers, they claim, because the individual has a sense of values against which to judge candidate appeal. In their view, the elector who is merely a rubber-stamp, casting a ballot only in accordance with static, predetermined group ties, may be guilty of arbitrary, whimsical behavior. If Jane Kelly, a blue-collar worker from South Boston, votes only for Roman Catholics because she is a Roman Catholic, or if Joseph Brown, a farmer from Vermont, votes only for Republicans because he is a Republican—

such habitual patterns are presumed *irrational.* Furthermore, the voter who responds to new ideas, and supports candidates because of the values they convey, has established a presumption of *rational* behavior.[80]

To test this hypothesis, we must examine the "Living Constitution" of voting behavior in federal elections—the implicit norms governing voter participation and voter choice—and its relationship to American political opinion. If electoral behavior is to check and balance group activism, minimal standards of electoral rationality have to be satisfied. To determine patterns of rational or irrational electoral content, we must address the following fundamental questions:

1. To what extent do citizens vote in federal elections? What kinds of citizens tend to participate, and what kinds tend not to? The latter can hardly check anybody, and in that sense their behavior could well be considered irrational.

2. To what extent do these voters cast ballots in predictable, routine fashion? Which variables account for the trends in electoral decision-making? Why? These inquiries will take us to the guts of the "rational voter" controversy.

The American electorate appears to have an abysmal voting record. In the last century, turnouts for presidential contests commonly exceeded 75 percent of the eligible population; today, the norm hovers around 60 percent, with both the Nixon-McGovern and Carter-Ford races attracting only about 55 percent of possible participants. Off-year congressional elections never attract even a 50 percent turnout, and federal primaries still less.

The conventional wisdom regarding who votes assumes a strong correlation between education and income on the one hand and franchise participation on the other. Naturally, we would expect schooling and affluence to be directly related; yet among those who never went beyond grade school, a better income enhances voter participation, as does college exposure among blue-collar wage earners. So each factor has its considerable impact; clearly, both greater information and a greater stake in the system encourage voting.

There are other stereotypes, too. Traditionally, men vote more often than women, ostensibly because they are better attuned to political affairs; the middle-aged vote more often than the young or the old, supposedly because they are up to their ears in political need and expectation; urban dwellers vote more often than rural dwellers, evidently because the agrarian life style is more conducive to a low-key, face-to-face style of politics; whites vote more often than blacks, ostensibly because they are better integrated into the mainstream of political affairs and have never encountered legal barriers to their participation; party identifiers vote more often than independents, allegedly because such loyalties prod them to make choices even when they see little other need to bestir themselves; finally, Republicans vote more often than Democrats, evidently because the "have-not" party attracts precisely those people who are more out of touch with the system, its rewards, and its rules.

However, some of these stereotypes are losing their vitality. For instance, the women's movement has had a measurable impact on voting propensities by sex. Men maintain an edge, but it is wafer-thin and stems largely from Southern folkways, which frown on females wielding the ballot. And the gap between white–black participation has also closed considerably, what with racist eligibility standards crumbling in Dixie and the civil rights movement raising the consciousness of blacks everywhere. In 1960, 82 percent of whites voted for President, compared with 53 percent of blacks; however, in 1972, the figures were 73 percent and 64 percent, respectively.[81]

Taken for granted today are a host of relationships between psychological profile and voter turnout. They are of interest because, even given the above-stated demographic variables, both the poor and the poorly educated do go to the polls in considerable numbers. Chief among those personal attitudes leading people to cast a ballot are (1) a sense of civic duty, (2) a concern about who will win the election, and (3) political efficacy—that is, a belief that one's participation affects the outcome. Of these, the "civic duty" theme is the most important, certainly a finding which would follow logically from my earlier assertion that civic duty is a cornerstone of American public opinion as a "Living Constitutional" phenomenon. Also of significance are such sociological characteristics as group affiliation. People who join clubs, churches, civic organizations, and labor unions display ties with the prevailing order of things—ties which are related positively to voting. Evidently, psychological "mind set" and formalized interpersonal linkages are products of family training and other early culturizing influences. In this sense they are virtually apolitical, yet their political ramifications are enormous because they encourage playing the democratic game by established rules.[82]

We must qualify these "givens," however, because of the alienation phenomenon. Many well-educated young people with a marked sense of personal efficacy simply eschew the voting process as "irrelevant." These "skeptics"[83] are individuals who were radicalized in the late 1960s and still believe that traditional partisan politics cannot solve the pressing problems of modern society. By refusing to vote, they are exercising a rational option of "no confidence"; moreover, the inability of the electoral mechanism to absorb citizens who have both a passion and a talent for politics must be considered at least a temporary breakdown in constitutional processes.

One reporter, in a bit of understatement, has told the story: "The outcome of elections in the United States is not viewed as desperately serious by most voters."[84] To be sure, certain dramatic political events, such as the drive for civil rights or the war in Vietnam, will activate discrete segments of the polity to vote or not to vote. And perhaps a more competitive party struggle would promote franchise participation. Thus the South, which usually has the poorest turnout, approached the national average in 1968 when the Nixon–Humphrey-Wallace race put a premium on its electoral votes. Nonetheless, whether ballots are cast or not cast seems, over time, to be the result of a mix between subtle psychological factors and not-so-subtle demographic factors. Although, as Key has pointed out, no one really understands why nineteenth-century Americans voted more often than do twentieth-century Americans,[85] it is perhaps a result of the enfranchisement of masses of people whose concern for political life does not match their need to feel that they *can* vote. Put bluntly, *voter participation per se* is not the stuff of rational politics.[86]

There are those political scientists who believe that the electoral process has lost its vigor because the two major parties have become inept and amorphous throughout much of the country; others say voter apathy is a sign of acquiescence in—if not satisfaction over—the way the system is performing its assigned duties, and they breathe a sigh of relief when millions of uninformed, uneducated, and uninterested citizens remain on the sidelines. For our purposes, though, we may conclude that if the controversial and highly publicized presidential sweepstakes of 1964 (Johnson-Goldwater), 1968 (Nixon Humphrey-Wallace), and 1972 (Nixon-McGovern) could not attract 65 percent of the eligible electorate, then voter participation hardly constitutes a meaningful check on the alleged excesses which contemporary candidates and their political-party-pressure-group allies have perpetrated on the system.

Turning now to the second major inquiry posed above, we find that a conventional wisdom has also evolved to explain voting trends in federal elections. The key, we are told, is *party identification.* Democrats vote for Democrats, and Republicans vote for Republicans. Most Democrats have never supported a Republican for President, and vice versa. And in congressional races, partisanship is even more manifest, because personality factors are less clearly visible. The norm, then, is straight-ticket voting, not split-ticket voting.

What causes voters to identify with one side or the other? Are average Democrats drawn to their party because it stands for specific policy preferences which they themselves favor? Are average Republicans drawn to their party because it espouses a generally conservative approach congenial with their outlook? Or perhaps our typical partisans are attracted to political groupings because they think the parties represent the interests of their own social class? The answer to all such questions, this literature tells us, is a resounding "no." Average party members find political issues a most formidable intellectual challenge and generally tune them out. They also find the terms "liberalism" and "conservatism" too theoretical and elusive. Finally, our average partisans are not motivated to establish a social rank for themselves, much less to base partisan affinities on such labels as "working class" or "middle class."

Party identification, the customary argument runs, is transmitted from parent to child in much the same way as religious identification is. So the average partisan's political identification is predicated not on any political commitment but on psychological and sociological factors relating to family interaction and indoctrination. And these party cues are reinforced by the fact that children are usually exposed to the same stresses and strains in the larger community as their parents. Eventually they get the message: such-and-such party is for folks like us.

So classical behavioral theory sees party identification as *the* "Living Constitutional" value dictating national voter trends; and its advocates note that for one hundred years (from the 1860s to the 1960s), approximately three-quarters of the electorate considered itself bound to one major party or the other. Moreover, because party preference constitutes a "standing decision" which determines voting behavior far in advance of any nominating convention or primary, the typical electoral choice is considered a product of irrational circumstance. This thesis, let me say, has never been refuted, at least when discussed in "politics as usual" contexts. But I should also note that the argument in no way undermines my earlier contention relating party constituency to "have" and "have-not" sentiment. The test of that thesis will come *when we see why individual voters made the commitment years earlier to join one party or the other.*

There has, of course, always been an "independent vote" to be accounted for; in fact, nonidentifiers are known to swing back and forth among presidential candidates, and they are of sufficient number generally to determine who will occupy the White House. A certain mythology has traditionally surrounded independents. The nonpartisan elector was once lionized as "rational," carefully investigating all sides of all issues and all aspects of candidate performance before casting a vote. Then, in the 1950s, the independent came to be viewed as a sort of clodhopper who knew much less about politics than the party member and whose vote was likely to be based on whimsy. Both these viewpoints are exaggerations. Some independents, it is true, are simply apolitical, even though they may wind up voting. However, there has always been a certain segment of our population—generally located somewhere in the upper middle class—that relates to such issues as "good government" or world peace but couldn't care less about partisan conflicts.[87] The upshot is that the typical independent has just as many opinions on issues as the typical partisan, scores just as high on political efficacy measures as the typical partisan, and is just as ideologically oriented as the typical partisan.[88]

Though party identification still seems to be the most crucial variable in voter choice, the politics of the past ten years has certainly weakened its punch, at least temporarily; moreover, as I shall elaborate momentarily, today's electoral turmoil is very difficult to explain if we invoke only the conventional wisdom recited above. In 1964 (the year of Johnson-Goldwater), Democratic identification reached a highwater mark of 51 percent, while the G.O.P. stood at 24 percent, and self-proclaimed independents at 22 percent. By 1968, the independent faction had risen to 29 percent, having passed the Republicans' continuing 24 percent. In 1972 (the year of Nixon-McGovern), the Democrats could corral only about 41 percent of the electorate, their lowest figure since World War II; the Republicans, Nixon's triumph notwithstanding, remained at 24 percent; but the independents now commanded 35 percent, their best showing since the modern two-party alignment came into existence. Comparable figures for the year of Carter–Ford (1976) were: Democrats, 46 percent; Republicans, 22 percent; independents, 32 percent.

The new voter is largely responsible for this trend.[89] As the two parties struggled unsuccessfully with Vietnam, busing, crime in the streets, and so on, the younger and more numerous generations became increasingly disenchanted with traditional loyalties. The most extreme data came from 1972, when 50 percent of all new voters labeled themselves independent, 27 percent as "weak Democrats" (a response no doubt occasioned by the usual intergenerational acculturation), and only 12 percent as Republicans. Since that time, G.O.P. strength could hardly have increased significantly in the wake of Watergate, while Carter's inability to carry the eighteen-to-twenty vote against Ford shows that the Democrats have yet to recoup their losses. Most of the mavericks couple youth with high scores on formal education and social-class standing; not surprisingly, then, they relate well to key issues and candidate positions. In sum, the "new independent" is better integrated into the American political universe than the "old independent" and is at least as well integrated with respect to knowledge and concern as the partisan identifier, if we put *electoral machinations* to one side.[90]

What effect has all this had on presidential voting? Generally speaking, *candidate perception* and *issue preference* are having a greater and greater impact on ballot choice, while *party identification* weighs less and less heavily. To understand this trend, we must first backtrack a bit and describe the role these three variables played prior to the tumultuous 1960s. The personal characteristics ascribed to presidential nominees traditionally have trailed only party affiliation in determining electoral results.[91] Charismatic qualities of the Roosevelts and Eisenhower provide ample testimony. Voters' perception of candidates' policy commitments tended to run third.

I must stress, however, that issues have always had a deeper, more subtle impact. Earlier, I said party identification was thought to stem almost entirely from nonpolitical, family sources; yet, at some distant past time, the family head must have made a decision to pledge allegiance to party X. Why? The standard explanation is the "realigning election" which often follows on the heels of a cataclysmic event.[92] Thus, the Civil War turned the Republican Party from minority to majority party, and the Great Depression did the same for Democrats. "Realigning elections" would surely include Jefferson's triumph in 1800 over the Federalists, McKinley's win over Bryan's "silver crusade" in 1896, and F.D.R.'s 1932 stampede. These events, indelibly etched into the electorate's subconscious, live on also through the dim perceptions of party competence. The Republicans are to this day shackled with the "party of Depression" label; they are still thought to be insensitive to needy groups within the community, such as the working poor and racial and religious minorities. The Democrats, meanwhile, can never seem to escape the charge of being the "war party," because they allegedly "got us into" world wars I and II.[93] So the nexus between party choice and issue position, while usually not proximate, has traditionally been ever present. And here is where the distinction between the "haves" and the "have-nots" assumes relevance, for these "realigning elections" occur because different interests suddenly realize that their place in the system requires a shift in party loyalty. No wonder *"the long-run social and political patterns in the American electorate appear related."*[94] But even so, candidate perception, because of its immediacy, carries greater clout in specific "one-on-ones."

Against this background, we can examine how voters recently have gone about selecting "Mr. President, Superstar." The election of 1960 was an old-fashioned competition in which party identification held overwhelming importance. Many church-going Protestant Democrats, however, did vote for Nixon rather than the Catholic Kennedy,[95] though not enough to compensate for the Democrats' majority status. The election of 1964 was the most issue-oriented contest since the Depression; Goldwater declared war on the "liberal consensus," and the average elector had no trouble deciphering the message. Yet candidate perception was even more significant in the final analysis, for the Arizona senator consistently was found to be impulsive and "trigger-happy." His shoot-from-the-hip rhetoric voiced while accepting the G.O.P. nomination ("Extremism in defense of liberty is no vice") probably doomed his chances from the outset. This election also saw blacks take their leave of the G.O.P. almost completely, and they have yet to return to any degree. Issues retained their 1964 vitality in 1968, what with Wallace's candidacy, which, again, the average voter understood. Furthermore, while the Democrats maintained their positive image as advocate of "underdog groups," the Johnson Administration's ineptness on the Vietnam question heightened traditional voter skepticism over the party's skill in foreign relations and doomed Humphrey's candidacy. Finally, in 1972, Nixon's "peace with honor" profile, combined with McGovern's weakness in handling such problems as the Eagleton vice presidential withdrawal, meant Democratic disaster. The Vietnam issue achieved even more visibility than in 1968, because the two aspirants disagreed so patently on the merits. Meanwhile, Nixon's experience and McGovern's supposedly amateurish approach guaranteed an important role for candidate characteristics as well. Never in our history have the races been so divided in a two-party presidential election as they were in 1972, for blacks simply could not identify with the Republicans or with Nixon. And never have the generations been so divided: 50 percent of those between eighteen and twenty-four voted for Nixon, but almost 70 percent of those over thirty-five voted for him; furthermore, 79 percent of Democrats between eighteen and twenty-four voted for McGovern, but only 46 percent of Democrats over 35 voted for him.[e]

[e] We await rigorous political science research into Carter-Ford electoral tendencies; though evidently voter race was every bit the cutting edge it had been in 1972, voter age was not. Carter-Ford certainly seems to have been a "reinstating election," as the Kennedy-Nixon contest was, in that the majority party regained the White House after a short-lived minority-party tenure. Party identification meant more in 1960 than in 1976, but further information is needed to determine its strength as against candidate perception and issue preference. For instance, did the typical Carter supporter vote for him because he was a Democrat, because he wanted to take strong action against unemployment, or because of his "non-Washington" image?

In summarizing these figures, one commentator has pointed to a fourfold increase in the impact of policy choice upon the presidential vote between 1956 and the 1968-1972 elections. Of course, the fact remains that party identification was still first, candidate image second, and issue positions third in all these contests, though party identification clearly has greater ideological overtones than it had twenty years ago. Today, the overwhelming bulk of voters realize that the Democrats represent economic liberalism and the Republicans represent economic conservatism, and the typical Democrat is clearly more amenable to federal-government action in this area than his Republican counterpart. These perceptions are a marked contrast to the vague, sweeping view of the Democrats as the "war party" and the Republicans as the "Depression party," but the shift does not alter this most basic of facts: one party is still seen as representing the "haves," while the other party is still seen as representing the "have-nots."[96]

What do these data tell us about voter rationality and the voter as independent check on group demands? The traditional notion that electors' ballots are knee-jerk responses conditioned by an inherited party identification provides much ammunition for the "irrational voter" school. More contemporaneous information, however, shows the electorate becoming increasingly responsive to differences in issue position of the candidates and their parties. Are voters more rational today than they used to be?

I think the key is *citizen grievance.* In Chapter 9 I said the struggle between political-party and pressure-group dominance should be perceived as a function of what citizens want, the nature of their demands, and the intensity with which these demands are felt. Under usual circumstances, people generally want Washington to let them alone; if they have a problem, they tend to act through the group closest to them that represents their interests. Meanwhile, they vote much as their fathers and mothers did. That vote is *irrational* in being mostly predetermined, but *rational* in the larger sense of being based on long-standing expectations about what the parties are like *along with the short-term consideration that a shift in partisan allegiance is unnecessary given the current state of affairs.* But in the 1960s something happened. Voters started making the *rational* decision that both parties were doing a lousy job. In other words, the nature of citizen grievance made many electors realize they should be more discriminating. Voters now have no greater mental agility than formerly, but the world—and the American constitutional environment—is changing.

Now in case anyone thinks we have entered some new era of "superrationality" based on citizen weighing and measuring of competing issue alternatives, let me point out the perils of what I would call the "upwards and onwards" fallacy. For one thing, "war and peace" issues are few and far between; Vietnam-type confrontations will not emerge every decade. For another thing, considering the survival instincts of our two parties, it will be some time before the Republicans run another Goldwater or the Democrats run another McGovern. And there is nothing unique about the sort of "overt rationality" in candidate selection we are getting nowadays. We must remember the electorate chose Woodrow Wilson in 1916 because "he kept us out of war," a result just as rational as selecting Nixon to bring us "peace with honor." And we must remember the electorate chose Eisenhower in 1952 because "he'll get us out of Korea," a result just as rational as selecting Washington because "he beat the Redcoats." So both issue orientation and candidate personality traits have encouraged voter reflection and response at various times in our history. More fundamentally, turning out the Hoover Administration because it could not cope with economic adversity was as rational as turning out the Federalists in 1800 because they had no program to help the "little man." Here we see the greater pull of issues over candidate nuances; in rare circumstances, policy questions can actually prompt a shift in long-term party identification through a realigning election.[97] I repeat the most interesting question: What does the crazy-quilt electoral politics of the past decade portend? Reaffirmation? Realignment? If realignment, what kind?

So the returns are mixed: voters are capable of both mindless reflex and well-reasoned choice. But the data show that rational calculation at the ballot box occurs in either-or elections, and these have not predominated in our pragmatic, nonideological politics. Evidently, voters can check and balance the excesses of partisan aggregations and their factional allies when the indiscretions take on a clear and unmistakable coloration, but to the extent that blunders are incremental and quantitative, the electorate is likely not to perceive them and so will fail to redress their harmful tendencies. That is one reason why the roll call of American chief executives is dotted with clumps of mediocrities; usually we get an outstanding President only when citizen grievances become unbearable. The "Living Constitution" of voting behavior contains probably not much more and surely no less than what the Framers anticipated: a fallible rank-and-file, more concerned with its own prospects and problems than with the nation's destiny, but possessing enough moxie to reject those who have lost touch with popular needs and to deflate the "extremist" candidate and the "extremist" policy that would threaten to unhinge the constitutional balance.[98]

NOTES

1. To this mixture we have added only the *nonelected* Supreme Court, which keeps the elected officials from stepping on one another's toes and enforces against them the individual freedoms I have already described.

2. The past master of "election as sports confrontation" reportage, certainly, is Theodore H. White, whose *Making of the President* series dominates the nonfiction best-seller list every four years.

3. *The Federalist*, No. 68.

4. Herbert Wechsler, "The Political Safeguards of Federalism: The Role of the States in the Composition and Selection of the National Government," in Arthur W. Macmahon, ed., *Federalism: Mature and Emergent* (New York: Russell & Russell, 1962), p. 104.

5. Letter from James Madison to George Hay, August 23, 1823, quoted in Max Farrand, *The Records of the Federal Convention* (New York: Henry Holt, 1937), vol. III, pp. 458–59.

6. Why? Assume that states A and B are each entitled to ten electoral votes, but A employs the district system and B employs the unit rule. If a candidate thinks his popularity is about equal in the two states, he will spend

much more time cultivating the voters in state B, where victory would mean a clean sweep for electors favorable to him.

7. His oft-cited expression for the common person; the phrase is readily applicable to mass political participation.

8. Wechsler, p. 100. The fact that each state, no matter what its population, is provided with one representative gives additional credence to the mixed "person-state" constituency the Founders seemingly endorsed.

9. *Wesberry v. Sanders,* 376 U.S. 1 (1964).

10. Art. I, Sect. 2. The Founders obviously thought all states would utilize bicameralism, but the Constitution does not require them even to have legislative assemblies!

11. This is the exact meaning of the "direct election" Seventeenth Amendment standard.

12. V. O. Key, Jr., *Politics, Parties, & Pressure Groups,* 5th ed. (New York: Thomas Y. Crowell, 1964), p. 620.

13. Stanley Kelley, Jr., et al., "Registration and Voting: Putting First Things First," *The American Political Science Review* 61 (1967), pp. 359-79.

14. *Dunn v. Blumstein,* 405 U.S. 331 (1972). Compare *Shapiro v. Thompson* (the "welfare waiting period" case), 394 U.S. 618 (1969).

15. The Justices have stretched things a bit since, approving Arizona's fifty-day durational criterion. *Marston v. Lewis,* 410 U.S. 679 (1973).

16. *Williams v. Mississippi,* 170 U.S. 213 (1898).

17. *Lassiter v. Northampton County Board,* 360 U.S. 45 (1959).

18. See also the next section, where I discuss Congress's attempt to give eighteen-year-olds the vote in *all* elections; and see also Chapter 11 for a discussion of civil rights policy.

19. *Oregon v. Mitchell,* 400 U.S. 112 (1970).

20. *Guinn v. United States,* 238 U.S. 347 at pp. 363-64 (1915).

21. *Lane v. Wilson,* 307 U.S. 268 at p. 275 (1939).

22. *Harper v. Virginia Bd. of Elections,* 383 U.S. 663 (1966).

23. Ibid., pp. 666, 668.

24. This is how Wallace Mendelson describes the term. See "From Warren to Burger: The Rise and Decline of Substantive Equal Protection," *The American Political Science Review* 66 (1972), pp. 1226-33. I employed the phrase somewhat differently in Chapter 6, when I said that the Justices, by creating the "separate but equal" standard, had indulged in "substantive equal protection." In my view, the term includes all judicial attempts to rip the equal protection clause from its historical moorings—that is, to give black and other "insular minorities" equality before and under the law both in form and in substance.

25. James MacGregor Burns, *The Deadlock of Democracy* (Englewood Cliffs, N.J.: Prentice-Hall, 1964), pp. 319-21

26. See generally Philip B. Kurland, *Politics, the Constitution, and the Warren Court* (Chicago: Univ. of Chicago Press, 1970).

27. Certainly the Framers did not share this optimism. If I had to guess, I would trace its roots to such disparate post-1800 social forces as the taming of the West and the "promised land" vision that made this country a haven for the immigrants who settled here.

28. *Oregon v. Mitchell.*

29. Ibid., p. 122, where Black cites with approval language first employed by Chief Justice Hughes in *Smiley v. Holm,* 285 U.S. 355 at p. 366 (1932).

30. Said Mr. Justice Stewart: "The state laws which [Congress has invalidated] do not invidiously discriminate against any discrete and insular minority" (*Oregon v. Mitchell,* p. 296)—by which I take it he meant Jews, Chicanos, American Indians, or people of a particular ethnic extraction.

31. *Gomillion v. Lightfoot,* 364 U.S. 339 (1960). The elegant description of the reconstituted Tuskegee comes from Mr. Justice Frankfurter's opinion.

32. R. G. Dixon, Jr., *Democratic Representation* (New York: Oxford Univ. Press, 1968), p. 460.

33. *Colegrove v. Green,* 328 U.S. 549 (1946).

34. 369 U.S. 186 (1962).

35. Ibid., p. 300.

36. 377 U.S. 533 (1964).

37. Ibid., p. 577.

38. Ibid., p. 562.

39. *Lucas v. Colorado Gen. Assembly,* 377 U.S. 713 (1964).

40. Dixon, pp. 250, 268.

41. *Lucas v. Colorado Gen. Assembly,* p. 750.

42. John R. Commons, *Representative Democracy* (New York: Bureau of Economic Research, n.d.), Ch. ii.

43. See *67th Minnesota State Senate v. Beens,* 406 U.S. 187 (1972), where the Court had to slap down a federal district panel for throwing out Minnesota's apportionment blueprint and then writing up its own master plan!

44. *Burns v. Richardson,* 384 U.S. 73 (1966).

45. *Wells v. Edwards,* 409 U.S. 1095 (1973).

46. *Avery v. Midland County,* 390 U.S. 474 (1968).

47. *Mahan v. Howell,* 410 U.S. 315 at p. 326 (1973).

48. *White v. Weiser,* 412 U.S. 783 (1973).

49. An outstanding analysis of the closed-open primary mishmash is Clarence A. Berdahl, "Party Membership in the United States," *The American Political Science Review* 36 (1942), pp. 16-50, 241-62.

50. *Nixon v. Herndon,* 273 U.S. 536 (1927).

51. *Nixon v. Condon,* 286 U.S. 73 (1932).

52. *Grovey v. Townsend,* 295 U.S. 45 (1935).

53. *United States v. Mosely,* 238 U.S. 383 (1915).

54. *United States v. Classic,* 313 U.S. 299 (1941).

55. *Smith v. Allwright,* 321 U.S. 649 (1944).

56. *Rosario v. Rockefeller,* 410 U.S. 752 (1973).

57. *Kusper v. Pontikes,* 414 U.S. 51 (1973).

58. The direct primary is given searching analysis, with negative conclusions reported in V. O. Key, Jr., *American State Politics* (New York: Alfred A. Knopf, 1956). For further criticism, see Burns, *The Deadlock of Democracy,* p. 239. Evidently, senators chosen via the open primary are just as committed to party orthodoxy as senators chosen via the closed primary, if their voting records are indicative. Ira Ralph Telford, "Types of Primary and Party Responsibility," *The American Political Science Review* 59 (1965), pp. 117-18. But the fundamental question, as I see it, is not which primary better induces legislative orthodoxy, but which primary better induces viable party organization at the grassroots and meaningful party-linked voter participation.

59. Compare Austin Ranney and Leon D. Epstein, "The Two Electorates: Voters and Nonvoters in a Wisconsin Primary," *The Journal of Politics* 28 (1966), pp. 598-616; Austin Ranney, "The Representativeness of Primary Electorates," *Midwest Journal of Political Science* 12 (1968), pp. 224-38; Austin Ranney, "Turnout and Representation in Presidential Primary Elections," *The American Political Science Review* 66 (1972), pp. 21-37.

60. For example, Frank J. Sorauf, *Party Politics in America* (Boston: Little, Brown, 1968), p. 273.

61. Republican conventions have never allowed state blocs to vote as units.

62. Compare *O'Brien v. Brown,* 409 U.S. 1 (1972) and *Cousins v. Wigoda,* 319 U.S. 477 (1975).

63. Denis G. Sullivan, Jeffrey L. Pressman, Benjamin I. Page, and John J. Lyons, *The Politics of Representation* (New York: St. Martin's Press, 1974), pp. 3-6.

64. Commission on Party Structure and Delegate Selection, *Mandate for Reform* (Washington, D.C.: Democratic National Committee, 1970), pp. 39-40.

65. Sullivan, Pressman, Page, and Lyons, Ch. 2.

66. *Congressional Quarterly Weekly Report* (December 14, 1974), pp. 3334-35.

67. Most of the states with very large blocs opted for the "district scheme" in order to avoid dividing their votes proportionally among candidates. Carter's grassroots strength was magnified thereby.

68. Recall that this was Mr. Justice Black's rationale in the *Mitchell* case.

69. M. Ostrogorski, *Democracy and the Party System in the United States* (New York: Macmillan, 1910), pp. 159-60.

70. Key, pp. 495-501.

71. *Congressional Quarterly Weekly Report* (July 6, 1974), pp. 1742-44.

72. I have taken the facts presented here from David Adamany and George Agree, "Election Campaign Financing: The 1974 Reforms," *Political Science Quarterly* 90 (1975), pp. 201-20. The Supreme Court's decision on political contributions discussed below is *Buckley v. Valeo,* 96 S.Ct. 612 (1976).

73. Robert S. Erikson and Norman R. Luttbeg, *American Public Opinion: Its Origins, Content, and Impact* (New York: John Wiley, 1973), Chs. 1 and 2. In preparing this section, I have relied considerably on their lucid account.

74. Take a similar issue, whether the United States should develop an ABM capability. In 1969, when debate over this program reached its peak, 56 percent of the public had formed no opinion on the matter (Erikson and Luttbeg, p. 26).

75. Erikson and Luttbeg, p. 5. For a comprehensive investigation of citizen involvement in political affairs, see Sidney Verba and Norman H. Nie, *Participation in America* (New York: Harper & Row, 1972).

76. Erikson and Luttbeg, pp. 41-42. The data which follow come from Ch. 2.

77. Erikson and Luttbeg, pp. 101-02.

78. V. O. Key, Jr., *Public Opinion and American Democracy* (New York: Alfred A. Knopf, 1961), pp. 43-49.

79. Erikson and Luttbeg, pp. 107-09.

80. The literature on American voting behavior is endless. In fact, when some thirty books, articles, and convention papers have been written in recent years arguing the positive relationship between issue preferences and presidential electoral opinion, one is moved to think the point of diminishing returns has been reached. See John H. Kessel, "Comment: The Issues in Issue Voting," *The American Political Science Review* 66 (1972), p. 459. An even hotter topic for discussion is the more general inquiry addressing voter rationality. Here again, commentary approaches excess, especially where theory is generated from the results of a single election. It is enough to compare and contrast Angus Campbell, Philip E. Converse, Warren E. Miller, and Donald E. Stokes, *The American Voter* (New York: John Wiley, 1960) and V. O. Key, Jr., *The Responsible Electorate* (Cambridge, Mass.: Harvard Univ. Press, 1966). Much of the so-called conventional wisdom cited below comes from research contained in the former study.

81. Gerald Pomper, *Voters' Choice* (New York: Dodd, Mead, 1975), pp. 70-71, 121. These data obviously are inflated when compared with overall voter turnout, but they are the best we have.

82. See generally Robert E. Lane, *Political Life* (Glencoe, Ill.: The Free Press, 1959) and Campbell, Converse, Miller, and Stokes, *The American Voter.*

83. Pomper, pp. 101-02.

84. William H. Flanigan, *Political Behavior of the American Electorate,* 2nd ed. (Boston: Allyn and Bacon, 1972), p. 15.

85. Key, *Political Parties,* p. 578.

86. Economists like to argue that "rational" people would hardly ever bother to vote in the typical national election, if only because the individual's ballot rarely makes any difference. But that is rationality in the abstract, not the rationality tempered by the "Living Constitutional" norms we are taught to revere.

87. Burns, pp. 211-12.

88. Flanigan, pp. 45-47.

89. See generally Norman H. Nie, Sidney Verba, and John R. Petrocik, *The Changing American Voter* (Cambridge, Mass.: Harvard Univ. Press, 1976).

90. Pomper, pp. 20-24, 31-34.

91. Flanigan, p. 121.

92. See the discussion in Key, *Political Parties,* pp. 534-36.

93. Donald E. Stokes, "Some Dynamic Elements of Contests for the Presidency," *The American Political Science Review* 60 (1966), pp. 19-28.

94. Flanigan, p. 71 (italics in text).

95. Angus Campbell, Philip E. Converse, Warren E. Miller, and Donald E. Stokes, *Elections and the Political Order* (New York: John Wiley, 1966), p. 89.

96. See Pomper, pp. 36, 93, 129, 148-50, 159-64, 197-203, and the numerous sources he includes, especially Stokes, "Some Dynamic Elements."

97. Richard W. Boyd, "Presidential Elections: An Explanation of Voting Defection," *The American Political Science Review* 63 (1969), p. 510.

98. For a splendid attempt to describe the balance of power among voters, political parties, and interest groups in this country (with conclusions somewhat more optimistic than my own), see E. Pendleton Herring, *The Politics of Democracy* (New York: W. W. Norton, 1940).

11

constitutional policy: academic jargon or the stuff of politics?

When we contemplate American national government, we usually contemplate a set of structural entities, each performing its accustomed offices, hewing to established procedural niceties, responding to public sentiment and pressure. But American national government includes more than "rules of the game," norms to delimit how and by whom public decisions will be formulated. Politics may be the study of power, of influence, of process, and of law, yet politics also encompasses the issues and values debated and decided on. Students of government must understand the *end product*, as well as the grand machinery that generated it. In this chapter, I will try to describe and evaluate these results in the light of the "Living Constitution."

Policy and *constitutional* policy

Like many scholarly disciplines, political science has its fads and fashions. During the 1960s, heavy research emphasis was placed on rigorous description of governmental *processes* and *decision-making*—that is, on the *behavior* of political actors rather than on the *issues* the actors were facing. Today, the shoe is on the other foot. Books and articles abound which characterize the *substance* of decisions made rather than the process invoked to make them, emphasizing especially the impact of these decisions on the political system. The term commonly used to convey the "what" of governmental accomplishment rather than the "how" is "policy."

Unfortunately, scholars use the term "policy" to signify a variety of different phenomena, thus destroying whatever precision and conceptual rigor the notion could provide. For example, *policy* has been defined to include everything government says and does on an official basis;[1] all verbal commands authorized by government;[2] all "general intentions" advocated by government;[3] all specific governmental choices designed to implement broad intentions;[4] all governmental programs designed to implement choices;[5] and all "purposive" governmental action, whether verbal or nonverbal, whether in the nature of plans, choices, or programs.[6]

For myself, I do not see how the "what" of decision-making can comprise either action without intent, or purpose without conduct. Very often, public officials do things or say things unrelated to any pattern or larger commitment, and very often they lay plans that never get off the drawing board. Neither random behavior nor lifeless motives constitute governmental "policy." Rather, the concept encompasses (1) the underlying *goals* of decision-making, (2) the *actions* taken on behalf of those goals, (3) the internal *logic, rationale,* or *plan* that purportedly links the decisions reached to the ends in view.[7]

However, I do not think policy necessarily presupposes any overarching grand strategy for all facets of racial politics, environmental politics, trade politics, or kindred terrain. Nor do I think policy necessarily presupposes any public declaration of the decision-maker's intentions. Nor do I think policy necessarily presupposes a deliberate choice of one approach over other, less satisfactory approaches.[8] These elements are usually present only when the policy-making process is highly structured, and such literal expressions are very often not the substance of checks-and-balances interplay.

Not unexpectedly, my conception of policy *flows directly from the theoretical focus underlying my approach to the study of governance.* That focus is the "Living Constitution." But what is the nexus between "policy" and "constitution"?

Remember, a constitution demarcates the explicit rules of a political game. Certainly that is how I have defined the Constitution of the United States with respect to our political game. But when we look back at the 1780s and reexamine the Framers' goals, the actions they took to implement those goals, and the thematic purposes transcending both behavior and result, is it not apparent that their creation, their "what," is policy? Thus:

> It is a matter of constitutional policy to have a President, a Congress, and a Supreme Court. It is a matter of constitutional policy that the President and members of Congress shall gain office through elections, and that members of the Supreme Court shall be appointed for life.[9]

Throughout my remarks, moreover, I have emphasized such implicit norms as "senatorial courtesy" and "government by whirlpools." These are just two aspects of the "Living Constitution," *and they too are policy.* It is true that significant customs and folkways are rarely authorized in any formal fashion; indeed, this would be a contradiction in terms. Yet they possess their own internal consistency and logic; they subsist because they enhance certain goals;

and they certainly comprise political action. If the official constitutional ban against ex post facto legislation is policy, if the Supreme Court's doctrine of "pure judicial review" is policy, then the "Living Constitution's" stress upon federal-state relations as "marble cake" is also in the nature of policy.

But when we view the Constitution today, we see it largely as a decision-making instrument. And we view the "Living Constitution" largely the same way. So, while these rules may have been the "what" of decision-making to the people who spawned them, they have become *process*—that is, the "how" of decision-making—to us. If I am right in considering policy to be *substance* rather than *procedure,* then we must not label either the Constitution or the "Living Constitution"—as I have thus far invoked that concept—with a new generic phrase, "constitutional policy." [10] Much greater clarity is afforded by christening virtually the entire package with the name "constitutional process." [11]

What then is constitutional policy? Like policy generally, it must be in the nature of output, or "what" stuff. And like policy generally, it must conform to the features specified above: *internally logical and purposive action designed to meet particular goals.* But policy is *constitutional* only when it attains constitutional dimension; it must be *durable, fundamental,* and *highly esteemed.* After all, our society venerates not only certain "rules of the political game" but the basic *ends* of statecraft and the basic *means* adopted to achieve those ends—in short, *taproot action blueprints* that a consensus thinks are *legitimate* and have *stood the test of time.* Professor Friedrich has said policy is more than a specific action; it is a *course of action.* That is, policy comprises *patterns* of governmental initiative and response. [12] I agree. Constitutional policy, then, involves *fundamental, durable,* and *highly esteemed* courses of action; it involves *fundamental, durable,* and *highly esteemed* patterns of the political "what." As defined here, constitutional policy is an integral portion of the "Living Constitution."

Constitutional policy can be divided into many classes and subgroups. For example, we could distinguish among institutional categories (executive policy, judicial policy, administrative policy), ideological categories (liberal policy, conservative policy), or substantive categories (environmental policy, transportation policy). [13] Although there is no agreement as to which are the most prudent and feasible, I think *substantive categories* are the most useful. They transcend concerns as to which link in the process chain authorized them (unlike institutional categories), and they transcend value biases (unlike ideological categories).

But another way to compare and contrast policies provides a more powerful theoretical understanding of the political dynamics flowing from policy content. Theodore Lowi has distinguished three significant types of *domestic* policy: distributive, regulatory, and redistributive. [14] A *distributive* policy is a gift or benefit or subsidy that government provides for the well-being of a particular class or interest—parity payments to farmers, grants-in-aid to cities, franchises to railroads, "pork barrel" to states. The theory envisions the government as a cornucopia from which can be taken all manner of "goodies," so pressure groups get into line to receive their helping. A *regulatory* policy is a coercive guideline or standard of behavior that must be obeyed, else punishment will follow. Antitrust statutes applied to steel manufacturers, contempt citations against radicals, interpretations of First Amendment rights, F.B.I. procedures enforcing *Miranda* warnings, and S.E.C. rules for marketing new stock issues—all are essentially regulatory. A *redistributive* policy is one by which the government takes perquisites or burdens from one class of interests and gives them to another class of interests. For example, progressive income taxes authorize a shift in financial load from less affluent to more affluent citizens, while welfare programs authorize a shift in responsibility for how poor people will subsist from personal obligation to taxpayer obligation. The premise underlying redistribution is that the "natural order of things" has not produced an equitable arrangement of powers and duties, so the state steps in and reshuffles the deck.

These categories are not self-identifying. Suppose the United States Army has a rule requiring that all homosexuals be discharged from military service; suppose further that the Supreme Court decides this *policy* is a bill of attainder and therefore unconstitutional. Would the new policy be distributive, redistributive, or regulatory? Has the Court conferred a bounty or a subsidy upon homosexuals, in the sense that they now possess rights which others have traditionally enjoyed? Or has the Court taken something away from the armed forces "establishment" and given it to homosexuals as a class? These analogies appear farfetched. Rather, the Court has invoked a neutral standard of fair play—a standard emphasizing how people conduct themselves, not who they are—and has extended this rule of thumb a bit further across the board. Such is the nature of regulatory policy.

In the following pages, I will focus on the three aspects of constitutional policy having the greatest significance for Americans at this time: *foreign* policy, *economic* policy, and *civil rights* policy. My central concern will be the means and ends of constitutional dimension that these policies have conveyed and convey today. Moreover, I will try to assess those policy spheres from the standpoint of distributive-regulatory-redistributive assumptions, paying special attention to whether this classificatory scheme helps us understand the nature of constitutional policy within the total "Living Constitutional" framework.

Foreign policy: America the unique?[15]

The national interest versus the "larger" interest

In Chapter 1, I said that the "Living Constitution" could not be ripped from the context of the larger American constitutional environment. It follows that national governmental policy cannot be ripped from the political environment that inspired it. And by "political environment" I mean here *the power relationships toward which public policy is directed.*

In any discussion of American foreign policy, political environment is crucial, because it very often lies outside American control. When the issues are domestic, the constitutional machinery is generally adequate to enforce whatever policy solutions society ordains. But in the international arena, policy is almost always directed toward events, conditions, and circumstances beyond the unilateral control of any nation, and there is not even widespread agreement on the explicit and implicit "rules of the game." Nonetheless, the basic norms that shape the international political environment are intertwined with our "Living Constitution" even though they involve people, places, and ideas alien to us.

Just as policy substance is influenced by political environment, so it is influenced by guiding premises. Two conflicting approaches respecting American foreign policy, predicated upon very different perceptions of the international arena, have received considerable attention in the literature. These world views are commonly known as the "idealist" and the "realist."

The idealist position holds that nation-state differences can be bridged by good works, good will, and good faith. Policy, idealism teaches, should stem from ethical considerations and should maximize cooperation rather than competition or struggle. [16] Our leadership has had intermittent infatuations with the idealist view. Woodrow Wilson's prevailing policy commitment was to "make the world safe for democracy," and in that spirit he advocated "open covenants openly arrived at." The covenant he hoped would ensure democracy's ultimate triumph was the League of Nations, a *program of action* derived from his overall policy preferences. World peace could be achieved by *collective security*, through which civilized nations, under the banner of League membership, would together resist all external aggression. But, of course, Americans were not ready to assume such obligations. Thirty years later, when the United States put the full weight of its prestige behind the United Nations, Wilsonian idealism seemed finally to have achieved a dominant position both here and abroad. The guiding policy principle was no longer democratic universalism, to be sure, for only the myopic could equate Stalin's monolith with freedom. Rather, the more modest substantive goal was a revised collective security, whereby threats to world peace would be countered by multilateral resistance on the part of all other nations, no matter what their ideological biases. And even though national selfishness seems as prominent in the 1970s as it was in the 1770s, hope among the idealists springs eternal. To quote a chief advocate, former Arkansas Senator (and Foreign Relations Committee chairman) J. W. Fulbright: "[We] regret the reversion to the old power politics, and . . . retain some faith in the validity and vitality of the United Nations idea." [17]

What Fulbright regrets, really, is the recent upsurge in support for the realist position. Essentially, the realists perceive the international environment as a jungle. In order to survive, a country must be the toughest, smartest animal in that jungle. Whereas idealists construct policy out of ethical and altruistic interests, the realists think there is only one interest—the *national interest.* In short, whatever is good for one's country almost always overrides everything else. [18]

It is difficult to document, but American foreign policy has probably been more influenced by hardheaded pragmatism than by head-in-the-sky morality. Did we eschew "entangling alliances" in our early years because mutual security smacked of the devious and the conspiratorial or because we thought unilateral action provided a better chance for survival? Did we fight Spain at the turn of the century because she had sunk one of our battleships, the *Maine,* in violation of international law or because we thought the Caribbean region lay within our sphere of influence? Did we employ a policy of "containment" to impede Soviet aggression in the late 1940s because Bolshevism was a totalitarian monstrosity or because we feared that Stalin's imperialistic designs would gobble up Western Europe and leave us without allies? In each case the "higher law" element was important, but historians seem to think the power factor was doubly important.

The great debate between idealists and realists does have its straw-man attributes. Ethical perfectionism might well be folly for a country negotiating with Attila the Hun, but, unless one is prepared to play saint, pure faith alone won't take us very far in personal relations either. Conversely, nation-states bent upon emulating the archvillains of history have been recognized, in the end, for their pernicious deeds, just as Caesar's assassins were themselves eventually unmasked. To be sure, the national leader does move in a universe in which the "rules of the game" are more elusive than those adhered to by any single political community. But this unique context need not activate a good-versus-evil dilemma. The proper policy orientation is to select the best moral choices that *circumstances permit.* Put another way, the goal of balancing national interest against larger interest would seem to be both attainable and ethically defensible.[19] That is the criterion against which the purposes and consequences of American constitutional policy in foreign affairs must be evaluated.

Foreign constitutional policies: 1787–1945

The single most pervasive and longstanding policy commitment Americans have entertained in foreign relations decision-making is probably *isolationism.* For more than 150 years, the preponderance of our leadership inveighed against international ties and responsibilities as a general principle and built countless policies and programs upon that implicit guidepost. Only since World War II has isolationism been exceptional policy rather than prevailing rule; indeed, there is some doubt as to whether the norm is dead or merely resting. In any event, isolationist policy was as much "Living Constitution" for Americans from 1787 to 1939 as, let us say, the nine-member Supreme Court.[a]

[a] The first Supreme Court had five Justices, and the number nine did not become standardized until after the Civil War. Franklin Roosevelt tried to "deconstitutionalize" the figure, but he failed. For the record, I also consider this custom "constitutional process" rather than "constitutional policy."

What did isolationism mean in its heyday? An important precedent was established when the French and English went to war in the 1790s. The United States had an alliance with France, which earlier had brought her navy to our rescue at Yorktown and ensured success for our revolution. Jefferson—the champion American idealist of those years—wanted us to honor that agreement in the name of human rights and popular revolutions everywhere. But George Washington, instead, issued the first of many presidential neutrality proclamations, declaring that the conflict was none of our business. And, later, his Farewell Address contained the cornerstone of isolationist constitutional policy:

> Europe has a set of primary interests, which to us have none, or a very remote relation. Hence she must be engaged in frequent controversies, the causes of which are essentially foreign to our concerns. Hence, therefore, it must be unwise in us to implicate ourselves, by artificial ties, in the ordinary vicissitudes of her politics, or the ordinary combinations and collisions of her friendships, or enmities.[20]

Washington pointed out the great geopolitical advantage of our "detached and distant situation," with the Atlantic Ocean as a buffer. The national interest, he said, required our country to build up its strength so that in later years our actions and words would be entirely respected. Finally, while economic health depended upon international trade, the United States should pursue commercial affairs with "as little *political* connection as possible." In short, isolationism never meant *total* isolation; it meant only a strict quarantine against *European political entanglements.*

Through the years, this definition was well lived up to. When the European nations went to war in 1914, Woodrow Wilson declared the conflict to be one "with which we have nothing to do, whose causes cannot touch us."[21] The usual neutrality declarations followed swiftly, but Germany's policy of unrestricted submarine warfare made our participation inevitable. Even then, technological advances had rendered traditional isolationism questionable. Yet our response to fascist aggression in the 1930s was much the same. Congress enacted no less than four neutrality statutes prior to Pearl Harbor, enunciating various embargoes against trading in armaments with belligerents regardless of their culpability. A new wave of idealism was in the making, however, spawned by Hitler's wanton persecution and destruction in Europe and brought to fervent desperation by Japan's sneak attack on us. The United States, said F.D.R., must help secure the "four essential freedoms" to peoples everywhere: freedom of speech, freedom of worship, freedom from want, and freedom from fear. To that end, the Allies—Great Britain, the U.S.S.R., China, and the U.S.A.—fought the Axis powers throughout the globe. The guiding policy was *unconditional surrender,* and surrender unconditionally Germany, Italy, and Japan did. But looming on the horizon was the "red menace"—first Russia, then China under Mao. Roosevelt's optimism turned out to be just another transient hope, while isolationism, as a "Living Constitutional" concept, has never recovered from the trauma of recognition that would shortly afflict us.

While self-restraint was the prevailing norm in dealing with "Europe's broils" for so many years, activism marked American foreign relations elsewhere. The oldest constitutional policy in that activist arsenal—a purposeful course of conduct still very much alive—is the *Monroe Doctrine.* When Spanish colonies in Latin America made a successful bid for independence, threats to retake those lands, echoing through the world's capitals, prompted President Monroe to issue his famous ultimatum of 1823:

> The American Continents, by the free and independent condition which they have assumed and maintain, are henceforth not to be considered subjects for future colonization by any European power. . . . In the wars of the European powers, in matters relating to themselves, we have never taken any part. . . . It is only when our rights are invaded, or seriously menaced, that we . . . make preparation for our defense. . . . With the existing Colonies . . . we have not interfered, and shall not interfere. But with the Governments who have declared their independence, and maintained it, and whose Independence we have . . . acknowledged, we could not view any interposition for the purpose of oppressing them . . . in any other light, than as the manifestation of an unfriendly disposition towards the United States.[22]

Monroe's dictum had its idealistic trappings—mainly cynicism about the machinations of European despots and sympathy toward South American patriots like Simón Bolívar. Yet the United States offered no tangible assistance whatsoever to these nations. Our primary interest lay in the improved commercial opportunities they afforded, but the United States was certainly not prepared to fight even over those markets. Did the expected invasion peter out, then, because continental powers feared the thunder of Monroe's rhetoric? Hardly. It was the British fleet, patrolling the Atlantic on behalf of British self-interest, that offered us the free hand we desired.

The Monroe Doctrine was in fullest flower during the early 1900s. When various Latin American nations defaulted on debts owed to Europeans, intervention by European powers loomed large. In Venezuela, considerable violence had resulted from such an intrusion. To forestall further foreign incursions, the irrepressible T.R. announced the *Roosevelt Corollary* to the Monroe Doctrine, warning Latin governments to keep their houses in order or the United States would do it for them. Under watchful White House stewardship, the Dominican Republic was converted into an American protectorate in the name of Caribbean tranquillity. Nor were Presidents Taft and Wilson any less feisty. Taft sent marines into Nicaragua when a revolution threatened American investors, whom the State Department initially had encouraged to compete there against European entrepreneurs. Taft's great fear was security for the Panama Canal. But Wilson's motivation was moral uplift. These unstable nations needed to be looked after for their own sakes, he believed, or they would never survive internal disorder and European designs. So our supervision of Nicaragua's finances intensified, while American troops were landed at Vera Cruz, Mexico, as a demonstration against President Huerta's autocratic regime. The Monroe Doctrine had now become a standard excuse for naked American imperialism.

Under Presidents Hoover and Franklin Roosevelt, the United States essayed a different approach to South of the Border relations, the *Good Neighbor Policy*. For a time, it even appeared that the Monroe Doctrine would have to share constitutional status with the new outlook. Revolutions rocked Latin America, but both Presidents rejected intervention. Many observers held their breath, expecting our vital interests to be seriously compromised, but no such trend developed. The premise of the Good Neighbor Policy was that all Western Hemisphere nations were equals, and its adherents hoped to work out cooperative strategies of mutual benefit. The Pan-American Union was conceived as a joint effort to promote economic and cultural unity, and most Latin countries banded together against the Axis during World War II. As we shall see, though, Good Neighborism has since had a spotty track record.

A third constitutional foreign policy of venerable standing is *Manifest Destiny*. Initially, this notion was merely an urge for elbowroom, stemming largely from feelings of inferiority in the power game. Conquer Canada, some said, or Great Britain will one day invade us from the north; conquer Florida as well, or Spain will forever threaten our southern flank. And, of course, the expansionist urge had its economic dimension, for entree to the Gulf of Mexico and control over the Mississippi River meant a gigantic boost in trade.

But by the 1840s, a cocky United States, smitten with "Oregon fever," had bigger ideas: "Our manifest destiny [is] to overspread and to possess the whole of the continent which Providence has given us," wrote one noted journalist.[23] Put bluntly, Manifest Destiny exemplified feelings of national greatness in world affairs, the idea that one's claim upon history has been staked out and merely awaits implementation. Put specifically, Manifest Destiny meant controlling all lands from the Atlantic to the Pacific that American power could command; later, the doctrine would justify island snatching in the Pacific to compete with the European island snatchers in achieving commercial success.

First came the establishment of American supremacy on the continental mainland. We conquered the Indian tribes, and indeed our claims were as valid as France's and Spain's in their respective colonies. We went on to gain control over Oregon via treaty, and indeed our claims were as valid as Great Britain's. Then we annexed an independent Texas, and indeed our claims were as valid as Mexico's. Finally, war erupted with the dictatorial Mexican government, a war we—but also our antagonists—could have avoided. We won and gobbled up the territory between Texas and California. Was it all inevitable? Yes, once we accepted the premises of Manifest Destiny, premises that have gripped countless nation-states bursting with unspent power.

Second came American exploitation of its new gateway to the Pacific. This version of Manifest Destiny received a boost from both Admiral Mahan's well-publicized thesis that expanded sea power was the key to global power and from Charles Darwin's "survival of the fittest" notion, which seemed to legitimize American hegemony over allegedly inferior island peoples. Before long, we annexed Hawaii (1898) and began jousting with Britain and Germany over tiny Samoa. At the same time, Manifest Destiny and the Monroe Doctrine became intertwined in Latin America. Our overall commercial strategy required an interoceanic canal, so we helped the Panamanian insurgents bring off their revolution against Colombia. Then, with Cuban exiles in Florida urging us on, we drubbed Spain easily; Puerto Rico and the Philippines were absorbed, while Cuba was turned into an American protectorate under the terms of the Platt Amendment, a Roosevelt Corollary without façade. So the United States had gained its canal in perpetuity (as the treaty terms recited), complete protection for the canal by ousting Spain from Caribbean waters, and a key outpost for Oriental trade, the Philippines. The only real surprise in retrospect was failure to annex Cuba, a "blunder" interventionists would later regret. For the edification of those who claimed the United States was simply another imperialist country, we then announced a policy whereby all nonbelievers within our new territorial jurisdiction would be Christianized!

Some idealists, of course, protested vehemently. William Jennings Bryan made imperialism a key issue in the 1900 presidential election, but William McKinley's "Don't haul down the flag!" theme was irresistible. A few years later, Woodrow Wilson, whose missionary zeal toward Latin Americans had won him no plaudits South of the Border, tried to replace Manifest Destiny with a new policy: *national self-determination.* By this he meant the right of each ethnic group to decide its own political fate. At Versailles, Wilson persuaded France not to establish control over western Germany because that would violate his self-determination principle. But the United States itself surrendered no territorial interests until the burst of idealism following Pearl Harbor. Shortly thereafter, the Philippines gained independence, and Hawaiians achieved statehood, changes advocated by overwhelming majorities in those islands. However, as I shall note shortly, much more circumspection is needed to stem the tide of Manifest Destiny.

A fourth constitutional policy was framed for Asia: the *Open Door.* Having obtained commercial outposts in the Pacific, American shipping interests began looking toward a brisk business in the largely untapped Chinese market; but this clumsy giant was also a ready-made target for predator European countries. When France, Russia, and Germany began to carve China up into spheres of influence, Secretary of State John Hay sent off protests to all concerned. The United States, he pontificated, insisted upon an Open Door—Chinese independence plus free and equal commercial opportunities at its many ports. Hay's notes did not actually challenge the foreign concessions already established; he was really seeking "equality within spheres." Of course, the United States could not possibly enforce any such policy. Indeed, Americans were willing neither to free the Philippines nor to open the trading door at Manila Harbor. We invoked the Open Door in China because we didn't have the clout to obtain our own sphere of influence there, and because we thought (erroneously) that the British also favored an Open Door and would stand behind our rhetoric with their navy. Yet, when the Europeans "answered evasively with faint gestures of approval,"[24] Hay announced victory for his aims. American public opinion lauded Open Doorism as both a diplomatic triumph and a victory for enlightenment over imperialism.

A few years later, President Taft improvised his own variation of the Open Door: *Dollar Diplomacy*. The United States government would help private enterprise penetrate China for profitable investment. The idea, said Taft, was to unite diplomacy, capital, and commerce for the peaceful development of Chinese potential, while reaping a fair profit for business and ripening our political ties with an underdog nation whose voice would one day be heard. If China were going to borrow money from German, French, and English bankers, why not from American bankers as well, especially when the political consequences loomed large? Wilson also tried the same general approach to blunt Japan's growing influence on the Asiatic mainland.

George Kennan has called the Open Door "a myth . . . destined to flourish in American thinking for at least a half-century."[25] The United States supposedly had saved China from rapacious enemies with its compassion, its sense of equality, and its financial resources. China was our friend, we believed, and grateful as well. No wonder that when we joined Chiang Kai-shek, dictatorial master of Chinese politics, in war against Japan in the 1940s, Americans saw the alliance as merely a reaffirmation of age-old cooperation between peace-loving peoples.

At least one other constitutional foreign policy seems to have captivated Americans over the long pull: *peaceful settlement of disputes*, the idea that when reasonable people sit down at the bargaining table, each with a willingness to give a little to get a lot, amicable relations will ensue, and important problems can be resolved. Generally speaking, this theme has been a vehicle for that unabashed moralistic fervor which now and again marks our foreign policy posture. But while idealism sometimes led us to dominate smaller countries for what we considered their own good, Britain and France could hardly be saved through exploitation. For them we reserved the "morality via international agreement" credo.

The Founding Fathers, let it be said, thought in no such terms. They were inured to a geopolitical universe in which the United States was surrounded by European enclaves in the Western Hemisphere. No wonder the term "common defense" precedes the term "general welfare" in the Constitution's Preamble as a transcendent value. It was only after 1812 that Americans became so wrapped up in domestic affairs, especially the taming of the frontier, that they forgot how to play the power game. When this country finally emerged from its shell, following victory over Spain in the late 1890s, the American people were in no mood to scrap isolationism, but they did want peace and order in the world. What they did not appreciate—and what their leaders did not appreciate—was Uncle Sam's unique capacity to rely on words, promises, and treaties. The United States could always retreat to its domain between the oceans; for

Britain, France, and Germany, however, there was only the reality of mutual borders and rivalries.[26]

The "peaceful settlement" motif achieved its highwater mark, not surprisingly, during the 1918–45 period. Wilson's "Fourteen Points" were shot through with such principles as mutual disarmament, mutual trade agreements, and mutual adjustment of colonial claims. More important, his conception of collective security—which he saw as humanity's only hope for survival—was predicated upon mutual accommodation, not to mention *mutual perceptions of aggression.* It is interesting to note that the Senate's refusal to join the League of Nations marked the first time a peace treaty had ever been rejected in the upper chamber.

The 1920s and 1930s found the United States off on a great crusade to regulate all manner of international strife. There was the Washington Five-Power Treaty, dealing with the number and magnitude of naval vessels; the London naval agreement, restricting the sizes of French, British, and American warships; and, without doubt the greatest monument to naiveté in international affairs, the Kellogg-Briand Pact, which pledged signatory nations to outlaw war. All that these agreements accomplished was to render us totally unprepared to meet Japan's naval thrusts in the Pacific and Germany's panzer thrusts on the European continent.

When the United States finally got its war machine in gear and led the drive which vanquished Nazism, the bottle of idealism filled once again. At long last, countless Americans believed, there would be one peaceful, harmonious world, not a cacophony of national squabbles. In this spirit, the United Nations was born. According to the United Nations Charter (constitution, that is), each member state would sit in the General Assembly and possess one vote. This body was not a legislative chamber as such but only a conference of diplomats. When people complain today that the General Assembly is strictly a debating society, they forget that it was meant to be little more. The big decisions were the province of the Security Council, whose members included the five "heavyweights" (the United States, the Soviet Union, France, Great Britain, and China) plus six other countries chosen by the General Assembly for two-year terms. The Security Council was intended to make binding determinations even with respect to war and peace, if all permanent members agreed. The veto was the brainchild of the Big Five acting in concert. "One nation, one vote" would have satisfied Americans no more than it would have satisfied the Russians, for the wealthy and powerful were determined to hold responsibilities commensurate with their strength. And why not, for what would the United Nations be without them? Finally, Article 52 of the United Nations Charter permitted regional arrangements, while Article 51 allowed nations participating in such arrangements the right to collective self-protection. But little public attention was drawn to those two provisions until world conditions had altered considerably.

The "new hope for mankind," then, was really a well-contrived compromise between national autonomy and world federalism, between hemispheric cooperation and collective security. In the parlance of political theory, the United Nations was only a confederation, but it could have been no more. The problem is that Americans were oversold, but they had oversold themselves because they wanted to believe in utopia. And when they soon found out what the real world was all about, a trauma of vast proportions inevitably resulted. That trauma has changed the very nature of the "Living Constitution."

Foreign constitutional policies: 1946–1976

Characterizing the fundamental norms of American foreign policy over the past thirty years is difficult. The problem is not to identify policies (we know what the courses of action and their purposes have been) so much as to answer larger questions of whether postwar initiatives are related to the taproot policies described above and whether they have attained *constitutional* dimension. There is at least one undisputed fact from which all further analysis must flow: contemporary American foreign policy has been forged in response to a grave sense of danger, a threat allegedly posed by international communism and its nation-state progenitor, the Soviet Union.

Some "revisionist" historians have claimed that the United States has been seeing ghosts. Russia, they argue, was hewing to its national interest during the late 1940s just as we were hewing to ours, and it is we who made of it a stalemated confrontation because of our procapitalist preconceptions.[27] Of course, intelligent people can read a set of facts in many ways, especially in hindsight. The question we must address is this: Did the United States formulate reasonable inferences in the light of generally accepted data?

When World War II ended, Uncle Sam possessed the most fearsome conventional military force ever assembled and held sole custody of the atomic bomb. If we had translated "national interest" to mean "Pax Americana," this country could have pushed and shoved without restraint. Instead, we broke up our arsenal through massive demobilization and offered to turn the A-bomb over to the United Nations. Was all this sheer altruism? No. We were also just plain tired of war. Meanwhile, the Soviet Union retained military control over Eastern Europe and prevented free elections in Rumania, Hungary, Poland, and the others, thus violating blatantly the pact signed at Yalta. When pro-Soviet governments were established in these nations, was not the ugly hand of despotism there for all to see? Indeed, had Stalin ever been elected in a competitive contest? But perhaps Winston Churchill was merely speaking from capitalist bias when, during his famous speech at Fulton, Missouri, in 1949, he said: "From Stettin in the Baltic to Trieste in the Adriatic, an iron curtain has descended across the Continent."[28] An iron curtain could be maintained, we finally realized, because there was not one vestige of a bill of rights in these nations. How, Americans asked, could the United States have been so stupid as to give the Russians important island bases in the Pacific simply for declaring war on Japan at the tail end of hostilities? How could we have been so naive as to help carve out an American island in occupied Berlin, an island the East Germans could isolate *and did isolate* whenever they wished? In reaction to the trauma of finally confronting the real postwar international environment was born a new constitutional policy, *containment.*

The American sense of Soviet betrayal fostered an overnight upsurge in "realist" conviction. George Washington had been an old-fashioned realist, of course, and he had adopted isolationism for precisely that reason. But Americans now realized isolationism was no longer viable. For one thing, sophisticated weapons made ocean barriers hardly serviceable as buffers. Surely, the Soviet Union would harness atomic energy within a few years. Second, Western Europe was in a state of economic and political disarray following the war. Should we retreat, the door would be wide open to Soviet advances. Clearly, then, a new realist strategy had to be contrived, a strategy not only emphasizing intervention but eschewing offensive military maneuvers.

The strategy our leadership sought was soon to be penned by Sovietologist George Kennan. He described Marxist-Leninist-Stalinist doctrine as a religion seeking converts through force. Because they believed in the long-term destiny of their credo, the Russian leaders were in no particular rush to brandish their strength. As skilled jungle fighters, they would retreat when necessary and wait for other weaknesses and opportunities. Therefore, said Kennan:

> The main element of any United States policy toward the Soviet Union must be that of a long-term, patient but firm and vigilant containment of Russian expansive tendencies. . . . The Soviet pressure against the free institutions of the Western world is something that can be contained by the adroit and vigilant application of counter-force at a series of constantly shifting geographical and political points, corresponding to the shifts and maneuvers of Soviet policy.[29]

Underlying Kennan's prescription was a belief that the international arena had become bipolar. To preserve equilibrium, one party's power must be apportioned to check the power asserted by the other party. At long last, then, the United States had adopted the most fundamental constitutional policy employed by influential nation-states in their international affairs: the *balance-of-power* principle.

President Truman got the containment policy off and running with an impassioned speech to the Congress. Greece was in desperate economic straits, and insurgent Communist forces were moving into high gear. Turkey's plight, though less serious, would be compelling should Greece fall. The chief executive's response was the *Truman Doctrine:* "I believe that it must be the policy of the United States to support free peoples who are resisting attempted subjugation by armed minorities or by outside pressures."[30] Noting that both countries had asked for American financial assistance, he persuaded Congress to appropriate the necessary funds.

The Truman Doctrine heralded an end to American noninvolvement in Europe. But did the policy forge new constitutional paths? Wasn't the Truman

Doctrine really the Monroe Doctrine writ large? On the one hand, the United States, as big brother, was protecting Venezuela and Nicaragua from France and Spain; on the other hand, the United States, as big brother, was protecting Greece and Turkey from the Soviet Union. If anything, the Monroe Doctrine was more radical because it entailed unilateral intervention. To be sure, the American conception of "vital national interest" had expanded extraordinarily, but given the premises of containment, the whole planet was now our stage.

The next step was the *Marshall Plan.* We feared that Communist parties, operating on orders from the Kremlin, would take advantage of the economic upheaval in war-ravaged Western Europe. Furthermore, old-fashioned American idealism generated a deep compassion for allies sunk in privation. So the Western countries were asked to submit requests for economic assistance to Washington, and Congress, through the European Recovery Program (E.R.P.) picked up the tab. In Italy's general election of 1948, the Communist Party—then, and now, the largest in the Western world—was decisively defeated, probably as a direct result of the Marshall aid package.

The final step was easily the most far-reaching, a mutual defense treaty ratified by the Atlantic-community democracies in 1949. Signatory nations included Canada, the United States, Great Britain, France, Italy, the Netherlands, Belgium, Luxembourg, Denmark, Norway, and Iceland. Later, Greece, Turkey, and West Germany were admitted. According to Article 5 of the North Atlantic Treaty Organization (N.A.T.O.):

> The Parties agree that an armed attack against one . . . shall be considered an attack against them all and consequently they agree that . . . each of them . . . will assist the Party or Parties so attacked by taking forthwith . . . such action as it deems necessary, including the use of armed force.[31]

Some have claimed that this provision is self-executing—that is, the United States must oppose by force an aggressor nation. But the words "such action as it deems necessary" would seem to preserve both Congress's traditional power to declare war and the President's discretionary authority as commander in chief. Still, the treaty was extreme departure, for it constituted our first formal peacetime military alliance. Collective security had failed. Collective self-defense seemed the next best prospect. The "cold war" was now in full swing.

But containment could rationalize hot war as well. When North Korea invaded South Korea, the United States, with full United Nations support,[b] rushed in troops to beat back the aggressor and reunify the entire Korean peninsula. The enemy's armies soon teetered on the brink of collapse, but Mao's newly organized regime in Peking dispatched "volunteers" to repulse the American force. Here was a grave moment of decision. The Chinese Communists had driven our old ally, Chiang Kai-shek, off the mainland onto his island refuge, Formosa (Taiwan). The United States said—and says today—that it

[b] The Soviet Union, boycotting U.N. sessions at that time, thus forfeited the opportunity to exercise its veto power.

stands ready to defend the Nationalist Chinese sanctuary against any Communist attack. But would the United States agree to employ Chiang's forces in Korea? Or would we somehow utilize our superior naval power or monopoly on atomic weaponry to intimidate Mao's war machine? The answer to all these questions was negative. A long drawn-out stalemate ensued, with General Douglas MacArthur, our commanding officer in Korea, protesting vainly against that approach and claiming the conflict could go on ad infinitum at a terrible cost in lives. "There is," he said, "no substitute for victory."[32] Later, after President Truman dismissed him for insubordination, MacArthur reiterated: "There is no policy—there is nothing, I tell you, no plan, or anything."[33] He was wrong. For him, war meant winning or losing, not the maintenance of equilibrium. But a new policy—containment—had taken form, with equilibrium as its basis.

The American people seemed ready for a more aggressive stance in the 1950s. Public opinion overwhelmingly disapproved MacArthur's ouster, and when General Eisenhower claimed he would go to Korea (undoubtedly with an eye toward staring the Chinese down), he was elected President by landslide proportions. Indeed, Eisenhower's Secretary of State, John Foster Dulles, talked a very tough game. Any Communist encroachment, he announced, would be met with "massive retaliation," by which was clearly meant nuclear counterattack. Furthermore, the United States would henceforth support a policy of "liberation," wherein revolutionaries looking to throw off Communist suppression could rely on American assistance. Finally, Dulles announced his overall strategy—the "brink of war" thesis. In foreign policy, a nation-state must be prepared to risk military confrontation, else its aims and efforts would carry no punch. The United States, he intimated, could be counted upon to take the gravest of chances to secure fundamental ends. Here, seemingly, was Manifest Destiny in contemporary dress: the United States would risk all to save oppressed peoples everywhere from Communist evil.

Our N.A.T.O. allies cringed at visions of unilateral American sallies and a European defense capability anchored in the nightmare of atomic warfare. But they needn't have worried. Dulles could talk, but the maintenance of equilibrium was still the order of the day, if only because the Russians had become a nuclear power. When, in 1956, Hungarian "freedom fighters" sought to lead their country onto the path of neutrality, the Soviet Union sent in tanks and crushed the "deviationists," while the United States stood aside, tacitly admitting that the conflict lay within the Communist orbit. Meanwhile, in the Middle East, Egypt's President Nasser nationalized the Suez Canal, prompting a military attack from Great Britain, France, and Israel, acting together. For the Soviets, this intervention constituted gross capitalist imperialism, but the Kremlin seemed powerless to take retaliatory action. Had the United States really shifted its foreign policy into high dudgeon against communism, Eisenhower would have let things take their own course. Instead, he talked about maintaining international law in true-blue American idealist fashion, and wound up siding with Russia and Egypt. Our allies were forced to retreat in disgrace.

Secretary Dulles also went the "containment" route by promoting N.A.T.O.-style alliances elsewhere. In that spirit, the United States tried to blockade communism in Asia with a new defense community, S.E.A.T.O. (the Southeast Asia Treaty Organization). Eight countries—the United States, Great Britain, France, Pakistan, Thailand, the Philippines, Australia, and New Zealand—joined in this arrangement, while Laos, Cambodia, and South Vietnam were included as protocol participants.[c] Finally, the *Eisenhower Doctrine,* as formalized in congressional legislation, pledged military assistance to any Middle Eastern country that asked for help in resisting aggression by "international communism." The doctrine was implemented in 1958 when the President sent 5,000 marines to Lebanon upon request, following bellicose threats against that nation by Iraq's volatile pro-Nasser regime.

In short, the United States, in the 1950s, had opted to contain not only Russia and China but "pro-Communist neutrals" such as Egypt, India, and Indonesia, for these nations might well threaten the many countries, whether democratic like Israel or undemocratic like Pakistan, identifying with the Western defense capability. Moreover, in a broader sense, even France and Great Britain were subject to containment, should they threaten the American conception of Russian-American equilibrium. As an empirical fact, then, Dulles's Manifest Destiny amounted to this: We, the United States, are the leaders of the "free world" and will act to preserve the balance of "free world" power as we construe that balance.

With John F. Kennedy's election, the scene shifted to Latin America. In the late 1940s, the Truman Administration had successfully pushed formation of the O.A.S. (Organization of American States), a N.A.T.O.-type alliance complete with "an attack against one is an attack against all" commitment. Of special interest was the fact that a two-thirds vote among members would be decisive, with no state holding unilateral veto power. Clearly, the O.A.S. seemed a fitting capstone to Good Neighborism in the international-security area. Yet, when a pro-Communist clique took control in Guatemala, the United States, acting alone, supported a successful coup d'état by Western-oriented rebels. Here again was evidence that containment policy carried no guarantee of alliance policy.

Under Kennedy, this country reemphasized the need for economic assistance to the Latin nations, defining their major problems as poverty and illiteracy rather than the threat of international communism. In that spirit, we undertook the *Alianza para el Progreso* (Alliance for Progress), promising $10 billion to combat those ills. Today, the alliance is but a dim memory; what the world recalls vividly is the manner in which Kennedy moved against Fidel Castro's Communist experiment. It was one thing for us to institute a naval blockade of Cuban shores in 1962, after Castro allowed Soviet Premier Khrushchev to set up ground-to-ground missile bases in our back yard. Kennedy directed the Russians to remove this weaponry or face the consequences, and most Latin nations breathed a sigh of relief when Khrushchev complied. With-

[c] That is, their independence was considered within the range of S.E.A.T.O.'s vital interests.

out doubt, Castro's Communist liaison had gone too far afield even for many of those who sympathized with his anti-American diatribes. However, one year earlier, Kennedy had allowed the Central Intelligence Agency to orchestrate an invasion by Cuban exiles with a view toward finalizing Castro's demise. Years later, the news would leak out that the C.I.A. had also made arrangements to assassinate Castro. While the fiasco at the Bay of Pigs (where the United States-sponsored insurrection was throttled, in part because Kennedy declined to provide the requisite air cover) temporarily made us look like a toothless wonder, it also showed that we could be as devious as anyone else playing in the foreign relations league.

Could the C.I.A.'s derring-do be justified as some new American policy designed to overthrow pro-Soviet revolutionary dictatorships in Latin America and substitute popularly chosen democratic institutions in their stead? Hardly. When another Communist, Salvador Allende, was elected head of state by the Chileans in the early 1970s, the C.I.A. was mobilized once again, this time to undermine Allende's administration. Though Castro still rules, Allende is now a martyred hero. But of larger significance to understanding American foreign policy, the complete picture shows that the Monroe Doctrine, with its various Platt Amendments and Roosevelt Corollaries, remains a dominant vehicle in our war against European influence in Latin American politics.

Cuba's presence as a Communist eyesore in our midst obscured developments unfolding abroad. American policy exemplified by the S.E.A.T.O. arrangement had anticipated containing Communist expansion at the borders of Laos and Cambodia. President Kennedy reasoned correctly, however, that both countries were too fragile and too easily subverted by Communist insurgents to be brought within the Western orbit. If these nations could be kept in the neutralist column, though, they would be a viable buffer between the Sino-Soviet sphere and South Vietnam, which Kennedy did think was defensible. To that end, American troops ("advisors," they were labeled euphemistically) trickled into Saigon for the purpose of propping up the dictatorial Diem regime in the face of Viet Cong guerrilla attack. By 1962, 8,000 servicemen were performing various support tasks throughout the country, and the figure had reached 16,000 when an assassin's bullet took J.F.K.'s life.

Lyndon Johnson was determined to make South Vietnam safe from communism. Yet the National Liberation Front—with assistance from the Soviet Union, China, and North Vietnam—refused to crumble. Indeed, there was hard evidence that some North Vietnamese forces had crossed the border to join in the fray. Slowly the civil war began to resemble an interstate conflict, so Johnson ordered bombings of military targets in North Vietnam and a wholesale increase of American ground forces in South Vietnam. Still, the enemy refused to fight a conventional war. American troops were ill-trained to counter terrorism and guerrilla hit-and-run tactics over a short haul, and American public opinion was ill-prepared to accept significant casualty rates for such purposes over a long haul. A stalemate reminiscent of Korea seemed inevitable, unless we elected to put our tail between our legs and retreat. In the end, 46,000

American soldiers would die in combat, and 150,000 more would suffer battlefield injuries requiring hospital care. There are many ways to assess such staggering costs, but criteria drawn from balance-of-power international politics will suffice here: not one soldier representing the legions of our "mortal enemies"—the Soviet Union and China—was killed or wounded during the fray.

The final act is a matter of common knowledge. Nixon, like Eisenhower before him, laid the political groundwork for meaningful negotiations. With much energy and almost as much publicity, Henry Kissinger and Le Duc Tho worked out the final peace arrangements. North Vietnam dropped its long-standing demand for a coalition government in Saigon, while the United States promised to remove its fighting force. However, this agreement attested to the failure of our policy by making no mention of Hanoi's 145,000 soldiers in South Vietnam, a permanent detriment to Saigon's pro-American status. Both sides committed numerous violations of the cease-fire pact in the next year or so, but General Thieu's regime continued to survive. Then, about eighteen months later, the North Vietnamese launched an all-out invasion. President Ford asked Congress for emergency aid, but none was forthcoming. The South Vietnamese government collapsed in a matter of days. The attempt to contain the uncontainable had failed.

Much has been written about *why* the United States fought in South Vietnam. Two policy themes recur again and again. The first is Woodrow Wilson's old shibboleth, *self-determination.* The South Vietnamese should be free to choose their own political leadership, Lyndon Johnson often remarked. The second is called the *domino theory.* If Saigon fell, it was said, then Laos would fall, Cambodia would fall, Thailand would fall, and so on and on. The domino analogy was hardly new; in 1947, the refrain ran, "If Greece falls, Italy will fall, France will fall . . ." But in the Asian context, both policies have a hollow ring. Thus, the 1954 Geneva accords, which guaranteed Vietnam reunification following France's exodus, had included the promise of a general election in 1956. That vote never came off, mostly because the United States thought the Communists might win. And, of course, the Thieu regime in Saigon was no more a democracy than the Diem regime that had preceded it. With respect to dominoism, the notion that South Vietnam's demise might commence an irreversible trend engulfing the Philippines, Burma, and India looks to be a non sequitur. As a matter of fact, when Sukarno, a "pro-Communist neutral," ruled Indonesia, during the 1950s, many believed that Chinese influence would take root there permanently. But Sukarno's death has brought about a clear shift to the political right in that country. Of course, dominoism could apply to a flimsy Laos and a flimsy Cambodia, which, indeed, have since been overrun by Communists, but why would these nations ever be included within America's defense perimeter? Self-determination and the domino theory clearly were superficial policy explanations for what we did in Southeast Asia. Our business there, as we saw it, was to contain the enemy—imperialist Communist statism. But only the most devout cold warrior could conclude in 1970 that containment did not require revision and refinement.

The first attempt at such reformulation was the *Nixon Doctrine.* Our foreign policy, the President announced, must henceforward be geared to avoid the sin of overinvolvement. Specifically, Nixon said that the United States would honor its treaty commitments and also provide a shield against aggression by a nuclear power where our vital interests were involved. But hostile acts of lesser scope must not prompt us to provide manpower in the field; American economic and military assistance would have to suffice. The Nixon Doctrine obviously raised as many questions as it answered, but this much seemed evident: containment would no longer be a reflex response, and most assuredly there would be no more Vietnams.

The most significant feature of the Nixon Doctrine was the new assumptions it made manifest. Containment had been predicated on the existence of a bipolar political and military universe. That universe, we now realized, had long since faded away. Our allies had evolved new and more independent policy postures as evidenced, say, by General de Gaulle's withdrawal of French troops from N.A.T.O. Meanwhile, Russia and China were berating each other at every turn, while their border resembled an eyeball-to-eyeball staredown between two poised pugilists. Even though the Soviets and the Americans possessed enough military clout to dismember everyone else, a *multipolar* political balance had emerged requiring a more flexible, less dogmatic, approach. While some American polemicists continue to discuss international politics as a struggle between the "free world" and the "Communist world," that dichotomy is hardly useful for operationalizing strategically viable plans and programs.

The Nixon Doctrine would seem also to signal a shift away from Manifest Destiny, for the United States now eschews the role of world police officer. Actually, though, what Nixon and Ford tried to do through their common foreign policy denominator, Secretary of State Kissinger, was to shift Manifest Destiny from a "cop on the beat" orientation to a "labor mediator" orientation. That is, the United States now employs its good offices to bring all manner of grievances to the bargaining table. Whether the rivals be Greece and Turkey feuding over Cyprus, or Israel and Egypt fighting in the Sinai, Kissinger was always there to help soothe the savage instinct on behalf of the larger equilibrium. This new Manifest Destiny, of course, travels the well-trodden American path of promoting the peaceful settlement of disputes. Moreover, it seems entirely consistent with the root assumptions governing containment, which, after all, has only been Manifest Destiny in modern role. But in the context of our relations with Russia and China, this shift away from confrontation toward accommodation creates a new and somewhat different focus for achieving an acceptable balance of power. That new focus is called *détente.*

Détente per se is hardly novel, but it does constitute America's leading foreign policy at this time. President Ford's definition stripped the concept of any magical allure:

> Détente means to me that two superpowers, who are strong militarily and economically, who represent differing political and governmental views, in-

stead of confronting one another, can consult with one another on a wide variety of areas of potential dispute, whether it's trade, whether it's military potential conflict (or whatever).[34]

Détente, then, is in the nature of traditional foreign policy; rival superpowers have for centuries been soft-pedaling their differences and accentuating their common interests when necessary. What is new about *this* détente are the factors that have brought it to the fore. The first is that, given the awesome nuclear arsenals assembled by the leading nations, conflict among the superpowers is a one-way ticket to oblivion. Sanity thus mandates discussion and compromise. The second factor is America's now acknowledged inability to reverse the course of history and make either Russia or China a Western democracy. Like it or not, this country must accept as valid Nikita Khrushchev's dictum that "peaceful coexistence" is inevitable.

Of course, a little friendly competition is compatible with the new posture. Thus, the United States and the Soviet Union bend every energy to see who can get to Mars first; who can demonstrate the greater support for black African nationalism; who can mobilize the more effective cadres in "swing" nations, as the "war" between their respective intelligence communities in Portugal during the mid-1970s shows; and even who can win the most gold medals at the Olympic Games. Perhaps deep down, each country dreams of the day when the other will collapse from its alleged internal contradictions. Meanwhile, it is hoped, détente will keep the two rivals from overreacting and causing trouble for themselves and everyone else. And neither is blind to the slowly unwinding Chinese "manifest destiny," which bids fair to make Peking eventually part of a three-cornered exercise in diplomatic pledge and counterpledge.

Just what has détente accomplished so far? I should begin by listing the essential agreements concurred in even before anyone was invoking the talisman "détente":

1. In 1963, a "hot line" was established between Moscow and Washington to avoid precipitous action caused by misunderstanding or error.

2. In 1963, the Soviet Union and the United States signed a treaty banning nuclear testing in outer space, in the atmosphere, and in the ocean. Underground experiments were still permitted, because the participants could not agree on a foolproof inspection system to monitor cheating.

3. In 1967, the two countries made a pledge not to use earthbound satellites as carriers for nuclear weapons.

4. In 1968, they initialed a nonproliferation treaty, thus promising not to transfer nuclear devices to nations who were lacking nuclear capability.

During the Kissinger era, détente included the following tangibles and intangibles, among others:

1. In 1971, the four countries administering Berlin—Russia, France, Great Britain, and the United States—agreed to honor unlimited access rights among themselves. In effect, East Germany and Russia were promising they would never again cut off land entry privileges to West Berlin, as they had done in the late 1940s, a blockade that had prompted the famous "Berlin Airlift." However, the infamous "Berlin Wall" still stands.
2. In 1972, the United States and China began to normalize relations. Mao's government was admitted to the United Nations shortly thereafter, and Americans were allowed to visit the mainland for the first time since World War II. Once again we commenced the long process of achieving an open door in China.
3. In 1972, the United States and Russia signed the SALT (Strategic Arms Limitation Treaties) agreements. The major breakthrough concerned antiballistic missiles (ABMs), a primary defense deterrent. Each nation could have only two such ABM complexes, one protecting their national capital and another protecting their prime field of *offensive* intercontinental weaponry.
4. In 1972, the United States and Russia pledged to pool resources in cancer research, environmental regulation, and outer space exploration.
5. In 1974, the two nuclear superpowers agreed to limit the total number of offensive strategic and delivery vehicles through 1985. Each country may now have no more than 2,400 ICBMs, submarine-launched missiles, and bombers. Moreover, only 1,320 of these can be armed with the dreaded MIRV (multiple independently targetable reentry vehicle), missiles capable of carrying many warheads programmed to hit different targets. On-site inspections are still taboo; however, reconnaisance satellites can detect at least some violations.
6. In 1974 and 1975, the United States sold millions of tons of wheat to the Soviets when their crops failed. We received no discernible quid pro quo, and the shipments, while good for American farmers, undoubtedly contributed to rampant inflation in this country.

Even with these several developments, it would be premature to label détente an American *constitutional* policy. After so many years of containment and cold war, many people, either inured to a posture of international confrontation or turned off by it, viewed Kissinger's efforts with suspicion if not distaste. The principal objection has been that détente is value-free, and this charge comes from both the political left and the political right. By "value-free" is meant ideologically neutral, ultrarealistic, lacking in humanistic appeal. The United States, critics argue, is concerned only with accommodation for the purpose of maintaining peace, tranquillity, and equilibrium. Why, political liberals ask, do we take a "business as usual" stance toward corporate investment in racist South Africa, and why did we fail to support vigorously Bangladesh's insurrection against despotic Pakistan? Why, political conservatives ask with equal vigor, do we now seem prepared to sacrifice hegemony over the Canal Zone simply because the Panamanians are making noises, and why did the SALT proviso allow the Soviets to retain a numerical advantage in ABMs? Skepticism prompted even the usually benign Congress to bestir itself. The legislature suspended military aid to Turkey after that nation invaded Cyprus and refused to grant the Soviet Union trade concessions until the Soviets liberalized their emigration rules for Jews. The Nixon-Ford (Kissinger) Administrations fought both moves. As I remarked several chapters ago, Congress has never bargained away its moralistic fervor, so these responses show the chink in détente's armor.

What, then, is the current state of American constitutional foreign policy? If containment is dead, what has replaced it? The answer seems to be that containment is *not* deceased, that détente really embodies attempts to bridge gaps where containment has been achieved or where containment is irrelevant. Hence, the United States would never allow China to invade India, or Russia (or the Arab nations) to overrun Israel. However, détente has meant a change in the logistics of containment as well. Détente means giving up cardboard alliances, as Kissinger demonstrated when he announced that S.E.A.T.O. was going out of business. Détente also means that the "military-industrial complex," which Eisenhower thought had become entirely too powerful, will no longer be an unchecked force, propelling us toward a greater and greater emphasis on national defense and international confrontation. The big corporations and the Pentagon have been unjustly accused of running the country; nonetheless, the President and Congress tended during the 1960s to think "big spend"-"big weapon"-"big intervention," so they allowed corporate heads, like Robert McNamara, and generals, like Maxwell Taylor, to provide the tactical approaches. But former Harvard professor Kissinger appears to have had enough ego to stare them all down![35] On the other hand, if the United States is going unilaterally to settle disputes between Israel and Egypt (as Kissinger took pride in doing), it cannot expect our N.A.T.O. allies to honor whatever bargains are struck when tensions heighten. That is one important reason why only two Western European countries allowed us to use their territory as a conduit for resupplying Israel during its 1973 struggle with the Arab states. Clearly, this new "labor mediator" orientation has a "we're number 1 in peace as well as strength" premise, which can undermine our relations with friends and even with enemies who feel left out.[36]

As one thinks through present-day foreign policies in the context of American constitutional policy, it is obvious that Professor Lowi's terms "distributive," "redistributive," and "regulatory," as I earlier described them, do not fit, by definition. These conceptual policy notions are inapplicable to an arena where unilateral sovereign power lacks the force and the legitimacy to work its will. But other sets of theoretical alternatives may be applied fruitfully to that arena. American foreign policy can be realistic or idealistic; it can be interventionist or isolationist; it can be collective or unilateral; finally, American foreign policy can strive for supremacy, concede supremacy to others, or seek equilibrium. The question is: How *does* one apply these models to the international role of the United States today and yesterday?

America's constitutional foreign policy has generally combined idealist rhetoric with realist action. In those moments when idealism predominated, the results have been mixed. For example, we have given billions in foreign aid since the Second World War to the so-called underdeveloped countries, in large measure because we thought economic stability and technical know-how bred democracy and a commitment to personal liberty. Such idealism has been misplaced, for not only do these nations fail to provide themselves the basics of a "free society," but they have made diplomatic war against individual freedom—for example, in branding Zionism a form of racism with their votes in the United Nations. The prime example, India, is a nation that for years preached the doctrine of third-world neutrality as the best defense against East-West power politics, a nation that idealists earnestly believed was a bastion of constitutional values, and a nation that, under the vise-like rule of Indira Gandhi, for a time turned both constitutionalism and political morality on their heads. Put simply, our purpose and our plan have overemphasized materialism and what it could accomplish. On the other side, the United States fought a war against the Axis powers based, in considerable degree, on moral revulsion against Nazi ideology. Would our statecraft possess *any* moral fiber at all—or, indeed, would our democratic society as an ethical alternative to totalitarianism even have survived—had we made a peace treaty with Hitler to "stop communism"? Yet realism has also spawned uneven results in the modern era, as the pluses of N.A.T.O. and the minuses of Vietnam clearly show. But over the past thirty years, our international posture has probably been even more pragmatic than usual, if only because the stakes have been higher.

America's constitutional foreign policy has tended to be isolationist rather than interventionist; however, *contemporary* American constitutional foreign policy has tended in the opposite direction. Still, isolationism is not moribund. There are data showing that most Americans today—especially younger people—want to back away from overseas commitments and concentrate on domestic problems.[37] And a few scholars are advocating an "informed isolationism," based not on idealistic miscalculation but on self-sufficiency and a need to protect the integrity of our domestic institutions, surely realistic criteria.[38] But containment with détente appended is as internationalist as containment unvarnished and unmodified. What the Nixon Doctrine has done is to cut out such overextensions as Vietnam without sacrificing international initiatives for global security.

America's constitutional foreign policy has been largely a study in the unilateral rather than the collective. Only during containment's heyday (1947–52) were Americans good team players in peacetime. Whether we be crusaders or hard-headed pragmatists, whether we be isolationists or meddlers, our spirit of individualism reflects itself at every turn. And when commentators say we should stop supporting dictators no matter who they are (Bloomfield), or treat United Nations decision-making as some noble alternative to our own selfish designs (Fulbright), they are also playing the great game of American individualism, because few others believe such things. Moreover, Kissinger's "labor mediation" is also part of this tradition.

"Go-it-aloneism" may constitute the most fundamental American constitutional policy in foreign affairs. We have invoked our independence sometimes to assert superiority and sometimes to pull in our horns. But as Walter Lippmann intimated years ago, we have traditionally ignored balance of power considerations, for such factors emphasize a rational adjustment of ends and means, of morality and power, in consultation with others.[39]

Recently, we have learned the value of international equilibrium without ever mastering the self-restraint of alliance policy. Containment at its best (N.A.T.O.) maximized balance of power interplay within a context of mutual understandings. Containment at its worst (Vietnam) maximized balance of power *alone*. Contemporary containment—guns plus mediation plus détente—assumes a military balance and tries to make that balance more civilized; but because the balance is bipolar, our allies wind up being read out of the decision-making process. As for political and economic power, contemporary policy assumes nation-state multipolarity, where the United States maintains an interest in preserving stability by playing ombudsman among competing factions. Our challenge at that level is "to evoke the creativity of a pluralistic world" by stimulating "an agreed concept of order."[40] I repeat: This is another way of rationalizing our role as "number 1" and converting Manifest Destiny into Pax Americana.

Americans have often dreamed of exporting their ideas and living standards. Today's aspirations would seem to settle for less. But there is enough in our current policy of "containment plus" to satisfy what is perhaps *the* taproot American constitutional foreign policy, the notion that this country has unique responsibilities and unique prerogatives among nation-states. The largest question, then, is whether that policy commitment preserves balance or forever dooms us to cause imbalance in the world.

Economic policy: betwixt individualism and collectivism

In the arena of domestic affairs, Americans worry more about pocketbook issues than about any others. Perhaps they cannot relate to environmental questions or free speech questions; but they certainly can relate to whether their paychecks are larger, whether unemployment poses a grave personal threat, whether they satisfy the eligibility standards for welfare, whether their businesses can meet payroll needs, and whether they should work for somebody else or strike out on their own. Purposive governmental action with respect to all these "making a living" problems is what I mean by economic policy.

The capitalist consensus[41]

If foreign policy, by constitutional definition, is a matter of vital *state* concern, economic matters are basically the concern of the *private* sector—producers and consumers, buyers and sellers, people generally. The federal government may be very active in regulating the marketplace, but because Washington possesses no *official constitutional duty*—that is, an obligation flowing from the document itself—to intervene, the level of responsibility is entirely different. Articulating economic policies requires a great measure of inference and insight, and systematizing them so that they form a constitutional-policy mosaic poses the greatest challenge of all.

The United States Constitution may be neutral with respect to foreign policies, but it is surely biased with respect to economic policies. Mr. Justice Holmes challenged that assertion when he wrote: "The Fourteenth Amendment does not enact Mr. Herbert Spencer's Social Statics. . . . A constitution is not intended to embody a particular economic theory, whether of paternalism . . . or of *laissez faire*."[42] Holmes's rebuff to capitalist interests invoking substantive due process as a shield against state regulation has now become established judicial doctrine, but it cannot be used to make the Framers economic neuters. Nor need one advocate Charles Beard's (or Karl Marx's) economic determinism to point out what good empirical research cannot ignore: the Founding Fathers were men of means who advocated what even today must be considered this nation's fundamental economic policy—*the ownership as private property of America's productive capacity,* goods and services alike. That doctrine is based on the notion of property as an integral *personal* attribute, wherein ownership becomes a source of liberty, dignity, and power essential to survival and happiness.

The Framers' debt to John Locke's individualism is exemplified by several constitutional freedoms they endorsed. Remember that life, liberty, and *property* cannot be taken without due process of law. This procedural guarantee shows that the Founding Fathers endorsed two significant assumptions: (1) people would hold property of value, property the state might attempt to confiscate by way of punishment; (2) property rights stood on a par with life and liberty in the sense that government could take none of them unless it satisfied the same minimal standards.

But the Constitution catalogues substantive property rights as well. The Fifth Amendment says the power of *eminent domain* can be asserted only where just compensation is provided.[d] Furthermore, the document restrains states

[d] By *eminent domain* is meant the sovereign's authority, recognized under common law, to seize private property for a public purpose such as, in our time, an interstate highway. The "just compensation" rule prohibits government from stripping people of their real estate, no matter how lofty the purpose, unless appropriate restitution is made.

from impairing the obligation of contracts. Contractual duties are the lifeblood of commerce, and to protect contracts is to protect property. The Framers did not want the states to meddle with these agreements and substitute their wisdom for the free play of private economic needs and interests. Nor did they dream that Congress had authority to enact sweeping laws impinging upon contracts; otherwise they might well have made the provision applicable to national action. These "rules of the game" express a clear policy preference for private-sector primacy in the world of economics, a preference still predominating today.

The "Living Constitution," moreover, has never assumed a neat line between the public (political) sector and the private (economic) sector. The constitutional policy prevailing in Hamilton's day and in our own is that the *federal government should foster American industry and trade.*

Prior to the Civil War, this policy was implemented by both legislative and judicial action, each branch using its unique set of tools. Congress's primary objective was to ensure American business vitality in the face of European competition, so it threw up high protective tariff barriers—a program well suited, incidentally, to our isolationist mood. The Supreme Court's primary objective was to keep the states from stifling interstate commerce by regulating national traffic on behalf of their own citizens or their own treasuries. One of the Justices' weapons was the "original package" doctrine. The Constitution forbids states to tax imports, but what are imports? Are they only commodities entering the United States and becoming taxable as soon as they reach an intended destination? The Court, per John Marshall, took a broader, nationalistic view. Imports retained their essential character until they became mixed up in the commerce of a particular state, usually only after they were sold or their form (original package) was altered drastically. State regulatory policy, including taxation, must await such transformation.[43] A more practical difficulty stemmed from state sponsorship of economic activity. Especially provocative were the monopolistic franchises given to in-state businesses, which prompted aggrieved states to sponsor their own monopolies in reprisal. So the Justices devised the "selective exclusiveness" principle. Pennsylvania, they said, could pass rules governing the use of Philadelphia Harbor, even though the requirements impinged upon commercial activity outside the state. However, if the subject matter of a regulation was "in [its] nature national, or admit[ted] only of one uniform system," then the Court said it would oust the states from the field, for interstate commerce was Congress's domain.[44] Today, the Justices give the states greater leeway, paying special attention to whether their rules *discriminate* against either interstate or foreign commerce. Where the regulation is even-handed, the state policy stands an excellent chance of surviving.[45] Yet neither the "original package" test nor "selective exclusiveness" is a dead letter. Both can be useful aids in gauging the consequences of state restrictions.[46] But from historical perspective, Congress's distributive policies (subsidy) and the Supreme Court's regulatory policies (coercion) created a "domestic common market," a free-trade haven, for American economic activity.

Until the Industrial Revolution, private property consisted largely of real estate, personal tangibles, and currency. Property "clothed with a public interest" (that is, business capital) was usually an extension of the individual entrepreneur. Merchants and artisans bought and sold for their own accounts; profits accrued only to them, and losses were mostly a personal disaster. Competition may have been encouraged and even underwritten by government policy, but competition seemed an eternal verity, incapable of suffocation.

If anything, the Industrial Revolution *increased* competition, at least initially, as the "robber barons" jousted for position and power. Innovative production and transportation facilities, derived from scientific discovery and technological refinement, meant new products inexpensively manufactured and sold, new services inexpensively distributed, and new markets inexpensively tapped. Profit-making possibilities became so fertile that they spawned revolutionary modes of economic organization and management. The result was proliferation of a unique arrangement that redefined marketplace conditions, the corporation.

The purpose of a corporation is to attract *capital*—that is, "the money devoted to more or less permanent investment in productive enterprise."[47] The company accomplishes this by selling stock—shares of ownership in the firm. Theoretically at least, those who own can oust those who govern; in other words, the board of directors, the corporation's policy-makers, sit at the tolerance of the stockholders. In small firms, theory and practice probably coincide. But in today's Wall Street environment, the widely scattered and uninformed "owners" are highly unlikely to vote out those who control General Motors, General Electric, or Xerox. A recurring question for students of the "Living Constitution" is: If corporate power cannot be checked by legally constituted property owners,[48] then who should check that power and under what conditions?

The inquiry does not simply resolve itself into a debate between those who favor political interests (public authority) and those who favor economic interests (private authority), because corporations possess quasi-political attributes. To begin with, every corporate charter must be approved by a state; therefore, public officials have the power to reject applications for licenses as inconsistent with community welfare. Moreover, the Supreme Court in its zeal to foster capital formation and expansion has thrown such a panoply of rights around the corporation that it even possesses *constitutional* status. Speaking in the *Dartmouth College* case,[49] John Marshall defined duly licensed corporate charters as binding contracts; thus, he said, the Constitution bars states from rewriting the terms of these agreements. Today the Court would not go so far; corporate licenses are still considered contracts, but the state cannot bargain away its police power responsibilities by making agreements with private parties. A state may even prescribe a moratorium on mortgage payments, where economic catastrophe has prevented debtors from satisfying their obligations.[50] But Marshall's ruling paved the way for widespread corporate expansion, and the late-nineteenth-century Court carried the capitalist ethic to the limits of logic by finding that if a corporation could make a contract, then it must be considered a *person* as that term is used in the Fourteenth Amendment, sheltered, like a flesh and blood person, from the winds of legislative caprice.[51]

This decision ushered in a new instrument of distributive constitutional policy—*substantive due process of law*—based on a new public philosophy—*laissez faire capitalism.* That gospel preached the separation of politics and economics as an inevitable attribute of constitutional liberty, and it was a natural outgrowth of business ascendency linked with national prosperity. There is considerable irony in the fact that this separatism should be extolled precisely when the state had taken capitalism's prime instrument, the corporation, to its bosom and blessed it with *constitutional* legitimacy. By contrast, church-state separation may be an implicit constitutional norm, but the state did not create the church!

The philosophic mainsprings of the capitalist credo were two-dimensional. Laissez faire was supposed to be economically feasible, because the law of supply and demand brought together low prices and high productive capacity, on the one hand, and substantial profits on the other. Furthermore, laissez faire was supposed to be spiritually rewarding, because, under the prevailing Protestant ethic, hard work and prudent financial management would lead to survival only of the fittest, a sure sign of ultimate salvation. But substantive due process *alone* shortly proved an inadequate policy instrument for fostering these values, for if government could not influence the marketplace, then the marketplace would tend toward monopoly.

Much has been written about what causes monopolies. Some say it is cutthroat competition: capitalists devour one another until only "King Beast" remains. Others say it is the trust arrangement: capitalists conspire with one another to reduce trade, thus creating a gigantic "fix," which eliminates competitors. Still others say the roots are simply flaws inherent in the capitalist system: monopolies stem from inevitable scientific and technical innovation, which allow a few entrepreneurs to corner the market; monopolies also stem from commercial activity that *cannot* be competitive due to unmanageable cost and efficiency factors (the so-called natural monopolies—gas and electric utilities, bus transportation, and telephone service). The clear purpose of the Sherman Antitrust Act (1890) and the Clayton Antitrust Act (1914) was to strike at what the legislature considered the chief source of monopoly—collusion. The former suppresses every "combination and conspiracy in restraint of trade"; the latter bars price discrimination among purchasers, price concessions, and intercorporate stock acquisitions where the effect "may be to substantially lessen competition or tend to create a monopoly." These statutes exemplified a new policy that has certainly acquired constitutional status: *government should break up "unnatural" monopolies and reinstitute competition.*

However, other anticapitalist features of capitalism also cried out for policy refinement, and Congress proved equal to the task. The Interstate Commerce Commission was created in 1887 to exercise supervisory power over the railroads. Since then, the airlines, the trucking industry, and the various utilities, among other businesses, have also been brought under the purview of governance by independent regulatory commission. With the exception of stock brokerage houses, these enterprises have a single feature in common: they are considered either "natural monopolies" or "natural oligopolies" (a term economists use to define enterprises in which only a few firms can subsist). Hence, a second constitutional policy emerges: *some measure of price control should obtain where monopolistic features are unavoidable.* At the same time, Congress passed various enactments outlawing unfair competition. The Federal Trade Commission Act (1914) regulated fraudulent and deceptive advertising, while the Robinson-Patman Act (1936) banned geographic discrimination in marketing. Such legislation has been called the Magna Carta of small businesses and represents a third constitutional policy: *competition must be ethical, and the law should punish excesses.* Many observers realize, however, that strict enforcement of the "ethical competition" norm may conflict with good-faith implementation of the antitrust laws, which, after all, treat competition as an end in itself.[52] The best way to conceive of these three policy norms, then, is as a set of mutually supportive regulatory aids aimed at inducing *capitalist equilibrium,* the slowly germinating constitutional policy that today underlies our political-economic system.

To what extent has equilibrium been attained by meaningful interpretation and implementation of the above programs? The record is, at best, spotty. Take the Sherman Act. In 1911 the Supreme Court drastically reduced that statute's scope by finding it forbade only *unreasonable* combinations in restraint of trade.[53] Naturally, only the Justices could construe definitively this new "rule of reason," and, given their 1920s flirtation with substantive due process (which continued to hang on as constitutional policy in spite of Congress's efforts at balancing capitalism's excesses), the law received little attention. To show what the Sherman Act can accomplish, however, one need only look at the Court's ruling that forced the big filmmakers (M.G.M., Warner Brothers, and others) to give up their ownership of movie houses.[54] This decision, handed down in 1948, has provided access to highly advantageous markets for a whole slew of independent producers, who have given the consumer such diverse fare as Ingmar Bergman's masterpieces and Russ Meyer's nonsense. But the "reasonableness" standard still lacks meaningful across-the-board definition, and corporations, both large and small, are far more pervasive today than they were in the 1890s.

The other regulatory schemes noted above have also had an equivocal impact on the "Living Constitution." Every corporation regulated by the Interstate Commerce Commission and the Civil Aeronautics Board, for example, is exempt from prosecution under the Sherman Act, as are labor unions, whose practices fall under National Labor Relations Board purview. But this seems to be *over*protection. Can't railroads compete? Can't labor unions compete? Can't a railroad compete with a truck line? Of course; but where they can compete, they can also *fail to compete,* thus coagulating their markets. At the least, many of these oligopolies have set substantially higher prices than would otherwise be permissible.[55] With regard to the Federal Trade Commission Act ban against unfair competition, this law possesses considerable potential, as has been shown recently when the Coors beer company was forced to distribute its beverage nationwide, thus terminating illegal marketing arrangements whereby Coors could be sold only in the Rocky Mountains area.[56] However, this and similar statutes are very hard to implement with consistency; the Robinson-Patman Act, for instance, has been called "replete with ambiguities and confusions."[57] Generally speaking, attempts to keep the free enterprise system on an even keel by "purifying" and revitalizing competition have failed to provide sustenance for the capitalist consensus.

The "Positive State"

As I have said before, the Great Depression worked extraordinary changes in American constitutional policy. An overwhelming majority now understood that the separation of politics and economics was absolutely impossible. The Depression killed laissez faire capitalism as conventional wisdom, and it killed due process in the marketplace as fundamental policy. However, it did not slay the private-property system, favored by the Constitution; or the corporate system, fostered for so many decades by national distributive policy; or the "negative watchman" regulatory policies dating from the Sherman Act, substantive rules through which government attempted to make the best of competition, and even the best of monopoly, functional.

The big shift in constitutional policy found the national "political branches" attempting to sustain capitalist equilibrium by formulating a wide variety of essentially *redistributive* instruments—the "Positive State." For example, elected officials funneled through the commerce power, the taxing power, and the spending power voluminous social service programs advertised as advancing the greater good—minimum wages, old age benefits, unemployment compensation. (There was also new regulatory policy supervising Wall Street, and new distributive policy ensuring subsidies to farmers.) Of even greater interest here, however, are the monetary and fiscal policies that took root.[e] Their purposes included overseeing the relationship between wages and prices, curtailing rampant inflationary and deflationary trends, expanding the gross national product, and combating unemployment. These various aims embody a new constitutional policy which may be stated as follows: *the government has an affirmative duty to manipulate the economy, thus promoting capitalist equilibrium by controlling the business cycle and providing for incremental egalitarianism.*

This policy reads like some bizarre amalgam of regulatory, distributive, and redistributive elements. True to the pragmatic New Deal temperament, that is surely the case. But what has been the *prime* purpose and effect? It seems

[e] A note on economic jargon: By "monetary policy" I mean the substantive norms which determine the value and amount of the nation's money supply; by "fiscal policy" I mean the substantive norms which define the nation's budgetary profile.

clear that the fundamental consideration underlying this innovative course of action is to give the average person a break by *humanizing* the private-property system and providing minimum living standards for all. And the Supreme Court has acceded to this policy without protest; indeed, the Justices will now accept any manner of economic legislation unless the statute is irrational.[58]

What governmental powers and programs sustain the new approach to economic balance through fiscal and monetary restraints? First, the "political branches" must be able to control what our currency is worth by authorizing a flexible medium of exchange. From 1900 until the Depression, the government was prepared to swap money for gold upon demand. Hence, private citizens could—and sometimes did—exchange a dollar's worth of currency for a dollar's worth of gold. The "gold standard" guaranteed great demand for American money throughout the world's capitals and markets, because the dollar bill could always be redeemed for its value in this precious metal. But the "Golden Dollar" rate of exchange obviously precluded floating more currency than the worth of bullion stored in Fort Knox, and "Positive State" philosophy argued that when the economy sputtered government should have the option of putting as much money on the market as was necessary to jack up buying and selling. In 1934 the United States went off the gold standard, and, to this day, the dollar cannot be "traded in" for any officially recognized commodity of exchange. The worth of our currency has ever since been determined by government fiat rather than the price of gold in the open market; F.D.R., with congressional approval, set its value at $35 per ounce of gold, and that standard abided for thirty-five years.

Second, the "political branches" must create devices for expanding and contracting the amount of money in circulation. The obvious way this can be accomplished is by spending or not spending. When Congress sees recession coming, it merely "primes the pump"—that is, juices up employment and purchasing power by deciding to build highways, airplanes, and the like. But passing laws is sometimes not fast enough, so a second tool has been relied upon, the Federal Reserve System. Established in 1913, this mechanism is composed of twelve banks located around the country. On orders from their board of governors, they can insert money into or withdraw money from the market, as economic conditions warrant. The Federal Reserve Board also decides what rates of interest their banks will charge other banks, and upon these policy judgments are predicated interest rates everywhere. Naturally, the higher the rate, the tougher it is to borrow money, and the tougher it is for businesses to expand operations or for a couple to buy a new home.

These substantive norms and institutional arrangements received formal acknowledgment when the President signed the Employment Act of 1946. This statute's stated purpose reads like a provision in Article I, Section 8, wherein are found Congress's delegated powers: "It is the continuing *policy* and *responsibility* of the *federal government* . . . to promote maximum employment, production and purchasing power" (italics mine).[59] The "political branches" were stating they had a "Living Constitutional" duty to make the capitalist system run in a manner consonant with the general welfare. The law created both a Council of Economic Advisers, to help the chief executive map economic strategies, and a Joint Congressional Committee on the Economic Report, to receive presidential recommendations and evaluate them with respect to necessary statutory action. But I must emphasize a redistributive bias, for the statute talks of guaranteeing "maximum employment," never "maximum profits." Furthermore, I must emphasize what may be a regulatory loophole, for the statute leaves with private, corporate enterprise virtually unfettered discretion over economic priorities in the marketplace. Nonetheless, the law certainly gave Franklin Roosevelt's "Positive State" official sanction.

Clearly, the Employment Act is predicated on a balance of power between government and business, an equilibrium rooted in pragmatic political considerations. But liberal Democrats also believed the "Positive State" was economically viable—that is, they believed the mesh between private power and public supervision could produce employment without significant inflation. This article of faith was based on a new economic philosophy, advanced initially by John Maynard Keynes.[60]

"Keynesian economics" teaches that unemployment (and depression) is caused by drops in *spending*. The cure for these afflictions lies in expanded *government* spending through *deficit financing*. In other words, Washington should deliberately unbalance its budget, because to spend only what is taken in through taxes does *not* increase total expenditures in the market. Thus, higher incomes and more jobs should result. However, cheaper money (inflation) should also result. Keynes understood this; therefore, he endorsed balanced budgets and a treasury surplus, absent "full employment."[61] When massive deficit financing for World War II ended the Great Depression, the Keynesian formula seemed indisputable.

Experience has shown, however, that these theories do not function smoothly within the context of "Positive State" constitutional policies. For one thing, "full employment" has proved elusive, except when the nation was fighting in Korea and Vietnam. For another thing, prosperity seems achievable only when Washington risks modest to high budget deficits. Since 1946 the national debt has risen from $269 billion to almost $500 billion. For a third thing, wages and prices chase one another to ever dizzier heights. In the 1950s, a 6 percent rise in the rate of inflation would have been considered volatile; in 1976, an 8 percent rise was considered encouraging. Economists used to posit a correlation between unemployment and deflation; but the United States today flirts with a full circle of horrors, excessive unemployment and excessive inflation. For yet a fourth thing, the United States spends considerably more money abroad than foreigners spend here, in large measure because of our far-flung military obligations and brisk tourist trade. This phenomenon has contributed significantly to economic stagnation at home and has twice inspired the "political branches" to *devalue the dollar* in the last decade, meaning our currency is now officially worth less in gold. Devaluation will, it is hoped, make our goods more competitive at the international level, but, of course, this strategy adds to domestic inflationary pressures, for it raises the price of everything we import. To make matters worse, imports have exceeded exports over the past five years, undoubtedly because of our great dependence on foreign oil. The situation is roughly this: let General Motors raise prices markedly, let the steel workers have a big boost in pay, let the Arab nations impose a boycott on petroleum sales, let the Federal Reserve Board make a mistake in interest rate policy, and the whole economy quivers and quakes.

Naturally, political liberals and conservatives disagree on how to attack these problems. Contemporary conservatives generally favor less government spending, lower taxes, greater incentives for business—in short, more reliance on the free market and less reliance on Keynesian preachments. Contemporary liberals generally favor steep and progressive taxation, federal work programs where necessary to reach "full employment," higher wage rates to encourage purchasing power—in short, more reliance than ever on government redistribution and less reliance on corporate initiatives.

Yet neither liberals nor conservatives have been dogmatic about seeking solutions, though their respective debts to pragmatism undoubtedly have different roots. After all, this is a period of "liberal consensus," so Presidents Nixon and Ford could not allow their free market predilections to go unchecked, lest they suffer severe popular disapproval. When the automobile companies upped prices unexpectedly in 1974, Ford reacted with dismay and outrage. The corporate sector retreated in a huff, as the Council on Wage-Price Stability (the President's "right arm" in these matters) ordered a rollback. Moreover, it was Nixon who imposed a freeze on all wages and prices and who set up (with congressional approval) independent machinery to oversee all boosts that seemed inflationary. These tribunals adopted the "5.5 policy" (no increases were permitted exceeding 5.5 percent of what the corporation was charging or what the worker was earning). Conservatives squirmed under the impact of such managed economics, but it was labor that really killed the Nixon program, when George Meany quit the Cost of Living Council, citing discriminatory practices.

Liberal inconsistencies in program and policy development tell us more about contemporary constitutional politics, because they stem from the majority's inability to contrive a systematic theory of "Positive State" powers and duties. The Employment Act of 1946 expresses a commitment to redistribution through extensive manipulation of the economic marketplace, but coherent manipulation requires planning, and liberals refuse to plan. Instead, they *delegate.* The Federal Reserve Board can raise or lower interest rates and expand or contract the flow of money *completely independent* of executive-legislative opinion. In short, *economic redistribution as constitutional policy contains a delegation-run-riot corollary.* And when meaningful regulatory policy looms large, *liberals delegate in spades.* They acquiesced in Nixon's price-wage regulatory policy for the same reason they supported N.I.R.A. regulatory policy in the 1930s: a coercive rule promulgated by labor-business-government partnership is not really threatening, because it has received interest-group ratification. In case anyone thinks all this is inevitable, one need only recall that Alexander Hamilton and John Marshall believed in distributive policy for property interests and contrived the rules to make it work.

There are other salient examples showing that the quest to achieve a more egalitarian balance has become as much fantasy as fulfillment. The fact is that liberal policy, despite its proegalitarian rhetoric, fosters corporate formulation and growth in a manner the old "robber barons" might well have extolled. What, for instance, is liberal policy with respect to antitrust enforcement? Certainly "bigness," which tends toward monopoly or lessens competition, is considered no sin. Did Presidents Kennedy and Johnson invoke the Sherman-Clayton arsenal against either the oil companies or the automobile manufacturers? President Ford's Attorney General brought suit to break up the largest firm of all, A.T.&T., but Ford is a midwestern Jeffersonian, not a "Positive State" economic egalitarian. Perhaps one reason why "combinations in restraint of trade" go unattacked in our time is that the government might be forced to prosecute its own creations. What, after all, is Amtrak? Liberal antitrust policy boils down to this: *unless corporations lose public confidence entirely* (as the oil companies bid fair to do), *they need not fear government attempts to break up monopolies.*

"Positive Staters" truly emulate the Hamiltonians of old, however, when they give generous subsidies to private-property interests; in our time, though, such interests are impersonal corporate entities. Take, for instance, the *capital gains tax.* Profits earned from selling stock or property are taxed at far lower rates than income earned through wages. As everyone knows, those who thrive on capital gains are the big investors, not those in the lower half of income distribution. Clearly, the capital gains device promotes corporate formation and expansion, and that may be just fine unless one believes in "Positive State" constitutional policy, with its egalitarian premises.

Some people might call this public–private sector love affair "capitalism," but capitalism presupposes that inefficient and incompetent producers will be driven from the marketplace. The fact is that not even New York City is incompetent enough to go bankrupt today; the federal government lent the city $2.3 billion in 1975 to save the community from this ignominious fate. One is almost tempted to opine that the rich, as well as the poor, are on welfare, and this phenomenon yields another corollary to "Living Constitutionalism" and the "Positive State": *big business deemed integral to mass production and consumption shall be subsidized.* Surely such gifts-without-strings also owe an intellectual debt to delegation-run-riot.

Let's pull these strands together. Liberalism does not quite know how to handle the corporation, in either constitutional theory or constitutional practice. The economic model Keynes pronounced has been replaced by a mishmash of political approaches that sometimes run into one another. Thus, liberal philosopher John Kenneth Galbraith says Washington must contrive public and private control centers such as "big labor" and "big federal budgets" to check capital[62]; liberal philosopher Arthur Schlesinger, Jr., argues that a partnership among government, business, and labor leaders must be encouraged[63]; liberal activists Fred Harris of Oklahoma and William Proxmire of Wisconsin clamor for vigorous antitrust enforcement. And the "Positive State" has unleashed a mishmash of economic initiatives as well. Redistributive policy remains the ultimate end, but the "liberal consensus" has decided to work through the corporate superstructure by plying it with distributive policy rather than to rip down the corporate superstructure by imposing regulatory policy. Evidently, then, corporations—perhaps even conglomerates—have acquired both the *durability* and the *legitimacy* to be classed as part of the "Living Constitution." But neither the corporation nor the "Positive State" has acquired the gloss of *accountability* one associates with nicely balanced political relationships in a system dedicated to reciprocal powers and duties.

Economic liberties in organizational America

Individuals as independent economic providers are a dying breed. Our citizenry is almost entirely employed or sponsored by impersonal corporations, impersonal service agencies, impersonal universities, or impersonal governments. Organizationalism runs rampant today because material wants are satisfied with optimal efficiency when groups are permitted free access to scientific and technical know-how.[64] (Today, even education is considered a "material want.") And current "Positive State" philosophy sees the federal government as merely another *group,* providing economic security to its assorted clients.[65] Computers tell Washington how best to parcel out largesse for the public's benefit, and computers tell corporations, created and nurtured by the state, how to maximize profits and cut losses.[66] In such a constitutional universe, where public and private structures and functions merge gently with one another, what happens to the individual and *personal* economic interests?

First, what "Positive State" policies have been developed to check governmental arbitrariness in the domain of property status? As one might expect, the Warren Court marked out certain limitations in this area. Its first innovative thrust occurred in the voting rights field; the Justices struck down a state poll tax as violating equal protection. The right to cast a ballot in state elections, they said, was nowhere guaranteed by the Constitution; however, once the state had provided for voting machinery, it could not condition electoral participation on an economic criterion—that is, paying a fee. Wealth, the Justices concluded, was an irrational touchstone for measuring voter credentials, and the equal protection clause was designed to ensure rational categories in prescribing legal privileges and obligations.[67] The Burger Court, taking this doctrine a step further, struck down a Texas law requiring all candidates entering primaries to tender filing fees.[68] However, when California amended its constitution to mandate a popular referendum in a community before any low-rent housing project could be constructed there, the Court refused to apply the equal protection rule. The provision, it said, abetted rather than retarded democratic participation.[69] In sum, the Justices will not allow poverty to keep citizens from voting or running for office, but they will not look behind electoral procedures to see if poor people could be unduly injured by the election returns.

A major breakthrough in the area of poverty law occurred in 1969, when the Court struck down state and *federal* residency requirements for obtaining welfare.[70] Several states, as well as the District of Columbia, refused to aid families with dependent children unless the recipients satisfied a one-year domiciliary standard. The Court said these statutes discriminated against needy recipients on the basis of where they lived, and the burden of proof was on the "Positive State" to show a *compelling interest* justifying any such categorization. No overriding interest could be displayed.

The Burger Court has applied this doctrine to void an Arizona one-year county residency requirement for medical care at public expense.[71] However, a one-year Iowa domiciliary standard for persons instituting divorce proceedings was found constitutional, and a Maryland welfare regulation setting an upper limit on how much money could be parceled out per family was also upheld against the challenge that large families (and thus the neediest families) were not being fairly provided for.[72] Evidently, the "evil" the Court has proscribed here is denial of minimal economic benefits to destitute out-of-staters.

A third line of decisions emanating from the Warren Court considered poverty status within the courthouse framework. The landmark case voided an Illinois law requiring defendants who requested an appellate hearing to supply—and to pay for—a complete transcript of trial court proceedings. Only those indigents sentenced to death received comparable records free of charge. A four-man plurality argued that a state was not obliged to have any appellate procedure, but if it did, economic status could not determine the benefits dispensed. In the criminal process, discrimination on account of wealth was as irrational as racial or religious discrimination.[73]

Based on this decision, the Burger Court knocked down a Texas law requiring those who couldn't pay traffic fines to be incarcerated until they "worked off" their debts at $5 a day. "Debtors' prison" conditioned penalties on economic status; hence it constituted an irrational classification under equal protection.[74] Furthermore, states cannot make persons suing for divorce pay a fee to have their cases heard. If the state allows individuals to vindicate their legal rights only through judicial determination, then the state cannot deprive indigents of equal access to those judicial processes.[75] These cases show the Justices giving special attention to statutory categories based on economic standing where weighty due process factors were implicated.

But the due process clauses carry their own protection against invidious loss of property interests. Before a state can cut off welfare payments to a particular individual, it must hold an evidentiary hearing wherein the recipient may present his side of things and impeach testimony put forward by adversary witnesses.[76] Furthermore, when teachers have tenure—that is, hold a contract for an indefinite period—they cannot be dismissed by a state school unless tendered a hearing; however, if the contract is for a fixed term, hearings need not be held justifying dismissal, once the contract has been fulfilled.[77] These holdings iterate that when someone has a legitimate claim of entitlement in some property interest—be it welfare or teacher employment in a public institution—the claim may not be dissolved without procedural due process.

Perhaps the most significant case handed down in the 1970s relating to economic issues, however, went *against* the claim of deprivation. Many states provide only a portion of the funding for their public school systems, the rest coming from the districts themselves. These schemes guarantee that considerably more money per pupil will be spent in affluent suburban communities than in less prosperous communities. Do these programs violate equal protection?

By a 5-4 tally, the Supreme Court upheld their constitutionality, with Justices Burger, Powell, Blackmun, Rehnquist, and Stewart outvoting Justices Douglas, Brennan, Marshall, and White. First, the majority found that wealth, unlike race or religion, was not a "suspect" classification, where an unusually formidable burden of proof lay on public officials to justify any and every distinction they had established. Sometimes categories based on economic status *in concert with some other important value* (the voting privilege or access to the judicial process) did establish a more strict equal protection standard, for in those circumstances, impecunity had been employed to deny citizens a meaningful benefit others more fortunate could enjoy. In this case, however, there was no evidence that all poor families were huddled in the less-affluent school districts. Furthermore, the alleged deprivation was a lower-quality education, not *no education whatsoever.* Second, the Justices could not believe that education was a fundamental right protected by the Constitution. Such rights included only those set out in the document explicitly (freedom of speech) or implicitly (the right to privacy). In short, the Court refused to make the state bear the burden of proof in justifying its funding mechanism. The issue was one of revenue collection and disbursal, where the usual burden lay on petitioners to show legislative irrationality. This they could not demonstrate, for if the local communities could be given certain privileges in educational self-government, then they could also be given certain fund-raising responsibilities.[78]

In the mid-1960s, Charles Reich coined the phrase "new property," by which he meant the funds pouring out of the "Positive State" cornucopia to fortify personal security against economic privation and to achieve economic equilibrium among clashing interest groups.[79] He feared that these "rights" were held conditionally, that they could be withdrawn at the whim of the state when the public interest demanded. Hence Reich proposed a constitutional policy treating publicly dispensed largesse as an *entitlement* rather than as a privilege—that is, he sought to *constitutionalize distributive policies.* The Supreme Court, however, has refused this invitation to resurrect substantive due process. In its view, a "noncontractual claim to receive funds from the public treasury enjoys no constitutionally protected status."[80]

What the Justices have attempted to do, then, is to contrive a more modest constitutional policy within the mainstream of egalitarian liberal thought. *Minimal national standards of fairness must control how government officials dis-*

pense their good works, so that economic discrimination is muted and economic values are respected. Poor people as an identifiable class cannot be fenced out of the voting process, the judicial process, or the welfare process; nor can people at large be deprived arbitrarily of property interests they hold as the result of expectations created by state action. These are essentially regulatory policies; they are the rudiments of an "economic Bill of Rights." But the Court has wisely left to the "political branches" the choice of what distributive or redistributive policies (the *right* to an education, the *right* to a job, the *right* to a home) should be granted at public expense and in what proportion.

To what extent have the Justices laid down policy regarding the constitutional liberties of private citizens, on the one hand, and *corporate* power on the other hand? The landmark decision involved a Jehovah's Witness who was convicted for distributing leaflets in the streets of a "company town"—that is, a community *owned* by a private firm for the benefit of its employees. The town's managers had told the pamphleteer to keep off their property or face arrest. The Court ruled that the state had surrendered sovereign power to the company, so the firm was a surrogate governmental institution with respect to town managerial affairs. Since the corporation owned the streets, the buildings, and the sanitation services, it was subject to the same constitutional restraints as any other town "government." Because communities cannot insulate their citizens from religious information, neither could the corporation.[81]

I have noted that public and private functions are becoming less and less distinct. The Jehovah's Witness case shows how a corporation—considered a *person* in American law—can assume the trappings of cityhood. What about a shopping center? Are such commercial districts really "private governments"? The Burger Court has answered this question negatively, holding that shopping center owners can oust from their property both pamphleteers protesting American involvement in Vietnam and picketers demonstrating against the labor practices of firms located there. These decisions in some measure undercut the Jehovah's Witness case, which also involved the dissemination of information in a quasi-public, quasi-private context.[82]

Rarely has the Court adjudicated a classic controversy between *personal* property rights and *corporate* property rights. However, in 1974 the Justices upheld an order by a private utility cutting off electrical service to homeowners because they weren't paying their bills. The company was a "natural monopoly," the only electrical power producer in the community, and all such cancellations were filed with a Pennsylvania state regulatory agency. Petitioner claimed that service could not be discontinued unless he were afforded a hearing, but the Court said the company performed no public functions, because energy service was traditionally a private undertaking. Moreover, if state approval of cancellation orders made electrical utilities governmental bodies, then federal regulation of countless private enterprises made them public agencies also, seemingly a dubious proposition.[83]

Adolph Berle has contended that corporations perform significant public functions; they are licensed by government because the "new capitalism" cannot survive without them. In other words, if laissez faire is dead and socialism is too monolithic for our taste, then "Positive State" supervision of corporate policy is the inevitable compromise. That supervision should include *constitutionalizing the corporation,* making it adhere to the same duties vis-à-vis private individuals as bind the state.[84] The Supreme Court has not adopted Berle's thesis. Prevailing constitutional policy constrains *only those corporations that perform traditional governmental functions.* All other corporations, including shopping centers and "natural monopolies," need honor *no* constitutional duties in their relations with individuals.

This discussion takes us back to the whole question of corporate *accountability,* a question in *regulatory policy.* The "Positive State" has failed to develop a set of correlative rights and duties to make the burgeoning corporate octopus accountable. Regulation ought to exist along two dimensions: (1) the corporation must not only be profitable but must provide goods and services beneficial to the general welfare; (2) the corporation must treat individuals fairly.[85] The first is a problem in *substantive economic policy* and involves the relationship between elected officials and corporations as quasi-private entities. These officials have failed to provide accountability, largely because of their commitment to "delegation-run-riot." However, *government* does *not* have carte blanche. Corporations are persons, and the state must regulate their behavior accordingly—that is, the public domain must tender the corporation equal protection and due process. The second dimension is a problem in *procedural economic policy* and involves the relationship between corporate property and personal property. The public sector will undoubtedly allocate more and more police power to private agencies in the economic sphere, because it can then both reduce spending and increase the tax base. Those corporations clothed with governmental functions will evade accountability if the principles of equal protection and due process do not restrain *their* actions. Quasi-public corporations must neither classify nor coerce individuals through subjective standards beyond challenge.

The "Living Constitution," expressing undoubtedly the will of the people, mandates a middle road between individualism and collectivism. That middle road will work only if a realistic balance between quasi-public and quasi-private corporate roles is formalized. These proposals provide the constitutional policy needed to achieve such equilibrium.

Civil rights policy: constitutional power and constitutional morality

We now turn to a discussion of civil rights—that is, the individual freedoms black Americans strive for. The struggle for civil rights and the policies thus generated have been an instant replay of all that is examplary and all that is frustrating about American constitutional politics, from the belief in general principles of personal dignity to the fragile accommodation of conflicting wills. The term *civil rights* conveys a special moral appeal—indeed, a moral necessity; yet our constitutional law has never created a special political mechanism to dispense *or even to define* those rights. Civil rights policy, then, is like any other policy worth fighting for, and, given the "rules of the game," not much more: the guts of civil rights policy is constitutional policy.

Not blacks, not whites, but Americans: abortive policy

Federal action in civil rights dates from the Confederate surrender. It is impossible to understand current steps taken to promote freedom for blacks unless one understands the steps taken in the nineteenth century, because the successes and failures of those years are with us today.

With Lincoln gone and the Supreme Court still reeling from its *Dred Scott* disaster, Congress assumed complete control over the constitutional status of black Americans. There was nothing subtle about prevailing legislative intentions. Congressional policy (and Radical Republican ideology) was simply this: *black people must be given immediately all personal freedoms white people enjoy.* At that time, civil rights truly possessed an unadulterated moral imperative, and there is little doubt the average Northerner supported Congress's every effort to make that moral conviction a constitutional reality. Put succinctly, the Stevens-Sumner policy was the essence of *regulation,* forcing whites to treat blacks as equals under the law.

The Radical Republicans began by passing the Thirteenth Amendment, which not only abolished slavery but also gave the Congress "power to enforce [that] article by appropriate legislation." This authority, Stevens and his allies thought, could be used to stamp out all surviving racist practices. To that end, Congress speedily adopted the sweeping Civil Rights Bill of 1866, which (1) said anyone born in the United States was a citizen of the United States, (2) declared blacks must be given the same freedoms whites enjoy "to inherit, purchase, lease, sell, hold, and convey real and personal property," and (3) said persons acting "under color of any law" who "willfully" deprive someone of constitutional liberties because of that person's race may be fined or imprisoned.

But could Congress by statute undo what the *Dred Scott* decision had said was a constitutional fact of life—namely, that blacks (even blacks who had never been slaves) were disqualified from holding American citizenship? And could the Thirteenth Amendment be stretched to authorize a federal criminal code for violating personal and property rights created by the states? These points troubled middle-of-the-roaders, so the Stevens forces pushed through the Fourteenth Amendment to assuage all doubts. That remarkable constitutional proposition first defined national citizenship, making it turn on whether the individual was born or naturalized in this country. Second, it said states could not abridge the "privileges or immunities" of United States citizens; could not deprive people of life, liberty, or property without due process; and could not deny people the equal protection of the laws. Third, Congress was again empowered to pass whatever legislation might be needed to implement these constraints. At the least, this meant Congress could stop states from tampering with the black citizen's privileges and immunities, access to due process, and right to equal protection. The first section of the provocative 1866 law had now become officially constitutionalized, while the latter two sections remain on the statute books.

The Fifteenth Amendment seemed icing on the cake. Federal and state governments were prohibited from interfering with the right to vote "on account of race, color, or previous condition of servitude," and Congress could pass laws necessary to effectuate that command as well. This language served as a predicate to the Enforcement Act of 1870, which, among other things, banned all conspiracies to harm or intimidate citizens in their enjoyment of federal rights, whether constitutional or statutory. That provision also survived.

Southern slavocrats responded to these rules with their own brand of law and order, Ku Klux Klan style. But cross burning, threats, and homicides only exacerbated the vengeful ardor of the Stevens consensus. In 1871, Congress passed the very tough Third Enforcement Act, dubbed by some the "Ku Klux Klan Act." All private conspiracies designed to impede the operations of federal and state government or to deprive individuals of their full benefits under the equal protection clause would now be severely punished. Federal troops were then sent southward in the wake of virtually every civil disturbance, under orders to "search and destroy" the local Klan brigade. Today, this law is important because it gives private individuals authority to sue in federal court anyone who has deprived them of their federal rights. This provision is really a civil counterpart to the criminal laws enacted in 1866 and 1870.

A final congressional thrust was mounted in 1875, guaranteeing to all persons, regardless of race, free access to *public accommodations*—that is, *privately* owned and operated inns, transportation facilities, theaters, parks, and the like, ostensibly open to the general public. The legislators had now done all in their power to codify civil rights and to punish offenders. But would congressional policy become *constitutional* policy? That was beyond even Stevens's control.

Constitutional policies, of course, are not contrived overnight. Sometimes several decades must pass before ideas and doctrines acquire the legitimacy needed to assume constitutional status. But less than ten years was required to bury the Reconstructionist consensus, and an invigorated Supreme Court played the role of undertaker. In a nutshell, the Justices said Congress could not subject private individuals to criminal sanctions for violating the Fourteenth Amendment freedoms of other private individuals. Thus was the "Ku Klux Klan Act" emasculated. Congress's power to implement the Fourteenth Amendment included only the power to shield persons from *state* action inhibiting their right to due process, equal protection, and the privileges and immunities of national citizenship.[86]

This line of decisions culminated in the *Civil Rights Cases,*[87] which must rank among the most important rulings the Court has ever handed down. There, the Justices nullified the 1875 statute banning racial discrimination in the most important public accommodations, saying that neither the Fourteenth Amendment nor the Thirteenth Amendment could justify this federal regulation of private property rights. The Fourteenth was inapplicable because it was binding only on state excesses. If private parties deprived blacks of their rights, they could be punished by the state; should the state shield or encourage such behavior, *then* the Congress could regulate the unconstitutional public action.

The Thirteenth gave the legislative branch authority to abolish the "badges and incidents of slavery," but

> it would be running the slavery argument into the ground to make it apply to every act of discrimination which a person may see fit to make as to the guests he will entertain, or as to the people he will take into his coach or cab or car, or admit to his concert or theatre.[88]

Therefore, Congress's power under this clause extended to vindicating those basic rights distinguishing freedom from slavery but not to adjusting interpersonal relations between the races.

This decision was followed by the well-known *Plessy v. Ferguson,* which allowed states to maintain "separate but equal" facilities for whites and blacks. These decisions framed a new federal civil rights policy for Americans: *government must accord blacks all privileges accorded whites, but racial intermingling was strictly optional; and private individuals need not accord blacks any rights at all.*[89] Of course, the Justices were only mirroring a new public philosophy with regard to racial justice. The Radical Republican policy of "instant integration" could not work unless the South were put under military rule and slavocracy torn out by the roots—a long-term commitment which public opinion was obviously unready to make. Dissenting in both the *Civil Rights Cases* and *Plessy,* Mr. Justice Harlan spoke as eloquently as any American has ever spoken about human rights, arguing that the Constitution is color-blind and that when businesses operate under licenses issued by the state, they are cloaked with the same duties delimiting state power itself. But he was more than sixty years ahead of his time.

Incrementalism and state-sponsored racism: transitional policy

The "state action-separate but equal" policy dominated the first half of this century. Yet during that same period, the Court evinced a growing skepticism about both principles. Two developments, discussed more fully elsewhere, demonstrate the point. One involved the infamous "white primary" rule, which kept blacks from voting in political-party electoral contests. The Justices crept up on this practice with the greatest deliberation, for they understood that to tie partisan affairs into state action might put internal party activities at the mercy of federal intervention. In the end, though, they bit the bullet and decided primaries were an integral part of the electoral process. The other issue was public school segregation. Here again, the Justices were circumspect insisting initially on similarity of academic tangibles (books, schoolrooms) but eventually demanding similarity of academic intangibles (reputation, faculty qualifications). The 1954 school desegregation decision climaxed this trend; having undercut the very foundation of "separate but equal," the Court could zero in on the "evils" which state-supported segregated education worked on black children by hiding them away in their own universe. It is important to understand that *Brown v. Board of Education*—even taken at face value—was no exercise in Radical Republican "instant integration." It was part and parcel of incremental policy accommodation, not some leap forward into uncharted realms.

But the full meaning of this incremental adjustment becomes clear only when we grasp what happened in the first several years after *Brown.* Yes, the *Brown* doctrine was swiftly extended from the public school building to other publicly owned facilities—beaches, golf courses, buses, and parks. Yes, "separate but equal" had been declared lifeless, and a new constitutional policy had been enunciated establishing *racially desegregated government instrumentalities.* Nonetheless, in the schools themselves "separate but equal" refused to die. In fact, it refused even to be budged in the deep South. Why?

After *Brown,* the Court issued a special opinion reciting how the plaintiffs could obtain relief.[90] The Justices said the defendant boards of education must make "a prompt and reasonable start" toward abolishing dual school systems, but they gave the federal district courts considerable latitude in developing unique decrees for each school system, including the power to approve delays where appropriate. To be sure, these local judges could take whatever action was necessary and proper to effect desegregation "with all deliberate speed," but the ramifications of the entire scenario from both a constitutional *process* and a constitutional *policy* standpoint were enormous. Put bluntly, the Supreme Court, inured to fighting racism with incremental weapons, could bring itself to smite segregation per se only by invoking a special dose of incremental policy, implemented by a process hitherto unknown in enforcing basic constitutional rights, the "delegation-run-riot" norm.

On top of that, the Justices underrated the resistance of countless white parents to sending their children to school with blacks. I have recounted much of the sorry tale before (see pp. 198, 258). The Supreme Court, when pushed to the wall, refuted direct interference with the *Brown* decision; but in 1964, political scientists found that while desegregation had occurred with considerable success in such states as Delaware and Missouri, it had achieved only token success in such states as Tennessee and Florida and none whatever in such states as Alabama and South Carolina. Their research shows that *political* factors—for example, high black voter registration—did not correlate nearly as well with desegregation in the South as various *economic* and *demographic* factors did—for example, high income levels attained by both races, high educational levels attained by blacks, and *urbanism.*[91] The new constitutional policy, then, really amounted to this: *public facilities must desegregate incrementally.*[92]

There is little doubt, of course, that the *Brown* decision generated civil rights enthusiasm on a broad scale. Congress, comatose since 1875, finally adopted the Civil Rights Act of 1957 despite intense Southern criticism, greatly enhanced by Southern seniority in both chambers. This legislation would probably have never been approved had it not been narrowly drawn to meet excesses clearly pernicious under constitutional law, keeping blacks as a class from exercising the franchise. Specifically, the act created a full-fledged division in the Justice Department charged with litigating civil rights complaints; it created the Civil Rights Commission, charged with investigating discrimination against blacks; and it authorized the Attorney General to go into federal court on behalf of individuals denied voting privileges because of race. Probably the most significant provision has turned out to be the establishment of the Civil Rights Commission, which, armed with the subpoena power, has collected and published voluminous documentation of racial deprivation in all its guises.[93] But from a larger focus, the act's importance was in setting precedent. Congress had finally entered the contemporary civil rights arena, though, like Supreme Court policy, the legislative response had only opened the door to additional incremental reform.

The 1957 statute made almost no dent in the real world of racial politics, if only because separate suits on behalf of separate individuals hardly maximized the Attorney General's resources. Therefore, Congress took another tentative step toward voting rights equity by passing the Civil Rights Act of 1960. This law gave the Justice Department authority to demonstrate that a "pattern of practice" in voter discrimination existed throughout a particular region, and empowered the courts in such cases to appoint a referee, who would work toward meaningful compliance through negotiation. The "pattern of practice" notion was an important conceptual breakthrough; however, the remedy of enforcement by referee proved to be very inefficient. Still, by 1964, 43 percent of all Southern blacks who met the minimum age standard had registered, and the figure dropped below 20 percent only in Alabama and Mississippi.[94] Progress in black voter participation far exceeded progress in school desegregation, because important *political* variables as well as economic and demographic variables were operative here. Generally, electoral discrimination had never been as deep-seated as educational discrimination, so conditions at the ballot box could rival the aforementioned economic factors as a means of spurring black political activism.[95]

Civil rights and federal police power: successful policy

Congress would doubtless have continued to root out civil rights violations with a tortoiselike inexorability but for the sudden emergence of a new black militancy, which produced wholesale changes in policy development, coerciveness, and clarity.

Until the early 1960s, the dominant black civil rights organization was the N.A.A.C.P. (National Association for the Advancement of Colored People). Founded in 1909 by Booker T. Washington, it had worked tirelessly through court litigation to make the intent of the Civil War constitutional amendments a reality.[96] These labors at long last received a coveted reward when the Supreme Court, responding to the impassioned appeals of N.A.A.C.P. chief counsel Thurgood Marshall, outlawed "separate but equal."

The social and political climate of the 1960s, however, apparently required a more forceful approach, for several reasons. One was impatience. Incremental responses to incremental federal policies became difficult to bear. But as events attest, there must have been more. For example, the N.A.A.C.P. seems to have come across as an "elitist" pressure group, heavily funded by white money and heavily influenced by whites on its board of directors. Many younger blacks believed racial dignity necessitated racial independence, and some even used acrimonious slogans such as "Black Power." Other younger blacks, while in no way condoning attacks on "whitey," agreed that only mass activism could achieve more than tokenism. A final reason may have been that in the age of television, charisma and image were the watchwords. The leader of this second group of younger blacks, Martin Luther King, Jr., would become the leader of the civil rights movement because he combined charisma, image, intelligence, and personal dignity. He also mobilized a distinctive method—civil disobedience—to confront discrimination through mass action while avoiding the violence that normally sprung from mass action. These attributes, plus a refusal to fight bigotry with "reverse bigotry," made him a natural leader in that hour of momentum.

If the activist movement was ignited by one particular episode, it may well have occurred in 1956, when a black woman, Rosa Parks, refused to sit in the back of a Montgomery, Alabama, bus, as city law then required.[97] This incident precipitated a successful, 381-day economic boycott of the entire Montgomery bus system by the black community, a protest that brought national attention to Dr. King, its chief organizer. In the next few years, television cameras traced a rising tide of rallies, demonstrations, marches, and arrests: Freedom Rides, in which students attempted to integrate privately owned transportation facilities, only to find themselves jailed for their trouble; the sit-ins, which found civil rights activists demanding service at segregated restaurants and lunch counters throughout the South, demonstrations which led to almost 4,000 arrests on charges of trespass and disturbing the peace; the March on Washington, during which 200,000 people gathered in the nation's capital and heard Dr. King deliver his famous "I have a dream" address. Such activities put tremendous pressure on Congress to enact sweeping ameliorative legislation, but action came only after President Kennedy's assassination, a tragedy so visible and so devastating that it jarred the nation's leaders into lashing out against the insanities and injustices that seemed to be running rampant.

The 1964 Civil Rights Act is the most far-flung attack on racist practices ever promulgated by American national government. In its sections relating to *public accommodations,* certainly the most politically volatile, the law banned discrimination against blacks in restaurants, cafeterias, movie theaters, gas stations, sports arenas, inns, hotels, and motels that "affect commerce." The only exception granted was for "Mrs. Murphy's" boarding houses—in other words, establishments offering five rooms or less for rent where the owner maintains residence. But the *Civil Rights Cases* had said that Congress could not outlaw discrimination by *private* businesses. How, then, could this 1964 enactment be constitutional?

The Supreme Court, indeed, had been asked to reexamine the entire "state action" rationale in the wake of criminal-trespass convictions arising from the sit-in demonstrations. It was an embarrassing moment for the Warren Court, clearly sympathetic to the civil rights movement but unprepared simply to throw out the *Civil Rights Cases.* The result was a terrible split: three Justices advocated bringing every business licensed by the state, including all *corporations,* within Fourteenth Amendment "state action" coverage; three other Justices steadfastly rejected this approach, asserting that private-property owners, unless somehow subsidized by state officialdom, could discriminate without regard to the equal protection clause; the three remaining Justices tried to steer a precarious middle course, finding in each case a way to avoid taking sides while searching out enough technicalities to reverse all convictions.[98] Hence, the contemporary Supreme Court never faced the naked question of whether police enforcement of general trespass laws against blacks trying peacefully to desegregate a public accommodation comprised state action.

Congress endeavored to avoid this thicket by invoking its extraordinarily broad control over interstate commerce. The idea was to treat racial injustice as a noxious social practice, subject to the same federal police power regulation adopted during T.R.'s Administration to ban impure foodstuffs and during F.D.R.'s Administration to ban goods produced by firms employing children. If the Supreme Court would uphold those efforts, then why wouldn't the Justices extend similar courtesies to a public accommodations statute?

As has so often been the case, the Supreme Court proved much braver when legitimizing "political branch" activism than when forging ahead on its own. First, the law was held binding upon a large Atlanta motel that advertised out of state and provided rooms mostly to out-of-staters. The Justices noted that the regulations were aimed at motels affecting commerce, by which was meant motels serving transient guests. The Justices also emphasized Congress's finding of fact, demonstrating the great inconvenience blacks encountered on the road in searching for hospitable lodgings.[f] Surely, legislative jurisdiction over interstate channels augmented by the necessary and proper clause was more than sufficient to remedy these inequities. Second, the law was held applicable to Ollie's Barbecue, a small Birmingham eaterie. While Ollie's had no direct connection with interstate traffic, the restaurant obtained 46 percent of its meat from a local supplier whose sources were out of state. The traditional constitutional test was whether Congress could conclude rationally that merchandise was being marketed across state lines contrary to particular social

[f] The Court might have recounted how Artie Shaw's all-white orchestra had been refused service again and again while touring in the South during the 1930s, because the band's female vocalist was the great Billie Holiday, and how the Jacksonville minor league baseball team had been refused service constantly during the 1953 season, because the club had just taken on a young outfielder named Henry Aaron.

standards. Because Congress's judgment *was* rational, relevant *intrastate* activity fell within the purview of the *interstate* regulation.[99] The courts have yet to find a restaurant or motel so unrelated to the national flow of commercial relations that it could discriminate against blacks with impunity.

Flushed with triumph, civil rights workers were not about to slacken their efforts. By now voter-registration drives blanketed the South but were running afoul of qualification requirements, fair in theory but highly discriminatory in practice. Thus, blacks with little formal education who could read and write were often denied ballot box access because they couldn't interpret constitutional and legal language to the satisfaction of state officials. Meanwhile, whites with no better credentials were given easier passages to construe and were graded with a lighter touch.

The result was another sweeping statute, the Civil Rights Act of 1965. This law suspended literacy tests for a five-year period in any state where less than 50 percent of voting age citizens had either failed to register or failed to cast ballots in the 1964 presidential election. The Attorney General was empowered to order into these areas registrars who could enroll otherwise qualified blacks forthwith. Evidence showed that six states fell under the 50-percent formula, and their election systems were for all practical purposes placed in federal receivership. The new rules, moreover, proved remarkably effective. Black registration jumped in Alabama from 19 percent to 51 percent, and in Mississippi from 6 percent to 59 percent.

A test case was brought before the Supreme Court, and the 1965 statute was upheld.[100] Legislative power under the Fifteenth Amendment embraced authority to pass all rationally contrived rules necessary and proper to ensure equality of voter participation by blacks. And when Congress, in 1970, not only extended these provisions for another five years but suspended state literacy tests throughout the nation, the Justices upheld this regulation as well.[101] Perhaps there was no evidence that a state like Oregon used such examinations as racist weapons, but Congress could reasonably assess lower registration and voting figures in states employing these tests as reflecting the unequal educational opportunities afforded blacks everywhere. In 1975, Congress made the ban against literacy criteria permanent and widened the 50-percent formula to embrace counties and cities where more than 5 percent of the voting-age citizenry comprised a "language minority" (that is, people of Spanish heritage, American Indians, Asian Americans, and Alaskan natives). If these groups were not participating because of English-language deficiencies, federal registrars would remedy the problem.

And what had the executive branch been doing all this time? Not a great deal. However, the 1964 Civil Rights Act gave the President a powerful weapon. The Department of Health, Education, and Welfare was told to terminate grants-in-aid in cases where the recipient public or private agency exercised discriminatory standards. Because all state-supported schools consume funds at the federal trough, H.E.W. could perhaps accomplish what the courts had failed to accomplish, desegregation in the South.

Under President Johnson's watchful eye, H.E.W. officials prepared, for elementary and secondary educational institutions, a set of guidelines requiring evidence that a plan of attack against discrimination had been drawn up and approved, plus evidence that specific grades had been desegregated. By January 1968, H.E.W. had cut off funds to 168 school districts for failure to comply[102]; by September 1968, the percentage of black students attending white-majority schools had risen from 2.14 to 20.3.[103] Throwing caution to the winds, H.E.W. even declared war on the previously untouchable de facto segregation patterns dominant throughout the North by ordering busing schemes to achieve racial balance within school districts, a blatant violation of language contained in the 1964 Civil Rights Act.

Perhaps spurred by Congress's aggressive civil rights stance and H.E.W.'s guidelines, the Supreme Court suddenly entered the fray with renewed vigor, using as its weapon the long-dormant Reconstructionist statutory scheme. The first case concerned the torture-murders of three civil rights workers in Mississippi. Three policemen and fifteen private citizens stood accused of depriving these victims of their constitutional right to life without according them even the rudiments of due process. The Justices held that these people were "acting under color of law" in violation of the 1866 statute because they were "acting under pretense of law."[104] In a far more controversial ruling, the Court upheld convictions under the 1870 law of private parties who allegedly planned to deprive blacks of their constitutional freedom of interstate travel.[105] On this point, Mr. Justice Harlan wrote a strong dissent, arguing the *constitutional right* at issue was freedom from *state abridgement* of interstate movement, because the Constitution *does not protect private individuals against action by other private individuals.*

The Court followed these decisions with a hotly debated ruling in the fair-housing area. A black couple had filed civil suit against white realtors, claiming they were denied the opportunity to purchase a home because of race. This, they said, was a violation of the 1866 provision giving blacks the same right as whites to purchase property. The Court decided that the statute was constitutional under the Thirteenth Amendment, because Congress's power to define and dispatch the "badges and incidents of slavery" included private racism as well as public racism.[106] The question the majority raised here and failed to answer is whether Congress can outlaw private racism per se in the economic marketplace, for if that option is now open, then the *Civil Rights Cases* are dead. A year later, as a fitting climax, the Justices returned to the school desegregation dilemma and said enough was enough. Southern public educational officials were ordered to provide racial equality forthwith.[107]

The 1960s, then, saw the three branches of national government join forces in a frontal attack on racial discrimination. Congress used its control over interstate commerce and its Fifteenth Amendment enforcement power to police public accommodations and voter participation; the President and the bureaucracy used their control over grant-in-aid administration to police public education; the Supreme Court used both the equal protection clause to help police the public schools, and Thaddeus Stevens's statutory legacy to help police private conduct aimed at disparaging civil rights. These regulatory policies have largely become constitutional policy.

The struggle for affirmative action: muddled policy

The civil rights movement in this country has hardly accomplished everything worth fighting for. Blacks have achieved neither political nor economic parity with whites, no matter how "parity" is defined. Virtually untouched by the new constitutional policies are the broad social problems posed by blacks huddled together in the central cities, fenced out of membership in the power structure. These policies also fail to resolve such tangible issues as employment and housing, and when it comes to de facto school segregation, the "Living Constitution" remains unaltered.

Civil rights organizations, of course, know all this; so do the audiences in Washington sensitive to their needs. But a dilemma in constitutional politics has caused those interests no end of concern: How can meaningful *regulatory policy* be contrived to address these imponderables?

The difficulties are thrown into sharp relief when we examine the search for a viable open-housing policy. Congress's final legislative salvo during the Johnson years was the Civil Rights Act of 1968, passed in the aftermath of Martin Luther King's assassination. This statute was intended to end discrimination in the sale and rental of living space except where a homeowner's intimate property rights were deemed preeminent. The law barred racial bias should mortgages be underwritten by either the Federal Housing Administration or the Veterans Administration; furthermore, it outlawed racist practices with respect to apartment buildings and most multifamily homes; and it forbade discrimination in the sale or rental of single-family units where a realtor served as intermediary. But this entire fair-housing code has been virtually impossible to implement. In theory, the law opened 80 percent of all living space to interracial occupancy, but in practice this goal is strictly illusory. The basic difficulties are economic and social. Most blacks don't have the money to escape the ghetto environment even if they want to, and those who have both the resources and the inclination find that most whites can't run fast enough to escape from the problems that are stereotypically associated with integrated communities. Segregated living patterns are on the rise, not on the decline.

The 1968 Civil Rights Act, then, is transitional policy. Federal regulation, as an engine for racial equity, is running out of fuel, and decision-making over the past several years seems to show a consensus that other policy premises must be mobilized. The new focus of the 1970s is *redistributive policy,* and the policy weapon utilized most often is called *affirmative action.*

Redistributive policy, of course, takes perquisites from one group and gives them to another. Redistribution is the primary economic premise of the contemporary "liberal consensus." In other words, property is siphoned from the affluent to the deprived in modest, incremental amounts. Naturally, blacks have benefited from financial redistribution because they lack economic resources, and, to the extent that blacks are an important cog in the liberal alliance, they certainly deserve a piece of the redistributive action. Perhaps, then, contemporary economic constitutional policy holds the key to ultimate civil rights implementation.

This hypothesis can be tested with regard to the intractable problem of equal employment. Presidents Kennedy and Johnson both achieved an unusually high level of public support for economic redistribution. To that end, they persuaded a receptive Democratic Congress to complement civil rights legislation with significant employee apprenticeship programs designed to turn poor, undereducated job seekers into competent workers performing useful services. The most costly have been On-the-Job Training, established in 1963, and the Neighborhood Youth Corps, established one year later. If these agencies were intended to give blacks a crack at obtaining and holding respectable employment, they have surely been failures. Neither program caters to a black clientele; the majority of workers they trained during the 1960s were white. Moreover, many blacks who "graduate" cannot find employment. Finally, those blacks who do obtain jobs often fail to hold them.[108] The lesson that emerges seems to be this: *if redistributive policy is to achieve civil rights, it is fruitless to shift perquisites from the prosperous to the poverty-stricken; they must be shifted from whites to blacks.* This policy is what I mean by "affirmative action."[109]

How has affirmative action worked in the employment field, and how does it contrast with traditional regulatory policy? The 1964 Civil Rights Act makes it illegal for any firm employing twenty-five or more workers to hire and fire on the basis of race, religion, national origin, or sex. The law also creates administrative enforcement machinery—the Equal Employment Opportunity Commission (E.E.O.C.). This is a straightforward regulatory approach that turns out to be only somewhat more successful than open-housing implementation, because the E.E.O.C. relies largely on compliance through mediation.

Federal contractors occupy a more vulnerable position, however; Washington can always send its business elsewhere if blacks are not accorded equal treatment. There have been executive orders in force forbidding racist practices by these employers since F.D.R.'s day; but, until 1969, they *mandated* only the usual antiracist and antisexist guidelines, though the government called this affirmative action.[110] Then the Nixon Administration developed the Philadelphia Plan, which compels government contractors to hire a certain percentage of black workers. This "quota" concept was first tried out in Philadelphia, whose population was 30 percent black but whose craft union membership was less than 5 percent black. To obtain a federal contract, businesses were told, they must recruit between 19 and 26 percent of their work force from the black community by 1973, depending on the industry. As of that date, the Philadelphia Plan was so successful that its use had spread to fifty-five of the nation's largest cities.

The building-trades unions have consistently opposed the Philadelphia Plan, as has George Meany's A.F.L.-C.I.O. They see the device as forcibly assigning jobs to blacks, thus evicting white workers. Of course, they are correct; that is what affirmative action is all about. Its distinctive feature, then, is *reverse racism,* and I do not employ this phrase pejoratively. The argument can reasonably be made that discrimination will persist until the state takes positive steps to even up the cards. In other words, banning racist practices does nothing to remedy the continuing effects of *past* racist practices. The N.A.A.C.P. abhors the Philadelphia Plan, claiming that the program pits black workers against white workers and was merely part of Nixon's grand strategy to break up the coalition of organized labor and civil rights groups.[111]

What is the situation regarding nonconstruction contractors—say, colleges and universities performing important research tasks for the federal government? They must file an "affirmative action program" detailing inventories of all workers broken down by job classification or by department, isolating the units in which women and minorities are unemployed or underutilized and setting up "goals and timetables" for rectifying these inadequacies. ("Underutilization" refers to the employment of fewer women or minorities in a job category "than would reasonably be expected by their availability.")

These rules specifically say "quotas" and "reverse discrimination" are illegal; they also say contractors should continue to recruit only qualified candidates. But this does not remove the guidelines from affirmative action policy. For one thing, a contractor must formulate corrective goals and timetables *even if there is no evidence the firm or school ever discriminated.* Thus, if the Physics Department at Yale included only white professors, it would be obligated to contrive appropriate remedial steps. For another thing, a contractor must compute the important "availability pool" by applying not only such criteria as the number of women and minorities possessing "requisite skills" but such factors as "the degree of training which the contractor is reasonably able to undertake *as a means of making all job classes available" to deprived groups.*[g] Finally, the goals and timetables must be specific, must be attainable, and may include "numbers or percentages." Taken together, these guidelines constitute the very essence of redistributive policy in the equal rights arena.[112]

Finally, we must investigate the intersection between affirmative action and the most politically sensitive universe of all, elementary and secondary public education. When last I discussed that context, the Supreme Court and H.E.W. were bearing down on de jure racial segregation. At long last, the Southern dual school system appeared doomed, and so it was. But the fight to eradicate discrimination did not abate. H.E.W. interpreted the Supreme Court's call for a unitary educational system as mandating the dissolution of

[g] If, for example, a prestige university recruits young faculty only from superior graduate schools, the university is expected to recruit minorities in proportion to the "national average" of minority candidates, not the percentage of minority candidates trained by the prestige graduate schools. And if a company has hired only a few blacks and women because there were only a few qualified applicants in the market, the company should now train black and women applicants.

racially identifiable schools. That is, desegregated learning institutions meant majority-white integrated institutions. Many district court judges agreed, and the result was massive busing orders throughout the South. This policy was upheld by the Supreme Court in 1971, the Justices ruling unanimously that lower federal courts had inherent power to establish quotas for racial balance in school districts with a history of de jure segregation.[113]

That holding spurred President Nixon, a long-time opponent of "forced busing" and an advocate of the "neighborhood school" concept, to offer his own public school civil rights package. The man who proposed and implemented a strict quota system for construction workers now asked Congress to enforce the Fourteenth Amendment by stopping all federal court-ordered busing for one year. During this cooling-off period, legislation could be formulated setting up uniform national desegregation standards, criteria ensuring the vitality of neighborhood education. Now if busing orders are merely discretionary remedies to resolve constitutional deprivations, then Congress can certainly enforce the equal protection clause by revising the lower courts' ability to issue them. But if busing to achieve racial balance is required under the equal protection clause, then Congress can stop it only by stripping the Supreme Court of its appellate jurisdiction in this area, a proposal even Nixon never espoused. The legislative branch ultimately rejected decisive action, so Nixon was forced to content himself with ousting H.E.W. from the "guidelines" business in the realm of de facto racism, where, as I indicated earlier, it had no authority to be in the first place.

The year 1974 cannot be labeled a vintage year for civil rights activism. It saw Congress pass a statute (the Educational Amendment Act) prohibiting federal agencies, including courts, from requiring busing except to the school closest or next closest to a student's home. It also saw the Supreme Court refuse to order cross-busing between Detroit and its suburbs on the ground that though de jure segregation could be shown within city limits, there was no proof implicating the suburbs in any racist practices.[114] And when District Judge W. Arthur Garrity found de jure discrimination throughout the Boston school system, widespread violence resulted in protest against Garrity's "solution," the busing of 17,000 students. One year later, the judge took the extraordinary step of placing South Boston High School under judicial receivership, vesting himself with authority to desegregate the facility as he sees fit. But sporadic violence persists.

The underlying policy conflict that has caused battle lines to harden revolves around affirmative action. Given the constraints of current Supreme Court doctrine, affirmative action prescribes that schools within a de jure *segregated district* must exhibit a mix of white and black students reflecting the overall district racial mix; otherwise the schools will be "racially identifiable." Where a city is more than 50 percent black (Detroit, for example), affirmative action policy would require at least most schools to have a black student majority; where a city is more than 50 percent white (Boston, for example), affirmative action policy would obligate at least most schools to maintain a white student majority. The 1954 *Brown* decision outlaws "separate but equal" and looks to desegregated education at the neighborhood level. That is regulatory policy. Voiding de facto segregation and substituting the neutral principle of distance from homesite to schoolsite to determine pupil placement would also be regulatory. But affirmative action necessitates ever more massive busing orders as the white-black student ratios (quotas) become more rigid. The quotas are designed to give black children the same educational experience white children receive, and if whites must be lifted from their residential enclaves and deposited in black schools far from home, then so be it. That is redistributive policy, and it is policy the Supreme Court has condoned.

The N.A.A.C.P. leads the fight for affirmative action in public education. After some years of losing the limelight to sit-ins, demonstrations, even riots, the cross-busing issue has given this venerable organization a new lease on life. It almost certainly has recaptured a large chunk of its black constituency by advocating a pro-busing, pro-quota system to cure both de jure and de facto racism. Curiously enough, however, the N.A.A.C.P. has painted itself precisely into the box it once fitted for Richard Nixon. While entirely justified in fearing a white labor-black labor split over building trades quotas, the group has caused the same kind of split over student quotas. Research shows most blacks want affirmative action in public education,[115] but the Caucasian blue-collar worker who votes Democratic and whose children may be bused into the ghetto has come to detest integration. No wonder N.A.A.C.P. support among whites has dropped to the point where 1976 presidential candidate Henry Jackson, an unreconstructed 1930s liberal, proclaimed loudly the virtues of a constitutional amendment to bar "forced busing."

The Burger Court seems unlikely to bless the N.A.A.C.P.'s conception of Fourteenth Amendment rights. On the "state action" question, the Justices refused to order the all-white Moose Lodge of Harrisburg, Pennsylvania, to serve black guests even though the club had been granted a state liquor license and was compelled thereby to satisfy all manner of state regulations.[116] If the Mooses' racist policy is here protected by the right of privacy, then the Court undoubtedly will not find state action lurking in de facto school segregation either.

Affirmative action remains, indeed, a study in jurisprudential uncertainty. When the Justices were asked to rule on a law school admissions policy giving extra points to academically inferior blacks and Chicanos so that those groups would attain "reasonable representation," the result was total confusion. Various civil rights groups defended the program; but in so doing, they once again rubbed an important ally in the liberal coalition the wrong way, this time Jewish organizations like the Anti-Defamation League. Remembering all too vividly how quotas had perpetuated anti-Semitism in years past, the league argued strongly for color-blind admissions. In the face of this split, only Mr. Justice Douglas reached the merits. He found the scheme unconstitutional, contending that all racist classifications, including "reverse racism," were suspect and, as a measure of capacity for legal study, invidious. However, a majority said the case should be dismissed because so much time had elapsed since petitioner's appeal was lodged that he had already registered for his third and final year in law school.[117] Such trepidation rarely presages the kind of breakthrough in constitutional doctrine that would be required to legitimize racial quotas for students, absent discriminatory conduct.

Affirmative action is muddled policy, then, because Congress has watered it down with antibusing amendments, because Presidents Nixon and Ford opposed "forced busing" without equivocation, because the liberal alliance is badly split over its virtues, and because the Supreme Court refuses to anoint the doctrine with unequivocal constitutional sanctity. Against such opposition, accusations by the N.A.A.C.P. and the Civil Rights Commission that the overarching commitment to racial integration is endangered because 71 percent of black students in Northern public schools attend segregated facilities border on political impotence.[118]

Political-behavior research lends credence to the premise that racial policy occupies a unique place in our "Living Constitutional" matrix. Generally speaking, if you give Americans more money, more education, and more power, you will alleviate their frustrations, reduce their anxieties, and make them good middle-class, law abiding citizens. This remedy hasn't worked for blacks, because they see American politics as a cheat depriving them of their dignity and personal esteem, and they use as evidence the fact that a vast majority of their people are mired in the ghetto, unable to get out no matter how hard they try.[119] Today's black elites will be militant blacks when the occasion arises. On the other hand, the more we transfer perquisites from whites to blacks, the angrier and more militant the whites become.

If this analysis is accurate, then the constitutional policy framework that stands the best chance of coping with race relations is *distributive policy*. Such policy, remember, entails bounties, subsidies, and inducements to promote the general welfare. Why not give a free college education to ghetto blacks who graduate in the top 5 to 10 percent of their high school class? Why not give the corporate giants tax write-offs for training blacks to find a place in the job market? The greater the number of blacks who succeed, the larger the write-off. Why not give willing black families x amount of money to relocate and build new communities for themselves beyond the invisible walls separating Roxbury from Newton and Harlem from Scarsdale? Why not a Northwest Ordinance for blacks? Finally, why not promote rationality in civil rights policy formation by putting all such programs under one institutional roof, a Cabinet-level Department of Black Affairs?

The kinds of steps I am suggesting are constitutional under the Thirteenth Amendment, because their purpose and effect are to eliminate the "badges and incidents of slavery." They would give much to blacks, and they would take few perquisites from whites. The distributive focus is not *the* answer, because there is none. But I think it comes much closer to addressing the empirical reality of the "Living Constitution" in the civil rights milieu than does either the regulatory or the redistributive approach.

As I review these pages and recall the subtitle of this chapter, I am struck by the significance of constitutional policy. The term describes the guiding principles of what American national government accomplishes. The spectrum of policy choice is a focal point for citizen participation and group action, because while technical programs seem overwhelming in their complexity, blueprints of action are comprehensible, if only because the issues they address possess symbolic meaning. That is especially the case with respect to *constitutional* policy, which, by definition, is a study of the durable, the fundamental, and the legitimate.

But constitutional policy cannot be extricated from the context of constitutional *process*. If the ends are what make politics worth fighting over, then the means convey all of the "fair play" that gives the Constitution a special "higher law" flavor. I have attempted in this book to describe what those two terms—constitutional process and constitutional policy—comprise and what they should comprise in America in the 1970s. I have tried to show the delicate mesh of substance and procedure, the latticed fence of check and double-check that limits power but also makes a home for responsible power. Most of all, I have tried to show that the balanced policy is the taproot anchoring and nourishing our "Living Constitution." To the extent that we do not live up to that guiding force in our politics, we plant the seed of government by whim, by caprice, by force of habit, by benighted despot, or by mindless mass.

NOTES

1. Robert H. Salisbury, *Governing America* (New York: Appleton-Century-Crofts, 1973), p. 61.

2. David Easton, *A Systems Analysis of Political Life* (New York: John Wiley, 1965), p. 358.

3. Ibid.

4. Salisbury, p. 62.

5. William Reitzel et al., *United States Foreign Policy, 1945-1955* (Washington, D.C.: Brookings Institution, 1956), p. 473.

6. Harold D. Lasswell and Abraham Kaplan, *Power and Society* (New Haven: Yale Univ. Press, 1950), p. 71.

7. This brings me very close to Vernon Van Dyke, "Process and Policy as Focal Concepts in Political Research," in Austin Ranney, ed., *Political Science and Public Policy* (Chicago: Markham, 1968), pp. 27-28.

8. See the definitions developed in Austin Ranney, "The Study of Policy Content: A Framework for Choice," in Ranney, pp. 7-8, and Randall B. Ripley, *American National Government and Public Policy* (New York: The Free Press, 1974), p. 8.

9. Van Dyke, p. 29.

10. That is the mistake I think Salisbury makes when he describes constitutional policy as "decision rules by which subsequent policy actions are to be determined." Robert H. Salisbury, "The Analysis of Public Policy: A Search for Theories and Roles," in Ranney, p. 159.

11. Naturally I would include under the latter rubric the fundamental patterns of interplay between political parties, pressure aggregations, and voters, on the one hand, and governmental agencies, on the other. Compare Salisbury, p. 165, Figure 1.

I do not intend, however, to thrust the terms "policy" and "process" into mutually exclusive boxes. Certainly the emerging "right of privacy," located in the penumbra of the Constitution, must be classified as "constitutional policy." After all, what does the freedom to obtain an abortion have to do with procedural norms or guarantees? And every once in a while, someone advocates reforms in our constitutional processes as a matter of sound policy. Should the policy proposal become institutionalized, it then becomes part of the decisional process.

12. Carl J. Friedrich, *Man and His Government* (New York: McGraw-Hill, 1963), p. 79.

13. Lewis A. Froman, Jr., "The Categorization of Policy Contents," in Ranney, p. 46.

14. T. J. Lowi, "American Business, Public Policy, Case-Studies, and Political Theory," *World Politics* 15 (1964), pp. 677-715.

15. The following general works have been helpful to me in preparing this section: Alexander De Conde, *A History of American Foreign Policy* (New York: Charles Scribner's Sons, 1963); Thomas A. Bailey, *A Diplomatic History of the American People,* 9th ed. (Englewood Cliffs, N.J.: Prentice-Hall, 1974); and George F. Kennan, *American Diplomacy, 1900-1950* (New York: Mentor Books, 1951).

16. See especially Dexter Perkins, *The American Approach to Foreign Policy,* rev. ed. (Cambridge, Mass.: Harvard Univ. Press, 1962) and Frank Tannenbaum, *The American Tradition in Foreign Policy* (Norman: Univ. of Oklahoma Press, 1955).

17. *Congressional Record,* 92nd Cong., 1st Sess. (April 14, 1971), p. S4787.

18. The best statement on behalf of realism is Hans J. Morganthau, *In Defense of the National Interest* (New York: Knopf, 1951).

19. See Arnold Wolfers, "Statesmanship and Moral Choice," *World Politics,* 1 (1949), pp. 175-95.

20. Quoted in Samuel Flaggs Bemis, *A Diplomatic History of the United States,* 4th ed. (New York: Henry Holt, 1955), p. 109.

21. Quoted in De Conde, p. 440.

22. Quoted in Bemis, pp. 210-11.

23. Quoted in De Conde, p. 169.

24. De Conde, p. 364.

25. Kennan, p. 37.

26. William Y. Elliott et al., *United States Foreign Policy* (New York: Columbia Univ. Press, 1952), pp. 15-16.

27. See such works as William Appleman Williams, *The Tragedy of American Diplomacy* (Cleveland: World, 1959).

28. Quoted in De Conde, p. 661.

29. Kennan, p. 99. His famous article is "The Sources of Soviet Conduct," *Foreign Affairs* 25 (1947), pp. 566-82.

30. The speech is reprinted in Henry T. Nash, *American Foreign Policy: Response to a Sense of Threat* (Homewood, Ill.: Dorsey Press, 1973), pp. 215-20.

31. Quoted in Nash, p. 34.

32. Quoted in De Conde, p. 709.

33. *Military Situation in the Far East,* Hearings Before the Senate Foreign Relations and Armed Services Committees, 82nd Cong., 1st Sess., Part 1 (May 3, 1951), p. 68.

34. "Meet the Press," television interview (November 8, 1975). For a scholarly treatment of détente and its various attributes, see Statement by the Honorable Henry A. Kissinger, Secretary of State, Before the Senate Foreign Relations Committee (September 19, 1974).

35. Lincoln P. Bloomfield, *In Search of American Foreign Policy* (New York: Oxford Univ. Press, 1974), pp. 89-99. President Eisenhower's farewell address, in which he claimed that a vast amalgamation of industrial and military power was overspreading our national and international politics, can be found in the *Department of State Bulletin* 44, (February 6, 1961), pp. 179-82.

36. Raymond Aron, *The Imperial Republic* (Cambridge, Mass.: Winthrop Publishers, 1974), p. xi.

37. Bloomfield, pp. 17-26.

38. Robert W. Tucker, *A New Isolationism* (New York: Universe Books, 1972).

39. Walter Lippmann, *U.S. Foreign Policy: Shield of the Republic* (Boston: Little, Brown, 1943).

40. Henry A. Kissinger, *American Foreign Policy* (New York: W. W. Norton, 1969), pp.

57-58. Kissinger also talks of building a "moral consensus" and standards of "political legitimacy" (p. 84). Just what these touchstones might be is never delineated.

41. I have found the following general works valuable in preparing this section: Merle Fainsod, Lincoln Gordon, and Joseph C. Palamountain, Jr., *Government and the American Economy,* 3rd ed. (New York: W. W. Norton, 1959); William Letwin, *A Documentary History of American Economic Policy Since 1789* (Garden City, N.Y.: Anchor Books, 1961); Arthur Selwyn Miller, *The Supreme Court and American Capitalism* (New York: The Free Press, 1968).

42. Dissenting in *Lochner v. New York,* 198 U.S. 45 (1905) at p. 75. Herbert Spencer's book, which Holmes alludes to in this passage, was a bible for those advocating individual autonomy.

43. *Brown v. Maryland,* 12 Wheat. 419 (1827).

44. *Cooley v. Board of Wardens,* 12 How. 299 (1852).

45. *Michelin Tire Corp. v. Wages,* 423 U.S. 276 (1976).

46. Some of the Court's decisions in this area make generalizations difficult. For an extension of the "original package" concept which seems dubious, see *Dept. of Revenue v. Beam Distilling Co.,* 377 U.S. 341 (1964). For a diminution of "selective exclusiveness" which seems untenable, see *Bob-Lo Excursion Co. v. Michigan,* 333 U.S. 28 (1948).

47. Adolph A. Berle, Jr., *Power Without Property* (New York: Harcourt, Brace, 1959), p. 28.

48. This hiatus in "political" responsibility is well described by Adolph A. Berle, Jr., and Gardiner C. Means, *The Modern Corporation and Private Property* (New York: Macmillan, 1934).

49. *Dartmouth College v. Woodward,* 4 Wheat. 518 (1819).

50. *Home Building & Loan Ass'n. v. Blaisdell,* 290 U.S. 398 (1934).

51. *Santa Clara County v. Southern Pacific Ry. Co.,* 118 U.S. 394 (1886).

52. The relationship between stiff competition and monopoly is discounted in Joseph A. Schumpeter, *Capitalism, Socialism and Democracy,* 3rd ed. (New York: Harper, 1950), pp. 87-106. Schumpeter notes another source of monopoly not as yet enumerated here, *governmental policy.* Is not the Tennessee Valley Authority (T.V.A.) a gigantic, interlocking trust or monopoly? In a sense, statutes forbidding unfair competition are really attempts to stabilize the market against competitive uncertainty, and prudent entrepreneurs well understand this fact. T. J. Lowi, *The Politics of Disorder* (New York: W. W. Norton, 1974), pp. 21-31.

53. *Standard Oil Co. v. United States,* 221 U.S. 1 (1911).

54. *United States v. Paramount Pictures,* 334 U.S. 131 (1948).

55. John Paul Stevens, "The Regulation of Railroads," *American Bar Association Section of Antitrust Law* 19 (1961), p. 361; "Exemptions from Antitrust Coverage," in "Policy Against Undue Limitations on Competitive Conditions: A Symposium," *American Bar Association Antitrust Law Journal* 37 (1968), p. 631.

56. *Adolph Coors Co. v. F.T.C.,* 497 F. 2d 1178 (1974).

57. Fainsod, Gordon, and Palamountain, p. 550.

58. *Williamson v. Lee Optical Co.,* 348 U.S. 483 (1955). An exception would be a statute that somehow violated a specific constitutional freedom, such as the First Amendment.

59. Quoted in Fainsod, Gordon, and Palamountain, pp. 805-06. The alternative policy positions favored by various interests advocating and opposing this legislative milestone are described in Stephen K. Bailey, *Congress Makes a Law* (New York: Columbia Univ. Press, 1950).

60. Keynes's most influential work was *The General Theory of Employment, Interest and Money* (New York: Harcourt, Brace, 1935).

61. There is general understanding that the "full employment" test has been satisfied when 96 percent of the total labor force is on the job. Berle, p. 122.

62. J. K. Galbraith, *American Capitalism: A System of Countervailing Power* (Boston: Houghton Mifflin, 1952).

63. A. M. Schlesinger, Jr., *A Thousand Days* (New York: Houghton Mifflin, 1965). For the best response by a contemporary conservative philosopher to these nagging problems, see the works of Milton Friedman, especially *Capitalism and Freedom* (Chicago: Univ. of Chicago Press, 1962).

64. Somewhat along the same line are William H. Whyte, *The Organization Man* (New York: Simon and Schuster, 1956) and Kenneth E. Boulding, *The Organizational Revolution* (New York: Harper & Row, 1953).

65. See Henry S. Kariel, *The Decline of American Pluralism* (Stanford, Calif.: Stanford Univ. Press, 1961) and T. J. Lowi, *The End of Liberalism* (New York: W. W. Norton, 1969).

66. For the impact of science on the constitutional order, see Don K. Price, *The Scientific Estate* (Cambridge, Mass.: Harvard Univ. Press, 1965).

67. *Harper v. Virginia Bd. of Elections*, 383 U.S. 663 (1966). See also the discussion in Chapter 6 with respect to equal protection and Chapter 10 with respect to voting rights.

68. *Bullock v. Carter*, 405 U.S. 134 (1972).

69. *James v. Valtierra*, 402 U.S. 137 (1971).

70. *Shapiro v. Thompson*, 394 U.S. 618 (1969).

71. *Memorial Hospital v. Maricopa County*, 415 U.S. 250 (1974).

72. *Sosna v. Iowa*, 419 U.S. 393 (1975); *Dandridge v. Williams*, 397 U.S. 471 (1970).

73. *Griffin v. Illinois*, 351 U.S. 12 (1956).

74. *Tate v. Short*, 401 U.S. 395 (1971).

75. *Boddie v. Connecticut*, 401 U.S. 371 (1971).

76. *Goldberg v. Kelly*, 397 U.S. 254 (1970).

77. *Perry v. Sindermann*, 408 U.S. 593 (1972); *Board of Regents v. Roth*, 408 U.S. 564 (1972).

78. *San Antonio School Dist. v. Rodriguez*, 411 U.S. 1 (1973). For research disapproving the theory of *substantive equal protection*, a conclusion shared by the Court in this case, see Wallace Mendelson, "From Warren to Burger: The Rise and Decline of Substantive Equal Protection," *The American Political Science Review* 66 (1972), pp. 1226-33.

79. Charles A. Reich, "The New Property," *The Yale Law Journal* 73 (1964), pp. 733-87; "The Law of the Planned Society," *The Yale Law Journal* 75 (1966), pp. 1227-70.

80. *Weinberger v. Salfi*, 95 S.Ct. 2457 at p. 2470 (1975).

81. *Marsh v. Alabama*, 326 U.S. 501 (1946).

82. *Lloyd Corp. v. Tanner*, 407 U.S. 551 (1972); *Hudgens v. N.L.R.B.*, 96 S.Ct. 1029 (1976).

83. *Jackson v. Metropolitan Edison Co.*, 419 U.S. 345 (1974).

84. Adolph A. Berle, Jr., "Constitutional Limitations on Corporate Activity—Protection of Personal Rights from Invasion Through Economic Power," *University of Pennsylvania Law Review* 100 (1952), pp. 933-55.

85. Miller, p. 143.

86. *United States v. Cruikshank*, 92 U.S. 542 (1876); *United States v. Harris*, 106 U.S. 629 (1882).

87. 109 U.S. 3 (1883).

88. Ibid., p. 24.

89. Exception: As I noted in Chapter 10, Congress has power under Article I, Section 4 to regulate the "times, places and manner" of choosing House and Senate members. *Anyone* trying to keep blacks from participating in that process runs afoul of federal statutes the Court has traditionally upheld. *Ex parte Yarbrough*, 110 U.S. 651 (1884). Furthermore, the necessary and proper clause allows Congress to punish anyone who attacks federal officials. See, for example, *Logan v. United States*, 144 U.S. 263 (1892). So the 1870 enactment outlawing conspiracies by private persons to deprive individuals of their federal rights were—*and are*—applicable to such situations.

90. This declaration became known as *Brown II*. Official citation: *Brown v. Bd. of Ed.*, 349 U.S. 294 (1955).

91. Donald R. Matthews and James W. Prothro, "Stateways versus Folkways: Criti-

cal Factors in Southern Reactions to *Brown v. Board of Education,*" in Gottfried Dietze, ed., *Essays on the American Constitution* (Englewood Cliffs, N.J.: Prentice-Hall, 1964), pp. 139-56. The authors point out correctly that voting rights for blacks might well have played a much greater role in speeding school desegregation in the Border states, whereas discriminatory literacy tests and the like made black voting power considerably less effective in the South itself.

92. The generally slow pace of public-agency desegregation has been summarized as follows: "Some cities and towns have not discontinued discrimination until pressured to do so by either protestors or some arm of the government." Harrell R. Rodgers, Jr., and Charles S. Bullock III, *Law and Social Change* (New York: McGraw-Hill, 1972), p. 57.

93. These reports have included the following: Commission on Civil Rights, *Voting* (Washington, D.C.: Government Printing Office, 1961); *Civil Rights* (Washington, D.C.: Government Printing Office, 1963); *Political Participation* (Washington, D.C.: Government Printing Office, 1968).

94. Rodgers and Bullock, p. 25.

95. Donald R. Matthews and James W. Prothro, "Social and Economic Factors and Negro Voter Registration in the South," *The American Political Science Review* 57 (1963), pp. 24-44; "Political Factors and Negro Voter Registration in the South," *The American Political Science Review* 57 (1963), pp. 355-67.

96. See Clement Vose's fine study *Caucasians Only: The Supreme Court, the NAACP, and the Restrictive Covenant Cases* (Berkeley: Univ. of California Press, 1959).

97. Some "new left" representatives date the inception of the entire counterculture movement from that moment. Mitchell Goodman, *The Movement Toward a New America* (Philadelphia: Pilgrim Press, 1970), p. x.

98. *Bell v. Maryland,* 378 U.S. 226 (1964); compare *Peterson v. Greenville,* 373 U.S. 244 (1963) and *Lombard v. Louisiana,* 373 U.S. 267 (1963).

99. *Heart of Atlanta Motel v. United States,* 379 U.S. 241 (1964); *Katzenbach v. McClung,* 379 U.S. 294 (1964).

100. *South Carolina v. Katzenbach,* 383 U.S. 301 (1966).

101. *Oregon v. Mitchell,* 400 U.S. 112 (1970).

102. Rodgers and Bullock, p. 83.

103. *Statistical Abstract of the United States* (Washington, D.C.: Government Printing Office, 1974), p. 124.

104. *United States v. Price,* 383 U.S. 787 (1966).

105. *United States v. Guest,* 383 U.S. 745 (1966).

106. *Jones v. Alfred H. Mayer Co.,* 392 U.S. 409 (1968). For a more recent decision combining the logic of the *Guest* and *Jones* cases, see *Griffin v. Breckenridge,* 403 U.S. 88 (1971).

107. *Alexander v. Holmes,* 396 U.S. 19 (1969).

108. *Rodgers and Bullock,* pp. 130-32.

109. The term is used often in legal and constitutional parlance, yet I have seen no generally agreed-upon definition. For a different view as to its elements, see Rodgers and Bullock, pp. 164-65.

110. Ibid., p. 125.

111. *Congress and the Nation,* vol. III, 1969-72, p. 711.

112. See Revised Order No. 4, *Federal Register,* 36, no. 234 (1971). For the academic-employment context, see "Higher Education Guidelines," Department of Health, Education, and Welfare (1972). The italics in this paragraph are mine.

113. This is the famous *Swann* decision, discussed in Chapter 6.

114. This is the famous *Milliken* decision, discussed in Chapter 6.

115. J. D. Aberbach and J. L. Walker, "Political Trust and Racial Ideology," *The American Political Science Review* 64 (1970), pp. 1208-09.

116. *Moose Lodge v. Irvis,* 407 U.S. 163 (1972).

117. *DeFunis v. Odegaard,* 94 S.Ct. 1704 (1974).

118. The figure for black students attending segregated public schools in the South is 54 percent. The Civil Rights Commission, true to hard-core affirmative action philosophy, defines an integrated facility as one that serves a majority-white student clientele. Commission on Civil Rights, *Twenty Years After Brown* (Washington, D.C.: Government Printing Office, 1975).

119. Compare Ada W. Finifter, "Dimensions of Political Alienation," *The American Political Science Review* 64 (1970), pp. 389–410, with Aberbach and Walker, "Political Trust and Racial Ideology."

bibliography

Books and Pamphlets

A.B.A. Project on Minimal Standards for Criminal Justice. *Fair Trial and Free Press,* 1966.

Abraham, Henry J. *The Judicial Process,* 2nd ed. New York: Oxford Univ. Press, 1968.

Advisory Commission on Intergovernmental Relations. *Fiscal Balance in the American Federal System.* Washington, D.C.: Government Printing Office, 1967.

Altshuler, Alan A., ed. *The Politics of the Federal Bureaucracy.* New York: Dodd, Mead, 1971.

Appleby, Paul. *Policy and Administration.* University: Univ. of Alabama Press, 1949.

Aron, Raymond. *The Imperial Republic.* Cambridge, Mass.: Winthrop Publishers, 1974.

Bailey, Stephen K. *Congress Makes a Law.* New York: Columbia Univ. Press, 1950.

Bailey, Thomas A. *A Diplomatic History of the American People,* 9th ed. Englewood Cliffs, N.J.: Prentice-Hall, 1974.

Bailyn, Bernard. *The Ideological Origins of the American Revolution.* Cambridge, Mass.: Harvard Univ. Press, 1967.

Banfield, Edward C. *The Unheavenly City.* Boston: Little, Brown, 1970.

Barber, James A., Jr. *Social Mobility and Voting Behavior.* Chicago: Rand McNally, 1970.

Barber, James David. *The Presidential Character.* Englewood Cliffs, N.J.: Prentice-Hall, 1972.

Barnard, Chester I. *The Functions of the Executive.* Cambridge, Mass.: Harvard Univ. Press, 1938.

Bauer, Raymond A.; Pool, Ithiel de Sola; and Dexter, Lewis A. *American Business and Public Policy.* New York: Atherton Press, 1963.

Beard, Charles A. *An Economic Interpretation of the Constitution of the United States.* New York: Macmillan, 1913.

Bemis, Samuel Flagg. *A Diplomatic History of the United States,* 4th ed. New York: Henry Holt, 1955.

Bentley, Arthur. *The Process of Government.* Chicago: Univ. of Chicago Press, 1908.

Berdahl, Clarence A. *War Powers of the Executive in the United States.* Urbana: Univ. of Illinois, 1921.

Berger, Raoul. *Executive Privilege: A Constitutional Myth.* Cambridge, Mass.: Harvard Univ. Press, 1974.

———. *Impeachment: The Constitutional Problems.* Cambridge, Mass.: Harvard Univ. Press, 1973.

Berle, Adolph A., Jr. *Power Without Property.* New York: Harcourt, Brace & World, 1959.

Berle, Adolph A., Jr., and Means, Gardiner C. *The Modern Corporation and Private Property.* New York: Macmillan, 1934.

Berns, Walter. "The Meaning of the Tenth Amendment." In Robert A. Goldwin, ed., *A Nation of States.* Chicago: Rand McNally, 1963, pp. 126–48.

Bernstein, Marver. *Regulating Business by Independent Commission.* Princeton, N.J.: Princeton Univ. Press, 1955.

Binkley, Wilfred E. *American Political Parties: Their Natural History,* 5th ed. New York: Alfred A. Knopf, 1965.

Black, Charles L., Jr. *Capital Punishment: The Inevitability of Caprice and Mistake.* New York: W. W. Norton, 1974.

Blackstone, Sir William. *Commentaries on the Laws of England.* Edited by William Carey Jones. San Francisco: Bancroft-Whitney, 1916.

Bloomfield, Lincoln P. *In Search of American Foreign Policy.* New York: Oxford Univ. Press, 1974.

Blumberg, Abraham. *Criminal Justice.* New York: Quadrangle Books, 1967.

Boulding, Kenneth E. *The Organizational Revolution.* New York: Harper & Row, 1953.

Brown, Robert E. *Charles Beard and the Constitution.* Princeton, N.J.: Princeton Univ. Press, 1956.

Bureau of the Census. *1970 Census Users' Guide.* Washington, D.C.: Government Printing Office, 1970.

Burns, James MacGregor. *The Deadlock of Democracy.* Englewood Cliffs, N.J.: Prentice-Hall, 1964.

Cahn, Edmond, ed. *Supreme Court and Supreme Law.* Bloomington: Indiana Univ. Press, 1954.

Campbell, Angus. "Surge and Decline: A Study in Electoral Change." In Angus Campbell, Philip E. Converse, Warren E. Miller, and Donald E. Stokes, *Elections and the Political Order.* New York: John Wiley, 1966.

Campbell, Angus; Converse, Philip E.; Miller, Warren E.; and Stokes, Donald E. *The American Voter.* New York: John Wiley, 1960.

Carmen, Ira H. *Movies, Censorship, and the Law.* Ann Arbor: Univ. of Michigan Press, 1966.

Carr, Robert K. *The Supreme Court and Judicial Review.* New York: Rinehart, 1942.

Casper, Jonathan D. *Lawyers Before the Warren Court.* Urbana: Univ. of Illinois Press, 1972.

Civil Service Commission. *Characteristics of the Federal Executive,* February 1968.

Clausen, Aage R. *How Congressmen Decide.* New York: St. Martin's Press, 1973.

Commager, Henry Steele, ed. *Documents of American History,* 5th ed. New York: Appleton-Century-Crofts, 1959.

Commission on Civil Rights. *Civil Rights.* Washington, D.C.: Government Printing Office, 1963.

Commission on Civil Rights. *Political Participation.* Washington, D.C.: Government Printing Office, 1968.

Commission on Civil Rights. *Twenty Years After Brown.* Washington, D.C.: Government Printing Office, 1975.

Commission on Civil Rights. *Voting.* Washington, D.C.: Government Printing Office, 1961.

Commission on Organization of the Executive Branch of the Government. *Concluding Report, A Report to the Congress.* Washington, D.C.: Government Printing Office, 1949.

Commission on Organization of the Executive Branch of the Government. *Final Report to the Congress.* Washington, D.C.: Government Printing Office, 1955.

Commission on Organization of the Executive Branch of the Government. *General Management of the Executive Branch, A Report to the Congress.* Washington, D.C.: Government Printing Office, 1949.

Commission on Organization of the Executive Branch of the Government. *Task Force Report, Personnel and Civil Service,* February 1955.

Commission on Party Structure and Delegate Selection. *Mandate for Reform.* Washington, D.C.: Democratic National Committee, 1970.

Commons, John R. *Representative Democracy.* New York: Bureau of Economic Research, n.d.

Cooley, Thomas M. *Principles of Constitutional Law,* 3rd ed. Boston: Little, Brown, 1898.

Corwin, Edward S. *The "Higher Law" Background of American Constitutional Law.* Ithaca, N.Y.: Cornell Univ. Press, 1957.

———. *The President: Office and Powers, 1787-1957.* New York: New York Univ. Press, 1957.

———. *The Twilight of the Supreme Court.* New Haven: Yale Univ. Press, 1934.

Cralle, Richard, ed. *The Works of John C. Calhoun.* Columbia, S.C.: A. S. Johnston, 1851.

Dahl, Robert A. *Congress and Foreign Policy.* New York: W. W. Norton, 1950.

Danelski, David J. *A Supreme Court Justice Is Appointed.* New York: Random House, 1965.

———. "The Chicago Conspiracy Trial." In Theodore L. Becker, ed., *Political Trials.* Indianapolis: Bobbs-Merrill, 1971, pp. 134-80.

———. "The Influence of the Chief Justice in the Decisional Process." In Herman C. Pritchett and Walter F. Murphy, eds., *Courts, Judges, and Politics,* 2nd ed. New York: Random House, 1974, pp. 525-34.

De Conde, Alexander. *A History of American Foreign Policy.* New York: Charles Scribner's Sons, 1963.

Dionisopoulos, P. Allen. *Rebellion, Racism, and Representation.* DeKalb: Northern Illinois Univ. Press, 1970.

Dixon, Robert G., Jr. *Democratic Representation.* New York: Oxford Univ. Press, 1968.

Dolbeare, Kenneth M. "The Federal District Court and Urban Public Policy." In Joel B. Grossman and Joseph Tanenhaus, eds., *Frontiers of Judicial Research.* New York: John Wiley, 1969, pp. 373-404.

Easton, David. *A Systems Analysis of Political Life.* New York: John Wiley, 1965.

Eckstein, Harry. *Pressure Group Politics.* Stanford, Calif.: Stanford Univ. Press, 1960.

Ehrlich, Eugen. *Fundamental Principles of the Sociology of Law.* New York: Russell and Russell, 1962.

Elazar, Daniel J. *American Federalism: A View from the States,* 2nd ed. New York: Thomas Y. Crowell, 1972.

———. *The American Partnership.* Chicago: Univ. of Chicago Press, 1962.

Eldersveld, Samuel J. *Political Parties: A Behavioral Analysis.* Chicago: Rand McNally, 1964.

Elliff, John T. *Crime, Dissent, and the Attorney General.* Beverly Hills, Calif.: Sage Publications, 1971.

Elliott, William Y., et al. *United States Foreign Policy.* New York: Columbia Univ. Press, 1952.

Erikson, Robert S., and Luttbeg, Norman R. *American Public Opinion: Its Origins, Content, and Impact.* New York: John Wiley, 1973.

Fainsod, Merle; Gordon, Lincoln; and Palamountain, Joseph C., Jr. *Government and the American Economy,* 3rd ed. New York: W. W. Norton, 1959.

Farrand, Max. *The Records of the Federal Convention.* New York: Henry Holt, 1937.

Faulkner, Robert K. *The Jurisprudence of John Marshall.* Princeton, N.J.: Princeton Univ. Press, 1968.

Fellman, David. *The Defendant's Rights.* New York: Rinehart, 1958.

Fenno, Richard F., Jr. *Congressmen in Committees.* Boston: Little, Brown, 1973.

———. *The Power of the Purse.* Boston: Little, Brown, 1966.

———. *The President's Cabinet.* Cambridge, Mass.: Harvard Univ. Press, 1959.

Fish, Peter G. *The Politics of Federal Judicial Administration.* Princeton, N.J.: Princeton Univ. Press, 1973.

Flanigan, William H. *Political Behavior of the American Electorate,* 2nd ed. Boston: Allyn and Bacon, 1972.

Frank, Jerome. *Courts on Trial.* Princeton, N.J.: Princeton Univ. Press, 1950.

———. *Law and the Modern Mind.* New York: Coward-McCann, 1930.

Frank, John P. "Review and Basic Liberties." In Edmond Cahn, ed., *Supreme Court and Supreme Law.* Bloomington: Indiana Univ. Press, 1954, pp. 109-39.

Friedman, Milton. *Capitalism and Freedom.* Chicago: Univ. of Chicago Press, 1962.

Friedrich, Carl J. *Man and His Government.* New York: McGraw-Hill, 1963.

Froman, Lewis A., Jr. "The Categorization of Policy Contents." In Austin Ranney, ed., *Political Science and Public Policy.* Chicago: Markham, 1968, pp. 41-52.

———. *The Congressional Process.* Boston: Little, Brown, 1967.

Galbraith, John Kenneth. *American Capitalism: A System of Countervailing Power.* Boston: Houghton Mifflin, 1952.

Galloway, George B. *History of the House of Representatives.* New York: Thomas Y. Crowell, 1962.

Gallup, George H. *The Gallup Poll.* New York: Random House, 1972.

Gerth, H. H., and Mills, C. Wright, eds. *From Max Weber: Essays in Sociology.* New York: Oxford Univ. Press, 1946.

Goldman, Sheldon, and Jahnige, Thomas P. *The Federal Courts as a Political System,* 2nd ed. New York: Harper & Row, 1976.

Goodman, Mitchell. *The Movement Toward A New America.* Philadelphia: Pilgrim Press, 1970.

Goodnow, Frank. *Politics and Administration: A Study in Government.* New York: Macmillan, 1900.

Graves, W. Brooks. *Intergovernmental Relations in the United States.* New York: Charles Scribner's Sons, 1964.

Griffith, Ernest. *Congress: Its Contemporary Role.* New York: New York Univ. Press, 1951.

———. *The Impasse of Democracy.* New York: Harrison-Hilton, 1939.

Grodzins, Morton. "Centralization and Decentralization in the American Federal System." In Robert A. Goldwin, ed., *A Nation of States.* Chicago: Rand McNally, 1963, pp. 1-23.

Grossman, Joel B. *Lawyers and Judges.* New York: John Wiley, 1965.

Halberstam, David. *The Best and the Brightest.* New York: Random House, 1972.

Hamilton, Alexander; Jay, John; and Madison, James. *The Federalist.* New York: Modern Library, n.d.

Harris, Richard. *Justice.* New York: E. P. Dutton, 1970.

Hartz, Louis. *The Liberal Tradition in America.* New York: Harcourt, Brace & World, 1955.

Heller, Walter W. *New Dimensions of Political Economy.* Cambridge, Mass.: Harvard Univ. Press, 1966.

Heller, Walter W.; Ruggles, Richard; et al. *Revenue Sharing and the City.* Baltimore: The Johns Hopkins Univ. Press, 1968.

Herring, E. Pendleton. *The Politics of Democracy.* New York: W. W. Norton, 1940.

Hinckley, Barbara. *The Seniority System in Congress.* Bloomington: Indiana Univ. Press, 1971.

Hirschfield, Robert S., ed. *The Power of the Presidency.* 2nd ed. Chicago: Aldine, 1973.

Holcombe, Arthur N. *The Constitutional System.* Chicago: Scott, Foresman, 1964.

Holt, John C. *Freedom and Beyond.* New York: E. P. Dutton, 1973.

Hook, Sidney. *Heresy, Yes—Conspiracy, No!* New York: J. Day, 1953.

Horwill, Herbert W. *The Usages of the American Constitution.* London: Oxford Univ. Press, H. Milford, 1925.

Hunt, Gaillard, ed. *The Writings of James Madison.* New York: G. P. Putnam's Sons, 1901.

Illich, Ivan D. *Deschooling Society.* New York: Harper & Row, 1971.

Jacob, Herbert. *Justice in America,* 2nd ed. Boston: Little, Brown, 1972.

James, Howard. *Crisis in the Courts,* rev. ed. New York: David McKay, 1971.

Javits, Jacob K. *Who Makes War?* New York: William Morrow, 1973.

Johnston, Henry P., ed. *The Correspondence and Public Papers of John Jay.* New York: G. P. Putnam's Sons, 1890-93.

Kallenbach, Joseph E. *The American Chief Executive.* New York: Harper & Row, 1966.

Kalven, Harry S., and Zeisel, Hans. *The American Jury.* Boston: Little, Brown, 1966.

Kariel, Henry S. *The Decline of American Pluralism.* Stanford, Calif.: Stanford Univ. Press, 1961.

Karlen, Delmar. *The Citizen in Court.* New York: Holt, Rinehart and Winston, 1965.

Kaufman, Herbert. "The Growth of the Federal Personnel System." In Wallace Sayre, ed., *The Federal Government Service,* 2nd ed. Englewood Cliffs, N.J.: Prentice-Hall, 1965, pp. 58-69.

Kelly, Alfred H. "Clio and the Court: An Illicit Love Affair." In Philip B. Kurland, ed., *The Supreme Court Review.* Chicago: University of Chicago Press, 1965, pp. 119-58.

Kelly, Alfred H., and Harbison, Winfred A. *The American Constitution,* rev. ed. New York: W. W. Norton, 1955.

Kennan, George F. *American Diplomacy, 1900-1950.* New York: Mentor Books, 1951.

Kennedy, Florynce. "The Whorehouse Theory of Law." In Robert Lefcourt, ed., *Law Against the People.* New York: Random House, 1971, pp. 81-89.

Key, V. O., Jr. *American State Politics.* New York: Alfred A. Knopf, 1956.

———. *Politics, Parties, and Pressure Groups,* 5th ed. New York: Thomas Y. Crowell, 1964.

———. *Public Opinion and American Democracy.* New York: Alfred A. Knopf, 1961.

———. *The Responsible Electorate.* Cambridge, Mass.: Harvard Univ. Press, 1966.

Keynes, John Maynard. *The General Theory of Employment, Interest and Money.* New York: Harcourt, Brace, 1935.

Kingdon, John W. *Congressmen's Voting Decisions.* New York: Harper & Row, 1973.

Kissinger, Henry A. *American Foreign Policy.* New York: W. W. Norton, 1969.

Koenig, Louis W. *The Chief Executive,* 3rd ed. New York: Harcourt Brace Jovanovich, 1975.

Konefsky, Samuel J. *John Marshall and Alexander Hamilton.* New York: Macmillan, 1964.

Kornhauser, William. *The Politics of Mass Society.* Glencoe, Ill.: The Free Press, 1959.

Kozol, Jonathan. *The Night Is Dark and I Am Far From Home.* Boston: Houghton Mifflin, 1976.

Krasnow, Erwin G., and Longley, Laurence D. *The Politics of Broadcast Regulation.* New York: St. Martin's Press, 1973.

Krislov, Samuel. *The Supreme Court in the Political Process.* New York: Macmillan, 1965.

Kurland, Philip B. *Politics, the Constitution, and the Warren Court.* Chicago: Univ. of Chicago Press, 1970.

Lane, Robert E. *Political Life.* Glencoe, Ill.: The Free Press, 1959.

Lasswell, Harold D., and Kaplan, Abraham. *Power and Society.* New Haven: Yale Univ. Press, 1950.

Leach, Richard H. *American Federalism.* New York: W. W. Norton, 1970.

Letwin, William. *A Documentary History of American Economic Policy Since 1789.* Garden City, N.Y.: Anchor Books, 1961.

Lewis, Anthony. *Gideon's Trumpet.* New York: Random House, 1964.

Lippmann, Walter. *U.S. Foreign Policy: Shield of the Republic.* Boston: Little, Brown, 1943.

Lipset, Seymour M. *Union Democracy.* Glencoe, Ill.: The Free Press, 1956.

Lodge, Henry Cabot, ed. *The Works of Alexander Hamilton,* 2nd ed. New York: G. P. Putnam's Sons, 1903.

Lowi, Theodore J. *The End of Liberalism.* New York: W. W. Norton, 1969.

———. *The Politics of Disorder.* New York: W. W. Norton, 1974.

Macmahon, Arthur, and Millett, John D. *Federal Administrators.* New York: Columbia Univ. Press, 1939.

MacRae, Duncan, Jr. *Dimensions of Congressional Voting.* Berkeley: Univ. of California Press, 1958.

Magrath, C. Peter. "The Obscenity Cases: Grapes of *Roth.*" In Philip B. Kurland, ed., *The Supreme Court Review.* Chicago: Univ. of Chicago Press, 1966, pp. 7-77.

Mainzer, Lewis C. *Political Bureaucracy.* Glenview, Ill.: Scott, Foresman, 1973.

Manley, John. *The Politics of Finance.* Boston: Little, Brown, 1970.

Mason, Alpheus Thomas. *The States Rights Debate: Antifederalism and the Constitution.* Englewood Cliffs, N.J.: Prentice-Hall, 1964.

———. *The Supreme Court From Taft to Warren.* Baton Rouge: Louisiana State Univ. Press, 1958.

Matthews, Donald R., and Prothro, James W. "Stateways Versus Folkways: Critical Factors in Southern Reaction to *Brown v. Board of Education.*" In Gottfried Dietze, ed., *Essays on the American Constitution.* Englewood Cliffs, N.J.: Prentice-Hall, 1964, pp. 139-56.

Mayhew, David L. *Congress: The Electoral Connection.* New Haven: Yale Univ. Press, 1974.

McCloskey, Robert G. *The American Supreme Court.* Chicago: Univ. of Chicago Press, 1960.

McConnell, Grant. *Private Power and American Democracy.* New York: Alfred A. Knopf, 1966.

McIlwain, C. H. *The American Revolution.* New York: Macmillan, 1923.

McKitrick, Eric L. *Andrew Johnson and Reconstruction.* Chicago: Univ. of Chicago Press, 1960.

Meiklejohn, Alexander. *Free Speech and Its Relation to Self-Government.* New York: Harper & Brothers, 1948.

Michels, Robert. *Political Parties.* London: Jarrold & Sons, 1915. Reprinted by The Free Press, Glencoe, Ill., 1949.

Milbrath, Lester W. *The Washington Lobbyists.* Chicago: Rand McNally, 1963.

Miller, Arthur Selwyn. *The Supreme Court and American Capitalism.* New York: The Free Press, 1968.

Mills, C. Wright. *The Power Elite.* New York: Oxford Univ. Press, 1956.

Morganthau, Hans J. *In Defense of the National Interest.* New York: Alfred A. Knopf, 1951.

Murphy, Walter F. *Elements of Judicial Strategy.* Chicago: Univ. of Chicago Press, 1964.

———. "In His Own Image: Mr. Chief Justice Taft and Supreme Court Appointments." In Philip B. Kurland, ed., *The Supreme Court Review.* Chicago: Univ. of Chicago Press, 1961, pp. 159-93.

Murphy, Walter F., and Tanenhaus, Joseph. *The Study of Public Law.* New York: Random House, 1972.

Myrdal, Gunnar. *An American Dilemma.* New York: Public Affairs Committee, 1944.

Nash, Henry T. *American Foreign Policy: Response to a Sense of Threat.* Homewood, Ill.: Dorsey Press, 1973.

Nathan, Richard P., et al. *Monitoring Revenue Sharing.* Washington, D.C.: Brookings Institution, 1975.

Navasky, Victor S. *Kennedy Justice.* New York: Atheneum, 1971.

Neubauer, David W. *Criminal Justice in Middle America.* Morristown, N.J.: General Learning Press, 1974.

Nicolay, John, and Hay, John, eds. *The Complete Works of Abraham Lincoln.* New York: F. D. Tandy, 1894.

Nie, Norman H.; Verba, Sidney; and Petrocik, John R. *The Changing American Voter.* Cambridge, Mass.: Harvard Univ. Press, 1976.

Olson, Mancur. *The Logic of Collective Action.* Cambridge, Mass.: Harvard Univ. Press, 1971.

Orfield, Gary. *Congressional Power: Congress and Social Change.* New York: Harcourt Brace Jovanovich, 1975.

Ostrogorski, M. *Democracy and the Party System in the United States.* New York: Macmillan, 1910.

Peltason, Jack W. *58 Lonely Men.* New York: Harcourt, Brace & World, 1961.

Perkins, Dexter. *The American Approach to Foreign Policy,* rev. ed. Cambridge, Mass.: Harvard Univ. Press, 1962.

Polsby, Nelson W. *Congress and the Presidency,* 3rd ed. Englewood Cliffs, N.J.: Prentice-Hall, 1976.

Pomper, Gerald. *Voters' Choice.* New York: Dodd, Mead, 1975.

Post, Charles G. *The Supreme Court and Political Questions.* Baltimore: The John Hopkins Univ. Press, 1936.

Price, Don K. *The Scientific Estate.* Cambridge, Mass.: Harvard Univ. Press, 1965.

Pritchett, C. Herman. *Civil Liberties and the Vinson Court.* Chicago: Univ. of Chicago Press, 1954.

———. *The Roosevelt Court.* New York: Macmillan, 1948.

Radway, Laurence I. *Foreign Policy and National Defense.* Glenview, Ill.: Scott, Foresman, 1969.

Randall, James G. *Constitutional Problems Under Lincoln.* Urbana: Univ. of Illinois Press, 1951.

Ranney, Austin, ed. *Political Science and Public Policy.* Chicago: Markham, 1968.

Reagan, Michael D. *The New Federalism.* New York: Oxford Univ. Press, 1972.

Reitzel, William, et al. *United States Foreign Policy, 1945–1955.* Washington, D.C.: Brookings Institution, 1956.

Report of the Commission on Obscenity and Pornography, The. New York: Bantam Books, 1970.

Report of the President's Committee on Administrative Management, 1937.

Richardson, James D. *Messages and Papers of the Presidents.* Washington, D.C.: Government Printing Office, 1896.

Richardson, Richard J., and Vines, Kenneth N. *The Politics of Federal Courts.* Boston: Little, Brown, 1970.

Riker, William H. *Federalism.* Boston: Little, Brown, 1964.

Ripley, Randall B. *American National Government and Public Policy.* New York: The Free Press, 1974.

———. *Congress: Process and Policy.* New York: W. W. Norton, 1975.

———. *Party Leaders in the House of Representatives.* Washington, D.C.: Brookings Institution, 1967.

———. *Power in the Senate.* New York: St. Martin's Press, 1969.

Rivlin, Alice M. *Systematic Thinking for Social Action.* Washington, D.C.: Brookings Institution, 1971.

Robinson, James. *The House Rules Committee.* Indianapolis: Bobbs-Merrill, 1963.

Rockefeller, Nelson A. *The Future of Federalism.* Cambridge, Mass.: Harvard Univ. Press, 1962.

Rodgers, Harrell R., Jr., and Bullock, Charles S., III. *Law and Social Change.* New York: McGraw-Hill, 1972.

Roosevelt, Theodore. *An Autobiography.* New York: Macmillan, 1916.

Rossiter, Clinton. *The American Presidency,* 2nd ed. New York: Harcourt, Brace & World, 1960.

Rourke, Francis E., ed. *Bureaucratic Power in National Politics.* Boston: Little, Brown, 1967.

Salisbury, Robert H. *Governing America.* New York: Appleton-Century-Crofts, 1973.

———. "The Analysis of Public Policy: A Search for Theories and Roles." In Austin Ranney, ed., *Political Science and Public Policy.* Chicago: Markham, 1968, pp. 151–75.

Sanford, Terry. *Storm Over the States.* New York: McGraw-Hill, 1967.

Schattschneider, E. E. *Party Government.* New York: Farrar and Rinehart, 1942.

Schick, Marvin. *Learned Hand's Court.* Baltimore: The Johns Hopkins Press, 1970.

Schlesinger, Arthur M., Jr. *A Thousand Days.* New York: Houghton Mifflin, 1965.

Schubert, Glendon. *Judicial Policy Making,* rev. ed. Glenview, Ill.: Scott, Foresman, 1974.

———. *The Judicial Mind.* Evanston, Ill.: Northwestern Univ. Press, 1965.

Schumpeter, Joseph A. *Capitalism, Socialism and Democracy,* 3rd ed. New York: Harper, 1950.

Schuyler, Robert L. *The Constitution of the United States.* London: Macmillan, 1923.

Seasholes, Bradbury, ed. *Voting, Interest Groups, and Parties.* Glenview, Ill.: Scott, Foresman, 1966.

Seidman, Harold. *Politics, Position, and Power: The Dynamics of Federal Organization,* 2nd ed. New York: Oxford Univ. Press, 1975.

Simon, Herbert. *Administrative Behavior,* 2d ed. New York: Macmillan, 1957.

Simon, James F. *In His Own Image.* New York: David McKay, 1973.

Solberg, Winton U. *The Federal Convention and the Formation of the Union of the American States.* New York: The Liberal Arts Press, 1958.

Sorauf, Frank J. *Party Politics in America.* Boston: Little, Brown, 1968.

Sorensen, Theodore C. *Kennedy.* New York: Harper & Row, 1965.

Storing, Herbert J., ed. *Essays on the Scientific Study of Politics.* New York: Holt, Rinehart and Winston, 1962.

Story, Joseph. *Commentaries on the Constitution.* Cambridge, Mass.: Brown, Shattuck, 1833.

Sullivan, Denis G.; Pressman, Jeffrey L.; Page, Benjamin I.; and Lyons, John J. *The Politics of Representation.* New York: St. Martin's Press, 1974.

Sundquist, James L. *Making Federalism Work.* Washington, D.C.: Brookings Institution, 1969.

———. *Politics and Policy.* Washington, D.C.: Brookings Institution, 1968.

Swisher, Carl B. *American Constitutional Development.* Boston: Houghton Mifflin, 1943.

Taft, William Howard. *Our Chief Magistrate and His Powers.* New York: Columbia Univ. Press, 1925.

Tannenbaum, Frank. *The American Tradition in Foreign Policy.* Norman: Univ. of Oklahoma Press, 1955.

Tiffany, Lawrence P., et al. *Detection of Crime.* Boston: Little, Brown, 1967.

Tocqueville, Alexis de. *Democracy in America.* London: Saunders and Otley, 1835.

Truman, David B. "Federalism and the Party System." In Arthur W. Macmahon, ed., *Federalism: Mature and Emergent.* New York: Russell & Russell, 1962. pp. 115–36.

———. *The Governmental Process.* New York: Alfred A. Knopf, 1951.

Tucker, Robert W. *A New Isolationism.* New York: Universe Books, 1972.

Turner, Julius. *Party and Constituency.* Baltimore: The Johns Hopkins Press, 1951.

Van Dyke, Vernon. "Process and Policy as Focal Concepts in Political Research." In Austin Ranney, ed., *Political Science and Public Policy.* Chicago: Markham, 1968, pp. 23-29.

Van Tyne, C. H. *The Causes of the War of Independence.* Boston and New York: Houghton Mifflin, 1922.

Verba, Sidney, and Nie, Norman H. *Participation in America.* New York: Harper & Row, 1972.

Vile, M. J. C. *The Structure of American Federalism.* New York: Oxford Univ. Press, 1961.

Vogler, David J. *The Politics of Congress.* Boston: Allyn and Bacon, 1974.

Vose, Clement. *Caucasians Only: The Supreme Court, the NAACP, and the Restrictive Covenant Cases.* Berkeley: Univ. of California Press, 1959.

Warren, Charles. *The Supreme Court in United States History.* Boston: Little, Brown, 1922.

Wasby, Stephen L. *The Impact of the United States Supreme Court: Some Perspectives.* Homewood, Ill.: Dorsey Press, 1970.

Wechsler, Herbert. "The Political Safeguards of Federalism: The Role of the States in the Composition and Selection of the National Government." In Arthur W. Macmahon, ed., *Federalism: Mature and Emergent.* New York: Russell & Russell, 1962, pp. 97-114.

Welch, Robert. *The Politician.* Belmont, Mass.: Belmont Publishing, 1964.

Wheare, K. C. *Federalism*, 3rd ed. New York: Oxford Univ. Press, 1953.

White, Leonard D. *The Jacksonians.* New York: Macmillan, 1954.

———. *The Jeffersonians.* New York: Macmillan, 1951.

White, William S. *Citadel.* New York: Harper, 1956.

Whyte, William H. *The Organization Man.* New York: Simon and Schuster, 1956.

Wildavsky, Aaron. *The Politics of the Budgetary Process,* 2nd ed. Boston: Little, Brown, 1974.

Williams, William Appleman. *The Tragedy of American Diplomacy.* Cleveland: World, 1959.

Willoughby, W. W. *The Constitutional Law of the United States.* New York: Baker, Voorhis, 1910.

Wilson, Woodrow. *Congressional Government.* Cleveland: World, 1963.

Wright, Benjamin F. *The Federalist.* Cambridge, Mass.: Harvard Univ. Press, 1961.

Yancey, William L. *The Moynihan Report and the Politics of Controversy.* Cambridge, Mass.: M.I.T. Press, 1967.

Zeigler, L. Harmon. *Interest Groups in American Society.* Englewood Cliffs, N.J.: Prentice Hall, 1964.

Articles and Periodicals

Aberbach, J. D., and Walker, J. L. "Political Trust and Racial Ideology." *The American Political Science Review* 44 (1970), 1199-1219.

Aberbach, Joel D., and Rockman, Bert A. "Clashing Beliefs Within the Executive Branch: The Nixon Administration Bureaucracy." *The American Political Science Review* 70 (1976), 456-68.

Adamany, David, and Agree, George. "Election Campaign Financing: The 1974 Reforms." *Political Science Quarterly* 90 (1975), 201-20.

Adrian, Charles. "State and Local Government Participation in the Design and Administration of Intergovernmental Programs." *The Annals* 359 (1965), 35-43.

Allison, Graham T. "Conceptual Models and the Cuban Missile Crisis." *The American Political Science Review* 63 (1969), 689-718.

Beany, William M., and Beiser, Edward N. "Prayer and Politics: The Impact of *Engel* and *Schempp* on the Political Process." *Journal of Public Law* 13 (1964), 475-503.

Beard, Charles A. "The Supreme Court—Usurper or Grantee." *Political Science Quarterly* 27 (1912), 1-35.

Berdahl, Clarence A. "Party Membership in the United States." *The American Political Science Review* 36 (1942), 16-50, 241-62.

Berle, Adolph A., Jr. "Constitutional Limitations on Corporate Activity—Protection of Personal Rights From Invasion Through Economic Power." *Univ. of Pennsylvania Law Review* 100 (1952), 933-55.

Birkby, Robert H. "The Supreme Court and the Bible Belt: Tennessee Reaction to the 'Schempp' Decision," *Midwest Journal of Political Science* 10 (1966), 304-19.

Black, Charles L., Jr. "A Note on Senatorial Consideration of Supreme Court Nominees." *The Yale Law Journal* 79 (1970), 657-64.

Black, Hugo L. "The Bill of Rights." *New York Univ. Law Review* 35 (1960), 865-81.

Blumberg, Abraham S. "The Practice of Law as a Confidence Game." *Law and Society Review* 1 (1967), 15-39.

Borosage, Robert, et al. "The New Public Interest Lawyers." *The Yale Law Journal* 79 (1970), 1069-1152.

Boyd, Richard W. "Presidential Elections: An Explanation of Voting Defection." *The American Political Science Review* 63 (1969), 498-514.

Bullock, Charles S., III. "House Careerists: Changing Patterns of Longevity and Attrition." *The American Political Science Review* 66 (1972), 1295-1300.

Cahn, Edmond. "Jurisprudence." *New York Univ. Law Review* 30 (1955), 150-69.

Carmen, Ira H. "One Civil Libertarian Among Many: The Case of Mr. Justice Goldberg." *Michigan Law Review* 65 (1966), 301-36.

———. "The President, Politics and the Power of Appointment: Hoover's Nomination of Mr. Justice Cardozo." *Virginia Law Review* 55 (1969), 616-59.

Chase, Harold W. "Federal Judges: The Appointing Process." *Minnesota Law Review* 51 (1966), 185-221.

Corwin, Edward S. "The Steel Seizure Case: A Judicial Brick Without Straw." *Columbia Law Review* 53 (1953), 53-66.

Curtis, Charles P. "The Ethics of Advocacy." *Stanford Law Review* 4 (1951), 3-23.

Dahl, Robert A. "Decision-Making in a Democracy: The Supreme Court as a National Policy-Maker." *Journal of Public Law* 6 (1958), 279-95.

Erikson, Robert S. "Malapportionment, Gerrymandering, and Party Fortunes in Congressional Elections." *The American Political Science Review* 66 (1972), 1234-45.

Fairman, Charles, and Morrison, Stanley. "Does the Fourteenth Amendment Incorporate the Bill of Rights?" *Stanford Law Review* 2 (1949), 5-173.

Falk, Stanley L. "The National Security Council Under Truman, Eisenhower and Kennedy." *Political Science Quarterly* 79 (1964), 403-34.

Fine, David J. "Federal Grand Jury Investigation of Political Dissidents." *Harvard Civil Rights Civil Liberties Review* 7 (1972), 432-99.

Finifter, Ada W. "Dimensions of Political Alienation." *The American Political Science Review* 64 (1970), 389-410.

Foote, Caleb. "Compelling Appearance in Court: Administration of Bail in Philadelphia." *Univ. of Pennsylvania Law Review* 102 (1954), 1031-79.

Frankfurter, Felix. "The Supreme Court in the Mirror of Justices." *Univ. of Pennsylvania Law Review* 105 (1957), 781-96.

Friendly, Fred W. "What's Fair on the Air?" *The New York Times Magazine* (March 30, 1975), pp. 11-12, 37-43, 46-48.

Friendly, Henry J. "The Bill of Rights as a Code of Criminal Procedure." *California Law Review* 53 (1965), 929-56.

Gilmour, Robert. "Central Legislative Clearance: A Revised Perspective." *Public Administration Review* 31 (1971), 150-58.

Glenn, Norvall D. "Class and Party Support in the United States: Recent and Emergent Trends." *Public Opinion Quarterly* 37 (1973), 1-20.

Goldman, Sheldon. "Johnson and Nixon Appointees to the Lower Federal Courts: Some Socio-Political Perspectives." *The Journal of Politics* 34 (1972), 934-42.

———. "Judicial Appointments to the United States Courts of Appeals." *Wisconsin Law Review* 1967 (1967), 186-214.

———. "Voting Behavior on the United States Courts of Appeals Revisited." *The American Political Science Review* 69 (1975), 491-406.

Goodwin, George, Jr. "Subcommittees: The Miniature Legislatures of Congress." *The American Political Science Review* 56 (1962), 596-604.

Hammond, Paul Y. "The National Security Council as a Device for Interdepartmental Coordination: An Interpretation and Appraisal." *The American Political Science Review* 54 (1960), 899-910.

Heller, Walter W. "Should the Government Share Its Tax Take?" *Saturday Review* (March 22, 1969), pp. 26-29.

Howard, J. Woodford, Jr. "On the Fluidity of Judicial Choice." *The American Political Science Review* 62 (1968), 43-56.

Huitt, Ralph K. "Democratic Party Leadership in the Senate." *The American Political Science Review* 55 (1961), 333-44.

———. "The Outsider in the Senate: An Alternative Role." *The American Political Science Review* 55 (1961), 566-75.

Huntington, Samuel P. "The Marasmus of the I.C.C.: The Commission, the Railroads, and the Public Interest." *The Yale Law Journal* 61 (1952), 467-509.

Jaffe, Louis. "The Effective Limits of the Administrative Process." *Harvard Law Review* 67 (1954), 1105-23, 1127-35.

Johnson, Richard M. "Compliance and Supreme Court Decision-Making." *Wisconsin Law Review* 1967 (1967), 170-85.

Kelley, Stanley, Jr., et al. "Registration and Voting: Putting First Things First." *The American Political Science Review* 61 (1967), 359-79.

Kennan, George F. "The Sources of Soviet Conduct." *Foreign Affairs* 25 (1947), 566-82.

Kessel, John H. "Comment: The Issues in Issue Voting." *The American Political Science Review* 66 (1972), 459-65.

Kirk, Russell. "The American Political Tradition." *National Review* (February 8, 1958), pp. 133-35.

Leiserson, Avery. "Political Limitations on Executive Reorganization." *The American Political Science Review* 41 (1947), 68-84.

Levy, Leonard. "The Right Against Self-Incrimination: History and Judicial History." *Political Science Quarterly* 84 (1969), 1-29.

Livingston, William S. "A Note on the Nature of Federalism." *Political Science Quarterly* 67 (1952), 81-95.

Llewellyn, Karl N. "The Constitution as an Institution." *Columbia Law Review* 34 (1934), 1-40.

Lowi, Theodore J. "American Business, Public Policy, Case-Studies, and Political Theory." *World Politics* 15 (1964), 677-715.

Maass, Arthur. "Congress and Water Resources." *The American Political Science Review* 44 (1950), 576-93.

Mann, Dean E. "The Selection of Federal Political Executives." *The American Political Science Review* 58 (1964), 81-99.

Masters, Nicholas A. "House Committee Assignments." *The American Political Science Review* 55 (1961), 345-57.

Matthews, Donald R. "The Folkways of the United States Senate: Conformity to Group Norms and Legislative Effectiveness." *The American Political Science Review* 53 (1959), 1064-89.

Matthews, Donald R., and Prothro, James W. "Political Factors and Negro Voter Registration in the South." *The American Political Science Review* 57 (1963), 355-67.

———. "Social and Economic Factors and Negro Voter Registration in the South." *The American Political Science Review* 57 (1963), 24-44.

McCloskey, Herbert, et al. "Issue Conflict and Consensus Among Party Leaders and Followers." *The American Political Science Review* 54 (1960), 406-27.

McCloskey, Robert G. "Deeds Without Doctrines: Civil Rights in the 1960 Term of the Supreme Court." *The American Political Science Review* 56 (1962), 71-89.

Mendelson, Wallace. "From Warren to Burger: The Rise and Decline of Substantive Equal Protection." *The American Political Science Review* 66 (1972), 1226-33.

———. "The Neo-Behavioral Approach to the Judicial Process." *The American Political Science Review* 57 (1963), 593-603.

Miller, Arthur S. "Notes on the Concept of the 'Living' Constitution." *The George Washington Law Review* 31 (1963), 881-918.

Miller, Warren E. "Presidential Coattails: A Study in Political Myth and Methodology." *Public Opinion Quarterly* 19 (1955-56), 353-68.

Miller, Warren E., and Stokes, Donald E. "Constituency Influence in Congress." *The American Political Science Review* 57 (1963), 45-56.

Murphy, Walter F. "Deeds Under a Doctrine: Civil Liberties in the 1963 Term." *The American Political Science Review* 59 (1965), 64-79.

Neustadt, Richard E. "Approaches to Staffing the Presidency: Notes on FDR and JFK." *The American Political Science Review* 57 (1963), 855-63.

———. "The Presidency and Legislation: The Growth of Central Clearance." *The American Political Science Review* 48 (1954), 641-71.

———. "The Presidency at Mid-Century." *Law and Contemporary Problems* 21 (1956), 609-45.

Note, "Trends in Legal Commentary on the Exclusionary Rule." *Journal of Criminal Law and Criminology* 65 (1974), 373-84.

O'Hanlon, Thomas. "The Unchecked Power of the Building Trades." *Fortune* (December 1968), pp. 102-07.

Pollack, Louis, et al. "The Congressional and Executive Roles in War-Making: An Analytical Framework." *Congressional Record* 116 (May 21, 1970), S7591-S7593.

Polsby, Nelson W. "The Institutionalization of the U.S. House of Representatives." *The American Political Science Review* 62 (1968), 144-68.

Polsby, Nelson W.; Gallaher, Miriam; and Rundquist, Barry Spencer. "The Growth of the Seniority System in the U.S. House of Representatives." *The American Political Science Review* 63 (1969), 787-807.

Ranney, Austin. "The Representativeness of Primary Electorates." *Midwest Journal of Political Science* 12 (1968), 224-38.

———. "Turnout and Representation in Presidential Primary Elections." *The American Political Science Review* 66 (1972), 21-37.

Ranney, Austin, and Epstein, Leon D. "The Two Electorates: Voters and Nonvoters in a Wisconsin Primary." *The Journal of Politics* 28 (1966), 598-616.

Reich, Charles A. "The Law of the Planned Society." *The Yale Law Journal* 75 (1966), 1227-70.

———. "The New Property." *The Yale Law Journal* 73 (1964), 733-87.

Roche, John P. "The Founding Fathers: A Reform Caucus in Action." *The American Political Science Review* 55 (1961), 799-816.

Rohde, D. W., and Shepsle, K. A. "Democratic Committee Assignments in the House of Representatives: Strategic Aspects of a Social Choice Process." *The American Political Science Review* 67 (1973), 889-905.

Rostow, Eugene V. "The Japanese-American Cases—A Disaster." *The Yale Law Journal* 54 (1945), 489-533.

Schmidhauser, John. "The Justices of the Supreme Court: A Collective Portrait." *Midwest Journal of Political Science* 3 (1959), 1-57.

Schubert, Glendon A. "The Rhetoric of Constitutional Change." *Journal of Public Law* 16 (1967), 16-50.

Schulman, Jay, et al. "Recipe for a Jury." *Psychology Today* (May 1973), pp. 37-44, 77-84.

Scigliano, Robert. "The Grand Jury, the Information, and the Judicial Inquiry." *Oregon Law Review* 38 (1959), 303-15.

Seligman, Lester G. "Presidential Leadership: The Inner Circle and Institutionalization." *The Journal of Politics* 18 (1956) 410-26.

Shapiro, Martin. "From Public Law to Public Policy, or the 'Public' in 'Public Law.' " *P.S.* 5 (1972), 410-18.

Stanga, John E., Jr. "Judicial Protection of the Criminal Defendant Against Adverse Press Coverage." *William & Mary Law Review* 13 (1971), 1-74.

Stevens, John Paul. "Exemptions from Antitrust Coverage," in "Policy Against Undue Limitations on Competitive Conditions: A Symposium." *American Bar Association Antitrust Law Journal* 37 (1968), 631.

———. "The Regulation of Railroads." *American Bar Association Section of Antitrust Law* 19 (1961), 361.

Stokes, Donald E. "Some Dynamic Elements of Contests for the Presidency." *The American Political Science Review* 60 (1966), 19-28.

Telford, Ira Ralph. "Types of Primary and Party Responsibility." *The American Political Science Review* 59 (1965), 117-18.

"Toward a More Responsible Two-Party System." Report of the Committee on Political Parties of the American Political Science Association, *The American Political Science Review* 44 (1950), Supplement.

Ulmer, S. Sidney. "Supreme Court Behavior and Civil Rights." *Western Political Quarterly* 13 (1960), 288-311.

Van Dyke, Jon M. "The Jury as a Political Institution." *The Center Magazine* (March 1970), pp. 17-26.

Vines, Kenneth N. "Federal District Judges and Race Relations Cases in the South." *The Journal of Politics* 26 (1964), 337-57.

Wald, Michael, et al. "Interrogations in New Haven: The Impact of *Miranda*." *The Yale Law Journal* 76 (1967), 1519-1648.

Whiteside, Thomas. "Annals of Television: Shaking the Tree." *The New Yorker* (March 17, 1975), pp. 41-91.

Wolanin, Thomas R. "Committee Seniority and the Choice of House Subcommittee Chairmen: 80th-91st Congresses." *The Journal of Politics* 36 (1974), 687-702.

Wolfers, Arnold. "Statesmanship and Moral Choice." *World Politics* 1 (1949), 175-95.

Wolfinger, Raymond E., and Heifetz, Joan. "Safe Seats, Seniority, and Power in Congress." *The American Political Science Review* 49 (1965), 337-59.

Wright, Benjamin F. "The Federalist on the Nature of Political Man." *Ethics* 59 (1949), no. 2, part II.

Wyzanski, Charles E., Jr. "A Trial Judge's Freedom and Responsibility." *Harvard Law Review* 65 (1952), 1281-1304.

the Constitution of the United States *

We the people of the United States, in Order to form a more perfect Union, establish Justice, insure domestic Tranquility, provide for the common defence, promote the general Welfare, and secure the Blessings of Liberty to ourselves and our Posterity, do ordain and establish this Constitution for the United States of America.

Article I

Section 1. All legislative Powers herein granted shall be vested in a Congress of the United States, which shall consist of a Senate and House of Representatives.

Section 2. The House of Representatives shall be composed of Members chosen every second Year by the People of the several States, and the Electors in each State shall have the Qualifications requisite for Electors of the most numerous Branch of the State Legislature.

No Person shall be a Representative who shall not have attained to the Age of twenty-five Years, and been seven Years a Citizen of the United States, and who shall not, when elected, be an Inhabitant of that state in which he shall be chosen.

[Representatives and direct Taxes shall be apportioned among the several States which may be included within this Union, according to their respective Numbers, which shall be determined by adding to the whole Number of free Persons, including those bound to Service for a Term of Years, and excluding Indians not taxed, three fifths of all other Persons.][1] The actual Enumeration shall be made within three Years after the first Meeting of the Congress of the United States, and within every subsequent Term of ten Years, in such Manner as they shall by Law direct. The Number of Representatives shall not exceed one for every thirty Thousand, but each State shall have at Least one Representative; and until such enumeration shall be made, the State of New Hampshire shall be entitled to chuse three, Massachusetts eight, Rhode-Island and Providence Plantations one, Connecticut five, New-York six, New Jersey four, Pennsylvania eight, Delaware one, Maryland six, Virginia ten, North Carolina five, South Carolina five, and Georgia three.

When vacancies happen in the Representation from any State, the Executive Authority thereof shall issue Writs of Election to fill such Vacancies.

The House of Representatives shall chuse their Speaker and other Officers; and shall have the sole Power of Impeachment.

Section 3. The Senate of the United States shall be composed of two Senators from each State, [chosen by the Legislature thereof,][2] for six Years; and each Senator shall have one Vote.

Immediately after they shall be assembled in Consequence of the first Election, they shall be divided as equally as may be into three Classes. The Seats of the Senators of the first Class shall be vacated at the Expiration of the second Year, of the second Class at the Expiration of the fourth Year, and of the third Class at the Expiration of the sixth Year, so that one-third may be chosen every second Year; [and if Vacancies happen by Resignation, or otherwise, during the Recess of the Legislature of any State, the Executive thereof may make temporary Appointments until the next Meeting of the Legislature, which shall then fill such Vacancies].[3]

No Person shall be a Senator who shall not have attained to the Age of thirty Years, and been nine Years a Citizen of the United States, and who shall not, when elected, be an Inhabitant of that State in which he shall be chosen.

The Vice-President of the United States shall be President of the Senate, but shall have no vote, unless they be equally divided.

The Senate shall chuse their other Officers, and also a President pro tempore, in the absence of the Vice-President, or when he shall exercise the Office of the President of the United States.

The Senate shall have the sole Power to try all Impeachments. When sitting for that purpose, they shall be on Oath or Affirmation. When the President of the United States is tried, the Chief Justice shall preside: And no person shall be convicted without the Concurrence of two thirds of the Members present.

Judgment in Cases of Impeachment shall not extend further than to removal from Office, and disqualification to hold and enjoy any Office of honor, Trust, or Profit under the United States: but the Party convicted shall nevertheless be liable and subject to Indictment, Trial, Judgment, and Punishment, according to Law.

Section 4. The Times, Places and Manner of holding Elections for Senators and Representatives, shall be prescribed in each state by the Legislature thereof; but the Congress may at any time by Law make or alter such Regulations, except as to the Places of Chusing Senators.

The Congress shall assemble at least once in every Year, and such Meeting shall [be on the first Monday in December,][4] unless they shall by Law appoint a different Day.

Section 5. Each House shall be the Judge of the Elections, Returns and Qualifications of its own Members, and a Majority

* The Constitution and all amendments are shown in their original form. Parts that have been amended or superseded are bracketed and explained in the footnotes.

1 Modified by the Fourteenth and Sixteenth amendments.

2 Superseded by the Seventeenth Amendment.

3 Modified by the Seventeenth Amendment.

4 Superseded by the Twentieth Amendment.

of each shall constitute a Quorum to do Business; but a smaller number may adjourn from day to day, and may be authorized to compel the Attendance of absent Members, in such Manner, and under such Penalties, as each House may provide.

Each House may determine the Rules of its Proceedings, punish its Members for disorderly Behavior, and, with the Concurrence of two thirds, expel a Member.

Each House shall keep a Journal of its Proceedings, and from time to time publish the same, excepting such Parts as may in their judgment require Secrecy; and the Yeas and Nays of the Members of either House on any question shall, at the Desire of one fifth of those Present, be entered on the Journal.

Neither House, during the Session of Congress, shall, without the Consent of the other, adjourn for more than three days, nor to any other Place than that in which the two Houses shall be sitting.

Section 6. The Senators and Representatives shall receive a Compensation for their Services, to be ascertained by Law, and paid out of the Treasury of the United States. They shall in all Cases, except Treason, Felony, and Breach of the Peace, be privileged from Arrest during their Attendance at the Session of their respective Houses, and in going to and returning from the same; and for any Speech or Debate in either House, they shall not be questioned in any other Place.

No Senator or Representative shall, during the Time for which he was elected, be appointed to any civil Office under the Authority of the United States, which shall have been created, or the Emoluments whereof shall have been increased, during such time; and no Person holding any Office under the United States shall be a Member of either House during his continuance in Office.

Section 7. All Bills for raising Revenue shall originate in the House of Representatives; but the Senate may propose or concur with Amendments as on other bills.

Every Bill which shall have passed the House of Representatives and the Senate, shall, before it become a Law, be presented to the President of the United States. If he approve he shall sign it, but if not he shall return it, with his Objections, to that House in which it shall have originated, who shall enter the Objections at large on their Journal, and proceed to reconsider it. If after such Reconsideration two thirds of that House shall agree to pass the bill, it shall be sent, together with the objections, to the other House, by which it shall likewise be reconsidered, and if approved by two thirds of that House, it shall become a Law. But in all such Cases the Votes of both Houses shall be determined by Yeas and Nays, and the Names of the Persons voting for and against the Bill shall be entered on the Journal of each House respectively. If any Bill shall not be returned by the President within ten Days (Sundays excepted) after it shall have been presented to him, the Same shall be a Law, in like Manner as if he had signed it, unless the Congress by their Adjournment prevent its Return, in which Case it shall not be a Law.

Every Order, Resolution, or Vote to which the Concurrence of the Senate and House of Representatives may be necessary (except on a question of Adjournment) shall be presented to the President of the United States; and before the Same shall take Effect, shall be approved by him, or being disapproved by him, shall be repassed by two thirds of the Senate and House of Representatives, according to the Rules and Limitations prescribed in the Case of a Bill.

Section 8. The Congress shall have Power To lay and collect Taxes, Duties, Imposts and Excises, to pay the Debts and provide for the common Defence and general Welfare of the United States; but all Duties, Imposts and Excises shall be uniform throughout the United States;

To borrow money on the credit of the United States;

To regulate Commerce with foreign Nations, and among the several States, and with the Indian Tribes;

To establish an uniform Rule of Naturalization, and uniform Laws on the subject of Bankruptcies throughout the United States;

To coin Money, regulate the Value thereof, and of foreign Coin, and fix the Standard of Weights and Measures;

To provide for the Punishment of counterfeiting the Securities and current Coin of the United States;

To establish Post Offices and post Roads;

To promote the Progress of Science and useful Arts, by securing for limited Times to Authors and Inventors the exclusive Right to their respective Writings and Discoveries;

To constitute Tribunals inferior to the Supreme Court;

To define and punish Piracies and Felonies committed on the high Seas, and Offenses against the Law of Nations;

To declare War, grant Letters of Marque and Reprisal, and make Rules concerning Captures on Land and Water;

To raise and support Armies, but no Appropriation of Money to that Use shall be for a longer Term than two Years;

To provide and maintain a Navy;

To make Rules for the Government and Regulation of the land and naval forces;

To provide for calling forth the Militia to execute the Laws of the Union, suppress Insurrections and repel Invasions;

To provide for organizing, arming, and disciplining the Militia, and for governing such Part of them as may be employed in the Service of the United States, reserving to the States respectively, the Appointment of the Officers, and the Authority of training the Militia according to the discipline prescribed by Congress;

To exercise exclusive Legislation in all Cases whatsoever, over such District (not exceeding ten Miles square) as may, by Cession of particular States, and the acceptance of Congress, become the Seat of the Government of the United States, and to exercise like Authority over all Places purchased by the Consent of the Legislature of the State in which the Same shall be, for the Erection of Forts, Magazines, Arsenals, dock-Yards, and other needful Buildings;—And

To make all Laws which shall be necessary and proper for carrying into Execution the foregoing Powers, and all other Powers vested by this Constitution in the Government of the United States, or in any Department or Officer thereof.

Section 9. The Migration or Importation of such Persons as any of the States now existing shall think proper to admit shall not be prohibited by the Congress prior to the Year one thousand eight hundred and eight, but a tax or duty may be imposed on such Importation, not exceeding ten dollars for each Person.

The privilege of the Writ of Habeas Corpus shall not be suspended, unless when in Cases of Rebellion or Invasion the public Safety may require it.

No Bill of Attainder or ex post facto Law shall be passed.

[No capitation, or other direct, Tax shall be laid unless in Proportion to the Census or Enumeration herein before directed to be taken.][5]

No Tax or Duty shall be laid on Articles exported from any State.

No Preference shall be given by any Regulation of Revenue to the Ports of one State over those of another: nor shall Vessels bound to, or from, one State, be obliged to enter, clear, or pay Duties in another.

No Money shall be drawn from the Treasury, but in Consequence of Appropriations made by Law; and a regular Statement and Account of the Receipts and Expenditures of all public Money shall be published from time to time.

No Title of Nobility shall be granted by the United States: And no Person holding any Office of Profit or Trust under them, shall, without the Consent of the Congress, accept of any present, Emolument, Office, or Title, of any kind whatever, from any King, Prince, or foreign State.

Section 10. No State shall enter into any Treaty, Alliance, or Confederation; grant Letters of Marque and Reprisal; coin Money; emit Bills of Credit; make any Thing but gold and silver Coin a Tender in Payment of Debts; pass any Bill of Attainder, ex post facto Law, or Law impairing the Obligation of Contracts, or grant any Title of Nobility.

No State shall, without the Consent of the Congress, lay any Imposts or Duties on Imports or Exports, except what may be absolutely necessary for executing its inspection Laws: and the net Produce of all Duties and Imposts, laid by any State on Imports or Exports, shall be for the Use of the Treasury of the United States; and all such Laws shall be subject to the Revision and Control of the Congress.

No State shall, without the Consent of Congress, lay any duty of Tonnage, keep Troops, or Ships of War in time of Peace, enter into any Agreement or Compact with another State, or with a foreign Power, or engage in War, unless actually invaded, or in such imminent Danger as will not admit of delay.

[5] Modified by the Sixteenth Amendment.

Article II

Section 1. The executive Power shall be vested in a President of the United States of America. He shall hold his Office during the Term of four years, and, together with the Vice-President, chosen for the same Term, be elected, as follows:

Each State shall appoint, in such Manner as the Legislature thereof may direct, a Number of Electors, equal to the whole Number of Senators and Representatives to which the State may be entitled in the Congress: but no Senator or Representative, or Person holding an Office of Trust or Profit under the United States, shall be appointed an Elector.

[The Electors shall meet in their respective States, and vote by Ballot for two persons, of whom one at least shall not be an Inhabitant of the same State with themselves. And they shall make a List of all the Persons voted for, and of the Number of Votes for each; which List they shall sign and certify, and transmit sealed to the Seat of the Government of the United States, directed to the President of the Senate. The President of the Senate shall, in the Presence of the Senate and House of Representatives, open all the Certificates, and the Votes shall then be counted. The Person having the greatest Number of Votes shall be the President, if such Number be a Majority of the whole Number of Electors appointed; and if there be more than one who have such Majority, and have an equal Number of Votes, then the House of Representatives shall immediately chuse by Ballot one of them for President; and if no Person have a Majority, then from the five highest on the List the said House shall in like Manner chuse the President. But in chusing the President, the Votes shall be taken by States, the Representation from each State having one Vote; a quorum for this Purpose shall consist of a Member or Members from two-thirds of the States, and a Majority of all the States shall be necessary to a Choice. In every Case, after the Choice of the President, the Person having the greatest Number of Votes of the Electors shall be the Vice-President. But if there should remain two or more who have equal votes, the Senate shall chuse from them by Ballot the Vice-President.][6]

The Congress may determine the Time of chusing the Electors, and the Day on which they shall give their Votes; which Day shall be the same throughout the United States.

No person except a natural-born Citizen, or a Citizen of the United States, at the time of the Adoption of this Constitution, shall be eligible to the Office of President; neither shall any Person be eligible to that Office who shall not have attained to the Age of thirty-five years, and been fourteen Years a Resident within the United States.

[In Case of the Removal of the President from Office, or of his Death, Resignation, or Inability to discharge the Powers and Duties of the said Office, the same shall devolve on the Vice-President, and the Congress may by Law provide for the Case of Removal, Death, Resignation, or Inability, both of the President and Vice-President, declaring what Officer shall then

[6] Superseded by the Twelfth Amendment.

act as President, and such Officer shall act accordingly, until the disability be removed, or a President shall be elected.][7]

The President shall, at stated Times, receive for his Services a Compensation, which shall neither be increased nor diminished during the Period for which he shall have been elected, and he shall not receive within that Period any other Emolument from the United States, or any of them.

Before he enter on the execution of his Office, he shall take the following Oath or Affirmation:—"I do solemnly swear (or affirm) that I will faithfully execute the Office of President of the United States, and will, to the best of my Ability, preserve, protect, and defend the Constitution of the United States."

Section 2. The President shall be Commander in Chief of the Army and Navy of the United States, and of the Militia of the several States, when called into the actual Service of the United States; he may require the Opinion, in writing, of the principal Officer in each of the executive Departments, upon any subject relating to the Duties of their respective Offices, and he shall have Power to Grant Reprieves and Pardons for Offenses against the United States, except in Cases of Impeachment.

He shall have Power, by and with the Advice and Consent of the Senate, to make Treaties, provided two thirds of the Senators present concur; and he shall nominate, and by and with the Advice and Consent of the Senate, shall appoint Ambassadors, other public Ministers and Consuls, Judges of the supreme Court, and all other Officers of the United States, whose Appointments are not herein otherwise provided for, and which shall be established by Law: but the Congress may by Law vest the Appointment of such inferior Officers, as they think proper, in the President alone, in the Courts of Law, or in the Heads of Departments.

The President shall have Power to fill up all Vacancies that may happen during the Recess of the Senate, by granting Commissions which shall expire at the End of their next Session.

Section 3. He shall from time to time give to the Congress Information of the State of the Union, and recommend to their Consideration such Measures as he shall judge necessary and expedient; he may, on extraordinary occasions, convene both Houses, or either of them, and in Case of Disagreement between them, with respect to the Time of Adjournment, he may adjourn them to such Time as he shall think proper; he shall receive Ambassadors and other public Ministers; he shall take Care that the Laws be faithfully executed, and shall Commission all the Officers of the United States.

Section 4. The President, Vice-President and all civil Officers of the United States, shall be removed from Office on Impeachment for, and Conviction of, Treason, Bribery, or other high Crimes and Misdemeanors.

Article III

Section 1. The judicial Power of the United States, shall be vested in one supreme Court, and in such inferior Courts as the Congress may from time to time ordain and establish. The Judges, both of the supreme and inferior Courts, shall hold their Offices during good Behaviour, and shall, at stated Times, receive for their Services, a Compensation, which shall not be diminished during their Continuance in Office.

Section 2. The judicial Power shall extend to all Cases, in Law and Equity, arising under this Constitution, the Laws of the United States, and treaties made, or which shall be made, under their Authority;—to all Cases affecting ambassadors, other public ministers and consuls;—to all cases of admiralty and maritime Jurisdiction;—to Controversies to which the United States shall be a Party;—to Controversies between two or more States;—[between a State and Citizens of another State;][8]—between Citizens of different States,—between Citizens of the same State claiming Lands under Grants of different States, and between a State, or the Citizens thereof, and foreign States, Citizens or Subjects.

In all Cases affecting Ambassadors, other public Ministers and Consuls, and those in which a State shall be Party, the supreme Court shall have original Jurisdiction. In all the other Cases before mentioned, the supreme Court shall have appellate Jurisdiction, both as to Law and Fact, with such Exceptions, and under such Regulations as the Congress shall make.

The trial of all Crimes, except in Cases of Impeachment, shall be by Jury; and such Trial shall be held in the State where the said Crimes shall have been committed; but when not committed within any State, the Trial shall be at such Place or Places as the Congress may by Law have directed.

Section 3. Treason against the United States, shall consist only in levying War against them, or in adhering to their Enemies, giving them Aid and Comfort. No Person shall be convicted of Treason unless on the Testimony of two Witnesses to the same overt Act, or on Confession in open Court.

The Congress shall have power to declare the Punishment of Treason, but no Attainder of Treason shall work Corruption of Blood, or Forfeiture except during the Life of the Person attainted.

Article IV

Section 1. Full Faith and Credit shall be given in each State to the public Acts, Records, and judicial Proceedings of every other State. And the Congress may by general Laws prescribe the Manner in which such Acts, Records and Proceedings shall be proved, and the Effect thereof.

Section 2. The Citizens of each State shall be entitled to all Privileges and Immunities of Citizens in the several States.

A Person charged in any State with Treason, Felony, or other Crime, who shall flee from Justice, and be found in another State, shall on demand of the executive Authority of the State from which he fled, be delivered up, to be removed to the State having Jurisdiction of the crime.

[7] Modified by the Twenty-fifth Amendment.

[8] Modified by the Eleventh Amendment.

[No Person held to Service or Labour in one State, under the Laws thereof, escaping into another, shall, in Consequence of any Law or Regulation therein, be discharged from such Service or Labour, but shall be delivered up on Claim of the Party to whom such Service or Labour may be due.][9]

Section 3. New States may be admitted by the Congress into this Union; but no new State shall be formed or erected within the Jurisdiction of any other State; nor any State be formed by the Junction of two or more States, or parts of States, without the Consent of the Legislatures of the States concerned as well as of the Congress.

The Congress shall have Power to dispose of and make all needful Rules and Regulations respecting the Territory or other Property belonging to the United States; and nothing in this Constitution shall be so construed as to Prejudice any Claims of the United States, or of any particular State.

Section 4. The United States shall guarantee to every State in this Union a Republican Form of Government, and shall protect each of them against Invasion; and on Application of the Legislature, or of the Executive (when the Legislature cannot be convened) against domestic Violence.

Article V

The Congress, whenever two-thirds of both Houses shall deem it necessary, shall propose Amendments to this Constitution, or, on the Application of the Legislatures of two-thirds of the several States, shall call a Convention for proposing Amendments, which, in either Case, shall be valid to all Intents and Purposes, as part of this Constitution, when ratified by the Legislatures of three-fourths of the several States, or by Conventions in three-fourths thereof, as the one or the other Mode of Ratification may be proposed by the Congress; Provided that no Amendment which may be made prior to the Year One thousand eight hundred and eight shall in any Manner affect the first and fourth Clauses in the Ninth Section of the first Article; and that no State, without its Consent, shall be deprived of its equal Suffrage in the Senate.

Article VI

All Debts contracted and Engagements entered into, before the Adoption of this Constitution, shall be as valid against the United States under this Constitution, as under the Confederation.

This Constitution, and the Laws of the United States which shall be made in Pursuance thereof; and all Treaties made, or which shall be made, under the Authority of the United States, shall be the supreme Law of the Land; and the Judges in every State shall be bound thereby, any Thing in the Constitution or Laws of any State to the Contrary notwithstanding.

The Senators and Representatives before mentioned, and the Members of the several State Legislatures, and all executive and judicial Officers, both of the United States and of the several States, shall be bound by Oath or Affirmation to support this Constitution; but no religious Test shall ever be required as a qualification to any Office or public Trust under the United States.

[9] Superseded by the Thirteenth Amendment.

Article VII

The Ratification of the Conventions of nine States shall be sufficient for the Establishment of this Constitution between the States so ratifying the same.

Done in Convention by the Unanimous Consent of the States present the Seventeenth Day of September in the Year of our Lord one thousand seven hundred and Eighty seven, and of the Independence of the United States of America the Twelfth. In Witness whereof We have hereunto subscribed our Names.

Articles in Addition to, and Amendment of, the Constitution of the United States of America, Proposed by Congress, and Ratified by the Legislatures of the Several States, Pursuant to the Fifth Article of the Original Constitution.

Amendment I[10]

Congress shall make no law respecting an establishment of religion, or prohibiting the free exercise thereof; or abridging the freedom of speech, or of the press; or the right of the people peaceably to assemble, and to petition the Government for a redress of grievances.

Amendment II

A well regulated Militia, being necessary to the security of a free State, the right of the people to keep and bear Arms shall not be infringed.

Amendment III

No Soldier shall, in time of peace, be quartered in any house, without the consent of the Owner, nor in time of war, but in a manner to be prescribed by law.

Amendment IV

The right of the people to be secure in their persons, houses, papers, and effects, against unreasonable searches and seizures, shall not be violated, and no Warrants shall issue, but upon probable cause, supported by Oath or affirmation, and particularly describing the place to be searched, and the persons or things to be seized.

Amendment V

No person shall be held to answer for a capital or otherwise infamous crime, unless on a presentment or indictment of a Grand Jury, except in cases arising in the land or naval forces, or in the Militia, when in actual service in time of War or public

[10] The first ten amendments were passed by Congress September 25, 1789. They were ratified by three-fourths of the states December 15, 1791.

danger; nor shall any person be subject for the same offence to be twice put in jeopardy of life or limb; nor shall be compelled in any criminal case to be a witness against himself, nor be deprived of life, liberty, or property, without due process of law; nor shall private property be taken for public use, without just compensation.

Amendment VI

In all criminal prosecutions, the accused shall enjoy the right to a speedy and public trial, by an impartial jury of the State and district wherein the crime shall have been committed, which district shall have been previously ascertained by law, and to be informed of the nature and cause of the accusation; to be confronted with the witnesses against him; to have compulsory process for obtaining witnesses in his favor, and to have the Assistance of Counsel for his defence.

Amendment VII

In suits at common law, where the value in controversy shall exceed twenty dollars, the right of trial by jury shall be preserved, and no fact tried by a jury, shall be otherwise reexamined in any Court of the United States, than according to the rules of the common law.

Amendment VIII

Excessive bail shall not be required, nor excessive fines imposed, nor cruel and unusual punishments inflicted.

Amendment IX

The enumeration in the Constitution, of certain rights, shall not be construed to deny or disparage others retained by the people.

Amendment X

The powers not delegated to the United States by the Constitution, nor prohibited by it to the States, are reserved to the States respectively, or to the people.

Amendment XI (1795) [11]

The Judicial power of the United States shall not be construed to extend to any suit in law or equity, commenced or prosecuted against one of the United States by Citizens of another State, or by Citizens or Subjects of any Foreign State.

Amendment XII (1804)

The Electors shall meet in their respective States and vote by ballot for President and Vice-President, one of whom, at least, shall not be an inhabitant of the same State with themselves; they shall name in their ballots the person voted for as President, and in distinct ballots the person voted for as Vice-President, and they shall make distinct lists of all persons voted for as President, and of all persons voted for as Vice-President, and of the number of votes for each, which lists they shall sign and certify, and transmit sealed to the seat of the government of the United States, directed to the President of the Senate;—The President of the Senate shall, in the presence of the Senate and House of Representatives, open all the certificates and the votes shall then be counted;—The person having the greatest number of votes for President, shall be the President, if such number be a majority of the whole number of Electors appointed; and if no person have such majority, then from the persons having the highest numbers not exceeding three on the list of those voted for as President, the House of Representatives shall choose immediately, by ballot, the President. But in choosing the President, the votes shall be taken by states, the representation from each state having one vote; a quorum for this purpose shall consist of a member or members from two-thirds of the states, and a majority of all the states shall be necessary to a choice. [And if the House of Representatives shall not choose a President whenever the right of choice shall devolve upon them, before the fourth day of March next following, then the Vice-President shall act as President, as in the case of the death or other constitutional disability of the President.] [12]—The person having the greatest number of votes as Vice-President, shall be the Vice-President, if such number be a majority of the whole number of Electors appointed, and if no person have a majority, then from the two highest numbers on the list, the Senate shall choose the Vice-President; a quorum for the purpose shall consist of two-thirds of the whole number of Senators, and a majority of the whole number shall be necessary to a choice. But no person constitutionally ineligible to the office of President shall be eligible to that of Vice-President of the United States.

Amendment XIII (1865)

Section 1. Neither slavery nor involuntary servitude, except as a punishment for crime whereof the party shall have been duly convicted, shall exist within the United States, or any place subject to their jurisdiction.

Section 2. Congress shall have power to enforce this article by appropriate legislation.

Amendment XIV (1868)

Section 1. All persons born or naturalized in the United States, and subject to the jurisdiction thereof, are citizens of the United States and of the State wherein they reside. No State shall make or enforce any law which shall abridge the privileges or immunities of citizens of the United States; nor shall any State deprive any person of life, liberty, or property, without due process of law; nor deny to any person within its jurisdiction the equal protection of the laws.

Section 2. Representatives shall be apportioned among the several States according to their respective numbers, counting the whole number of persons in each State, excluding Indians

[11] Date of ratification.

[12] Superseded by the Twentieth Amendment.

not taxed. But when the right to vote at any election for the choice of electors for President and Vice-President of the United States, Representatives in Congress, the Executive and Judicial officers of a State, or the members of the Legislature thereof, is denied to any of the male inhabitants of such State, being twenty-one years of age, and citizens of the United States, or in any way abridged, except for participation in rebellion, or other crime, the basis of representation therein shall be reduced in the proportion which the number of such male citizens shall bear to the whole number of male citizens twenty-one years of age in such State.

Section 3. No person shall be a Senator or Representative in Congress, or elector of President and Vice-President, or hold any office, civil or military, under the United States, or under any State, who, having previously taken an oath, as a member of Congress, or as an officer of the United States, or as a member of any State legislature, or as an executive or judicial officer of any State, to support the Constitution of the United States, shall have engaged in insurrection or rebellion against the same, or given aid or comfort to the enemies thereof. But Congress may by a vote of two-thirds of each House, remove such disability.

Section 4. The validity of the public debt of the United States, authorized by law, including debts incurred for payment of pensions and bounties for services in suppressing insurrection or rebellion, shall not be questioned. But neither the United States nor any State shall assume or pay any debt or obligation incurred in aid of insurrection or rebellion against the United States, or any claim for the loss or emancipation of any slave; but all such debts, obligations, and claims shall be held illegal and void.

Section 5. The Congress shall have the power to enforce, by appropriate legislation, the provisions of this article.

Amendment XV (1870)

Section 1. The right of citizens of the United States to vote shall not be denied or abridged by the United States or by any State on account of race, color, or previous condition of servitude—

Section 2. The Congress shall have power to enforce this article by appropriate legislation.

Amendment XVI (1913)

The Congress shall have power to lay and collect taxes on incomes, from whatever source derived, without apportionment among the several States, and without regard to any census or enumeration.

Amendment XVII (1913)

The Senate of the United States shall be composed of two Senators from each State, elected by the people thereof, for six years; and each Senator shall have one vote. The electors in each State shall have the qualifications requisite for electors of the most numerous branch of the State legislatures.

When vacancies happen in the representation of any State in the Senate, the executive authority of such State shall issue writs of election to fill such vacancies: *Provided,* That the legislature of any State may empower the executive thereof to make temporary appointments until the people fill the vacancies by election as the legislature may direct.

This amendment shall not be so construed as to affect the election or term of any Senator chosen before it becomes valid as part of the Constitution.

Amendment XVIII (1919)[13]

Section 1. After one year from the ratification of this article the manufacture, sale, or transportation of intoxicating liquors within, the importation thereof into, or the exportation thereof from the United States and all territory subject to the jurisdiction thereof for beverage purposes is hereby prohibited.

Section 2. The Congress and the several States shall have concurrent power to enforce this article by appropriate legislation.

Section 3. This article shall be inoperative unless it shall have been ratified as an amendment to the Constitution by the legislatures of the several States, as provided in the Constitution, within seven years from the date of the submission hereof to the States by the Congress.

Amendment XIX (1920)

The right of citizens of the United States to vote shall not be denied or abridged by the United States or by any State on account of sex.

Congress shall have power to enforce this article by appropriate legislation.

Amendment XX (1933)

Section 1. The terms of the President and Vice-President shall end at noon on the 20th day of January, and the terms of Senators and Representatives at noon on the 3d day of January, of the years in which such terms would have ended if this article had not been ratified; and the terms of their successors shall then begin.

Section 2. The Congress shall assemble at least once in every year, and such meeting shall begin at noon on the 3d day of January, unless they shall by law appoint a different day.

Section 3. If, at the time fixed for the beginning of the term of the President, the President elect shall have died, the Vice-President elect shall become President. If a President shall not have been chosen before the time fixed for the beginning of his term, or if the President elect shall have failed to qualify, then the Vice-President elect shall act as President until a President shall have qualified; and the Congress may by law provide for the case wherein neither a President elect nor a Vice-President elect shall have qualified, declaring who shall then act as President, or the manner in which one who is to act shall be se-

[13] Repealed by the Twenty-first Amendment.

lected, and such person shall act accordingly until a President or Vice-President shall have qualified.

Section 4. The Congress may by law provide for the case of the death of any of the persons from whom the House of Representatives may choose a President whenever the right of choice shall have devolved upon them, and for the case of the death of any of the persons from whom the Senate may choose a Vice-President whenever the right of choice shall have devolved upon them.

Section 5. Sections 1 and 2 shall take effect on the 15th day of October following the ratification of this article.

Section 6. This article shall be inoperative unless it shall have been ratified as an amendment to the Constitution by the legislatures of three-fourths of the several States within seven years from the date of its submission.

Amendment XXI (1933)

Section 1. The eighteenth article of amendment to the Constitution of the United States is hereby repealed.

Section 2. The transportation or importation into any State, Territory, or possession of the United States for delivery or use therein of intoxicating liquors, in violation of the laws thereof, is hereby prohibited.

Section 3. This article shall be inoperative unless it shall have been ratified as an amendment to the Constitution by conventions in the several States, as provided in the Constitution, within seven years from the date of the submission hereof to the States by the Congress.

Amendment XXII (1951)

No person shall be elected to the office of the President more than twice, and no person who has held the office of President, or acted as President, for more than two years of a term to which some other person was elected President shall be elected to the office of the President more than once.

But this Article shall not apply to any person holding the office of President when this Article was proposed by the Congress, and shall not prevent any person who may be holding the office of President, or acting as President, during the term within which this Article becomes operative from holding the office of President or acting as President during the remainder of such term.

Amendment XXIII (1961)

Section 1. The District constituting the seat of Government of the United States shall appoint in such manner as the Congress may direct:

A number of electors of President and Vice-President equal to the whole number of Senators and Representatives in Congress to which the District would be entitled if it were a State, but in no event more than the least populous State; they shall be in addition to those appointed by the States, but they shall be considered, for the purposes of the election of President and Vice-President, to be electors appointed by the State; and they shall meet in the District and perform such duties as provided by the twelfth article of amendment.

Section 2. The Congress shall have power to enforce this article by appropriate legislation.

Amendment XXIV (1964)

Section 1. The right of citizens of the United States to vote in any primary or other election for President or Vice-President, for electors for President or Vice-President, or for Senator or Representative in Congress, shall not be denied or abridged by the United States or any State by reason of failure to pay any poll tax or other tax.

Section 2. The Congress shall have power to enforce this article by appropriate legislation.

Amendment XXV (1967)

Section 1. In case of the removal of the President from office or of his death or resignation, the Vice-President shall become President.

Section 2. Whenever there is a vacancy in the office of the Vice-President, the President shall nominate a Vice-President who shall take office upon confirmation by a majority vote of both Houses of Congress.

Section 3. Whenever the President transmits to the President pro tempore of the Senate and the Speaker of the House of Representatives his written declaration that he is unable to discharge the powers and duties of his office, and until he transmits to them a written declaration to the contrary, such powers and duties shall be discharged by the Vice-President as Acting President.

Section 4. Whenever the Vice-President and a majority of either the principal officers of the executive department or of such other body as Congress may by law provide, transmit to the President pro tempore of the Senate and the Speaker of the House of Representatives their written declaration that the President is unable to discharge the powers and duties of his office, the Vice-President shall immediately assume the powers and duties of the office as Acting President.

Thereafter, when the President transmits to the President pro tempore of the Senate and the Speaker of the House of Representatives his written declaration that no inability exists, he shall resume the powers and duties of his office unless the Vice-President and a majority of either the principal officers of the executive department or of such other body as Congress may by law provide, transmit within four days to the President pro tempore of the Senate and the Speaker of the House of Representatives their written declaration that the President is unable to discharge the powers and duties of his office. Thereupon Congress shall decide the issue, assembling within forty-eight hours for that purpose if not in session. If the Congress, within twenty-one days after receipt of the latter written declaration, or, if Congress is not in session, within twenty-one days after Congress is required to assemble, determines by two-thirds vote of both Houses that the President is unable to discharge the powers and duties of his office, the Vice-President shall continue to discharge the same as Acting President; otherwise, the President shall resume the powers and duties of his office.

Amendment XXVI (1971)

Section 1. The right of citizens of the United States, who are eighteen years of age or older, to vote shall not be denied or abridged by the United States or by any State on account of age.

Section 2. The Congress shall have power to enforce this article by appropriate legislation.

Presidents and Vice Presidents of the United States

President	Vice President
George Washington 1789-97	John Adams 1789-97
John Adams 1797-1801	Thomas Jefferson 1797-1801
Thomas Jefferson 1801-09	Aaron Burr 1801-05
	George Clinton 1805-09
James Madison 1809-17	George Clinton 1809-13
	Elbridge Gerry 1813-17
James Monroe 1817-25	Daniel D. Tompkins 1817-25
John Quincy Adams 1825-29	John C. Calhoun 1825-29
Andrew Jackson 1829-37	John C. Calhoun 1829-33
	Martin Van Buren 1833-37
Martin Van Buren 1837-41	Richard M. Johnson 1837-41
William H. Harrison 1841	John Tyler 1841
John Tyler 1841-45	
James K. Polk 1845-49	George M. Dallas 1845-49
Zachary Taylor 1849-50	Millard Fillmore 1849-50
Millard Fillmore 1850-53	
Franklin Pierce 1853-57	William R. King 1853-57
James Buchanan 1857-61	John C. Breckinridge 1857-61
Abraham Lincoln 1861-65	Hannibal Hamlin 1861-65
	Andrew Johnson 1865
Andrew Johnson 1865-69	
Ulysses S. Grant 1869-77	Schuyler Colfax 1869-73
	Henry Wilson 1873-77
Rutherford B. Hayes 1877-81	William A. Wheeler 1877-81
James A. Garfield 1881	Chester A. Arthur 1881
Chester A. Arthur 1881-85	
Grover Cleveland 1885-89	T.A. Hendricks 1885-89
Benjamin Harrison 1889-93	Levi P. Morton 1889-93
Grover Cleveland 1893-97	Adlai E. Stevenson 1893-97
William McKinley 1897-1901	Garret A. Hobart 1897-1901
	Theodore Roosevelt 1901
Theodore Roosevelt 1901-09	Charles Fairbanks 1905-09
William H. Taft 1909-13	James S. Sherman 1909-13
Woodrow Wilson 1913-21	Thomas R. Marshall 1913-21
Warren G. Harding 1921-23	Calvin Coolidge 1921-23
Calvin Coolidge 1923-29	Charles G. Dawes 1925-29
Herbert C. Hoover 1929-33	Charles Curtis 1929-33
Franklin Delano Roosevelt 1933-45	John Nance Garner 1933-41
	Henry A. Wallace 1941-45
	Harry S Truman 1945
Harry S Truman 1945-53	Alben W. Barkley 1949-53
Dwight D. Eisenhower 1953-61	Richard M. Nixon 1953-61
John F. Kennedy 1961-63	Lyndon B. Johnson 1961-63
Lyndon B. Johnson 1963-69	Hubert H. Humphrey 1965-69
Richard M. Nixon 1969-74	Spiro T. Agnew 1969-73
	Gerald R. Ford 1973-74
Gerald R. Ford 1974-77	Nelson Rockefeller 1974-77
Jimmy Carter 1977-	Walter F. Mondale 1977-

index

index of court cases

A 7
B 8
C 9
D 0
E 1
F 2
G 3
H 4
I 5
J 6